Preventing and Remediating Reading Difficulties

Bringing Science to Scale

edited by Barbara R. Foorman

YORK
PRESS

Baltimore

This book was manufactured in the United States of America.

Typography by Type Shoppe II Productions Ltd.
Printing and Binding by Data Reproductions Corporation
Cover design by Joseph Dieter, Jr.

Library of Congress Cataloging-in-Publication Data

Preventing and remediating reading difficulties : bringing science to
scale / edited by Barbara R. Foorman.
        p. cm.
Includes bibliographical references and index.
   ISBN 0-912752-75-0
   1. Reading--Remedial teaching--United States--Case studies. 2.
Learning disabled children--Education (Elementary)--United States--Case
studies. I. Foorman, Barbara R.
   LB1050.5.P74 2003
   372.43--dc21
                                    2003010736

Acknowledgements

This book is the result of a June 12–15, 2002 symposium held on the "big" island of Hawaii sponsored by The Dyslexia Foundation (formerly the National Dyslexia Research Foundation). It was an honor to be asked by William H. Baker, Director of TDF, to organize this conference, although the truth is that Will and his assistant, Phil Pasho, did most of the organizational work, and for that I am extremely grateful. From my own staff, I wish to acknowledge the outstanding support of my Executive Assistant, Michele Hoffman, whose sense of humor and gentle persistence were instrumental in obtaining abstracts and drafts of presentations from speakers prior to the symposium and completed chapters after the symposium. Appreciation is also extended to Jennifer Griffin for stepping in at the last minute and coming to Hawaii to help with logistics, and to my colleague, Jack Fletcher who gave another speaker's presentation when she was unable to attend the symposium at the last moment.

Will Baker and I extend our deep appreciation to the following for their help in making this symposium possible: The Chany Trust, The Park Foundation, The Orchid Hotel, Scientific Learning, Johnson Family Foundation; and Helen U. Baker, Dr. Ed Kame'enui, Colleen Osborne, Dr. Paula Tallal, Fran Thompson, Mr. and Mrs. Brooks Firestone and Firestone Vineyards, and an anonymous donor for their financial support.

Finally, I thank Elinor Hartwig at York Press for her undivided attention to bringing this book out within a year of the symposium conference and my husband, Justin Leiber, and daughter, Casey Leiber, for their patience with my workaholic tendencies.

Dedication

To my mother, Marjorie McCarthy Robins, who encouraged my intellectual pursuits and my father, G. Kenneth Robins, who encouraged my athletic pursuits.

Contents

Introduction

The chapters in this book resulted from a symposium sponsored by The Dyslexia Foundation on the "big" island of Hawaii during June 12–15, 2002. The theme of the symposium was "Ingredients of effective preventions and interventions for children at-risk of reading difficulties or with identified reading disabilities." Researchers in neuroscience, psychology, educational psychology, and special education participated in the symposium and presented empirical evidence of the components of effective interventions. The emphasis on the ingredients, the components, or the elements of interventions that work helps us focus on the quality of the implementation necessary to achieve and maintain treatment gains. Only by "unpacking" our interventions and showing which components are effective for which children at which stage of reading development (Lyons and Moats 1997) can we fully address the challenge of the No Child Left Behind Act of 2001. The phrase "scientifically based research" is mentioned 111 times in the Act and has now achieved acronym status (SBR) in state applications for Reading First funds to prevent reading difficulties in primary-grade classrooms (Feuer, Towne, and Shavelson 2002). It behooves researchers to articulate the elements of successful preventions and interventions so that educators can replicate, sustain, and bring to scale evidence-based reading instruction. To that end, these chapters are presented in five sections, with a final coda on scaling reading interventions.

SECTION I. EARLY LEARNING AND DEVELOPMENT OF READING-RELATED SKILLS

The chapters in the first section focus on the plasticity of early learning and development and recent developments in assessment of reading-related phonological processes. The chapter by Papanicolaou and colleagues gives precise meaning to the notion of reading as "brain-based learning." Using the non-invasive procedure of Magnetic Source Imaging, they capture the time course of brain activation as child and adult readers process letters and words. They have imaged dyslexic children before and after effective intervention and shown on a case-by-case basis the normalized brain activation. They also show the aberrant dyslexic profile in kindergarten children identified as at-risk with the Texas Primary Reading Inventory (Foorman, Fletcher, and Francis in press). This profile is characterized by lack of engagement of the posterior portion of the left superior temporal region and an increase in the homologous right hemisphere region. The at-risk children received intervention in Grade 1 and the increase in left temporoparietal activity predicted change in letter-sound knowledge between kindergarten and first grade. These findings highlight the importance of early intervention. The fact that effective early reading interventions alter neural circuitry is clear evidence of the plasticity of neural systems.

Chapters by Lonigan and Wagner and colleagues emphasize the importance of phonological processing skills in emergent readers. Lonigan reviews studies indicating that children from lower socio-economic status (SES) are at risk of later reading difficulties because of slower development of the emergent literacy skills of oral language development, phonological processing, and print knowledge, and because of the high degree of stability of these skills. Lonigan argues that without effective preschool interventions children from lower SES backgrounds will not arrive at school ready to benefit from the reading instruction they receive. Wagner and his colleagues use the example of a preschooler who figures out how to isolate an initial phoneme half way through a phonological processing task (e.g., what is the first sound of "bat"?) and then completes all subsequent items correctly to discuss recent developments in assessment. These developments are possible because of advances in (a) theories of cognition and learning, (b) psychometrics, and (c) computer technology. Theories of cognition and learning provide increasing detail about how knowledge is represented, organized, and processed in many domains. Accordingly, methods exist to link assessment to tasks that are precisely designed, to observations of cognitive performance, and to inferences about what a person knows and does (Pellegrino, Chudowsky, and Glaser 2001). Advances in psychometrics under a general model called hierarchical Bayesian network (Pellegrino, Chudowsky, and Glaser 2001) allow items to be weighted differentially according to informational value and to link progress on classroom-level assessment to target scores on year-end achievement tests.

SECTION II. IDENTIFYING SOURCES OF RISK FOR READING DIFFICULTIES

Authors of all three chapters in this section agree that experiential factors are the primary source of risk for reading difficulties. Vellutino and his colleagues present data on a two-year follow-up of the difficult to remediate and readily remediated poor readers in his earlier study of children in kindergarten and Grade 1 (Vellutino et al. 1996). Follow-up results confirm previous findings that reading difficulties in most middle- and upper-middle class children are caused by experiential and instructional deficits rather than basic cognitive deficits, thereby underscoring the need for early identification and intervention. However, Vellutino also reports the existence of a small but significant number of children with phonological deficits that may be of constitutional origin who will require intensive and individualized remedial assistance beyond the intervention in order to become functionally independent readers.

Both Tom Nicholson and Bill Tunmer and his colleagues present data from New Zealand that address the source of the relatively large variability in reading scores in international studies of literacy achievement. They attribute the variability to Matthew effects triggered by constructivist and whole-language approaches to classroom reading instruction coupled with Reading Recovery tutorials (Clay 1993), which fail to respond adequately to the gaps in literacy-related skills children bring to school that stem primarily from social-class differences in home literacy environments. Both Nicholson and Tunmer et al. report results of phonological and alphabetic interventions that remediated children's reading skills and eliminated the achievement gap between children of different social classes.

SECTION III. EARLY READING INTERVENTIONS

Prevention is the best intervention, as chapters by Deborah Simmons and Ed Kame'enui and colleagues, Carolyn Denton and Patricia Mathes, and Benita Blachman and colleagues clearly show. A critical question for these early interventions in grades K-2 is the relative mix of isolated phonological and alphabetic skills versus connected text reading.

Simmons and Kame'enui and colleagues present findings of a two-year longitudinal study in which they examined the efficacy of prevention in kindergarten and the conditions needed to sustain reading success in first grade, using small-group instruction with existing school personnel in seven schools ($n = 96$). Supplemental kindergarten interventions that emphasized phonological skills and alphabetic instruction put the majority of children in the normal range who started the year in the bottom quartile of fall predictors. A nagging question is what would be the outcome of a no treatment control, if such a group had been included? To study maintenance and stability of kindergarten intervention, 59 children who met beginning of Grade 1 benchmarks participated in a two-phrase intervention, with mid-year adjustment. Some students received maintenance intervention throughout the year, others were monitored throughout the year, and others switched in February from monitor to intervention or intervention to monitor. The most important finding was that children who began the year with higher oral reading fluency reached end-of-year benchmarks sooner and maintained this learning trajectory regardless of supplemental instruction. The authors conclude that classroom instruction can be sufficiently good to maintain skill development without supplemental instruction. Such was the case with the explicit alphabetic instruction in the eight Title 1 schools we studied (Foorman et al. 1998).

Denton and Mathes describe findings from Grade 1 interventions in six non-Title 1 urban schools. They identified children at risk of reading difficulties based on the Texas Primary Reading Inventory (Foorman et al. in press) at the end of kindergarten and randomly assigned them to one of three conditions in Grade 1: Proactive Reading ($n = 82$), Responsive Reading ($n = 83$), or Enhanced Classroom ($n = 93$). In the Enhanced Classroom condition, classroom teachers received professional development on using assessment results to differentiate instruction. Throughout the year, the teachers received progress-monitoring graphs depicting words correct per minute on benchmark stories for each child in the study. The children in the Proactive and Responsive interventions received an additional 40 minutes of daily tutoring in groups of three delivered by a certified teacher from October to May. Proactive Reading is a prescriptive approach based on Open Court Reading (SRA/McGraw-Hill 2000), adopted by the school district. In Responsive Reading teachers adjust instruction in response to student needs, rather than following a prescribed scope and sequence. Responsive Reading uses leveled text rather than the decodable texts of Proactive Reading. Both approaches provide explicit alphabetic code instruction, but Responsive Reading provides less time practicing phonological and alphabetic skills in isolation and more time applying these skills to connected text reading and writing. Preliminary data analyses show that students in all three groups did well. Only 16% of students in the Enhanced Classroom condition remained below the 30th percentile on the Woodcock-Johnson III Basic Skills Cluster (WJ-III; Woodcock, McGrew, and Mather 2001) at the end of the year. In Proactive Reading, only one child out of 82 failed to reach the average range on the WJ-III; in Responsive Reading, only 8 out of 83 students failed to reach the average range.

Differences between Proactive and Responsive Reading were not significant, on average. Denton and Mathes conclude that combinations of classroom prevention and secondary intervention can be highly effective in reducing the percentages of children needing tertiary intervention in special education to less than 2%. Responsive Reading will be a popular approach for teachers who eschew prescriptive approaches and it will be important to study how it can be brought to scale in Title 1 schools, along with Proactive Reading, with quality implementation.

Blachman and colleagues describe the evolution of a kindergarten and Grade 1 classroom prevention program into a remedial program for second and third graders. The results of the prevention program are well known (Blachman et al. 1999): 10 to 13 hours of phonological awareness training in kindergarten, followed by 30 minutes daily of explicit alphabetic coding instruction and text reading using decodable text and stories from basal readers was sufficient to move treatment children in Grade 1 significantly ahead of control children on measures of phonemic awareness, alphabetic knowledge, and word recognition. Effects were maintained through second grade. It is important to note that these gains were made with regular classroom teachers during regular classroom instruction. The remedial program was tested on 69 second and third graders who were below the 25th percentile on the Woodcock Reading Mastery Test-Revised (Woodcock 1987) and were randomly assigned to treatment or control conditions. The treatment consisted of 50 minutes of one-to-one tutoring, five days a week, delivered by certified teachers who had received 45 hours of initial training by Blachman and Tangel. Training continued throughout the year in monthly meetings. Fidelity was monitored by listening to audiotapes collected weekly. Lessons consisted of the alphabetic coding, decodable text, and leveled text reading used in the Grade 1 program, but additional work on multisyllabic words, fluency, and spelling dictation was added once facility with closed syllables was achieved. Preliminary results (see Blachman et al. 2002) show that treatment children significantly outperformed controls on standardized measures of word reading, reading rate, spelling, and passage comprehension at the end of the one-year intervention as well as one year later. Additional analyses divided intervention students into those with high and low initial status (i.e., those above and below the 15th percentile). Both groups made equivalent gains; in other words, the gap remained the same.

All three chapters on early reading interventions show the potential of classroom prevention in kindergarten and in Grade 1, coupled with supplementary intervention in Grades 1 to 3 with certified teachers, as a vehicle for nearly eliminating reading failure in the primary grades. These are enormously important findings. Rather than "stabilizing reading failure" as is evident with the tertiary interventions in special education (Torgesen et al. 2001), we can prevent reading failure by (a) improving classroom instruction and, (b) by providing a double dose of reading in small-group or tutorial interventions. In both cases, the elements of reading instruction are the same critical elements of phonemic awareness and phonemic decoding skills, fluency in word recognition and text processing, construction of meaning, vocabulary, spelling, and writing (Foorman and Torgesen 2001).

SECTION IV. INSTRUCTIONAL CONDITIONS NECESSARY FOR REMEDIATING READING DIFFICULTIES IN OLDER CHILDREN

In Section IV, Joe Torgesen and colleagues discuss components of successful interventions with students in upper elementary and middle school. Sharon Vaughn and Sylvia Linan-Thompson, as well as Lynn and Doug Fuchs, discuss issues of grouping size and assessment, with a focus on Grade 2.

Torgesen and colleagues present an overview of results from five of their intervention studies with children in late elementary and middle school. Samples varied in their average levels of initial word reading skill: Two samples were at the 2nd percentile; two samples were at the 10th percentile; and one sample was at the 30th percentile. Interventions were either The Lindamood Phoneme Sequencing Program for Reading, Spelling, and Speech (Lindamood and Lindamood 1998) or Spell Read P.A.T. (Phonological Auditory Training; MacPhee 1998). Both programs stress phonemic awareness and phonemic decoding, but Spell Read P.A.T allocates a greater percentage of instructional time to fluency-oriented practice and writing. Results showed similarities and differences across samples. All five interventions produced substantial gains in reading performance relative to average children. These gains tended to close the gap in phonemic decoding, but not in the area of reading fluency. Reading comprehension skills improved to levels close to the general verbal ability of the students. Torgesen and his colleagues conclude that older students with mild reading disabilities (i.e., around the 30th percentile) can be brought into the normal range of skills in phonemic decoding, text reading accuracy and fluency, and comprehension with 60 hours of remedial intervention. However, for older students who start around the 10th percentile, 100 hours will be needed to bring skills into the average range, and the fluency gap will be closed somewhat, but the skills still remain substantially impaired. Students starting at the 2nd percentile can develop average phonemic decoding skills and show strong gains in text reading accuracy and comprehension with intensive intervention. However, the fluency gap is likely to remain. Given that gains in reading fluency were significantly correlated with initial word reading skill for all samples, Torgesen and his colleagues suggest that limitations in sight word vocabulary impede automatic recognition of individual words. Underlying this limitation, for some students, may be an inability to form orthographic representations (Wolf and Bowers 1999).

Vaughn and Linan-Thompson present two studies with second graders that shed light on two critical elements of reading interventions—group size and duration of treatment. In the first study, effects of group size (1:1, 1:3, 1:10) on reading outcomes were examined by controlling for treatment across group size. Gains across the 11 weeks of daily supplemental reading instruction differed by group size: There were no significant differences between 1:1 and 1:3; however, students in both 1:1 and 1:3 outperformed students in 1:10. This result is highly significant given the enormous expense of tutoring students individually, as happens in the Reading Recovery approach (Elbaum et al. 2000), and the knowledge that small-group intervention can be just as effective as one-to-one intervention. In the second study, Vaughn and Linan-Thompson show the wisdom of basing treatment duration on a priori established criteria for exit. Forty-five second graders in the bottom 20% of their grade received the same research-based intervention used in the first study in group ratios of 1:3. Students met exit criteria at varying times: 10-, 20-, and 30-week exit, or no exit. Significantly, all groups exhibited the greatest gains in oral reading fluency during the first 10 weeks.

The issue of grouping for instruction is also examined in the chapter by Lynn and Doug Fuchs. They wondered if general educators instructed in diagnostic analysis of curriculum-based measurement (CBM) would make instructional adaptations to enhance student learning. Accordingly, they randomly assigned 28 second grade teachers in four high-poverty and three middle-class schools to one of four conditions: (1) no instructional consultation and no CBM (i.e., control), (2) instructional consultation (i.e., consultation only); (3) instructional consultation with CBM (i.e., CBM), and (4) instructional consultation with CBM with diagnostic analysis (i.e., CBM + diagnostic analysis). Curriculum-based measurement consisted of one-minute oral reading of benchmark stories. Teachers in the CBM and CBM + diagnostic analysis groups shared weekly fluency graphs charting progress in words correct per minute over time. Students in need of decoding instruction in both CBM conditions were given a computerized decoding test. Only teachers in the CBM + diagnostic analysis group received recommendations about comprehension, fluency, and decoding instruction and information about specific decoding deficits. Every third week, research assistants met with all teachers to provide script-guided consultations in how teachers might consider the needs of their students. Teachers in the CBM condition examined features of their CBM class report. These 3-week sessions occurred five times across the 15-week study from October to March. Fidelity to condition was good and overlap between Instructional Plan Sheets and observed instruction was 82%. Both CBM groups exhibited greater specialized adaptations relative to the consultation-only group and the diagnostic analysis added value in increasing instructional differentiation. However, the instances of instructional adaptations were few and tended to address all struggling readers with one simultaneous instructional action, which may or may not have been appropriate. Not surprising, effects on student achievement gains were modest. Teachers in the CBM groups were more likely to describe student difficulties in terms of reading performance, whereas consultation-only teachers often attributed difficulties to factors beyond their control. Fuchs and Fuchs conclude that the appropriate role for assessment within regular education may be to signal the need for secondary or tertiary intervention, which others are responsible for implementing. However, results from the CBM + diagnostic condition suggest that further professional development for general educators in how to translate results of early reading assessment to differentiated instruction is warranted.

SECTION V. RE-MEDIATING ORAL AND WRITTEN LANGUAGE UNDERSTANDING

Cole and Griffin (1983) remind us that implicit in the idea of remediating reading difficulties is the renegotiation of how oral language mediates written language understanding. The three chapters in this section underscore this point by emphasizing the importance of understanding (a) sound-to-spelling relations (i.e., encoding) as well as spelling-to-sound (i.e., decoding), (b) morphological units, and (c) word meanings to learning to read.

Maryanne Wolf and her colleagues see reading remediation as a rearrangement of the perceptual, cognitive, linguistic, and motoric regions of the brain so that all regions operate in the parallel, automatic fashion we refer to as fluent reading. They argue that one of the best predictors of the efficiency of the processes underlying reading fluency is the naming speed task. Wolf and her colleagues have developed a multi-componential approach to fluency instruction called RAVE-O (Retrieval, Automaticity, Vocabulary-Elaboration, Enrichment with Language, and Orthography). RAVE-O emphasizes (1) accuracy and automaticity of sublexical and lexical processes, (2) increased rate in word attack, word identification, and comprehension, and (3) a transformed attitude towards language. This transformation stresses not only the need for automaticity in phonological, orthographic, semantic, syntactic, and morphological systems but also the importance of teaching explicit links among these linguistic systems. RAVE-O is taught in combination with a program that teaches systematic, phonological analysis and blending (Lovett, Steinbach, and Frijters 2000). Preliminary results with severely impaired second and third grader readers show promising gains in reading accuracy, speed, and comprehension.

Virginia Berninger and her colleagues posit that awareness of morphology is an important instructional component above and beyond phonological awareness and the alphabetic principle. This is a highly reasonable proposition because English is, in fact, morphophonemic (Chomsky and Halle 1968), that is, spellings preserve meaning at the expense of phonology. For example, we write vineyard, not vinyard. The morphological treatment that Berninger et al. developed for upper-elementary grade students involves writing and identifying words using bases and affixes, and sorting and comparing words based on morphemic units. They developed a parallel phonological treatment as well. Common components across treatments consist of practice with spelling-phoneme associations and fluency and comprehension work. Twenty children who had just completed grades 4, 5, or 6 were randomly assigned to receive either the phonological or the morphological treatments in groups of ten for 30 hours over a three-week period during the summer. Both groups tended to make modest gains, on average, on reading and spelling measures. Importantly, the phonology group made no gain on speeded word reading and spelling, whereas the morphology group made some gains here. Berninger et al. reason that instruction in morphemic units may help to smooth the connections between orthographic, phonological, and morphological processes for dyslexic readers, whereas normal readers are able to smooth these connections through orthographic and phonological instruction alone.

In the final chapter in this section, my colleagues and I describe a vocabulary enrichment project (VEP) for African American third and fourth graders similar to the vocabulary improvement project that McLaughlin et al. (2000; see Lively et al. 2003) developed for English language learners. We point out that in spite of the consensus regarding the importance of vocabulary development during the elementary school years (Snow, Burns, and Griffin 1998), there is a surprising dearth of research on effective vocabulary instruction (NICHD 2000). The "before reading" vocabulary instruction in the basal readers is inadequate, as was evident in the extremely low and stable receptive vocabulary scores in the 1300 kindergarten through Grade 4 students participating in our longitudinal study in 17 high poverty schools in Houston, Texas and in Washington, D.C. These students' word identification and passage comprehension skills improved to be solidly at national average, but their receptive vocabulary scores remained at the 15th percentile, on average, with only 3.5% and 6% of instructional time devoted to vocabulary instruction in Grades 1 and 2. As the students began to read more widely across the curriculum in upper elementary grades, we worried that low vocabulary size would retard reading comprehension. Consequently, we wrote a vocabulary enrichment program (VEP) for the third and fourth grade teachers participating in our study. We developed a five-day lesson plan, similar to those designed by Beck, Perfetti, and McKeown (1982) and Lively et. al. (2003), but we used literature based on African American heroes and heroines and targeted words from level 4 of the Dale and O'Rourke (1981) Living Word Vocabulary. Instructional techniques included: context activities; morphological elements such as prefixes, suffixes, and word roots; synonyms/antonyms; inferencing and summarizing skills, paraphrasing, and deep processing activities; multiple meanings; dictionary skills, word games, semantic feature analysis, and figurative language. Fifteen Grade 3 teachers and 10 Grade 4 teachers received two-days of after-school training and follow-up coaching in the classroom. The program continued for 20 weeks, with fidelity observations twice a month.

Results confirmed what others have found: upper elementary school students learn the vocabulary words taught but results do not transfer to distal measures of reading comprehension. In Grade 3, we found significant pretest to posttest gains in VEP classrooms compared to non-VEP classrooms for vocabulary words taught, but no significant differences on reading measures. In Grade 4, we found that teachers who implemented the VEP program regularly and did so more closely to protocol had classrooms with higher language skills at the end of the year. A major reason for the uneven implementation of VEP in Grade 4 in Houston classrooms was competition from the curriculum designed to prepare students for the state accountability test. One-third of reading/language instruction was devoted to this curriculum daily from the fall until the writing test in February and the reading test in April. We conclude that vocabulary instruction needs to begin at the very beginning of schooling—in preschool—if the gap between rich and poor children is to be closed (Foorman et al. 2002). We recommend that teachers target 8 to 15 words each school day, using instructional strategies that move from contextualized definitions to deep understanding of word meanings found in multiple contexts that serve to maintain understanding.

SECTION VI. CODA

In the final chapter, Carolyn Denton and Jack Fletcher ask how findings from research on effective interventions can be scaled into widespread practice. They provide a five-phase model for scaling and sustaining educational interventions: (1) development of the intervention; (2) empirical evaluation of the intervention; (3) tests of robustness and generalizability; (4) scaling up and sustaining; and (5) networking. Within the scaling phase they include steps of (a) dissemination, (b) decision, (c) implementation, (d) transition, (e) confirmation, and (f) institutionalization.

When one looks at examples of interventions that have successfully scaled, one also sees the power of top-down mandates, of manualized procedures and products, and of teacher-empowerment movements. The potency and sustainability of the theme of teacher empowerment is apparent in the success of whole-language, literature-based, and guided-reading approaches. These approaches exist and thrive in reaction to the perceived stranglehold of the basal reader on beginning reading instruction. Capitalizing on this empowerment mood are publishers of professional books such as Heinemann and trade books such as Wright and Rigby and professional organizations such as Reading Recovery. Occasionally academic leaders steer teacher empowerment towards reflection on practice, as Howard Gardner (1983) has done with the idea of multiple intelligences, E.D. Hirsch (1996) has done with the core knowledge curriculum, Henry Levin (1988) has accomplished in Accelerated Schools, and Ted Sizer (1984) has done at the high school level in the Coalition of Essential Schools.

Interventions with top-down mandates and manualized procedures and products tend to thrive in the inner city where the reality of teacher turnover, lack of home literacy, and second language issues quickly dispel the rhetoric of teacher empowerment. Success for All (Slavin and Madden 2001) is an example of a school reform model that has become institutionalized as districts' Title 1 program and has developed an organization that provides curriculum, teacher professional development, facilitators, tutors, and parental support staff. These same components have recently been integrated into implementations of the basal program Open Court Reading (SRA/McGraw-Hill 2000) in California.

Factors affecting scaling of interventions lie at the level of students, teachers, schools, districts, states, and nations. For the first time in the history of the United States, the federal legislation of the No Child Left Behind Act of 2001 holds educators at all levels accountable for educational performance. The scientific evidence brought forth in this book regarding effective classroom preventions and supplementary interventions for reading difficulties can contribute to the knowledge base needed to pursue this national challenge and opportunity.

ACKNOWLEDGEMENT

Supported in part by grant R01-HD30995, Early Interventions for Children with Reading Problems, from the National Institute of Child Health and Human Development (NICHD).

REFERENCES

Beck, I. L, Perfetti, C. A., and McKeown, M. G. 1982. Effects of long-term vocabulary instruction on lexical access and reading comprehension. *Journal of Educational Psychology* 74:506–21.

Blachman, B. A., Schatschneider, C., Fletcher, J. M., Francis, D. J., Clonan, S., Shaywitz, B. E.,and Shaywitz, S. E. 2002. Effects of intensive reading remediation for second and third graders and a one year follow-up. Manuscript in preparation.

Blachman, B. A., Tangel, D. M., Ball, E. W., Black, R., and McGraw, C. K. 1999. Developing phonological awareness and word recognition skills: A two-year intervention with low-income, inner-city children. *Reading and Writing: An Interdisciplinary Journal* 11:239–73.

Chomsky, N., and Halle, M. 1968. *The Sound Pattern of English*. New York, NY: Harper & Row.

Clay, M. M. 1993. *Reading Recovery: A Guidebook for Teachers in Training*. Portsmouth, NH: Heinemann.

Cole, M., and Griffin, P. 1983. A socio-historical approach to re-mediation. *The Quarterly Newsletter of the Laboratory of Comparative Human Cognition* 5:69–74.

Dale, E., and O'Rourke, J. 1981. *Living Word Vocabulary*. Chicago: World Book/Childcraft International.

Elbaum, B., Vaughn, S., Hughes, M. T., and, Moody, S. W.. 2000. How effective are one-on-one tutoring programs in reading for elementary students at risk for reading failure? A meta-analysis of the intervention research. *Journal of Educational Psychology* 924:605–19.

Feuer, M. J., Towne, L., and Shavelson, R. J. 2002. Scientific culture and educational research. *Educational Researcher* 31:4–14.

Foorman, B. R., Anthony, J., Seals, L., and Mouzaki, A. 2002. Language development and emergent literacy in preschool. To appear in Ian Butler's Language Development & Disorders in Childhood, a special issue of *Seminars in Pediatric Neurology* 9:172–830.

Foorman, B. F., Fletcher, J. M., and Francis, D. J. In press. Early reading assessment. In *Testing American's School Children*, ed. W. Evans. Stanford: Hoover Press.

Foorman, B. R., Francis, D. J., Fletcher, J. M., Schatschneider, C. and Mehta, P. 1998. The role of instruction in learning to read: Preventing reading failure in at-risk children. *Journal of Educational Psychology* 90:37–55.

Foorman, B. R., and Torgesen, J. K. 2001. Critical elements of classroom and small-group instruction promote reading success in all children. *Learning Disabilities Research and Practice*, 16:202–11.

Gardner, H. 1983. Frames of Mind. New York: Basic Books.

Hirsh, E. E. 1996. *The Schools We Need and Why We Don't Have Them*. New York: NY, Doubleday.

Levin, H. M. 1988. *Accelerated Schools for At-risk Students*. New Brunswick, NJ: Center for Policy Research in Education.

Lindamood, P. and Lindamood, P. 1998. *The Lindamood Phoneme Sequencing Program for Reading, Spelling, and Speech: The LiPS Program*. Austin, TX: PRO-ED.

Lively, T., August, D., Snow, C., and Carlo, M. 2003. *Vocabulary Improvement Program for English Language Learners and Their Classmates*. Baltimore, Maryland: Brookes Publishing.

Lovett, M. W., Steinbach, K. A., and Frijters, J. C. 2000. Remediating the core deficits of developmental reading disability: A double-deficit perspective. *Journal of Learning Disabilities* 33:334–58.

Lyons, G. R. and Moats, L. 1997. Critical conceptual and methodological considerations and reading intervention research. *Journal of Learning Disabilities* 30:579–88.

MacPhee, K. 1998. *Spell Read P.A.T.* Charlottetown, Canada: Learning Systems, Inc.

McLaughlin, B., August, D., and Snow, C. 2000. *Vocabulary knowledge and reading comprehension in english language learners: Final performance report*. California: Office of Educational Research and Improvement.

National Institute of Child Health and Human Development. 2000. *National Reading Panel Report*. Washington, D.C.: National Institutes of Health.

Open Court Reading 2000. *Collections for Young Scholars*. Peru, IL: SRA/McGraw-Hill.

Pellegrino, J. W., Chudowsky, N., and Glaser, R. 2001. *Knowing What Students Know: The Science and Design of Educational Assessment*. Washington, D.C.: National Academy Press.

Sizer, T. R. 1984. Horace's *Compromise: The Dilemma of the American High School*. Boston, MA: Houghton Mifflin.

Slavin, R. E., and Madden, N. A. 2001. Success for All: An overview. In R. Slavin and N. Madden (Eds.), *Success for All: Research and Reform in Elementary Education.* (pp. 3–15). Mahwah, NJ: Lawrence Erlbaum Associates.

Snow, C. E., Burns, M. S., and Griffin, P. (Eds.) 1998. *Preventing Reading Difficulties in Young Children.* Washington, D.C.: National Academy Press.

Torgesen, J. K., Alexander, A. W., Wagner, R. K., Rashotte, C. A., Voeller, K. S., and Conway, T. 2001. Intensive remedial instruction for children with severe reading disabilities: Immediate and long-term outcomes from two instructional approaches. *Journal of Learning Disabilities* 34:33–58.

Vellutino, F. R., Scanlon, D. M., Sipay, E., Small, S., Pratt, A., Chen, R., and Denckla, M. 1996. Cognitive profiles of difficult-to-remediate and readily remediated poor readers: Early intervention as a vehicle for distinguishing between cognitive and experiential deficits as basic causes of specific reading disability. *Journal of Educational Psychology* 88:601–38.

Wolf, M., and Bowers, P. 1999. The "double-deficit hypothesis" for the developmental dyslexias. *Journal of Educational Psychology* 91:1–24.

Woodcock, R. 1987. *Woodcock Reading Mastery Tests.* Circle Pines, MN: American Guidance Service.

Woodcock, R. W., McGrew, K. S., and Mather, N. 2001. *Woodcock-Johnson III.* Itasca, IL: Riverside Publishing.

Conference Participants

Virginia Berninger, Ph.D.
University of Washington
Educational Psychology
322 P Miller Hall
P.O. Box 353600
Seattle, WA 98195
206-616-6372
vwb@u.washington.edu

Benita Blachman, Ph.D.
Syracuse University
Reading & Language Arts
Syracuse, NY 13244
315-443-1870
Blahman@syr.edu

Carolyn Denton, Ph.D.
University of Texas
Houston Health Science Center
Center for Academic & Reading
  Skills
7000 Fannin UCT 2443
Houston, TX 77030
713-500-3812
Carolyn.A.Denton@uth.tmc.edu

Jack Fletcher, Ph.D.
University of Texas
Houston Health Science Center
Center for Academic & Reading
  Skills
7000 Fannin UCT 2478
Houston, TX 77030
713-500-3683
Jack.Fletcher@uth.tmc.edu

Barbara R. Foorman, Ph.D.
Universitiy of Texas
Houston Health Science Center
Center for Academic & Reading
  Skills
7000 Fannin UCT 2443
Houston, TX 77030
713-500-3685
Barbara.R.Foorman@uth.tmc.edu

Lynn Fuchs, Ph.D.
Vanderbilt University
Box 328 Peabody
Nashville, TN 37203
615-322-8156
lynn.fuchs@vanderbilt.edu

Deborah Simmons, Ph.D.,
and Ed Kame'enui, Ph.D.
University of Oregon
170 College of Education
Eugene, OR 97403
541-346-1644
dsimmons@oregon.uoregon.edu
ekamee@oregon.uoregon.edu

Christopher Lonigan, Ph.D.
Florida State University
Department of Psychology
One University Way
Tallahassee, FL 32306
850-644-7241
lonigan@psy.fsu.edu

Tom Nicholson, Ph.D.
University of Auckland
Education Department
1011 Fisher International Building
18 Waterloo Quadrant
New Zealand
+64-9-373-7599 ext. 7372
t.nicholson@auckland.ac.nz

Andrew Papanicolaou, Ph.D.
  University of Texas
  Houston Health Science Center
  1333 Moursund Street
  TIR H114
  Houston, TX 77030
  713-797-7571
  Andrew.C.Papanicolaou@
    uth.tmc.edu

Joseph Torgesen, Ph.D.
  Florida State University
  Departament of Psychology
  Tallahassee, FL 32306
  850-644-1707
  torgesen@psy.fsu.edu

William Tunmer, Ph.D.
  Massey University
  College of Education
  Private Bag 11-222
  Palmerston North New Zealand
  +64-6-356-9909 ext. 8962
  W.Tunmer@massey.ac.nz

Sharon Vaughn, Ph.D.
  University of Texas
  Texas Center for Reading &
    Language
  Campus Mail Code: D4900
  Austin, TX 78712
  512-232-2320
  srvaughnum@aol.com

Frank Vellutino, Ph.D.
  Universtiy at Albany
  Educational Psychology & Stat
  1400 Washington Avenue
  Albany, NY 12222-0001
  518-442-3780
  frv@csc.albany.edu

Richard Wagner, Ph.D.
  Florida State University
  Department of Psychology
  One University Way
  Tallahassee, FL 32306-1270
  850-644-1033
  rkwagner@psy.fsu.edu.

Maryanne Wolf, Ph.D.
  Tufts University
  Center for Reading & Language
  Miller Hall
  Medford, MA 02155-7019
  617-627-3815
  maryanne.wolf@tufts.edu

Collaborators

Douglas Fuchs, Ph.D.
 Vanderbilt University
 Special Education
 110 Magnolia Circle
 Nashville TN 37235
 615-322-8252
 doug.fuchs@Vanderbilt.edu

Deborah Simmons, Ph.D.
 University of Oregon
 Development of Educational
  Achievement
 5225 University of Oregon
 Eugene, OR 97403
 541-346-3486
 dsimmons@oregon.uoregon.edu

Mike Stoolmiller, Ph.D.
 University of Oregon
 Education Annex
 5225 University of Oregon
 Eugene, OR 97403
 541-346-1017

Beth Harn, Ph.D.
 California State University, Fresno
 5241 N. Maple Avenue
 Fresno CA 93740
 559-278-4240

Joanne Carlisle, Ph.D.
 University of Michigan
 School of Education
 610 East University Avenue
 Ann Arbor MI 48109
 734-615-1267
 jfcarl@umich.edu

Sharolyn Pollard-Durodola, M.Ed.
 Univesity of Texas
 Center for Academic & Reading Skills
 7000 Fannin UCT 2443
 Houston TX 77030
 713-500-3817
 Sharolyn.D.Pollard-
  Durodola@uth.tmc.edu

Jack Fletcher, Ph.D.
 University of Texas
 Developmental Pediatrics
 7000 Fannin UCT 2478
 Houston TX 77030
 713-500-3683
 Jack.Fletcher@uth.tmc.edu

Robin Morris, Ph.D.
 Georgia State University
 Department of Psychology
 758 Urban Life
 Atlanta GA 30303
 404-651-1637
 psyrdm@langate.gsu.edu

Sylvia Linan-Thompson, Ph.D.
 University of Texas—Austin
 Department of Special Education
 Campus Mail Code: D4900
 Austin TX 78712
 512-471-5716
 sylviat@mail.utexas.edu

Beth O'Brien, Ph.D.
 Tufts University
 Child Development
 Eliot Pearson Center
 Medford MA 02155
 617-627-3833
 beth.obrien@tufts.edu

Michael D. Coyne, Ph.D.
University of Connecticut
Educational Psychology
Gentry Building—Unit 2064
Storrs CT 06269
260-486-8326

Donna Scanlon, Ph.D.
University of Albany
Reading Husted 134
1400 Washington
Albany NY 12222
518-442-3775
dslenmont.aol.com

Katharine Donnelly Adams, M.A.T.
Tufts University
Child Development
Miller Hall
210 Packard Avenue
Medford MA 02155
617-627-4137
katharine.donnelly@tufts.edu

Terry Joffe, M.A.T.
Tufts University
Child Development
Miller Hall
210 Packard Avenue
Medford MA 02155
617-627-6083
terry.joffe@tufts.edu

William E. Nagy, Ph.D.
Seattle Pacific University
Education
Peterson 409
Seattle WA 98119
206-281-2253
wnagy@spu.edu

James Joecard, Ph.D.
University of Albany
Psychology
Social Science 248C
1400 Washington
Albany NY 12222
518-442-4864
jjj20@cnsunix.albany.edu

Sheilia M. Clonan, Ph.D.
Syracuse University
Reading & Language Arts
Syracuse NY 13244
315-43-4765
smclonan@syr.edu

Jason Anthony, Ph.D.
University of Houston
Psychology
4800 Calhoun Road
Houston TX 77204
713-743-2062
janthony@uh.edu

Latrice Seals, M.Ed.
WETA-TV
26 Research Director
2775 S. Quincy Street
Arlington VA 22206
703-998-2440
Iseals@weta.com

Jennifer Thomson, Ph.D.
University of Washington
Educational Psychology
Box 353600
Seattle WA 98195
206-616-6377
thomsonj@u.washington.edu

Diana Hoffer, M.Ed.
University of Washington
Educational Psychology
Box 353600
Seattle WA 98195

Sylvia Abbott, Ph.D.
University of Washington
Educational Psychology
Box 353600
Seattle WA 98195

Robert Abbott, Ph.D.
University of Washington
Educational Psychology
Box 353600
Seattle WA 98195
206-616-6308
abbottr@u.washington.edu

Todd Richards, Ph.D.
University of Washington
Radiology
Box 357115
Seattle WA 98195
206-598-6725
toddr@u.washington.edu

Elizabeth Aylward, Ph.D.
University of Washington
Radiology
Box 357115
Seattle WA 98195
206-221-6610
eaylward@u.washington.edu

Christopher Schatschneider, Ph.D.
Florida State University
Psychology
315D Psychology Building
Tallahassee FL
850-644-4323
schatschneider@psy.fsu.edu

Panagiotis G. Simos, Ph.D.
University of Texas
Neurosurgery
1333 Moursund Street
Houston TX 77030
713-797-7576
Panagiotis.G.Simos@uth.tmc.edu

David J. Francis, Ph.D.
University of Houston
Psychology
4800 Calhoun Road
Houston TX 77204
713-743-8533
dfrancis@eh.edu

Eduardo M. Castillo, Ph.D.
University of Texas
Neurosurgery
1333 Moursund Street
Houston TX 77030
713-797-7575
eduardo.m.castillo@uth.tmc.edu

Shirin Sarkari, Ph.D.
University of Texas
Neurosurgery
1333 Moursund Street
Houston TX 77030
713-7979-7582
Shirin.Sarkari@uth.tmc.edu

Maureen Lovett, Ph.D.
Toronto Hospital for Sick Children
416-813-6329
mwl@sickkids.ca

Andrea E. Muse, B.A.
Florida State University
Psychology
209 Psychology Building
Tallahassee FL 32306
850-644-2040
amuse2@hotmail.com

Tamara L. Stein, Ph.D.
Florida State University
Psychology
209 Psychology Building
Tallahassee FL 32306
850-644-2040

Kelly C. Cukrowicz, M.A.
Florida State University
Psychology
209 Psychology Building
Tallahassee FL 32306
850-644-5227

Erin R. Harrell, M.A.
Florida State University
Psychology
209 Psychology Building
Tallahassee FL 32306
850-644-2040
erinharrelll@hotmail.com

Carol A. Rashotte, Ph.D.
Florida State University
Psychology
208 Longmire Building
Tallahassee FL 32306
850-644-4563
crashott@psy.fsu.edu

Corine S. Samwel, M.A.
Florida State University
Psychology
214 Stone Building
Tallahassee FL 32306
850-644-4838
samwell@psy.fsu.edu

James W. Chapman, Ph.D.
Massey University
College of Education
Private Bag 1-222
Palmerston North, New Zealand
+64-6-356-9909

Jane E. Prochnow, M.Ed.
Massey University
College of Education
Private Bag 11-222
Palmerston North, New Zealand
+64-6-356-9909
J.E.Prochnow@massey.ac.nz

Ann Alexanader, M.D.
Morris Child Development Center
700 NW 91 Street
Suite B-200
Gainesville, FL 32606
352-332-2629

Jane Alexander
Morris Child Development Center
3700 NW 91 Street
Suite B-200
Gainesville, FL 326016
352-332-2629

Kay MacPhee, M.Ed.
Spell Read P.A.T.
134 Kent Street
Charlottetown, PE C1A 8R8
902-892-9645
kmacphee@spellread.com

Section • I

Early Learning and Development of Reading Related Skills

Chapter • 1

Early Development and Plasticity of Neurophysiological Processes Involved in Reading

Andrew C. Papanicolaou, Panagiotis G. Simos, Jack M. Fletcher, David J. Francis, Barbara Foorman, Eduardo M. Castillo, and Shirin Sarkari

One of the core problems in children with dyslexia is difficulty learning how the printed word maps onto spoken language. A functional deficit in the brain circuits that support linguistic processing is suspected. Until recently, however, no information existed regarding the functional status of this circuit during the early stages of reading acquisition. We recently completed a series of studies addressing key issues in the pathophysiology of dyslexia using magnetic source imaging protocols that have been validated against external neuroanatomical modalities and used clinically in our laboratory. These studies include two involving children learning to read, including a study of at-risk children who received intervention in Grade 1. An intervention study of older children with dyslexia has also been completed. Prior to discussing these three studies, some background on language, reading, and dyslexia will be provided.

LANGUAGE AND READING

Research on dyslexia in our laboratory builds upon other research on the brain mechanisms mediating word recognition and reading. Regional specialization for processes involved in reading develops onto an advanced network of brain areas involved in linguistic operations. This network shows signs of specialization soon after birth (Entus 1977; Hahn 1987; Hiscock 1988; Molfese and Betz 1988), although the complete commitment of various component areas supporting language may not be complete until puberty (Dennis 1988; St. James-Roberts 1979). Reading, on the other hand, is a relatively late achievement in the course of human development. It is built upon naturally recurring human capabilities for oral language, but also depends on skills that do not appear to be directly related to those normally involved in understanding oral language, such as phonological awareness (Liberman 1998). Phonological awareness is a metacognitive understanding that words have internal phonological structures. In order to learn to read, the child must bridge the gap between spoken and written language by developing an explicit understanding of the segmented nature of speech (Blachman 1997). Although this structure is implicit, it is not necessary to be aware of the internal structure of speech in order to speak and comprehend oral language. But an explicit understanding is essential to recognizing and comprehending print (Lukatela and Turvey 1998).

These issues are well understood at a behavioral level. The relationship of oral and written language through the phonological awareness bridge is a "big idea" in science (Stanovich 2000). What we know about beginning reading is the accumulation of over 30 years of research from the early 1970s and recently cited as an example of how scientific knowledge evolves over time in a report from the National Research Council on science and education (Shavelson and Towne 2002). However, until recently, little was known regarding the development of neurophysiological processes associated with reading acquisition. Nonetheless, as with the acquisition of any new skill, the spatial extent of task-specific cortical engagement would be expected to change with age (Castro-Caldas et al. 1998; Poldrak et al. 1998). Therefore, a progressive increase in the degree of left hemisphere specialization of these regions for reading-related processes could be hypothesized that contrasts with oral language, where hemispheric representation predominantly in the left hemisphere of most individuals appears to be established very early in development.

The development of these neural mechanisms mediating word recognition and reading may be much more dependent on experience than oral language. Why else would we have cultures in which people speak but have no orthography, or have illiteracy in a literate society? Thus, most children likely require some form of instruction in order to learn to read. It is likely that when instruction is provided and the child becomes proficient, changes in the areas of the brain that support language will become apparent. Similarly, if a child does not become proficient, what happens at the level of the brain? Do these networks fail to develop at all, develop in different areas of the brain, or show some other form of aberrant development?

Perhaps of greater practical impact is the question of the plasticity of these mechanisms. If specialization has resulted in a functionally aberrant brain circuit for reading, is it possible to change it to a circuit capable of sustaining a functional level of reading skill? An alternative hypothesis would postulate the existence of a critical period for the acquisition of reading skills, beyond which the neural networks supporting reading functions show no plasticity. Any improvement in reading may simply reflect compensatory processes and the engagement of brain other than those seen in typically achieving readers.

A direct approach to the study of cortical specialization of language and reading involves the recording of brain activity during performance of tasks designed to engage the cognitive operations under investigation. Describing the cerebral mechanisms that support reading involves clarifying the exact temporal characteristics and anatomical distribution of neurophysiological activity that reflect inter-neuronal signaling within and between different brain areas. This goal requires:

1. Information regarding brain areas that show increased levels of neurophysiological activation during reading tasks;
2. Real-time data regarding the temporal course of regional activation;
3. Information on how brain activity measures relate to individual performance in these tasks; and
4. Independent confirmation, preferably from invasive functional brain mapping, that areas activated during a particular task are essential for the performance of that task.

In the remainder of this chapter, we discuss a program of research using magnetic source imaging for these purposes. All four goals have been met, along with applications to children and adults varying in age and level of reading proficiency.

FUNCTIONAL NEUROIMAGING STUDIES OF INDIVIDUALS
WITH READING DISABILITIES (RD)

Over the past ten years, significant research activity has occurred in the use of functional neuroimaging to identify the brain mechanisms supporting good and poor reading (Eden and Zeffiro 1998; Pugh, Mencl, Jenner et al. 2000). These studies consistently report decreased activation in the left temporoparietal areas during tasks involving phonological analysis of print (Rumsey et al. 1992, Rumsey et al. 1997; Shaywitz et al. 1998). Studies using functional magnetic resonance imaging (fMRI) and positron emission tomography have been completed, largely with adults. The fMRI studies converge in demonstrating that adults with reading difficulties engage posterior brain regions, including the angular gyrus, the superior temporal gyrus, and striate and extrastriate regions of the occipital lobe to a lesser extent than controls (Eden and Zeffiro 1998; Rumsey et al. 1992; 1997; Shaywitz et al. 1998). Moreover, when compared with non-impaired readers, adults with reading problems may show compensatory hemodynamic changes in tasks that require phonological analysis of print in right temporoparietal areas and in the inferior frontal gyrus (Shaywitz et al. 1998). The presumed reliance on the anterior circuit has not been observed as consistently in children with dyslexia (Shaywitz et al. 2002). Studies using positron emission tomography agree only in part with these findings. Gross-Glenn et al. (1991) and Rumsey et al. (1992, 1997) found reduced activity in left temporoparietal areas in adults with RD during reading tasks. Both studies, however, failed to find evidence of increased involvement of the anterior circuit in adults with dyslexia.

Functional imaging methods, like fMRI, that measure changes in hemodynamics (blood flow), lack the requisite resolution to show the sequence of regional activation in real time. These modalities derive evidence regarding functional interactions among different brain regions involved in reading from cross-correlations in the task-related degree of activation among active regions. Some evidence of reduced functional connectivity between the angular gyrus and temporal lobe areas in the left hemisphere in adults with dyslexia has been found using this method (Pugh, Mencl, Shaywitz et al. 2000). Adults with dyslexia consistently demonstrated disruption in the connectivity of the left hemisphere during tasks that make varying demands on phonological processing. No evidence for such a disruption was noted when visual-orthographic coding was required. Pugh, Mencl, Shaywitz et al. (2000) concluded that when heavy demands for phonological processing are made by the experimental task, a reading circuit that involves right hemisphere areas is engaged to compensate potentially for the disrupted left hemisphere circuit.

MAGNETIC SOURCE IMAGING STUDIES OF DYSLEXIA

More recent studies have examined children with dyslexia. The first reports involved the latest in non-invasive functional imaging techniques, magnetoencephalography, also known as magnetic source imaging (MSI) (Papanicolaou 1998). This modality records the magnetic flux associated with electrical currents in activated sets of neurons. It allows tracking of brain activity in real time. Unlike evoked electrical potentials of the sort recoding in an electroencephalogram, the sources of this activity can be accurately estimated as they are not distorted by differences in conductivity between the brain, skull, and scalp. Deduction of the sources from the measured magnetic field distribution is simple. Both the spatial and temporal aspects of the activity can be determined with remarkable accuracy (0.1 to 1 cm and 1 msec respectively). The location of these activity sources is estimated and co-registered onto structural images of the brain (MRI), which allows for visualization of the activated brain regions (Papanicolaou 1998).

Like other functional neuroimaging, the procedures for imaging with MSI begin with the presentation of auditory or visual stimuli. With MSI, stimulation results in regional increases in neuronal signaling in large neuronal aggregates that, in turn, generate electrical currents and magnetic fields. With recurring presentations of stimuli, these signals can be recorded as evoked potentials and event-related fields (ERFs) on the head surface. The event-related fields, much like evoked potentials, are waveforms that represent temporal variations in brain activity time-locked to the presentation of stimuli. Some of the waveforms occur consistently across different experimental conditions and, as in electrophysiological records, are known as "components." There are two basic components: (a) early, extending up to 150 ms following stimulus onset; and (b) late, lasting several hundred milliseconds after stimulus onset. Early components reflect activation of the primary sensory cortex (Nakasato et al. 1997; Seki et al. 1996). Late components have been shown to reflect activation of the association cortex (Rogers et al. 1991; 1993; Simos, Basile, and Papanicolaou 1997).

Magnetic source imaging fulfills the four criteria proposed above for functional imaging studies of higher cognitive functions. It possesses adequate temporal and anatomical resolution not only to identify which areas of the brain are active, but when in real time these areas are activated. Moreover, there is ample evidence of the concurrent validity of individual MSI protocols and more invasive brains maps from direct, invasive methods. For example, MSI-derived hemispheric asymmetries associated with auditory word recognition representing cerebral dominance for language correspond almost perfectly (over 90% agreement) with the results of a standard invasive procedure used clinically to determine hemispheric dominance (Wada test) in over 80 consecutive epilepsy patients (Breier et al. 1999; Maestu et al. 2002; Papanicolaou et al. in press). A difference is that MSI can be done in almost all patients, while the invasive nature of the Wada test precludes assessment of cerebral dominance for language and other functions in some patients. In addition, we have reported precise concordance between MSI-derived maps of language-specific activity within the dominant hemisphere, and the results of direct electrocortical stimulation for the exact spatial localization of the receptive and expressive language cortex (Castillo et al. 2001; Simos, Breier, Wheless et al. 2000; Simos et al. 1999). Moreover, MSI data regarding the timing of activity in left hemisphere temporal lobe areas correlate strongly with individual performance (reading speed) (Simos, Breier et al. 2002). Keep in mind that in all these studies, results can be based on data from individual participants. There is no need to average across participants or to use subtraction methods as in hemodynamically based methods.

In our laboratory all MSI recordings are made with a multichannel neuromagnetometer (4-D Neuroimaging, Magnes 2500) consisting of 148 magnetometers arranged to cover the entire head. It is housed in a magnetically shielded chamber used to reduce environmental noise that may interfere with the recording of biological signals. Because the typical recording session, during which the participant must remain still, rarely exceeds ten minutes, it is possible both to repeat measurements to establish reliability of results, and to test very young children.

A variety of tasks have been used, including reading of real words, pseudowords, and text. Variables like word frequency, and speed of presentation can also be manipulated. Until recently, all functional brain imaging of the mechanisms for reading (including MSI studies), has been performed long after the potentially critical period of reading acquisition has lapsed. No data were available on the emergence of either the typical or the aberrant brain circuits associated with learning to read. The prevention of reading problems is more desirable and cost-effective than lengthy intervention programs following a delayed diagnosis. Using MSI, the studies described below attempt to map brain regions involved in complex cognitive functions in individual children and adults. The critical question is the identification of typical and aberrant neural mechanisms that support reading across the ranges of age and proficiency.

INITIAL MSI STUDIES

The general outline of the spatio-temporal profile of neurophysiological activity associated with the brain mechanism that supports reading has been described by several MSI studies with both adults and children during the performance of both silent and overt reading tasks (Breier et al. 1998, Breier, Simos, Zouridakis, and Papanicolaou 1999; Simos et al. 2001). In adult readers, this profile features initial activation in the occipital visual areas (within the first 150 ms after the onset of the printed stimulus), followed by activity in the occipito-temporal and ventral temporal cortices (between 150-300 ms predominantly in the left hemisphere), and finally by virtually simultaneous activation of posterior superior temporal, inferior parietal, and sometimes inferior frontal regions (again, predominantly in the left hemisphere). The spatiotemporal activation profile observed in older children without reading difficulties is similar to the one found in adults with one notable exception, namely the lack of the hemispheric asymmetry (left > right) in the degree of activation of visual association areas in the ventral surface of the temporal lobe.

In addition to normative studies of reading in typically achieving children and adults, we have performed MSI studies of children 7 years and older with dyslexia, identified using research-based criteria involving word recognition and phonological processing (Fletcher et al. 1994). For these studies, the activation profiles of children with dyslexia were recorded during tasks that involved silent reading of words and pseudowords (Papanicolaou et al. in press; Simos, Breier, Fletcher et al. 2000; Simos, Fletcher et al. 2000). For example, in Simos, Breier, Fletcher et al. (2000), children viewed four blocks of 25 pseudoword pairs (e.g., "Yoat" and "Wote") and determined whether the stimuli in each pair rhymed. Each pseudoword was shown for 1500 ms with a one-second interval separating the paired words. An inter-stimulus interval ranging from 1500 to 2300 ms separated each pair in a randomly determined order. The words were 4 to 5 letters long and orthographically dissimilar so that comparisons would not be made on the basis of the child's orthographic knowledge.

The brain activation profiles clearly varied with proficiency. For typically achieving readers, the profile paralleled that described above, involving sequential activation of the primary and secondary visual areas about 100 to 150 milliseconds after the pseudowords were presented. Then the basal surface of the temporal lobes was activated for about 150 to 300 milliseconds. Finally, the superior temporal gyrus (STGp), inferior parietal areas (supramarginal and angular gyri), and inferior frontal regions, predominantly in the left hemisphere, were activated almost simultaneously.

For children with dyslexia, the activation patterns are temporally similar, but involve homotopic activation of the same temporoparietal areas in the right hemisphere. The patterns are especially anatomically distinct in the third phase of activation. Thus, there is little activation of the left STGp and inferior parietal areas, with predominant activation of the same regions in the right hemisphere.

Although these results were highly consistent across individual children, they do not address the question of the plasticity of these mechanisms. It is interesting that we obtain essentially normal activation patterns for an auditory word recognition task. This task activates similar areas of the left hemisphere, after engagement of the auditory cortex, as the visual (reading) tasks. These findings imply that these areas of the left hemisphere perform in the manner that would be expected for some non-reading tasks. But are these mechanisms for reading malleable? For example, do they emerge as children learn to read? Do they change when people with dyslexia receive an intense intervention that results in improved proficiency?

In the remainder of this chapter, we review preliminary evidence obtained with MSI that bears on these three interrelated issues: (1) What is the developmental course that leads to the establishment of the activation profile seen in older proficient children and adults? (2) What is the developmental course that leads to the establishment of the aberrant activation profile seen in older children with reading difficulties? (3) To what extent can intervention alter the developmental course of the aberrant activation profile seen in older children with dyslexia?

Study 1. Emergence of activation profiles specific to reading

In our first study, we examined whether the aberrant brain activation profile observed in older children with dyslexia is already present during the early stages of reading acquisition. (For a report of preliminary findings see Simos, Fletcher, Foorman et al. 2002.) Thirty children were identified as at-risk for reading difficulties at the end of kindergarten based on the Texas Primary Reading Inventory (Foorman, Fletcher, and Francis in press) and some additional screening measures. In essence, these children have little knowledge of letter sounds, little development of phonological awareness, and no word reading abilities. These children were compared to 15 children who had good development of letter sound knowledge, phonological awareness, and some ability to read words.

An MSI study was conducted at the end of the kindergarten year while each child performed a letter-sound pronunciation task. This task could be adequately performed by all children, in contrast to word reading tasks that many of the at-risk children could not perform. The at-risk children displayed a markedly different activation profile than the not-at-risk children. This aberrant profile was characterized by the lack of engagement of the posterior portion of the left superior temporal region, and an increase in activation in the homologous right hemisphere region (see figure 1). This profile was very similar to that observed consistently in older children with severe reading difficulties (Simos, Breier, Fletcher et al. 2000; Simos, Fletcher et al. 2000). Timing data, also presented in figure 1, indicated that children in the at-risk group engaged the right superior temporal area soon after the letter stimulus was presented, but that activity in this area may not be sustained long enough to ensure access to the letter-sound representation. These differences are clearly apparent in figure 1 and preceded by several years the age at which formal diagnoses of a reading disability are typically made (Grade 3 and above).

Study 2. Growth of activation profiles specific to reading

A subset of the children who participated in Study 1 was tested one year later after they had completed first grade. All children identified as at-risk received either an enhanced classroom intervention or a small group pull-out intervention in Grade 1, with over 90% showing rapid development of reading ability into the average range (see Denton and Mathes, this volume). Brain activation profiles in the subset who volunteered were obtained using identical procedures as in the previous year. Thus far, data from 10 children in the at-risk group and six children in the not-at-risk group have been collected.

A significant developmental change in the degree of left hemisphere temporoparietal activity was evident in both groups of children, although it appeared to be more pronounced in the atrisk children. This effect was still evident when regional activity was normalized with respect to total brain activity in order to

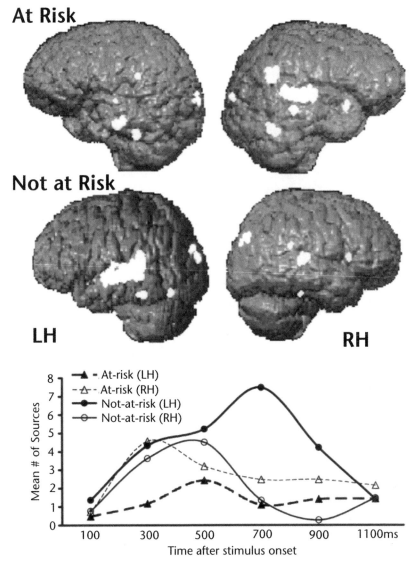

Figure 1.   Upper panel: MSI activation profiles from a typical at-risk child (upper set of images), and from a child in the not-at-risk group (lower set of images), during the letter-sound task. Note the abundance of activity in the left superior temporal gyrus in the latter case and the scarcity of such activity in the former case. Children in the two groups are indistinguishable with respect to activity in any other brain area. Lower panel: Average degree of activity in the left (solid markers) and right superior temporal gyrus (white markers) for the two groups of children as a function of time after the onset of the visual letter stimuli ($n = 30$ for the at-risk and $n = 15$ for the not-at-risk group).

control for potential changes in overall brain activation with maturation (see figure 2). Moreover, the amount of activation in the inferior frontal region was significantly greater in the at risk than in the not-at-risk children, in agreement with fMRI findings (Shaywitz et al. 2002). Despite this reduction, the relative degree of left temporoparietal activity was a significant predictor of letter-sound pronunciation latencies in kindergarten and first grade, F (1, 15) = 17.43, $p < .001$, $R2 = .52$. Adding the degree of right temporoparietal activation did not significantly improve the prediction of change, F (1, 15) = 9.75, $p < .003$, $R2 = .54$. As figure 2 shows, the activation profiles of the at-risk children have shifted to patterns that predominantly involve the left hemisphere and resemble those of the not-at-risk children.

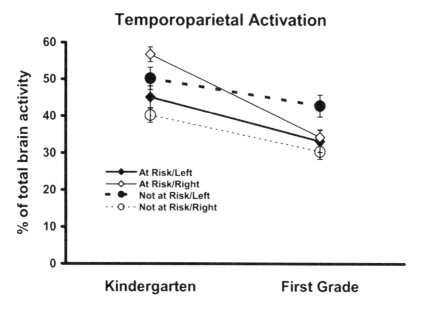

Figure 2.   Average degree of activity in the left and right superior temporal and supramarginal gyri (temporoparietal cortex) in the group of children at risk for developing reading problems (solid lines) and in the not-at-risk group (dashed lines). Longitudinal data from a total of 16 children were obtained at the end of kindergarten and one year later at the end of first grade. The degree of activity was adjusted with respect to activity in the entire brain to control for potential age-related differences in overall brain activity. Notice the reduction in left temporoparietal activity and the less pronounced decrease in activation of the right temporoparietal region. These changes appear to be more pronounced in children who had mastered key pre-reading skills at the end of kindergarten. Vertical bars represent standard error of the mean.

Study 3. Plasticity of reading-related activation profiles in older dyslexic children

If difficulty in mentally converting print into sound representations is associated with failure to engage the left temporoparietal region, then intense training focusing on the development of these skills should lead to the establishment of function to this area in association with significant improvement in reading skills. Eight children (aged 8–17 years) were scanned while performing a pseudoword reading task before and after a reading intervention (Simos, Fletcher et al. 2002). Following the results of a study by Torgesen et al. (2001), in which severely disabled readers showed marked improvement with 8 weeks of intense intervention, we provided up to 80 hours of one-to-one instruction using either the Lindamood Phonemic Sequencing ($n = 2$; Lindamood and Lindamood 1998) or Phono-graphix ($n = 6$; McGuiness and McGuiness 1998) programs in an 8 week period. Both interventions focused on the development of phonological decoding skills. Before enrolling in the intervention program, all eight children had decoding skills below the 19th percentile (actually below the 3rd percentile in 6 of the 8 participants). At baseline, MSI showed the typical "dyslexia-specific" profile featuring little or no activity in left superior temporal areas and strong activation of homotopic areas in the right hemisphere (see figure 3). In all 8 cases, the intervention resulted in marked improvement in phonological decoding abilities (range = 38th–60th percentile), paired with a dramatic increase in left superior temporal lobe activation and a moderate decline in activation of the corresponding right hemisphere areas. These results support the idea that intervention results in the normalization of aberrant brain patterns, reflecting the influence of the environment (instruction) as necessary in these children to establish the neural mechanisms supporting word recognition. They suggest that the patterns seen in children and adults with dyslexia are compensatory, but valuable.

CONCLUSIONS AND IMPLICATIONS

Based on the findings from the three studies outlined above, the following conclusions can be derived. First, the vast majority of children with serious reading problems show, during engagement in reading tasks, a distinct brain activation profile that is uncom-

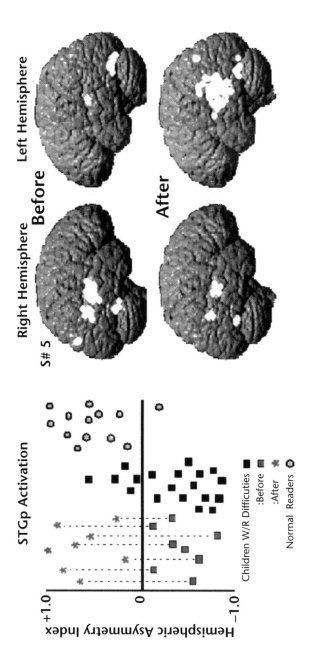

Figure 3. Left: The distribution of individual hemispheric asymmetry indices (Left -Right) / (Left + Right) for the degree of activation in the superior temporal gyrus for children who experience severe reading difficulties (squares) and fluent readers (open circles) during performance of the pseudoword reading task. The scores of the eight children in the former group, who successfully completed an 8-week intensive instruction program, are represented by stippled squares (before instruction) linked with asterisks (after instruction). Note the shift of asymmetry indices from negative to positive values reflecting the marked increase in left superior temporal gyrus activation in all cases. All eight children showed dramatic improvement in their phonological decoding skills after receiving 8 weeks of intensive remedial instruction. Right: Individual activation maps from a representative case, a 10-year old child, scanned before and after instruction using the Phonographix program

mon among children who have never experienced reading difficulties. It remains to be seen if this profile is independent of other
conditions, such as attention deficit/hyperactivity disorder
(ADHD) or other forms of learning disability that show a high degree of comorbidity with dyslexia. However, the pattern is seen in
individuals with dyslexia regardless of comorbid ADHD or math
disability. Second, this profile is observed in a variety of tasks that
involve phonological decoding regardless of whether the task involves reading of real words or pseudowords. Third, it appears that
neurophysiological activity in the left superior temporal regions,
as revealed by MSI, reflected the engagement of brain operations
that are indispensable components of the brain mechanism for
reading. If these operations are not engaged properly, as in the
case of dyslexia or young children learning to read, reading performance and the capacity to acquire reading skills is severely compromised. There are strong indications that these operations are
predominantly involved in phonological processing of print.
Fourth, the aberrant neural circuit that underlies severe reading
problems in older children with dyslexia appears to be present
during the early stages of reading acquisition, at a much earlier age
than previously believed. Fifth, individual differences in the degree of specialization of the left temporoparietal region account
for a significant proportion of individual variability in mastering
alphabetic knowledge. Sixth, systematic reading instruction that
promotes the development of phonological awareness and decoding skills can drastically alter the aberrant activation profile found
in children with dyslexia and those at-risk of reading difficulties.

These findings have important implications for current views
regarding the pathophysiology and optimal management of
dyslexia. Brain imaging data from children at the end of kindergarten show that it is possible to detect signs of an aberrant brain
circuit responsible for reading before the level of actual ability in
reading is established. The fact that neural signs of dyslexia are
present very early in the reading acquisition process highlights the
importance of early intervention. They also imply that instruction
plays a critical role in establishing the brain mechanisms necessary
for proficient reading.

Our findings are also consistent with current cognitive models of reading acquisition and dyslexia, pointing to the critical role
of basic knowledge of the correspondence between letters and
sounds in learning to read. The results concur with views of reading as a trait that is normally and quantitatively distributed in the
population (Shaywitz et al. 1992). Thus, reading difficulties most
likely represent variations in normal development as opposed to a

specific pathological condition. Moreover, reading difficulties in many individuals can be overcome by intervention that is sufficiently intense. When successful intervention occurs, our evidence suggests that neural systems are altered and that these neural systems are much more plastic than was believed in the past.

Finally, the results have important implications for views of neural plasticity as well as views of how environmental factors impact the brain. According to one hypothesis, recruitment of brain areas already specialized for linguistic operations occurs naturally during the early stages of reading acquisition. This hypothesis predicts that little, if any, change is evident in the degree of activity in left temporoparietal regions as children master the alphabetic principle. According to an alternative hypothesis, recruitment of cortical areas that are already specialized for linguistic processing is a time-intensive process that requires extensive experience with print. This hypothesis predicts a significant increase in the engagement of left temporoparietal areas during the primary grades. Our data (Studies 1 and 2) partially supports the former hypothesis. Areas such as the superior temporal gyrus and the supramarginal gyrus in the left hemisphere are also involved in the phonological processing of aural language, as predicted by this hypothesis. Even children who initially experience difficulties in mastering essential skills that are precursors of reading ability (such as knowledge of letter sounds) typically show dramatic changes in the degree of commitment of left temporoparietal areas. When tested at the end of first grade, the brain activation profiles of these children become virtually indistinguishable from those of children never considered to be at risk for developing reading problems.

Although preliminary, the data presented here suggest that instruction like that provided in many classrooms is sufficient to promote development of a "normal" brain circuit that supports reading. However, in a smaller proportion of children, this process does not take place in the regular classroom and the brain circuit that is specialized for reading does not emerge. In those cases, intense remedial instruction that promotes the development of decoding and word recognition skills may jumpstart the normal maturation process of functional brain specialization. Although it is common to describe the children and adults who are poor readers as "disabled," the fact that our preliminary data suggests that the brain activation profiles associated with poor reading are malleable and change with instruction may indicate that instruction plays a significant role in the development of neural systems that are specialized for reading.

In our studies, good instruction, as provided by classroom teachers as well as by teachers who were provided additional professional development in supplemental and remedial approaches to reading instruction, resulted in functional neural changes. Such a result is hardly surprising because learning has occurred and the brain should change in ways that reflect this learning. Two aspects of these findings stand out. First, MSI is sensitive to these dynamic changes in brain function on a case-by-case basis. Second, good instruction is always brain-based. The interventions focused on the elements critical to learning to read (phonologic and alphabetic skills and practice reading text) and was provided by teachers in school settings. Under these conditions, effective instruction appeared to change the brain in ways essential to support the task of learning to read.

ACKNOWLEDGMENTS

Supported in part by NICHD Grant HD38346-01, and NSF Grant REC-9979968 to Dr. Papanicolaou.

REFERENCES

Blachman, B. A. 1997. Early intervention and phonological awareness: A cautionary tale. In *Foundations of Reading Acquisition and Dyslexia: Implications for Early Intervention*, ed. B. A. Blachman,. Mahwah, NJ: Lawrence Erlbaum Associates.

Breier, J. I., Simos, P. G, Zouridakis, G., Wheless, J. W., Willmore, L. J., Constantinou, J. E., and Papanicolaou, A. C. 1999. Language dominance determined by magnetic source imaging: A comparison with the Wada procedure. *Neurology* 53:938–45.

Breier, J. I., Simos, P. G., Zouridakis, G., and Papanicolaou, A. C. 1998. Relative timing of neuronal activity in distinct temporal lobe areas during a recognition memory task for words. *Journal of Clinical and Experimental Neuropsychology* 20:782–90.

Breier, J. I., Simos, P. G., Zouridakis, G., and Papanicolaou, A. C. 1999. Temporal course of regional brain activation associated with phonological decoding. *Journal of Clinical and Experimental Neuropsychology* 21:465–76.

Castillo, E. M., Simos, P. G., Venkataraman, V., Breier, J. I., Wheless, J. W. 2001. Mapping of expressive language cortex using Magnetic Source Imaging. *Neurocase* 7:419–22.

Castro-Caldas, A., Peterson, K. M., Reis, A., Stone-Elander, S., and Ingvar, M. 1998. The illiterate brain. Learning to read and write during childhood influences the functional organization of the adult brain. *Brain* 121:1053–63.

Dennis, M. 1988. Language in the young damaged brain. In *Clinical Neuropsychology and Brain Function* (APA Master Lecture Series) eds. T. Boll and B. K. Bryant. Washington DC: APA.

Eden G. F., and Zeffiro T. A. 1998. Neural systems affected in developmental dyslexia revealed by functional neuroimaging. *Neuron* 21:279–82.

Entus, A. K. 1977. Hemispheric asymmetry in processing of dichotic ally presented speech and nonspeech sounds in infants. In *Language Development and Neurological Theory*, eds. S. J. Segalowitz and F. A. Gruber, New York: Academic Press.

Fletcher, J. M., Shaywitz, S. E., Shankweiler, D. P., Katz, L., Liberman, I. Y., Stuebing, K. K., Francis, D. J., Fowler, A., and Shaywitz, B. A. 1994. Cognitive profiles of reading disability: Comparisons of discrepancy and low achievement definitions. *Journal of Educational Psychology* 85:1–18.

Foorman, B. F., Fletcher, J. M., and Francis, D. J. in press. Early reading assessment. In *Testing American's School Children*, ed. W. Evans, Stanford: Hoover Press.

Gross-Glenn, K., Duara, R., Barker, W. W., Loewenstein, D., Chang, J. Y., Yoshii, F., Apicella, A. M., Pascal, S., Boothe, T., Sevush, S. 1991. Positron emission tomographic studies during serial word-reading by normal and dyslexic adults. *Archives of Neurology* 13:531–44.

Hahn, W. K. 1987. Cerebral lateralization of function: From infancy through childhood. Psychological Review 101:376–92.

Hiscock, M. 1988. Behavioral asymmetries in normal children. In *Brain Lateralization in Children*, Eds. D. L. Molfese and S. J. Segalowitz. New York: Guilford.

Liberman, A. M. 1998. Why is speech so much easier than reading? In *Reading and Spelling: Development and Disorders*, eds. C. Hulme and Joshi R. M. Malatesha. Mahwah, NJ: Lawrence Erlbaum Associates.

Lindamood, P. and Lindamood, G. 1998. *The Lindamood Phoneme Sequencing Program (3rd ed.)*. Austin, TX: PRO-ED.

Lukatela, G., and Turvey, M. T. 1998. Reading in two alphabets. *American Psychologist* 53:1057–72.

Maestu, F., Ortiz, T., Fernandez, A., Amo, C., Martin, P., Fernandez, S., Sola, R. G. 2002. Spanish language mapping using MEG: A validation study. *Neuroimage* 17:1579–86.

McGuiness, C., and McGuiness, G. 1998. *Reading Reflex*. New York, NY: Simon and Schuster.

Molfese, D. L., and Betz, J. C. 1988. Electrophysiological indices of the early development of lateralization for language and cognition, and their implications for predicting later development. In *Brain Lateralization in Children*, eds. D. L. Molfese and S. J. Segalowitz, New York: Guilford.

Nakasato, N., Kumabe, T., Kanno, A., Ohtomo, S., Mizoi, K., and Yoshimoto, T. 1997. Neuromagnetic evaluation of cortical auditory function in patients with temporal lobe tumors. *Journal of Neurosurgery* 86:610–18.

Papanicolaou, A. C. 1998. *Fundamentals of Functional Brain Imaging*. Lisse, The Netherlands: Swets and Zeitlinger.

Papanicolaou, A. C., Simos, P. G., Breier, J. I., et al. In press. MEG: A method comparable to the Wada procedure for language laterality assessment. *Epilepsia*.

Papanicolaou, A. C., Simos, P. G., Breier, J. I., Fletcher, J. M., Foorman, B. R., Francis, D. J., Castillo, E. M., and Davis, R. In press. Brain mechanisms for reading in children with and without dyslexia: A review of studies of normal development and plasticity. *Developmental Neuropsychology*.

Poldrak, R. A., Desmond, J. E., Glover, G. H., and Gabrieli, J. D. 1998. The neural basis of visual skill learning: An fMRI study of mirror reading. *Cerebral Cortex* 8:1–10.

Pugh, K. R., Jenner, A. R., Mencl, W. E, et al. submitted. Contrasting silent word recognition with overt pronunciation of printed words and pseudowords.

Pugh, K. R., Mencl, W. E., Jenner, A. R., Katz, L., Frost, S. J., Lee, J. R., Shaywitz, S. E., and Shaywitz, B. A. 2000. Functional neuroimaging studies of reading and reading disability (developmental dyslexia). *Mental Retardation and Developmental Disability Research* 6:207–13.

Pugh, K. R., Mencl, W. E., Shaywitz B. A., Shaywitz S. E., Fulbright R. K., Constable R. T. Skudlarski, P., Marchione, K. E., Jenner A. R., Fletcher, J. M., Liberman, A. M., Shankweiler, D. P., Lacadie, C. and Gore, J. C. 2000 The angular gyrus in developmental dyslexia: task-specific differences in functional connectivity within posterior cortex. *Psychological Science* 11:51–6.

Rogers, R. L., Basile, L. F., Papanicolaou, A. C., and Eisenberg, H. M. 1993. Magnetoencephalography reveals two distinct sources associated with late positive evoked potentials during visual oddball task. *Cerebral Cortex* 3:163–69.

Rogers, R. L., Baumann, S. B., Papanicolaou, A. C., Bourbon, T. W., Alagarsamy, S., and Eisenberg, H. M. 1991. Localization of the P3 sources using magneto- encephalography and magnetic resonance imaging. *Electroencephalography and Clinical Neurophysiology* 79:308–21.

Rumsey, J. M, Andreason, P., Zametkin, A. J., Aquino, T., King, A. C., Hamburger, S. D., Pikus, A., Rapoport, J. L., and Cohen, R. M. 1992. Failure to activate the left temporoparietal cortex in dyslexia. An oxygen-15 positron emission tomographic study. *Archives of Neurology* 49:527–34.

Rumsey, J. M., Nace, K., Donahue, B., Wise, D., Maisog, J. G., and Andreason, P. 1997. A positron emission tomographic study of impaired word recognition and phonological processing in dyslexic men. *Archives of Neurology* 54:562–73.

Seki, K., Nakasato, N., Fujita, S., Hatanaka, K., Kawamura, T., Kanno, A., and Yoshimoto, T. 1996. Neuromagnetic evidence that the P100 component of the pattern reversal visual evoked response originates in the bottom of the calcarine fissure. *Electroencephalography and Clinical Neurophysiology* 100:436–42.

Shavelson, R. J. and Towne, L. 2002. *Scientific Research in Education*. National Research Council. Washington, DC: National Academy Press.

Shaywitz, S. E., Escobar, M. D., Shaywitz, B. A., Fletcher, J. M., Makuch, R. 1992. Evidence that dyslexia may represent the lower tail of normal distribution of reading ability. *New England Journal of Medicine* 326: 145–50.

Shaywitz, B., Shaywitz, S., Pugh, K. R., Mencl, W. E., Fulbright, R. K., Skudlarski, P., Constable, R. T., Marchione, K. E., Fletcher, J. M., Lyon, G. R., and Gore, J. C. 2002. Disruption of posterior brain systems in children with developmental dyslexia. *Biological Psychiatry* 52:101–10.

Shaywitz, S. E., Shaywitz, B. A., Pugh, K. R., Fulbright, R. K., Constable, R. T., Mencl, W. E., Shankweiler, D. P., Liberman, A. M., Skudlarski, P., Fletcher, J. M., et al. 1998. Functional disruption in the organization of the brain for reading in dyslexia. *Proceedings of the National Academy of Science* 95:2636-41.

Simos, P. G., Basile, L. F., and Papanicolaou, A. C. 1997. Source localization of the N400 response in a sentence-reading paradigm using evoked magnetic fields and magnetic resonance imaging. *Brain Research* 762:29–39.

Simos, P. G., Breier, J. I., Fletcher, J. M., Bergman, E., and Papanicolaou, A. C. 2000. Cerebral mechanisms involved in word reading in dyslexic children: A Magnetic Source Imaging approach. Cerebral Cortex 10:809–16.

Simos, P. G., Breier, J. I., Fletcher, J. M., Foorman, B. R., Castillo, E. M., and Papanicolaou, A. C. 2002a. Brain mechanisms for reading words and pseudowords: An integrated approach. *Cerebral Cortex* 12:297–305.

Simos, P. G., Breier, J. I., Fletcher, J. M., Foorman, B. R., Mouzaki, A., and Papanicolaou, A. C. 2001. Age-related changes in regional brain activation during phonological decoding and printed word recognition. *Developmental Neuropsychology* 19:191–210.

Simos, P. G., Breier, J. I., Wheless, J. W., Maggio, W. W., Fletcher, J. M., Castillo, E. M., and Papanicolaou, A. C. 2000. Brain mechanisms for reading: The role of the superior temporal gyrus in word and pseudoword naming. *NeuroReport* 11:2443–7.

Simos, P. G., Fletcher, J. M., Bergman, E., Breier, J. I., Foorman, B. R., Castillo, E. M., Davis, R. N., Fitzgerald, M., and Papanicolaou, A. C. 2002. Dyslexia-specific brain activation profile becomes normal following successful remedial training. *Neurology* 58:1203–13.

Simos, P. G., Fletcher, J. M., Foorman, B. R., Francis, D. J., Castillo, E. M., Davis, R. N., Fitzgerald, M., Mathes, P. G., Denton, C., and Papanicolaou, A. C. 2002. Brain activation profiles during the early stages of reading acquisition. *Journal of Child Neurology* 17:159–63.

Simos, P. G., Papanicolaou, A. C., Breier, J. I., Fletcher, J. M., Foorman, B. R., Bergman, E., Fishbeck, K., and Papanicolaou, A. C. 2000. Brain activation profiles in dyslexic children during nonword reading: A magnetic source imaging study. *Neuroscience Letters* 290:61–65.

Simos, P. G., Papanicolaou, A. C., Breier, J. I., Wheless, J. W., Constantinou, J. E. C., Gormley, W. B., and Maggio, W. W. 1999. Localization of language-specific cortex by using magnetic source imaging and electrical stimulation mapping. *Journal of Neurosurgery* 91:787–96.

Stanovich, K. E. 2000. *Progress in Understanding Reading: Scientific Foundations and New Frontiers.* New York, NY: Guilford Press.

St. James-Roberts, I. 1979. Neurological plasticity, recovery from brain insult, and child development. In *Advances in Research on Child Development,* ed. H. W. Reese, (Vol. 14). New York: Academic Press.

Torgesen, J. K., Alexander, A. W., Wagner, R. K., Rashotte, C. A., et al. 2001. Intensive remedial instruction for children with severe reading disabilities: Immediate and long-term outcomes from two instructional approaches. *Journal of Learning Disabilities* 34:33–58.

Chapter • 2

Development and Promotion of Emergent Literacy Skills in Children At-Risk of Reading Difficulties

Christopher J. Lonigan

Learning to read is an important milestone in children's development. Reading skills provide a critical foundation for children's academic success. Children who read well read more and, as a result, acquire more knowledge in numerous domains (Cunningham and Stanovich 1998; Echols et al. 1996; Morrison, Smith, and Dow-Ehrensberger 1995). Nagy and Anderson (1984, p. 328) estimated that the number of words read in a year by a middle-school child who is an avid reader might approach 10,000,000, compared to 100,000 for the least motivated middle-school reader. By virtue of the sheer volume read, increased knowledge of the vocabulary and content domains (e.g., science or history) included in the texts would be expected. In contrast, children who lag behind in their reading skills receive less practice in reading than other children (Allington 1984), miss opportunities to develop reading comprehension strategies (Brown, Palincsar, and Purcell 1986), often encounter reading material that is too advanced for their skills (Allington 1984), and acquire negative attitudes about reading itself (Oka and Paris 1986). Such processes may lead to what Stanovich (e.g., 1986) has termed a "Matthew effect," (i.e., the rich get richer while the poor get poorer). Those children with poor reading skills fall further and further behind their more literate peers in reading as well as in other academic areas (Chall, Jacobs, and Baldwin 1990), which become increasingly dependent on reading across the school years.

Children with limited reading-related skills rarely catch-up to their peers (Baydar, Brooks-Gunn, and Furstenberg 1993; Stevenson and Newman 1986; Torgesen et al. 1997; Tramontana, Hooper, and Selzer 1988) and many continue to experience difficulties throughout their school years and into adulthood. Juel (1988), for instance, reported that the probability that children would remain poor readers at the end of the fourth grade if they were poor readers at the end of the first grade was .88. Children who are poor readers are frequently referred to special education classes (Lentz 1988), and of those who experience the most serious reading problems, 10 to 15% drop out of high school, and only 2% complete a four-year college program. Surveys of adolescents and young adults with criminal records and/or histories of substance abuse report that about 50% have reading difficulties (NICHD 2000).

EMERGENT LITERACY AND RISK FOR READING DIFFICULTIES

Emergent literacy includes the skills, knowledge, and attitudes that are presumed to be developmental precursors to conventional forms of reading and writing (Whitehurst and Lonigan 1998). From an emergent literacy perspective, reading, writing, and oral language skills are seen as developing concurrently and share an interdependent relationship from an early age even in the absence of formal literacy instruction. Consequently, an emergent literacy perspective views "pre-reading" behavior occurring during the preschool years as authentic and legitimate aspects of literacy. This chapter focuses on three domains of emergent literacy skills: oral language, phonological sensitivity, and print awareness. These skills both develop during the preschool period and have predictive links to later reading acquisition.

An increasing number of children enter kindergarten classrooms with low levels of emergent literacy skills in the areas of oral language, phonological processing, and print knowledge, primarily because the home and preschools where they spend most of their time do not provide optimal support for the development of these skills. Moreover, the problem is compounded by risk factors such as poverty, community violence, racial discrimination, and adult illiteracy. Children from low-income families are at high risk for reading difficulties (Dubrow and Ipolito 1994; Juel et al. 1986; Smith and Dixon 1995). They are likely to be slow in developing oral language skills (Juel, Griffith, and Gough 1986; Hart and Risley 1996; Lonigan and Whitehurst 1998; Whitehurst 1996), letter knowledge, and phonological processing skills prior to school entry (Bowey 1995; MacLean, Bryant, and Bradley 1987). These socio-economic status (SES) linked differences in phonological processing skills are related to later differences in children's word decoding skills (e.g., Raz and Bryant 1990).

Emergent literacy skills other than oral language, phonological processing, and print knowledge have been described in the literature, including understanding the conventions of print (e.g., left-to-right and top-to-bottom orientation of print, difference between pictures and print on a page; Clay 1979) and the functions of print (e.g., that print tells a story or gives directions; Purcell-Gates 1996; Purcell-Gates and Dahl 1991), faculty with environmental print (e.g., recognizing product names from signs and logos), as well as emergent reading and emergent writing (i.e., pretending to read or write; Pappas and Brown 1988; Purcell-Gates 1988; Sulzby 1986, 1988). However, evidence for the independence or predictive significance of these abilities is either negative or currently lacking. That is, although these abilities are sometimes associated with later reading when considered in isolation, research either has not generally supported a direct causal link between them and later decoding skills (Gough 1993; Masonheimer, Drum, and Ehri 1984) or has found that these behaviors appear to be better conceptualized as proxy measures for letter knowledge, phonological sensitivity, and oral language, and more exposure to print and other literacy-related activities (e.g., Lonigan, Burgess, and Anthony 2000; Purcell-Gates 1996).

Oral Language Skills. Reading is a process of translating visual codes (i.e., text) into meaningful language. In the earliest stages, reading in an alphabetic writing system involves decoding letters into corresponding sounds and linking those sounds to single words. In more advanced stages, reading involves a complex synthesis of linguistic meaning from both intra- and inter-textual sources of information. There are clear links between vocabulary, oral linguistic skills, and all levels of a child's reading development. The National Research Council (Snow, Burns, and Griffin 1998) maintained that most reading problems could be prevented by, among other things, increasing children's oral language skills, and the National Reading Panel (NICHD 2000) concluded that "vocabulary is critically important in oral reading instruction." Empirical research supports these conclusions by demonstrating positive correlations between individual differences in oral language skills and later differences in reading (e.g., Bishop and Adams 1990; Pikulski and Tobin 1989). Children who have larger vocabularies and greater understanding of spoken language have higher reading scores.

The connection between oral language and reading appears to depend on the child's developmental levels in both language development and literacy. Studies indicate that children's vocabulary skills have a significant impact on decoding skills early in the process of learning to read, but that the influence of vocabulary fades with development (e.g., Wagner et al. 1997). Vocabulary skill also appears to be related to the acquisition of phonological sensitivity, as defined below, in both preschool (Burgess and Lonigan 1998; Chaney 1992; Lonigan et al. 2000; Lonigan, Burgess, Anthony, and Barker 1998) and early elementary school children (e.g., Bowey 1994; Wagner et al. 1993; Wagner et al. 1997), suggesting that vocabulary development sets the stage for the emergence of phonological sensitivity (Fowler 1991; Metsala 1999; Metsala and Walley 1998).

In contrast to young children's vocabulary skills, their semantic and syntactic abilities are most likely to be important later in the sequence of learning to read, when children are reading for meaning (e.g., see Gillon and Dodd 1994; Mason 1992; Share and Silva 1982;(in references as 1987) Snow et al. 1991; Tunmer and Hoover 1992; Tunmer, Herriman, and Nesdale 1988; Vellutino, Scanlon, and Tanzman 1991). Dickinson and colleagues (e.g., Dickinson and Snow 1987; Dickinson and Tabors 1991; Snow 1983) have proposed also that children's understanding of text and story narratives is facilitated by the acquisition of decontextualized language (i.e., language used to convey novel information to audiences who may share only limited background knowledge with the speaker or who may be physically removed from the things or events described).

For older children, the relation between reading and language comprehension is direct and bi-directional. Children with more semantic knowledge are better able to comprehend what they are reading (Gillon and Dodd 1994; Mason 1992; Snow et al. 1991; Tunmer and Hoover 1992), and those who read more frequently and fluently develop larger vocabularies and more conceptual and factual knowledge (Cunningham and Stanovich 1998). Thus, for older children, reading generates knowledge, and knowledge supports reading comprehension.

Phonological Processing Skills. Phonological processing plays a key role in the acquisition of reading and spelling in alphabetic languages. Phonological processing is the sensitivity to, manipulation of, or use of the sounds in words, and it involves three interrelated abilities: phonological sensitivity, phonological access, and phonological memory (Adams 1990; Wagner and Torgesen 1987). *Phonological sensitivity* is the ability to detect and manipulate the sounds in oral language. This is apparent in a child's ability to identify words that rhyme, blend spoken syllables or phonemes together to form a word, delete syllables or phonemes from spoken words to form a new word, or count the number of phonemes in a spoken word. Phonological sensitivity can develop without any exposure to print or letters, and it progresses from sensitivity to large and concrete units of sound (e.g., syllables) to small and abstract units of sound (phonemes) (Adams 1990; Anthony et al. 2002; Lonigan et al. 1998; 2000). *Phonological memory* refers to short-term memory for sound-based information (Baddeley 1986) and is measured by immediate recall of verbally presented material. *Phonological access* is the efficiency of retrieval of phonological information from permanent memory. Evidence from a significant body of research indicates that there is a core phonological deficit in most poor readers, and there are often deficits in other reading-related skills (e.g., vocabulary) depending on how discrepant their reading level is from their general cognitive and academic functioning (Stanovich and Siegel 1994).

Print Knowledge. Knowledge of the alphabet at school entry is one of the single best predictors of eventual reading achievement (Adams 1990; Stevenson and Newman 1986). In alphabetic writing systems, decoding text involves the translation of units of print (graphemes) to units of sound (phonemes), and writing involves translating units of sound into units of print. At the most basic level, this task requires the ability to distinguish letters. A beginning reader who cannot recognize and distinguish letters of the alphabet will have difficulty learning the sounds those letters represent (Bond and Dykstra 1967; Mason 1980). In addition to its direct role in facilitating text decoding, letter knowledge plays a role in the development of phonological sensitivity, both prior to and after the initiation of formal reading instruction. Higher levels of letter knowledge are associated with children's abilities to detect and manipulate phonemes (Bowey 1994; Stahl and Murray 1994). Wagner, Torgesen, and Rashotte (1994; Wagner et al. 1997) found that individual differences in kindergarten and first grade children's letter knowledge were significantly predictive of growth in phonological sensitivity over a one- to two-year period. Likewise, Burgess and Lonigan (1998) found that preschool children's letter knowledge was a unique predictor of growth in phonological sensitivity across one year.

Development of Phonological Processing Skills

Compared to the sizable body of research supporting the significance of phonological processing abilities, print knowledge, and oral language for the development of reading in grade school children (e.g., Metsala and Ehri 1998; Snow, Burns, and Griffin. 1998), there has been far less systematic research concerning the development and predictive utility of these emergent literacy skills in preschool children. However, an emerging body of evidence highlights that phonological processing abilities and print knowledge are present during the preschool period (Chaney 1992; Lonigan et al. 1998), are stable individual differences from the late-preschool period forward (Burgess and Lonigan 1998; Lonigan, Burgess, and Anthony 2000; Wagner et al. 1997), and are predictive of beginning reading and spelling (Lonigan, Burgess, and Anthony 2000; MacLean, Bryant, and Bradley 1987).

Almost all research on phonological processing skills in preschool children has examined phonological sensitivity. The question of the significance of children's early phonological sensitivity for later reading is complicated by controversy concerning the structure and significance of preschool phonological sensitivity. For instance, several authors have argued that various tasks designed to measure phonological sensitivity tap separate and independent abilities (e.g., Muter et al. 1997; Muter and Snowling 1998; Yopp 1988). Advocates of this separate phonological abilities model generally stress the importance of phoneme manipulation skills (i.e., phonemic awareness) in literacy because it is at the level of the phoneme that graphemes correspond to speech sounds and because individual phonemes do not have separable physical reality (e.g., Liberman et al. 1967; Morais 1991; Nation and Hulme 1997; Tunmer and Rohl 1991). Significantly, this narrow conceptualization of phonological awareness excludes those skills that involve manipulation of linguistic units larger than a phoneme and those skills that involve detection rather than production or manipulation of phonological information (e.g., Morais 1991).

The significance of this debate for the study of emergent literacy is that phonological sensitivity tasks that involve manipulation of phonemes are too difficult for the majority of preschool children. In contrast, supraphoneme sensitivity tasks that involve detection or manipulation of larger linguistic units (e.g., syllables, onset-rime) are within the developmental capacities of many preschool children (Lonigan et al. 1998). We have addressed this issue in a number of studies (Anthony and Lonigan 2002; Anthony et al. 2002). In several samples of 2- to 6-year-old children, we used confirmatory factor analysis (CFA) to compare plausible theoretical and atheoretical model variations that could account for children's performance across tasks that required children to detect, blend, or elide words, syllables, onset-rimes, or phonemes. These analyses have indicated that a single-factor model provides an accurate characterization of the data (see Schatschneider et al. 1999, for a similar result using a different methodology). The conclusion supported by these analyses is that all of these tasks—regardless of level of linguistic complexity or operation involved—are indicators of the same underlying ability. The results support a developmental conceptualization of phonological sensitivity in which children's phonological sensitivity develops in a progressive fashion with sensitivity to smaller and smaller units of sound across the preschool period (Adams 1990).

Beyond structural studies of preschool phonological sensitivity, a number of studies have examined the predictive utility of phonological sensitivity for young children's early reading abilities. These studies have demonstrated that children's early phonological sensitivity is predictive of beginning reading and spelling (Bradley and Bryant 1985; Bryant et al. 1990; Goswami 1986; Goswami and Bryant 1990 1992; Lonigan, Burgess, and Anthony 2000; MacLean, Bryant, and Bradley 1987). For example, Lonigan et al. (Lonigan, Burgess, and Anthony 2000) examined the distinctiveness and predictive significance of phonological sensitivity, print knowledge, and oral language in a one-year longitudinal study of 2- to 5-year-old children from higher SES backgrounds. All children completed phonological sensitivity measures, tests of oral language, tests of print awareness, and other emergent literacy measures (e.g., concepts about print) at an initial assessment and 12 to 18 months after the initial assessment. The older group of children also completed two measures of single-word decoding at the follow-up. At each assessment, and for older and younger groups of children, CFAs supported the distinctiveness of different emergent literacy and literacy domains (i.e., phonological sensitivity, oral language, print awareness, decoding). Structural equation modeling revealed moderate levels of developmental continuity in emergent literacy skills from early preschool to late preschool and high levels of developmental continuity in these skills from the late preschool period (i.e., age 4) to early-grade school (i.e., kindergarten and first grade; see table I). For older preschoolers, a phonological sensitivity latent variable predicted approximately 50% of

Table I   Correlations of preschool emergent literacy skills with emergent literacy and decoding skills in kindergarten and first grade

	Time 2 Variables	Letter Knowledge	Reading	Concepts of Print
Phonological Sensitivity	1.00	.48	.60	.44
Environmental Print	.59	.42	.51	.18
Letter Knowledge	.64	.80	.51	.37
Concepts of Print	.60	.35	.40	.62

Note. $N = 96$; all variables, except the Concepts of Print variable, were represented as latent variables; all correlations were significant at $p < .01$; adapted from Lonigan, Burgess, and Anthony (2000).

the variance in text decoding skills measured when the children were 5 and 6 years of age. A letter knowledge latent variable was the only other emergent literacy skill that added to the prediction of decoding. These results highlight the importance of both phonological sensitivity and print knowledge for the development of later reading skills.

CHILDREN AT-RISK FOR READING DIFFICULTIES

The studies summarized above demonstrate that preschool emergent literacy skills—particularly phonological sensitivity—are powerful and unique predictors of later decoding skills in children from higher SES families. Children from lower SES families are at significant risk of reading difficulties. Evidence suggests that low levels of emergent literacy skills represent significant risk factors for later reading difficulties in children from lower SES families. A substantial body of evidence indicates that there are sizable differences in oral language skills between children from lower SES families and their higher SES counterparts. In part, this discrepancy in oral language skills appears to be related to a paucity of language stimulation in the homes of children from lower SES families (Hart and Risley 1996).

Several studies have highlighted SES-linked differences in phonological sensitivity skills that place children from lower SES families at-risk of reading difficulties (Bowey 1995; Raz and Bryant 1990). In a cross-sectional study (Lonigan et al. 1998), we compared the performance of 250 children from higher income families to 170 children from lower income families on measures of phonological sensitivity. All of the children were between the ages of two and five years, and all children completed four tests of phonological sensitivity that assessed their ability to detect, blend, or elide words, syllables, onset-rimes, or phonemes as well as measures of oral language ability (e.g., *Peabody Picture Vocabulary Test— Revised, Expressive One-Word Picture Vocabulary Test—Revised*). Because of significant differences on the oral language measures, analyses examined language-corrected scores on the phonological sensitivity measures. Data from two of the phonological sensitivity tasks for children from the higher and lower SES groups are presented in figure 1. Two conclusions are evident in these data. First, children from lower SES families have significantly less well-developed phonological sensitivity than children from higher SES families. Second, children from lower SES families appear to experience significantly less growth in phonological sensitivity skills during the preschool years compared to their higher SES counterparts.

As a follow-up to these cross-sectional results, Lonigan (2002a) examined the growth and stability of phonological processing skills and print knowledge in a one-year longitudinal study of 325 3- to 5-year-olds attending Head Start. These children averaged 48 months of age at study entry (SD = 7.10); the majority of the children (95%) were African American, and 55% were girls. All children completed multiple measures of phonological processing skills (sensitivity, access, memory), print knowledge, and oral

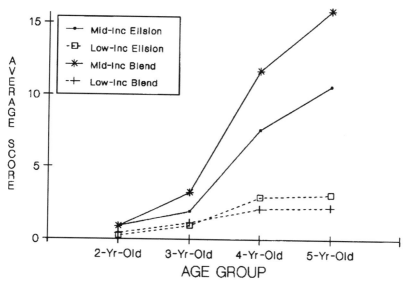

Figure 1. Differences in phonological sensitivity skills for children from lower and higher SES families from 2- to 5-years of age.

language three times during the Head Start year. Where appropriate, multiple measures of the same construct were combined into a latent variable. Mean scores on the emergent literacy variables at each of the three assessments conducted during the Head Start years are shown in table II. As can be seen in the table, there was growth in emergent literacy skills from Head Start entry (September) to the end of the academic year (May). For instance, children experienced average approximate growth of 1.3 items on phonological sensitivity tests and 1.5 items on phonological memory tests. During the Head Start year, the children learned approximately 4.4 letter names, .45 letter sounds, and 8 words assessed by the expressive vocabulary measure. Although there was some growth in these skills, the degree was less than that demonstrated by children from middle-income families (e.g., Lonigan, Burgess, and Anthony 2000; Lonigan 2002b). As shown in table III, which lists the 3-month and 9-month stability correlations for latent and

Table II　Descriptive Statistics for Average Score in Emergent Literacy Skills at Three Assessment Points Across a Head Start Year

Construct	Assessment 1 September		Assessment 2 January		Assessment 3 May	
	Mean	(SD)	Mean	(SD)	Mean	(SD)
Phonological Sensitivity	2.63	(1.04)	3.22	(1.33)	3.92	(1.52)
Phonological Access (RON)	69.70	(28.98)	55.55	(18.81)	51.85	(17.48)
Phonological Memory	9.31	(3.81)	11.27	(4.40)	10.86	(3.88)
Letter-name Knowledge	3.51	(6.72)	5.56	(8.19)	7.92	(9.40)
Letter-sound Knowledge	0.29	(0.92)	0.59	(1.28)	0.76	(1.51)
Print Concepts	3.01	(1.86)	3.44	(2.26)	4.74	(2.60)
Expressive Vocabulary	16.06	(8.57)	22.67	(10.77)	24.23	(10.47)
Word Reading	0.02	(0.16)	0.04	(0.19)	0.05	(0.29)

Table III　Cross-time stability coefficients for emergent literacy skills across three assessment points in a Head Start year

Assessment Intervals	September to January	January to May	September to May
Phonological Sensitivity	.95	.90	.82
Phonological Access (RON)	.94	.93	.91
Phonological Memory	.77	.65	.58
Letter-name Knowledge	.77	.80	.54
Letter-sound Knowledge	.24	.39	.23
Print Concepts	.43	.44	.30
Expressive Vocabulary	.70	.76	.74
Word Reading	.50	.56	.52

observed variables representing oral language, phonological processing, and print knowledge, the majority of emergent literacy skills are highly stable across the Head Start year. This level of stability indicates that the rank ordering of children in terms of the emergent literacy skills they demonstrate changes very little as a function of their experiences in Head Start.

INTERVENTIONS FOR PRESCHOOL CHILDREN AT-RISK OF READING DIFFICULTIES

The studies summarized above indicate that children from lower SES families are at risk of later reading difficulties because of overall slower development of emergent literacy skills and the high degree of stability of these skills. Importantly, the lower level and high degree of stability of emergent literacy skills in children from lower income families suggests the need for powerful interventions to increase these skills and reduce the risk for later reading difficulties. Indeed, these data suggest that in the absence of effective and powerful interventions, children from lower SES families are unlikely to arrive at school ready to benefit from the reading instruction they will receive.

Shared Reading Interventions

A number of interventions have been developed to enhance children's oral language skills through shared reading. The most widely researched and validated of these interventions is called dialogic reading (Whitehurst and Lonigan 1998). Dialogic reading involves several changes in the way adults typically read books to children. Central to these changes is a shift in roles. During typical shared reading, the adult reads and the child listens, but in dialogic reading the child learns to become the storyteller. The adult assumes the role of an active listener, asking questions, adding information, and prompting the child to increase the sophistication of descriptions of the material in the picture book. A child's responses to the book are encouraged through praise and repetition, and more sophisticated responses are encouraged by expansions of the child's utterances and by more challenging questions from the adult reading partner. For 2- and 3-year-olds, questions from adults focus on individual pages in a book, asking the child to describe objects, actions, and events on the page (e.g., "What is this? What color is the duck? What is the duck doing?"). For 4- and 5-year-olds questions increasingly focus on the narrative as a whole or on relations between the book and the child's life (e.g., "Have you ever seen a duck swimming? What did it look like?").

Dialogic reading has been shown to produce larger effects on the oral language skills of children from middle- to upper-income families than a similar amount of typical picture book reading (Arnold et al. 1994; Whitehurst et al. 1988). Studies conducted with children from lower SES families attending child care demonstrate that child care teachers, parents, or community volunteers using a six-week small-group center-based or home dialogic reading intervention can produce substantial positive changes in the development of children's language as measured by standardized and naturalistic measures (Lonigan et al. 1999; Lonigan and Whitehurst 1998; Valdez-Menchaca and Whitehurst 1992; Whitehurst, Arnold, et al. 1994) that are maintained for six months following the intervention (Whitehurst, Arnold, et al. 1994). A large scale longitudinal study of the use of dialogic reading over a year of a Head Start program for 4-year-olds showed large effects on emergent literacy skills at the end of Head Start that were maintained through the end of kindergarten; however, these positive effects did not generalize to reading scores at the end of second grade (Whitehurst, Epstein, et al. 1994; Whitehurst et al. 1999).

Phonological Skills Interventions

Experimental studies of programs designed to teach children phonological sensitivity have shown positive effects on children's reading and spelling skills (e.g., Ball and Blackman 1988; Bradley and Bryant 1985; Lundberg, Frost, and Petersen 1988; Torgesen, Morgan, and Davis 1992; Uhry and Shepherd 1992). Phonological sensitivity training programs that included letter knowledge training (e.g., Ball and Blackman 1988; Bradley and Bryant 1985) have generally produced larger gains than phonological sensitivity training alone. The majority of these programs teach children how to categorize objects on the basis of certain sounds (e.g., initial phonemes). Other programs have explicitly taught children phonemic analysis and synthesis skills. For example, Torgesen, Morgan, and Davis (1992) reported on a 7-week group training program that taught children both analysis (e.g., identify initial, final, or middle sounds in words) and synthesis skills (e.g., say words after hearing their phonemes in isolation). Graduate students worked with groups of three children using a limited word list for all activities. Analysis training began by having children identify pictures that started with a specific sound (e.g., "What words for pictures begin the /k/ sound, 'car,' 'cat,' 'hat,' 'bat'?") or ended with a specific rime (e.g., "What words for pictures ended with the 'at' sound: 'hat,' 'bat,' 'hut,' 'map'?"). Training progressed until children could identify words with specific phonemes in initial, middle, and final positions (e.g., pick the pictures for hat, cat, and bat when asked for words that have the /a/ sound in the middle, say the /a/ in "bat" when asked for the middle sound, or say the /t/ in cat when asked for the last sound), and then required them to segment the words into the constituent phonemes (e.g., "Say all the sounds you hear in the word 'bat'."). Synthesis training began by having children blend onset and rime to form a word (e.g., "What word is /b/...'at'?"), and progressed until children could say what a word was when said as its individual phonemes (e.g., blend the sounds /t/... /r/... /u/... /k/, spoken individually, into the word "truck"). Training in both analysis and synthesis resulted in larger gains in both phonological sensitivity and a reading analogue task than training in synthesis skills alone. Both training groups performed better than a group of control children who had listened to stories, engaged in discussions about the stories, and answered comprehension questions for an equivalent period.

Whereas most phonological sensitivity training studies have been conducted with children at the beginning stages of learning to read (i.e., kindergarten or first grade), Byrne and Fielding-Barnsley (1991a) reported positive effects for a groups of preschool children (mean age = 55 months) exposed to 12 weeks of their *Sound Foundations* program (Byrne and Fielding-Barnsely 1991b). The *Sound Foundations* program consisted of teaching children six phonemes in the initial and final positions of words by drawing attention to the sound in words, discussing how the sound is made by the mouth, reciting rhymes with the phoneme in the appropriate position, and encouraging children to find objects in a poster that had the sound in the initial (or final) position. Worksheets in which children identified and colored items with the phoneme in the correct position were used, and the letter for the phoneme was displayed. A final stage of training introduced children to two card games that required matching objects on the basis of initial or final phonemes. The children exposed to this program demonstrated greater increases in phonological sensitivity than a group of control children exposed to storybook reading and a semantic categorization program (Byrne and Fielding-Barnsley 1991a). Significantly, some of these gains were maintained through the first and second grades (Byrne and Fielding-Barnsley 1993; 1995).

Computer assisted instruction (CAI). Teacher-directed interventions can produce increases in children's phonological sensitivity. However, interventions examined to date require significant teacher time, and some early childhood educators would question the developmental appropriateness of some of the activities (e.g., Neuman, Copple, and Bredekamp 2000). Some evidence points to the potential effectiveness of software designed to teach phonological sensitivity skills to children (Barker and Torgesen 1995; Foster et al. 1994; Olson et al. 1997; Wise et al. 1998). For instance, Foster et al. (1994) conducted two experiments in which preschool and kindergarten children who were mainly from middle-income families were randomly assigned to receive either their standard school curriculum or between five and eight hours of exposure to *DaisyQuest*, a computer program designed to teach phonological sensitivity in the context of an interactive adventure game. Children in the experimental group in both studies demonstrated significant and large gains in phonological sensitivity skills compared to the children in the no-treatment control group. Barker and Torgesen (1995) examined the effectiveness of the *DaisyQuest* program with a group of at-risk first grade children who were randomly assigned to either an experimental or control group. Children in the experimental group received approximately eight hours of exposure to the program, and children in the control group received an equal amount of exposure to computer programs designed to teach early math skills or other reading skills. Exposure to the *DaisyQuest* program resulted in significant improvements in children's phonological sensitivity and word identification skills compared to the control group.

Although these studies suggest that CAI for phonological sensitivity might be a means of increasing the phonological sensitivity of preschoolers at-risk for reading difficulties, children in the studies above were either from middle-income families or were older than preschool age.

Whether a CAI intervention would be effective for preschoolers at-risk for reading difficulties is unclear. Two studies have examined the efficacy of CAI phonological sensitivity training for preschool children from lower income families. In the first study, Lonigan et al. (in press) randomly assigned 41 children attending Head Start to either a CAI phonological sensitivity intervention group or a control group that received nothing in addition to the standard Head Start curriculum. The children averaged 55.1 months of age ($SD = 6.07$). The majority of children were African American (85.4%), and 66% were girls. All children were pre- and post-tested on measures of phonological sensitivity, print awareness, and oral language.

Children assigned to the CAI group worked individually on a portable computer with two instructional programs, *DaisyQuest* and *Daisy's Castle*. Both programs employed high-quality digitized speech and colorful graphic images to engage children in a series of interactive tasks within an overall adventure game context. At each step of the programs, instructions about the current tasks were provided, and a brief tutorial followed requiring the children to respond actively. At any point in the progression of the programs, children were able to review the instructions. Children in the CAI group received instruction and practice on seven phonological sensitivity tasks (recognizing rhyming words, matching words on the basis of similar first sounds, matching on the basis of last sounds, matching on the basis of middle sounds, recognizing words presented in onset-rime format, recognizing words presented as individual phonemes, and counting the number of phonemes in words). Trained research assistants worked on an individual basis with several children each day providing additional instruction as needed. Throughout the intervention period, children worked at their own pace and could return to earlier levels if they desired. Intervention activities occurred for approximately 15 to 20 minutes, four to five days a week, for approximately 10 weeks.

There were no differences between the groups in terms of growth in oral language or letter knowledge—two emergent literacy skills not targeted by the intervention. In contrast, results indicated that children in the CAI groups experienced significantly more growth in phonological sensitivity skills than did the children in the control group. In a repeated measures analysis, the pre- to post-test by intervention group interactions were significant for the rhyme oddity, rhyme matching, word elision, and syllable/phoneme elision tests. The interactions were not significant for the word blending, syllable/phoneme blending, multiple choice blending, or multiple choice elision tests. These results are shown in figure 2 in terms of pre- to post-test difference scores for the CAI and control groups.

These findings indicate that CAI can produce significant gains in the phonological sensitivity skills of preschool children from lower SES groups. The absence of an active control group leaves open the question of whether it was the additional interaction (e.g., one-to-one interaction with the research assistants) children received while engaged in CAI training that was responsible for their gains. Additionally, as noted above, studies with older children suggest that combining training in phonological sensitivity with training in print knowledge produces larger effects for phonological sensitivity skills. Therefore, Lonigan and Driscoll, (2001) conducted a second CAI study that provided both an active control group and a contrast between training in phonological sensitivity, training in letter knowledge, and combined training.

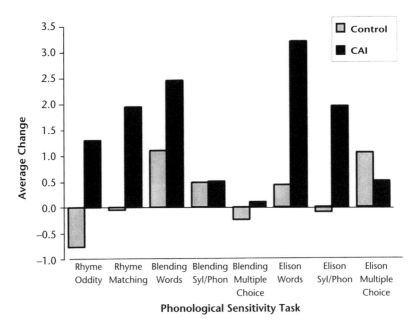

Figure 2.   Average pretest to post-test differences scores on phonological sensitivity measures for CAI intervention group and control group.

In this study, 120 children from low-SES families attending either sub-sidized preschools or the school districts pre-K program were randomly assigned to one of four CAI groups: CAI training in (a) phonological sensitivity only, (b) letter knowledge only, (c) combined phonological sensitivity and letter knowledge, or (d) math (control).

Computer assisted instruction intervention activities for all four groups occurred for approximately 15 to 20 minutes, four to five days a week, for approximately 10 weeks. Trained research assistants worked on an individual basis with several children each day providing additional instruction as needed. As with the Head Start CAI study, children in the two groups receiving phonological sensitivity training worked individually on a portable computer with the instructional programs, *DaisyQuest* and *Daisy's Castle*. In addition, children's CAI activities alternated with the instructional program *Earobics*. Children in the two groups receiving letter knowledge training worked at a portable computer with *Curious George ABC Adventure* software that was alternated with *Sesame Street ABC* software. Children in the CAI math control group worked at a portable computer with *Blues Clues Math* software. Children in the combined phonological sensitivity and letter knowledge group alternated phonological sensitivity and letter knowledge programs by session. Throughout the intervention period, children worked at their own pace and could return to earlier levels if they desired.

All children were pre- and post-tested on measures of phonological sensitivity, print awareness, and oral language. For purposes of analyses, scores on tests were converted to z-scores based on the full sample and converted to a standard score with a mean of 100 and a standard deviation of 15. Composite variables were created among tests measuring the same construct (e.g., phonological sensitivity, print knowledge). Results for the four groups on the phonological sensitivity composite variable are shown in figure 3, and results for the print knowledge composite variable are shown in figure 4 (note that the graphs show deviations from the average for the entire group of children). Significant group-by-time interactions indicated that there was differential growth in children's skills depending on CAI group. For both phonological sensitivity skills and print knowledge, children in the phonological sensitivity only and combined groups experienced significantly more growth than children in the letter knowledge only and math groups. Although significant effects were obtained, the effects

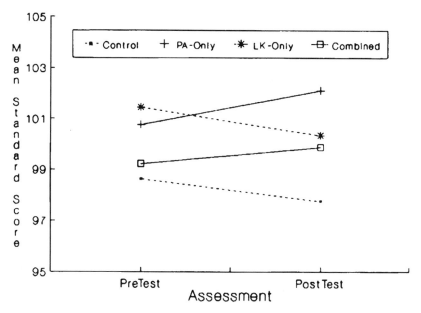

Figure 3.   Mean pretest and post-test composite phonological sensitivity scores for preschool children in four CAI intervention conditions. Standard scores were based on z-scores within time and across all groups; hence, scores show deviation from average performance of all children.

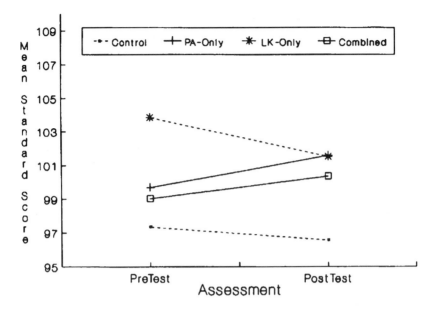

Figure 4.   Mean pretest and post-test composite print knowledge scores for preschool children in four CAI intervention conditions. Standard scores were based on z-scores within time and across all groups; hence, scores show deviation from average performance of all children.

were smaller than they were in the Head Start study. This result might have been a result of children in the second study entering with better emergent literacy skills than the children in the Head Start study, or these results might reflect the fact that the pre-K programs from which these children were drawn generally had a more coherent and literacy focused curriculum than that in place at Head Start.

Taken together, these findings indicate that CAI can be an effective means of promoting the phonological sensitivity and print knowledge skills of children from lower SES backgrounds who are at-risk of reading difficulties. Other data collected throughout both studies indicated that children enjoyed the CAI activities. Data concerning the longer term effects of training (i.e., were the gains maintained?) were not collected. Significantly, although CAI was effective and liked by the children, it did not result in significant reductions in teacher time because children needed one-to-one attention to navigate the instructional activities or have the activities explained to them. Consequently, it is unlikely that CAI can be used as a primary means of promoting these emergent literacy skills in preschool children who are at-risk of reading difficulties. Computer assisted instruction may be useful as an augmentative activity in the context of other interventions.

COMPREHENSIVE EMERGENT LITERACY INTERVENTION

The studies summarized above indicate that interventions targeting separate emergent literacy skills (oral language, phonological sensitivity) can be effective. Data suggest, however, that emergent literacy skills are relatively modular. Long-term dialogic reading effects on oral language do not extend to decoding (Whitehurst et al. 1999). Such a finding is not surprising given data from longitudinal studies that indicate that phonological processing and print knowledge skills—and not oral language—predict early decoding (e.g., Lonigan, Burgess, and Anthony 2000).

Whitehurst's recent work (Storch and Whitehurst 2002) addresses the relations (described above) between oral vocabulary size and phonological sensitivity in pre-readers, and the relation between oral language and reading among beginning readers. Their findings suggest that the relation is indirect (i.e., mediated by phonological sensitivity skills acquired in the preschool period). Whitehurst and colleagues followed several hundred children from low-income families at entry into Head Start at age four to the end of 2nd grade. Measures of emergent literacy skills were collected at Head Start exit and at kindergarten exit and reading ability and oral language ability were measured at the end of 1st and 2nd grade. There were three notable findings: First, there was striking continuity in emergent literacy skills from pre-K to kindergarten. Individual differences among children on these skills were set by age four and were quite stable thereafter. Second, phonological processing and print knowledge skills in kindergarten predicted reading in 2nd grade directly and with greater strength than reading in 1st grade predicted reading in 2nd grade. Thus, emergent literacy skills in kindergarten are as important, or more important, than a child's actual reading success in 1st grade in predicting later reading outcomes. Third, the relation of oral language skills with phonological processing and print knowledge skills was very strong in the pre-K period, but this relation weakened in kindergarten and was nonsignificant in 1st and 2nd grade. Thus, during early elementary school when children are learning to read, their knowledge of language and concepts and their reading and pre-reading skills are modular: Having a larger vocabulary in first grade does not directly help a child learn to read. The influence of vocabulary is indirect, mediated by a child's early acquisition of phonological processing and print knowledge skills.

Evaluations of emergent literacy interventions have shown relatively short-term effects. Whitehurst's (see Whitehurst and Lonigan 1998) results show, for interventions that produce significant improvement in children's skills, a catch-up or equalization effect that may reduce the tangible impact of the program over time. Early literacy interventions are not inoculations against later reading difficulties; rather, they provide important building blocks for additional educational experiences, reading acquisition, and ultimate academic success. Similarly, single-faceted interventions are unlikely to overcome the myriad emergent literacy delays experienced by children from lower income families. Research on emergent literacy suggests the desirability of a sequenced approach to intervention. Oral language skills provide the basis for development of phonological processing skills, and print knowledge is critical for the development of both decoding skills and phonological sensitivity. Consequently, literacy curricula for young children should first focus on improving their oral language skills. Other emergent literacy skills such as phonological sensitivity and print knowledge need to be taught explicitly in preschool and early grade school.

Historically, curricula for preschool have not focused on preacademic skills. Consequently, there have been few evaluations of multi-faceted or comprehensive interventions for children at-risk of reading difficulties. Lonigan and Torgesen (1999) designed a preschool emergent literacy intervention study that was designed to evaluate the optimal combinations of intervention activities focused on oral language, phonological sensitivity, and print knowledge. The study involves a randomized comparison of five combinations of intervention activities. Intervention followed a sequenced approach designed to target oral language skills first, followed by a focus on phonological sensitivity, letter knowledge, or both. All intervention activities were add-on; that is, all children continued to receive their typical pre-K curriculum. Intervention activities were conducted in small groups of three to five children. Children in the study were randomly assigned to either (a) a control group that received the pre-K curriculum used in their preschool, (b) an intervention group that received dialogic reading plus phonological sensitivity training, (c) an intervention group that received dialogic reading plus letter knowledge training, (d) an intervention group that received dialogic reading plus both phonological sensitivity and letter knowledge training, or (e) an intervention group that received standard shared reading plus both phonological sensitivity and letter knowledge training.

All children completed pretest measures of phonological sensitivity, print awareness, oral language, and other skills (September). Children completed additional assessments of these skills at mid-year (February) and immediately post-intervention (May). Preliminary results support the efficacy of these pre-literacy interventions. Figure 5 shows the results for each emergent literacy skill domain for the first cohort of 140 children. The figure shows that children receiving an active intervention for oral language or phonological sensitivity experienced significantly more growth in the skills in the targeted domain than children not receiving active intervention in that domain—despite the ongoing high-quality pre-K curriculum. Answers concerning the benefits of sequencing and combining intervention will require completion of data collection for the full sample.

SUMMARY AND CONCLUSIONS

Children's skill levels in three areas of emergent literacy are significant contributors to how easily, quickly, and well children will learn how to read. There are substantial differences between children from different SES groups in each of these three areas. Children from lower SES backgrounds are at significant risk for difficulties in learning to read because of their lower level of emergent literacy skills in

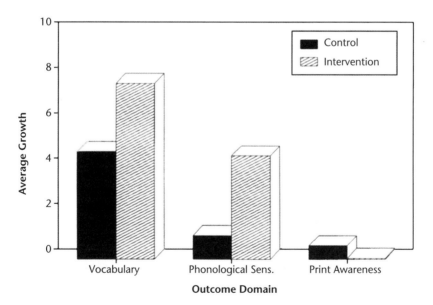

Figure 5.   Average standard score difference from pretest to post-test on oral language, phonological sensitivity, and print knowledge composite variables for children receiving an active intervention in that skill domain and children not receiving an active intervention in that skill domain.

terms of oral language, phonological processing, and print knowledge. Although there is growth in emergent literacy skills during the preschool period for children from lower SES backgrounds, this growth is less rapid than observed in children from higher SES backgrounds. For both groups of children, skill levels across emergent literacy domains are very stable across the preschool period and into early grade school. In the absence of effective intervention, children from lower SES backgrounds are very likely to have difficulties in learning to read because there is a mismatch between their skills and the skills needed to benefit from reading instruction. Although there appear to be effective interventions for improving children's emergent literacy skills, the long-term efficacy of such interventions is mostly unknown. Emergent literacy skills are modular. It is likely that effective intervention will need to address performance in all three areas (oral language, phonological processing, print awareness).

ACKNOWLEDGMENTS

Preparation of this work was supported in part by grants from the National Institute of Child Health and Human Development (HD/MH38880, HD30988, HD36067, HD36509) and the Administration for Children and Families (90YF0023). Views expressed herein are the authors' and have not been cleared by the grantors.

REFERENCES

Adams, M. J. 1990. *Learning to Read: Thinking and Learning about Print.* Cambridge, MA: MIT Press.

Allington, R. L. 1984. Content, coverage, and contextual reading in reading groups. *Journal of Reading Behavior* 16:85–96.

Anthony, J. L., and Lonigan, C. J. 2002. The nature of phonological sensitivity: Converging evidence from four studies on preschool and early grade school children. Manuscript submitted for publication.

Anthony, J. L., Lonigan, C. J., Burgess, S. R., Driscoll, K., Phillips, B. M., and Bloomfield, B. G. 2002. Structure of preschool phonological sensitivity: Overlapping sensitivity to rhyme, words, syllables, and phonemes. *Journal of Experimental Child Psychology* 82:65–92.

Arnold, D. H., Lonigan, C. J., Whitehurst, G. J., and Epstein, J. N. 1994. Accelerating language development through picture book reading: Replication and extension to a videotape training format. *Journal of Educational Psychology* 86:235–43.

Baddeley, A. 1986. Working Memory. NY: Oxford University Press.

Ball, E. W. and Blachman, B. A. 1988. Phoneme segmentation training: Effect on reading readiness. *Annals of Dyslexia* 38:208–25.

Barker, T. A. and Torgesen, J. K. 1995. An evaluation of computer-assisted instruction in phonological awareness with below average readers. *Journal of Educational Computing Research* 13:89–103.

Baydar, N., Brooks-Gunn, J., and Furstenberg, F. F. 1993. Early warning signs of functional illiteracy: Predictors in childhood and adolescence. *Child Development* 64:815–29.

Bishop, D. V. M. and Adams, C. 1990. A prospective study of the relationship between specific language impairment, phonological disorders and reading retardation. *Journal of Child Psychology and Psychiatry and Allied Disciplines* 31:1027–50.

Bond, G. L. and Dykstra, R. 1967. The cooperative research program in first-grade reading instruction. *Reading Research Quarterly* 2:5–142.

Bowey, J. A. 1995. Socioeconomic status differences in preschool phonological sensitivity and first-grade reading achievement. *Journal of Educational Psychology* 87:476–87.

Bradley, L. and Bryant, P. 1985. *Rhyme and Reason in Reading and Spelling.* Ann Arbor, MI: University of Michigan Press.

Bryant, P. E., MacLean, M., Bradley, L. L., and Crossland, J. 1990. Rhyme and alliteration, phoneme detection, and learning to read. *Developmental Psychology* 26:429–38.

Burgess, S. R., and Lonigan, C. J. 1998. Bidirectional relations of phonological sensitivity and prereading abilities: Evidence from a preschool sample. *Journal of Experimental Child Psychology* 70:117–41.

Byrne, B. and Fielding-Barnsley, R. 1995. Evaluation of a program to teach phonemic awareness to young children: A 2- and 3-year follow-up and a new preschool trial. *Journal of Educational Psychology* 87:488–503.

Byrne, B. and Fielding-Barnsley, R. F. 1991a. Evaluation of a program to teach phonemic awareness to young children. *Journal of Educational Psychology* 82:805–12.

Byrne, B. and Fielding-Barnsley, R. F. 1991b. *Sound Foundations.* Artarmon, New South Wales, Australia: Leyden Educational Publishers.

Byrne, B. and Fielding-Barnsley, R. F. 1993. Evaluation of a program to teach phonemic awareness to young children: A one year follow-up. *Journal of Educational Psychology* 85:104–11.

Chall, J. S., Jacobs, V., and Baldwin, L. 1990. *The Reading Crisis: Why Poor Children Fall Behind.* Cambridge, MA: Harvard university Press.

Chaney, C. 1992. Language development, metalinguistic skills, and print awareness in 3-year-old children. *Applied Psycholinguistics* 13:485–514.

Clay, M. M. 1979. *Reading: The Patterning of Complex Behavior.* Auckland, NZ: Heinemann.

Cunningham, A. E., and Stanovich, K. E. 1998. Early reading acquisition and its relation to reading experience and ability 10 years later. *Developmental Psychology* 33:934–45.

Dickinson, D. K., and Snow, C. E. 1987. Interrelationships among prereading and oral language skills in kindergartners from two social classes. *Early Childhood Research Quarterly* 2:1–25.

Dickinson, D. K., and Tabors, P. O. 1991. Early literacy: Linkages between home, school, and literacy achievement at age five. *Journal of Research in Childhood Education* 6:30–46.

Dubow, E. F., and Ippolito, M. F. 1994. Effects of poverty and quality of the home environment on changes in the academic and behavioral adjustment of elementary school-age children. *Journal of Clinical Child Psychology* 23:401–12.

Echols, L. D., West, R. F., Stanovich, K. E., and Zehr, K. S. 1996. Using children's literacy activities to predict growth in verbal cognitive skills: A longitudinal investigation. *Journal of Educational Psychology* 88:296–304.

Foster, K. C., Erickson, G. C., Foster, D. F., Brinkman, D., and Torgesen, J. K. 1994. Computer administered instruction in phonological awareness: Evaluation of the DaisyQuest Program. *Journal of Research and Development in Education* 27:126–37.

Fowler, A. E. 1991. How early phonological development might set the stage for phoneme awareness. In *Phonological Processes in Literacy*, eds. S. A. Brady and D. P. Shankweiler. Hillsdale, NJ: Lawrence Erlbaum Associates.

Gillon, G., and Dodd, B. J. 1994. A prospective study of the relationship between phonological, semantic and syntactic skills and specific reading disability. Reading and Writing: *An Interdisciplinary Journal* 6:321–45.

Goswami, U. 1986. Children's use of analogy in learning to read: A developmental study. *Journal of Experimental Child Psychology* 42:73–83.

Goswami, U., and Bryant, P. E. 1990. Phonological Skills and Learning to Read. Hillsdale, NJ: Lawrence Erlbaum Associates.

Goswami, U., and Bryant, P. E. 1992. Rhyme, analogy, and children's reading. In Reading Acquisition, eds. P. B. Gough, L. C. Ehri, and R. Treiman. Hillsdale, NJ: Lawrence Erlbaum Associates.

Gough, P. B. 1993. The beginning of decoding. *Reading and Writing: An Interdisciplinary Journal* 5:181–92.

Juel, C. 1988. Learning to read and write: A longitudinal study of 54 children from first through fourth grades. *Journal of Educational Psychology* 80:437–47.

Juel, C., Griffith, P. L., and Gough, P. B. 1986). Acquisition of literacy: A longitudinal study of children in first and second grade. *Journal of Educational Psychology* 78:243–55.

Lentz, F. E. 1988. Effective reading interventions in the regular classroom. In *Alternative Educational Delivery Systems: Enhancing Instructional Options for All Students*, eds. J. L. Graden, J. E. Zins, and M. J. Curtis. Washington DC: National Association of School Psychologists.

Liberman, A. M., Cooper, F. S., Shankweiler, D., and Studdert-Kennedy, M. 1967. Perception of the speech code. *Psychological Review* 74:431–61.

Lonigan, C. J., and Driscoll, K. 2001. Efficacy of a computer-assisted instruction emergent literacy program. Unpublished data. Florida State University.

Lonigan, C. J. 2002a. Development of emergent literacy skills across the Head Start year. Paper presented at the 6th Head Start Research Conference; Washington, DC.

Lonigan, C. J. 2002b. Growth and stability of emergent literacy skills of preschool children. Unpublished data. Florida State University.

Lonigan, C. J., Anthony, J. L., Bloomfield, B. G., Dyer, S. M., and Samwel, C. S. 1999. Effects of two preschool shared reading interventions on the emergent literacy skills of children from low-income families. *Journal of Early Intervention* 22:306–22.

Lonigan, C. J., Burgess, S. R., and Anthony, J. L. 2000. Development of emergent literacy and early reading skills in preschool children: Evidence from a latent variable longitudinal study. *Developmental Psychology* 36:596–613.

Lonigan, C. J., Burgess, S. R., Anthony, J. L., and Barker, T. A. 1998. Development of phonological sensitivity in two- to five-year-old children. *Journal of Educational Psychology* 90:294–311.

Lonigan, C. J., Driscoll, K., Phillips, B. M., Cantor, B.G., Anthony, J.L., and Goldstein, H. in press. Evaluation of a computer-assisted instruction phonological sensitivity program with preschool children at-risk for reading problems. *Journal of Early Intervention.*

Lonigan, C. J., and Torgesen, J. K. 1999. Preschool pre-literacy intervention for children at-risk of reading difficulties. Unpublished grant proposal. Florida State University.

Lonigan, C. J., and Whitehurst, G. J. 1998. Examination of the relative efficacy of parent and teacher involvement in a shared-reading intervention for preschool children from low-income backgrounds. *Early Childhood Research Quarterly* 17:265–92.

Lundberg, I., Frost, J., and Petersen, O. 1988. Effects of an extensive program for stimulating phonological awareness in preschool children. *Reading Research Quarterly* 23:263–84.

MacLean, M., Bryant, P., and Bradley, L. 1987. Rhymes, nursery rhymes, and reading in early childhood. Merrill-Palmer Quarterly 33:255–82.

Mason, J. M. 1980. When children do begin to read: An exploration of four year old children's letter and word reading competencies. *Reading Research Quarterly* 15:203–27.

Mason, J. M. 1992. Reading stories to preliterate children: A proposed connection to reading. In *Reading Acquisition*, eds. P. B. Gough, L. C. Ehri, and R. Treiman. Hillsdale, NJ: Lawrence Erlbaum Associates.

Masonheimer, P. E., Drum, P. A., and Ehri, L. C. 1984. Does environmental print identification lead children into word reading? *Journal of Reading Behavior* 16:257–71.

Metsala, J. L. 1999. Young children's phonological awareness and non-word repetition as a function of vocabulary development. *Journal of Educational Psychology* 91:3–19.

Metsala, J.L., and Ehri, L., eds. 1998. *Word Recognition in Beginning Literacy.* Mahwah, NJ: Lawrence Erlbaum Associates.

Metsala, J. L., and Walley, A. C. 1998. Spoken vocabulary growth and the segmental restructuring of lexical representations: Precursors to phonemic awareness and early reading ability. In *Word Recognition in Beginning Literacy*, eds. J. L Metsala and L. C. Ehri. Mahwah, NJ: Lawrence Erlbaum Associates.

Morais, J. 1991. Constraints on the development of phonological awareness. In *Phonological Processes in Literacy*, eds. S. A. Brady and D. P. Shankweiler. Hillsdale, NJ: Lawrence Erlbaum Associates.

Morrison, F. J., Smith, L., and Dow-Ehrensberger, M. 1995. Education and cognitive development: A natural experiment. *Developmental Psychology* 31:789–99.

Muter, V., and Snowling, M. 1998. Concurrent and longitudinal predictors of reading: The role of metalinguistic and short-term memory skills. *Reading Research Quarterly* 33:320–37.

Muter, V., Hulme, C., Snowling, M., and Taylor, S. 1997. Segmentation, not rhyming, predicts early progress in learning to read. *Journal of Experimental Child Psychology* 65:370–98.

Nagy, W. E., and Anderson, R. C. 1984. How many words are there in printed school English? *Reading Research Quarterly* 19:304–30.

Nation, K., and Hulme, C. 1997. Phonemic segmentation, not onset-rime segmentation, predicts early reading and spelling skills. *Reading Research Quarterly* 32:154–67.

NICHD 2000. *Report of the National Reading Panel: Teaching Children to Read.* Washington, DC: U.S. Department of Health and Human Services.

Oka, E., and Paris, S. 1986. Patterns of motivation and reading skills in underachieving children. In *Handbook of Cognitive, Social, and Neuropsychological Aspects of Learning Disabilities,* Vol. 2, ed. S. Ceci. Hillsdale, NJ: Lawrence ErlbaumAssociates.

Olson, R. K., Wise, B. W., Ring, J., and Johnson, M. 1997. Computer-based remedial training in phoneme awareness and phoneme decoding: Effects on post-training development of word recognition. *Scientific Studies of Reading* 1:235–53.

Pappas, C. C., and Brown, E. 1988. The development of children's sense of the written story language register: An analysis of the texture of "pretend reading." *Linguistics and Education* 1:45–79.

Pikulski, J. J., and Tobin, A. W. 1989. Factors associated with long-term reading achievement of early readers. In *Cognitive and Social Perspectives for Literacy Research and Instruction,* eds. S. McCormick, J. Zutell, P. Scharer, and P. O'Keefe. Chicago: National Reading Conference.

Purcell-Gates, V. 1988. Lexical and syntactic knowledge of written narrative held by well-read-to kindergartners and second graders. *Research in the Teaching of English* 22:128–60.

Purcell-Gates, V. 1996. Stories, coupons, and the TV Guide: Relationships between home literacy experiences and emergent literacy knowledge. *Reading Research Quarterly* 31:406–28.

Purcell-Gates, V., and Dahl, K. L. 1991. Low-SES children's success and failure at early literacy learning in skills-based classrooms. *Journal of Reading Behavior* 23:1–34.

Raz, I. S., and Bryant, P. 1990. Social background, phonological awareness and children's reading. *British Journal of Developmental Psychology* 8:209–25.

Schatschneider, C., Francis, D. J., Foorman, B. R., Fletcher, J. M., and Mehta, P. 1999. The dimensionality of phonological awareness: An application of item response theory. *Journal of Educational Psychology* 91:439–49.

Share, D., and Silva, P. 1987. Language deficits and specific reading retardation: Cause or effect? *British Journal of Disorders of Communication* 22:219–26.

Smith, S. S. and Dixon, R. G. 1995. Literacy concepts of low- and middle-class four-year-olds entering preschool. *Journal of Educational Research* 88:243–53.

Snow, C. E. 1983. Literacy and language: Relationships during the preschool years. *Harvard Educational Review* 53:165–89.

Snow, C. E., Barnes, W. S., Chandler, J., Hemphill, L., and Goodman, I. F. 1991. *Unfulfilled Expectations: Home and School Influences on Literacy.* Cambridge, MA: Harvard University Press.

Snow, C. E., Burns, M. S., and Griffin, P., eds. 1998. *Preventing Reading Difficulties in Young Children.* Washington, D.C.: National Academy Press.

Stahl, S. A., and Murray, B. A. 1994. Defining phonological awareness and its relationship to early reading. *Journal of Educational Psychology* 86:221–34.

Stanovich, K. E. 1986. Matthew effects in reading: Some consequences of individual differences in the acquisition of literacy. *Reading Research Quarterly* 21:360–407.

Stanovich, K. E., and Siegel, L. S. 1994. Phenotypic performance profile of children with reading disabilities: A regression-based test of the phonological-core variable-difference model. *Journal of Educational Psychology* 86:24–53.

Stevenson, H. W., and Newman, R. S. 1986. Long-term prediction of achievement and attitudes in mathematics and reading. *Child Development* 57:646–59.

Storch, S. A., and Whitehurst, G. J. 2002. Oral language and code-related precursors to reading: Evidence from a longitudinal structural model. *Journal of Educational Psychology* 38:934–47.

Sulzby, E. 1986. Writing and reading: Signs of oral and written language organization in the young child. In *Emergent Literacy: Reading and Writing*, eds. W. H. Teale and E. Sulzby. Norwood, NJ: Ablex.

Sulzby, E. 1988. A study of children's early reading development. In *Psychological Bases for Early Education*, ed. A. D. Pelligrini. Chichester, England: Wiley.

Torgesen, J. K., Morgan, S., and Davis, C. 1992. Effects of two types of phonological awareness training on word learning in kindergarten children. *Journal of Educational Psychology* 84:364–70.

Torgesen, J., Wagner, R., Rashotte, C., Alexander, A., and Conway, T. 1997. Preventive and remedial interventions for children with severe reading disabilities. *Learning Disabilities: An Interdisciplinary Journal* 8:51–62.

Tramontana, M. G., Hooper, S., and Selzer, S. C. 1988. Research on preschool prediction of later academic achievement: A review. *Developmental Review* 8:89–146.

Tunmer, W. E., and Hoover, W. A. 1992. Cognitive and linguistic factors in learning to read. In *Reading Acquisition*, eds. P. B. Gough, L. C. Ehri, and R. Treiman. Hillsdale, NJ: Lawrence Erlbaum Associates.

Tunmer, W. E., and Rohl, M. 1991. Phonological awareness and reading acquisition. In *Phonological Awareness in Reading: The Evolution of Current Perspectives*, eds. D. Sawyer and B. Fox. New York: Springer-Verlag.

Tunmer, W. E., Herriman, M. L., and Nesdale, A. R. 1988. Metalinguistic abilities and beginning reading. *Reading Research Quarterly* 23:134–58.

Uhry, J. K., and Shepherd, M. J. 1993. Segmentation/spelling instruction as part of a first-grade reading program: Effects on several measures of reading. *Reading Research Quarterly* 28:218–33.

Valdez-Menchaca, M. C., and Whitehurst, G. J. 1992. Accelerating language development through picture book reading: A systematic extension to Mexican day-care. *Developmental Psychology* 28:1106–14.

Vellutino, F. R., Scanlon, D. M., and Tanzman, M. S. 1991. Bridging the gap between cognitive and neuropsychological conceptualizations of reading disability. *Learning and Individual Differences* 3:181–203.

Wagner, R. K., and Torgesen, J. K. 1987. The natural of phonological processing and its causal role in the acquisition of reading skills. *Psychological Bulletin* 101:192–212.

Wagner, R. K., Torgesen, J. K., and Rashotte, C. A. 1994. Development of reading-related phonological processing abilities: New evidence of bidirectional causality from a latent variable longitudinal study. *Developmental Psychology* 30:73–87.

Wagner, R. K., Torgesen, J. K., Laughon, P., Simmons, K., Rashotte, C. A. 1993. The development of young readers' phonological processing abilities. *Journal of Educational Psychology* 85:1–20.

Wagner, R. K., Torgesen, J. K., Rashotte, C. A., Hecht, S. A., Barker, T. A., Burgess, S. R., Donahue, J., and Garon, T. 1997. Changing relations between phonological processing abilities and word-level reading as children develop from beginning to skilled readers: A 5-year longitudinal study. *Developmental Psychology* 33:468–79.

Whitehurst, G. J. 1996. Language processes in context: Language learning in children reared in poverty. In *Research on Communication and Language Disorders: Contribution to Theories of Language Development*, eds. L. B. Adamson and M. A. Romski. Baltimore, MD: Brookes.

Whitehurst, G. J., Epstein, J. N., Angell, A. C., Payne, A. C., Crone, D. A. and Fischel, J. E. 1994. Outcomes of an emergent literacy intervention in Head Start. *Journal of Educational Psychology* 86:542–55.

Whitehurst, G. J., Falco, F., Lonigan, C. J., Fischel, J. E., DeBaryshe, B. D., Valdez-Menchaca, M. C., and Caulfield, M. 1988. Accelerating language development through picture-book reading. *Developmental Psychology* 24:552–58.

Whitehurst, G. J. and Lonigan, C. J. 1998. Child development and emergent literacy. *Child Development* 68:848–72.

Whitehurst, G. J., Zevenbergen, A. A., Crone, D. A., Schultz, M .D., Velting, O. N., and Fischel, J. E. (1999). Outcomes of an emergent literacy intervention from Head Start through second grade. *Journal of Educational Psychology* 91:261–72.

Wise, B. W., Olson, R. K., Ring, J., and Johnson, M. 1998. Interactive computer support for improving phonological skills. In *Word Recognition in Beginning Literacy*, eds. J. L Metsala and L. C. Ehri. Mahwah, NJ: Lawrence Erlbaum Associates.

Yopp, H. K. 1988. The validity and reliability of phonemic awareness tests. *Reading Research Quarterly* 23:159–77.

Chapter • 3

How to Assess Reading-Related Phonological Abilities

Richard K. Wagner, Andrea E. Muse, Tamara L. Stein, Kelly C. Cukrowicz, Erin R. Harrell, Carol A. Rashotte, and Corine S. Samwel

Learning to read English is perhaps the most important outcome of primary schooling in English-speaking countries. Accomplishing this outcome requires accessing the printed form of the words of English oral language. These printed forms can represent, to varying degrees for different words, aspects of a word's pronunciation, meaning, and origin (Crowder and Wagner 1991; Rayner and Polletsek 1989).

One determinant of the ease with which children learn to read is a set of related abilities that involve processing the speech sounds that spoken words are composed of (Share and Stanovich 1995; Wagner et al. 1997). We refer to these abilities as reading-related phonological abilities (Wagner and Torgesen 1987). The root of the word phonological, and the related phone, phoneme, phonics, and even telephone, is the Greek *phone* which means sound or voice. Children who have difficulty learning to read commonly have deficits in one or more aspect of phonological processing, and interventions for the purpose of preventing or remediating early reading problems target phonological skills among other skills (Foorman et al. 1998; Foorman, Francis, Fletcher et al. 1997; Foorman, Francis, Shaywitz et al. 1997; Torgesen et al. 2001; Torgesen et al. 1999).

The purpose of this chapter is to review what is known about the optimal assessment of reading-related phonological abilities. The chapter is divided into three major parts. The first part is devoted to describing an assessment framework and some general issues. The second part is devoted to applying the framework to assessing two reading-related phonological processes: phonological awareness and phonological memory. The third part is devoted to mentioning some recent developments that have the potential to change the way we assess reading-related phonological processes in the foreseeable future.

A FRAMEWORK FOR ASSESSMENT

The optimal assessment of any construct, including that of reading-related phonological abilities, is best considered within an assessment framework that addresses five relevant issues.

Optimal for What Purpose?

Assessment is never a purposeless activity. Common purposes for educational assessment include (a) screening to identify problems before they develop or problems that have not been detected, (b) monitoring progress during the academic year and from year to year, (c) determining whether a desired outcome has been attained, (d) and diagnosis of specific strengths and weaknesses. Each of these purposes in turn can exist in the context of basic research, applied research, or educational application.

Characteristics of optimal assessment can vary as a function of purpose. For example, efficiency and economy are characteristics of assessments that are critical for screening because of the large number of individuals that must be assessed. In contrast, efficiency and economy might need to be sacrificed for the purpose of diagnosis when a relatively detailed account of strengths and weaknesses is needed to plan an intervention.

A Construct-Centered versus Task-Centered Approach

The early days of psychological assessment, particularly in the context of diagnosis of functional consequences of brain damage or disease, were characterized by a task-centered approach to assessment. As a result of trying out different tasks on individuals with brain injury or illness, tasks were identified that differentiated these individuals from controls. An example is the Corsi block task, in which a set of black squares is arrayed in a random pattern on a black background. The examiner touches a series of blocks, and the patient's task is to mimic the examiner by touching the same blocks in the same order. On average, individuals with brain damage or disease perform more poorly on the Corsi block task than do individuals without known brain damage or disease.

In domains that are characterized by significant accumulated knowledge, assessment shifts from a task-centered approach to a construct-centered approach. A construct-oriented approach begins with a specification of the target construct in terms of a signature complex of skills, knowledge, or other attributes. The nature of the target construct then guides the selection or construction of assessment tasks (Messick 1992).

The advantage of a construct-centered approach over a task-centered approach is that it leverages accumulated scientific knowledge in a way that is difficult to do with a task-centered approach. The assessment is embedded in a knowledge base that facilitates interpretation and use of assessment results. Task-centered approaches can result in the identification of interesting tasks that may have practical utility but for which an understanding of what the task actually measures remains illusive. A construct-centered approach facilitates establishing the construct validity of assessments in particular because the assessment derives from an identified construct.

Fortunately, reading is a domain that is characterized by a substantial accumulation of knowledge and thus lends itself to a construct-centered approach to assessment. In fact, the topic of this chapter, namely, the assessment of reading-related phonological abilities, provides an example of a construct-centered approach to assessment.

Ancillary Determinants of Performance

At best, the target construct of interest will be only one of a number of potential determinants of performance. Consider the phonological awareness task of elision. The task typically requires an individual to delete a speech segment from a word and then pronounce what remains. For example, "Say bland. Now say bland without the /b/ sound." The correct response is land. Successful performance involves the target construct of phonological awareness, because an awareness of the speech sounds that make up bland is required to perform the task.

However, successful task performance requires a number of other ancillary abilities. Adequate hearing and perception are required to hear the stimulus correctly. Attending to what the examiner is saying as opposed to the other noises that invariably will be present requires selective attention, and if the item is embedded in a larger set of items or tasks, sustained attention will be required. Remembering the item while performing the required operations requires phonological memory and working memory. Performing elision requires a cognitive strategy. Producing the correct response requires the ability to generate the required speech/motor output. Lexical knowledge, in the form of knowing the spellings of words, can affect task performance, if one uses the strategy of visualizing the spelling of "bland" and then deleting the letter "b." Metacognitive aspects of performance such as correctly monitoring whether you are getting the items right or not and employing an appropriate trade-off between speed and accuracy can influence task performance. Finally, general verbal ability and personality attributes such as willingness to attempt difficult items also can influence performance.

Composite Versus Discrete Measures

The issue of composite versus discrete measures refers to the extent to which one or more construct and ancillary determinants of performance are combined into a single composite measure or are separated into discrete measures.

The obvious advantage of discrete measures over composite measures is the smaller set of abilities that are likely to be responsible for performance, and potential targets for intervention designed to improve performance. However, our decision about whether to favor discrete or composite measures needs to be informed by the nature of our target construct and our purpose for assessment.

For example, consider the case of screening kindergarten children for risk for reading failure. The target construct of risk for reading failure is fairly broad. Deficiencies in phonological awareness and early literacy are two obvious sources of risk for reading failure, but deficiencies in attention, memory, and verbal ability also can contribute to the subsequent development of reading problems. Given the breadth of the construct, and the value of efficiency and economy when the purpose of assessment is screening, one or more composite measures might be optimal. Conversely, for many research and diagnostic contexts, the target constructs are likely to be defined more narrowly, and the need to minimize extraneous effects of ancillary determinants of performance is greater. Under these circumstances, an array of discrete measures is likely to be optimal.

For most assessment situations other than screening, discrete measures are preferred over composite measures. In practice, attempts to design discrete measures are characterized by trade-offs. Consider the previously mentioned task of elision in which the child is required to drop the /b/ sound from the word "bland" to produce "land." Our current interest includes assessing phonological awareness and other reading-related abilities in preschool-age children. Tasks such as elision are difficult for some preschool-age children to perform. The memory load is considerable, and responding requires making a verbal response to an adult. To reduce the effects of these ancillary determinants of performance, we have created multiple-choice versions of elision in which the child responds by picking out the correct picture from four alternatives. Memory load is reduced because pictures of the initial item and the four response alternatives are provided in front of the child as they are attempting the elision item. The response of pointing to a picture as opposed to verbalizing a response seems to elicit responses from children who are reluctant to respond verbally. However, the presence of four response alternatives increases the strategic complexity and level of attention required to do the task.

A related example is using nonwords rather than words to reduce the effects of lexical knowledge on task performance. Using well-constructed nonwords as opposed to common real words does appear to reduce, although not eliminate entirely, the influence of lexical knowledge on language tasks. However, the memory demands increase as it is more difficult to maintain nonwords in memory than it is common real words, and willingness to respond may be reduced because some young children are not comfortable having to try to pronounce nonwords.

ASSESSING READING-RELATED PHONOLOGICAL ABILITIES

The focus of this chapter is on two phonological constructs that have been of interest to researchers seeking to understand how children learn to read and why some children fail to learn to read (Wagner and Torgesen 1987).[1]

---

1. Wagner and Torgesen (1987) identified retrieval of phonological codes from long-term memory as the third reading-related phonological processing ability of interest. Much of the processing of written and spoken language involves retrieving phonological codes or pronunciations associated with letters, word segments, or whole words. The efficiency with which phonological codes are retrieved may influence the success with which phonological coding is used in decoding printed words (Wolf, 1991). The most commonly used measure that taps retrieval of phonological codes from long-term memory is a rapid naming task that requires children to say the names of common objects, colors, digits, or letters as

Phonological awareness refers to awareness of and access to the sound structure of one's oral language (Mattingly 1972). All words in the English spoken language can be produced by combining members of a set of roughly 43 distinct sounds or phonemes. Although almost 9 trillion (8,796,093,033,208) possible combinations of 43 phonemes are possible, only a relatively small number actually are represented in spoken English, and many members of this limited set are common to multiple words (e.g, "cat," "rat," "hat," "sat"). Because this sound structure is represented partially in printed English, phonological awareness provides a leg up for children learning to read.

Phonological memory refers to coding information in a speech-sound based (i.e., phonological) representation for efficient short-term storage (Baddeley 1986). Phonological memory is used, for example, when you remember a phone number you just looked up and are about to dial. We used to believe that a speech-sound based short-term store was involved fundamentally in all language activities including reading. This view has given way in the face of mounting evidence that a surprising amount of language processing can occur outside the confines of a traditional short-term memory (Wagner 1996). Nevertheless, individual and developmental differences in phonological memory appear to play more of a role when beginning readers attempt to decode words. Presumably, as readers attempt to sound out words, efficient phonological memory helps the beginning reader by storing sounds they retrieve from permanent storage that are associated with letters and letter patterns in the to-be-decoded word. In addition, an intriguing empirical fact is that for preschool- and perhaps even kindergarten-age children, measures of phonological memory and phonological awareness appear to be assessing essentially the same source of individual differences.

Much has been learned about how best to measure reading-related phonological processes over the past several decades of research. Nevertheless, less than optimal measures of reading-related phonological processes are commonly used in both research and practice. The goal of this part of the chapter is to summarize some

---

rapidly as possible. Although rapid naming tasks measure aspects of phonological code retrieval, much of performance is determined by ancillary abilities, particularly when continuous naming tasks using letters as stimuli are given to children who are able to read. Under these conditions, much of the variance in performance may represent letter knowledge, which in turn can be a byproduct of reading experience. Because of space limitations and the desire to feature some new developments in the measurement of phonological awareness and memory, assessing retrieval of phonological codes from long-term memory will not be addressed in the present chapter. Wagner Measuring Phonological Abilities page 12.

lessons learned about ways to measure reading-related phonological processes optimally.

Measuring Phonological Awareness

Common phonological awareness tasks include the previously mentioned elision ("Say *bland* without the /b/ sound"), segmentation ("Say *bland* one sound at a time"), blending ("What word do these sounds make: /b/ /l/ /a/ /n/ /d/?"), counting ("How many sounds do you hear in the word *bland*?"), and reversal ("Say *tab* backwards"). Although a complete account of performance on phonological awareness tasks is beyond the scope of this chapter, in simple terms, performance on measures of phonological awareness varies as a function of the cognitive operations required and the linguistic characteristics of the units on which the operations are performed (Golinkoff 1978; Schatschneider et al. 1999; Treiman 1992). For example, the cognitive operations required for counting segments or detecting rhyme or alliteration are less demanding that those required for segmenting or reversing the order of segments. With respect to linguistic characteristics of the unit being operated on, in general, larger units such as syllables are easier to operate on than are smaller units such as individual phonemes.

The literature that is relevant to understanding what determines performance on phonological awareness tasks is extensive. However, the literature is less than fully informative because nearly all of the studies address a single or at most a couple of variables, and because most of the variables are correlated in language samples, interpretation of the results can be problematical. Thus, word frequency tends to be negatively correlated with number of phonemes and number of syllables, with longer words being less frequent. Position within a syllable is correlated with phoneme category, with consonants occurring in initial and final positions more frequently than in medial positions. These correlated variables can make it difficult to construct stimuli that differ on a variable of interest but are equated on other variables that might affect performance. Consequently, whether a given variable has an independent effect on performance is not clear.

For example, Yopp (1988) carried out a factor analysis of phonological awareness tasks and concluded that two factors were necessary to account for the results. The factors were called simple and complex phonological awareness. What differentiated complex from simple phonological awareness was the extent to which sounds had to be stored in working memory while the operations were being carried out. Tasks that loaded primarily on the complex phonological awareness factor tended to be more difficult than tasks that loaded primarily on the simple phonological awareness factor. However, Stahl and Murray (1994) analyzed Yopp's data and found that item difficulty was correlated nearly perfectly (r = .95) with linguistic complexity, a variable Yopp had neglected to control. When Stahl and Murray generated new stimuli that controlled for linguistic complexity, only a single factor was necessary to account for correlations among phonological awareness tasks.

Garon (1998) carried out a study designed to examine the independent effects of a number of variables on phonological awareness task performance. These variables are listed in table I. A number of these variables represented aspects of linguistic complexity broadly defined.

Hierarchical word structure refers to the level of the units to be manipulated in the hierarchical structure of the syllable. Syllables can be described at four tiers or levels: Syllable, onset-rime, vowel-coda, and phoneme. Consider the first syllable of the spoken word "grasping," which is "grasp." At the highest, syllable-level tier, "grasp" is represented as the whole syllable "grasp." At the second, onset-rime level tier, syllables are represented by their onset and rime. An onset is the initial consonant or consonant cluster, and the rime is the vowel and any following consonant or consonant clusters. For the present example, the onset is "gr" and the rime is "asp." At the third, vowel-coda level tier, the rime is broken into the vowel and the coda, with the coda representing

Table I   Variables Believed to Influence Performance on Phonological Awareness Tasks Examined by Garon (1998)

1. Hierarchical Word Structure
    a. Syllable-Level Tier
    b. Onset-Rime Level Tier
    c. Vowel-Coda Level Tier
    d. Phoneme-Level Tier
2. Postvocalic Phonemes
3. Difficulty of Target Phoneme
    a. Manner of Articulation
    b. Place of Articulation
    c. Voicing
    d. Position
    e. Sound Represented by Letter Name
4. Word Length
5. Task

the sounds of the trailing consonant or consonant cluster. At this level, the rime "asp" is broken into the sound of the short vowel /a/ and the sound of the consonant cluster "sp." Finally, at the fourth and lowest phoneme-level tier, the coda is broken into separate consonants if necessary, and the syllable "grasp" is represented by the individual phonemes /g/ /r/ /a/ /s/ and /p/. The hierarchical view of syllable structure is supported by both linguistic and behavioral (Mackay 1972; Treiman 1983, 1985, 1986, 1995; Treiman and Danis 1988) evidence. In general, it is easier to operate on units in the higher-level tiers relative to the lower-level tiers. However, the magnitude of the effects of syllable structure can vary for different children and different stimuli (Christensen 1997; Carlisle 1991).

Postvocalic phonemes refers to the fact that consonants, particularly liquids (/l/ and /r/) and nasals (/n/, /m/, /ng/), tend to adhere to the vowels they follow (Stemberger 1983; Treiman 1984) to a much greater extent than they adhere to the vowels they precede (Treiman 1986).

The difficulty of the target phoneme refers to the fact that some phonemes are easier to distinguish and manipulate than others. Five variables that may contribute to phoneme difficulty were examined. The first three, manner of articulation, place of articulation, and voicing, refer to how phonemes are generated by our vocal tract. Manner of articulation describes what is done to produce sounds. Six manners of articulation—stops, fricatives, affricatives, nasals, liquids, and glides—vary in the extent to which air is constricted. Stops are produced by nearly completely stopping and then releasing the flow of air in the vocal tract; glides are produced by less constriction of air in the vocal tract. Place of articulation refers to where in the vocal tract the air is most obstructed. The eight places of articulation are bilabial, labiodental, dental, alveolar, palato-aveolar, palatal, velar, and glottal. These labels refer to which part of the vocal apparatus is constricted: Labial refers to lips; dental to teeth; alveolus to the pit at the front of the roof of the mouth; palate to the roof of the mouth; velum to the soft, rear portion of the palate; and glottis to the space between the vocal cords in the upper part of the larynx or voice box. For example, the sound /p/ is a bilabial, produced by constricting the air flow with the lips. The sound /g/ is a velar, produced by constricting the air flow by pressing the back of the tongue to the velum or rear portion of the roof of the mouth. Voicing refers to whether the vocal cords are vibrating when the sound is produced. The sound of the /p/ is an unvoiced bilabial; the sound of the /b/ is a voiced bilabial. Phoneme position within a word also affects phoneme difficulty. In general, the initial position is the least difficult, followed by final position, then medial position (Stage and Wagner 1992; Stanovich, Cunningham, and Cramer 1984; Treiman and Baron 1981). Other orderings of difficulty by position occasionally are reported (e.g., McBride-Chang 1995), but discrepancies in results may reflect uncontrolled variance in correlated variables such as phoneme category. Stage and Wagner (1992) found the expected ordering of initial, final, and medial position on item difficulty in an invented spelling task after controlling for phoneme category. Sounds that correspond to letter names (e.g., b) are easier than sounds that do not (e.g., w) (Treiman, Tincoff, and Richmond-Welty 1996).

Word length in number of phonemes has an effect on the difficulty of phonological awareness task items (McBride-Chang 1995; Treiman and Weatherston 1992). What is unclear is the extent to which the increase in difficulty of phonological awareness task items is due to aspects of phonological awareness per se as opposed to correlated variables including increased memory load and the fact that longer words are less frequent in general.

Word frequency affects performance on phonological awareness tasks. Performance on nonword items is poorer than on comparable real word items (Treiman 1996). The measure of word frequency used by Garon (1998) was the average bigram frequency for all of the bigrams (i.e., letter pairs) in a word.

In addition to the linguistic variables just described, Garon (1998) also contrasted two phonological awareness tasks, elision of a target segment and complete segmentation. These tasks were chosen because it was possible to construct stimuli for both of them that manipulated a variable of interest while controlling for linguistic variables that might influence performance.

Participants in the study were 70 first-grade children who were at risk for reading poorly based on their performance on two screening measures, namely, number of words read per minute and elision. Two analyses were done. The first analysis examined main effects of the variables previously described without controlling for the effects of other variables. This analysis was done for the purpose of comparing the results to the results of prior studies that tended to evaluate the effects of individual variables in isolation. The second analysis was a simultaneous regression analysis that showed the independent effects of each variable when the effects of other variables were controlled statistically.

The results of examining the effects of variables one at a time were consistent with the existing literature. Significant effects on item difficulty were found for eight variables: level of word structure; postvocalic phoneme; manner of articulation; place of articulation; voicing, position within a syllable; sound contained in letter name; and task. Of particular interest was which variables affected item difficulty when the other variables were controlled. Three variables had significant independent effects: level of word structure; postvocalic phoneme; and task. The effects of level of word structure were consistent with expectations based on which tier the segments were from. Postvocalic phonemes were more difficult, and elision was easier than segmentation

Recommendations. If the goal is to measure phonological awareness, simpler tasks such as elision, sound matching, and blending, are better than more complex tasks such as phoneme reversal or "pig-Latin" because the more complex tasks increase the cognitive complexity and memory requirements of the task. Items should vary in the level of word structure the target segments are from. For preschool-age children, it can be helpful to include both pictured, multiple-choice, and verbal free-response items.

Measuring Phonological Memory

If the goal is to provide the best measure of the construct of phonological memory and minimize the effects of extraneous variables, tasks should be chosen or constructed to minimize the effects of memory strategies and of ancillary cognitive operations. Perhaps the most commonly used measure of phonological memory is digit span. Strings of digits are repeated and the examinee's task is to repeat the string back in the correct order. To minimize the effects of extraneous variables for digit span, it is better to only use forward span as opposed to combining measures of forward span and backward span, because backward span introduces more cognitive complexity and involvement of working memory. It also can be helpful to use presentation rates equal to or ideally greater than one item per second to discourage rehearsal strategies. Even under these circumstances, digit span is of limited use for very young children because they do not know digits. Digits also are similar to letters in that they are encountered frequently in books. Consequently, correlations between phonological memory when measured by digit span and reading can be inflated by individual differences in reading experience.

A more recent phonological memory measure that avoids these limitations is nonword repetition (Gathercole and Baddeley 1989). This task requires examinees simply to listen to a nonword and then repeat it. The nonwords become increasingly longer and more complex. An example of a very easy item is "balope." An example of a very challenging item is "dookershatupietazawm."

Stone and Brady (1995) gave a variety of measures including nonword repetition to poor third-grade readers and control groups of age matched and reading-level matched children. Nonword repetition distinguished the less-skilled third graders from the other two groups. Nonword repetition performance accounted for 12% of the variance in reading ability when word attack was the criterion variable and 14% of the variance in reading ability when word identification was the criterion variable. These results reflect nonword repetition's contribution after age, verbal cognition, and the other phonological processing variables had been partialled out. Nonword repetition did not contribute significantly to the variance when passage comprehension was the criterion variable. Muter and Snowling (1998) reported that nonword repetition at ages five and six predicted reading accuracy at age nine after accounting for full scale IQ scores ($ß = .41$, $p < .05$ at age 5 and $ß = .40$, $p < .05$ at age 6). Nonword repetition performance at ages 5 and 6 also predicted nonword reading ability at age 9 after accounting for full scale IQ scores ($ß = .37$, $p < .05$ at age 5 and $ß = .39$, $p < .05$ at age 6). However, Gathercole and Baddeley (1993) did not find relations between nonword repetition and reading in a longitudinal study of children from ages four to eight, after controlling for age and nonverbal intelligence. Nonword repetition may also have an indirect effect on reading acquisition through its facilitation of vocabulary acquisition (Gathercole and Baddeley 1989, 1993).

The nonword repetition task is simple with respect to administration and the respondent's task is straightforward, merely to repeat the nonword. Where complexity arises is in deciding which nonwords to include. Technically, merely changing a single sound can turn a word into a nonword (e.g., "bicycle" to "picycle"), and that used to be the preferred method for generating nonwords. The reason for using nonwords as opposed to words is to minimize lexical knowledge and emphasize processing the phonological representation of the item. Presumably, changing "bicycle" to "picycle" resulted in an item with no lexical referent, and thus avoided any role of lexical knowledge. We now know that this view is incorrect. Lexical knowledge of words like "bicycle" and "pie" can be used in processing nonwords that share sound segments. For example, Dollaghan, Biber, and Campbell (1993, 1995) created 24 pairs of nonwords. Each member of a given pair differed by one phoneme in the stressed syllable. This change resulted in one member of the pair having a stressed syllable that corresponded to a word. The stressed syllable of the other member of the pair did not correspond to a word. An example of such a pair is "tay'-mo" and "day'-mo." Both are nonwords, but the stressed syllable of "daymo" is the word "day" whereas the stressed syllable of "taymo" (i.e., "tay) is not. Nonwords with stressed syllables corresponding to real words were repeated significantly more accurately than those with stressed syllables that did not correspond to real words. Findings such as these prompted Dollaghan and Campbell (1998) to develop guidelines for constructing a nonword repetition task that is less likely to utilize lexical representations already stored in the long-term memory.

In a related but different domain, Treiman, Goswami, and Bruck (1990) examined the influence of lexical representations on nonword reading as opposed to repetition. The nonwords examined were all of the form consonant-vowel-consonant (CVC). What they manipulated was the VC part of the nonwords. Half of the nonwords contained VC's that had many "neighbors" in the English language, meaning that there are several words that differ from the nonword by one letter in the initial position of the syllable. The other half had few, if any, neighbors. For example, the nonword 'tain' has several neighbors (main, rain, train, etc.) whereas 'goan' has few neighbors (not many real words end in 'oan'). The results were that the nonwords with real word neighbors were read significantly more accurately than nonwords sharing their VC's with few or no English words. This finding was consistent across groups of first graders, third graders, and college students. More lexicalization errors were made on the high-frequency VC's, implying that reading of these nonwords may be influenced by long-term memory processes. It is also interesting to note that poor third grade readers performed better than first graders on nonwords with high-frequency VC's, but worse on nonwords with low-frequency VC's.

We developed criteria to be used in constructing and evaluating nonwords based on guidelines from Dollaghan and Campbell (1998) and the results of Treiman, Goswami, and Bruck (1990). These criteria, which are presented in table II, are intended to result in nonwords that (a) minimize lexical processing and maximize phonological processing, (b) are pronounceable in the sense of not incorporating phonemes a child is not likely to be able to articulate, and (c) encourage reliable scoring.

We applied these criteria to the nonwords found in two published tests of nonword repetition. Gathercole et al. (1994) published *The Children's Test of Nonword Repetition-Revised*. Sample nonwords from this test include tirroge, merhayba, goodallower, yarsteth. Of the eight criteria for constructing and evaluating nonwords, the average number passed for nonwords on Gathercole et al.'s test was

Table II   Criteria for Constructing and Evaluating Nonwords

1. No consonant clusters.
2. Only CVC-type syllables.
3. No syllables are words.
4. Phonemes can be articulated by intended age of respondent.
5. Only tense vowels (all long vowel sounds, short o, and io, aw)
6. Consonants assigned to syllables that occur at frequencies less than 35 percent.
7. No phoneme is repeated in a nonword.
8. VC units of stressed syllables are low in frequency.

between two and three criteria. *The Comprehensive Test of Phonological Processing* (CTOPP) (Wagner, Torgesen, and Rashotte 1999) also includes a nonword repetition test. Examples of items include pate, nigong, lisashrul, and viversoomouj. The average number of criteria passed by the nonwords on the CTOPP was between five and six. The extent to which adherence to these criteria makes a functional difference in what the nonword repetition measures in practice is not known. However, Andrea Muse is beginning a study that will answer this question. She is comparing nonword repetition performance for items that vary in adherence to the criteria, including a nonword repetition test that contains nonwords that adhere to all eight criteria. Examples of nonwords that adhere to all eight criteria are dape, meeg, tawfoig, vafoimub, chahoigesobe.

Recommendations.   Phonological memory is best assessed using more than a single task, with each task designed to minimize the influence of rehearsal strategies. One way to do this is to minimize the time available for using rehearsal strategies. Nonword repetition, digit span when digits are presented to children at a rate one per second or better, and sentence memory where individual sentences are heard and then repeated verbatim, all satisfy this requirement. Digit span reversed introduces ancillary cognitive operations beyond those involved in phonological memory. Using nonwords rather than intact sentences as stimuli also reduces extraneous effects of non-phonological language abilities including semantic knowledge, grammar, and syntax.

RECENT DEVELOPMENTS IN ASSESSMENT

Assessments have changed in surprisingly modest ways in the past century. The IQ tests developed in the early 1900s bear strong resemblance to IQ tests used today. This resemblance has several likely explanations. Conceptions about basic abilities such as those assessed by IQ tests have changed little over this time period (Sternberg and Detterman 1986). The psychometric models that underlie many current tests are similar to those of early tests, as are basic assessment practices. The test theory that dominates existing educational measurement has been characterized as the application of 20th century statistics to 19th century psychology (Mislevy 1993). However, three synergistic advances provide the opportunity for a new generation of assessments that are likely to be fundamentally different and more useful than existing assessments. These advances are in the sciences of thinking and learning, psychometrics, and technology.

Advances in the Sciences of Thinking and Learning

Cognitive models now exist for performance on key tasks, including reading, that describe the representations and operations at a level of detail and understanding that was not the case even a couple of decades ago. Current theories of thinking and learning address how knowledge is represented, organized, and processed.

The methods used in the contemporary cognitive sciences to design tasks that are linked to underlying models of knowledge and cognitive processing, to structure observations of cognitive performance, and to draw inferences about what people know and do are directly transferable to the context of assessment (Pellegrino, Chudowsky, and Glaser 2001).

Advances in Psychometrics

One reason that many tests seem to look pretty much the same is the psychometric "bottleneck." Psychometrics refers to the science and technology of test construction. The fundamental psychometric models rely on techniques such as factor analysis and item analysis that have been in widespread use for decades. These models have constrained the content and format of tests in important ways. For example, high internal consistency reliability is a desirable characteristic of tests. Internal consistency reliability refers to the extent to which all items on a subtest or a test are measuring the same thing. The need to maximize internal consistency reliability, and related characteristics such as high item-total score correlations, results in tests that are limited in the range of information that is collected. To get high internal consistency reliability, and to maximize other traditional indicators of test quality, test items need to look pretty much the same and have relatively limited formats and modes of response.

Recent advances in psychometrics potentially can relieve the psychometric bottleneck. The traditional psychometric models, including item response theory models, classical item analysis, factor analysis, and latent variable and latent class models, all turn out to be special cases of a much more flexible, general model called a hierarchical Bayesian network (Pellegrino, Chudowsky, and Glaser 2001). The importance of this development is that the more general model does not impose the constraints that characterize the traditional psychometric models. Consider two examples of this freedom from previous constraints.

A score on most assessments is simply the number of items answered correctly. This number is obtained by simply adding up the correct responses, thereby weighting each item equally. But items are not always equally informative. Passing difficult items can be more informative than missing easy items. There are many possible reasons that a child might miss an item, but a correct response (provided guessing is ruled out) indicates that the child is able to do the task. In our work with preschool children, we sometimes have a child who figures out a way to do a task half-way through. The fact that they were able to do more difficult items is more informative about their ability than is the fact that they missed the beginning, easier items.

For a second example, the kind of assessment information that is generated and needed in the classroom on a weekly basis is essential for planning instruction, but it may or may not be relevant to prediction of more distal criteria such as performance on a year-end, high-stakes assessment. The general Bayesian network allows us to link classroom-level assessment information to year-end assessment, thereby informing the teacher whether students are making the progress needed to make a target level of performance on the year-end assessment. An analogy is the use of bar code readers in stores. Prior to bar codes, stores were periodically shutdown so an inventory could be carried out. Bar code readers make this practice obsolete, because reading bar codes during check-out provides a real-time inventory on a daily basis. This in turn makes ordering inventory more accurate and results in fewer out-of-stock items than used to be the case.

Advances in Technology

The key advance in technology is the widespread availability of computers. The insight that traditional psychometric models were special cases of a general Bayesian network would have had little practical value were it not possible to do the math required for generating and implementing a general Bayesian network. Programs for doing so serve the role of the bar code reader, allowing the input of a wide variety of assessment and other relevant information and generating probabilities that children will achieve desired outcomes.

It is important to note that the advances just described in the sciences of thinking and learning, in psychometrics, and in technology provide only the potential for genuinely new, more powerful and useful forms of assessment. Capitalizing on this opportunity will require an investment on the part of funding agencies and the research community before practical applications become commonplace.

ACKNOWLEDGMENTS

The work described in this chapter has been supported by grant number HD23340 from the National Institute of Child Health and Human Development.

REFERENCES

Baddeley, A. D. 1986. *Working Memory*. Oxford, England: Clarendon Press

Carlisle, J. F. 1991. Questioning the psychological reality of onset-rime as a level of phonological awareness. In *Phonological Processes in Literacy*, eds. S. A. Brady and D. P. Shankweiler. New Jersey: Lawrence Erlbaum Associates.

Christensen, C. A. 1997. Onsets, rhymes, and phonemes in learning to read. *Scientific Studies of Reading* 1(4):341–58.

Crowder, R. G., and Wagner, R. K. 1991. *The Psychology of Reading*. New York: Oxford University Press.

Dollaghan, C., Biber, M., and Campbell, T. 1993. Constituent syllable effects in a nonsense-word repetition task. *Journal of Speech and Hearing Research* 36:1051–4.

Dollaghan, C., Biber, M, and Campbell, T. 1995. Lexical influences on nonword repetition. *Applied Psycholinguistics* 16:211–22.

Dollaghan, C., and Campbell, T. 1998. Nonword repetition and child language impairment. *Journal of Speech-Language and Hearing Research* 41:1136–46.

Foorman, B. R., Francis, D. J., Fletcher, J. M., Schatschneider, C., and Mehta, P. 1998. The role of instruction in learning to read: Preventing reading failure in at-risk children. *Journal of Educational Psychology* 90:37–55.

Foorman, B. R., Francis, D. J., Fletcher, J. M., Winikates, D., and Mehta, P. 1997. Early interventions for children with reading problems. *Scientific Studies of Reading* 1:255–76.

Foorman, B. R., Francis, D. J, Shaywitz, S. E., Shaywitz, B. A., and Fletcher, J. M. 1997. The case for early reading interventions. In *Foundations of Reading Acquisition and Dyslexia: Implications for Early Intervention*, ed. B. Blachman. Mahwah, NJ: Lawrence Erlbaum Associates.

Garon, T. L. 1998. Elements of linguistic complexity and their effect on children's performance on phonological awareness tasks. Unpublished doctoral dissertation: Florida State University.

Gathercole S. E., and Baddeley, A. D. 1989. Evaluation of the role of phonological STM in the development of vocabulary in children: A longitudinal study. *Journal of Memory and Language* 28:200–213.

Gathercole, S. E., and Baddeley, A. D. 1993. Phonological working memory: A critical building block for reading development and vocabulary acquisition. *European Journal of Psychology of Education* 8:259–72.

Gathercole, S., Willis, C., Baddeley, A., and Emslie, H. 1994. The Children's Test of Nonword Repetition: A test of phonological working memory. *Memory* 2:103–27.

Golinkoff, R. M. 1978. Phonemic awareness skills and reading achievement. In *The Acquisition of Reading*, eds. P. Murray and J. Pikulski. Baltimore, MD: University Park Press.

Mackay, D. G. 1972. The structure of words and syllables: Evidence from errors in speech. *Cognitive Psychology* 3:210–27.

Mattingly, I. G. 1972. Reading, the linguistic process, and linguistic awareness. In *Language by Ear and by Eye*, eds. J. F. Kavanagh and I. G. Mattingly. Cambridge, MA: MIT Press.

McBride-Chang, C. 1995. What is phonological awareness? *Journal of Educational Psychology* 87:179–92.

Messick 1992. The interplay of evidence and consequences in the validation of performance assessments. *Educational Researcher* 23:13–23.

Mislevy, R. J. 1993. Foundations of a new test theory. In *Test Theory for a New Generation of Tests*, eds. N. Frederiksen, R. J. Mislevy, and I. I. Bejar. Hillsdale, NJ: Lawrence Erlbaum Associates.

Muter, V. and Snowling, M. 1998. Concurrent and longitudinal predictors of reading: The role of metalinguistic and short-term memory skills. *Reading Research Quarterly* 33:320–37.

Pellegrino, J. W., Chudowsky, N., and Glaser, eds. 2001. *Knowing What Students Know: The Science and Design of Educational Assessment.* Washington, DC: National Academy Press.

Rayner, K., and Polletsek, A. 1989. The Psychology of Reading. Englewood Cliffs, NJ: Prentice Hall.

Schatschneider, C., Francis, D. J., Foorman, B. R., Fletcher, J. M., and Mehta, P. 1999. The dimensionality of phonological awareness: An application of item response theory. *Journal of Educational Psychology* 91: 439–49.

Share, D. L., and Stanovich, K. E., 1995. Cognitive processes in early reading development: Accommodating individual differences into a model of acquistion. *Issues in Education: Contributions from Educational Psychology* 1:1–57.

Stage, S. A., and Wagner, R. K. 1992. Development of young children's phonological and orthographic knowledge as revealed by their spellings. *Developmental Psychology* 28(2):287–96.

Stahl, S. A., and Murray, B. A. 1994. Defining phonological awareness and its relationship to early reading. *Journal of Educational Psychology* 86(2):221–34.

Stanovich, K. E., Cunningham, A. E., and Cramer, B. B. 1984. Assessing phonological awareness in kindergarten children: Issues of task comparability. *Journal of Experimental Child Psychology* 38:175–90.

Stemberger, J. P. 1983. The nature of /r/ and /l/ in English: Evidence from speech errors. *Journal of Phonics* 11:139–47.

Stone, B. and Brady, S. 1995. Evidence for phonological processing deficits in less-skilled readers. *Annals of Dyslexia* 45:51–78.

Torgesen, J. K., Alexander, A. W., Wagner, R. K., Rashotte, C. A., Voeller, K. K. S., and Conway, T. 2001. Intensive remedial instruction for children with severe reading disabilities: Immediate and long-term outcomes from two instructional approaches. *Journal of Learning Disabilities* 34(1):33–58.

Torgesen, J. K., Wagner, R. K., Rashotte, C. A., Rose, E., Lindamood, P., Conway, T., and Garvin, C. 1999. Preventing reading failure in young children with phonological processing disabilities: Group and individual responses to instruction. *Journal of Educational Psychology* 91:1–15.

Treiman, R. 1983. The structure of spoken syllables: Evidence from novel word games. *Cognition* 15:49–74.

Treiman, R. 1984. Individual differences among children in reading and spelling styles. *Journal of Experimental Child Psychology* 37:463–77.

Treiman, R. 1985. Onsets and rimes as units of spoken syllables: Evidence from children. *Journal of Experimental Child Psychology* 39:161–81.

Treiman, R. 1986. The division between onsets and rimes in English syllables. *Journal of Memory and Language* 25:476–91.

Treiman, R. 1992. The role of intrasyllabic units in learning to read and spell. In *Reading Acquisition*, eds. P. B. Gough, L. C. Ehri, and R. Treiman. Hillsdale, NJ: Lawrence Erlbaum Associates.

Treiman, R. 1995. Errors in short-term memory for speech: A developmental study. *Journal of Educational Psychology* 21(5):1197–208.

Treiman, R. 1996. Children's phonological awareness: Confusions between phonemes that differ only in voicing. *Journal of Experimental Child Psychology*. (volume and page numbers?)

Treiman, R., and Baron, J. 1981. Segmental analysis ability: Development and relation to reading ability. *Reading Research: Advances in Theory and Practice* 3:159–98.

Treiman, R., and Danis, 1988. Short-term memory errors for spoken syllables are affected by the linguistic structure of the syllables. *Journal of Experimental Psychology: Learning, Memory and Cognition* 14:145–52.

Treiman, R., and Weatherston, S. 1992. Effects of linguistic structure on children's ability to isolate initial consonants. *Journal of Educational Psychology* 84(2):174–81.

Treiman, R., Goswami, U., and Bruck, M. 1990. Not all nonwords are alike: Implications for reading development and theory. *Memory and Cognition* 18:559–67.

Treiman, R., Tincoff, R., and Richmond-Welty, D. E. 1996. Letter names help children to connect print and speech. *Developmental Psychology* 32:505–14.

Wagner, R. K. 1996. From simple structure to complex function: Major trends in the development of theories, models, and measurements of memory. In *Attention, Memory*, and Executive Function, eds. R. Lyon and N. Krasnegor. Baltimore, MD: Brookes.

Wagner, R. K., and Torgesen, R. K. 1987. The nature of phonological processing and its causal role in the acquisition of reading skills. *Psychological Bulletin* 101(92):191–212.

Wagner, R. K., Torgesen, J. K., and Rashotte, C. A. 1999. *Comprehensive Test of Phonological Processing.* Austin, TX: PRO-ED.

Wagner, R. K., Torgesen, R. K., Rashotte, C. A., Hecht, S. A., Barker, T. A., Burgess, S. R., Donahue, J., and Garon, T. 1997. Changing relations between phonological processing abilities and word-level reading as children develop from beginning to skilled readers: A 5-year longitudinal study. *Developmental Psychology* 33(3):468–79.

Yopp, H. K. 1988. The validity and reliability of phonemic awareness tests. *Reading Research Quarterly* 23(2):159–77.

Section • II

Identifying Sources of Risk for Reading Difficulties

Chapter • 4

Toward Distinguishing Between Cognitive and Experiential Deficits as Primary Sources of Difficulty in Learning to Read:

A Two Year Follow-Up of Difficult to Remediate and Readily Remediated Poor Readers

Frank R. Vellutino, Donna M. Scanlon, and James Jaccard

BACKGROUND

In a recently published paper (Vellutino et al. 1996), we reported initial findings from a six year longitudinal study that addressed the question of whether currently employed "psychometric-exclusionary" approaches to diagnosing specific reading disability (dyslexia) tend to inflate the number of children classified as "reading disabled" beyond reasonable proportions (see

Clay 1987 for an excellent commentary on this issue). Estimates of the incidence of reading disability have ranged between 10% and 20% of the population of school children (National Advisory Committee on Dyslexia and Related Disorders 1969; see also Shaywitz et al. 1992). Yet, our own research and clinical experience suggested that these estimates are inordinately high and we intuited that early reading difficulties in most impaired readers are caused by inadequacies in pre-school literacy experience and/or inadequate instruction, rather than by neurodevelopmental disorder in cognitive abilities underlying the ability to learn to read, as is generally assumed to be the case (see Vellutino, Scanlon, and Tanzman 1998; Ysseldyke and Christensons 1988 for discussions of this issue). Thus, the primary objective of the study was to evaluate the validity of this intuition.

To accomplish this objective, we evaluated literacy development in severely impaired readers (n = 118) and normally achieving readers (n = 65) from their entry into kindergarten (before their reader group membership was determined) through the end of fourth grade. These two groups were sub-samples taken from a much larger population of middle to upper middle class children (n = 1407) initially assessed at the time they entered kindergarten. Reader status was determined in these groups in mid-first grade using measures of word level reading skills, intelligence, and exclusionary criteria typically used to define specific reading disability (e.g. uncorrected deficits, emotional disorder, frequent absences from school, socioeconomic disadvantage, etc.). Through random selection, the majority of the impaired readers from this group (n = 76) were assigned to receive daily one-to-one tutoring that was tailored to their individual needs[1]. The impaired readers who were not given daily one-to-one tutoring received whatever remediation was available at their home schools. For some of the children (n = 26), school-based remediation involved 2 to 4 days of small group instruction and for others (n = 16) it involved 2 or 3 days of one-to-one tutoring. The normally achieving readers were also subdivided into two groups using the group's Full Scale IQ as the cut point. This yielded a group of normally achieving readers with an average IQ, and a group of normally achieving readers with an above average IQ.

Reading achievement was periodically assessed for both the impaired and the normally achieving reader groups from the beginning of kindergarten through the end of fourth grade. Reading-

---

[1]Because 2 of the children given daily one-to-one tutoring moved out of the area, the final sample of these children consisted of 74 participants.

related cognitive abilities were also assessed in kindergarten and again in first and third grades. These included language and language-based abilities such as vocabulary knowledge, syntactic competence, rapid naming, and verbal memory, in addition to visual and executive processing abilities. Verbal and non-verbal intelligence were also assessed to evaluate the relationship between reading achievement and intelligence. In addition, at kindergarten entry, we evaluated literacy skills such as knowledge of the alphabet, phoneme awareness, and knowledge of print concepts. These assessments provided an indication of the children's home and preschool literacy experiences. To evaluate the possibility that early reading difficulties in many poor readers may be caused by limitations in early literacy instruction, we systematically observed the kindergarten language arts programs in all of the schools from which our poor and normal reader groups were selected.

On the basis of results from previous intervention studies (e.g. Clay 1985; Iversen and Tunmer 1993; Pinell 1989; Wasik and Slavin 1993), we expected that daily one-to-one tutoring would facilitate at least average level reading ability in most of the impaired readers. We also expected that reading-related cognitive abilities, especially phonological abilities, would tend to be deficient in the children who were found to be the most difficult to remediate, relative to the cognitive abilities of children who were found to be readily remediated and those of the normally achieving readers. These expectations were, in the main, confirmed.

Whereas the number of tutored children who would have qualified for "disabled reader" status prior to implementation of our intervention program represented approximately 9% of the first grade population from which our poor reader sample was selected, (n = 1284 after attrition), the number of children who would have been placed in this category was substantially reduced after only one semester of one-to-one tutoring and represented only 3% of this population when all children scoring below the 30th percentile on a norm referenced measure of print decoding were included in the count. When only the lowest achieving and most difficult to remediate children were counted—that is, those scoring below the 15th percentile on the reading outcome measure—this figure was reduced to 1.5%[2]. And in accord with

---

[2]The procedures we used for calculating percentage estimates for the number of children who would have qualified for a diagnosis of "specific reading disability" before and after remedial intervention have been discussed in Vellutino et al. (1996), but they are worth repeating here. The before intervention estimate was obtained by dividing the number of children from our kindergarten sample who were

our expectations, the most difficult to remediate children were found to perform below the level of both the readily remediated readers and the normally achieving readers on measures of phonological skills such as phoneme awareness, verbal memory, and rapid naming. Moreover, the performance of the readily remediated readers approached that of the normally achieving readers on these measures as well as on the reading outcome measures, and the children in the former group no longer qualified as "disabled readers." The poor and the normal (average IQ) reader groups were not found to differ, however, on measures of visual, semantic, and syntactic skills.

The possibility that early reading difficulties might be due, in some measure, to deficiencies in home and pre-school literacy experiences was supported by our finding that virtually all children in our poor reader sample were found to have poorly developed foundational literacy skills such as letter name knowledge and phoneme awareness at the time they entered kindergarten. That early reading difficulties may also be due to deficiencies in early literacy instruction was supported by our finding that children were more likely to experience success in beginning reading and less likely to be identified as poor readers if their kindergarten language arts program placed sufficient emphasis on helping them develop both word level and text level skills (Scanlon and Vellutino 1996, 1997; Vellutino et al. 1996). It was also found that the impact of various instructional activities varied in accord with

---

identified as impaired readers in mid-first grade (n = 118), by the total number of children from our kindergarten sample who were yet available in mid-first grade after attrition (n = 1284). This yielded approximately 9% (118/1284) as the estimate of the percent of children in the population who could have been classified as "disabled readers" using the type of psychometric-exclusionary criteria typically used in our schools.

However, this figure was based on a total (n = 118) that included the number of impaired readers given daily one-to-one remediation by project staff (n = 76), as well as the number of impaired readers given school based remediation (n = 42). To obtain a more accurate population estimate, excluding the children given school-based remediation, we multiplied the number of children in the total population of available children (after attrition) by the percentage of identified poor readers who received daily one-to-one tutoring by project staff (76/118 = 64.4%; 1,284 x 64.4% = 827). Using this figure as the base, the number of tutored children who scored below the 15th percentile on the Basic Skills Cluster (BSC) after one semester of remediation was estimated to be only 1.5% (12/827) of the total population from which these children were drawn. The total number of tutored children who scored below the 30th percentile on the BSC after the same amount of remediation was estimated to be only 3% (25/827) of the population from which they were drawn. Both of these percentages represent significant reductions in the estimate of the percent of children in the population who would have qualified for the diagnosis of "specific reading disability" compared with the 9% estimate obtained before remedial intervention was implemented.

the competencies that the child demonstrated at kindergarten entry.

Finally, we found that neither verbal nor non-verbal tests of intelligence discriminated between the impaired readers and the normally achieving readers of average intelligence. Neither did they discriminate between the impaired readers who were found to be difficult to remediate and the impaired readers who were found to be readily remediated. In addition, IQ-achievement discrepancy scores were not significantly correlated with initial growth in reading in poor readers having equivalent amounts of remediation (Vellutino, Scanlon, and Lyon 2000), suggesting that IQ scores do not predict initial response to remedial intervention, as might be supposed. At the same time, we found that the average IQ and the above average IQ normally achieving readers performed at virtually equivalent levels on measures of word level reading skills. Taken together, these results suggest that individual differences in intelligence are not strongly correlated with individual differences in basic print decoding skills (i.e., word identification and letter-sound decoding). They, therefore, add to the growing body of evidence questioning the use of intelligence tests scores to define specific reading disability, particularly the IQ-achievement discrepancy (Aaron 1997; Fletcher et al. 1994; Francis et al. 1996; Siegel 1988, 1989; Stanovich and Siegel 1994; Vellutino, Scanlon, and Lyon 2000).

In the present paper, we summarize and briefly discuss results that were not yet available at the time the Vellutino et al. (1996) paper was published. In that paper, we reported and discussed emergent literacy and reading achievement data obtained in periodic assessments of our target groups performed from the beginning of kindergarten through the end of second grade, which included assessments performed before initiation of our remedial intervention program and assessments performed after termination of the intervention program. In the present paper, we extend these findings insofar as we report and discuss the reading achievement data obtained in assessments conducted at the end of third and fourth grades. Similarly, in the Vellutino et al. (1996) paper, we reported and discussed results on measures of reading-related cognitive abilities obtained in assessments of these abilities performed in kindergarten and first grade, and contrasted the performance of children found to be difficult to remediate with the performance of children found to be readily remediated, relative to that of normally achieving readers. In the present paper, we contrast these groups on comparable measures obtained in assessments performed in third grade. We also report and discuss selected findings from hierarchical regression analyses evaluating reading growth in these groups.

A BRIEF REVIEW OF THE INTERVENTION PROGRAM

The intervention program used in the Vellutino et al. (1996) study was designed to be comprehensive and balanced. It involved activities designed to facilitate development of word level skills such as phoneme awareness, phonological decoding using letter-sound relationships and larger orthographic units, sight word identification, and written spelling. It also involved instruction designed to facilitate development of text processing skills, for example, discussion before reading a text to activate prior knowledge and generate predictions, guidance, and practice in the strategic use of both context and decoding cues to direct and check efforts to identify unfamiliar words, collaborative discussion of text meaning to facilitate reading for meaning, and writing for purposes of communication.

As we indicated earlier, each child received daily one-to-one tutoring for one or two school semesters, depending on individual progress. The remedial activities presented in each session, as well as the degree of emphasis placed on given activities, were tailored to that child's individual needs in accord with his or her strengths, weaknesses, and existing knowledge. However, approximately half of each session was spent helping the child acquire facility in various word level skills, while the other half was devoted to the reading of new texts and the re-reading of familiar texts to help the child acquire increasingly greater fluency in text processing and to foster deliberate and interactive use of both word level and text processing skills (see Vellutino and Scanlon, 2002 for a more detailed description of our intervention program).

The remedial instruction implemented in our intervention program was provided by teachers (n = 14) who were certified in either reading or elementary education. All but one had at least two years of teaching experience. Initial training of these teachers consisted of a 30-hour seminar supplemented by assigned readings that encompassed both theoretical and practical issues in reading and reading disability research. Fidelity of treatment was ensured by having the tutors record each remedial session on audiotape and 1 out of every 10 of these tapes was randomly selected for review by project staff responsible for implementing the study. Feedback and consultation to facilitate adjustments in teaching strategies were provided weekly. Bi-weekly meetings were also held with all of the tutors to discuss relevant issues and problems and to share ideas in the interest of improving instruction.

As we pointed out in a previous section, the intervention component of our study was designed to aid in distinguishing between impaired readers whose reading difficulties are caused primarily by basic cognitive deficits and impaired readers whose reading difficulties are caused primarily by experiential and instructional deficits. Thus, we did not compare our approach with other approaches and we did not attempt to evaluate the relative effectiveness of any given component of the intervention. However, the children who were (randomly) assigned to the school-based contrast condition mentioned earlier provided us with at least a rough barometer of the effectiveness of our program. The reader is reminded that most of these children received 2 to 4 days of small group instruction and the remainder received 2 or 3 days of one-to-one tutoring. We compared the performance of these groups with the performance of the children who received daily one-to-one tutoring from project staff on the Basic Skills Cluster (BSC) of the *Woodcock Reading Mastery Test-Revised* (WRMT-R, Woodcock 1987), which combines the Word Identification and Word Attack subtests of the WRMT-R. As might be expected, daily one-to-one tutoring was found to be generally more effective than small group instruction insofar as a larger percentage of children who received daily one-to-one tutoring was brought to at least an average level of reading achievement after one semester of remediation (67.1% versus 54%). However, for children who received 2 or 3 days of school-based one-to-one tutoring, the percentage of those who were brought up to the average range was about the same as the percentage of those who received daily one-to-one tutoring. Further, when compared with children who received only small group instruction, larger percentages of those who received any amount of one-to-one tutoring scored above the 45th percentile on the BSC (45% for daily one-to-one tutoring; 44% for 2 or 3 days of one-to-one tutoring; 19% for 2 to 4 days of small group instruction). Conversely, a smaller percentage of children who received daily one-to-one tutoring scored below the 15th percentile on the BSC: 15% for daily one-to-one tutoring; 25% for both 2 or 3 days of one-to-one tutoring and 2 to 4 days of small group instruction.[3] These results are in keeping

---

[3]It should be noted that the standard score mean for the *Woodcock Reading Mastery Tests-Revised* is 100 and the standard deviation is 15. Note, in addition, that the 15th percentile corresponds with a standard score of 84, the 30th percentile corresponds with a standard score of 92, and the 45th percentile corresponds with a standard score of 98. Thus, children who scored at or above the 30th percentile on these tests were solidly within the average range, while children who scored below the 15th percentile were at least one standard deviation below the mean.

with results obtained in other intervention studies (DeFord et al. 1988; Hiebert and Taylor 2000; Huck and Pinnell 1986; Iversen and Tunmer 1993: Pinnell 1989; Santa and Høien 1999; Torgesen, Wagner, and Rashotte 1999; Torgesen 2000; Wasik and Slavin,1993) and we feel reasonably comfortable in suggesting that our intervention program was adequate for its intended purpose.

SUMMARY OF MAJOR FINDINGS

Because the children who were assigned to the school-based contrast group received lesser amounts of remediation than the children assigned to the daily tutoring group and because unequal amounts of remediation would have complicated contrasts of difficult to remediate and readily remediated readers, the children who received school-based remediation were not included in the analyses comparing the former groups reported in the Vellutino et al. (1996) paper, and they were not included in any of the analyses to be reported in the present paper. In addition, the children who received daily one-to-one tutoring were tentatively partitioned into more or less difficult to remediate groups on the basis of estimated growth in reading from their entry into kindergarten through the fall of second grade. This procedure effectively equated the groups for the amount of remediation they received (each group had received approximately 15 weeks of tutoring) while providing us with a statistically defensible means for differentiating the tutored children in terms of their initial response to remediation. Growth in reading was estimated by calculating slopes produced by regressing Rasch-based "W" scores from the Basic Skills Cluster (BSC) of the *Woodcock Reading Mastery Test-Revised* (WRMT-R, Woodcock 1987) on time of assessment in months since kindergarten entry. Individual growth rates were computed for each child based on four assessment points: beginning of kindergarten, mid-first grade, end of first grade, and beginning of second grade. (Note that the 15 weeks of remediation occurred in the period from mid-first grade to end of first grade.) The slopes for the tutored children were then rank ordered and thereafter partitioned so as to form four (approximately) equal sized groups designated as follows: very limited growth (VLG); limited growth (LG); good growth (GG) and very good growth (VGG). To evaluate the relationship between reading achievement and intelligence in the normally achieving readers, we compared the normal readers whose intelligence test scores were in the average range (AvIQNorm) with the normal readers who had above average intelligence test scores (AbAvIQNorm) on all measures of reading achievement.

As we indicated earlier, reader group contrasts in the present paper will focus on results from assessments of reading achievement through the end of fourth grade and results from assessment of reading-related cognitive abilities undertaken in third grade. Brief descriptions of the third grade test battery appear in figure 1. It can be seen that the tests included in this battery evaluate essentially the same types of cognitive abilities evaluated by the kindergarten and first grade test batteries described in Vellutino et al. (1996), in particular, phoneme awareness, rapid naming, confrontational naming, verbal fluency, vocabulary, verbal concept development, language comprehension, syntactic awareness, verbal memory, and visual processing ability (see figure 2 for descriptions of the kindergarten battery). In the next section, we discuss results obtained on the selection measures and thereafter discuss results obtained on the achievement and cognitive measures.

A. Intellectual Ability
　　1. Wechsler Intelligence Scale for Children-Revised (WISC-R) was administered to all subjects.
B. Achievement Measures
　　1. Letter-Word Identification subtest of the Woodcock-Johnson Tests of Achievement - read letters and words presented in isolation.
　　2. Passage Comprehension subtest of the Woodcock-Johnson Tests of Achievement - read brief passages and supply the missing word.
　　3. Word Identification subtest of the Woodcock Reading Mastery Test - Revised (WRMT-R) - read words presented in isolation.
　　4. Word Attack subtest of the WRMT-R - decode orthographically legal nonsense words.
　　5. Spache Diagnostic Reading Scales - read connected text and answer comprehension questions (based primarily on explicitly stated information). This measure yields two indices of reading comprehension and one index of skill in word identification:
　　　　a. Independent Reading Level - Highest text level at which student should be able to read independently.
　　　　b. Instructional Reading Level - Highest text level at which student should be able to read with instructional support.
　　　　c. Word Lists - Number of words accurately identified in isolation.
C. Language Measures
　　1. Phonological Processing
　　　　a. Phonemic Segmentation
　　　　　- Initial Deletion - say the word that remains after deleting the initial sound in the word (e.g., mat - at).
　　　　　- Final Deletion - say the word that remains after deleting the final sound (e.g., place - play).
　　　　　- Articulation - say the different sounds in minimally contrasting word pairs (e.g., for the word fat and cat, say /f/ and /k/).
　　　　b. Phonological Memory - remember and say six nonsense syllables following each of eight presentation/recall trials. Children counted for 6 seconds between presentation and recall attempts.
　　2. Syntactic/Grammatical Processing
　　　　a. Token Test (Subtests IV and V) - comprehend and respond to spoken directions (e.g., Touch the large red square and the small yellow circle).

Figure 1.　Third Grade Test Battery

      b. Grammatic Comprehension subtest of the Test of Language Development - Intermediate, 2nd Edition (TOLD-I:2) - listen to sentences and decide whether they are grammatically well formed (e.g., John always forget where he lives).

      c. Grammaticality Judgment - listen to sentences and decide whether they are grammatically well-formed (e.g., The girl eated some cake.)

      d. Oral Cloze - listen to paragraphs from which a word has been deleted. Supply the missing word based on sentential constraints and story themes.

      e. Word Order subtest of the TOLD-I:2 - listen to a randomly ordered string of words and construct a grammatically well-formed sentence using all of the words presented and only those words.

3. Semantic Processing

      a. Vocabulary subtest of the WISC-R - define spoken words.

      b. Similarities subtest of the WISC-R - detect and characterize similarities in verbally presented concepts.

4. Naming and Verbal Fluency

      a. Rapid Automatized Naming (Letters, Numbers, Colors, Objects) - name the items in a 5 X 10 array as quickly as possible. Each item type is presented in a separate array. Score is the total number of seconds required to name all of the items in a given array.

      b. Rapid Articulation - Repeat five different pairs of words seven times as quickly as possible. Score reported is mean time, in seconds, to repeat pairs seven times.

      c. Word Fluency

      Semantic fluency - given a semantic category, name as many items in that category as possible within one minute. Two categories were provided: animals and food. Score reported is the total of the number of unique acceptable items provided for each category.

      Phonological fluency - given an initial letter, name as many items that begin with that letter as possible within one minute. Three initial letters were provided (C, L and F). Score reported is the total of the number of unique acceptable items provided for each category

      d. Boston Naming Test - evaluates the ability to retrieve names of items presented pictorially.

5. General Language Processing

      a. Listening Comprehension component of the Spache Diagnostic Reading Scales–evaluates ability to answer main idea and factual questions about narrative text presented auditorily.

6. Verbal Memory

      a. Digit Span subtest of the WISC-R - evaluates recall of randomly presented digits. Child recalls digits either in the order in which they were presented or in reversed order.

      b. Memory for Words - evaluates memory for concrete and abstract words under immediate and delayed recall conditions.

      c. Word Ordering subtest of the TOLD-I:2 - listen to a randomly ordered string of words and construct a grammatically well-formed sentence using all of the words presented and only those words. (or see Syntactic processing)

      d. Phonological Memory - remember and say six nonsense syllables following each of eight presentation/recall trials. Children counted for 6 seconds between presentation and recall attempts. (or see Phonological processing)

D. Visual Processing Skills

1. Performance Scale of the WISC-R - The subtests on this scale measure a variety of visual processing abilities (e.g., visual recognition, visual coding, visual-spatial analysis and synthesis, visual-spatial reasoning, visual-motor coordinations, etc.)

2. Visual Memory - remember dot patterns presented on a 3 X 3 or 3 X 4 matrix and reproduce each pattern on a magnetic drawing board using a round magnet equal in size to the dots on the stimulus matrix.

Figure 1.   continued

A. Conceptual Development (estimated) - Subtests of the Wechsler Preschool and Primary Scale of Intelligence-Revised (WPPSI-R, Wechsler, 1989) and Concrete Operations.
  1. Information subtest of the WPPSI–R - asks child questions evaluating general knowledge.
  2. Block Design subtest of the WPSSI–R - requires that the child assemble blocks to reproduce abstract geometric designs under time constraints; evaluates visual-spatial analysis and reasoning ability.
  3. Concrete Operations - measures of conservation, seriation and class inclusion were administered to determine whether the child had attained the concrete operational stage of conceptual development (Piaget, 1952).
B. Concepts of Print
  1. Print Awareness - assesses understanding of the communication value of print. For example, the child is asked to indicate which would be the best way to find out what is in a can: read the label or open the can.
  2. Print Conventions - assesses understanding of left/right sequencing of words, the concept of word and letter, etc.
C. Achievement Measures
  1. Rudimentary Reading Skills - measured by subtests of the Woodcock Reading Mastery Test-Revised
      a. Letter Identification
      b. Word Identification (naming whole words on sight)
      c. Word Attack (pronouncing nonsense words)
  2. Arithmetic
      a. WPPSI-R Arithmetic subtest - evaluates ability to solve "story problems" presented auditorily.
      b. Experimental test evaluating basic number concepts and simple arithmetic operations. Subtests included:
        (1) Counting by 1s
        (2) Counting by 2s
        (3) Number Identification (identifying numbers on sight).
D. Language Measures
  1. Phoneme Segmentation
      a. Initial Deletion - say the word that remains after deleting the initial sound of a word (e.g., cup - up).
      b. Final Deletion - say the word that remains after deleting the final sound of a word (e.g., plate - play).
      c. Articulation - vocalize the different sounds in minimally contrasted word pairs (/f/ and /c/ for fat and cat).
  2. Syntactic/Grammatical Processing - The Linguistic Concepts subtest of the Clinical Evaluation of Language Fundamentals-Revised (Semel, Wiig, & Secord, 1987)- children hear sentences directing them to perform certain operations in order ("Point to the red line after you point to the blue one.").
  3. Semantic Development - Peabody Picture Vocabulary Test-Revised (Dunn & Dunn, 1981)- evaluates recognition of vocabulary words depicted pictorially.
  4. Naming and Fluency
      a. Rapid Automatized Naming - requires child to name simple objects presented in a 5 x 10 array as quickly as possible. Score reported is total amount of time taken (in seconds) to complete the array.
      b. Rapid Articulation - requires child to repeat word pairs as quickly as possible. Score reported is mean time (in seconds) to complete seven repetitions.
  5. Verbal Memory and Visual-Verbal Learning
      a. Sentence Memory - child hears sentences and must repeat each verbatim.

Figure 2.   Kindergarten Test Battery

      b. Word Memory - child hears strings of randomly ordered words and must repeat each verbatim.

      c. Visual-Auditory Learning subtest from the Woodcock Reading Mastery Test-Revised - child learns to associate novel symbols with words and learns to "read" sentences made up of these symbols.

E. Visual Skills

    1. Visual-Spatial Reasoning - The Block Design subtest from the WPPSI-R evaluates analysis and synthesis of spatial relations, visual-spatial reasoning, visual-motor coordination, etc. Child assembles blocks to reproduce geometric designs.

    2. Visual Memory - Child is asked to reproduce dot patterns from memory on a magnetic drawing board. Patterns are either labelable (e.g., dots form a "T") or non-labelable (randomly arrayed).

F. Executive Functions (Attention, Concentration, Planning and Vigilance)

    1. Visual matching (Matching Familiar Figures Test-Modified) - the child is asked to find the identical match for a line drawing in a group of four similar drawings.

    2. Visual Search (Target Search Test) - the child is asked to look at a large group of geometric designs and put a line through all those that are identical to a target design.

Figure 2.   continued

Selection Measures

Table I presents results on the selection measures. Note first that the children in each of the tutored groups performed well below the children in both of the normal reader groups on all of the reading measures, but were comparable to the children in the average IQ normal reader group (AvIQNorm) on the intelligence measures. Thus, the children in the tutored groups would have qualified for "disabled reader" status on the basis of these results alone. At the same time, there were no significant differences between the tutored groups on any of the intelligence measures, indicating that the child's IQ did not predict his or her initial response to remediation, as we reported earlier. It can also be seen that the two normal reader groups have almost identical means and standard deviations on the word identification and word attack measures, which we also reported earlier. Note also that children who manifested the greatest amount of initial growth in reading when provided with intervention (GG and VGG groups) performed somewhat better on the word identification measure than did the children who manifested the least amount of initial growth in reading (VLG and LG groups), but all four groups were equally deficient on the word attack measure. Given that the word identification standard scores of the better performing groups were

Table I. Means and Standard Deviations obtained by Tutored Poor Readers Grouped in Accord With Growth in Reading Over Time and by Normal Readers on the Reading and Intelligence Measures Administered for Sample Selection Prior to Intervention (First Grade-Winter).

		Normal Readers		Tutored Groups			
		AvIQNorm n=28	AbAvIQNorm n=37	VLG n=19	LG n=18	GG n=18	VGG n=19
Verbal IQ	M	106.14	121.51	100.89	101.11	104.11	105.42
	SD	6.70	8.57	14.47	10.19	10.46	12.01
Performance IQ	M	107.00	119.03	102.32	102.67	106.11	105.26
	SD	9.03	5.97	9.84	9.59	13.35	9.43
Full IQ	M	106.89	122.86	101.37	101.94	105.56	105.58
	SD	6.57	5.33	10.17	7.66	12.53	10.24
Word Identification Standard Scores	M	116.64	117.00	80.89	86.22	93.17	93.74
	SD	13.98	13.24	6.47	9.80	5.67	6.39
Word Attack Standard Scores	M	102.21	103.14	74.58	77.50	76.89	80.05
	SD	11.68	10.84	7.77	8.91	5.62	7.40
Basic Skills Cluster Standard Scores	M	110.79	111.32	77.68	81.83	86.17	87.74
	SD	9.83	10.50	6.18	7.07	4.11	5.72

NOTE: Tutored Children are grouped by slopes for W scores obtained on the Basic Skills Cluster of the WRMT-R from Kindergarten through Fall of second grade. The word identification and word attack means and standard deviations are derived from the WRMT-R subtests evaluating these skills.

Key
VLG   - Very Limited Growth
LG   - Limited Growth
GG   - Good Growth
VGG   - Very Good Growth
AvIQNorm - Average IQ normal readers
AbAvIQNorm - Above average IQ normal readers

in the low average range, this disparity could be taken as an indication that several of the children in these latter groups had acquired some functional (albeit limited) strategies for word identification despite their deficiencies in letter-sound decoding.

Reading Achievement Measures

We reported in Vellutino et al. (1996) that approximately 70% of the tutored children were brought to an average level of reading achievement after one semester of daily one-to-one remedial instruction. A question that naturally arises is whether the positive effects of this instruction would diminish over time, a phenomenon sometimes referred to as "wash out" effects. A related question is whether such wash out effects would differentiate children initially judged to be difficult to remediate and children initially judged to be readily remediated. To address these questions, we calculated percentages, at each assessment period, for the total number of tutored children not lost through attrition whose standard scores on the WRMT-R Word Identification, Word Attack, and Basic Skills Cluster (BSC) was at or above a standard score of 90, which is well within the average range (see footnote 3)[4]. We performed the same calculations for the Passage Comprehension subtest from the Woodcock-Johnson Psycho-educational Battery (Woodcock and Johnson 1989, 1990) from which we had data for first and third grade. As an additional measure of reading comprehension, we calculated, for each assessment period at which data were available (Grades 1 to 4), the percentage of children whose grade equivalent scores on the Spache Diagnostic Reading Scales Silent Reading subtest (Spache 1981) were at least at grade level. These results are presented in table II.

It can be seen that 69% to 78% of the tutored children performed within the average range on the WRMT-R measures of basic word level skills at the end of first grade after one semester of remedial instruction. However, the percentages decline between first and fourth grade, the largest declines occurring at the beginning of second grade and the end of fourth grade. The sharp decline at the beginning of second grade was no doubt a summer "drop off" effect, which was more pronounced in the VLG and LG groups than in the GG and VGG groups (see figure 3). The sharp

---

[4]We opted to use a standard score of 90 in these analyses rather than percentile scores of 15 and/or 30 as used previously (Vellutino et al. 1996) because standard scores appear to be a more commonly used metric in reports that have appeared in the literature recently.

Table II. Percentages for Tutored Children Achieving Criterion Level Scores on the Reading Outcome Measures at Different Time Periods.

Grade	Word Identification	Word Attack	Standard Scores > 90*		
			Basic Skills Cluster	Woodcock Passage Comprehension	Reading Comprehension Grade Equivalents at Grade Level**
First(Spring) (n=74)	78%	69%	73%	50%	23%
Second(Fall) (n=74)	54%	49%	51%		
Second(Winter) (n=74)	61%	54%	58%		
Second(Spring) (n=74)	68%	58%	65%		73%
Third(Spring) (n=70)	64%	57%	61%	83%	67%
Fourth(Spring) (n=69)	46%	61%	54%		62%

Key

*Standard Scores for the Word Identification, Word Attack, and Basic Skills Cluster measures are taken from the Woodcock Reading Mastery Tests-Revised. Standard scores for the Passage Comprehension measure are taken from the Woodcock-Johnson Psychoeducational Battery.

**Grade Equivalent Scores are taken from the Silent Reading component of the Spache Diagnostic Silent Reading Scales.

Note that McNemar's (1955) Z test for correlated proportions was used to assess whether given percentage differences are statistically significant ($p < .05$). The number of contrasts was minimized by testing the smallest differences first. Percentage differences that are statistically significant ($p < .05$) are as follows: Word Identification-all differences greater than 16%; Word Attack-all differences greater than 10%; Basic Skills Cluster-all differences greater than 10%; Passage Comprehension- all differences equal to or greater than 33%; Reading Comprehension-all differences equal to or greater than 6%.

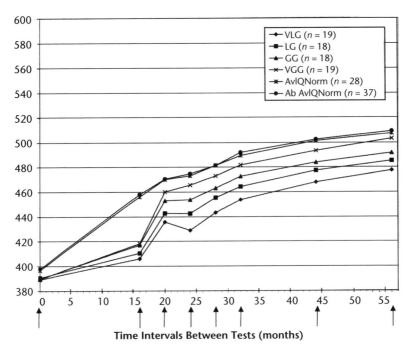

Figure 3. Growth Curves for Mean W Scores on the WRMT-R Basic Cluster Subtest for Normal and Tutored Poor Readers

decline at the end of fourth grade is especially pronounced in the case of the Word Identification subtest of the WRMT-R—from 78% of the tutored children scoring within the average range at the end of first grade to 46% percent scoring within this range at the end of fourth grade, which is a 32% drop off. This contrasts with an 8% drop off on the Word Attack subtest of the WRMT-R—from 69% scoring within the average range at the end of first grade to 61% scoring within this range at the end of fourth grade. Thus, combining the two measures produced a 19% drop off on the Basic Skills Cluster—from 73% scoring within the average range at the end of first grade to 54% scoring within this range at the end of fourth grade.

This is a puzzling pattern of results because until fourth grade, performance on the word identification measure was 5% to 10% greater than performance on the word attack measure. We suggest that the dramatic decline in the number of tutored children scoring in the average range on the fourth grade assessment of skill in word identification was an artifact of the difficulty level of the words presented on the Word Identification subtest of the WRMT-R (relative to the unique properties of the normative sample beyond second grade) rather than a manifestation of "backward sliding" in word identification ability. We make this suggestion because there was also a sharp decline in the standard scores of the normal readers beyond second grade (in first grade SS = 118.14 AvIQNorm; SS = 119.16 AbAvIQNorm; in fourth grade SS = 106.62 AvIQNorm; SS = 108.67 AbAvIQNorm). In addition, the percentages for tutored children obtaining criterion scores on the reading comprehension measures increased sharply beyond first grade: from 50% to 83% for Passage Comprehension; from 23% to between 62% and 73% for Spache Reading Comprehension. Given that facility in word identification is a prerequisite determinant of performance in reading comprehension, we think it would be incorrect to conclude that the sharp decline in the word identification standard scores of the tutored children between the end of first grade and the end of fourth grade signifies a true decline in the children's standing on word identification skill (relative to their normally achieving peers), between first and fourth grade or even between second and fourth grade, since the decline was evident among normal readers across these grades.

Nevertheless, it is clear that beyond first grade, there was a significant decrease in the number of tutored children whose standard scores on the three measures of basic word level skills were within the average range, despite the fact that there were significant increases in the number of children scoring within the average range or at grade level on the reading comprehension measures. This raises the question of whether the same pattern of results would be observed more often in the tutored children who showed the least amount of growth in reading during the initial period of remediation, relative to those who showed the greatest amount of growth in reading during this period. To address this question, we calculated, for each of the tutored groups, the same percentages on each of the reading measures that we calculated for the tutored groups combined. These results are presented in table III.

As is evident, the initial decline in percentages tends to be more precipitous in the VLG and LG groups than in the GG and VGG groups, and the percentage of children falling within the average range on the various measures is substantially lower in the former than in the latter groups at all grade levels. Indeed, in the VGG group, 95% to 100% of the children scored at least within the average range on the different measures of word level skills in both first and fourth grades and there was very little fluctuation between these grades. In contrast, only 26% to 37% of the children in the VLG group scored within the average range on these measures at the end of first grade and only 10% to 21% of the

Table III. Percentages for Tutored Children by Group Achieving Criterion Level Scores on the Reading Outcome Measures at Different Time Periods.

Grade	Standard Scores > 90 Very Limited Growth Group (VLG)				
	Word Identification	Word Attack	Basic Skills Cluster	Woodcock Passage Comprehension	DRS Silent Reading Comprehension (% at Grade Level)
First(Spring) (n=19)	37%	37%	26%	16%	5%
Second(Fall) (n=19)	0%	11%	0%		
Second(Winter) (n=19)	5%	11%	5%		
Second(Spring) (n=19)	11%	5%	10%		26%
Third(Spring) (n=19)	21%	32%	16%	67%	32%
Fourth(Spring) (n=19)	11%	21%	10%		42%

Table III. cont.

			Limited Growth Group (LG)		
Grade	Word Identification	Word Attack	Basic Skills Cluster	Woodcock Passage Comprehension	DRS Silent Reading Comprehension (% at Grade Level)
First(Spring) (n=18)	78%	56%	67%	44%	17%
Second(Fall) (n=18)	17%	17%	11%		
Second(Winter) (n=18)	56%	50%	44%		
Second(Spring) (n=18)	61%	61%	67%		78%
Third(Spring) (n=15)	50%	47%	60%	75%	71%
Fourth(Spring) (n=15)	27%	53%	33%		60%

Table III.   cont.

			Good Growth Group (GG)		
Grade	Word Identification	Word Attack	Basic Skills Cluster	Woodcock Passage Comprehension	DRS Silent Reading Comprehension (% at Grade Level)
First(Spring) (n=18)	100%	89%	100%	72%	39%
Second(Fall) (n=18)	100%	67%	94%		
Second(Winter) (n=18)	89%	72%	89%		
Second(Spring) (n=18)	100%	78%	83%		89%
Third(Spring) (n=17)	76%	58%	76%	88%	82%
Fourth(Spring) (n=17)	47%	71%	71%		47%

Table III.   cont.

	Very Good Growth Group (VGG)				
Grade	Word Identification	Word Attack	Basic Skills Cluster	Woodcock Passage Comprehension	DRS Silent Reading Comprehension (% at Grade Level)
First(Spring) (*n*=19)	100%	95%	100%	68%	32%
Second(Fall) (*n*=19)	100%	100%	100%		
Second(Winter) (*n*=19)	95%	84%	95%		
Second(Spring) (*n*=19)	100%	89%	100%		100%
Third(Spring) (*n*=19)	100%	89%	95%	100%	84%
Fourth(Spring) (*n*=18)	100%	100%	100%		100%

Note that because these percentages were obtained to provide additional information as to the derivation of the drop-off effects observed in the tutored combined groups, significance levels for each of the tutored groups were not of primary interest, and they were not computed.

children in this group scored within this range at the end of fourth grade. Percentages for children in the GG group are closer to those of children in the VGG group from first to fourth grade, but the percentages for average level scores on the different measures decline unevenly in this group—from between 89% and 100% at the end of first grade to between 47% and 71% at the end of fourth grade. Percentages for children in the LG group tend to be closer to those of children in the GG group than to those of children in the VLG group, but they fluctuate more than in any of the groups. Thus, it would appear, from these percentage differences, that the children who manifested the greatest amount of initial growth in the acquisition of word level skills in response to remediation were better able to consolidate and maintain their gains than were the children who showed lesser amounts of initial growth in the acquisition of these skills in response to remediation. However, this conclusion is qualified to some extent by the mean performance levels achieved by these respective groups on the various word level measures from the end of first grade through the end of fourth grade when the project ended. Because of space constraints, we table results only for the BSC. Table IV presents these results (see also figure 3)[5].

It can be seen that the means for the VLG and LG groups are closer to the cut-off score of 90 than are the means for the GG and VGG groups, which predicts that the percentages of children obtaining this cut-off score would be more labile in the former than in the latter groups. Moreover, the magnitudes of the mean change scores in the LG and GG groups are not appreciably different. And, whereas the mean initial drop off is of the largest magnitude in the VLG group, it is of the smallest magnitude in the VGG group. Thus, consolidation of initial gains was probably most difficult for children in the VLG group and least difficult for children in the VGG group.

We should point out, however, that 67% of the children in the VLG group and 75% of the children in the LG group obtained a standard score of at least 90 on the *Woodcock—Johnson Passage*

---

[5]It is worth noting that when we used a less stringent cut off to determine percentages of children in given groups who scored within the average range on each of the reading measures—that is, a standard score of 85 or better on the *Woodcock Reading Mastery-Revised* (WRMT-R) and *Woodcock-Johnson Tests* (which is the low end of the average range), 75% of the tutored children scored at or above this cut-off on the Word Identification subtest of the WRMT-R at the end of fourth grade, 72% did so on the Word Attack subtest, and 68% did so on the Basic Skills Cluster composite. Similarly, 93% of the tutored children scored at or above the Woodcock-Johnson Passage Comprehension subtest at the end of third grade.

Table IV. Means and Standard Deviations of Various Reader Groups on Basic Skills Cluster of Woodcock Reading Mastery Test - Revised (WRMT-R) Administered from First Through Fourth Grade.

Reader Group		Basic Skills Grade 1 Spring	Basic Skills Grade 2 Fall	Basic Skills Grade 2 Winter	Basic Skills Grade 2 Spring	Basic Skills Grade 3 Spring	Basic Skills Grade 4 Spring
VLG	MEAN	86.26	74.68	78.32	80.95	80.95	79.37
	SD	5.48	5.26	6.19	10.15	12.46	10.80
	N	19	19	19	19	19	19
LG	MEAN	91.39	85.33	88.11	90.17	89.60	86.13
	SD	4.05	3.71	5.85	6.49	8.23	8.76
	N	18	18	18	18	15	15
GG	MEAN	99.11	94.28	95.50	97.17	95.24	91.94
	SD	3.95	3.36	6.02	6.98	7.03	6.40
	N	18	18	18	18	17	17
VGG	MEAN	105.26	104.26	103.32	105.68	103.53	102.67
	SD	4.85	6.09	7.58	6.35	7.78	6.76
	N	19	19	19	19	19	18
AvIQNorm	MEAN	113.43	111.78	111.62	112.62	110.77	106.86
	SD	13.54	13.76	11.94	11.21	10.65	9.50
	N	28	27	26	26	22	21
AbAvIQNorm	MEAN	113.57	112.75	112.50	114.63	111.52	108.97
	SD	12.17	13.62	12.79	10.18	9.00	9.87
	N	37	36	36	35	31	30

Comprehension Test at the end of third grade (see table III). Similarly, 42% of the children in the VLG group and 60% of the children in the LG group scored at least at grade level on the silent reading comprehension component of the *Spache Diagnostic Reading Scales* (see table III) at the end of fourth grade. These percentages approach those obtained by children in the GG and VGG groups on the same measures for the same grade levels (respectively, 88% and 47% GG group; 100% and 100% VGG group). Average level performance on the reading comprehension measures is also reflected in the mean comprehension scores obtained by these groups at the end of third and fourth grades (see table V). These results are important because they suggest that despite their weaknesses in de-contextualized word identification and phonological decoding, most of the children in the two lowest reading groups had acquired functional reading comprehension skills by the end of fourth grade.

In light of the foregoing results, we cautiously suggest that our intervention program facilitated the acquisition of functional reading skills in the majority of impaired readers who were exposed to the program, notwithstanding significant declines in the percentages of children who scored within the average range (or performed at grade level) on the various reading outcome measures, after the intervention program ended. However, the average level of performance of children in the VLG and LG groups was substantially below that of children in the GG and VGG groups on all of the reading outcome measures administered from the end of first grade (after one semester of remediation) through the end of fourth grade when the project terminated (see tables IV and V). And, whereas all of the children in the VLG and LG groups received two consecutive semesters of remediation, approximately half the children in the GG group and all of the children in the VGG group received only one semester of remediation. Thus, the children in the VLG and LG groups generally proved to be more difficult to remediate than the children in the GG and VGG groups, particularly the children in the VLG group.

We pointed out in an earlier section of this paper that the children who were difficult to remediate were found to perform below the children who were readily remediated as well as below normal readers on language-based measures administered in kindergarten and first grade, especially those that depend heavily on phonological coding, for example, tests evaluating phoneme awareness, verbal memory, and rapid naming (Vellutino et al. 1996). These groups were not found to differ, however, on tests evaluating visual, semantic and, syntactic competencies. These re-

Table V. Means and Standard Deviations of Various Reader Groups on Measures of Reading Comprehension Administered from First through Fourth Grade.

		Woodcock-Johnson Passage Comprehension Standard Scores		Spache Diagnostic Reading Scales Silent Reading Comprehension Grade Equivalent Scores			
		Grade 1	Grade 3	Grade 1	Grade 2	Grade 3	Grade 4
VLG	MEAN	84.63	93.61	.08	2.03	2.95	4.28
	SD	7.85	8.93	.37	.84	.84	1.26
	N	19	18	19	19	19	19
LG	MEAN	85.65	94.75	.34	2.81	3.73	4.63
	SD	8.42	9.28	.66	.48	1.18	1.37
	N	17	16	18	18	17	15
GG	MEAN	93.41	101.12	.69	3.27	3.85	4.46
	SD	9.15	9.43	.90	.76	.98	1.27
	N	17	17	18	18	17	17
VGG	MEAN	93.79	108.74	.77	3.31	4.02	5.33
	SD	9.96	8.48	.96	.63	1.01	.62
	N	19	19	19	19	19	18
AvIQNorm	MEAN	111.56	109.87	2.20	3.84	4.38	5.36
	SD	12.36	10.93	1.02	.88	.95	1.11
	N	25	23	27	26	24	21
AbAvIQNorm	MEAN	114.24	120.26	2.68	4.81	5.48	6.07
	SD	9.87	7.94	1.11	1.47	1.26	1.01
	N	33	31	37	36	32	30

sults were essentially replicated in the follow-up assessments administered in third grade.

Results From the Third Grade Cognitive Battery

Table VI presents effect sizes for cognitive measures included in the third grade battery that produced statistically significance differences between given groups following multivariate analysis of variance on tasks evaluating similar skills and abilities. The SPSS statistical software package was used for data analysis and the SPSS Bonferroni t test procedure was used for post hoc pair-wise comparisons between means. This procedure automatically controls overall error rate by setting the error rate for each test to the experiment-wise error rate divided by the total number of tests. The experiment-wise error rate for contrasts among the six reader groups was $p = .05$ (adjusted per contrast error rate = .05/15 = .003). Note also that for all measures, effect sizes were computed relative to the normally achieving readers of average intelligence. Accordingly, the means and standard deviations derived from this group are presented for each of the measures tabled. For the sake of economy, we present superscripts marking significant differences only for contrasts involving the tutored groups and the average IQ normal reader group (AvIQNorm), but it can be inferred that significant differences favoring the AvIQNorm group also favor the above average IQ normal reader group (AbAvIQNorm). Note also that there were no statistically significant differences between the average and the above average IQ normal reader groups on any of the measures that appear in table VI.

Before discussing these results, however, we should point out that with one exception, the AvIQNorm group did not differ significantly from any of the tutored groups on the various measures of intelligence administered in third grade (Wechsler intelligence Scale for Children-Revised, Wechsler 1974), nor did the tutored groups differ significantly from each other on any of these measures. The only exception was a statistically significant difference between the AvIQNorm group and the VLG group on the WISC-R Verbal IQ (AvIQNorm VIQ = 110.72, SD = 11.41; VLG VIQ = 99.05, SD = 11.55), although the difference between the Verbal IQs of the VGG and the VLG groups was marginally significant (VGG VIQ = 108.68, SD = 10.20). These differences could certainly be due to chance and/or regression to the mean, but they could also reflect growing disparities between increasingly fluent and less fluent readers in the acquisition of knowledge and skills that depend, in part, on reading ability (Stanovich 1986; Vellutino, Scanlon, and

Table VI. Effect sizes for cognitive variables in third grade.

Measure		Normal Readers		Tutored Groups			
		AvIQNorm n=28	AbAvIQNorm n=32	VLG n=19	LG n=16	GG n=17	VGG n=19
Phoneme Segmentation[a]	M	26.17	0.53	-1.01	-0.94	-0.97	-0.50
	SD	4.61					
RAN Objects Time[a]	M	46.98	-0.46	1.21	0.15	0.23	0.22
	SD	7.73					
RAN Colors Time[a]	M	42.50	0.16	1.43	0.39	0.39	0.25
	SD	8.86					
RAN Letters Time[a,d]	M	27.01	-0.15	1.81	0.79	1.06	-0.06
	SD	4.45					
RAN Numbers Time	M	28.53	-0.01	0.98	0.58	0.57	0.04
	SD	7.19					
Boston Naming Test[a]	M	40.86	0.47	-1.54	-0.77	-0.59	-0.65
	SD	4.62					
WISC-R Digit Span[a,b,c]	M	11.05	0.00	-1.24	-1.07	-0.97	-0.70
	SD	2.36					
Immediate Recall Concrete Words	M	21.55	0.85	-0.63	-0.23	-0.18	-0.05
	SD	4.16					
Immediate Recall Abstract Words	M	20.32	0.39	-0.81	-0.24	-0.23	-0.37
	SD	4.90					
Syntactic Word Order[a]	M	12.35	0.49	-1.32	-0.75	-0.96	-0.61
	SD	2.50					
Phonological Memory[d,e]	M	22.36	0.45	-1.02	-0.64	-0.85	0.27
	SD	6.11					

Table VI. continued

Measure		Normal Readers		Tutored Groups			
		AvIQNorm n=28	AbAvIQNorm n=32	VLG n=19	LG n=16	GG n=17	VGG n=19
Token Sentence Comprehension IV[a]	M	9.27	0.25	-1.19	-1.01	-0.74	-0.43
	SD	1.03					
Token Sentence Comprehension V	M	18.55	0.24	-0.65	-0.66	-0.56	-0.19
	SD	2.13					

Effect Sizes were computed relative to the average IQ normal reader mean and standard deviation.

Note: The cognitive variables tabled were those that were found to be statistically significant in contrasts involving the different tutored groups and the average IQ normal readers. In all cases, differences that were found to be statistically significant in contrasts involving the average IQ normal readers and given tutored groups were also found to be statistically significant in contrasts involving those groups and the above average IQ normal reader group. However, for the sake of economy we did not mark these differences with superscripts. There were no statistically significant differences observed between the two normal reader groups on any of the measures tabled.

[a]Significant differences between the AvIQNorm versus the VLG group.
[b]Significant differences between the AvIQNorm versus the LG group.
[c]Significant differences between the AvIQNorm versus the GG group.
[d]Significant differences between the VGG versus the VLG group.
[e]Significant differences between the VGG group versus the GG group.

Spearing 1995; Vellutino, Scanlon, and Tanzman 1988). Nevertheless, the absence of reliable differences between any of these groups on the non-verbal and composite measures of intelligence (respectively, WISC-R Performance IQ and Full Scale IQ; Wechsler 1974) provides additional confirmation for our contention that neither observed differences between the tutored children and the normal readers in beginning reading achievement nor the differential response of the tutored children to remedial intervention can be explained by individual or group differences in intelligence (Vellutino et al. 1996; Vellutino et al. 2000). We turn now to comparisons of these groups on the third grade cognitive battery.

It can be seen in table VI that statistically significant differences were observed between the VLG group and the AvIQNorm group on the phoneme segmentation measure. None of the other group differences was found to be statistically significant based on the Bonferroni t. However, it should be noted that the VLG, LG, and GG groups performed at comparable levels on the phoneme segmentation measure and that all three groups generally performed below the AvIQNorm group on this measure (see effect sizes). A similar pattern of results was observed at the end of second and fourth grades, except for significant differences between the GG group and the two normal reader groups at these grade levels (data not shown). Thus, by the end of third grade, a substantial proportion of the tutored children continued to demonstrate weaknesses in phoneme segmentation skills. These results are consistent with the observation of significant differences between the tutored and normal reader groups on measures of these skills, both at sample selection and at the end of first grade (Vellutino et al. 1996).

On the rapid automatized naming (RAN) tasks, statistically significant differences were observed between the AvIQNorm and VLG groups on all but RAN Number Naming, and between the VLG and VGG groups on RAN Letter Naming (table VI). No other group differences were found to be statistically significant on the RAN measures, although once again, the effect sizes for the LG and GG groups on RAN Letter Naming suggest that at least some of the children in these groups found this task to be more challenging than did the normal readers, in accord with the pattern of results obtained on the third grade phoneme segmentation measure. Results on RAN Letter Naming parallel results reported for these children when they were in first grade (Vellutino et al. 1996).

On the confrontational naming (Boston Naming) task, the AvIQNorm group performed significantly better than the VLG group, but not significantly better than the other tutored groups.

Further, the effect sizes for the LG and GG groups were more similar to that of the VGG group than to that of the VLG group. However, there were no statistically significant differences among the tutored groups on the confrontational naming task. These results essentially replicate results obtained on the first grade assessment, although on that assessment, the VGG group was found to perform better than the VLG group on this task (Vellutino et al. 1996).

Statistically significant reader group differences were also observed on the verbal memory tasks (table VI). On the digit span task, the normal reader groups performed significantly better than the VLG, LG, and GG groups, but not significantly better than the VGG group. However, the tutored groups did not differ on this task. On the working memory task (Syntactic Word Order), the AvIQNorm group performed significantly better than the VLG group, but no better than the other three tutored groups. The tutored groups did not differ among themselves on the working memory task and the effect sizes were moderate to large for all of the groups. On the phonological memory task, the VGG group performed significantly better than the VLG and GG groups, but no better than the LG group. Somewhat surprisingly, and despite some fairly large effect sizes, the performance of the AvIQNorm group was not significantly different from that of any of the tutored groups on the phonological memory task. However, the AbAvIQNorm group performed significantly better than all but the VGG group on this task. Note also that with the exception of statistically significant differences between the AbAvIQNorm group and the VLG group on immediate recall of concrete words and both immediate and delayed recall of abstract words, there were no significant differences between and among the other groups on the memory for words measures.

The pattern of results on the verbal memory tasks is quite similar to the pattern of results obtained on such tasks on the kindergarten and first grade assessments (Vellutino et al. 1996) insofar as the normal readers generally performed better than the VLG group, but not consistently better than the VGG group. At the same time, the VGG group often performed better than the VLG group on one or another of the verbal memory tasks, as observed in the earlier assessments.

Finally, both of the normal reader groups performed significantly better than the VLG group on one of the measures of sentence comprehension presented in table VI (Token Sentence Comprehension IV), but no other group differences were found to be statistically significant on this test. There were no significant reader group differences on the second measure of sentence comprehension presented in table VI (Token Sentence Comprehension V), except for those involving the AbAvIQNorm group and the VLG, LG, and, GG groups respectively (significance levels not shown). Yet effect sizes for the tutored groups, on both of these measures, were generally below those of the normal reader groups. These results were essentially the same as those reported in Vellutino et al. (1996), except that the normal readers were found to perform better than the VLG group on Token Sentence Comprehension IV and V and the VGG group was found to perform better than the VLG group on Token Sentence Comprehension V.

In contrast to the reader groups differences observed on the cognitive measures presented in table VI, there were no statistically significant differences between the AvIQNorm group and any of the tutored groups on measures of semantic and phonological fluency, vocabulary and verbal concept development, syntactic competence, general language (listening) comprehension, and visual processing abilities (data not shown). Neither were there any significant differences between the tutored groups themselves on these measures (data not shown). The magnitudes of effect sizes among the tutored groups ranged from small to moderate size, and their signs were, in most (though not all) instances, negative. However, magnitude was not always linearly related to reader group membership, although the top reading groups (VGG and GG) generally performed above the bottom reading groups (VLG and LG) on most of the language-based measures.

Finally, the, AbAvIQNorm group performed significantly better than the tutored groups on many of these measures though not reliably so (data not shown). In addition, the AbAvIQNorm group performed better than the AvIQNorm group on the general language comprehension measure as well as on one of the visual processing measures, the WISC-R Block Design (data not shown). These results are generally in accord with those reported in Vellutino et al. (1996), except for significant differences reported in the previous paper between the AvIQNorm group and the VLG group on the general language comprehension measure and on one of the syntax measures (oral cloze), and between the VLG and VGG groups on the general language comprehension measure.

Results From Growth Curve Analyses

To evaluate at least some of the factors that may have influenced growth in reading ability in the tutored and normally achieving readers, we regressed Rasch-based W scores from the Basic Skills

Cluster (BSC) of the WRMT-R on time in months using the hierarchical linear modeling program (HLM) initially developed by Bryk and Raudenbush (1992) to estimate growth parameters (see also Raudenbush and Bryk 2002). Reading growth was evaluated over eight measuring points: beginning of kindergarten, winter of first grade, spring of first grade, fall of second grade, winter of second grade, spring of second grade, spring of third grade, and spring of fourth grade. Hierarchical linear modeling is, of course, the preferred approach to modeling change over time because it allows one to separate variability in individual growth from variability in person level characteristics (e.g., cognitive abilities, educational history, etc.) as determinants of individual growth parameters. However, in preliminary analyses we conducted, it became evident that neither a linear nor a polynomial regression model provided an adequate fit to our data, largely because of discontinuous shifts in the growth trajectories of the tutored children, that were (apparently) associated with the intervention they received (see figure 3). We then decided to use a form of piecewise linear regression known as "spline regression" to estimate growth parameters (Marsh and Cormier 2002; Pindyck and Rubinfeld 1998). As stated by Marsh and Cormier (2002), "a piecewise linear spline model can be defined as a regression model that consists of a continuous explanatory variable defined over specified segments of the domain of that variable and a dependent variable that is a continuous function of that explanatory variable over all segments, but with different slopes in each of the separate segments" (p.9). Because of its demonstrated ability to accommodate even dramatic shifts in slope (Marsh and Cormier 2001), spline regression seemed appropriate for modeling our data.

In spline regression models, the regression line is divided at certain strategic join points called "spline knots," using dummy coding procedures to adjust for breaks in the line to do so[6]. Because we were interested in modeling changes in the regression slopes of the tutored children, relative to those of the normal readers, before, during, and after remedial intervention, we used three spline knots to divide the regression line into four segments: the period before intervention (beginning of kindergarten to winter of first grade—0 to 16 months); the period encompassing first grade

---

[6]The dummy coding procedure used for segmenting the regression line in spline regression models is described in greater detail in Marsh and Cormier (2002). In general, it involves creating separate dummy variables for the time periods demarcated by each "spline knot" and then using these dummy variables to create spline adjustment variables that eliminate breaks in the regression line.

intervention (winter to spring of first grade—16 to 20 months); the summer hiatus period (spring of first grade to fall of second grade—20 to 24 months); and the long-term follow up period (fall of second grade to spring of fourth grade—24 to 56 months). Accordingly, the HLM analyses provided us with regression coefficients for the intercept, and separate coefficients for the slope of the regression line for each of the four segments, along with coefficients for changes from one segment to the next.

Two separate sets of analyses were conducted: one that included both the normally achieving and tutored readers (n = 139); and a second that included only the tutored readers (n = 74)[7]. Note that in both analyses, the first segment in the spline analysis had only two time points so that analyses of correlates of slope differences in this segment represent analyses of correlates of raw change. An alternative approach models covariate adjusted change based on predicting reading levels at time 2 while holding constant reading levels at time 1. Such analyses address a somewhat different question than correlates of raw change. Our focus in this chapter is on correlates of raw change. We might also point out that, for most children, the beginning of kindergarten is truly the "zero point" for word level skills and the significant intercepts that emerged in the analyses reported below were probably produced by a very small number of children. Thus, we doubt that results would have been appreciably different if we had held reading at time 1 constant in these analyses.

Table VII presents parameter estimates for both an unconditional model for the combined groups that used only time in months and the spline adjustment variables (spline knots) segmenting the regression line as first level predictors (panel A), and a conditional model for the combined groups that used dummy variable coding for reader group differences as a second (person) level predictor (panel B). It can be seen (panel A) that all of the parameter estimates for the regression of time on the BSC W scores are statistically significant as are all but one of the variance components. The significant intercept is meaningful because it represents the beginning (zero point) of data collection. It indicates that some children entered kindergarten with substantial print decoding skills (i.e., significantly different from zero). The average

---

[7]Preliminary analyses suggested that there is some degree of autocorrelation in the residuals, which, of course, would distort the magnitude of the standard errors. However, this circumstance would not appreciably affect parameter estimates that are highly significant, and, thus, the results reported above provide us with at least a "bird's eye view" of the reading growth parameters which characterize the target groups in this study.

Table VII. Growth curve parameters for basic skills cluster W scores of normal reader groups and tutored groups for four time periods: before intervention, during first grade intervention, during the summer hiatus, and from fall of second grade to the end of fourth grade.

Panel A: Unconditional Model for Combined Groups ($n=139$).

Time Periods	Intercept	Slopes	Slopes Change
Before Intervention (0–16 months)	393.52**	2.50**	
First Grade Intervention (16–20 months)		6.09**	3.59**
Summer Hiatus (20–24 months)		1.56**	–4.53**
Second to Fourth Grade (24–56 months)		.93**	–.63*

Standard Deviations for Parameter Estimates	
Intercept	9.18**
Slope (0–16 months)	1.24**
Slope Change (16–20 months)	3.77**
Slope Change (20–24 months)	2.62**
Slope Change (24–56 months)	1.07

Panel B: Conditional Model: Reader Group as Predictor.

Time Periods	Intercept	Slopes	Slopes Change
Before Intervention (0–16 months)			
Normal	397.63**	3.71**	
Tutored	389.89**	1.43**	
Differences	7.74**	2.28**	
First Grade Intervention (16–20 months)			
Normal		3.11**	–.60
Tutored		8.70**	7.27**
Differences		–5.59**	–7.87**
Summer Hiatus (20–24 months)			
Normal		1.80**	–1.31**
Tutored		1.33**	–7.37**
Differences		.47	6.06**
Second to Fourth Grade (24–56 months)			
Normal		.71*	–1.09**
Tutored		1.11**	–.22
Differences		–.40	–.87*

Table VII. continued

Standard Deviations for Parameter Estimates	
Intercepts	8.45**
Slope (0–16 months)	.52**
Slope Change (16–20 months)	.67
Slope Change (20–24 months)	.72
Slopes Change(24–56 months)	1.15

*< .05, **< .01.

Note that a separate analysis involving only the tutored groups (Unconditional Model) produced no statistically significant variability on any of the parameter estimates.

rate of growth in these skills increased significantly during the period from kindergarten to winter of first grade, prior to initiation of the first grade intervention program. However, there was a sharp increase in the average rate of growth of print decoding skills during the period encompassing the first grade intervention program, which was (ostensibly) associated with sharp increases in individual growth rates among the children who received remedial intervention (see figure 3). This was followed by a sharp decline in the average growth rate over the summer months and a more gradual decline during the months encompassing the follow-up period from second to fourth grade. The statistically significant variance components indicate that there was substantial variability in the growth parameters of the different individuals in the sample, with the exception of that corresponding with the rate of reading growth from second to fourth grade. The standard deviation for this coefficient did not achieve statistical significance suggesting that individual growth rates during this period did not deviate significantly from the average growth rate.

The general overview of reading growth provided by panel A is qualified by the pattern of differences that emerged when reader group was used as the person level predictor (panel B). First, note that although the average intercept was significantly larger in the normal than in the tutored readers (as would be expected), both intercepts are significantly different from zero, which indicates that there were some children in both groups who entered kindergarten with some degree of facility in print decoding. Second, it is apparent that the rate of growth in print decoding was significantly greater in the normal readers than in the tutored readers before the first grade intervention program was initiated. However, there was a dramatic increase in the average growth rate of the tutored children during the four-month period following initiation of the first grade intervention program, which was quite likely a positive effect of the remediation these children received during this period. In contrast, there was a slight (though non-significant) decline in the normal readers' growth rate during the first grade intervention period and their rate of growth was significantly smaller than that of the tutored readers during this period. Yet, there was a sharp decline in the average growth rate of the tutored readers during the summer hiatus, though the drop-off was apparently more pronounced in the children who were found to be difficult to remediate (see figure 3). There was also a significant decline in the average growth rate of the normal readers, but it was statistically less than that of the tutored readers. It should be noted, however, that, overall, both the normal readers and the tutored children demonstrated some growth over the summer months and that their growth rates tended to be similar. The average growth rates of both groups continued on a downward trend from second through fourth grade when the project ended, but the magnitude of the decline achieved statistical significance only in the normal readers and both groups continued to be on a positive trajectory. In fact, the slopes for both groups during this period were statistically significant and similar to one another.

Finally, compared with the unconditional model (panel A), the conditional model using reader group as a person-level predictor accounted for most of the variability in the slopes for both the first grade intervention period (82%) and the period encompassing the summer hiatus (73%). In fact, neither of the residual variances for these periods was statistically significant, after controlling for reader group differences in reading growth. In contrast, there was variability yet to be explained in the case of both the intercept and the slope for the period before initiation of the intervention program, although the conditional model explained more variance in the pre-intervention slope (58%) than in the intercept (8%).

The pattern of reader group differences in the parameter estimates produced by the conditional model just discussed leads naturally to the question of what factors may be influential in accounting for such differences. Our data suggest that remedial intervention is one such factor and we cautiously suggest that the remedial assistance the tutored children received was influential in bringing at least some of them closer to the normal readers in terms of their rate and level of reading growth following intervention (see figure 3). Our data also suggest that pre-first grade literacy skills, reading-related cognitive abilities, and classroom instruction may also be important factors in accounting for reader group differences in rate and level of reading growth, as we discussed earlier and elsewhere (Scanlon and Vellutino 1996, 1997; Vellutino et al. 1996).

Indeed, we suspect that some of the unexplained variability in the pre-intervention slopes and intercepts of the tutored and normal readers may well be partly explained by one or more of these factors. Although we do not have the data required to model the predictive value of classroom instruction, we do have data that allow us to model the predictive value of commonly used measures of pre-first grade literacy skills and reading-related cognitive abilities. As we indicated earlier, both the tutored and the normally developing readers were given a battery of tests evaluating pre-first grade (emergent) literacy skills and reading-related cognitive abilities in kindergarten and comparable batteries evaluating reading-related cognitive abilities were administered in first and third grades. Because of space constraints, we limit our discussion to results from growth curve analyses using only the kindergarten measures as person level predictors and present selected findings from these analyses (see figure 2 for description of kindergarten battery). We should point out, however, that comparable results were obtained in the analyses using the first grade measures as predictors. Because there was a great deal of redundancy in the first and third grade cognitive batteries, we did not conduct growth curve analyses using the third grade measures as predictors.

Our strategy in obtaining the parameter estimates of interest was to first conduct bivariate regression analyses to eliminate variables that did not account for significant variance in any of the growth parameters. We then conducted simultaneous (multivariate) regression analyses with variables that we judged, on theoretical and intuitive grounds, to share variance by virtue of their relationship to common latent abilities (e.g., pre-first grade literacy skills, verbal and non-verbal abilities, etc.). We then gradually eliminated those that did not account for unique variance in any of these parameters until arriving at a small set that accounted for unique variance in one or more of them. In the case of the bivariate regression analyses involving both the tutored and normal readers, we should point out that except for tests evaluating controlled and focused attention, virtually all of the measures in the kindergarten battery accounted for significant variance in most of the growth parameters modeled, save for the slope for the final (follow-up) measuring period (24 to 56 months). Thus, we present regression coefficients only for the final set that emerged from the simultaneous analyses. In the case of the bivariate regression analyses involving only the tutored children, only a small set of predictors accounted for significant variance in the growth parameters modeled, so we present results for both the bivariate and simultaneous analyses. It should be noted that five of the variables used as predictors are composite measures created by combining tests having similar factor structures: Letter/Number Naming, Print Concepts and Awareness, Verbal Memory, General Language, and Visual Processing[8].

Tables VIII and IX present results from these analyses. Table VIII presents results from analyses involving both the tutored children and the normal readers (n = 139) and table IX presents results from analyses involving only the tutored children (n = 74). As is evident from table VIII, a small set of kindergarten predictors accounted for unique variance in one or more of the growth parameters except for the slope corresponding with the follow-up measurement period. Two of the pre-first grade literacy measures—Phoneme Awareness and Letter/Number Naming—predicted initial level of performance in print decoding and accounted for 58% of the variance in this parameter. This circumstance is reflected in positive and highly significant coefficients for the intercept, suggesting that children who entered kindergarten with some degree of facility in letter naming, number naming, and phoneme analysis had somewhat better print decoding skills than children who had little or no facility in these areas. Similarly, growth in print decoding before first grade intervention was predicted by Letter/Number Naming, Verbal Memory, and Speech Articulation (accounting for 23% of the variance) indicating that children with better developed skills in these areas (more often the normal readers) had higher initial growth rates than children whose skills in these areas were less well developed. In contrast, Letter/Number Naming, Verbal Memory, and Speech Articulation were negatively (and significantly) associated with rate of growth in print decoding during the first grade intervention period (accounting for 27% of the variance), which is consistent with the observation that individual growth rates in the normal readers were significantly less,

---

[8]These composite variables were created on the basis of both exploratory and confirmatory factor analysis, which revealed that the measures we combined were significantly correlated with the same latent constructs. The Letter/Number Naming measure consisted of the Letter Identification subtest of the WRMT-R and an experimental test of number naming. The Print Concepts and Awareness measure consisted of experimental tests of print concepts and print awareness as described in figure 3. The General Language measure consisted of the syntactic and picture vocabulary tests described in figure 3. The Verbal Memory measure consisted of the experimental tests of word memory and sentence memory described in figure 3 and the Visual Processing measure consisted of experimental tests evaluating memory for the spatial locations of visual designs comprised of dots, along with the Block Design subtest of the WISC-R, all of which are also described in figure 3.

Table VIII.   Multiple regression coefficients for kindergarten variables predicting growth curve parameters for combined normal reader and tutored groups before, during, and after first grade intervention (n=139).

Measure	Intercept	Slopes			
		Before Intervention (0–16 mo)	First Grade Intervention (16–20 mo)	Summer Hiatus (20–24 mo)	Second to Fourth Grade (24–56 mo)
Phoneme Awareness	.405**	−.012	.008	−.008	.010
Articulation Accuracy	.001	.012*	−.040*	.040	−.013
Verbal Memory	−.028	.023**	−.076**	.064	−.015
Letter/ Number Naming	.233**	.050**	−.148**	.115**	−.022
Standard Deviations for Parameter Estimates					
Intercept				3.83**	
Slope (0-16 months)				0.96**	
Slope Change (16-20 months)				2.75**	
Slope Change (20-24 months)				1.64	
Slope Change (24-56 months)				1.01	

*<.05, **<.01.

Note that statistical significance for the various parameters was determined using robust standard errors that adjust for heteroscedasticity and non-normality in the parameter estimates (Raudenbush & Bryk, 2002).

on average, than individual growth rates in the tutored children during this period. Letter/Number naming alone predicted the sharp decline in growth rate during the summer hiatus (37% of the variance), and the residual variability for this parameter was no longer statistically significant, relative to the unconditional model. The positive sign of the coefficient for the summer hiatus is consistent with the finding that the decline in rate of growth in reading during this period was less in the normal readers than in the tutored children.

Results from the bivariate regression analyses involving only the tutored children complement the foregoing findings, but because the unconditional model for this group produced no statistically significant variability on any of the parameter estimates (we suspect because of low power associated with the small sample size, among other things), results should be interpreted with caution.

Table IX. Bivariate and multiple regression coefficients for kindergarten variables predicting growth curve parameters for tutored children before, during, and after first grade intervention (*n*=74).

Bivariate Regression Analyses

Measure	Intercept	Slopes			
		Before Intervention (0–16 mo)	First Grade Intervention (16–20 mo)	Summer Hiatus (20–24 mo)	Second to Fourth Grade (24–56 mo)
RAN Objects	–.035*	–.003	–.005	.010	–.003
Articulation Speed	–.034*	–.003	–.016	–.003	.022*
Letter/ Number Naming	.079**	.014**	.001	.007	–.021
Print concepts & Awareness	.057*	.001	.005	.009	–.019
Visual-Verbal Learning	.018	.009*	–.025	.023	–.010

Multiple Regression Analysis

Measure	Intercept	Slopes			
		Before Intervention (0–16 mo)	First Grade Intervention (16–20 mo)	Summer Hiatus (20–24 mo)	Second to Fourth Grade (24–56 mo)
Articulation Speed	–.019	.000	–.018	–.002	.020*
Letter/ Number Naming	.071**	.015**	–.006	.006	–.013

*<.05, **<.01.

RAN = rapid automatic naming

Note that statistical significance for the various parameters was determined using robust standard errors that adjust for heteroscedasticity and non-normality in the parameter estimates (Raudenbush & Bryk, 2002).

Nevertheless, it is of some significance that five of the kindergarten measures accounted for significant variability in one or more of the parameter estimates and that the measure that was found to be the strongest and most consistent predictor in the combined groups analyses—that is, Letter/Number Naming—also tended to be the strongest and most consistent predictor in the analyses involving only the tutored children. Two measures of pre-first grade literacy skill—Letter/Number Naming and Print Concepts and Awareness—predicted initial level of performance in print decoding, as did measures evaluating rapid naming of objects and speech articulation speed. Letter/Number Naming also predicted pre-intervention growth rates along with Visual-Verbal Learning (a task that simulates beginning reading). Essentially the same pattern of results was observed in the combined groups analysis insofar as tests evaluating language-based abilities and foundational literacy skills such as alphabetic knowledge were found to be the strongest predictors of both initial levels of performance in print decoding and pre-intervention growth rates in both sets of analyses. None of the kindergarten measures predicted growth rates during the first grade intervention or summer hiatus periods, but again, this could have been due, in part, to low power and limited variability. Articulation Speed was the only kindergarten measure to predict growth rates during the second to fourth grade follow-up period. The positive sign for this coefficient indicates that children who took more time to perform the speech articulation task in kindergarten also tended to have higher rates of reading growth during the follow-up period than children who took less time to complete the speech articulation task in kindergarten[9].

The multiple regression analysis produced essentially the same pattern of results as the bivariate regression analysis, but Letter/Number Naming and Articulation Speed were the only measures that contributed unique and independent variance in these analyses.

SUMMARY AND CONCLUSIONS

Results reported in the present paper extend initial findings from the longitudinal study discussed in Vellutino et al. (1996) and reaffirm the major conclusions drawn from those findings. One such conclusion was that an impaired reader's initial growth in reading,

---

[9]Because this finding is atypical, it warrants some comment. First note that most of the coefficients involving articulation speed as a predictor had negative signs, which suggests that tutored children who had faster rates of articulation in kindergarten demonstrated a trend toward higher levels and rates of reading growth than tutored children who had slower rates of articulation in kindergarten. Note also that the more difficult to remediate tutored children tended to lose more ground than the less difficult to remediate tutored children during the summer hiatus. As a result, the reading growth rates of the more difficult to remediate children tended to be steeper and more accelerated than the reading growth rates of the less difficult to remediate children after the summer hiatus, especially during the period encompassing the beginning of second grade to the end of second grade (see figure 3). Because of this, the overall slope values for the entire follow-up period (second through fourth grade) were generally greater in the more difficult to remediate children than in the less difficult to remediate children. Thus, if children in the former groups also had higher values on the articulation measure (reflecting slower rates of speech) than children in the latter groups, then the positive coefficient obtained when this measure predicted reading growth during the follow-up period would be explained.

in response to remedial intervention, could be taken as a reasonably good barometer of that child's ability to acquire functional reading skills, and, thereby, his or her eligibility for classification as a "disabled reader." A related conclusion was that the child's initial response to remedial intervention could be effectively and profitably used as a "first cut diagnostic" to distinguish between cognitive versus experiential and/or instructional factors as primary causes of early reading difficulties.

Analyses of the follow up data provide additional confirmation for both of these conclusions. Additional confirmation for the first conclusion is provided by the finding that the tutored children who made the most initial reading growth, in response to remedial intervention, had smaller drop off effects and stronger reading skills during the period following the initial period of remediation than the tutored children who made the least initial reading growth, in response to remedial intervention. Additional confirmation for the second conclusion is provided by results on the third grade cognitive battery insofar as the types of language-based skills and abilities that were found to distinguish between the normally achieving readers and the most difficult to remediate readers on this battery, also distinguished between these groups on the kindergarten and first grade cognitive batteries. And, whereas some of these measures also distinguished between the most difficult to remediate and most readily remediated readers on the third grade battery as well as on the kindergarten and first grade batteries, they did not reliably distinguish between the most readily remediated readers and the normally achieving readers on any of these batteries, suggesting that the cognitive abilities of the readily remediated readers were comparable to those of the normal readers. Thus, results from the third grade cognitive battery reaffirm our earlier conclusion that an impaired reader's response to remediation can help determine whether that child's reading difficulties are caused primarily by basic (neurodevelopmental) deficits in reading-related cognitive abilities or by limitations in early literacy experience and/or early literacy instruction (Vellutino et al. 1996). Of course, subnormal scores on measures of pre-first grade literacy skills and/or reading-related cognitive abilities, in given cases, may be caused by neurodevelopmental deficits of one description or another, but they may also be caused by limitations in experience and instruction, suggesting that decisions as to causality and prognosis in an individual case may be most confidently made on the basis of both remedial intervention and relevant assessment procedures used in concert with one another.

Still more support for these conclusions is provided by results from the growth curve analyses. These analyses generally showed that kindergarten literacy skills and reading-related cognitive abilities, especially language-based abilities, predicted both entry level print decoding skills and initial rates of growth in reading. This was found to be the case in the analyses involving both the normally achieving and tutored readers as well as in the analyses involving only the tutored readers. Kindergarten literacy skills and reading-related cognitive abilities were also found to predict reading growth after initiation of the first grade intervention program, although this pattern was more prominent in the combined groups analyses than in the analyses involving only the tutored children. In the combined groups analysis, children who obtained low scores on the cognitive measures in kindergarten (presumably the tutored children), manifested significantly greater reading growth during the intervention period, and dropped off more sharply during the summer hiatus period, than did children who obtained higher scores on the kindergarten cognitive measures. In the analysis involving only the tutored children, only one measure (Articulation Speed) predicted reading growth after initiation of the remedial intervention program, although this could have been a result of low power associated with the small sample size, in addition to low variability among the growth rates of these children.

Nevertheless, it is clear that the types of measures that often distinguished between the more and less skilled readers on the kindergarten, first, and third grade batteries, also predicted individual reading growth both before and after remedial intervention. Moreover, the differential patterns of reading growth observed in the normally achieving and tutored readers, before, during, and after intervention (table VII panel B), make it evident that the reading growth trajectories of impaired readers can be dramatically altered with appropriate intervention. Thus, it would seem that it is only by plotting a child's growth under such circumstances that we can have confidence in our ability to identify that child's long term instructional needs.

A third and related conclusion articulated in Vellutino et al. (1996) was that early identification of children "at risk" for beginning reading difficulties may help to prevent long term reading difficulties by flagging children who are likely to have difficulty learning to read. This conclusion seemed warranted by the finding that the children identified in first grade as problem readers were generally found to have relatively weak foundational literacy skills such as knowledge of the alphabet and phoneme awareness on entry into kindergarten, as well as relatively weak language-based skills such as verbal memory and rapid naming. The present findings reinforce this conclusion. Results from the growth curve analyses are especially reinforcing insofar as they show that this same assortment of skills and abilities predicted initial level of skill in print decoding and differential patterns of reading growth both before and after remedial intervention. The data generally suggest that children who entered kindergarten with adequate literacy skills and literacy-related cognitive abilities had higher initial growth rates than children who entered kindergarten with weaknesses in these areas. Moreover, Letter/Number Naming proved to be the strongest and most consistent predictor in both the combined groups analysis and the analysis involving only the tutored children. This finding is of interest because it suggests that entry-level literacy skills may carry somewhat greater weight as determinants of early reading achievement than do reading-related cognitive abilities. Indeed, fluency in letter naming also distinguished between the most difficult to remediate and least difficult to remediate tutored children as well as between the former group and the normally achieving readers in first grade and continued to do so in third grade (see Scanlon and Vellutino 1997 for comparable findings). Thus, early identification of children at risk for early reading difficulties using early literacy skills to identify such children initially would seem to be a worthwhile undertaking, especially if an attempt is made to provide them with remedial intervention that reduces the probability that they will experience early and/or long term reading difficulties. We are currently conducting a study that evaluates the utility of such intervention and initial findings are salutary (Scanlon et al. 2000).

Finally, based on their finding that measures of verbal and non-verbal intelligence did not discriminate either between the tutored groups and the normally achieving readers of average intelligence or between any of the tutored groups themselves, as well as on the finding that such measures did not predict beginning reading achievement in normal readers, Vellutino et al. (1996) concluded that the correlation between IQ scores and scores on measures of basic print decoding skills was not strong enough to warrant continued use of IQ scores to diagnose specific reading disability in terms of expected level of reading achievement. The present results reinforce this conclusion. Except for a statistically significant difference between the most difficult to remediate readers (VLG group) and the normally achieving readers on the WISC-R Verbal IQ (which could reflect regression to the mean), none of the contrasts between the various tutored groups and the average IQ normal readers produced significant group differences on any of the intelligence measures administered on the third grade assessment.

In sum, results from the follow up assessments of reading achievement and reading-related cognitive abilities in the target children initially studied by Vellutino et al. (1996) complement results reported in their paper, and reaffirm the major conclusions drawn from these results. The combined data sets suggest that reading difficulties in most middle to upper middle class children are caused by experiential and instructional deficits rather than basic cognitive deficits and speak for the utility of using early identification and early intervention as the primarily vehicles for evaluating the locus and origin of early reading difficulties and preventing long term reading difficulties. However, it is also clear from the combined data sets, especially the results from the follow up assessments, that there are small but significant numbers of children who will require intensive and individualized remedial assistance for a period of time beyond that provided by the intervention project in order for them to become functionally independent readers. The data also suggest that the reading difficulties of such children are caused primarily by language-based deficits, especially phonological deficits that may well be of constitutional origin. Results from growth curve analyses modeling reading growth before and after remedial intervention are of special interest because they suggest that it is possible, through intervention, to alter differences in the growth rates of poor and normally achieving readers in statistically reliable ways. Thus, before remedial intervention, the slope for rate of reading growth in normal readers was found to be significantly greater than that for poor readers. During intervention, the slope for reading growth was found to be significantly greater in the poor readers, and after intervention the growth rates for the two groups were not statistically different. This pattern of results suggests that it is possible to "close the gap" in reading skills between many children who experience early reading difficulties and their normally achieving peers.

ACKNOWLEDGMENTS

The data for this study were collected as part of a project implemented under the auspices of a special center grant awarded to the Kennedy Krieger Institute of Johns Hopkins University by the National Institute of Child Health and Human Development (#P50HD25806). Martha B. Denckla was the principal investigator overseeing the various projects initiated under the grant. The research reported in this paper was part of Project IV (The Reading and Language Project) implemented under a subcontract directed by Dr. Frank R. Vellutino and Dr. Donna M. Scanlon of the Child Research and Study Center of the University at Albany. The authors wish to express their sincere gratitude to the teachers, students, secretarial and administrative staff in participating schools. Many, many thanks also go to our colleagues Dr. Edward Sipay, Sheila Small, and Diane Fanuele who devoted years of their lives to this project!

REFERENCES

Aaron, P. G. 1997. The impending demise of the discrepancy formula. *Review of Educational Research* 67:461–502.

Bryk, A. S., and Raudenbush, S. W. 1992. *Hierarchical Linear Models for Social and Behavioral Research: Application and Data Analysis Methods.* Newbury Park, CA: Sage.

Clay, M. M. 1985. *The Early Detection of Reading Difficulties, 3rd edition.* Auckland, New Zealand: Heinemann.

Clay, M. M. 1987. Learning to be learning disabled. *New Zealand Journal of Educational Studies* 22:155–73.

DeFord, D., Pinnell, G. S., Lyons, C., and Young, P. 1988. *Reading Recovery: Volume IX, Report of the follow-up studies.* Columbus, OH: Ohio State University.

Dunn, L. M., and Dunn, L. M. 1981. *Peabody Picture Vocabulary Test-Revised.* Circle Pines, MN: American Guidance Service.

Fletcher J. M., Shaywitz, S. E., Shankweiler, D. P., Katz, L., Liberman, I. Y., Steubing, K. K., Francis, D. J., Fowler, A. E. and Shaywitz, B. A. 1994. Cognitive profiles of reading disability: Comparisons of discrepancy and low achievement definitions. *Journal of Educational Psychology* 86:6–23.

Francis, D. J., Shaywitz, S. E., Steubing, K. K., and Shaywitz, B. A. 1996. Developmental lag versus deficit models of reading disability: A longitudinal, individual growth curve analysis. *Journal of Educational Psychology* 88(1):3–17.

Hiebert, E. H., and Taylor, B. M. 2000. Beginning reading instruction: Research on early interventions. In *Handbook of Reading Research: Volume III*, eds. M. L. Kamil, P. B. Mosenthal, P. David Pearson, and R. Barr. Mahwah, NJ: Erlbaum.

Huck, C. S., and Pinnell, G. S. 1986. *The Reading Recovery Project in Columbus, Ohio, Pilot Year, 1984–85.* Columbus, OH: Ohio State University.

Iversen, S., and Tunmer, W. 1993. Phonological processing skills and the Reading Recovery program. *Journal of Educational Psychology* 85:112–26.

Marsh, L. C., and Cormier, D. R. 2002. *Spline Regression Models.* Sage Publications Inc. Thousand Oaks, CA.

McNemar, Q. 1955. *Psychological Statistics (2nd ed.).* New York: John Wiley & Sons, Inc.

National Advisory Committee on Dyslexia and Related Disorders 1969. *Reading Disorders in the United States.* Washington, DC: Government Printing.

Pindyck, R. S., and Rubinfeld, D. L. 1998. *Econometric Models and Economic Forecasts (4th ed.).* New York: Irwin/McGraw-Hill

Pinnell, G. S. 1989. Reading recovery: Helping at risk children learn to read. *Elementary School Journal* 90:161–84.

Raudenbush, S. W., and Bryk, A. S. 2002. *Hierarchical Linear Models. (2nd Edition).* Thousand Oaks, CA: Sage.

Santa, C. M., and Høien, T. 1999. An assessment of Early Steps: A program for early intervention of reading problems. *Reading Research Quarterly* 34:54–79.

Scanlon, D. M., and Vellutino, F. R. 1996. Prerequisite skills, early instruction, and success in first grade reading: Selected results from a longitudinal study. *Mental Retardation and Developmental Disabilities* 2:54–63.

Scanlon, D. M., and Vellutino, F. R. 1997. A comparison of the instructional backgrounds and cognitive profiles of poor, average, and good readers who were initially identified as at risk for reading failure. *Scientific Studies of Reading* 1(3):191–215.

Scanlon, D. M., Vellutino, F. R., Small, S. G.and Fanuele, D. P. 2000. Severe reading difficulties: Can they be prevented? A comparison of prevention and intervention approaches. Paper presented at the Annual Conference of The American Educational Research Association, New Orleans, April, 2000.

Semel, E., Wiig, E. H., and Secord, W. 1987. *Clinical Evaluation of Language Fundamentals-Revised.* San Antonio, TX: Psychological Corporation.

Shaywitz, S. E., Escobar, M. D., Shaywitz, B. A., Fletcher, J. M., and Makuch, R. W. 1992. Evidence that dyslexia may represent the lower tail of a normal distribution of reading ability. *New England Journal of Medicine* 326:145–50.

Siegel, L. S. 1988. Evidence that IQ scores are irrelevant to the definition and analysis of reading disability. *Canadian Journal of Psychology* 42(2):201–15.

Siegel, L. S. 1989. IQ is irrelevant to the definition of learning disabilities. *Journal of Learning Disabilities* 22:469–78.

Spache, G. D. 1981. *Diagnostic Reading Scales.* Monterey, CA: CTB/ McGraw-Hill.

Stanovich, K. E. 1986. Matthew effects in reading: Some consequences of individual differences in the acquisition of literacy. *Reading Research Quarterly* 21:360–407.

Stanovich, K. E., and Siegel, L. S. 1994. Phenotypic performance profile of children with reading disabilities: A regression-based test of the phonological-core variable-difference model. *Journal of Educational Psychology* 86(1):24–53.

Torgesen, J. K. 2000. Individual differences in response to early interventions in reading: The lingering problem of treatment resisters. *Learning Disabilities Research and Practice* 15(1):55–64.

Torgesen, J. K., Wagner, R. K., and Rashotte, C. A. 1999. Preventing reading failure in young children with phonological processing disabilities: Group and individual responses to instruction. *Journal of Educational Psychology* 91:579–94.

Vellutino, F. R., and Scanlon, D. M. 2002. The interactive strategies approach to reading intervention. *Contemporary Educational Psychology.*27:573–635.

Vellutino, F. R., Scanlon, D. M., and Lyon, G. R. 2000. Differentiating between difficult to remediate and readily remediated poor readers: More evidence against the IQ Achievement discrepancy definition of reading disability. *Journal of Learning Disabilities* 33(3):223–38.

Vellutino, F. R., Scanlon, D. M., and Spearing, D. 1995. Semantic and phonological coding in poor and normal readers. *Journal of Experimental Child Psychology* 59:76–123.

Vellutino, F. R., Scanlon, D. M., and Tanzman, M. S. 1988. Lexical memory in poor and normal reader: Developmental differences in the use of category cues. *Canadian Journal of Psychology* 42:216–41.

Vellutino, F. R., Scanlon, D. M., and Tanzman, M. S. 1998. The case for early intervention in diagnosing specific reading disability. *Journal of School Psychology* 36(4):367–97.

Vellutino, F. R., Scanlon, D. M., Sipay, E. R., Small, S. G., Pratt, A., Chen, R., and Denckla, M. B. 1996. Cognitive profiles of difficult to remediate and readily remediated poor readers: Early intervention as a vehicle for distinguishing between cognitive and experiential deficits as basic causes of specific reading disability. *Journal of Educational Psychology* 88:(4):601–38.

Wasik, B. A., and Slavin, R. R. 1993. Preventing early reading failure with one-to-one tutoring: A review of five programs. *Reading Research Quarterly* 28:179–200.

Wechsler, D. 1974. Wechsler Intelligence Scale for Children-Revised. New York: Psychological Corporation.

Wechsler, D. 1989. *Wechsler Preschool and Primary Scale of Intelligence-Revised*. New York: Psychological Corporation.

Woodcock, R. W. 1987. *Woodcock reading mastery tests-revised*. Circle Pines, MN: American Guidance Services.

Woodcock, R. W., and Johnson, M. B. 1989,1990. *Woodcock-Johnson Psycho-educational Battery-Revised*. Allen, TX: DLM Teaching Resources.

Ysseldyke, J., and Christensons, S. L. 1988. Linking assessment to intervention. In *Alternative Educational Delivery Systems*, eds. J. L. Graden, J. E. Zins, and M.J. Curtis. Washington, DC: National Association of School Psychologists.

Chapter • 5

Preventing Negative Matthew Effects in At-Risk Readers:
A Retrospective Study

William E. Tunmer, James W. Chapman, and Jane E. Prochnow

We begin this paper by presenting some puzzling findings. Although New Zealand generally ranks well in international surveys of literacy achievement, the variability in test scores is consistently very high in comparison to other countries. For example, in the recently released study of literacy achievement among 15-year-olds carried out by the Organization for Economic Cooperation and Development (2001), New Zealand's mean reading scores (within the margin of error) were in the top two to eight countries of the OECD. However, of the top eight countries (five of which were English speaking countries) New Zealand had the highest percentages of students performing at the highest and lowest levels. Similarly, in the last international study of literacy achievement conducted by the International Association for the Evaluation of Educational Achievement (IEA), New Zealand had the largest variation in achievement of any of the 32 participating countries (Elley 1992). The majority of poor readers were from low-income backgrounds with an over-representation of Maori students (Wagemaker 1993).

Recent research in New Zealand revealed disparities between children of different backgrounds in important literacy-related skills at school entry, such as phonological sensitivity, letter-name knowledge, and understanding of concepts about printed language (Gilmore 1998; Nicholson 2000b). Group differences in literacy achievement steadily increase over the first years of schooling (Crooks and Caygill 1999; Nicholson 2000b), throughout high school (Nicholson 1995; Nicholson and Gallienne 1995), and into adulthood (Ministry of Education 1997). Crooks and Caygill (1999) reported that of the 15 curriculum areas assessed in the National Education Monitoring Project (NEMP), the difference in performance between 8-year-old Maori and non-Maori students was greatest for reading, with a mean effect size of –.52. The pattern of results remained the same when socio-economic factors were controlled, although the mean effect size was reduced to –.34. Relatedly, results from the international survey of adult literacy (Ministry of Education 1997) indicated that proportionately almost twice as many Maori adults scored in the bottom two achievement levels of the study as did non-Maori adults. Home language is not a contributing factor to these performance differences as very few Maori learn to speak Maori as a first language, and only a small proportion learn Maori as a second language (Crooks and Caygill 1999).

The relatively wide gap in literacy achievement in New Zealand is puzzling for two reasons. First, New Zealand is a very small country with a unified national education system. There are no separate states, provinces, or school districts in New Zealand. Although there is some degree of management at the local school level, almost everything else relating to literacy education is controlled centrally by the Ministry of Education, including the setting and monitoring of the national curriculum and the production of beginning reading materials and instructional guides for beginning reading teachers. As well, the two major intervention programs for struggling readers, Reading Recovery and Resource Teachers: Literacy, are funded and monitored on a national basis (Greaney 2002). Consequently, compared with other countries like the United States or Canada, there is considerably less variation in the reading methods and instructional strategies used in regular classroom reading programs and in nationally implemented intervention programs. Second, it is well established that reading difficulties are associated with various socio-economic factors, such as residing in low-income families, living in poor neighborhoods, having parents with limited education and low levels of literacy, and attending schools in which literacy achievement is chronically low (Snow, Burns, and Griffin 1998). However, while poverty certainly exists in New Zealand, the degree of poverty and the difference in material wealth between low- and middle-income families are not nearly as great as in other countries, such as the United States.

STRATEGIES FOR REDUCING THE GAP

Three strategies have been proposed for preventing reading failure and reducing the unacceptably large gap in literacy achievement between Maori and Pakeha (i.e., non-Maori) children (Wilkinson, Freebody, and Elkins 2000). These are (1) doing "more of the same" (but better), (2) focusing greater attention on accommodating cultural differences, and (3) changing the method of teaching literacy.

Doing More of the Same

Those who argue for doing more of the same are strongly opposed to making any substantial changes to current literacy practices in New Zealand (Elley 1996, 1997; Ministry of Education 1999; Smith 1997, 2000; Smith and Elley 1994). Instead, they recommend placing greater emphasis on addressing the needs of struggling readers, largely by providing professional development to teachers on what is regarded as "best practice" (vaguely specified) in working with children most at risk for underachievement (Ministry of Education 1999). As part of this strategy, each school would be provided with an expert literacy adviser to ensure ongoing access to quality professional development opportunities, to provide literacy leadership within the school, and to evaluate the effectiveness of school literacy programs, including those for children needing additional support. Reading Recovery, however, would remain as the nationally implemented intervention program for children failing to respond adequately to formal reading instruction after 12 months of schooling (see Nicholson 2002, for a more detailed discussion of the development of the National Literacy Strategy in New Zealand).

Ironically, the development and rapid expansion of whole language and Reading Recovery in New Zealand during the 1980s and 1990s provides the strongest argument against the "more of the same" strategy for reducing the gap in literacy achievement (see Openshaw 2002, for a historical analysis of the development of Reading Recovery). Survey data indicate that every year since 1991 a staggering 20% to 25% of all six-year-old children received expensive, intensive, one-to-one Reading Recovery tutoring after only their first year in school (Kerslake 2000). Most of these children had made little or no progress toward gaining independence in reading despite having been immersed in a print-rich environment for an entire year.

Reading Recovery was designed to complement regular classroom literacy instruction in New Zealand, which is predominantly whole language in orientation with theoretical underpinnings compatible with the reading theories of Ken Goodman (1967, 1986) and Frank Smith (1978). In the book experience approach used in most New Zealand classrooms, children are taught what they need to know to learn to read incidentally (i.e., "as the need arises") through frequent encounters with absorbing reading materials. According to Smith and Elley (1994), two leading proponents of the whole language approach in New Zealand, "children learn to read themselves; direct teaching plays only a minor role" (p. 87). The focus of this approach, then, is on learning to read by reading, with minimal attention being given to the development of essential word-level skills and strategies. Instead, beginning readers are urged to use preceding passage content, sentence context cues, and picture cues as the primary strategies for identifying unfamiliar words in text. Connelly, Johnston, and Thompson (2001) noted that the shift from emphasis on words in teaching reading to an emphasis on the story and book "has become more prevalent in the last twenty years and there has been increasing concern that children are able to predict reading responses from story and sentence contexts" (p. 433).

If, as we argue below, the whole language approach is particularly disadvantageous to at risk readers, then it is perhaps no accident that the rapid expansion of Reading Recovery and whole language in New Zealand almost exactly coincided with the increasing disparity between New Zealand readers. Given that Reading Recovery is essentially a more intensive version of what occurs in regular New Zealand classrooms (Thompson 1993), it would not seem to be an effective strategy to place children who are failing to learn to read into a remedial reading program that uses the same methods that most likely contributed to their failure in the first place. In support of these claims are the results of a longitudinal study of Reading Recovery that we carried out in New Zealand (Chapman, Tunmer, and Prochnow 2001). We found that Reading Recovery failed to improve significantly the literacy development of children considered to have succeeded in the program. These children showed no signs of accelerated reading performance, and one year after completion of the program, they were performing at around one year below age-appropriate levels (see Tunmer and Chapman, in press a, for a more detailed critique of Reading Recovery).

Accommodating Cultural Differences

Accommodating cultural differences is another strategy that has been proposed for reducing the literacy achievement gap (Au 1998, 2000; McNaughton 1995). There seems to be little disagreement that teachers should adjust their teaching to accommodate student differences in cultural background (Ministry of Education 1999). However, this may be easier said than done. As Snow, Burns, and Griffin (1998) pointed out, "Cultural differences are entrenched in history and social institutions and are not easily amenable to educators' manipulations" (p. 243).

Despite these difficulties, several researchers have attempted to examine the effects of modifying teaching approaches to build upon the diverse range of knowledge and literacy practices found in the homes of children from minority cultures. This research is based on the assumption that early school literacy problems can be reduced by adjusting teaching practices so that they better match the cultural patterns and styles of learning of children of diverse backgrounds. McNaughton (1995), for example, claimed that more effective forms of instruction are those that provide bridges between home and school by allowing children from minority cultures to engage in literacy learning activities in the classroom that draw on familiar family literacy practices. Other examples of "culturally responsive instruction" include making learning experiences more personally meaningful to students of diverse backgrounds by engaging them in activities that relate to their interests and experiences outside of school; using instructional materials that present minority cultures in an authentic manner, including presenting culturally relevant content in culturally familiar social contexts; and improving community involvement in literacy learning by promoting stronger connections among schools, parents, and the community (Au 1998, 2000). These links should go in both directions with schools learning more about family literacy practices and how to build upon them, and families learning more about what they can do to support their children's literacy learning in school.

Perhaps most importantly, teachers should hold high expectations for students from minority cultures. Au (2000) argued that, "There should not be a different set of standards for students of diverse backgrounds, but there should be a recognition that these students may require more powerful instruction and additional time to meet the standards" (p. 844). Some teachers from the dominant culture have low expectations of success for children of diverse backgrounds that stem from racist attitudes and deficit views of minority children's intelligence, linguistic competence, and home environment (Nicholson 2000a).

Although attention to most of these factors would appear to be important, if not essential, in teaching students of diverse backgrounds, there is little or no evidence in support of the specific hypothesis that the poor literacy achievement of students from minority cultures is largely the result of the failure of mainstream schools to modify their teaching approaches so that they better match the home literacy practices of these children, which in many cases are very limited or nonexistent. In general there are three criticisms of this hypothesis. First, cultural/ethnic differences are often confounded with socio-economic variables that are themselves associated with reading difficulties in young children. For example, in New Zealand the majority of Maori students come from low-income families, live in low-income neighborhoods, and attend schools with relatively high proportions of students with similar disadvantages (Crooks and Caygill 1999). Although both socio-economic and cultural factors appear to be important, it is difficult to determine the relative contributions of each to reading achievement differences.

Second, although research indicates that culturally accommodated instruction may result in greater student participation and school satisfaction, there is little or no evidence that such instruction positively influences reading achievement (Snow, Burns, and Griffin 1998). Projects reporting positive effects typically include many components, some of which are not culture specific, such as general principles of effective teaching and classroom organization. In such circumstances it is impossible to determine whether culturally based factors or more general factors are responsible for the positive effects on student achievement (see Snow et al. 1998, for further discussion).

Finally, as we argue below, the problem of how to reduce the gap in early literacy achievement may have less to do with modifying classroom instruction to match home literacy practices and more to do with addressing the specific needs of children struggling to learn to read in an alphabetic orthography regardless of the cultural group or social class to which they belong. There is no evidence to suggest that direct instruction in essential reading skills cannot be done in a culturally sensitive manner.

Rather surprisingly, support for this view comes from one of the strongest proponents of culturally responsive instruction, Katherine Au (1998, 2000), who drew attention to the disadvantages of using the whole language approach with students of diverse backgrounds, or what she called the "mainstream constructivist orientation" (p. 306). Au (1998) argued that,

In a mainstream constructivist orientation, the tendency is to propose general principles applicable to all students, although individual differences may be considered. This point of view fails to
acknowledge that a given set of learning opportunities may benefit
mainstream students while working to the detriment of students of
diverse backgrounds within the same classroom. (p. 307)

Au (1998) further stated that,

Because the emphasis in constructivist approaches tends to be on
process rather than product, educators with a mainstream constructivist orientation may see it as their role to act as facilitators of students' learning, responding to students' work but not transmitting
knowledge . . . . Educators with this orientation may be reluctant to
provide students with instruction on specific skills. (p. 313)

The concerns expressed by Au (1998) regarding the use of the
whole language approach are particularly applicable to New
Zealand. Wilkinson, Freebody, and Elkins (2000) concluded that
New Zealand faces a dilemma in meeting the challenge of equity
in literacy education because of its child-centered pedagogy:

New Zealand's literacy practices have a history of association with a
developmental constructivist bias in teaching and learning. There is
a general commitment to the centrality of the child in teaching and
to a view of learning as proceeding from the child along developmentally appropriate pathways under guidance or support of the
teacher; direct instruction of specific knowledge and skills according
to prespecified routines finds little favour. (p. 12)

The clear implication of these observations is that the "learn
to read by reading" approach to teaching literacy that is predominant in New Zealand schools is not a culturally responsive form of
instruction and may even be a major contributing factor to cultural reproduction within New Zealand society (Tunmer,
Prochnow, and Chapman 1999).

Changing the Method of Teaching Literacy

In claiming that changing the method of teaching literacy is the
best strategy for reducing the relatively high level of disparity between New Zealand readers, we are not suggesting that such a strategy alone will act as a "silver bullet" for bringing about equity in
New Zealand literacy education. Although many children from
low-income backgrounds do not struggle to learn to read, and a significant number from middle-class backgrounds do, the odds are
generally stacked against low-income children because they live in
families that are under varying degrees of financial and social
stresses; for example, unemployment, single parent households,

large families, poor living conditions (Crooks and Caygill 1999; Nicholson 1997, 1999, 2002). As a consequence, fewer resources are available for books, study materials, learning aids, and private study areas, and less adult time is available for engaging children in important literacy-related activities prior to school entry. In addition, low-income children are more likely to attend schools with fewer resources; with a lower ability composition; with lower levels of academic self-concept, achievement motivation, and school satisfaction; with higher levels of learning, emotional, and behavioral problems; with a higher proportion of disrupted class time; and with less qualified, experienced, and motivated staffs (Crooks and Caygill 1999; Nicholson and Gallienne 1995; Snow, Burns, and Griffin 1998).

Although changing the methodology of literacy instruction would not be expected to overcome all of the disadvantages associated with living in low-income families and neighborhoods, our contention is that the whole language approach to teaching literacy makes the situation considerably worse than it otherwise would be by failing to provide at risk children with explicit instruction in alphabetic coding and related skills (see Foorman et al. 2000, for a similar view). Instead, whole language is predicated on the assumption that "reading and writing are best acquired 'naturally' in the same way that we learn to speak and listen" (Smith and Elley 1994, p. 81). If children are immersed in a print-rich environment in which the focus is on the meaning of print, they will readily acquire reading skills, according to this view.

An alternative conceptualization is that the acquisition of a complex skill like reading is a developmental process that occurs over time and involves qualitatively different (but perhaps overlapping) stages or phases (Ehri 1997; Juel 1991; Spear-Swerling and Sternberg 1996). In this view consideration must be given to *cognitive entry behaviors*, which are the existing knowledge, skills, and strategies that students have at the outset of learning something new. Literacy-related skills and experiences of children at school entry vary enormously. These skills include familiarity with "book" or "decontextualized" language (promoted by adult storybook reading); knowledge of letter names and sounds; sensitivity to the subcomponents of spoken words (referred to as *phonological awareness*; see Blachman 2000); understanding of concepts and conventions of printed language; and ability to produce invented spellings (e.g., writing *color* as KLR). Vellutino et al. (1996) have drawn attention to the importance of differences in these entry-level skills, arguing that:

> . . . any given level of reading achievement is a by-product of a complex interaction between one's endowment and the quality of one's

literacy experience and instruction, such that the child who is endowed with an adequate mix of the cognitive abilities underlying reading ability is better equipped to profit from experience and instruction in learning to read than is the child who is endowed with a less than adequate mix of these abilities. Indeed, the optimally endowed child may be able to profit from less than optimal experience and instruction, whereas the inadequately endowed child may have difficulty profiting from even optimal experience and instruction. (p. 602)

There is considerable evidence that children from low-income backgrounds begin school with significantly lower levels of literacy-related skills and experiences than children from more advantaged backgrounds (Nicholson 1997; Snow, Burns, and Griffin 1998). The differences are especially large for phonological awareness, which is the best single predictor of future reading achievement at school entry (Share et al. 1984; Tunmer et al. 1998). Bowey (1995), for example, found a strong relationship between socio-economic status and preschool phonological awareness even after controlling for the effects of IQ and general verbal ability (vocabulary knowledge and grammatical understanding). Recent research in New Zealand has revealed disparities between children of different backgrounds in entry-level phonological sensitivity, letter-name knowledge, invented spelling ability and understanding of concepts about printed language (Gilmore 1998; Nicholson 2000b).

Home literacy environment has been suggested as the major contributing factor to these differences in entry-level pre-reading skills (Nicholson 1999; Snow, Burns, and Griffin 1998). Because economic disadvantage is associated with lower levels of formal education and adult literacy, the parents of children from low-income families are less likely than middle-income parents to demonstrate a high positive regard for literacy and may feel less confident about engaging in strategic communication with schools and teachers about how to support their children's early literacy development (especially if there are cultural and ethnic differences as well). Moreover, as a consequence of financial and social stresses, low-income parents may have less time available to engage their children in the amount of verbal interaction necessary for the development of higher levels of vocabulary knowledge and oral language proficiency (which, in turn, are related to subsequent reading growth; Hoover and Tunmer 1993; Tunmer and Hoover 1992, 1993) and in the kinds of activities that promote the development of preliterate phonological awareness. The latter include looking at books and playing games that increase knowledge of letter names and their relation to sounds in words (e.g., "s" is for snake; see Murray, Stahl, and Ivey 1996), playing rhyming and sound analysis games and being read books that increase phonological sensitivity (e.g., pig Latin, I spy, nursery rhymes, Dr Seuss books; see Bryant et al. 1989), and manipulating movable letters to form preconventional spellings of words (e.g., FRE for fairy). Exposure to such activities may be particularly important to children who enter whole language programs, which are based on the mistaken assumption that phonologically based skills and knowledge of the alphabetic principle are of limited value in learning to read, and possibly even a hindrance (see, for example, Smith and Elley 1994, p. 143).

When literacy-related activities in the home environment are passed from one generation to the next, as they often are, they become what sociologists call *literate cultural capital*. As the prominent New Zealand sociologist Nash (1997) argued, families located within the existing economic class structure "are engaged in long term actions with the strategic purpose (broadly known to them) of enabling their offspring to maintain their economic, cultural, and social position [and] schools are involved in this process by affording recognition to the skills acquired through a literacy-focused socialisation . . ." (p. 13). In their empirical work, Nash and Harker (1992) reported that literate cultural capital was significantly associated with reading achievement. With respect to differential performance in the Maori population, they concluded that, "A considerable proportion of working class Maori pupils come to have relatively poor reading scores because schools as they are constituted are unable to transcend the effects of [Maori pupils'] somewhat less than literacy-dominated home environments (this is, of course, the result of the mono-cultural nature of the schools) . . . [and] this relatively poor level of reading then begins to shape and confirm class and ethnically specific expectations pupils form about their eventual social and labour market destination . . ." (p. 10).

The suggestion that differences in home literacy environment are a major cause of social class differences in school literacy achievement is highly controversial (see, for example, Taylor et al. 2000). As Nash (2002) noted:

> Many people regard the argument as a "deficit" theory and set their minds against it for that reason alone. This response is akin to burying one's head in the sand. (p. 243)

We agree with Nash (2002) and maintain that the argument we (and others) are putting forward is not another example of deficit theory, where educational failure is explained largely in terms of relatively fixed characteristics that reside within the child or the child's home, such as the intelligence the child possesses, the language the child speaks, or the culture from which the child comes. Stubbs (1980) distinguishes "deficit" from "disadvantage" and argues that the latter term is more appropriate because it implies that there is nothing wrong with the children. Rather, it is only their social experience that puts them at a disadvantage because it is different from what is expected from mono-culturally oriented schools. Not all children enter school with an abundance of literate cultural capital.

In support of this distinction, consider the following example. Imagine two 5-year old children of similar physical ability who are about to begin taking swimming lessons. Child A comes from a family that has a small swimming pool in their backyard (or perhaps lives in a neighborhood where some of the families have swimming pools, or where there is an accessible and affordable community pool). This child has already spent a fair amount of time in the water moving around, putting her head under the water, learning not to breathe in while doing so, possibly opening her eyes under water, and in general becoming fairly comfortable in the water though not having learned to swim. Perhaps also the parents of Child A, who place a high value on learning to swim, have purchased a paddle board for their child to hold on to as she kicks her way around the pool. And perhaps also her parents have taught her how to float in the water because they know that people who are tense in the water tend to sink. However, Child B got none of this for whatever reasons. Would it make sense to say that Child B has a deficit? Or would it make better sense to say that Child A is advantaged, and that Child B is disadvantaged if taught by a method of teaching swimming that *assumes* that all children at the beginning of instruction are comfortable in the water, know how to float, and know how to kick?

Stubbs' (1980) use of the term "disadvantage" is particularly relevant to the mainstream constructivist (i.e., whole language) orientation to literacy teaching, where it is assumed that children mostly "learn to read themselves" when immersed in a print-rich environment (Smith and Elley 1994, p. 87). The emphasis in whole language and Reading Recovery on the use of text-based strategies over word-based strategies stems from the incorrect assumption that skilled reading is a process in which minimal word-level information is used to confirm language predictions (Clay 1991; Goodman 1967; Smith 1978). On the basis of this assumption, whole language proponents concluded that the development of reading ability is largely a matter of learning to rely increasingly on the syntactic and semantic redundancies of language to generate hypotheses about the text yet to be encountered. As Smith and Elley (1994) argued, children ". . . learn to read with minimal input from the text, predicting and confirming and making sense as they go" (p. 142). The teaching approach of urging beginning readers to use sentence context as the primary strategy for identifying unfamiliar words in text, and the theoretical assumptions about reading that underlie this approach, have been strongly promoted by the Ministry of Education in New Zealand through its various publications (*Reading in Junior Classes*, 1991; *The Learner as Reader*, 1996; *Reading and Beyond*, 1997).

This view of reading, however, has been rejected by the scientific community. Pressley (1998), for example, stated that "the scientific evidence is simply overwhelming that letter-sound cues are more important in recognizing words than either semantic or syntactic cues" (p. 16), and that heavy reliance on the latter is a "disastrous strategy" for beginning readers (p. 32). Several studies have shown that children with reading problems are much more likely to rely on sentence context to identify words than normally developing readers (for further arguments and evidence, see Tunmer and Chapman 1998, 2002, in press b, c). Liberman and Liberman (1992) claimed that most children (perhaps up to 75%) will independently discover the enormous value of taking advantage of the alphabetic code in identifying words, which they must do to achieve progress in reading, regardless of the method of instruction to which they are exposed. The use of letter-sound relationships is the basic mechanism for acquiring word-specific knowledge, including knowledge of irregularly spelled words (Ehri 1992, 1997; Gough and Walsh 1991; Tunmer and Chapman 1998).

To discover mappings between spelling patterns and sound patterns, children must be able to segment spoken words into subcomponents. For beginning readers who have difficulty detecting phonological sequences in words, progress in reading will be impeded. Stanovich (1996) succinctly described the chain of events that leads to reading failure: "Impaired language segmentation skills lead to difficulties in phonological coding which in turn impede the word recognition process which underpins reading comprehension" (p. 155).

Children from low-income backgrounds are particularly susceptible to early reading difficulties because they often lack the necessary preschool exposure to the kinds of language play activities and early literacy experiences that promote the development of preliterate phonological awareness (Blachman 2000). This in turn may trigger negative Matthew (poor-get-poorer) effects in reading (Stanovich 1986). At risk children who do not possess a sufficient level of phonological sensitivity at the outset of formal reading instruction (and who are not provided with supplementary teaching to overcome their weakness in the phonological domain) most likely will not await phonological development, but instead will be forced to rely increasingly on ineffective word identification strategies, such as using picture cues, partial word-level cues, and contextual guessing. Reliance on such counterproductive strategies would almost certainly be exacerbated by an instructional approach like whole language in which beginning readers are specifically encouraged to use text-based strategies over more effective word-based strategies.

Many at risk children will rely on ineffective strategies to such an extent and for such a long time (years in some cases) that the strategies become consolidated and difficult to "unlearn." Because of their deficient word identification skills, these children not only receive less practice in reading but soon begin to confront materials that are too difficult for them, which (not surprisingly) results in avoidance of reading. As a consequence, they are prevented from taking advantage of positive Matthew (rich-get-richer) effects in reading. As children become better readers, both the amount and difficulty of the material they read increases, which leads to increased knowledge of letter-sound patterns (which improves word identification skills) and to further development of vocabulary knowledge, syntactic knowledge, and general knowledge (all of which improve reading comprehension skills).

As a result of repeated learning failures, many struggling readers also develop negative self-perceptions of ability and therefore do not try as hard as other children because of their low expectations of success (Chapman and Tunmer 1997, 2003; Chapman, Tunmer, and Prochnow 2000). For some of these children, especially boys, the sense of failure and feelings of frustration, coupled with the need to disguise their inability to perform reading tasks, become so great that they begin to exhibit classroom behavior problems (Prochnow et al. 2001). What began as a relatively small difference in reading-related skills and knowledge at the beginning of school, then, soon develops into what Stanovich (1986) described as a downward spiral of achievement deficits and negative motivational and behavioral spin-offs (i.e., negative Matthew effects).

In summary, a clear (and testable) explanation for why New Zealand continues to have such a large spread of scores in international studies of literacy achievement is that these differences are largely the result of Matthew effects triggered by a mainstream constructivist orientation to teaching reading that fails to respond adequately to differences (not deficits!) in essential reading-related (especially phonologically based) skills and knowledge at school entry that stem primarily from social class differences in home literacy environment. Evidence in support of this claim comes from a five-year longitudinal study in New Zealand by Nicholson (2000b), who found that differences in phonological awareness skills, letter-name knowledge, and invented spelling ability between low- and middle-income children at school entry were associated with a steadily increasing gap between the two groups in reading accuracy, reading comprehension, and spelling over the next five years. Relatedly, we (Chapman, Tunmer, and Prochnow 2001) found in a longitudinal study of beginning literacy development in New Zealand that children selected by their schools for Reading Recovery were, without exception, experiencing severe difficulties in detecting sound sequences in words (i.e., phonological awareness) and in relating letters to sounds (i.e., alphabetic coding) during the year preceding entry into the program. Participation in Reading Recovery did not appreciably reduce these deficiencies, and the failure to remedy these problems severely limited the immediate and long-term effectiveness of the program. The few children who received some benefit from Reading Recovery were more advanced in phonological processing skills at the beginning of the program than children who derived little or no benefit from the program, and progress in learning to read following participation in Reading Recovery was strongly related to phonological processing skills at discontinuation from the program.

Further evidence in support of our claim is provided by a recent meta-analysis of studies examining the effects of whole language instruction on the literacy achievement of children from low-income backgrounds (Jeynes and Littell 2000). Overall, the results indicated that less advantaged children benefitted less from whole language instruction than from basal instruction, leading the authors to conclude that "using a whole language approach with low-SES children could widen the gap between advantaged and disadvantaged students" (p. 31). In support of this conclusion are results from a study by Foorman et al. (1998) of the effects of different methods of beginning reading instruction on the reading growth of at risk beginning readers. They found that degree of explicitness of instruction in the alphabetic code and related skills was positively associated with amount of improvement in reading, and that more explicit instruction in alphabetic coding was more effective than less explicit approaches with children who had lower levels of phonological processing skills at the beginning of the year. Of particular importance was the finding that direct instruction in alphabetic coding resulted in less disparity between students in reading achievement at the end of the year than less explicit approaches to teaching spelling-sound patterns.

To examine further these issues in the New Zealand educational context, we designed a study to answer two questions. First, if beginning reading teachers incorporated into their literacy programs supplementary materials and procedures designed to help children develop awareness of sound sequences in spoken words and make greater use of letter-sound patterns in reading unfamiliar words, would this produce significantly greater gains in reading achievement than the standard whole language approach to literacy instruction? Second, would the incorporation of these materials and teaching strategies reduce the gap in beginning reading achievement between Maori and Pakeha (i.e., European) children?

METHOD

Sample and Design

A retrospective study was carried out in which a representative sample of seven schools was selected from 22 schools that three years earlier had participated in a longitudinal study in which the literacy development of 152 children was closely followed from school entry to the middle of year 3. Children in New Zealand commence school on or around their fifth birthday, and formal reading instruction begins at that time. To control for amount of prior schooling, the children selected for participation in the original study had almost reached their fifth birthday or had turned 5 years of age during the preceding summer break, and therefore had entered school for the first time at the beginning of a new school year.

The seven schools selected for program modification were located in a range of socio-economic areas. In New Zealand, schools are rated from a decile of 1 (low) to 10 (high) according to the socio-economic community the school serves. The decile ratings of the selected schools ranged from 1 to 10, with one school at each of levels 1, 3, 4, 5, 7, 9 and 10. A total of 80 children from 13 classrooms in the seven target schools satisfied the same criteria for selection as the children in the original study. The mean age of the children at school entry was 5 years, 1 month (range = 4 years, 11 months to 5 years, 3 months).

A comparison group of 63 children was formed by selecting children from the original sample who had attended the target schools three years earlier. The mean age of the comparison group children at school entry was 5 years, 1 month (range = 5 years, 0 months to 5 years, 3 months). The classroom reading programs of these children strongly adhered to the whole language philosophy of teaching reading (for detailed descriptions of the New Zealand version of whole language, see Connelly, Johnston, and Thompson 2001; Smith and Elley 1994; Thompson 1993; Tunmer and Chapman 1999).

Instruments

The children in the program modification schools were tested at four of the same testing points as the children in the original longitudinal study (beginning, middle and end of year 1 and end of year 2) with a selection of tests from the original test battery, especially those that assessed phonological processing skills. The tests, which were given at developmentally appropriate testing times, included measures of letter identification, phonological sensitivity (as measured by onset-rime segmentation, sound matching, and phoneme segmentation), knowledge of letter-sound patterns (as measured by pseudoword decoding), ability to use orthographic analogies, invented spelling ability, conventional spelling ability, context free word identification ability (as measured by two tests), reading book level, and children's reported word identification strategies.

Letter identification was assessed at school entry by means of the Letter Identification task in the *Diagnostic Survey* (Clay 1985). Children were required to give the name or sound of 26 uppercase and 28 lowercase letters, two of which appeared in varying fonts. Scoring was based on the number of letters correctly identified by name or sound. The reliability estimate for this scale was .97.

The *onset-rime segmentation* task was developed by Calfee (1977) and was administered at the beginning and middle of year 1. The task was to delete the initial consonant onset from a presented word and to say aloud the vowel-consonant rime that remained, where an onset is the initial consonant or consonant cluster of a syllable, and rime is the vowel and any following consonants. For instance, to the word *mice*, the correct response was "ice"; to the word *rope*, the correct answer was "ope." The task comprised four training lists and six transfer lists. The difficulty level increased through the lists. For the last two transfer lists, half of the words were real and half synthetic (e.g., *kend, mox, jad*). Scoring was based on the number of correct responses to items presented in the six transfer trials, with a maximum possible score of 53. The internal reliability coefficient for this scale was .96.

The *sound matching* task was an adaptation of a task developed by Bryant et al. (1989). This task, which was administered at the middle of year 1, comprised two parts; an onset matching task and a rime matching task. In the onset matching task, the child was asked to indicate which two of three orally presented words sounded the same "at the beginning" (e.g., *hair, pin, pig*). In the rime matching task, the child was asked to indicate which two of three orally presented words sounded the same "at the end" (e.g., *snail, nail, boot*). For both tasks a series of practice items was included, and picture support was provided for each test item in order to reduce memory load. Scores for the sound matching task comprised the total number correct for the onset matching task (maximum = 9) plus the total number correct for the rime matching task (maximum = 9), giving a maximum possible score of 18. The internal reliability estimate for this scale was .78.

Phoneme segmentation ability was assessed at the end of year 1 by means of a modified version of a phoneme counting task developed by Tunmer, Herriman, and Nesdale (1988). The children were required to use counters to represent the sounds in orally presented pseudowords of varying length. The task was presented in the form of a game in which the children were asked to identify the sounds in "funny sounding names of children who live in far away lands." One demonstration item was given, followed by four practice items with corrective feedback. Scoring was based on the number of items correctly segmented, giving a total possible score of 24. The internal reliability coefficient for this scale was .83.

An adapted version of a *pseudoword decoding* task developed by Richardson and DiBenedetto (1985) was used to measure knowledge of letter-sound patterns at the middle and end of year 1 and end of year 2. Thirty monosyllabic pseudowords from Section 3 of their Decoding Skills Test were presented in the form of a game in which the children were asked to try to read the "funny sounding names of children who live in far away lands." The pseudowords were presented in order of increasing difficulty, ranging from simple consonant-vowel-consonant patterns (e.g., *jit, med, dut*) to blends, digraphs, and vowel variations (e.g., *prew, thrain, fruice*). Two practice items with corrective feedback were given followed by the 30 test items with no corrective feedback. When the child incorrectly pronounced an item, the mispronunciation was recorded using the pronunciation key provided by Richardson and DiBenedetto. The items were scored according to the total number of sounds pronounced correctly in each item, provided the sounds in the item were blended into a single syllable. The total number of possible points was 101, and the internal reliability estimate for this scale was .99.

Invented spelling was assessed at the middle and end of year 1. The children were asked to write 18 words that were read aloud by the experimenter, first in isolation, then in a sentence. The 26 letters of the alphabet were displayed across the top of the children's response page. Each word that the children wrote received a score from 1 to 4. Maximum points were awarded for correct conventional spellings. Three points were awarded if all the sounds in the word were represented with letters, although unconventionally (e.g., *kik* for *kick*, *fil* for *fill*, *sid* for *side*). Two points were awarded if more than one phoneme (but not all) was represented with phonetically related or conventional letters (e.g., *sd* for *side*, *lup* for *lump*). One point was awarded where the initial phoneme was represented with the correct letter (e.g., *f* for *fat*). The total number of possible points was 72, and the internal reliability estimate for this measure was .94.

An *analogical transfer* task devised by Greaney, Tunmer, and Chapman (1997) was used to measure the children's ability to take advantage of orthographic analogies when reading words containing common rime spelling units. The children were asked to read 72 monosyllabic words that were presented in 18 rows of four words each. The 72 words comprised 18 groups of words, each of which contained a common rime spelling unit (e.g., *at* in *cat*, *hat*, *bat*, *fat*). Half the words were presented contiguously (e.g., *tail*, *mail*, *sail*, *jail*), and half were presented noncontiguously such that no two words containing a common rime spelling unit appeared in any one row (e.g., *bank*, *side*, *may*, *meat*). The words presented contiguously and noncontiguously were counterbalanced across participants. The first word of each of the rows containing contiguously presented words was a frequently occurring word that children could easily recognize. The remaining three words in each row were chosen to vary widely in frequency of occurrence to increase the likelihood that some of the words would not be immediately recognized by the children. Scoring was based on the number of words read correctly in the two presentation conditions. The internal reliability for this task was .98.

Context free *word identification* ability was assessed by means of a combination of Forms A, B, and C of the Ready to Read Word Test (Clay 1985) at the beginning, middle, and end of year 1, and the Burt Word Reading Test, New Zealand Revision (Gilmore, Croft, and Read 1981) at the middle and end of year 1 and end of year 2. The Ready to Read Word Test comprised 45 words selected from the most frequently occurring words in the 12 "little" books of the New Zealand *Ready to Read Series*. Scoring was based on the number of words read correctly by each child. The internal reliability coefficient for this test was .90.

The Burt Word Reading Test is a standardized test in which children are presented with a list of 110 words of increasing difficulty and asked to look at each word carefully and read it aloud. Testing continued until 10 successive words were read incorrectly or not attempted. Scoring was based on the number of words read correctly. The Burt Test has a reliability coefficient of .97. Of particular relevance to the present study, which did not include a standardized measure of reading comprehension ability, Blaiklock (1997) reported that the Burt Test correlated highly with word recognition accuracy in connected text ($r = .94$) and reading comprehension ability ($r = .85$), as assessed by means of the Neale Analysis of Reading Ability—Revised (Neale 1988).

Reading book level, as assessed by the children's classroom teachers at the end of years 1 and 2, was included as an estimate of reading progress. Children were assigned to the book level in which they were able to attain a word recognition accuracy rate of 90% to 94%. There are 26 book levels, the characteristics of which are more fully described by Iversen and Tunmer (1993). Reading book level has been criticized as an unreliable measure of reading achievement that yields inflated estimates of children's progress (Chapman, Tunmer, and Prochnow 2001; Elbaum et al. 2000; Tunmer and Chapman in press a).

Spelling of common words was assessed at the end of year 2 by means of 20 words from the *Spell-Write Manual* developed for use in New Zealand schools by Croft (1983). Five words from each of the four word lists in the manual were randomly selected for inclusion in this task. The words were clustered in groups of 5, and in increasing difficulty. The reliability estimate for this scale was .92.

Children's *reported word identification strategies* were obtained by asking each child the following question toward the end of year 1: "When you are reading on your own and come across a word that you don't know, what do you do to try to figure out what the word is?" The children's responses were coded according to whether reference was made to the use of word-based strategies, reference was made to the use of text-based strategies, or no response was given. Examples of word-based strategies were "sound it out," "think of the sounds," "hear all the letters," "listen to what the letters are." Examples of text-based strategies were "guess," "think, guess what the word is," "read it over again," "read on," "have a look at the picture," "put my finger on the book and try other words and get a word that makes sense," "miss it out and go to the end and go back and guess a word that makes sense." Responses were independently rated by two research assistants. There were very few differences in categorization of responses, and these were resolved by discussion.

Modified Literacy Teaching Program

In designing and evaluating intervention programs there are many factors to consider (Lyon and Moats 1997; Tunmer et al. 2002). Lyon and Moats (1997) noted that all "real-world" interventions will have strengths and weaknesses, no matter how elegantly designed:

> In conducting intervention research, there are clear trade-offs with respect to experimental control and ecological validity. For example, the more control that is exerted over teacher and school effects, the more difficult it is to generalize the results of the study to typical classroom settings. (p. 585)

Because our ultimate goal was to affect change in regular classroom literacy practices, a deliberate decision was made to have the supplementary instruction delivered by the classroom teachers themselves rather than specially trained researchers brought to the school. Accordingly, our approach was to work collaboratively with the beginning reading teachers in the 13 new entrant classrooms of participating schools to adapt, deliver, and test supplementary teaching strategies and materials designed to help all children, but especially those at risk for failure, to derive greater benefit from regular classroom instruction.

An important feature of our program was the emphasis placed on professional development. Hiebert and Taylor (2000) concluded from a review of research on early reading interventions that opportunities for teachers to learn are an essential part of successful early intervention projects, especially in initiating changes in the profiles of struggling beginning readers (p. 478). Teachers need to know what they are doing and why they are doing it, and be able to respond to the individual differences and needs of their students rather than teaching in narrow, formulaic ways. With these considerations in mind, a full-time researcher was assigned to the project to provide ongoing support throughout the school year to all participating teachers in the use of the supplementary teaching materials and strategies. The researcher visited the 13 classrooms on a rotating basis, and assisted the teachers in implementing the program by explaining, demonstrating, and modeling effective use of the materials and instructional strategies.

Toward the end of the year preceding the implementation of the program, we met with the teachers and principal of each participating school to explain the rationale for the next phase of our research project. We indicated that the data from the longitudinal study we had carried out in their school (and the other participating schools) showed that many beginning readers were having trouble detecting sound sequences in spoken words and in relating letter patterns to sound patterns, and that these problems were strongly related to subsequent delays or difficulties in learning to read (data from actual cases in each participating school were presented to illustrate the pattern of results we obtained). We then suggested to the teachers and principal that incorporating some additional materials (that we would provide free of charge) and instructional strategies into their beginning literacy program might help their children, especially those at risk, to derive greater benefit from the school's literacy program, and thus make the program more effective. We presented material from three commercially available literacy instruction packages that were designed to help children develop awareness of sound sequences in spoken words and to make greater use of letter-sound patterns in reading unfamiliar words. Because the packages had been developed in Australia and England, we explained to the teachers that their role would be to work collaboratively with the research team to determine whether the packages could be successfully adapted for use in New Zealand classrooms. The teachers agreed to use the resources with the support of the full-time researcher and to provide ongoing comments and written evaluations of their usefulness, including recommendations for adaptations.

Minimal teacher training was required to use the three packages because each was specifically designed for use by classroom teachers and included information about teaching strategies, use of the instructional materials, and the sequencing and pacing of recommended activities. Immediately prior to the implementation of each program (which occurred at a particular point during the school year; see below), the researcher presented the teachers at each participating school with a detailed overview of the program, made suggestions as to how the program could be implemented in their classrooms, and modeled the use of the materials and instructional procedures. On subsequent visits to the school the researcher provided further support to the teachers by answering questions and working directly with students to demonstrate the effective use of the program's materials and learning activities. At different times during the project the teachers in each of the schools were invited to a lunch hosted by the research team to share their experiences in using the supplementary materials and instructional strategies with teachers at other participating schools. Throughout the project the authority and professionalism of the participating teachers were recognized and respected.

Components of the three selected packages were used by the teachers of year 1 students over the course of a four-term school year (each term lasted approximately 10 weeks). *Sound Foundations* (Byrne and Fielding-Barnsley 1991b) was used during the first term, *Rhyme and Analogy* (Goswami 1996) during the second term, and *Jolly Phonics* (Lloyd 1992) during the third and fourth terms. The selection of the three packages was based on the assumption that the degree of explicitness and detail with which phonologically related knowledge, skills, and strategies are taught is particularly important. Although a naturalistic, informal, whole language approach to reading instruction (in which word analysis activities arise incidentally from the child's responses during text reading) may be suitable for many children (mainly those with an abundance of literate cultural capital at school entry), other children (especially those at risk) appear to require a more highly structured, systematic approach with particular attention focused on the development of phonologically based skills and strategies.

Sound Foundations is a thoroughly researched program (Byrne and Fielding-Barnsley 1991a, 1993, 1995; Byrne, Fielding-Barnsley, and Ashley 2000) that aims to increase young children's sensitivity to the phonological components of words (the beginning and end sounds) through activities that focus on sound-sharing among spoken words. Most attention is focused on nine phonemes; three continuant consonants (*s, sh, l*), four stop consonants (*m, p, t, g*) and two short vowels (*a* as in *bat, e* as in *bet*). For each of these sounds there are a variety of activities. The first involves the use of large, durable, brightly colored posters depicting scenes with objects beginning with the same sound (*sea, seal, sailor,* etc.) and other posters with objects ending with the same sound (*bus, horse, octopus,* etc.). Accompanying each poster are three reproducible worksheets containing drawings of objects and characters. On each worksheet about half the items begin (or end) with the critical sound and the child's task is to find and color the target items.

Two card games are included in the package. In "Sound Dominoes" two pictured objects appear on each card and the child's task is to join cards sharing beginning sounds (or ending sounds in a second version of the game). In "Snap" one pictured object appears on each card and children (as many as eight) take turns placing their next card face up on a pile and saying "snap" when the new card matches the top one in the pile for initial sound (or final sound in a second version of the game, or beginning or final sound in a third version). The teachers used the posters, worksheets, and card games to teach the nine key sounds (in beginning and ending positions), with a new sound being introduced each week in the order recommended in the *Sound Foundations* manual. The *Sound Foundations* materials and teaching activities were used by the teachers for at least 60 minutes each week during the first term.

Rhyme and Analogy (Goswami 1996), which was used during the second term, is based on Goswami's work on the role of orthographic analogies in learning to read (see Goswami 2000, for a review of research). The ability to segment spoken words into phonemic units is preceded by the ability to divide words into onsets and rimes (Treiman 1992). Because onsets and rimes are more accessible to beginning readers, especially to children as young as New Zealand beginning readers, an initial focus on teaching orthographic units corresponding to onsets and rimes was considered to be a useful first step in making children more aware of sublexical relationships between written and spoken words.

The *Rhyme and Analogy* package comprises three components. First, an alphabet frieze (and tabletop poster version of the same material) shows the letters of the alphabet and four common digraphs (*ch, sh, th, wh*), each presented with a colorful illustration of an object beginning with the sound represented by the letter or digraph (e.g., a picture of a shoe accompanies *sh*). The frieze and poster are used to help children recognize letter shapes and learn letter sounds. Second, 60 reproducible worksheets are used to develop children's knowledge of the alphabet by having them practice letter formation, identify and categorize the initial sounds of illustrated objects, and make connections between initial sounds and letters.

The third and most important component of *Rhyme and Analogy* are four sets of cards that can be used to play more than 50 games designed to develop children's awareness of onset and rime, and to help children recognize and use common rime spelling patterns in their reading and spelling. The first deck contains 120 initial sound (i.e., onset) picture cards (four picture cards for each letter of the alphabet and for each of the common digraphs) that are used to increase children's sensitivity to the beginning sounds of spoken words. The second deck contains 120 letter cards (four cards for each letter and digraph, presented in lower case) that are used to develop knowledge of letter sounds and, when used in conjunction with initial sound picture cards, to encourage children to make connections between letters and initial sounds. The third deck contains 64 rhyme picture cards (16 families of pictured objects that rhyme) that are used to develop children's sensitivity to rime units in spoken words. The fourth deck contains 64 rhyme word cards (each with a printed word that matches one of the rhyme picture cards in the third deck) that are used to encourage children to make connections between rimes in spoken words and rime spelling patterns in printed words (e.g., "ip" in "ship," "zip," "lip," "chip," and ip in ship, zip, lip, chip). The teachers reported that the card games were easily integrated into their regular classroom literacy activities and were particularly helpful in developing beginning readers' knowledge of basic letter-sound patterns (i.e., initial letter sounds and rime spelling units).

Two components of the *Jolly Phonics* package were used during the third and fourth terms. These were the *Phonics Handbook* and the seven *Finger Phonics* books. A distinctive feature of the program is that children are taught the main letter or letter pattern corresponding to each of the 42 sounds of English, not just the alphabet sounds (i.e., sounds represented by individual letters like *s*, *t*, and *o*, as well as those represented by digraphs like *ai*, *oo*, *th*, *ng*, and *ch*). The program therefore provided a review and extension of the letter-sound patterns that were taught in the *Rhyme and Analogy* program.

Jolly Phonics uses a multi-sensory approach that incorporates visual, aural and tactile teaching techniques. The Phonics Handbook provides over 100 reproducible sheets for teaching the 42 letter-sound patterns and the structured blending of letter sounds. For each of the 42 letter sounds a "sound sheet" is provided with a suggested storyline (e.g., "Pack a hamper—children suggest food taken—they sit down and lay out the picnic—start eating—little child feels tickling on arm and says *a a a a a ants*—they jump and leave the angry ants"), an action (teacher shows the letter a and children wiggle their fingers above their elbow as if ants were crawling on them, and say *a, a, a!*), a picture to color (e.g., two angry ants), and a line to practice writing the letter(s) on. Training in blending sounds begins by having the children listen to the separate sounds of three-letter words (e.g., "duh-ah-guh") and then calling out the appropriate word (e.g., "dog"). The *Phonics Handbook* also includes lists of words for the children to cut up and put into "sound boxes" to be taken home for additional blending practice.

The seven *Finger Phonics* books each contain six letter sounds presented in a textured format that allows the child to feel the letter shape. Also included in each book are illustrations of the actions the children learn to associate with each letter sound, and illustrations of objects (and their associated printed words) containing the sound in different positions in words. The back pages of each book give additional practice in matching sounds to letters and in word-building activities involving the manipulation of word segments.

The teachers reported that the *Jolly Phonics* materials and procedures were most easily and effectively used when working with groups of four to six children. They further indicated that the children responded very enthusiastically to the program, especially the storylines and associated actions. Each week the teachers spent about an hour working with each group, and normally introduced three new letter sounds in the order recommended in the *Phonics Handbook*.

The materials and procedures from the three packages that were incorporated into the year 1 literacy programs of the seven participating schools did not represent a return to a rigid, skill-and-drill approach to literacy instruction in which word-level skills are largely taught in isolation as part of an overall lock-step approach to literacy instruction. Instead, the instructional approach that we encouraged the teachers of beginning readers to adopt was based on two assumptions. First, there needed to be a balance between activities that facilitated the acquisition of declarative, or factual, knowledge and those that facilitated the acquisition of procedural, or "how to," knowledge (i.e., strategies). Skill-and-drill approaches tend to place too much emphasis on teaching factual knowledge, such as that a particular letter or letter sequence (e.g., *tion*) makes a particular sound (e.g., /shun/), without giving sufficient attention to developing within beginning readers an understanding of how and when to apply such knowledge. In contrast, strategy training fosters the development of procedural knowledge by encouraging beginning readers to become *active* problem solvers with regard to graphic information, which includes adopting a "set for diversity" (Gaskins et al. 1988) that enables them to make use of irregular and polyphonic spelling patterns (e.g., *ear* as in *bear* and *hear*, *own* as in *clown* and *flown*, where children generate alternative pronunciations of the word until one is produced that matches a word in their vocabulary and is appropriate to the sentence context). Emphasis was therefore placed on developing *self-improving* strategies for acquiring spelling-sound relationships (because there are too many to acquire by direct instruction; Gough and Hillinger 1980) rather than on just teaching individual spelling patterns per se, as in the skill-and-drill approach. Juel (1991) argued that a little explicit phonics instruction may go "a long way" in facilitating the process by which children induce untaught spelling-sound relationships (p. 783). We therefore hypothesized that as the reading attempts of beginning readers became more successful, they would begin making greater independent use of letter-sound information (possibly supplemented with text-based cues) to identify unfamiliar words from which additional spelling-sound relationships could be induced without explicit instruction (Juel and Minden-Cupp 2000; Share 1995; Share and Stanovich 1995; Tunmer and Chapman in press b). As Juel and Minden-Cupp (2000) suggested, "the critical question may be how teachers can most efficiently help children gain enough skill to successfully enter the world of print so that, in a sense, they can then read enough to become their own teachers" (p. 462).

Second, balance also needed to be achieved in the instructional components included in the modified beginning reading programs, especially between learning new skills and actually using them. Beginning readers must be given plenty of opportunities to use their newly acquired word-level skills and strategies to identify unfamiliar words while reading *connected text*. Although beginning readers should receive explicit and systematic instruction in letter-sound patterns and word identification strategies outside the context of reading connected text, they must also be taught how to use this information during text reading through demonstration, modeling, direct explanation and guided practice. It cannot be assumed that beginning readers who are successful in acquiring word analysis skills will automatically transfer them when attempting to read connected text (Lyon and Moats 1997). Some children, especially struggling readers, must be made aware that successful attempts in identifying unfamiliar words in text are a direct consequence of the appropriate and effortful application of taught skills and strategies. For this reason we stressed to the teachers during the final term of the school year the importance of giving students consistent and accurate feedback to encourage them in their reading and writing efforts, to help them identify appropriate strategies, and to help them recognize the effort needed to achieve success in reading and writing tasks. The intention of the "feedback scripts" that we developed and modeled for the teachers was to make the children more aware of the cause-effect links between what they do on the reading or writing task and the outcome achieved, and to promote a positive sense of reading-related self-efficacy (Chapman and Tunmer 2003). For example, a feedback message for the successful accomplishment of a difficult reading task emphasized the adoption of a strategy, together with the application of effort (e.g., "Well done, Tony! You looked carefully at all the letters in that word and you sounded them out. You worked hard on that!"). For a task that did not result in a satisfactory outcome, the feedback emphasized the use of an appropriate strategy together with perseverance (e.g., "Good try, Maria, but you missed the middle sounds of that word. If you work out the beginning sounds, and then look carefully at the middle sounds and keep on until you have finished all the sounds in the word, you'll be able to figure it out.").

RESULTS AND DISCUSSION

Presented in table I are the means and standard deviations for measures taken at the beginning, middle and end of year 1 and at the end of year 2 as a function of type of program. t-tests were carried out to determine whether there were any significant differences between the means of children in the original and modified beginning literacy programs. The results indicate that the two comparison groups performed at similar levels on letter identification, onset-rime segmentation, and word identification at school entry. The children in both groups performed at floor levels on the word identification measure, usually only recognizing the word *I* (which is also an upper case letter) and possibly one other word.

At the middle of year 1, the children in the modified program scored more highly than the children in the original program on all measures. However, only two reached significance, sound matching and invented spelling, both of which were phonological processing measures. By the end of the year the differences between the means for all measures except reading book level (which, as noted earlier, is a somewhat unreliable measure) had reached significance, including two standardized measures of reading achievement (i.e., the Clay and Burt tests). Of particular importance were the very robust differences favoring the modified program group on all phonological processing measures (i.e., phoneme segmentation, invented spelling, pseudoword decoding, and analogical transfer). The materials and procedures from the three packages that were incorporated into the reading programs of the 13 intervention classrooms were clearly having a cumulative positive effect on the development of children's phonologically related skills and strategies, which in turn were beginning to generalize to standardized measures of reading achievement.

An important aspect of intervention research is determining whether any positive effects obtained from the intervention are maintained after the intervention is completed. The data presented in table I indicate that by the end of year 2 the gains made

Table I.   Tests of differences between means of original and modified beginning literacy programs for all measures

Variable	Maximum score	Type of Program				p
		Original		Modified		
		M	D	M	SD	
Beginning of Year1		(*n* = 63)		(*n* = 80)		
Letter identification	54	20.1	18.0	25.4	17.4	ns
Onset-rime segmentation	53	31.9	15.5	34.6	12.5	ns
Word identification (Clay)	45	1.5	3.6	2.4	2.5	ns
Middle of Year 1		(*n* = 62)		(*n* = 77)		
Letter identification	54	44.6	11.9	45.3	10.0	ns
Sound matching	18	13.8	3.2	15.2	2.8	<.01
Onset-rime segmentation	53	40.5	14.2	42.4	12.4	ns
Invented spelling	72	31.9	17.8	38.1	14.6	<.05
Pseudoword decoding	101	28.3	24.2	33.1	24.1	ns
Word identification (Clay)	45	17.2	14.0	18.0	12.0	ns
Word identification (Burt)	110	9.3	9.2	11.0	8.3	ns
End of Year 1		(*n* = 61)		(*n* = 74)		
Phoneme segmentation	24	12.6	7.1	17.6	4.7	<.001
Invented spelling	72	39.9	16.6	47.5	11.3	<.001
Pseudoword decoding	101	40.6	25.1	59.7	22.4	<.001
Analogical transfer	72	19.1	22.4	35.1	21.6	<.001
Word identification (Clay)	45	29.1	13.0	35.2	10.2	<.01
Word identification (Burt)	101	17.5	11.9	20.7	10.4	<.05
Burt reading age (yrs., mos.)	12;0	<6;0	–	6;1	–	–
Reading book level	26	10.9	5.1	11.8	5.0	ns
End of Year 2		(*n* = 58)		(*n* = 60)		
Pseudoword decoding	101	68.7	21.1	86.5	14.9	<.001
Analogical transfer	72	48.7	21.4	66.4	7.2	<.001
Spelling common words	20	11.9	5.4	14.8	4.6	<.01
Word identification (Burt)	110	31.9	13.1	45.6	15.3	<.001
Burt reading age (yrs., mos.)	>12;0	7;1	–	8;3	–	–
Reading book level	26	20.0	4.7	21.3	4.6	<.10

by the children in the modified program (which was completed at the end of year 1) over the children in the original program were not only maintained, but had increased to an average difference in reading age of 14 months. Convergent evidence that these gains can be attributed to greater knowledge and use of letter-sound patterns comes from the children's responses to the question concerning their preferred word identification strategy given at the end of year 1. Presented in table II are the frequency and percentage for each response category as a function of type of beginning literacy program. For the children in the modified program, there was a clear shift toward reporting the use of word-based strategies, from 54% to 76%, with a corresponding decline in text-based responses, such as those referring to sentence context or picture cues.

The second aim of the study was to determine whether supplementary materials and procedures designed to help children develop phonological awareness and alphabetic coding skills would reduce the gap in reading achievement between Maori and Pakeha (i.e., European) children. To answer this question we divided the children in the original and modified literacy programs into Pakeha and Maori subgroups (the few children who did not belong to either of these ethnic groups were not included in the analysis). Although there was at least one Maori student in the sample from each of the seven schools that implemented the modified beginning literacy program, the majority of Maori students attended low decile schools (65% in deciles 1 to 5, 35% in deciles 6 to 10) with the largest percentage (29%) attending a decile 1 school. In contrast, the majority of Pakeha children were in higher decile schools.

For the Pakeha and Maori children in the original longitudinal study, the means, standard deviations and tests of significant differences for all measures included in the retrospective study are presented in table III. The results show significant differences between the two groups on all measures at all testing points. Particularly noteworthy are the large group differences on all phonological processing measures from school entry to the end of year 2 (i.e., onset-rime segmentation, sound matching, phoneme segmentation, pseudoword decoding, analogical transfer, invented spelling). These findings support our claim that the mainstream constructivist orientation to teaching reading in New Zealand fails to respond adequately to differences in essential phonologically

Table II. Frequency and percentage for each response category of reported word identification strategies as a function of type of beginning literacy program

Response Category	Original Program		Modified Program	
	n	%	*n*	%
Word-based strategies	33	54.1	55	76.4
Text-based strategies	24	39.3	12	16.7
No response	4	6.6	5	6.9
Total	61	100.0	72	100.0

Table III.   Tests of differences between means of Pakeha and Maori children in original longitudinal study

Variable	Maximum Score	Ethnicity				
		Pakeha		Maori		
		M	SD	M	SD	p
Beginning of Year1		(*n* = 114)		(*n* = 27)		
Letter identification	54	24.9	17.9	11.0	14.6	<.001
Onset-rime segmentation	53	32.2	15.9	22.9	16.0	<.01
Word identification (Clay)	45	2.5	5.7	0.6	0.8	<.001
Middle of Year 1		(*n* = 112)		(*n* = 24)		
Letter identification	54	46.5	11.3	29.1	18.8	<.001
Sound matching	18	14.0	3.6	11.5	3.5	<.01
Onset-rime segmentation	53	39.8	14.0	32.1	14.6	<.01
Invented spelling	72	32.4	18.6	12.7	17.2	<.001
Pseudoword decoding	101	31.2	23.4	12.0	15.1	<.001
Word identification (Clay)	45	19.7	14.2	10.9	12.5	<.01
Word identification (Burt)	110	10.5	9.6	4.3	5.8	<.001
End of Year 1		(*n* = 109)		(*n* = 24)		
Phoneme segmentation	24	12.7	7.0	7.0	7.9	<.001
Invented spelling	72	40.2	16.2	21.9	19.0	<.001
Pseudoword decoding	101	44.9	24.7	18.3	25.1	<.001
Analogical transfer	72	20.4	21.9	10.5	19.0	<.05
Word identification (Clay)	45	30.1	13.0	17.8	16.0	<.001
Word identification (Burt)	101	18.8	12.1	9.4	11.2	<.001
Burt reading age (yrs., mos.)	>12;0	<6;0	–	<6;0	–	–
Reading book level	26	11.3	5.4	7.0	5.6	<.001
End of Year 2		(*n* = 102)		(*n* = 22)		
Pseudoword decoding	101	70.8	18.3	48.4	26.6	<.001
Analogical transfer	72	51.4	19.3	29.3	28.9	<.001
Spelling common words	20	11.5	5.1	8.1	7.3	<.05
Word identification (Burt)	110	32.7	12.3	20.6	14.5	<.001
Burt reading age (yrs., mos.)	>12;0	7;2	–	6;3	–	–
Reading book level	26	20.6	4.3	15.2	7.7	<.01

related skills and knowledge during the initial years of schooling. After two years of schooling the Maori children were performing on average 9 months below age-appropriate levels in reading (as measured by the Burt test) and 11 months below the Pakeha children in the sample.

Effect sizes were calculated to provide data for comparing the performance of Pakeha and Maori children. For each measure, the mean score obtained by Pakeha students was subtracted from the mean score obtained by Maori students, and the difference was divided by the standard deviation of the scores obtained by the Pakeha students. In this procedure, Pakeha mean effect sizes were set at 0 to form a benchmark against which to compare Maori mean effect sizes. When the mean effect sizes for the measures taken at each testing point were computed and plotted against time, the standard negative Matthew effect of increasing group differences was revealed, as illustrated in figure 1 (see the line representing the performance of Maori children in standard beginning reading programs). Consistent with these findings are the results presented in table IV showing large differences in reported word identification strategies between Pakeha and Maori children at the end of year 1. The Pakeha children were three

Table IV. Frequency and percentage for each response category of reported word identification strategies as a function of ethnicity (original program)

Response Category	Pakeha		Maori	
	n	%	n	%
Word-based strategies	68	61.8	5	20.8
Text-based strategies	32	29.1	12	50.0
No response	10	9.1	7	29.2
Total	110	100.0	24	100.0

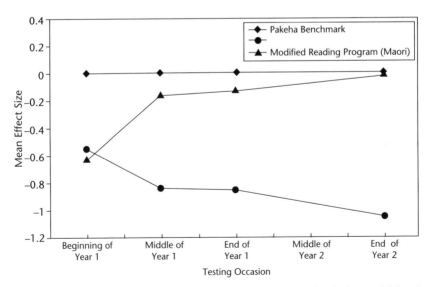

Figure 1.   Mean effect sizes comparing performance of Pakeha and Maori children as a function of type of beginning literacy program and testing occasion.

times more likely than Maori children to report using word-based strategies to identify unfamiliar words in text.

For the Pakeha and Maori children in the program modification study, the means, standard deviations and tests of significant differences for all measures are presented in table V. At school entry, the differences between the two groups were very similar to those in the original longitudinal study. However, at all subsequent testing points there were no significant differences between

Table V. Tests of differences between means of Pakeha and Maori children in retrospective program modification study

Variable	Maximum Score	Pakeha M	SD	Maori M	SD	p
Beginning of Year1		(*n* = 56)		(*n* = 17)		
Letter identification	54	28.8	16.9	15.4	13.8	<.01
Onset-rime segmentation	53	36.7	11.8	28.8	13.1	<.01
Word identification (Clay)	45	2.6	2.7	1.4	1.2	<.01
Middle of Year 1		(*n* = 55)		(*n* = 15)		
Letter identification	54	46.2	9.1	42.5	11.4	ns
Sound matching	18	15.3	2.9	14.5	2.7	ns
Onset-rime segmentation	53	43.4	12.0	44.4	9.3	ns
Invented spelling	72	38.1	14.5	37.8	14.0	ns
Pseudoword decoding	101	33.0	23.4	31.3	28.5	ns
Word identification (Clay)	45	18.8	12.1	16.0	11.6	ns
Word identification (Burt)	110	11.3	8.7	9.9	6.8	ns
End of Year 1		(*n* = 54)		(*n* = 13)		
Phoneme segmentation	24	17.6	4.5	17.2	5.8	ns
Invented spelling	72	47.1	11.1	47.3	13.2	ns
Pseudoword decoding	101	59.3	22.3	57.1	26.6	ns
Analogical transfer	72	35.5	20.7	32.4	27.2	ns
Word identification (Clay)	45	35.6	9.6	33.4	11.5	ns
Word identification (Burt)	101	20.9	11.2	19.8	11.5	ns
Burt reading age (yrs., mos.)	>12;0	6;2	–	6;1	–	–
Reading book level	26	12.1	4.9	10.7	5.5	ns
End of Year 2		(*n* = 43)		(*n* = 12)		
Pseudoword decoding	101	85.6	16.8	87.8	9.3	ns
Analogical transfer	72	66.2	7.8	65.8	6.5	ns
Spelling common words	20	14.4	4.7	15.6	3.9	ns
Word identification (Burt)	110	45.6	14.3	45.9	18.1	ns
Burt reading age (yrs., mos.)	>12;0	8;3	–	8;3	—	–
Reading book level	26	21.9	4.7	20.0	3.6	ns

any of the measures taken. The mean effect sizes shown in figure 1 indicate that the initial gap between Maori and Pakeha children at school entry had closed by the end of year 2 (see the line representing the performance of Maori children in modified beginning reading programs). Consistent with these findings are the results presented in table VI showing no major differences between Pakeha and Maori children in reported word identification strategies. By the end of year 1, both groups reported a strong preference for using word-based strategies to identify unfamiliar words in text. These results suggest that the phonologically related materials and procedures incorporated into the reading programs of the 13 intervention classrooms were effective in eliminating the gap in reading achievement between Maori and Pakeha students.

CONCLUSIONS

We began this paper by drawing attention to some puzzling findings. Despite having a very homogeneous education system with a uniform approach to reading instruction and intervention, New Zealand has for several years now consistently shown comparatively high levels of variability in the test scores from international surveys of literacy achievement. Three strategies have been proposed for preventing reading failure and reducing the unacceptably large amount of disparity between New Zealand readers: doing more of the same, accommodating cultural differences, and changing the method of teaching reading. On the basis of an analysis of the arguments and evidence in support of each of these positions, we concluded that the third strategy is most supportable. We hypothesized that New Zealand's relatively large spread of scores in international studies of literacy achievement is largely the result of Matthew effects triggered by a mainstream constructivist orientation to teaching reading that fails to respond adequately to differences in essential reading-related skills and

Table VI: Frequency and percentage for each response category of reported word identification strategies as a function of ethnicity (modified program)

Response Category	Pakeha		Maori	
	n	%	*n*	%
Word-based strategies	40	75.5	11	84.6
Text-based strategies	11	20.7	0	0.0
No response	2	3.8	2	15.4
Total	53	100.0	13	100.0

knowledge at school entry that stem primarily from social class differences in home literacy environment.

Two predictions were derived from this hypothesis. First, incorporating into beginning literacy programs supplementary materials and procedures designed to help children develop awareness of the sound components of spoken words and make greater use of letter-sound patterns in reading unfamiliar words should produce significantly greater gains in reading achievement than the standard whole language approach to literacy instruction. Second, the use of these materials and teaching strategies should reduce or eliminate the gap in beginning reading achievement between Maori and Pakeha children. To test these predictions a retrospective study was carried out in which a representative sample of seven schools was selected from 22 schools that three years earlier had participated in a longitudinal study of beginning literacy development. The target children in the program modification schools were tested at four of the same testing points as the children in the original longitudinal study with tests that assessed phonological processing skills and literacy achievement.

Two major findings emerged from the study. First, incorporating into existing classroom literacy programs materials and procedures designed to increase beginning readers' phonological awareness and alphabetic coding skills resulted in an average difference in reading age of 14 months over standard literacy programs by the end of year 2. Second, the use of the supplementary materials and teaching strategies eliminated the gap in beginning reading achievement between Maori and Pakeha children by the end of the second year of schooling. These findings are very encouraging because they suggest that relatively small changes to the predominant approach to teaching literacy in New Zealand will greatly increase the overall effectiveness of beginning reading instruction and substantially reduce the number of reading failures, especially among Maori children. Provided that our findings are a reasonably accurate depiction of reality (i.e., are replicable and generalizable), a disturbing implication of our findings is that the mainstream constructivist (learn-to-read-by-reading) orientation to beginning literacy instruction in New Zealand is functionally discriminatory.

There are, however, limitations of the study that need to be considered before any firm conclusions can be drawn. First, the sample size was somewhat small, especially the number of Maori students who participated in the program modification study (initially 17 students but only 12 by the end of the study). A study involving a larger number of children needs to be carried out.

Second, this was not an experimental study. Perhaps the positive effects obtained for the modified program group over the untreated comparison group were largely the result of Hawthorne effects. However, there are two counter arguments to this possibility. First, the positive effects obtained in the study were very specific in nature and followed a particular sequence. As can be seen in table 1, there were only two positive effects at the middle of year 1, the most significant one being for a measure of phonological awareness, which, it could be argued, reflected the focus of the intervention up to that point. By the end of year 1, there were very robust effects for all phonological processing measures but only modest effects for the standardized measures of reading achievement. However, by the end of year 2, the robust effects obtained for the phonological processing measures had not only been maintained, but had generalized to a robust effect for reading achievement. In short, the positive effects seem to emerge in the order predicted by theory (Stanovich 1996): phonological awareness skills are essential for the development of alphabetic coding skills which in turn are essential for the development of word recognition skills. This pattern of results cannot be easily explained in terms of Hawthorne effects. The second counter argument is that the findings from the retrospective study are consistent with other intervention studies carried out in New Zealand that are more experimental in nature. Greaney, Tunmer and Chapman (1997), for example, found in a carefully designed study that even children with persistent reading problems, most of whom had been referred on from Reading Recovery, were able to derive long-term benefits from explicit instruction in phonological processing skills.

Another limitation of the study is that we do not know if the positive effects obtained at the end of year 2 were maintained in subsequent years, especially the elimination of the gap in reading achievement between Pakeha and Maori children. We cannot conclude that the intervention program implemented in year 1 resulted in a "vaccination effect" guaranteeing freedom from future reading problems. Research reviewed by Hiebert and Taylor (2000) indicates that the gains made from early reading interventions are necessary, but not sufficient for success in the middle grades. As they put it, at risk children are "not out of the woods yet" as the initial positive effects of early interventions often decrease in subsequent grades (p. 477). Although early reading intervention programs like the one we initiated may help at risk children to acquire basic literacy skills, further support for these children may be required to help them develop the higher order comprehension strategies necessary for reading the kinds of informational texts that are introduced in the middle grades and beyond (Hiebert and Taylor 2000; Pressley 1998, 2000).

The findings from the retrospective study have important implications for educational practice in New Zealand. The children with lower levels of literacy-related skills at school entry clearly benefitted the most from the intervention. The mean scores on the Burt test for the Pakeha children increased from 32.7 in the original longitudinal study to 45.6 in the program modification study, whereas the mean scores for the Maori children increased from 20.6 to 45.9. In general the amount of explicit instruction required to develop adequate levels of phonological awareness and alphabetic coding skills varies considerably across beginning readers.

Recent research by Juel and Minden-Cupp (2000) suggests that organizing instruction to cater for the differing phonological processing skill needs of new entrants is essential for maximizing the effectiveness of beginning literacy instruction. They studied in depth the widely varying instructional practices of teachers in four first-grade classrooms, each of which comprised a high proportion of at risk students. Juel and Minden-Cupp (2000) reported two major findings. First, differential instruction appears to be a particularly important feature of beginning literacy instruction:

> One of the most provocative findings from this study is the indication that differential instruction may be helpful in first grade. All teachers used homogenous reading groups. The more time incoming students with comparatively fewer early literacy skills spent in these groups—as opposed to whole-class instruction—the better they did. Further, the two classrooms that were most successful in getting them off to a good start in first grade had the most differentiated word recognition instruction . . . . In fact, the classroom . . . that had the very highest success both overall and with the low group had considerably different instruction across the groups. As compared with the other low groups, and with the other reading groups within this classroom, the focus of the low group was squarely on phonics . . . (pp. 482–483).

Second, training in phonological processing skills is critical for some children, but less so for others:

> Certainly the finding from the current study that appeared the most clear-cut . . . was that children who entered first grade with few literacy skills benefited from a heavy dose of phonics. However, children who possessed middle-range literacy skills on entering first grade benefited from a classroom with more trade book reading and time for writing text . . . . Children who entered first grade with some reading ability did exceptionally well in a classroom that included a less structured phonics curriculum and more reading of trade books and writing of text . . . (p. 484).

The important question to ask at this point is what kinds of home literacy environments and social class backgrounds did these children most likely come from that enabled them to benefit more from a book experience (i.e., whole language) approach, which is the approach that is predominantly used in New Zealand schools? As we see it, the critical issue facing the New Zealand Ministry of Education is whether they will continue to pursue a policy of actively promoting a largely unidimensional approach to literacy teaching that helps make schools contributing agents to cultural reproduction within New Zealand society. We hope not.

ACKNOWLEDGMENTS

This study is part of a research project funded by the New Zealand Ministry of Education, contract No. ER/299/5, and a Massey University post-doctoral fellowship. We are grateful to Heather Ryan for her professionalism in the implementation of the project and the collection of data.

REFERENCES

Au, K. H. 1998. Social constructivism and the school literacy learning of students of diverse backgrounds. *Journal of Literacy Research* 20:297–319.
Au, K. H. 2000. A multicultural perspective on policies for improving literacy achievement: Equity and excellence. In *Handbook of Reading Research.* Vol. 3, eds. M. L. Kamil, P. B. Mosenthal, P. D. Pearson, and R. Barr. Mahwah, NJ: Lawrence Erlbaum Associates.
Blachman, B. A. 2000. Phonological awareness. In *Handbook of Reading Research.* Vol. 3, eds. M. L. Kamil, P. B. Mosenthal, P. D. Pearson, and R. Barr. Mahwah, NJ: Lawrence Erlbaum Associates.
Blaiklock, K. E. 1997. Bring back the Burt: Some comments on the value of word recognition tests for the assessment of reading. *New Zealand Reading Forum* 2:13–16.
Bowey, J. A. 1995. Socioeconomic status differences in preschool phonological sensitivity and first-grade reading achievement. *Journal of Educational Psychology* 87:476–87.
Bryant, P., Bradley, L., MacLean, M., and Crossland, J. 1989. Nursery rhymes, phonological skills, and reading. *Journal of Child Language* 16:407–28.
Byrne, B., and Fielding-Barnsley, R. 1991a. Evaluation of a program to teach phonemic awareness to young children. *Journal of Educational Psychology* 83:451–55.
Byrne, B., and Fielding-Barnsley, R. 1991b. *Sound Foundations: An Introduction to Prereading Skills.* Sydney, Australia: Peter Leyden Educational.
Byrne, B., and Fielding-Barnsley, R. 1993. Evaluation of a program to teach phonemic awareness to young children: A 1-year follow-up. *Journal of Educational Psychology* 85:104–11.
Byrne, B., and Fielding-Barnsley, R. 1995. Evaluation of a program to teach phonemic awareness to young children: A 2- and 3-year follow-up

and a new preschool trial. *Journal of Educational Psychology* 87:
488–503.

Byrne, B., Fielding-Barnsley, R., and Ashley, L. 2000. Effects of preschool
phoneme identity training after six years: Outcome level distinguished
from rate of response. *Journal of Educational Psychology* 92:659–667.

Calfee, R. C. 1977. Assessment of independent reading skills: Basic research and practical applications. In *Toward a Psychology of Reading,*
eds. A. S. Reber, and D. L. Scarborough. Hillsdale, NJ: Lawrence
Erlbaum.

Chapman, J. W., and Tunmer, W. E. 1997. A longitudinal study of beginning reading achievement and reading self-concept. *British Journal of
Educational Psychology* 67:279–91.

Chapman, J. W., and Tunmer, W. E. 2003. Reading difficulties, reading-
related self-perceptions, and strategies for overcoming negative self-
beliefs. *Reading and Writing Quarterly* 19:5–24.

Chapman, J. W., Tunmer, W. E., and Prochnow, J. E. 2000. Early reading-
related skills and performance, reading self-concept, and the development of academic self-concept: A longitudinal study. *Journal of
Educational Psychology* 92:703–08.

Chapman, J. W., Tunmer, W. E., and Prochnow, J. E. 2001. Does success
in the Reading Recovery program depend on developing proficiency in
phonological processing skills? A longitudinal study in a whole language instructional context. *Scientific Studies of Reading* 5:141–76.

Clay, M. M. 1985. *The Early Detection of Reading Difficulties.* Auckland,
New Zealand: Heinemann.

Clay, M. M. 1991. *Becoming Literate: The Construction of Inner Control.*
Auckland, New Zealand: Heinemann.

Connelly, V., Johnston, R., and Thompson, G. B. 2001. The effects of
phonics instruction on the reading comprehension of beginning readers. *Reading and Writing: An Interdisciplinary Journal* 14:423–57.

Croft, C. 1983. *Teachers Manual for Spell-Write: An Aid to Writing, Spelling
and Word Study.* Wellington, New Zealand: New Zealand Council for
Educational Research.

Crooks, T., and Caygill, R. 1999. New Zealand's National Educational
Monitoring Project: Maori student achievement, 1995–1998. Paper presented at the combined annual conference of the New Zealand Association for Research in Education and the Australian Association for
Research in Education, Melbourne, Australia, November.

Ehri, L. 1992. Reconceptualizing the development of sight word reading
and its relationship to recoding. In *Reading Acquisition,* eds. P. Gough,
L. Ehri, and R. Treiman. Hillsdale, NJ: Lawrence Erlbaum Associates.

Ehri, L. C. 1997. Sight word learning in normal readers and dyslexics. In
*Foundations of Reading Intervention and Dyslexia: Implications for Early Inter-
vention,* ed. B. Blachman. Mahwah, NJ: Lawrence Erlbaum Associates.

Elbaum, B., Vaughn, S., Hughes, M., and Moody, S. 2000. How effective
are one-to-one tutoring programs in reading for elementary students at
risk for reading failure? A meta-analysis of the intervention research.
Journal of Educational Psychology 92:605–19.

Elley, W. B. 1992. *How in the World do Students Read?* Hamburg, Germany:
International Association for the Evaluation of Educational Achievement.

Elley, W. B. 1996. The phonics debate. *Set: Research Information for Teachers* 1, Article 7.

Elley, W. B. 1997. A perspective on New Zealand reading programmes. In *Language/Literacy Education: Diversity and Challenge. Report on the New Zealand Council for Teacher Education Language/Literacy Teacher Education Conference*, ed. J. Biddulph. Hamilton, New Zealand: School of Education, University of Waikato.

Foorman, B. R., Fletcher, J. M., Francis, D., and Schatschneider, C. 2000. Response: Misrepresentation of research by other researchers. *Educational Researcher* 29:27–37.

Foorman, B. R., Francis, D. J., Fletcher, J. M., Schatschneider, C., and Mehta, P. 1998. The role of instruction in learning to read: Preventing reading failure in at-risk children. *Journal of Educational Psychology* 90:37–55.

Gaskins, I. W., Downer, M. A., Anderson, R., Cunningham, P. M., Gaskins, R. W., Schommer, M., and the Teachers of the Benchmark School. 1988. A metacognitive approach to phonics: Using what you know to decode what you don't know. *Remedial and Special Education* 9:36–41.

Gilmore, A. M. 1998. *School Entry Assessment*. Wellington, New Zealand: Ministry of Education.

Gilmore, A., Croft, C., and Reid, N. 1981. *Burt Word Reading Test: New Zealand Revision*. Wellington, New Zealand: New Zealand Council for Educational Research.

Goodman, K. S. 1967. Reading: A psycholinguistic guessing game. *Journal of the Reading Specialist* 4:126–35.

Goodman, K. S. 1986. *What's Whole in Whole Language: A Parent-Teacher Guide*. Portsmouth, NH: Heinemann.

Goswami, U. C. 1996. *The Oxford Reading Tree Rhyme and Analogy Programme*. Oxford, UK: Oxford University Press.

Goswami, U. C. 2000. Phonological and lexical processes. In *Handbook of Reading Research*. Vol. 3, eds. M. L. Kamil, P. B. Mosenthal, P. D. Pearson, and R. Barr. Mahwah, NJ: Lawrence Erlbaum Associates.

Gough, P., and Hillinger, M. 1980. Learning to read: An unnatural act. *Bulletin of the Orton Society* 30:179–96.

Gough, P. B., and Walsh, M. 1991. Chinese, Phoenicians, and the orthographic cipher of English. In *Phonological Processes in Literacy*, eds. S. Brady and D. Shankweiler. Hillsdale, NJ: Lawrence Erlbaum Associates.

Greaney, K. T. 2002. School remedial reading programmes: Supporting children with reading difficulties. In *Learning to Read in Aotearoa New Zealand*, eds. P. Adams and H. Ryan. Palmerston North, New Zealand: Dunmore Press.

Greaney, K. T., Tunmer, W. E., and Chapman, J. W. 1997. Effects of rime-based orthographic analogy training on the word recognition skills of children with reading disability. *Journal of Educational Psychology* 89:645–51.

Hiebert, E. H., and Taylor, B. M. 2000. Beginning reading instruction: Research on early interventions. In *Handbook of Reading Research*. Vol. 3, eds. M. L. Kamil, P. B. Mosenthal, P. D. Pearson, and R. Barr. Mahwah, NJ: Lawrence Erlbaum Associates.

Hoover, W., and Tunmer, W. E. 1993. The components of reading. In *Reading Acquisition Processes*, eds. G. Thompson, W. Tunmer, and T. Nicholson. Clevedon, UK: Multilingual Matters.

Iversen, S. A., and Tunmer, W. E. 1993. Phonological processing skill and the Reading Recovery program. *Journal of Educational Psychology* 85:112–25.

Jeynes, W. H., and Littell, S. W. 2000. A meta-analysis of studies examining the effect of whole language instruction on the literacy of low-SES students. *The Elementary School Journal* 101:21–33.

Juel, C. 1991. Beginning reading. In *Handbook of Reading Research*. Vol. 2, eds. R. Barr, M. Kamil, P. Mosenthal, and P. D. Pearson. New York: Longman.

Juel, C., and Minden-Cupp, C. 2000. Learning to read words: Linguistic units and instructional strategies. *Reading Research Quarterly* 35:458–492.

Kerslake, J. 2000. Annual monitoring of Reading Recovery: The data for 1999. *The Research Bulletin* pp. 21–26. Wellington, New Zealand: Ministry of Education.

Liberman, I. Y., and Liberman, A. M. 1992. Whole language versus code emphasis: Underlying assumptions and their implications for reading instruction. In *Reading Acquisition*, eds. P. Gough, L. Ehri, and R. Treiman. Hillsdale, NJ: Lawrence Erlbaum Associates.

Lloyd, S. 1992. *Jolly Phonics*. Essex, UK: Jolly Learning.

Lyon, G. R., and Moats, L. C. 1997. Critical conceptual and methodological considerations in reading intervention research. *Journal of Learning Disabilities* 30:578–88.

McNaughton, S. 1995. *Patterns of Emergent Literacy: Processes of Development and Transition*. Auckland, New Zealand: Oxford University Press.

Ministry of Education 1997. *Adult Literacy in New Zealand: Results from the International Adult Literacy Survey*. Wellington, New Zealand: Author.

Ministry of Education 1999. *Report of the Literacy Taskforce*. Wellington, New Zealand: Author.

Murray, B. A., Stahl, S. A., and Ivey, M. G. 1996. Developing phoneme awareness through alphabet books. *Reading and Writing: An Interdisciplinary Journal* 8:307–22.

Nash, R. 1997. Deficit theory and the family resource framework: Parkyn revisited. *New Zealand Journal of Educational Studies* 32:13–23.

Nash, R. 2002. Family resources and reading: Literacy practices, cognition and school success. In *Learning to read in Aotearoa New Zealand*, eds. P. Adams and H. Ryan. Palmerston North, New Zealand: Dunmore Press.

Nash, R., and Harker, R. 1992. Working with class: The educational expectations and practices of class-resourced families. *New Zealand Journal of Educational Studies* 27:3–20.

Neale, M. M. 1988. *Neale Analysis of Reading Ability—Revised*. Camberwell, Victoria, Australia: Australian Council for Educational Research.

Nicholson, T. 1995. Research note: More news on rich and poor schools, and the news is still not good. *New Zealand Journal of Educational Studies* 30:227–28.

Nicholson, T. 1997. Closing the gap on reading failure: Social background, phonemic awareness, and learning to read. In *Foundations of Reading Acquisition and Dyslexia: Implications for Early Intervention*, ed. B. A. Blachman. Mahwah, NJ: Lawrence Erlbaum Associates.

Nicholson, T. 1999. Literacy in the family and society. In *Learning to Read: Beyond Phonics and Whole Language*, eds. G. B. Thompson and T. Nicholson. New York: Teachers College Press.

Nicholson, T. 2000a. *Reading the Writing on the Wall: Debates, Challenges and Opportunities in the Teaching of Reading*. Palmerston North, New Zealand: Dunmore Press.

Nicholson, T. 2000b. What makes for a better start in literacy? The results of a 5-year study a preliminary report. Paper delivered at a pre-world congress seminar on policy, research and practice, Auckland, New Zealand, July.

Nicholson, T. 2002. The social and policy contexts of reading: Contemporary literacy policy in Aotearoa New Zealand. In *Learning to Read in Aotearoa New Zealand*, eds. P. Adams, and H. Ryan. Palmerston North, New Zealand: Dunmore Press.

Nicholson, T., and Gallienne, G. 1995. Struggletown meets Middletown: A survey of reading achievement levels among 13-year-old pupils in two contrasting socio-economic areas. *New Zealand Journal of Educational Studies* 30:15–24.

Openshaw, R. 2002. The social and political contexts of early intervention programmes: A case study of Reading Recovery. In *Learning to Read in Aotearoa New Zealand*, eds. P. Adams and H. Ryan. Palmerston North, New Zealand: Dunmore Press.

Organization of Economic Cooperation and Development 2001. *Knowledge and Skills for Life: First Results from PISA 2000*. Paris, France: OECD Publications.

Pressley, M. 1998. *Reading Instruction that Works: The Case for Balanced Teaching*. New York: Guilford Press.

Pressley, M. 2000. What should comprehension instruction be the instruction of? *In Handbook of Reading Research*. Vol. 3, eds. M. L. Kamil, P. B. Mosenthal, P. D. Pearson, and R. Barr. Mahwah, NJ: Lawrence Erlbaum Associates.

Prochnow, J. E., Tunmer, W. E., Chapman, J. W., and Greaney, K. T. 2001. A longitudinal study of early literacy achievement and gender. *New Zealand Journal of Educational Studies* 36:221–36.

Reading in Junior Classes 1991. Wellington, New Zealand: Ministry of Education.

Reading and Beyond 1997. Wellington, New Zealand: Ministry of Education.

Richardson, E., and DiBenedetto, B. 1985. *Decoding Skills Test*. Parkton, MD: York Press.

Share, D. L. 1995. Phonological recoding and self-teaching: Sine qua non of reading acquisition. *Cognition* 55:151–218.

Share D. L., Jorm, A. F., MacLean, R., and Matthews, R. 1984. Sources of individual differences in reading acquisition. *Journal of Educational Psychology* 76:1309–24.

Share, D. L., and Stanovich, K. E. 1995. Cognitive processes in early reading development: Accommodating individual differences into a model of acquisition. *Issues in Education* 1:1–57.

Smith, F. 1978. *Understanding Reading*. New York: Holt, Rinehart and Winston.

Smith, J. 1997. Whole language and its critics: A New Zealand perspective. *The Australian Journal of Language and Literacy* 20:156–62.

Smith, J. W. 2000. The Literacy Taskforce in context. In *Literacy in New Zealand: Practices, Politics and Policy Since 1900*, eds. J. Soler and J. Smith. Auckland, New Zealand: Pearson Education.

Smith, J. W. A., and Elley, W. B. 1994. *Learning to Read in New Zealand*. Auckland, New Zealand: Longman Paul.

Snow, C. E., Burns, M. S., and Griffen, P. (eds.) 1998. *Preventing Reading Difficulties in Young Children*. Washington, DC: National Academy Press.

Spear-Swerling, L., and Sternberg, R. J. 1996. *Off track: When Poor Readers Become "Learning Disabled".* Boulder, CO: Westview Press.

Stanovich, K. E. 1986. Matthew effects in reading: Some consequences of individual differences in the acquisition of literacy. *Reading Research Quarterly* 21:340–406.

Stanovich, K. E. 1996. Toward a more inclusive definition of dyslexia. *Dyslexia* 2:154-66.

Stubbs, M. 1980. *Language and Literacy: The Sociolinguistics of Reading and Writing.* London: Routledge and Kegan Paul.

Taylor, B. M., Anderson, R. C., Au, K. H., and Raphael, T. E. 2000. Discretion in the translation of research to policy: A case from beginning reading. *Educational Researcher* 29:16–26.

The Learner as Reader 1996. Wellington, New Zealand: Ministry of Education.

Thompson, G. B. 1993. Reading instruction for the initial years in New Zealand schools. In *Reading Acquisition Processes*, eds. G. B. Thompson, W. E. Tunmer, and T. Nicholson. Clevedon, UK: Multilingual Matters.

Treiman, R. 1992. The role of intrasyllabic units in learning to read and spell. In *Reading Acquisition*, eds. P. Gough, L. Ehri, and R. Treiman. Hillsdale, NJ: Erlbaum.

Tunmer, W. E., and Chapman, J. W. 1998. Language prediction skill, phonological recoding ability, and beginning reading. In *Reading and Spelling: Development and Disorders*, eds. C. Hulme and R. M. Joshi. Mahwah, NJ: Lawrence Erlbaum Associates.

Tunmer, W. E., and Chapman, J. W. 1999. Teaching strategies for word identification. In *Learning to Read: Beyond Phonics and Whole Language*, eds. G. B. Thompson and T. Nicholson. New York: Teachers College Press and International Reading Association.

Tunmer, W. E., and Chapman, J. W. 2002. The relation of beginning readers' reported word identification strategies to reading achievement, reading-related skills, and academic self-perceptions. *Reading and Writing: An Interdisciplinary Journal* 15:341–58.

Tunmer, W. E., and Chapman, J. W. in press a. The Reading Recovery approach to preventative early intervention: As good as it gets? *Reading Psychology.*

Tunmer, W. E., and Chapman, J. W. in press b. The relation of metalinguistic abilities, phonological recoding skill and the use of sentence context to beginning reading development: A longitudinal study. In *Handbook of Orthography and Literacy*, eds. R. M. Joshi and P. G. Aaron. Mahwah, NJ; Lawrence Erlbaum Associates.

Tunmer, W. E., and Chapman, J. W. in press c. The use of context in learning to read. In *Handbook of Literacy*, eds. P. Bryant and T. Nu(es. Dordrecht, The Netherlands: Kluwer Academic.

Tunmer, W. E., Chapman, J. W., Greaney, K. T., and Prochnow, J. E. 2002. The contribution of educational psychology to intervention research and practice. *International Journal of Disability, Development and Education* 49:11–29.

Tunmer, W. E., Chapman, J. W., Ryan, H., and Prochnow, J. E. 1998. The importance of providing beginning readers with explicit training in phonological processing skills. *Australian Journal of Learning Disabilities* 3:4–14.

Tunmer, W. E., Herriman, M., and Nesdale, A. R. 1988. Metalinguistic abilities and beginning reading. *Reading Research Quarterly* 23:134–58.

Tunmer, W. E., and Hoover, W. A. 1992. Cognitive and linguistic factors in learning to read. In *Reading Acquisition*, eds. P. G. Gough, L. C. Ehri, and R. Treiman. Hillsdale, NJ: Erlbaum.

Tunmer, W. E., and Hoover, W. A. 1993. Components of variance models of language-related factors in reading disability: A conceptual overview. In *Reading Disabilities: Diagnosis and Component Processes*, eds. M. Joshi, and C. K. Leong. Dordrecht, The Netherlands: Kluwer.

Tunmer, W. E., Prochnow, J. E., and Chapman, J. W. 1999. Science can inform educational practice: The case of literacy. *New Zealand Annual Review of Education* 9:133–56.

Vellutino, F., Scanlon, D., Sipay, E., Small, S., Pratt, A., Chen, R., and Denckla, M. 1996. Cognitive profiles of difficult-to-remediate and readily remediated poor readers: Early intervention as a vehicle for distinguishing between cognitive and experiential deficits as basic causes of specific reading disability. *Journal of Educational Psychology* 88:601–38.

Wagemaker, H., ed. 1993. *Achievement in Reading Literacy: New Zealand's Performance in a National and International Context*. Wellington, New Zealand: Ministry of Education.

Wilkinson, I. A. G., Freebody, P., and Elkins, J. 2000. Reading research in Australia and Aotearoa/New Zealand. In *Handbook of Reading Research*. Vol. 3, eds. M. L. Kamil, P. B. Mosenthal, P. D. Pearson, and R. Barr. Mahwah, NJ: Lawrence Erlbaum Associates.

Chapter • **6**

Risk Factors in Learning to Read

Tom Nicholson

RISK FACTORS IN LEARNING TO READ
AND WHAT TO DO ABOUT THEM

Children from low-socioeconomic (low-SES) backgrounds are sometimes referred to as "Struggletown" children (McAlman 1984). They do not have the "cultural capital" (Bourdieu 1974) of children from high socioeconomic (high-SES) backgrounds (Nicholson 1997a and b, 1999a , 2000). They come from poor families and often from dysfunctional ones. Some children have parents who are nice to them, while others are not so lucky. In New Zealand Alan Duff is a Maori writer who has tried to confront the issue of violent homes through his novels and by starting a program for poor children called Books in Homes. In Duff's (1990) novel that later became a movie, *Once Were Warriors*, the children of Jake Heke were raised in a violent home situation. All disposable income seemed to be spent on Jake's drinking habits. There were no books in the Heke home. As Jake's wife, Beth, put it, "It occurred to Beth that her own house—no, not just her own house but every house she'd ever been in—was bookless. The thought struck her like one of Jake's punches" (p. 10).

Many children from low-SES homes go to school hungry or without any lunch (Turner, Connolly, and Devlin 1992) or else do not go to school at all. In contrast, children from middle-class homes are more likely to attend school regularly and to be well fed (e.g., will bring lunch to school with them). As a result, they receive more consistent schooling and are able to give their school tasks more attention.

Parents with little money struggle to keep their children well fed and lack financial resources needed to provide their children with school textbooks and other study materials. Orr (1995) reported the results of an interview survey of 500 Australian families who had children attending high school. All families were receiving financial assistance. The findings revealed that 60% of the children in the sample of 500 had not progressed beyond a 10-year-old level. The pressures faced by these children were revealed in interviews. One comment was, "They say to me, 'Your family is poor and we don't want to hang around germs.'" Another comment was, "They would tease me because of the clothes I was wearing so then I got a uniform . . . . Now they just tease me because I wasn't born in Australia" (p. 21).

Yet for all these difficulties there are many pupils from low-SES backgrounds who come from homes where they are well fed and cared for, and have supportive parents. There are many instances in the literature of children from humble backgrounds who have become successful readers and writers. Abraham Lincoln, President of the United States during the American Civil War, came from a background of rural poverty. D. H. Lawrence became a famous novelist, though his father was a coal miner. What was it that enabled these people to be successful? In this chapter I argue that many people, including myself, have come from poor backgrounds yet have succeeded in schools. It is not a sufficient explanation in itself to argue that children of the poor are doomed to failure. If some can succeed then many more can as well.

Children from low-SES backgrounds start school with significantly lower levels of phonemic awareness skills than do children from high-SES backgrounds. Wallach et al. (1977) found that 5-year-old children from low-income backgrounds in the United States had much more difficulty with easy phonemic awareness tasks (e.g., finding a picture of something that starts with a particular phoneme) than did middle class children of the same age. Dickenson and Snow (1987) found social class differences among 5-year-olds on simple tasks such as deciding whether "Nat" rhymed with "feet" or "fat" or giving the first sound of a word, such as "d" for "dog." Raz and Bryant (1990), in England, also reported social class differences, after a year in school, on tasks such as picking the odd one out of a string of spoken words (e.g., "hug," "dig," "pig," "wig," where "hug" is the odd one out). Bowey (1995), in Australia, also found social class differences when she used tasks similar to those of Wallach et al. (1977).

Juel (1988) followed a group of 129 low-SES pupils in Austin Texas, through Grades 1 to 4. She found that pupils who became poor readers all entered school with low levels of phonemic awareness. These poor readers, after four years in school, had still not achieved reading levels attained by average and good readers after only two years in school. Juel (1994) found that getting off to a slow start in learning to read and spell will have negative Matthew effects in that poor readers and spellers fall further and further behind as they pass through each school grade.

Stanovich (1986) summarized research showing the negative effects of attending schools where most of the pupils are from low-income backgrounds. Teacher expectations will be lower, classroom discipline more of a problem, teachers are harder to recruit, and those who are recruited tend to be less experienced. There are negative effects of being in a class where most of the children are low-achievers. Pupils who need extra help with reading are less likely to get it if most of their classmates also need help with reading. Pupils make better progress academically in classrooms where the average level of achievement is high than in classrooms where academic levels are low (Rutter 1983; Nicholson and Gallienne 1995; Share et al. 1984).

Bernstein (1974) has made the point more strongly, that for children from low-SES backgrounds, "we offer these children grossly inadequate schools with less than able teachers. No wonder they fail—for the 'more' tend to receive more, while the socially defined 'less' receive less and become less." (p. 151). To some extent this statement is accurate. It is difficult to recruit teachers to low-SES schools. Teachers are not easily attracted to work in an area where you see graffiti everywhere, with gutted cars parked on front lawns, where there are no gardens or flowers growing because people can't afford these luxuries, and where you are likely to have your house burgled or your belongings stolen while you are at work. On the other hand, Bernstein's statement may be too strong. My experience with low-SES schools is that they are usually in pleasant surroundings and there is a real willingness among teaching staff to help low-SES children. However this does not seem to be sufficient to enable them to close the gap between these children and their high-SES peers.

It can be argued that children in low-SES areas have too many social problems for schools to make any difference. These children come to school with fewer literacy skills and concepts than high-SES children (Gilmore 1998). They lack the middle class language "code" that seems to be necessary to succeed in schools (Bernstein 1974; Nash 2002). There is a view, called social reproduction theory, that low-SES children, whose parents probably struggled at school themselves, will repeat their parents' own experiences (Bourdieu 1974). Society replicates itself so that the rich will stay rich and the poor will stay poor, and schools are a conservative force in reproducing the social structure.

Yet it does not have to be this way. A number of studies have reported that low-SES children can get off to a much better start in school with a phonological approach to reading. This approach does not assume a weight of pre-reading skills at school entry. The approach assumes that children have few of these skills and it starts by teaching the alphabet and the sounds that each letter makes. In contrast, the whole language approach appears to depend for success on skills that middle-class children have and low-income children lack (Nicholson 1999a).

Some researchers argue that whole language benefits middle class children rather than children from low-income backgrounds (Adams 1990; Chall, Jacobs, and Baldwin 1990). Whole language is the mandated approach in New Zealand schools, but which part of society does it best serve? Whole language relies on children teaching themselves to read. The approach immerses children in the language of books and encourages children to learn to read by reading, using contextual guessing, picture clues, and initial letter cues to acquire phonological recoding skills. Tunmer and Chapman (1999), however, have found that the contextual guessing strategy only works well for children who have good phonological recoding skills. Phonological recoding refers to knowledge of the letter-sound correspondence rules of a language. Phonological recoding ability in English is evidenced by ability to decode pseudowords (e.g., MAZ or BUFKIBBER), and by ability to produce "invented" spellings that show understanding of the letter-sound correspondences of the written form of language (e.g., spelling CAKE as CAEK). Good readers can use their phonological recoding skills in combination with context to identify words they have not come across before. Yet poor readers have to rely on context to compensate for their lack of phonological recoding skills. Nicholson (1991) has found that while poor readers embrace contextual guessing to work out words, good readers have such high levels of phonological recoding skills that they are just as good at reading words in isolation as they are in context. The whole language approach assumes that the school is building on the literacy skills that have been acquired in the home. Yet this assumption cannot be made for many low-SES children.

Many low-SES children start school with very little knowledge of the alphabet and low levels of phonemic awareness. Yet phonological recoding skill depends on knowledge of the alphabet and phonemic awareness (Juel, Griffith, and Gough 1986). In addition, phonological recoding as well as depth of vocabulary and general knowledge helps good readers acquire more new words and infer more meanings of words than poor readers (Nicholson and Whyte 1992). As a result, low-SES children suffer a double whammy in a whole language approach compared with high-SES children. First, they are poorly equipped to infer phonological recoding rules through reading because they start school lacking in alphabet knowledge and phonemic awareness. Second, they are less able to increase their vocabulary and general knowledge compared with good readers because they have less well developed decoding skills, vocabulary, and general knowledge.

A phonological approach sidesteps this problem by teaching how to decode words without guessing, and this puts children in a strong position once a word is decoded during reading to figure out its meaning from context and to add this new word to their mental dictionaries. The phonological approach helps the child gain an increased vocabulary whereas the guessing approach forces the child to rely always on an existing mental vocabulary.

In support of this argument, there are a number of studies that have used the phonological approach with success. Wallach and Wallach (1979) taught 98 Grade 1 pupils from inner city schools on Chicago's South Side. The pupils received 10 weeks of daily, half hour instruction (25 hours) in a one-to-one situation with parent tutors. The program included teaching of phonemic awareness and letter-sound rules. The control group received no extra instruction. The researchers found significant gains in word recognition and reading comprehension compared with a control group from the same schools.

Williams (1980) worked with 63 learning disabled pupils from Central and North Harlem, aged 7 to 12 years. Classroom teachers taught the program for 26 weeks, for 30 minutes each day (65 hours), in small groups of 2 to 5 pupils at a time. The control group was selected from similar schools, and received no extra instruction. The experimental group was taught phonemic awareness and letter-sound rules. The initial study was a trial run. A second study, using random assignment to experimental and control groups, was then carried out. The results of both studies showed that the trained pupils were significantly better than the controls in reading, as measured by real word and pseudoword reading.

Whitehurst et al. (1994) worked with 94 preschool children who were enrolled in Head Start programs (eligibility is only for pupils from low-income families). The children received training in phonemic awareness as well as interactive book reading experiences at home, which involved parents reading to their children in a way that encouraged child participation. A control group of 73 pre-schoolers received no extra instruction. The program ran all year, but the phonemic awareness instruction only ran for 20 weeks, carried out by the pupils' teachers three times each week (a total of 20 hours). The results of the study showed that the trained pupils were better than the untrained controls in knowledge of print concepts, writing, and oral language. There was an improvement in phonemic awareness but only for recognizing the first sound of words.

Blachman et al. (1994) followed up an earlier study with a similar design (Ball and Blachman 1991), teaching phonemic awareness and letter-sound correspondence skills to 84 kindergarten (5-year-old) children from low-SES areas of upstate New York. A control group of 75 children received no extra instruction. The program ran for 11 weeks, with 15 to 20 minutes of instruction 4 times each week (a total of 11 hours). The children were trained in small groups. The findings of the study were that the trained children were significantly better than the control children in phonemic segmentation skills, letter name knowledge, and the reading of short regular words and pseudowords. The children in the trained group were also better than the control children in spelling. A follow-up of these children in first grade, when they received a second round of similar instruction, showed that they retained their advantage in spelling (Tangel and Blachman 1995).

Foorman et al. (1998) worked with 285 first-grade children in Houston, Texas. The children were from low-SES backgrounds. Sixty percent were African-American, 20% were Hispanic. They were taught in small groups, outside the classroom, across 19 different schools. Children were taught with either a direct instruction approach, which was heavily phonics based, a less direct approach, which used phonemic awareness and onset-rime phonics, or an incidental approach, which was intended to be like whole language in emphasis. The findings were that children who received the direct phonics instruction were able to read words faster than children who received the whole language, indirect approach. Only 16% of the children in the phonics group did not improve in reading compared to 44% of the onset-rime phonics group and 44% of the whole language group. Children taught with phonics scored close to the national average in terms of decoding ability. The children taught with direct phonics had higher reading comprehension scores, though this advantage was not statistically significant. This showed that comprehension was not compromised in the phonics approach.

To summarize, there is every reason low-SES children should be able to succeed at school even though they do not have the same levels of "cultural capital" that high-SES children have on entry to school. A lot depends on the reading instruction provided to low-SES children. A whole language approach succeeds better with children who start school with high levels of technical knowledge (e.g., knowledge of the alphabet, phonological awareness) and with high levels of vocabulary and general knowledge. On the other hand, the whole language approach will disadvantage low-SES children because they do not have this level of "cultural capital" and it is very difficult, through direct instruction in school, to raise quickly levels of vocabulary and general knowledge that have been built up over several years in a middle-class home. A better approach is to give low-SES children decoding skills to enable them to teach themselves new words through reading and in this way acquire new vocabulary and general knowledge. Low-SES children are more likely to make better progress if they are given phonological decoding instruction from the outset, which enables them to work out words on their own without guessing, which, in turn, makes it easier for them to increase their vocabulary through reading, and in turn improve their reading comprehension.

The rest of this chapter is in three parts. First we look at longitudinal data showing emerging literacy gaps between low- and high-SES children through the first five years of school. Second, we use the longitudinal data to explore the "simple view" of how children learn to read and write (Juel, Griffith, and Gough 1986). Data will be presented to show that the cultural capital of a high-SES background is not the crucial factor in reading and writing success. What matters more is getting off to a good start at school with high entry levels of alphabet knowledge and phonemic awareness, and a quick learning trajectory into phonological recoding skills. Finally, we look at data on the results of an 18-month evaluation of an after-school reading tuition program for children with reading difficulties.

A LONGITUDINAL STUDY: HOW THE RICH GET RICHER AND THE POOR GET POORER

This longitudinal study was originally a study of the effects of phonemic awareness instruction on a low-SES experimental group compared with a low-SES control group. At the time, the study included a high-SES group of children of the same age to act as a comparison. The results showed small but positive effects of the phonemic awareness instruction on invented spelling and pseudoword reading (Nicholson 1996, 1997a). However follow up assessments of the children in years 2 and 5 showed that the initial effects of the intervention had washed away. As a result, the assessment data for the experimental and control groups were pooled together to form one low-SES group and re-analysed in order to look at the long-term progress of the low-SES children. The re-analysis also included the high-SES children who served as a comparison group in year 1 but who were also re-assessed in years 2 and 5.

Participants

We assessed children in year 1. There were 111 children in total, 88 from six schools in low-SES areas of Auckland, and 23 from one school in a high-SES area. The participants had only been at school for a few months. Average age was 5.27 years for the low-income children and 5.26 years for the middle-income children. In the final term of year 1, we located 94 of the original 111 children (low-SES = 71, high-SES = 23). Average age was 5.9 years. In the final term of year 2, we located 78 of the children (low-SES = 57, high-SES = 21). Average age was 7.0 years. In the final term of year 5, we located 46 of the children (low-SES = 33, high-SES = 13). Average age was 9.9 years

The missing children in years 1 and 2 were nearly all from low-SES schools. This number of dropouts in just a few months is typical of schools in low-income areas, where families move in and out of the community (see "Hundreds of school children missing" 1996). In the high-SES school by comparison, there was no attrition rate during year 1 and a small attrition rate in year 2. There was a much bigger attrition rate in year 5 for both groups. This dropout rate was high, but it was not unusual for longitudinal studies involving children from low-SES backgrounds. Juel (1988) reported a similar high dropout rate from 129 to 54 over four years.

The low-SES children were from six different decile 1 schools in Auckland. Decile 1 is the lowest category in a scale used by the Ministry of Education to determine levels of government funding for schools. The high-SES children came from one decile 10 school. Decile 10 is the highest category on the scale (Norris, Bathgate, and Parkin 1994). We did not gather ethnicity data at the beginning of the study, only in the year 5 follow-up where we located 46 of the original children. The children in the six low-SES schools were mostly of Pacific Island (45%) or Maori (36%) descent with a small minority of European (12%) and Asian (6%) descent, whereas the children in the middle-income school were mostly of European descent (92%) with a small minority of Asian children (8%).

Measures

We used the GKR phonemic awareness test (Roper 1984, reprinted in Nicholson, 1999b). The test has 42 items and assesses six phonemic awareness skills including blending, segmenting, deletion and substitution. Juel, Griffith, and Gough (1986) reported that the test has good internal consistency (Cronbach alphas greater than 0.7).

Verbal ability was assessed with the *Peabody Picture Vocabulary Test - Revised* (PPVT-R; Form L, Dunn and Dunn 1981). Only standard scores are reported here.

Letter knowledge was assessed using the Clay (1985) alphabet knowledge measure. The total score is 52, with 26 uppercase and 26 lowercase letters.

Spelling was assessed with two measures. The first was a test of invented spelling (Tunmer and Chapman 1995). The test gives points for phonemic similarity to the test words, ranging from 1 to 4. The total score is 72 points.

The second measure of spelling ability was the *Wide Range Achievement Test of Spelling* (WRAT-S; Jastak, Bijou, and Jastak 1993). Alpha internal consistency reliability for the test at the 5-year-old level is 0.89 according to the WRAT manual.

Reading was assessed with tests of real word reading, pseudoword reading, and text reading. The *Burt Word Reading Test* (Gilmore, Croft, and Reid 1981) is a test of real word reading standardized in New Zealand. The test-retest reliabilities for this test are 0.97. The text reading measure was the *Neale Analysis of Reading Ability Revised* (Neale 1988) that assesses reading accuracy and comprehension. The test-retest reliabilities (parallel forms) were 0.98 for accuracy and 0.94 for comprehension.

The pseudoword reading measure used in year 1 was made up of 30 single syllable nonsense words (Richardson and Di Benedetto 1985). Children received points for the number of phonemes in each pseudoword pronounced correctly. The Bryant (1975) *Test of Basic Decoding Skills* with 50 items, consisting of single and multiple syllable pseudowords was administered in years 2 and 5 and scored for number of words read correctly. These tests assess children's phonics knowledge: simple consonant-vowel-consonant correspondences, consonant and vowel blends and digraphs, and syllabication.

We also used a writing task. Each pupil was given a single blank page and told to write a story about an unusual picture that depicted a car accident, with an ambulance driven by an astronaut and an alligator. The task was allocated 10 minutes. Each story was given a holistic score, using the same criteria as in Juel et al. (1986). The score depended on the extent to which the story related to the picture, and whether or not there was a plot. Two raters independently assessed all stories. Inter-rater agreement was $r = .97$ using the Pearson r statistic.

Results

The statistical analyses used two-tailed t-tests. Because there were a considerable number of t-tests, the conservative Bonferroni adjustment was used, with significance levels set at p < .002.

Beginning of year 1. The mean age for low-SES children in the first year of school was 5.27 years ($SD = .25$) while the mean age for high-SES children was 5.26 years ($SD = .20$). There was no significant difference in the ages of the two groups, $t(109) = 0.21, p > .05$

There were significant language differences at school entry between children from low-SES and high-SES backgrounds. The PPVT standard score for receptive language for the low-SES group was 75.75 (SD = 19.48) and for the high-SES group was 105.30 ($SD = 6.87$), $t (109) = 6.87, p < .001$.

As shown in table I, there were also significant differences between the two groups in alphabet knowledge, phonemic awareness, invented spelling, and pseudoword reading.

In each SES group there was a wide range of scores. Not all low-SES children did poorly. In the low-SES group, phonemic awareness ranged from zero to 19, and 20 children out of 88 (23%)

Table I. Social Class Differences at School Entry - Group Means and Standard Deviations

Measure	Group				Independent Samples t-tests	
	Low-SES N = 88		High-SES N = 23		t-test (t)	df
	M	SD	M	SD		
Alphabet	20.31	17.48	40.87	11.90	5.32*	109
Phonemic Awareness	3.42	3.88	8.70	5.89	5.16*	109
Invented Spelling Points (Low-SES N = 77)	2.68	7.13	22.87	12.25	9.94*	98
Pseudoword Reading Points	1.58	6.74	8.04	9.05	3.80*	109

Note. *$p < .002$

scored at or above the high-SES average score of 9. Alphabet knowledge ranged from zero to 51 and 20 children out of 88 (23%) scored at or above the high-SES average of 41. Peabody Picture Vocabulary Test standard scores ranged from very low to 118 and there were 22 children (25%) with a PPVT standard score of 90 or above.

In the high-SES group, there was also a range of scores. Not all high-SES children did well. Phonemic awareness ranged from zero to 21. There were 4 children out of 23 (17%) who scored either the same as or else below the low-SES average of 3. Alphabet knowledge ranged from13 to 51. There were 2 children (9%) who scored below the low-SES average of 20. Peabody Picture Vocabulary Test scores ranged from 88 to 134. There were 22 children (96%) with a PPVT score of 90 or above.

End of Year 1. Assessments carried out at the beginning of the last school term of year 1 also showed significant differences between low-SES and high-SES children, as shown in table II. There was a PPVT standard score difference for receptive language but the difference was not so great as at the beginning of year 1, mean standard score for low-SES ($N = 58$) was 82.90 ($SD = 14.75$) and for high-SES was 105.32 ($SD = 12.10$), $t(79) = 5.95$, $p <001$.

The children in the low-SES group at the end of year 1 had attained levels of alphabet knowledge, phonemic awareness and invented spelling skills that the high-SES children had already

Table II. Social Class Differences at End of Year 1 - Group Means and Standard Deviations

Measure	Group				Independent Samples t-tests	
	Low-SES N = 71		High-SES N = 23		t-test (t)	df
	M	SD	M	SD		
Alphabet	41.99	12.51	50.48	2.95	3.22*	92
Phonemic Awareness	12.20	9.91	23.61	6.42	5.17*	92
Invented Spelling Points (Low-SES N = 77)	24.59	19.13	44.00	14.64	4.45*	92
Burt Words Correct	8.80	7.52	18.91	8.12	5.50*	92
Story Writing	2.89	1.89	4.80	1.67	4.32*	91
WRAT Spelling Words Correct	1.45	1.57	2.74	1.36	3.49*	87

Note. *$p < .002$

achieved when assessed at the beginning of year 1. The low-SES raw scores for Burt word reading were below average for their age, while the high-SES children's scores were average for their age.

To find the best predictor of reading success in year 1 of school, a series of partial correlations were carried out. The school entry PPVT vocabulary measure was correlated with Burt reading after partialing out school entry alphabet and GKR phonemic awareness scores. The partial correlation of PPVT with Burt reading was not significant, $r = .20$, $N = 89$, $p = .06$. The same partial correlation analysis was done for the GKR measure and the result was significant, $r = .21$, $N = 89$, $p = .04$. The same pattern was followed for the alphabet measure. The correlation was significant, $r = .64$, $N = 89$, p = .000. Knowledge of the alphabet had a higher correlation with Burt word reading than the other two measures.

End of Year 2.   Assessments carried out at the beginning of the last school term of year 2 showed significant differences between low-SES and high-SES children. These are shown in table III. At this time children in the study were 7.0 years of age. Burt word reading frequencies showed that 75% of low-SES children were reading below the 7-year-old level, and 25% were reading below a 6-year-old level. In contrast, 14% of the high-SES children were reading below a 7-year-old level and none were reading below a 6-year-old level. The pattern of differences was similar for other reading measures. The gap between the two SES groups on the Burt word reading measure was 1.2 years.

This does not mean that all low-SES children were failing. A frequency analysis showed that the range was between 5.0 and 9.9 years. There were 14 out of 57 (25%) at a 7-year level or above for

Table III.   Social Class Differences at End of Year 2 - Group Means and Standard Deviations

Measure	Group				Independent Samples t-tests	
	Low-SES N = 57		High-SES N = 21		t-test (t)	df
	M	SD	M	SD		
Burt Reading Age	6.69	.92	7.89	.98	5.01*	76
Neale Accuracy Reading Age	6.47	1.02	8.01	1.21	5.90*	76
Neale Comprehension Reading Age	6.58	1.06	7.97	1.10	5.32*	76
WRAT Spelling Words Correct	4.30	2.71	7.10	3.71	3.64*	76

Note. *$p < .002$

Neale reading accuracy. For reading comprehension the range was between 5.0 and 9.3. There were 21 out of 57 (37%) at a 7-year level or above. A check of beginning year 1 scores for the high achieving low-SES children showed that, on average, their scores for alphabet, phonemic awareness, and PPVT vocabulary were higher than those of their low-SES classmates, and closer to the beginning year 1 scores of high-SES children.

Likewise, not all high-SES children were succeeding. For reading accuracy the range was between 6.2 and 9.8 years. There were 5 out of 21 (24%) of the high-SES group who were reading below a 7-year level for accuracy. For reading comprehension the range was between 6.2 and 10.5 years, and 3 (14%) were reading below average for reading comprehension. A check of beginning year 1 scores for alphabet, phonemic awareness, and PPVT vocabulary showed that, on average, their scores were lower than those of their high-SES classmates.

To find out the best predictors of reading success in year 2 of school, a series of partial correlations were again carried out. The end of year 1 PPVT measure was correlated with Burt reading at end of year 2 after adjusting for end of year 1 alphabet and GKR scores. The partial correlation with Burt reading at end of year 2 was not significant, $r = .24$, $N = 62$, $p = .06$. The same partial correlation analysis was done for GKR and was significant, $r = .63$, $N = 62$, $p = .000$. The same analysis was done for the alphabet measure and was significant, $r = .33$, $N = 62$, $p = .009$. These results indicated that phonemic awareness had a higher correlation with Burt word reading than the other two measures.

End of Year 5.   Assessments carried out at the beginning of the last school term of year 5 showed significant differences between low-SES and high-SES children, as shown in table IV, except for WRAT spelling ($p = .006$), which did not meet the conservative Bonferroni criterion ($p = .002$). At this time children in the study were 9.90 years of age. Burt word reading frequencies showed that 67 % of low-SES children were reading below the 10-year-old level, and 52% were reading below the 9-year-old level. In contrast, 15% of the high-SES children were reading below the 10-year-old level, and 8% were reading below the 9-year-old level. The pattern of differences between the two SES groups was similar for other reading measures. The gap between the two SES groups had increased since the year 2 assessments. The gap on the Burt word reading measure was 2.1 years.

Not all low-SES children were failing. For Neale reading accuracy, scores ranged from 5.50 to 12.50 years. There were 10 out of 33 (30%) who were reading at a 10-year-old level or above. For

Table IV.   Social Class Differences at End of Year 5 - Group Means and Standard Deviations

Measure	Group				Independent Samples t-tests	
	Low-SES N = 33		High-SES N = 13		t-test (t)	df
	M	SD	M	SD		
Burt Reading Age	9.12	1.87	11.21	1.61	3.55*	44
Neale Reading Age	9.18	1.75	11.12	1.26	3.65*	44
Neale Comprehension Reading Age	8.45	1.50	10.56	1.53	4.28*	44
WRAT Spelling Standard Score	92.45	12.16	104.54	14.81	2.87	44

Note. *$p < .002$

Neale reading comprehension the range of scores was from 7.08 to 12.50 years. There were 6 out of 33 (18%) who were reading at or above a 10-year-old level for reading comprehension.

Not all high-SES children were succeeding. The range of scores was between 8.25 and 12.50 for Neale accuracy. Among the high-SES children there were 2 out of 13 (15%) who were reading below the 10-year-old level for reading accuracy. The range of scores was between 7.08 and 12.50 for reading comprehension. There were 5 out of 13 (38%) who were reading below the 10-year-old level.

Summary

These results showed significant differences in school entry reading and writing skills between low- and high-SES children from first months of school. The long-term effects were that the initial gaps were not closed, and, in fact, became wider. Although there were significant differences in vocabulary knowledge between these different SES groups, as indicated by PPVT vocabulary scores, the results also showed that these differences were not as important as the reading related skills of alphabet knowledge, phonemic awareness and phonological recoding. Schools were unable to close the reading and writing gaps. For example, the low-SES children took most of year 1 to get to the point that high-SES children were at when they were assessed at the beginning of the year. The results showed that in relation to reading and writing the rich got richer and the poor got poorer.

THE SIMPLE VIEW OF READING

In this part of the chapter we look at what variables are most important in learning to read and write, using the longitudinal data reported in the previous section. Although many variables correlate with reading and writing, it is important to have a theory that explains why some variables are more important than others. The theory we will consider is the simple view of literacy acquisition (Juel, Griffith, and Gough 1986). This theory states that ethnicity, intelligence, and oral language initially influence the development of phonemic awareness. The mediating role of personal variables, language, and home background influence initial levels of phonemic awareness skills when children start school. The combination of phonemic awareness and exposure to print through reading is necessary to acquire cipher knowledge, that is, knowledge of the letter-sound rules of English.

Exposure to print through reading is also a source of lexical knowledge, that is, knowledge of irregular spellings. With both cipher and lexical knowledge, the child will acquire skills of word recognition and spelling. Word recognition combined with language comprehension accounts for reading comprehension. Spelling ability combined with ideas accounts for writing (see Juel 1994 and Nicholson 1999b for more detail on the simple view).

Cipher knowledge

Year 1. The simple view of reading would predict that in Year 1 the development of cipher knowledge depends on phonemic awareness. In the longitudinal study reported above, the measure of cipher knowledge used was pseudoword reading. Simple correlations showed that the best predictor of pseudoword reading at the beginning of year 1 was phonemic awareness ($r = .61$), followed by alphabet ($r = .40$) and PPVT vocabulary ($r = .30$). A stepwise regression was carried out with beginning of year 1 pseudoword reading as the dependent measure, entering beginning of year PPVT, alphabet and GKR in that order. The results ($N = 110$) showed that GKR had the most predictive value, ($r = .61$), accounting for 38 % of the variance. Peabody Picture Vocabulary Test and alphabet did not add to the variance accounted for.

Simple correlations with end of year pseudoword reading showed $r = .48$ for alphabet, $r = .51$ for PPVT, and $r = .78$ for phonemic awareness. A stepwise regression was carried out with end of year 1 pseudoword reading as the dependent measure, entering end of year PPVT, alphabet, and GKR in that order. The results $N = 80$ showed that GKR phonemic awareness had predictive value ($r = .78$) over and above PPVT and alphabet, accounting for 60 % of the variance. Peabody Picture Vocabulary Test and the alphabet measure did not account for further variance.

Word recognition

End of Year 1. A stepwise regression was carried out using Burt word reading scores at the end of year 1 as the dependent measure, with PPVT, alphabet, GKR, and pseudoword reading variables entered in that order. The results showed that the pseudoword reading measure was the strongest predictor, $r = .82$, accounting for 67 % of the variance. Alphabet and GKR increased the predictive value to $r = .83$ and $r = .87$ respectively. The three variables together accounted for 75 % of the variance. The PPVT did not add to the variance.

End of Year 2. A stepwise regression was carried out using Neale Reading Accuracy at the end of year 2 as the dependent variable ($N = 65$). The predictors entered were end of year 1 PPVT, alphabet, year 2 GKR, and year 2 Bryant pseudoword reading scores in that order.

The results showed that the best predictor was the Bryant pseudoword reading score, r = .84, accounting for 70 % of the variance. Alphabet increased the predictive value to r = .89. PPVT increased the correlation to r = .91. The combination of the three measures accounted for 82 % of the variance.

End of Year 5. A stepwise regression at year 5 with Neale reading accuracy as the dependent measure $N = 38$, and with end of year 1 PPVT and year 5 Bryant pseudoword reading entered in that order, showed Bryant to be the better predictor $r = .85$, accounting for 72 % of the variance. The PPVT increased the predictive value to $r = .92$ accounting for an extra 12 % of variance. The two measures together accounted for 84 % of the variance

Reading comprehension

End of Year 2. A stepwise regression was carried out for Neale reading comprehension, with PPVT and Burt word reading entered as predictor variables in that order. The better predictor was Burt word reading, r = .84, accounting for 70% of the variance. Peabody Picture Vocabulary Test increased the predictive value to $r = .85$, accounting for a further 2% of variance.

End of Year 5. A stepwise regression ($N = 38$) was carried out for Neale reading comprehension, with PPVT and Burt reading scores entered in that order. The better predictor was Burt word reading r = .86, accounting for 75% of the variance. The PPVT increased the predictive value to r = .91, accounting for an additional 8 % of the variance. The combination of the two measures accounted for 83% of the variance.

Invented spelling

Beginning of Year 1. Invented spelling requires the child to have awareness of the sequence of sounds in spoken words, that is, phonemic awareness, and be able to represent each phoneme with its corresponding grapheme. Thus, GKR and alphabet knowledge should account for invented spelling. A stepwise regression (N = 99) with beginning of year 1 invented spelling as the dependent measure showed GKR was the strongest predictor (r = .73) of invented spelling, accounting for 54% of the variance. Alphabet knowledge increased the correlation to r = .79, accounting for an additional 8 % of the variance. The PPVT increased the correlation further to r = .80, accounting for a further 2% of the variance.

End of Year 1. A stepwise regression with end-of-year 1 invented spelling as the dependent measure (N = 80), entering end of year PPVT, alphabet, and GKR scores in that order, showed that the GKR phonemic awareness test was the most powerful predictor (r = .86), accounting for 74% of the variance, with alphabet knowledge increasing slightly the predictive value (r = .89), contributing an additional 5% of the variance. The PPVT did not account for any additional variance.

End of Year 2. A stepwise regression with end of year 2 invented spelling as the dependent measure (N = 65) was carried out. End of year 1 PPVT, end-of-year alphabet, and year 2 GKR scores were entered in that order. The GKR measure was the strongest predictor (r = .77) of invented spelling, accounting for 60% of the variance. The PPVT measure increased the predictive value to r = .84, accounting for an additional 10% of the variance.

Traditional Spelling

End of Year 2. A measure of conventional spelling used in the longitudinal study was the WRAT spelling test. Conventional spelling relies on cipher knowledge as represented by invented spelling ability. A stepwise regression was carried out using end of Year 2 WRAT spelling raw scores as the dependent measure. Variables entered were PPVT, alphabet, and invented spelling in that order. The results showed that invented spelling was a strong predictor of WRAT spelling ($r = .70$), accounting for 49% of variance. Alphabet knowledge increased the predictive value to $r = .72$, adding an extra 3% of variance. The PPVT did not account for additional variance.

Writing

End of Year 1.   The simple view predicts that writing is made up of spelling and ideas. In the longitudinal study the PPVT vocabulary measure was used as a surrogate for "ideas." For year 1 the spelling measure was invented spelling. A stepwise regression was carried out using end of year 1 story writing ($N = 79$) as the dependent variable. End-of-year PPVT, and invented spelling were entered in that order. The better predictor variable was invented spelling ($r = .86$), accounting for 73% of the variance. The PPVT did not account for further variance.

End of Year 2.   A stepwise regression was carried out for story writing assessed at end of year 2. The predictor variables were WRAT spelling and PPVT. Again, the better predictor variable was WRAT spelling, $r = .59$, accounting for 34% of the variance. The PPVT scores did not add additional variance.

SUMMARY

Although there is a view that success in school depends on the language that children bring to school, the correlation and regression results from the longitudinal study did not support that view. The analyses indicated that PPVT language knowledge did contribute to reading and writing development, but in a much smaller way than did skills more directly related to reading and writing: alphabet knowledge, phonological awareness, invented spelling, and pseudoword reading.

THE EFFECTS OF AN AFTER-SCHOOL INTERVENTION FOR CHILDREN WITH READING DISABILITIES

The University of Auckland after-school reading program has been in operation for two years. The program offers free tuition to children with reading disabilities. It emphasizes a phonological approach to reading, which is different from the mainstream whole language approach. The focus of each lesson is on phonological recoding, both in reading and in spelling. The program is located in one of the classrooms of an elementary school in inner city Auckland. Children attending the program tend to come from the local area in which the school is situated which is low-SES, but some come from high-SES areas as well.

The lessons are divided into four parts: sight word reading, phonics, spelling, and text reading. It teaches children more than 50 letter-sound correspondences as well as strategies for breaking down and decoding long words (e.g., syllabication, structural analysis). The program also stresses accurate and fluent sight word reading skills. Spelling is practiced and spelling strategies are taught. The reading lessons also include some reading of age-appropriate text. The tutors consist of teachers who are between jobs and teacher trainees. The tutors receive training through the university. They follow a set lesson plan, but the content of the lesson depends on the reading level of the child. Tutors keep a logbook for each lesson. The manager of the program monitors the logbooks.

The after-school reading program is funded by private sponsorship and is supported with free teaching materials from commercial publishers: *Smart Kids*, *Sunshine Books*, and *Nelson-PM Library*. Children attend the program between 3:30 PM and 5:30 PM. Reading lessons last for one hour. Most children attend one lesson a week, but some receive two lessons a week or more.

Parents usually enroll their children, though some schools recommend children to the program. Tutors give the children a range of reading and spelling assessments at entry, and the same assessments at exit. The children receive one-to-one tutoring, and are assessed at mid-year and end-of-year. Sometimes a reading test is given in mid-term to assess progress. In each year of the program so far, many of the children have attended a 3-week daily summer school program run by the University, and then continued on with after-school lessons.

Phase 1 of the program

In the first year, the program ran from March to December. There were 34 children in the program, 23 boys and 11 girls. Two thirds of the enrollments were boys. From parent information sheets, we found that 10 out of 21 (48%) children had been in Reading Recovery. This is a government run program that gives one-to-one tutoring to 6-year-olds, but does not stress phonological recoding strategies. Out of 28 children, 10 (36%) were European, 5 (18%) were Maori and 13 (46%) were Pacific Island. Out of 25 parents, 10 (40%) were in professional jobs and the rest were in trades, semi-skilled jobs, or unemployed/not known.

We were able to assess 15 of the children for receptive language using the PPVT. Standard scores ranged from 58 to 125. The average was 84.33. Age levels at entry ranged from 6.00 to 11.83 years. Average age was 8.60 years at entry and 9.17 years at exit. Children spent from 3 to 10 months in the program, but most spent 7 months.

A number of the children, when quizzed about their attitudes to reading before starting the program, had negative feelings about reading. For example, one child was asked, "How do you feel when it is your turn to read to the teacher?" He said: "Sad because the other kids laugh at me—shame me." Another child said, "Sad. I'm afraid of being told off."

The program used the same assessment measures as were used for the longitudinal study. At entry, all children were behind their chronological age on the Burt reading test, but by the end of the year, 10 of the children (29%) were at or above their chronological age. On entry to the program, Burt word reading scores ranged from 4.33 years below chronological age to 0.08 years below. On exit at the end of the first year, children ranged from 3.92 years behind chronological age to 1.83 years above their age. On entry to the program 71% of the children were a year or more behind in reading. On final testing, this figure had dropped to 35%. On average the children were initially 1.68 years behind in reading, but by time of final testing they were 0.83 years behind.

Assessment results were analyzed by using paired sample *t*-tests. The results showed that children made significant gains on nearly all reading and spelling measures. Burt word reading in-

Table V.   After-School Reading Program Year 1 - Group Means and Standard Deviations

Measure	Group				Paired Samples t-tests	
	Pretest		Posttest		t-test (t)	df
	M	SD	M	SD		
Burt Reading Age	6.92	1.17	8.34	1.77	8.85*	33
Neale Reading Age	6.99	0.81	7.74	1.29	5.03*	29
Neale Comprehension Reading Age	7.08	1.01	8.10	1.76	4.28*	28
WRAT Spelling Standard Score	84.73	12.02	88.80	10.35	2.37	29

Note. *$p < .002$

creased from 6.92 to 8.34 years, a gain of 17 months. Neale reading accuracy increased from 6.99 to 7.74 years, a gain of 9 months. Neale reading comprehension increased from 7.08 to 8.10 years, a gain of 12 months.

Phase 2 of the program

At time of writing only the mid-year results were available. There were 31 children, 23 boys and 8 girls. Three quarters of enrollments were boys. There were 20 new enrollments, and 11 children who continued from the previous year. Parent information about the children indicated that 16 out of 23 (70%) had been through Reading Recovery. Parent information also indicated that of 25 parents, 11 (44%) had professional jobs while the remainder were in trades, semi-skilled jobs, or were unemployed/not known. Data on 25 of the children indicated that 15 (58%) were European (Pakeha), 3 (12%) were Maori, and 7 (27%) were Pacific Island. We were able to assess 21 of the children for receptive language using the PPVT test. Standard scores ranged from 55 to 131. The average score was 91.24. Chronological ages at entry ranged from 6.00 to 12.58 years. Average age was 9.06 years. Average age at mid-year was 9.38 years. At mid-year, most children had spent 4 months in the program.

The assessment measures used in the program were the same as in the longitudinal study. The only additional measure was the Schonell spelling test (Schonell 1950). At entry on the Burt word reading test children were reading from 5.08 years behind to 0.67 years above their chronological age. At mid-year, children were from 3.58 behind their age to 2.50 years above their chronological age. At entry, 2 out of 31 (6 %) were reading at or just above average on the Burt test though they were below average on our other reading measure, the Neale test. At mid-year, 7 out of 30 (23%) were reading at or above average on the Burt.

On entry to the program 55% of the children were a year or more behind in reading. On final testing, this figure had dropped to 37%. On entry, the children were 1.46 years behind in reading, but by time of final testing the figure was 0.71 years.

Paired sample t-tests at mid-year showed that children made significant gains in reading and spelling measures. Results for Burt word reading showed improvement from 7.60 years to 8.67 years, a gain of nearly 13 months. Neale reading accuracy improved from 7.38 years to 8.16 years, a gain of 9 months. Neale reading comprehension improved from 7.47 to 8.28 years, a gain of nearly 10 months. Children's spelling ages improved from 7.17 to 7.92 on the Schonell spelling test, a gain of 9 months.

Table VI.   After-School Reading Program Year 2 - Group Means and Standard Deviations

Measure	Group				Paired Samples t-tests	
	Pretest		Posttest		t-test (t)	df
	M	SD	M	SD		
Burt Reading Age	7.60	1.46	8.68	2.05	6.10*	29
Neale Reading Age	7.38	0.96	8.16	1.62	4.51*	23
Neale Comprehension Reading Age	7.47	1.33	8.28	1.97	3.42*	23
Schonell Spelling Age	7.17	1.11	7.92	1.06	7.38*	23

Note. *$p < .002$

An interesting development during the second year of the program was an offer of free visual assessments for all the children in the program from a private optometry firm, Barry and Beale, in Auckland. Of the 16 children who took advantage of the assessments, 6 (38%) required spectacles. Five of the children required spectacles for reading and one for all near and distance viewing. The provision of glasses for reading may have influenced the results for some of these children. One child in particular seemed to make dramatic gains in reading, and this may have been because he simply was better able to see the print. In order to separate out this possibility, the results were re-analyzed without the children who had been prescribed glasses. The pattern of results was still the same. Nevertheless, the optometry results suggest that visual examinations should be required for children who are having difficulties with reading. Such problems can easily affect children's progress since reading requires visual acuity at a close distance.

What is it that enabled the after-school program to work?

The results indicated that the key to the success of the after-school program was the teaching of phonological recoding skills. This had positive effects on reading accuracy and spelling and also improved reading comprehension. Reading comprehension depends not just on decoding skills but also vocabulary and general knowledge. Although the program did not teach these things directly, it provided decoding skills essential for their development since it enabled pupils to read text more easily, and text reading is a source of vocabulary learning and general knowledge. The improvement in decoding skills enabled these children to concentrate on the meaning of what they were reading, which in turn improved their comprehension of text (Tan and Nicholson 1997; Nicholson 1998).

DISCUSSION

The first part of the chapter presented longitudinal data showing "rich get richer" and "poor get poorer" effects between children from high- and low-SES backgrounds. The data showed that there is no level playing field when children start school. Some children are much better prepared to learn to read and spell when they walk through the school gate on their first day. They are ready to put their pre-reading skills into learning how to read and spell. The most striking differences between low-income and middle-income children from day 1 were in knowledge of the letters of the alphabet, phonemic awareness, and vocabulary knowledge. Low-SES children were disadvantaged in pre-reading skills relative to high-SES children as soon as they started school. It took them all of year 1 of school to reach the point where middle-income children were at the start of year 1. Even worse, they fell further behind in reading and spelling as they proceeded through the school years. To give an example, results for the Burt word reading measure showed that the gap between the low- and high-SES groups at the end of year 2 was 1.2 years. By the end of year 5 the gap was 2.1 years.

The low-SES children were below average for their age in reading and spelling, but with effective instructional interventions it seems likely that they could achieve levels of reading and spelling appropriate for their age. The view that children from poverty areas are "illiterate" is not correct. By year 5, when they were nearly 10 years of age, the low-income children in this study were reading at an early 9-year level. They could read, but not to the level of the average reader of that age. Even so, to be reading below average for their age is a real disadvantage in terms of making academic progress at school.

An interesting aspect of the results was that differences in vocabulary knowledge in year 1, as measured by PPVT, was not a major predictor of learning to read in years 1 and 2. There is a view that the language sophistication children bring to school from the home is the key to their academic success in reading and writing (e.g., Bernstein 1974—see also an updated view by Nash 2002). There is no question that children with high levels of language are well placed to succeed in school. They understand the language of school and they have a better understanding of middle class language skills, of the tools of trade of teachers, such as children's books, alphabet blocks, pencil and paper activities, and so on. They have extensive experience with the formal language of books through listening to stories read to them at home.

Yet the partial correlation results of this study indicated that entry language knowledge was not the most important predictor of reading success. The best predictors of success were alphabet knowledge, GKR phonemic awareness, and pseudoword reading.

Some children at the end of year 1 were already feeling negative toward reading. This was apparent in their answers to a questionnaire. One question was, "How often do you read at home?" A child replied, "Never. I hate reading now." This was from a 5-year-old still in the first year of school. Another question was, "How do you feel when you come to a new word while reading?" A child replied, "I cry." Another said, "Sad because if you don't know it the teacher might growl you." Another question was, "Would you rather clean up your room or read?" One child said, "Clean up my room, 'cause I *can* clean up my room, but I can't read." To the question, "How do you feel when it's your turn to read to the teacher?" one child said, "Sad, because the teacher gives you a growling."

Some of the questions probed support at home, and it was clear that there was very little in the way of literacy resources in some homes. We asked one child, "How do you feel when someone reads you a story at home?" The child said, "No one ever reads me a story at home." Another child said, "Mum reads to me, not often, no one else does." We asked another child, "How many children's books do you have at home?" The child said she had no books at all and commented, "I never get to get any books." Another child said she had between five and ten books. When asked why, she said, "Because I've been good. My mum buys them, she's got the moneys [sic], she paid it." When the same child was asked whether she liked to read, she said, "No. Mum likes me to read, but I read ugly. 'Cause I don't know how to read."

For many children, negative feelings about reading occur in the first year of school, and this is a significant concern in that negative attitudes can inhibit their self-confidence.

The second part of the chapter explored the reasons for success in reading and writing. The data analysis indicated that in the first years of school, reading comprehension is determined very much by word recognition skills. These skills in turn depend on the development of phonological recoding skills (cipher knowledge). This knowledge in turn depends on alphabet knowledge and phonemic awareness. Writing depends on spelling and "ideas." However, in the first few years of school, it seems that writing is strongly predicted by spelling. Spelling, in turn, is strongly predicted by invented spelling, which, in turn, is predicted by phonemic awareness skills.

The third part of the chapter presented data from an after-school tutoring program to show that for children who have fallen behind, tutoring in phonological recoding improves their reading and spelling. The after-school tutoring program was based at a low-decile school in inner city Auckland. Many of the children had already gone through a Reading Recovery program, yet were still behind in reading. Likewise, quite a few children had slipped through the net and not been through Reading Recovery at all. About half the children were Pakeha, and half were Maori and Pacific Island. The children were from a range of SES backgrounds. The tutoring program emphasized phonological recoding skills. The results showed that many of these children, who came to the program with major reading difficulties, made dramatic improvements in their reading and spelling skills.

Phonological teaching of reading could make a huge difference to children if they received this kind of instruction from their first days of school. In the last few decades there has been a reluctance to do this. Instead, to reduce the failure rate, New Zealand and other countries have introduced interventions such as Reading Recovery (Clay 1994) to provide extra tutoring for children falling behind. Reading Recovery is a one-to-one tutoring program for 6-year-olds but the emphasis is not on explicit instruction in phonological recoding. In the United States, at least 1,000,000 children have been through Reading Recovery. In New Zealand, at least 100,000 children have been through the program. Yet it would be a lot cheaper simply to change teaching practices. As DeLemos (2002) puts it, "The adoption of effective classroom practices is, in comparison with strategies such as the reduction of class size or the implementation of intervention programs such as Reading Recovery, much more cost effective. Teachers have to be trained and employed. It costs no more to train teachers to use effective teaching practices than it costs to train them to use ineffective teaching practices." (p. 35)

The results presented in this chapter indicate that the phonological approach is a highly effective teaching approach for children from a range of SES backgrounds who do not respond to the whole language approach. Given the importance of reading and writing, the results reported in this chapter converge on the fact that many children do not benefit from the whole language approach, that, in fact, they get further and further behind their peers as the years pass. The data reported here also show that these children can benefit from an emphasis on phonological recoding skills. The intervention program described in this chapter where children received after-school tutoring that emphasized phonological decoding suggests that intensive teaching of a phonological approach is what is sorely needed to get at-risk children off to a better start in school.

ACKNOWLEDGMENTS

The chapter is a re-analysis and extension of longitudinal data previously reported at conferences and presented as technical reports (Nicholson 1997a; Nicholson, Ell, and McIntosh 1999; and Nicholson 2000). The year 1 data were originally collected for a different study and have been summarized in a book chapter (Nicholson 1997b).

Thanks to Sheryll McIntosh for data entry and help with the original longitudinal data, as well as data related to the tutoring program at The University of Auckland Reading Centre.

REFERENCES

Adams, M. J. 1990. *Beginning to Read*. Cambridge, MA: MIT Press.
Ball, E. W., and Blachman, B. A. 1991. Does phoneme awareness training in kindergarten make a difference in early word recognition and developmental spelling? *Reading Research Quarterly* 26: 49–66.
Bernstein, B. 1974. Class, Codes, and Control. Vol.1. Theoretical Studies Toward a Sociology of Language. London: Routledge and Kegan Paul.
Blachman, B. A., Ball, E. W., Black, R. S., and Tangel, D. M. 1994. Kindergarten teachers develop phonemic awareness in low-income, inner-city classrooms. Does it make a difference? *Reading and Writing: An Interdisciplinary Journal*, 6:1–18.
Bourdieu, P. 1974. The school as a conservative force. In *Contemporary Research in the Sociology of Education*, ed. J. Eggleston. London: Methuen.
Bowey, J. A. 1995. Socioeconomic status differences in preschool phonological sensitivity and first-grade reading achievement. *Journal of Educational Psychology* 87:476–87.
Bryant, N. D. 1975. *Bryant Test of Basic Decoding Skills*. New York: Teachers College Press.
Chall, J. S., Jacobs, V. A., and Baldwin, L. E. 1990. *The Reading Crisis: Why Poor Children Are Left Behind*. Harvard, MA: Harvard University Press.
Clay, M. M. 1985. *The Early Detection of Reading Difficulties*. Auckland, New Zealand: Heinemann.
Clay, M. M. 1994. *Reading Recovery*. Auckland, New Zealand: Heinemann
DeLemos, M. 2002. *Closing the Gap Between Research and Practice: Foundations for the Acquisition of Literacy*. Melbourne, Australia: Australian Council for Educational Research.
Dickenson, D. K., and Snow, C. E. 1987. Interrelationships among pre-reading and oral language skills in kindergartners from two social classes. *Early Childhood Research Quarterly* 2:1–25.
Duff, A. 1990. *Once Were Warriors*. Auckland, New Zealand: Tandem Press.
Dunn, L. M., and Dunn, L. M. 1981. *Peabody Picture Vocabulary Test - Revised*. Circle Pines, MN: American Guidance Service.

Foorman, B. R., Francis, D. J., Fletcher, J. M., Schatschneider, C., and Mehta, P. 1998. The role of instruction in learning to read: Preventing reading failure in at-risk children. *Journal of Educational Psychology* 90:37–55.

Gilmore, A. 1998. *School Entry Assessment.* Wellington, New Zealand: Ministry of Education

Gilmore, A., Croft, C., and Reid, N. 1981. *Burt Word Reading Test - Revised.* Wellington, New Zealand: New Zealand Council for Educational Research.

"Hundreds of school children missing." 1996. *Manukau Courier,* March 7.

Jastak, J. F., Bijou, S. W., and Jastak, S. 1993. *The Wide Range Achievement Test- Revised.* Wilmington, DE: Guidance Associates.

Juel, C.1988. Learning to read and write: A longitudinal study of 54 children from first through fourth grades. *Journal of Educational Psychology* 80: 437–47.

Juel, C. 1994. *Learning to Read in One Elementary School.* New York: Springer-Verlag.

Juel, C, Griffith, P. L., and Gough, P. B. 1986. Acquisition of literacy: A longitudinal study of children in first and second grade. *Journal of Educational Psychology* 78:243–55.

McCalman, J. 1984. *Struggletown: Portrait of an Australian Working-class Community, 1900–1965.* Ringwood, Victoria: Penguin.

Nash, R. 2002. Family resources and reading: Literacy practices, cognition, and school success. In *Learning to Read in Aotearoa New Zealand,* eds. P. Adams and H. Ryan. Palmerston North, New Zealand: Dunmore Press.

Neale, M. D. 1988. *Neale Analysis of Reading Ability - Revised.* Hawthorn, Victoria: Australian Council for Educational Research.

Nicholson, T. 1991. Do children read words better in context or in lists? A classic study revisited. *Journal of Educational Psychology* 83:444–50.

Nicholson, T. 1996. Can the poor get richer? The effects of phonemic awareness and letter-sound correspondence instruction on the reading and writing development of children from low-income backgrounds. Unpublished report, The University of Auckland, New Zealand.

Nicholson, T. 1997a. Does phonemic awareness training improve the literacy skills of low-SES children? Paper presented at biennial meeting of European Association for Research on Learning and Instruction, Athens, Greece, September.

Nicholson, T. 1997b. Closing the gap on reading failure: Social background, phonemic awareness and learning to read. In *Foundations of Reading Acquisition and Dyslexia,* ed. B. A. Blachman. Mahwah, NJ: Lawrence Erlbaum Associates.

Nicholson, T. 1998. *The flashcard strikes back.* The Reading Teacher 52:188–192.

Nicholson, T. 1999b. *At the Cutting Edge. Recent Research on Learning to Read and Spell for Success.* Wellington, New Zealand: New Zealand Council for Educational Research.

Nicholson, T. 1999a. Family, literacy and society. In *Learning to Read. Beyond Phonics and Whole Language,* eds. G.B. Thompson and T. Nicholson. New York: Teachers College Press.

Nicholson, T. 2000. *Reading the Writing on the Wall.* Palmerston North, New Zealand: Dunmore Press.

Nicholson, T., and Gallienne, G. 1995. Struggletown meets Middletown: Reading achievement levels among 13-year-old students in low and middle socioeconomic areas. *New Zealand Journal of Educational Studies* 30:15–23.

Nicholson, T., Ell, F., and McIntosh, S. 1999. The rich get richer and the poor get poorer. A longitudinal study of children's literacy development. Paper presented at the annual meeting of the Australian Association of Special Education, Sydney, Australia, September.

Nicholson,T., and Whyte, B. 1992. Matthew effects in learning new words while listening to stories. In *Literacy Research, Theory and Practice: Views from Many Perspectives*, eds. C. K. Kinzer and D. J. Leu. Chicago: National Reading Conference.

Norris, M., Bathgate, M., and Parkin, M. 1994. Development of a socioeconomic indicator for schools. Paper presented the annual meeting of the New Zealand Association for Research in Education Conference, Dunedin, December.

O'Connor, R. A., Jenkins, J. R., and Slocum, T. A. (1995). Transfer among phonological tasks in kindergarten: Essential instructional content. *Journal of Educational Psychology* 87:202–17.

Orr, E. 1995. *Australia's Literacy Challenge: The Importance of Education in Breaking the Poverty Cycle for Australia's Disadvantaged Families.* Sydney, Australia: The Smith Family.

Raz, I. T., and Bryant, P. 1990. Social background, phonological awareness and children's reading. *British Journal of Developmental Psychology* 8:209–25.

Richardson, E., and DiBenedetto, B. 1985. *Decoding Skills Test.* Parkton, MD: York Press.

Roper, H. D. 1984. Spelling, word recognition and phonemic awareness among first grade children. Unpublished doctoral dissertation, University of Texas at Austin.

Rutter, M. 1983. School effects on pupil progress: Research findings and policy implications. *Child Development* 54:1–29.

Share D. L., Jorm, A. F., MacLean, R., and Matthews, R. 1984. Sources of individual differences in reading acquisition. *Journal of Educational Psychology* 76:1309–24.

Schonell, F. J. 1950. *Diagnostic and Attainment Testing: Including a Manual of Tests, Their Nature, Use, Recording and Interpretation.* Edinburgh: Oliver & Boyd.

Stanovich, K. E. 1986. Matthew effects in reading: Some consequences of individual differences in the acquisition of literacy. *Reading Research Quarterly* 21:210–14.

Tan, A., and Nicholson, T. 1997. Flashcards revisited: The effects of automaticity training on poor readers' comprehension of text. *Journal of Educational Psychology* 89:276–88.

Tangel, D. M., and Blachman, B. A. 1995. Effect of phoneme awareness instruction on the invented spelling of first grade children: A one-year follow-up. *Journal of Reading Behavior* 27:153–85.

Tunmer, W. E., and Chapman, J. W. 1995. Invented spelling test. Unpublished manuscript, Massey University, Palmerston North, New Zealand.

Tunmer, W. E., and Chapman, J. W. 1999. Teaching strategies for word identification. In *Learning to Read: Beyond Phonics and Whole Language*, eds. G. B. Thompson and T. Nicholson. New York: Teachers College Press & International Reading Association.

Turner, A., Connolly, G., and Devlin, M. 1992. Food related needs in a sample of Otara and Manurewa families. Report for the Health Promotion Unit, Auckland Area Health Board. Auckland, New Zealand: Manukau City Council.

Wallach, M. A., and Wallach, L. 1979. Helping disadvantaged children to read by teaching them phoneme identification skills. In *Theory and Practice of Early Reading*, Vol.3, eds. L.A. Resnick and P.A. Weaver. Hillsdale, NJ: Lawrence Erlbaum Associates.

Wallach, L., Wallach, M. A., Dozier, M. G., and Kaplan, N. E. 1977. Poor children learning to read do not have trouble with auditory discrimination but do have trouble with phoneme recognition. *Journal of Educational Psychology* 69:36–39.

Whitehurst, G. J., Epstein, J. N., Angell, A. L., Payne, A. C., Crone, D. A., and Fischel, J. E. 1994. Outcomes of an emergent literacy intervention in Head Start. *Journal of Educational Psychology* 86:542–55.

Williams, J. P. 1980. Teaching decoding with an emphasis on phoneme analysis and phoneme blending. *Journal of Educational Psychology* 72:1–15.

Section • III

Early Reading Interventions

Chapter • 7

Accelerating Growth and Maintaining Proficiency:
A Two-Year Intervention Study of Kindergarten and First-Grade Children at Risk for Reading Difficulties

Deborah C. Simmons, Edward J. Kame'enui, Mike Stoolmiller, Michael D. Coyne, and Beth Harn

The "promise of prevention" is that we can significantly decrease the incidence (i.e., number of new cases) and prevalence (i.e., number of existing cases) of children who experience reading difficulties by intervening early, systematically, differentially, and intensively (National Research Council 1998, Simeonsson 1994). This promise lies at the very heart of the current "Reading First" initiative (*No Child Left Behind* 2002, Title I, Part B, Student Reading Skills Improvement Grants, Subpart 1, Reading First, pp. 178–212). In fact, Reading First unwittingly represents a significant national campaign to prevent reading difficulties in young children who gain their primary reading instruction in complex "host environments" known as schools (Simmons et al. 2002). This unprecedented national commitment and promise are predicated on at least four basic assumptions: First, the condition of early reading risk and reading disabilities is identifiable. Second, early reading difficulties or disabilities are preventable. Third, there is a "generative base . . . and research substrate . . . to be mined by astute primary preventionists" (Cowen 1982, p. 132) in beginning reading for immediate application in schools. Fourth, the effects of prevention endure beyond periods of intervention and further intensive intervention is no longer required (Coyne et al. in preparation).

In this chapter, we focus on the basic assumptions of prevention, and the types and levels of instruction necessary to prevent identified conditions of reading risk from becoming reading difficulties or disabilities. This examination of prevention is based on a four-year longitudinal study of 96 children who completed kindergarten intervention and the 77 children who continued and completed a Grade 1 follow-up intervention study. Our particular interests are in the features of instruction that accelerate reading growth in kindergarten children and whether supplemental intervention is necessary to maintain reading proficiency in Grade 1. We discuss findings in terms of the effects, stability, and sustainability of reading performance over a two-year intervention. Specifically, we address two primary questions:

1. What are the effects of systematically varied kindergarten interventions on the phonologic and alphabetic understanding of kindergarten children who enter school at risk of reading difficulty?

2. Is supplemental intervention in Grade 1 necessary to maintain adequate levels of reading performance of children who responded strongly to a kindergarten intervention?

We begin with a brief discussion of the definition of prevention and the essential elements of prevention as a system. Next, we summarize the methods and results of a kindergarten intervention using absolute and normative standards of reading performance. We conclude with the methods and results of a Grade 1 intervention with particular emphasis on whether reading difficulties were prevented.

DEFINING PREVENTION: A CONCEPT OR SYSTEM?

At the very heart of prevention is the simple proposition that a prevention is designed "to keep something from happening." Its operational specificity is revealed narrowly and conspicuously in the long-term empirical effects of specific instructional strategies and curricular programs that actually prevent reading difficulties for children in the early years of reading development. But what does the prevention of reading difficulty look like if it works? Exactly how many children must benefit from a prevention program, treatment, or strategy before it is deemed preventive? Is prevention an all or nothing proposition? Or is it merely an unwieldy and provocative construct that serves host to a range of ideas, activities, and commitments from prevention as a "national goal and agenda" as in Reading First, to prevention as an epidemiological model in which the distribution of a defined risk condition (e.g., reading problems or disabilities) in the population is identified, potential risk factors targeted and prioritized, and comprehensive preventive strategies implemented and sustained to promote the well-being of children, youth, and adults (Simeonsson 1994). Though the term prevention permeates virtually every large-scale consensus report (e.g., National Research Council 1998, National Reading Panel 2000), and is readily embraced by practitioners (American Federation of Teachers 1999, Learning First Alliance 1998), researchers (Adams 1990, Foorman and Torgesen 2001) and policy makers (e.g., *No Child Left Behind* 2002), the need for common understanding of the dimensions of prevention prevails.

The framework we use to conceptualize the outcomes of prevention is drawn from the public health domain and literature (Caplan and Grunebaum 1967, cited in Simeonsson 1994) and consists of three different levels: primary, secondary, and tertiary.

The litmus test of preventive intervention (Torgesen 2000) is that *all* children with identifiable reading risk would attain adequate reading proficiency by a designated time period (e.g., end of Grade 3). At the primary prevention level, children with indicators of early reading risk might be "selected" (Simeonsson 1994) to receive targeted intervention to prevent them from becoming new cases of reading disabilities. At the secondary level, prevention may serve a mediating role that prevents a condition from being fully "manifested" (Simeonsson 1994). This level of support is less intensive than what would have been required to attain or sustain adequate levels of reading proficiency. Finally, tertiary prevention is concerned with reducing the complications associated with an existing and identified problem or condition. According to the National Research Council (1998), "Programs, strategies, and interventions at this level have an explicit remedial or rehabilitative focus. If children demonstrate inadequate progress under secondary prevention conditions, they may need instruction that is specially designed and supplemental—special education, tutoring from a reading specialist—to their current instruction" (p. 16). In the next section, we review three intervention studies that focused on the goal of primary prevention.

Specifying the Features of Kindergarten and Grade 1 Primary Prevention Instruction

Over the past decade, critical components of effective intervention for children with reading risk have been identified and methods of reducing the incidence and prevalence of serious reading difficulties tested empirically (e.g., Foorman and Torgesen 2001, Lovett, Lacerenza, and Borden 2000). Central to prevention is instruction that is strategic, explicit, intensive, and timely (Foorman and Torgesen 2001, Vellutino et al. 1996). Primary prevention holds that instruction, if carefully designed and delivered within a specified "window" of time, is sufficient to correct or remove the phonological and alphabetic deficits of a significant percentage of children who are initially identified as at risk for reading failure, making further intensive intervention at a subsequent time during reading development unnecessary. Early intervention, in this sense, acts like a "jump-start" (O'Connor 2000, p. 43).

This view of prevention draws heavily from Stanovich and Share's (Stanovich 1986, Share and Stanovich 1995, Share 1995) conceptualization of reading acquisition. According to this model, there are reciprocal effects of establishing strong phonological and alphabetic skills. Early and timely establishment of these skills facilitates the building of fully specified orthographic representations in memory, which then become the foundation for successful acquisition of later reading skills such as word-reading automaticity and text-reading fluency.

Three studies have particular bearing on the "window of opportunity" for jump-starting the acquisition of early reading skills and preventing reading risk from becoming reading difficulty. Vellutino et al. (1996) documented that 67% of children (79 of 118) who performed in the bottom 9% of their kindergarten cohort could be brought within average ranges of first-grade reading achievement with one semester of one-to-one daily instruction that focused on word identification, reading connected text, phonemic awareness, phonetic decoding and writing skills. At the end of Grade 2, 41% of the total sample still performed below the 30th percentile on a word identification measure (Vellutino cited in Torgesen 2000). Moreover, they documented that "children who attained the most accelerated rate of growth in reading subskills . . . approached the level of the normal readers and maintained their advantage" (p. 629). Although children in the tutored group approached performance levels of the average group, there was the general tendency for average-achieving students to maintain an advantage over children who began the study with the lowest performance profiles. An important implication the authors drew from these results was that of identifying children earlier and intervening in kindergarten on the rudimentary phonologic and alphabetic skills. They hypothesized that a jump-start on foundational skills may help accelerate reading success in Grade 1 and lessen the severity of reading difficulty.

In a second study of prevention effects, O'Connor (2000) investigated the efficacy of layers of intervention intensity for 59 students who constituted the lowest 40% of students on a battery of vocabulary, letter identification, memory, rapid naming, phonological, and reading measures. After a year of whole-class instruction and one-to-one tutoring in kindergarten, O'Connor concluded that 28% of participating students who received continuous intervention responded poorly. At the end of first grade, after a combination of small-group and one-to-one intensive interventions, seven students performed more than 1 standard deviation below the mean on Woodcock Johnson subtests. O'Connor followed children into second grade and concluded that most of the children with disabilities and several others who were provided only "status quo" reading instruction lost ground in comparison with children not at risk.

Torgesen et al.'s (1999) longitudinal study of 138 children from kindergarten through Grade 2 further documented the importance of preventive, explicit, code-based reading instruction. For two and a half years, children identified in the bottom 12% of their kindergarten cohort received four 20-minute sessions of one-to-one tutoring per week beginning in the second semester of kindergarten. At the end of second grade, students in the most explicit instructional condition outperformed those in the other conditions on measures of phonemic awareness, phonemic decoding, and context-free word recognition. Despite the magnitude of improvement, 30% of students in the strongest condition performed below the 30th percentile on a measure of word attack and 36% below the 30th percentile on word identification. Due to the absence of strong effects on passage comprehension, the authors identified the need to examine the "balance" between word-level and comprehension skills.

From these studies, we derive four primary conclusions. First, the potential effectiveness of early reading intervention for the majority of children identified as at reading risk in kindergarten is clear and compelling. Interventions that provided small-group and one-to-one, explicit code-based interventions brought the majority of children within average ranges of reading performance (O'Connor 2000, Torgesen et al. 1999, Vellutino et al. 1996). Second, despite the effectiveness of the instruction, in each study there remained children who failed to attain adequate levels of proficiency on word reading at the end of intervention. Third, students who attained the most accelerated levels of achievement maintained adequate levels of reading proficiency yet lagged behind average-achieving peers. Fourth, students who attained lower levels of proficiency may not maintain adequate reading skills without a supplement or booster intervention.

In our study, we sought to further understand findings of prevention studies. We examined (a) the design and delivery of instruction that brings the greatest number of kindergarten children to levels of phonological and alphabetic proficiency and (b) the need for supplemental intervention in Grade 1 to maintain desirable levels of reading achievement. Moreover, we address these issues in the context of schools as complex host environments. Toward that end, interventions were delivered by school personnel in small-group contexts. Finally, we describe the methods and results of two years of a longitudinal study investigating the types and levels of intervention that will allow children identified as at risk to attain and maintain adequate levels of reading achievement.

SUMMARY OF YEAR 01 RESEARCH

In the first year, we examined the relative effectiveness of three interventions—two that varied systematically in levels of instructional emphasis on the alphabetic code or comprehension, and a third that employed an explicit, code-based commercial reading program. We attempted to determine whether instruction that varied in terms of emphasis (i.e., phonologic and alphabetic only vs. phonologic, alphabetic, semantic and listening comprehension) would produce differential results on early reading outcomes. Because preventing reading difficulties was of primary interest, our focus centered on determining the elements and emphases of early reading intervention that produced the greatest practical benefit.

One hundred thirteen children who performed in the bottom quartile of all kindergarteners in 7 schools on letter naming fluency and initial sound fluency were randomly assigned to one of three interventions (Code Emphasis, Code and Comprehension Emphasis, or the code element from a Commercial Program. All schools received Title I funding, and the percentage of free- and reduced-lunch services ranged from 32 to 63%. Participating children were primarily White (84%) and Latino/Hispanic (14%). Participating students received a 30-minute, small-group, pull-out, 21-week supplement to their typical kindergarten instruction provided primarily by educational assistants. Of the 30 intervention groups, 26 were delivered by educational assistants and 4 by certified teachers.

Code Emphasis (CE).   The CE intervention focused on strategic and systematic instruction of phonemic awareness and alphabetic understanding and consisted of two 15-minute components delivered consecutively in daily, 30-minute lessons. In the first 15 minutes, instruction established and reinforced the phonologic skills of (a) first and last sound isolation, (b) sound blending, and (c) sound segmentation. Fundamental alphabetic skills and strategies of (a) letter name identification, (b) letter sound identification, (c) letter sound blending to read consonant-vowel-consonant (CVC) words, (d) selected irregular word reading, and (e) sentence reading of controlled text were also taught. The second 15 minutes extended phonologic and alphabetic skills through instruction in handwriting (e.g., letter dictation and formation), integrated phonologic and alphabetic tasks, and spelling.

Code and Comprehension Emphasis (CCE).   The CCE intervention distributed emphasis across two areas of reading: code (i.e., phonologic and alphabetic) and comprehension (i.e., vocabulary, narrative text structure, story retell) and consisted of two 15-minute, consecutive segments per day. The first 15 minutes were the same lessons as the CE intervention and focused on high-priority phonologic and alphabetic skills. The second 15 minutes had two primary foci: (a) receptive and expressive knowledge of vocabulary that appeared in storybooks, and (b) expanded knowledge and development of story structure and story retell. One half of the CCE intervention was allocated to code-based features and the other half to vocabulary and comprehension.

Commercial Program (CP).   This intervention served as a comparison group representative of commercial reading programs characterized as explicit and systematic with a strong emphasis on phonologic and alphabetic development. This group used the Sounds and Letters module of the *Open Court Reading* (Adams et al. 2000) comprehensive reading program. Like the CE condition, the entire 30 minutes of instructional time was allocated to code-emphasis activities.

Changes in children's performance were assessed in the following domains with the corresponding measures: (a) phonological awareness (Dynamic Indicators of Basic Early Literacy Skills [DIBELS]: phonemic segmentation fluency) (Good, Kaminski, and Smith 2002), (b) nonsense or pseudoword reading (DIBELS: nonsense word fluency (Good and Kaminski 2002) and *Woodcock Reading Mastery Test* word attack subtest), and word reading (*Woodcock Reading Mastery Test* word identification subtest) (Woodcock 1987), (c) general receptive vocabulary (*Peabody Picture Vocabulary Test - Revised*) (Dunn and Dunn 1981), (d) targeted expressive vocabulary, and (e) listening comprehension using an experimental measure to tap story retell and story comprehension.

We focus our discussion of results on measures most directly related to early reading proficiency of code-based tasks. Data collection points varied by measure (pre/post or alternate-form growth measures) and by the appropriateness of the measure for kindergarten children at specific points in time. Measurement periods included: (a) monthly growth assessment on selected measures of phonological awareness and alphabetic understanding, and (b) post-test only measures of word attack and word reading deemed too difficult for fall of kindergarten.

Did Children With Early Reading Risk Attain Adequate Levels of Reading Proficiency?

The 96 children began the kindergarten year in the bottom 25 percent of their grade-level cohort and at some level of risk for reading difficulty. On average, they identified fewer than 3 letter names and recognized less than 7 first sounds in words in the fall of kindergarten. For comparative purposes, two children from each kindergarten class, forty-six children total, were randomly selected from the total sample of students scoring at or above the 50th percentile on DIBELS letter naming and initial sound fluency measures in September of kindergarten. Thirty-seven of these children remained at the end of kindergarten and will be referenced as the above-average (AA) comparison group. Means and standard deviations of the three intervention groups and the above-average comparison group are found in table I.

Though the idea of early identification and intervention is generally endorsed, the critical point in time when children are best identified for intervention has inherent costs and tradeoffs. O'Connor and Jenkins (1999) documented that fall risk indicators in kindergarten are less reliable than spring indicators and resulted in an overprediction rate of 12% of children. Identifying children who

Table I.   Descriptive Statistics on Screening Measures Across Intervention and Above-Average Comparison Groups for Students Completing Study

Interventions Small groups	Students Assigned to Interventions			Above Average Students
	CE (n=32)	CCE (n=34)	CP (n=30)	AA (n=37)
	Initial Sounds Fluency			
M	7.16	6.68	5.63	17.95
SD	4.02	3.49	3.36	2.95
	Letter Naming Fluency			
M	2.78	2.53	2.13	14.59
SD	2.83	2.39	1.74	3.65

Note: CE = Code Emphasis; CCE = Code and Comprehension Emphasis; CP = Commercial Program

are false positives (i.e., identified as at risk but do not develop reading disability) is a potential cost of fall kindergarten identification. However, O'Connor and Jenkins (1999) observed that fall screening procedures rarely miss children who later develop reading disability. With this caveat noted, we administered screening measures in October, consciously aware that there may be a percentage of children identified to receive intervention who may not actually require additional instruction. We, however, did not want to overlook children who may be at potential risk for later reading difficulties.

To examine whether children attained levels of early reading proficiency, we used two indicators: (a) end-of-year benchmarks on DIBELS growth measures, and (b) reading achievement as indexed by the Basic Skills composite on the WRMT-R. Scores on phonemic segmentation fluency and nonsense word fluency measures indicated that the average performer in each of the three intervention groups and the AA group met established end-of-year kindergarten benchmarks of 35 phonemes per minute and 20 letter-sounds per minute (Good, Simmons, and Kame'enui 2001). One-way analyses of variance indicated a significant main effect for group on the May phonemic segmentation fluency (PSF) measure, $F(3,135) = 5.245$, $p = .002$ and the May nonsense word fluency (NWF) measure, $F(3,134) = 4.548$, $p = .005$. Planned comparisons among the 3 randomized intervention groups using the Tukey-Kramer method (critical point = 2.37 for the studentized range statistic, q, for alpha = .05 and 3 simultaneous contrasts) indicated that the CE group was significantly higher than the CP group on both NWF ($q = 3.11$) and PSF ($q = 2.41$) and significantly higher than the CCE group on the NWF measure ($q = 2.94$).

Planned comparisons of each intervention group to the AA group using the Tukey-Kramer method (critical point = 2.37 for q for alpha = .05 and 3 simultaneous contrasts) indicated that the CP group was significantly lower than the AA group on both PSF (q = –2.56) and NWF (q = –3.53) (See table II for descriptive statistics).

A criterion score of 20 or more letter sounds on the NWF measure was established as the benchmark for spring-of-kindergarten alphabetic proficiency. The terminal benchmark for NWF is 50 letter sounds per minute by midyear of Grade 1 (Good et al. 2001). A noteworthy difference emerged between the percent of students in the AA comparison, CE, CCE, and CP groups meeting benchmark levels by the end of intervention. In May, 88% of students in the CE group identified 20 or more letter sounds in one minute compared to 65% and 63% of students in the CCE and CP groups respectively. This finding is particularly impressive given that 86% of students in the AA comparison group achieved the 20 NWF benchmark. Chi-square analyses indicated a significant relation among groups and attainment of benchmark, $x^2(3 \ df)$ = 9.55, p = .023. Figure 1 illustrates the observed mean growth trajectories on nonsense word fluency from January through May.

Performance on end-of-year standardized reading measures revealed a strong response to intervention across groups with mean scores falling well within average ranges. On the Basic Skills Cluster of the WRMT - R (word attack and word identification subtests composite), respective means for groups were: CE: M = 109.31

Table II. **Descriptive Statistics of PSF and NWF End-of Kindergarten Performance by Group**

	Students Assigned to Interventions			Above Average Students
Interventions Small groups	CE (n=32)	CCE (n=34)	CP (n=30)	AA (n=37)
May Phonemic Segmentation Fluency[a]				
M	47.84	41.44	36.43	49.62
SD	14.42	17.61	17.54	9.88
May Nonsense Word Fluency[b]				
M	39.38	29.38	25.03	39.68
SD	17.48	17.81	13.60	25.74

Note: [a]Phoneme Segmentation Fluency (Good, R. H., Kaminski, R. A., and Smith, S. 2002)
[b]Nonsense Word Fluency (Good, R. H. and Kaminski, R. A. 2002)

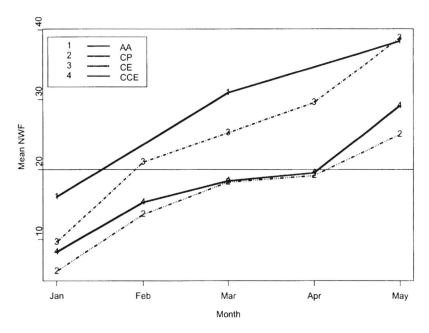

Figure 1.   Observed Mean nonsense word growth trajectories in relation to above average students.

$(SD = 9.79)$; CCE: $M = 104.47$, $(SD = 9.51)$; CP: $M = 100.13$, $(SD = 14.47)$, and AA: $M = 111.97$, $(SD = 15.27)$. One-way analysis of variance indicated a significant main effect for group, $F(3,129) = 9.175$, $p < .001$. Planned comparisons among the 3 intervention groups using the Tukey-Kramer procedure (critical point $q = 2.37$ for alpha $= .05$ and 3 simultaneous contrasts) indicated that the CE group was significantly higher than the CP group ($q = 3.28$). Planned comparisons of each intervention group to the AA group using the Tukey-Kramer procedure (critical point $q = 2.37$ for alpha $= .05$ and 3 simultaneous contrasts) indicated that the CP ($q = -4.91$) and CCE ($q = -3.43$) groups were significantly lower than the AA group.

Because we were further interested in responsiveness to intervention (Byrne, Fielding-Barnsley, and Ashley 2000, Vellutino et al. 1996), we conducted a duration-to-benchmark survival or event history analysis (Willett and Singer 1991). This method allowed us to address the following question: "At what point in time did students in the intervention groups attain established levels of proficiency on measures of validated importance to early reading success?" Because the PSF and NWF measures have established phonemic and alphabetic proficiency levels with predictive validity for later reading proficiency (Good, Simmons, and Kame'enui 2001), event history analyses were deemed appropriate. A criterion score of 20 or greater on the NWF measure was established as the benchmark for spring-of-kindergarten proficiency, allowing for the examination of survival functions for each intervention group from January to May, 2000. As shown in figure 2, the CE intervention was positively influenced by the NWF performance quite early, while students in the other intervention groups took longer to reach benchmark level. Using median survival times, students in the CE group (*Mdn* = 2.0, *SE* = .28) reached the benchmark sooner (approximately February) than did the students in either the CCE (*Mdn* = 4.0, *SE* = .60) (i.e., April) or the CP (*Mdn* = 4.0, *SE* = 59) (i.e., April) group. Differences among the survival functions across groups were also supported by the log-rank (Mantel-Cox) statistic, which was significant at $p < .05$.

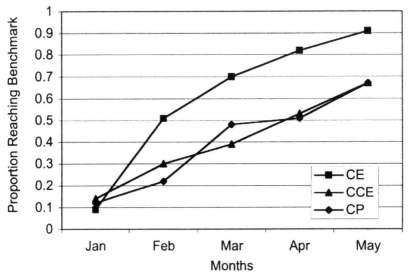

Figure 2.   Duration to goal on nonsense word fluency.

To place the effects of intervention in perspective, the probability that the 96 students in the three intervention groups would attain average levels of reading performance (i.e., at or above the 30th and 50th percentiles) on the word attack and word identification subtests of the Woodcock Reading Mastery Test follow:

Criterion	Probability
≥ 30th percentile on word attack	87/96 = .91
≥ 30th percentile on word identification	79/96 = .82
≥ 50th percentile on word attack	73/96 = .76
≥ 50th percentile or word identification	68/96 = .71

If we use at or above the 30th percentile criterion as an indicator for adequate reading performance (Torgesen et al. 2001), the kindergarten intervention did not prevent reading difficulties for all children. Each child in each intervention group did not reach designated benchmarks or attain average levels of performance. On average, 9 to 18% of students remained below the 30th percentile at the end of kindergarten on word attack and word identification measures, respectively. For specific intervention conditions, the percentages of children who did not reach the 30th percentile on the WRMT-R word attack and word identification subtests are shown in table III.

To gain an appreciation for the power of the interventions, we used Torgesen et al.'s (2001) algorithm for estimating population prevalence (percent in actual sample who did not reach criterion X percentage of students sampled) and found that 2.25% of children in the population would not reach or exceed the 30th percentile in word attack skills if any of the three interventions was used with all children. If the CE intervention was applied, 1.5% would remain at risk. For word identification, 4.5% of the population would remain below the 30th percentile using any of the three treatments. If the CE intervention was implemented, 2.25% would perform below the 30th percentile. From another perspective, the CE intervention resulted in a 54% reduction rate in children who performed below the 30th percentile on word attack compared to the CP intervention. For word identification, the reduction rate for the CE and CP intervention comparison was 73%.

SUMMARY OF YEAR 02 RESEARCH: SUSTAINING AND ACCELERATING READING PROFICIENCY

Though end-of-kindergarten performance levels indicated we fell short of preventing reading difficulty among the sample of kindergarten children, we were highly encouraged with the response and

Table III. Percentages of Children Below the 30th Percentile at the End of Kindergarten by Group

Measures		Interventions		Above Average Students
	CE	CCE	CP	AA
WRMT-AT < 30th%	6%	9%	13%	3%
WRMT-ID < 30th%	9%	12%	33%	3%

Note: WRMT-AT = Woodcock Reading Mastery Test - Word Attack subtest
WRMT-ID = Woodcock Reading Mastery Test - Word Identification subtest

level of performance across interventions. Our investigation in Year 02 examined the levels and adjustments to intervention necessary to sustain average reading performance for students who attained adequate levels of reading proficiency at the end of kindergarten. At the heart of the study was whether children benefited adequately from supplemental kindergarten intervention to maintain adequate growth from general education instruction in first grade. Or, put another way, is intervention necessary to sustain adequate rates of performance in Grade 1 for children who entered with adequate levels of performance?

Of the original 96 students in Year 01, 77 completed our Year 02 study. Fifty-nine of the 77 children who received intervention in kindergarten performed at adequate levels of reading proficiency on PSF (35 or higher) and NWF (20 or higher) in October of Grade 1. This subset of 59 students will be the focus of this section. As a reference, a score of 35 on PSF and 20 on NWF in October of Grade 1 corresponded to a standard score of 107.54 on word attack and 99.73 on word identification on the WRMT-R in this sample of 59 children. Additionally, a score of 35 on PSF references the 45th percentile in a national sample of 36,865 children and 20 NWF the 33rd percentile in a sample of 36,708 children (Good et al. 2002).

DO THE EFFECTS OF KINDERGARTEN INTERVENTION MAINTAIN FROM END OF KINDERGARTEN TO BEGINNING OF GRADE 1?

One of the first questions investigated was whether students who met designated benchmarks at the end of kindergarten were the same students who met benchmarks in fall of Grade 1 (i.e., 35 PSF and 20 NWF). The chi-square test of spring-of-kindergarten to fall-of-Grade 1 benchmark attainment ($x^2 = 62.14$, $df = 1$, $p < .001$) was highly significant, suggesting that performance was stable from one measurement point to the next. Of the 55 students who met the May kindergarten dual benchmark, 47 met the fall of first-grade benchmark. Of the 30 students who did not reach the end-of-kindergarten benchmark, 22 did not meet the beginning of Grade 1 benchmarks. The odds of the fall Grade 1 benchmark status being the same as spring of kindergarten benchmark status were just over 16 to 1. The strength of the relation between spring of kindergarten and fall of Grade 1 performance was further documented through multiple regression analysis which indicated that 52% of the variance in October fall NWF was predicted by spring of kindergarten PSF and NWF, multiple $R = .72$. Likewise, 47% of fall of Grade 1 PSF was accounted for by spring of kindergarten PSF and NWF.

An Examination of Maintenance: Phase I

To study the conditions necessary to maintain adequate achievement levels, we used a two-phase intervention design. From November through mid-February (50 instructional sessions), students who met fall benchmarks were randomly assigned to either maintenance intervention (*n* = 30 assigned but 2 dropped out) or a monitor condition (*n* = 31). The purpose of this intervention was to provide students with additional support in maintaining reading-related skills associated with phonological awareness and alphabetic skills as well as developing the more complex reading skills of automatic word reading and text-reading fluency.

Maintenance Intervention. The first 15 minutes of the intervention focused on enhancing phonological awareness and alphabetic skills and consisted of instruction from the *Write Well* program (Sprick and Howard 2000). This program emphasizes phonologic and alphabetic skills through practice spelling and writing. The major components include (a) reviewing letter-sound correspondences and letter combinations, (b) orally segmenting teacher-dictated words into individual phonemes and sequentially writing the letters that correspond with each phoneme to spell words, (c) decoding words to confirm spellings, and (d) spelling whole words and sentences from dictation. The second 15 minutes of the intervention focused on (a) word reading practice with both regular and sight words, (b) teacher-supported group readings of storybooks, and (c) partner readings of storybooks. Additional design features included multiple readings of storybooks with controlled, decodable text, and scaffolded instruction progressing from sound-by-sound decoding of individual words to independent reading of whole storybooks. School-based personnel including four certified teachers and 26 paraprofessionals implemented the maintenance intervention. Instruction was delivered in small groups (i.e., 3–5 students) for 30-minute sessions during the regular school day.

Monitor Condition. Students in the monitor condition received their school-designed curriculum and reading programs and did not participate in additional research-specified intervention. Commercial programs in the seven schools included *Open Court, Reading Mastery* (Englemann and Bruner 1995), and *Read Well* (Sprick, Howard, and Fidanque 1998).

Midyear Analyses and Instructional Adjustments

In February a range of reading measures was individually administered including PSF and NWF, oral reading fluency (ORF) (Marston and Deno 1987), and word attack, word identification, and passage comprehension subtests of the WRMT-R. The mean performance of both groups exceeded the benchmark levels on PSF and NWF and were above the 50th percentile on the three target subtests of the WRMT-R. Results of independent t-tests indicated that none of the February monitor versus maintenance intervention comparisons were significantly different ($p > .05$). Means and standard deviations by condition are summarized in table IV.

February analyses provided preliminary evidence that, on average, the quality and quantity of general education instruction, coupled with children's starting point in fall of Grade 1, were sufficient to maintain adequate levels of reading achievement. The absence of a significant difference between groups who received 50 additional sessions of intervention from those who did not suggests that students "held their own" based on implementation of research-based reading practices in general education in Grade 1 (e.g., *Open Court, Reading Mastery*). These are indeed encouraging findings. Nonetheless, analyses of performance within the monitor and maintenance conditions revealed marked variability in individual level and slope of performance.

ADJUSTING INSTRUCTION BASED ON PERFORMANCE: PHASE II

Individual performance of students in each group was analyzed and a criterion of 20 correct words per minute (CWPM) on February oral reading fluency measures was applied as a decision rule to identify students who would continue (ORF < 20) or discontinue

Table IV. **Means and Standard Deviations of February DIBELS and WRMT-R Measures by Condition**

Reading Measures	Conditions			
	Monitor ($n = 31$)		Maintenance Intervention ($n = 28$)	
	M	(SD)	M	(SD)
PSF	51.74	(10.26)	51.57	(10.59)
NWF	58.00	(19.85)	58.64	(27.94)
ORF	31.77	(25.54)	35.36	(31.98)
Word Attack SS	113.48	(5.80)	113.21	(8.19)
Word Identification SS	109.94	(8.02)	109.86	(11.37)
Passage Comprehension SS	102.48	(7.88)	102.82	(8.79)

Note: PSF = Phonemic Segmentation Fluency, NWF = Nonsense Word Fluency, ORF = Oral Reading Fluency, SS = Standard Score

(ORF = 20) maintenance intervention. A criterion of 20 CWPM was established, as it represents one-half of the minimum annual goal of 40 CWPM. Of the 31 children in the Monitor condition, 16 or 52% achieved the criterion; of the 28 children in the Maintenance Intervention, 10 or 36% attained the criterion; overall, 26 of 59 children or 44% reached the 20 CWPM criterion.

Students who met the 20 CWPM criterion in February, on average, had already exceeded the end-of-year target of 40 correct words per minute in February (M = 56.27, SD = 29.60) and were considered to have solid beginning reading skills sufficient to maintain average reading performance without additional intervention. Their corresponding average standard score on the WRMT-R Basic Skills Cluster was 114.77 (SD = 7.89). Of particular interest was the finding that 16 of the 26 students in the monitor condition from November through February maintained strong performance without continued instructional support.

Conversely, 33 students (56% of the total sample) in February read fewer than 20 correct words per minute, (M = 15.52, SD = 6.37) and had a mean standard score of 108.33 (SD = 8.25) on the Basic Skills Cluster of the WRMT-R. Clearly, these students were within adequate reading proficiency as indexed by a normative-referenced measure. Their average number of correct words per minute, however, was slightly below the 20 correct words per minute we established as indicative of satisfactory progress in mid-first grade. We will return to this seeming discrepancy between what constitutes adequate performance between criterion and normative-referenced measures.

To address individuals' response to intervention in February, we disaggregated and reconfigured the two original fall groups into four. Students in the original Monitor group and the Maintenance Intervention group who read less than 20 words correct per minute were identified and either continued or began intervention. We refer to these groups as Monitor-Intervention and Intervention-Intervention groups, respectively. Students who received intervention from November through February and reached or exceeded the 20 correct words per minute criterion were discontinued from further additional intervention and are referred to as Intervention-Monitor group. Students originally assigned to monitor condition who met the 20 CWPM benchmark remained in monitoring only and are referenced as the Monitor-Monitor condition (See table V).

Figures 3 and 4 depict monthly nonsense word reading fluency (September to May) and oral reading fluency (October to May) mean growth trajectories of the four groups. Perhaps the most striking pattern revealed in this graphic was that despite

Table V.   Adjusted Intervention Groups in February of Grade 1

Group	Intervention Characteristics
Monitor-Intervention	• Monitored from November to February • Less than 20 CWPM in February • Intervention from February to May
Intervention-Intervention	• Intervention from November to February • Less than 20 CWPM in February • Intervention from February to May
Intervention-Monitor	• Intervention from November to February • 20 or more CWPM in February • Monitor from February to May
Monitor-Monitor	• Monitor from November to February • 20 or more CWPM in February • Monitor from February to May

Note: CWPM = Correct Words Per Minute

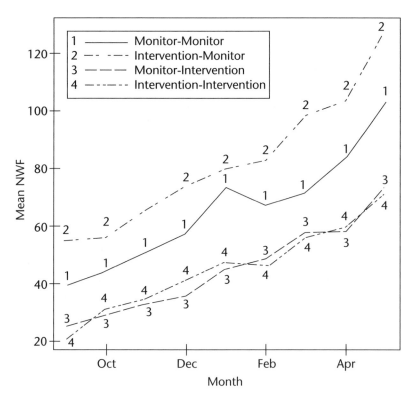

Figure 3.   Nonsense word trajectories of four groups based on February raw-score adjustments.

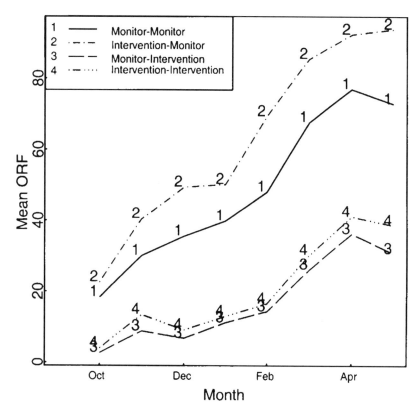

Figure 4.   Oral reading fluency trajectories of four groups based on February CWPM raw-score adjustments.

random assignment to treatment and the between-group comparability at the outset of the study, the retrospective creation of groups based on February performance revealed clear differences among the starting points of students within their respective groups. Trajectories 1 and 3 represent the 31 students originally assigned to the Monitor condition. Trajectories 2 and 4 represent the 28 students in the Maintenance Intervention. On oral reading fluency, for example, irrespective of original assignment, students who were discontinued from intervention in February read 20 correct words per minute in October of Grade 1 while their peers who did not reach the 20 CWPM criterion in February and hovered slightly above zero CWPM in October.

Figures 3 and 4 likewise depict end-of-year outcomes on nonsense word and oral reading fluency. Students who received no additional intervention beyond February, on average, read 80.85 (*SD* = 36.21) correct words per minute (CWPM), and attained a mean standard score of 116.54 (SD = 9.40) on the Basic Skills Cluster of the WRMT-R in May of Grade 1. As a point of reference, the mean correct words per minute for the 28 students in the AA comparison group was 71.21 (SD = 36.21), and their Basic Skills Cluster standard score was 115.57 (SD = 12.08).

End of year progress for students who received intervention from February through May (Groups 3 and 4) was markedly lower, M ORF = 34.91, (SD = 13.41) and corresponds to the 29th percentile in a national sample of 30,221 first-grade students (Good et al. 2002).

Using a multi-level model and a Bonferroni adjusted alpha level to keep Type I error at .05 for 3 group comparisons (.05 / 3 = .017), analyses of slopes for the four groups on ORF from October to May revealed significantly lower monthly growth rates for the Monitor-Intervention and Intervention-Intervention groups as compared to the Monitor-Monitor group (5.30 vs. 8.59, t = −3.24, p = .001 and 4.65 vs. 8.59, t = −3.72, p = .001 respectively) but a non-significant higher monthly growth rate for the Intervention-Monitor group as compared to the Monitor-Monitor group (10.55 vs. 8.59, t = 1.64, p = .101). Analyses of slopes for the four groups on NWF from September to May revealed non-significantly lower monthly growth rates for the Monitor-Intervention and Intervention-Intervention groups as compared to the Monitor-Monitor group (5.54 vs. 7.08, t = −1.27, p = .205 and 5.71 vs. 7.08, t = −1.08, p = .280 respectively) and a non-significant higher monthly growth rate for the Intervention-Monitor group as compared to the Monitor-Monitor group (8.62 vs. 7.08, t = 1.07, p = .283).

For end-of-year achievement on normative-reference measures, a between-groups, one-way analysis of variance on all 6 first grade groups (the AA group, the 4 groups achieving benchmark levels in the fall and the group that did not achieve benchmark levels in the fall) indicated a significant effect on May word identification, $F(5, 99)$ = 9.410, p < .001, and May passage comprehension, $F(5, 99)$ = 13.22, p < .001. Planned comparisons among the 4 groups achieving benchmark levels in the fall using the Tukey-Kramer procedure (critical point = 2.61 for alpha .05 and 6 simultaneous contrasts) revealed that the Intervention-Monitor group was significantly higher than the Intervention-Intervention group, q = 2.84 and q = 2.78, for word identification and passage comprehension respectively. Planned comparisons of the AA group to each of the 4 groups achieving benchmark levels in the fall using the Dunnett procedure (critical point = 2.51 for Dunnett's statistic, d, for alpha .05 and 4 simultaneous contrasts) indicated that the Intervention-Intervention group was significantly lower than the AA group on word identification ($d = -2.66$) and the Intervention-Intervention ($d = -3.58$) and Monitor-Intervention ($d = -3.16$) groups were both lower than the AA group on passage comprehension. Planned comparisons of the group that did not achieve benchmark levels in fall to each of the 4 groups achieving benchmark levels in the fall using the Dunnett procedure (critical point = 2.49 for alpha = .05 and 4 simultaneous contrasts) revealed that all 4 groups were significantly higher than the below benchmark group (d ranged from 2.90 to 5.30) for word identification and for passage comprehension (d ranged from 3.45 to 5.68). This comparison confirmed that students who entered first grade with higher scores and consequently received no additional intervention maintained the magnitude of difference over students who entered with lower scores and received intervention from November through May.

Were Interventions Sufficient to Maintain Adequate Reading Performance?

Performance on end-of-year standardized reading measures revealed strong levels of performance across groups with mean scores within the average to above-average ranges. Means for each of the groups exceeded the 50th percentile on the word attack, word identification, and passage comprehension subtests (See table VI). Probabilities that the 59 students in the combined sample would attain average levels of reading performance on the word attack, word identification, and passage comprehension subtests of the Woodcock Reading Mastery Test follow.

Criterion	Probability
≥ 30th percentile on word attack	59/59 = 1.00
≥ 30th percentile on word identification	56/59 = .95
≥ 30th percentile on passage comprehension	55/59 = .93
≥ 50th percentile on word attack	55/59 = .93
≥ 50th percentile on word identification	50/59 = .85
≥ 50th percentile on passage comprehension	46/59 = .78

If we use the criterion of 30th percentile or above as an indicator for adequate reading performance (Torgesen 2000), the instructional interventions did not prevent reading difficulties for all participants. For word identification, 3 of the 59 (5%) students fell below the 30th percentile cut score; 4 students or 7% fell below the 30th percentile in passage comprehension.

Table VI. Means and Standard Deviations of End-of-First Grade WRMT-R Subtests by Condition

Reading Measures	Condition							
	Monitor/Monitor		Intervention/Monitor		Monitor/Intervention		Intervention/Intervention	
	Mean	(SD)	Mean	(SD)	Mean	(SD)	Mean	(SD)
Word Attack	118.38	(8.61)	119.01	(10.84)	113.47	(8.04)	112.20	(9.64)
Word Identification	113.48	(9.74)	118.14	(10.38)	107.80	(8.41)	105.61	(10.05)
Passage Comprehension	106.50	(7.54)	109.90	(6.19)	101.53	(6.62)	100.94	(7.90)

What Factors Contribute to End-of-Grade-1 Success?

We now examine factors that account for and predict successful Grade 1 performance for children who enter kindergarten in the bottom quartile of performance on phonologic and letter naming measures. We used discrete time event history analysis to model the time it took (in months, 7 altogether) a child to reach the benchmark level of 40 or more correct words per minute on unpracticed, grade-level text. This score of 40 CWPM in our full sample of 77 students corresponded to a standard score of 107.3 on the Basic Skills cluster of the WRMT-R. The correlation coefficient between the two measures in May of Grade 1 was .73. In a sample of 30,221 first graders, a series of 40 CWPM corresponds to the 34th percentile on spring first grade oral reading fluency (Good et al. 2002).

To identify the factors most responsible for the variability in the time to reach benchmark, we conducted separate univariate analyses on all candidate predictors. We then estimated four separate models where each set of predictors came from one of four points in time: fall of kindergarten, winter of kindergarten, spring of kindergarten, and fall of Grade 1. Our goal was to identify the best predictors from each period. Data from all children in the sample (the 59 students who met fall of Grade 1 benchmarks and the 18 students who did not) were used in this analysis except for 4 children who were already above the benchmark level in October of Grade 1. To put effects sizes into perspective, the estimated coefficient for a predictor can be exponentiated to get the multiplicative change in the odds of making benchmark for each one unit increase of the predictor. One minus the exponentiated coefficient times 100 is the percentage change in the odds of making benchmark.

In fall of kindergarten, the best additive predictor proved to be a 1-minute letter dictation task modified from Berninger et al. (1997). The letter-dictation score was strongly significant and increased the odds by 43% for every unit increase. Therefore, a child 1 standard deviation (2.35) above the mean of 3.28 letters written in 1 minute is 5.4 times more likely to make benchmark than a child 1 standard deviation below the mean.

Results for winter of kindergarten predictors indicated that only nonsense word fluency was significant and each unit increase raised the benchmark rate by 14%. A child 1 standard deviation (10.73) above the mean of 20.06 is 16.1 times more likely to make benchmark than a child 1 standard deviation below the mean.

Results for the end of kindergarten indicated that two variables were significant, letter naming fluency (M 32.53; $SD = 16.48$)

and oral reading fluency on decodable text (M = 8.09; SD = 7.94). A two standard deviation increase raises the odds of making benchmark by 3.3 and 4.8 for letter naming and oral reading, respectively. Results for the fall of Grade 1 also showed several predictors to be important including October oral reading fluency (M = 5.93; SD = 7.42), (14% increase in odds per unit, 7.4 increase for 2 SD shift), fall word identification raw score (M = 11.5; SD = 8.48), 16% increase in odds per unit, 13.0 increase for 2 SD shift) and fall rapid automatized naming (M = 50.42; SD = 14.47) (7% increase in odds per unit, 7.6 increase for 2 SD shift).

Effects from the fall of first grade were considerably stronger than kindergarten effects. None of the significant predictors from kindergarten were significant in the presence of the fall of Grade 1 predictors. Fall of Grade 1 group assignment had a significant impact on the time to benchmark; the two randomly assigned groups that achieved benchmark levels in the fall of Grade 1 were not significantly different from each other (.092, t = .50, p = .615). However, the contrast of the average of these two groups versus the group that did not achieve benchmark levels in the fall was significant (-.84, t = −3.40, p = .001). The significant contrast between the pooled high achieving groups and the low achievers was mediated by nonsense word fluency from October of first grade, one of the selection variables used to create the groups (group contrast = −.44, t = −1.55, p = .122; NWF = .08, t = 4.60, p < .001). The other selection variable, phonemic segmentation, was not significant (−.01, t = −.82, p = .411). In turn, the three final predictors in the fall of first grade model mediated the effect of nonsense word fluency (NWF = .03, t = 1.41, p = .160; October ORF = .13, t = 2.10, p = .037; Word ID = .14, t = 2.41, p = .016; rapid automatized naming = .06, t = 2.34, p = .012). Thus, it would appear that word identification, oral reading fluency and rapid automatized naming would be better selection variables for identifying reading risk in the fall of Grade 1 for children who were also at risk during kindergarten than nonsense word fluency or phonemic segmentation.

THE PROMISE OF PREVENTION: ATTAINING AND MAINTAINING PROFICIENCY

The promise of prevention is that early reading instruction, if carefully designed with the right combination of phonologic, alphabetic, and orthographic elements and strategically delivered within a specified "window" of time, can reduce if not prevent the need for further intervention for children initially identified as at risk for reading failure. Intervention studies validate that large pro-

portions of children can attain average levels of reading achievement with intensive intervention (e.g., O'Connor 2000, Torgesen
et al. 1999, Vellutino et al. 1996). In this two-year longitudinal
study, we investigated the efficacy of primary prevention in
kindergarten and the conditions necessary to sustain adequate
reading performance in Grade 1. Of particular relevance was the
viability of providing early reading interventions in conditions
that approximate the realities of schools; that is, in small groups
with existing personnel.

The first question addressed how to optimize effects of
kindergarten intervention. Specifically, what emphasis of code and
comprehension instruction for children with identified phonologic
and letter naming risk best accelerates rates of learning to read?
Teachers in the CE condition spent 100% of their time on code-
based activities. In contrast, teachers in the CCE condition divided
their time amongst phonologic, alphabetic, vocabulary, and comprehension dimensions. The CP group spent 100% of its time on
code emphasis instruction that was less explicit than the CE group.
Findings from the kindergarten intervention offer promise that supplemental interventions that emphasize the phonologic and alphabetic dimensions of the alphabetic writing system can put the
majority of children who performed in the bottom quartile of fall
predictor indicators on solid footing at the end of kindergarten.
Only 9% of the children designated with reading risk performed
below the 30th percentile on the WRMT word attack and 18% on
measures of word identification at the end of kindergarten. Average
end-of-kindergarten performance indicated strong response by all intervention groups on the Basic Skills Cluster of the WRMT-R, with
the mean of the least effective intervention a respectable standard
score of 100.

Two previous kindergarten intervention studies provide a
basis for comparison. Torgesen et al.'s (1999) longitudinal study of
the bottom 12% of children identified as at-risk in kindergarten
who received the most effective form of one-to-one tutoring for
the second half of the kindergarten year attained a raw score of .76
on the word attack subtest and a score of 2.7 (SD = 3.1) words on
the WRMT word identification subtest at year's end. By comparison, the mean raw scores of students in our strongest kindergarten
intervention for word attack and word identification respectively
were 10.81 (SD = 7.36) and 7.50 (SD = 4.51).

O'Connor (2000) worked with the lowest performing 40% of
kindergarten students and found that children she characterized as
high-gain, at-risk students had a standard score of 89.4 (SD = 6.2)
on the Woodcock Johnson letter-word identification subtest. For

comparative purposes, students in the CE condition of our study attained a standard score of 109.31 (*SD* = 9.79) on the word identification measure of the WRMT-R.

We offer these comparators with due caution as it is difficult to generalize findings across early intervention studies for obvious reasons (e.g., sample selection, criterion selection measures, interventions). Vellutino et al. (1996), for example, sampled from the bottom 9% of students, Torgesen et al. (1999) the bottom 12%, O'Connor the lowest 40%, and this study the bottom 25%. This matter, nonetheless, has bearing if we are to address the dimensions of prevention more precisely. What levels of performance, on what measures, and at what point in time should be used to identify children who are at risk?

To evaluate the extent to which students attained adequate levels of proficiency, we also compared end-of-kindergarten performance to a cohort of above-average achievers from the same local schools. Despite significant differences between the above-average and at-risk groups in October (e.g., 15 letters vs. 3; 18 first sounds vs. 7), analyses indicated that in the most powerful intervention (CE), there were no reliable differences from the above-average cohort on measures of PSF, NWF, or word identification and word attack at the end of kindergarten. Overall, this finding suggests instructional emphasis mattered and positioned exiting kindergarten children with performance proficiencies that endured well into Grade 1.

Of further interest in our kindergarten study was not *whether* children reached particular outcome levels but *when* they reached these levels. Efficiency of instruction and corresponding response to intervention have particular relevance for children who enter kindergarten with low levels of proficiency on predictor measures. As Vellutino et al. (1996) documented, the acceleration rate of learning provides further information on students who will attain adequate levels of reading proficiency. Duration to benchmark analyses indicated that performance on NWF fluency in March of kindergarten strongly related to successful attainment of 40 CWPM at the end of Grade 1. Students who read 31 letter sounds per minute in March were 16 times more likely to reach the 40 CWPM criterion at the end of Grade 1. Students in the CE group reached the NWF kindergarten benchmark of 20 letter sounds per minute two months earlier than students in the other conditions.

For end of kindergarten, oral reading fluency on decodable text and letter naming fluency emerged as the strongest predictors. Specifically, students who read 16 correct words per minute were almost 5 times more likely to reach the end-of-Grade-1 criterion of 40 correct words per minute than students who read no words correctly. Likewise, students who could name 50 letter names in one minute were 3 times more likely to reach the end-of-Grade-1 benchmark than students who could identify 16 letter names per minute. Duration to benchmark analyses are an indicator for when children will reach critical benchmarks. These findings are relevant to the response to remediation (Vellutino et al. 1996) and learning rate (Bryne, Fielding-Barnsley, and Ashley 2000) methods that are increasingly the foci of research involving children identified as nonresponders or treatment resisters. Methods and measures designed to study the level and rate of response in a timely and instructionally sensitive manner have critical bearing on the design of optimal interventions (Good, Simmons, and Kame'enui 2001).

Though end of kindergarten outcomes were our initial focus, the stability and sustainability of those effects were of equal interest. If children attain adequate levels of reading proficiency, what does it take to maintain proficiency and what factors predict successful end-of-first-grade outcomes? To address this question, 59 children who met beginning-of-Grade-1 benchmarks engaged in a two-phase intervention study with instructional adjustments at midyear. Because of the mid-course instructional adjustments in response to student performance, the answer to how much intervention is required becomes necessarily complex. A central finding of this study is that children who enter with higher entry scores on oral reading fluency attain end-of-year benchmarks earlier and maintain this learning trajectory irrespective of supplemental intervention. We now know that students who read approximately 13 correct words per minute in October of Grade 1 are 5 times more likely to reach the end-of-first-grade benchmark of 40 correct words per minute than students who read zero correct words per minute. A fundamental question for schools, however, is how to determine whether students will require further intervention. From the present study, we can conclude that all 16 students who read on average 13 correct words in October scored above the 30th percentile on word attack, word identification, and passage comprehension without additional intervention. Moreover, all but one student read 40 correct words per minute in May of Grade 1. It appears that the general education reading program was sufficiently rich and robust that children not only derived adequate benefit but did not require supplemental intervention.

The lesson we learned from this study is that a nomothetic orientation based on averaged group data (see Fuchs et al. 2002) masked the individual differences that may require tailored interventions. Despite this rather obvious conclusion, few studies have employed "differentiated" and "dynamic" instructional designs. Vellutino et al. (1996) employed individualized instructional plans while O'Connor (2000) used layers of intervention to accommodate individual performance and response to intervention. This, however, is an understudied but essential next step if we are to advance our understanding of how to maximize reading growth. In this study, we adjusted intervention for more than 50% of children based on their February performance. Fifteen children who were originally assigned to the monitor intervention group began fluency-based interventions in February. Of the 33 students who participated in intervention from February through May, 100% performed at or above the 30th percentile on word attack, 90% on word identification, and 87% on passage comprehension. Sixty-three percent met the oral reading fluency criterion of 40 correct words per minute. The question that remains is whether these students would have attained adequate levels of proficiency without intervention. Unfortunately, to answer this question would have required us to withhold intervention for some students.

The finding that all but 3 children would be above the critical criterion on word identification, and all but 4 above the critical criterion on passage comprehension is of particular importance as previous investigations have difficulty effecting adequate passage comprehension growth (Foorman et al. 1998, Torgesen, et al. 1999). We must, however, put these findings in context. The sample in this study represented 59 of the 77 students who responded strongly to kindergarten intervention and entered first grade with adequate phonologic and alphabetic skills. Conclusions regarding comprehension outcomes are, therefore, yoked to entry-level performance in fall of Grade 1.

Limitations and Implications for Practice

This study corroborates previous findings that explicit reading intervention in kindergarten can bring the majority of children who perform low on early reading indicators within average ranges of performance. In the absence of a no-treatment control group, we cannot definitively conclude that this level of response could not have occurred by chance. This limitation notwithstanding, there is ample evidence from well-conducted research indicating that in the absence of intervention many children do not catch up (Foorman et al. 1998, Lovett, Lacerenza, and Borden 2000, Torgesen et al. 1999). The question of importance then becomes when to intervene. If we do not intervene in kindergarten, do we fail to capitalize on a critical window of opportunity (Vellutino et al. 1996) *or* can we compensate with highly intensive reading interventions in Grade 1? This question begs a response.

A second factor requires further investigation that involves the use of benchmark cut scores to gauge levels of reading proficiency. In fall of Grade 1, we used a combination of 35 on PSF and 20 on NWF to identify children who had reached adequate levels of proficiency. Though informed by prior research (Good et al. 2000), the cut scores we used to determine whether children required further intervention were determined before we had benefit of the national sample of more than 30,000 students per benchmark level (Good et al. 2002). This information now allows us to make more selective decisions using percentile rankings. For instance, we now know that an NWF score of 55 in fall of Grade 1 corresponds to the 30th percentile, while a score of 20 relates to the 33rd percentile. As schools face tough decisions regarding how many children can receive primary prevention, reliable indicators become increasingly important. Duration to event analyses from the current study indicated that oral reading fluency and word identification may serve as more reliable predictors of children who are on adequate learning trajectories in the fall of Grade 1. Oral reading fluency is not typically administered in fall of Grade 1, therefore, we have no national comparison with our current work. The word identification measure from the *Woodcock Reading Mastery Test*, though a highly reliable and valid measure, may not be feasible for individual administration to all children because of the time commitment.

We selected 20 correct words per minute in midyear of Grade 1 based on analysis of prior performance. This score corresponded to the 39th percentile from our national database. Sharpening the precision of these scores can substantially increase their decision-making utility in future intervention research. As we move toward more dynamic measurement and instructional adjustments to better address individual differences, reliable means of making these decisions with parsimonious and sensitive measures is another focus of importance. Through this study, we were able to discern that 40 CWPM on oral reading fluency corresponded to a score of 107 on the Basic Skills Cluster of the WRMT-R and the 34th percentile from a national sample.

Finally, perhaps one of the most encouraging findings is that significant and meaningful results can be obtained *in the complex environment of schools*. We began with a premise that if primary prevention worked, it would prevent the need for intervention or lessen the need for intensive intervention. Though we cannot draw firm conclusions as to whether reading disability was prevented, we feel confident that the sequence of explicit and systematic kindergarten intervention coupled with systematic monitoring and instructional adjustments in first grade represent a reasonable and effective plan for schools to pursue. Moreover, we are confident that schools can implement these methodologies. The findings of this study were realized in the context of schools that are implementing research-based reading programs, that are collecting formative progress measures on all children, and that invest seriously in professional development. These conditions notwithstanding, prior to this study, these seven schools were not systematically providing intervention in kindergarten. Today, because of these findings and research agenda, these schools are all providing these interventions in kindergarten. Perhaps this is yet another positive dimension of maintenance we failed to anticipate.

REFERENCES

Adams, M. J., Bereiter, C., Brown, A., Campione, J., Carruthers, I., Case, R., Hirshberg, J., McKeough, A., Pressley, M., Roit, M., Scardamalia, M., and Treadway Jr., G. H. 2000. *Open Court Reading.* Columbus, OH: SRA.

Adams, M. J. 1990. *Beginning To Read: Thinking and Learning About Print.* Cambridge, MA: MIT Press.

American Federation of Teachers. 1999. *Building on the Best, Learning from What Works: Seven Promising Reading and English Language Arts Programs.* Washington DC: Author.

Berninger, V. W., Vaughan, K. B., Abbott, R. D., Abbott, S. P., Rogan, L. W., Brooks, A., Reed, E., and Graham, S. 1997. Treatment of handwriting problems in beginning writers: Transfer from handwriting to composition. *Journal of Educational Psychology* 89:652–66.

Byrne, B., Fielding-Barnsley, R., and Ashley, L. 2000. Effects of preschool phoneme identity training after six years: Outcome level distinguished from rate of response. *Journal of Educational Psychology* 92:659–67.

Cowen, E. L. 1982. Primary prevention research: Barriers, needs and opportunities. *Journal of Primary Prevention* 2(3):131–37.

Coyne, M., Simmons, D., Kame'enui, E., and Harn, B. in preparation. Beginning Reading Intervention as Inoculation or Insulin: An Examination of the First Grade Reading Performance of Strong Responders to Kindergarten Intervention.

Dunn, L., and Dunn, L. 1981. *Peabody Picture Vocabulary Test—Revised.* Circle Pines, MN: American Guidance Service.

Englemann, S., and Bruner, E. C. 1995. *Reading Mastery: Rainbow Edition.* Columbus, OH: SRA.

Foorman, B. R., and Torgesen, J. 2001. Critical elements of classroom and small-group instruction promote reading success in all children. *Learning Disabilities Research & Practice* 16:203–12.

Foorman, B. R., Francis, D. J., Fletcher, J. M., Schatschneider, C., and Mehta, P. 1998. The role of instruction in learning to read: Preventing reading failure in at-risk children. *Journal of Educational Psychology* 90:37–55.

Fuchs, D., Fuchs, L. S., Thompson, A., Al Otaiba, S., Yen, L., Yang, N. J., and Braun, M. 2002. Exploring the importance of reading programs for kindergartners with disabilities in mainstream classrooms. *Exceptional Children* 68:295–311.

Good, R. H., and Kaminski, R. A. 2002. Nonsense Word Fluency. In *Dynamic Indicators of Basic Early Literacy Skills (6th ed.)*, eds. R. H. Good and R. A. Kaminski. Eugene, OR: Institute for the Development of Educational Achievement. Available: http://dibels.uoregon.edu/.

Good, R. H., Kaminski, R. A., and Smith, S. 2002. Phoneme Segmentation Fluency. In *Dynamic Indicators of Basic Early Literacy Skills (6th ed.)*, eds. R. H. Good and R. A. Kaminski. Eugene, OR: Institute for the Development of Educational Achievement. Available: http://dibels.uoregon.edu/.

Good, R. H., Wallin, J. U., Simmons, D. C., Kame'enui, E. J., and Kaminski, R. A. 2002. *System-Wide Percentile Ranks for DIBELS Benchmark Assessment* (Tech. Rep. No. 9). Eugene, OR: University of Oregon.

Good, R. H., Simmons, D. C., and Kame'enui, E. J. 2001. The importance and decision-making utility of a continuum of fluency-based indicators of foundational reading skills for third-grade high-stakes outcomes. *Scientific Studies of Reading* 5:257–88.

Good, R., Kaminski, R., Shinn, M., Bratten, J., Shinn, M., and Laimon, D. 2000. *Technical Report #7: Technical Adequacy and Decision Making Utility of DIBELS*. Eugene, OR: University of Oregon, Early Childhood Research Institute.

Learning First Alliance. 1998. Every child reading: An action plan of the Learning First Alliance. *American Educator* 1-2:52–63.

Lovett, M. W., Lacerenza, L., and Borden, S. L. 2000. Putting struggling readers on the PHAST Track: A program to integrate phonological and strategy-based remedial reading instruction and maximize outcomes. *Journal of Learning Disabilities* 33:458–76.

Marston, D., and Deno, S. L. 1987. *Tests of Oral Reading Fluency: Measures for Screening and Progress Monitoring in Reading*. Minneapolis, MN: Children's Educational Services, Inc.

National Reading Panel. 2000. *Teaching Children To Read: An Evidence-Based Assessment of the Scientific Research Literature on Reading and its Implications for Reading Instruction: Reports of the Subgroups*. Bethesda, MD: National Institute of Child Health and Human Development.

National Research Council. 1998. *Preventing Reading Difficulties in Young Children*. Washington, DC: National Academy Press.

No Child Left Behind, 2002, Title I, Part B, Student Reading Skills Improvement Grants, Subpart 1, Reading First.

O'Connor, R. 2000. Increasing the intensity of intervention in kindergarten and first grade. *Learning Disabilities Research & Practice* 15:43–54.

O'Connor, R. E., and Jenkins, J. R. 1999. Prediction of reading disabilities in kindergarten and first grade. *Scientific Studies of Reading* 3:159–97.

Share, D. L. 1995. Phonological recoding and self-teaching: Sine qua non of reading acquisition. *Cognition* 55:151–218.

Share, D. L., and Stanovich, K. E. 1995. Cognitive processes in early reading development: Accommodating individual differences into a model of acquisition. *Issues in Education: Contributions from Educational Psychology* 1:1–57.

Simeonsson, R. J. 1994. Promoting children's health, education, and well-being. In *Risk, Resilience, & Prevention*, ed. R. J. Simeonsson. Baltimore: Paul H. Brookes.

Simmons, D. C., Kame'enui, E. J., Good, R. H., Harn, B. A., Cole, C., and Braun, D. 2002. Building, implementing, and sustaining a beginning reading improvement model school by school and lessons learned. In *Interventions for Academic and Behavior Problems II: Preventive and Remedial Approaches*, eds. M. Shinn, G. Stoner, and H. M. Walker. Bethesda, MD: National Association of School Psychologists.

Sprick, M. M., and Howard, L. M. 2000. Write *Well: Spelling*. Longmont: CO: Sopris West.

Sprick, M. M., Howard, L. M., and Fidanque, A. 1998. *Read Well*. Longmont, CO: Sopris West.

Stanovich, K. E. 1986. Matthew effects in reading: Some consequences of individual differences in the acquisition of literacy. *Reading Research Quarterly* 21:360–406.

Torgesen, J. K., Alexander, A. W., Wagner, R. K., Rashotte, C. A., Voeller, K. K. S., and Conway, T. 2001. Intensive remedial instruction for children with severe reading disabilities: immediate and long-term outcomes from two instructional approaches. *Journal of Learning Disabilities* 34:33–58,78.

Torgesen, J. K. 2000. Individual differences in response to early interventions in reading: The lingering problem of treatment resisters. *Learning Disabilities Research & Practice* 15:55–64.

Torgesen, J. K., Wagner, R. K., Rashotte, C. A., Rose, E., Lindamood, P., Conway, T., and Garvan, C. 1999. Preventing reading failure in young children with phonological processing disabilities: Group and individual responses to instruction. *Journal of Educational Psychology* 91:579–93.

Vellutino, F. R., Scanlon, D. M., Sipay, E. D., Small, S. G., Pratt, A., Chen, R., and Denckla, M. B. 1996. Cognitive profiles of difficult-to-remediate and readily remediated poor readers: Early intervention as a vehicle for distinguishing between cognitive and experiential deficits as basic causes of specific reading disability. *Journal of Educational Psychology* 88:601–38.

Willett, J. B., and Singer, J. D. 1991. How long did it take? Using survival analysis in educational and psychological research. In *Best Methods for the Analysis of Change: Recent Advances, Unanswered Questions, Future Directions*, eds. L. M. Collins and J. L. Horn. Washington, DC: American Psychological Association.

Woodcock, R. 1987. *Woodcock Reading Mastery Test—Revised*. Circle Pines, MN: American Guidance Service.

Chapter • **8**

Intervention for Struggling Readers:
Possibilities and Challenges

Carolyn A. Denton and Patricia G. Mathes

In recent years, unprecedented attention has been given to the goal of universal literacy, and there have been substantial gains in our understanding of how to prevent reading difficulties in the great majority of children (Snow, Burns, and Griffin 1998; Langenberg et al.. 2000). Nevertheless, large numbers of American students struggle to become competent readers (U.S. Department of Education 2001) and many are placed in special education for a learning disability in reading (Shaywitz 1996). Currently, learning disability (LD) is the most commonly identified type of disability for public school students in the United States (Lyon et al. 2001), and nearly 80% of students with identified LD are so labeled because they have not learned to read efficiently (Commission on Excellence in Special Education 2002). Lyon and his colleagues (2001) have hypothesized that the need for special education services within the category of learning disability could be dramatically reduced if schools identified children early for risk of reading difficulties and implemented intensive, systematic intervention. Even so, there is ongoing debate about when reading difficulty constitutes a learning disability and who should and should not receive special services for reading problems (Gresham 2001; Jenkins and O'Connor 2001).

Traditionally, educators and researchers have sought to identify categories of struggling readers with various specific deficiencies, with the hope of finding specific treatments that would remediate the problems of students in each group (Vaughn, Gersten, and Chard 2000). This conception implies that some reading subprocesses are inherently different in these readers from those processes used by "normal" readers (Grigorenko 2001). An alternate view is that dyslexia is a matter of quantity rather than quality. In this paradigm, reading ability exists on a continuum, with the least proficient readers occupying the lower tail of the distribution (Grigorenko 2001). In this chapter we explore this conceptualization of reading ability and disability and its implications for the identification of students who have severe reading disabilities or dyslexia. We then discuss practical implications of the implementation of a model of prevention and intervention based on the conception of reading ability and disability as variability in the format and duration of instruction required by individual students to become successful readers. Finally, we outline some of the components of a research agenda necessary to provide the foundation for such a model.

IDENTIFYING STUDENTS WHO HAVE READING DISABILITIES

Traditionally, the presence or absence of reading disability in American school children has been defined in absolute terms, as unexpected underachievement characterized as a discrepancy between achievement and intellectual aptitude, usually demonstrated through a difference between scores on an IQ test and a norm-referenced test of reading achievement. For the most part, only students who meet these criteria currently qualify for special education services under the LD label. In this context, reading disability is perceived as a finite condition that can be identified through the administration of objective tests. Inherent in the discrepancy model is the perception that differences in IQ and aptitude test scores can reliably detect real differences in students who have "true" reading disabilities and students whose low reading achievement is not due to dyslexia. In the current paradigm, many struggling readers who do not demonstrate the discrepancy do not qualify for supplemental assistance, even though they may experience serious reading problems.

Unfortunately, we have learned that the aptitude-achievement discrepancy model does not, in fact, discriminate reliably between students who respond quickly to quality intervention and those who have more severe difficulties that require extended and intensive services (Fletcher et al. 1992; Lyon et al. 2001; Stanovich 1991; Stuebing et al. in press). Studies indicate that there is, at best, a tenuous relationship between IQ and intervention outcomes (Foorman et al. 1997; Foorman et al.1998; Francis et al. 1996; Hatcher and Hulme 1999; Torgesen et al. 1999; Vellutino, Scanlon, and Lyon 2000).

Contributing to the lack of validity of the discrepancy model is the fact that it tends to favor students with higher IQ scores, as it is difficult for a student with a low average IQ to exhibit achievement scores low enough to produce the discrepancy. Further, excluding cultural deprivation in the current definition of LD can result in the withholding of services to students from impoverished backgrounds, although there is no evidence that reading problems resulting from a lack of environmental stimulation and those caused by an assumed neurological problem can be discriminated. In fact, recent studies of brain activation patterns of children with serious reading problems from both affluent and impoverished environments evidence similar neurological dysfunction, suggesting that a reading problem is a reading problem, regardless of its source (i.e., environmental or genetic) (Simos et al. 2002). Furthermore, factors associated with inadequate instruction, emotional disturbance, and poverty may actually cause differences in neurological and cognitive development that lead to severe learning difficulties (Lyon et al. 2001). Genetic and neurological research has demonstrated that, although some individuals have a genetic predisposition for the development of reading difficulties or dyslexia, the presence and the severity of their difficulties are mediated to a large degree by their environments (Grigorenko 2001). All of these factors call into question the validity of a model that categorizes students as having or not having a disability on the basis of discrepant test scores. This is not to negate the concept of learning disability. There certainly are a number of individuals with severe learning disabilities that impede their acquisition of literacy. However, there is no evidence that these students can be reliably identified through discrepant test scores.

An Alternative Model

In response to the poor validity of the current model for identifying learning disability, it has been proposed that reading disability may be characterized as poor response to high quality instruction (Gresham 2001). As such, reading ability and disability are viewed as existing within a continuum of needs. As asserted by Foorman and Torgesen (2001), at-risk status is not only a product of conditions inherent within the student, but is always associated with a "mismatch between child characteristics and the instruction that is provided" (p. 206). Reframing reading ability as a continuum of need for support in literacy acquisition has the potential of prompting educators to respond to struggling readers according to their demonstrated learning requirements, rather than according to the category to which they have been assigned.

Practically interpreted, the continuum of need implies that some children learn to read very easily, requiring little or no formal instruction, while others require instruction of substantially greater explicitness and intensity. Juel and Minden-Cupp (2000) observed that, in the four classrooms they studied, students who entered first grade with high levels of reading proficiency had little need for extended explicit instruction, but benefitted most from a reading program including high levels of engaged practice reading trade books. Other children require explicit instruction within their classrooms, and still others need more intense supplemental instruction offered in addition to their classroom reading programs. A smaller group of students need instruction of even greater intensity and duration in order to acquire adequate reading skills (Foorman and Torgesen 2001). In a conceptualization of reading ability and disability in terms of varying instructional needs, only those children who require very intense instruction of long duration would be considered reading disabled. The need for this intense instruction would be determined by continuously assessing each child's response to high quality reading instruction. Under such a model, student needs would be determined using ongoing, frequent measures of word recognition, fluency, vocabulary, and comprehension, as well as subskills that correlate strongly with reading development (Stuebing et al. in press).

The Three-Tier Model

This response-to-instruction approach has been depicted as having three tiers, as illustrated in figure 1. On the first tier, classroom-level general education instruction is enhanced to reflect the tenets of empirically validated best practices in reading (see Snow et al. 1998; Langenberg et al. 2000). Children who still experience difficulty after receiving quality classroom-level instruction move into more intense second-tier intervention. In the three-tier intervention model, only after these two levels of intervention have proven inadequate would a child be considered to have a reading disability, requiring tertiary intervention. Presumably, at this

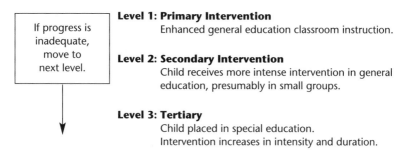

Level 1: Primary Intervention
>Enhanced general education classroom instruction.

Level 2: Secondary Intervention
>Child receives more intense intervention in general education, presumably in small groups.

Level 3: Tertiary
>Child placed in special education.
>Intervention increases in intensity and duration.

If progress is inadequate, move to next level.

Figure 1:   The three-tier model for preventing reading disability

point special education services would be provided (Gresham 2001; Mathes and Denton 2002; Vaughn and Linan-Thompson 2002). Each of these three tiers of intervention will be discussed below.

The First Tier: Enhanced Classroom Instruction.   Under this three-tier model, all children would be provided with adequate classroom reading instruction in the earliest years of school. Recent consensus documents and research syntheses have identified the critical content for early reading instruction (e.g., Langenberg et al. 2000; Rayner et al. 2001; Snow et al. 1998). These documents suggest that this critical content includes provisions for emergent readers to develop phonological awareness, letter-knowledge, and skills required to implement phonetic decoding strategies within contextual constraints, in order to accurately identify novel words in print. For children who enter school at risk for reading difficulties, an effective curriculum needs to directly address the acquisition of accurate and quick word recognition skills, speed and ease of reading connected text, extensive engagement with authentic literature, and strategies for enhancing the deep processing of text.

The Second Tier: Supplemental Secondary Intervention.   Although high quality classroom-level instruction has been shown to be adequate to support the development of a large proportion of students, some continue to demonstrate the need for further support (Foorman et al. 1998). In the three-tier model, children whose rates of progress in literacy acquisition demonstrate the need for more explicit or extended instruction, despite inclusion in high quality early reading instruction, would be identified as at-risk for reading difficulties and receive supplemental second-tier instruction. The determination of the need for supplemental intervention would be made in the early stages of literacy acquisition, in kindergarten or first grade, before reading problems become intractable. Students who do not learn to read well in first grade rarely catch up to their peers on their own (Francis et al.1996; Juel 1988; Torgesen and Burgess 1998). Foorman and Torgesen (2001) describe effective intervention for students at-risk for reading failure as being more intense, more explicit, more comprehensive, and more supportive (with more careful and consistent instructional scaffolding) than can usually be effectively implemented within regular classroom reading programs.

The Third Tier: Intervention of Extended Duration and Intensity. In the three-tier model, children who continued to acquire reading at a slow rate after the provision of second-tier supplemental instruction would receive intervention of longer intensity and duration, and would be eligible for special education services. Continued support beyond the initial acquisition of reading skill would be available to all students as needed, to ensure continued academic growth into the upper grades (e.g., Mathes and Torgesen 1998). Thus, all students who are identified as at-risk for possible reading problems would be provided with intervention within general education. Only children who did not make adequate progress would be considered for a reading disabilities label. This label would not be based on IQ-achievement discrepancies, but rather on inadequate response to quality intervention (Gresham 2001; Torgesen et al. 2001).

KEY QUESTIONS

Although this provision of intervention to students according to a continuum of needs is intuitively appealing, the complete model has yet to be evaluated empirically, although research of this type is underway (D. M. P. Kamps, personal communication June 4, 2002; S. R. Vaughn, personal communication February 8, 2002). Many questions must be addressed before such a model can be successfully implemented on a large scale. Some of these include: (a) What percentage of students with reading difficulties are likely to respond adequately to intervention at each level? (b) What criteria should be used to indicate that students have made sufficient progress and no longer require secondary intervention? and (c) How long should students be provided with secondary intervention before the determination is made that tertiary intervention is warranted?

What percentage of students with reading difficulties are likely to respond adequately to intervention at each level?

Primary Intervention. Research suggests that the Primary classroom level of intervention is adequate to reduce substantially the large numbers of struggling readers in our schools. For example, Foorman and her colleagues (1998) found that classroom-level explicit instruction in phonological awareness and the alphabetic principle, along with opportunities to apply skills in reading and writing, brought the majority of students in grades 1 and 2 in eight high-poverty schools to national averages. Similarly, peer tutoring based on a program combining practice in alphabetic decoding and engaged reading has shown robust results as a classroom-level intervention (Allor et al. 2000; Mathes et al. in press; Mathes et al. 1998; Mathes, Torgesen, and Allor 2001).

In our own research, we have observed that at-risk students in an enhanced classroom condition made strong progress, although their scores were significantly lower than students who received our secondary interventions (Mathes et al. 2003). In this tier 1 intervention, we monitored the oral reading fluency progress of each at-risk student in our study every three weeks, and provided easily interpretable graphs of student progress to classroom teachers, intervention teachers, principals, and parents. In addition, we provided inservice training to classroom teachers in the use of assessment data to plan differentiated instruction and in partner reading routines (Mathes et al. 2001), and we offered consultation relating to literacy instruction to teachers if needed. This was done in the context of curricular materials and district staff development that were well aligned with scientifically based best practices in early reading instruction.

Table I presents the findings of studies that illustrate the power of solid classroom-level instruction in the prevention of reading problems. In total, these studies demonstrate that nationally, if core classroom instruction conformed to empirically proven best practice, only about 6% or less of children should be expected to experience reading problems requiring secondary intervention.

Secondary Intervention. The prevalence of reading difficulty can be further reduced through supplemental secondary intervention, delivered in addition to high quality primary level instruction within general education, either by the classroom teacher or by additional general education personnel such as reading specialists. Such instruction might be delivered in the students' classroom or in another location within the school. Currently, researchers have

Table I.   Impact of high quality classroom level instruction on the percentage of children who require secondary reading services defined as reading below the 30th percentile after intervention

Study	Hours of Instruction	Student/ Teacher Ratio	Reading %ile for Initial Identification of Risk Status	% of Lowest Readers Reading Below 30th %ile After Intervention	% of Students Reading Below 30th %ile after Intervention Extrapolated to The Total Population
Foorman et al., 1998	174	Classroom	18	30%	5%
Mathes et al., 2001	35	Classroom (Peer tutoring)	25	31%	6%
Allor et al., 2002	35–55	Classroom (Peer tutoring)	25	29%	6%
Mathes et al., in press	35	Classroom (Peer tutoring)	25	18%	5%

described several models of successful secondary-level interventions. For example, Torgesen et al. (1997) identified children in kindergarten who had poor phonological awareness. By second grade, secondary intervention that included explicit, systematic instruction in phonological awareness and phonetic decoding brought 75% of these children to grade-level performance in phonetic reading skills. Vellutino and colleagues (1996) identified middle-class children with very low word recognition skills at the beginning of grade 1. After one semester of intervention, 70% were reading at grade level. After two semesters, over 90% were at grade level.

Table II presents examples of the effect of secondary intervention alone on the numbers of children who can be expected to have severe reading difficulties requiring tertiary (special education) services. In examining this table, it is important to note the teacher to child ratio and the number of hours of instruction because it is likely that the number of students who remain poor readers is related to both the duration and intensity of the intervention. Intensity is increased as the number of students in a group decreases.

Combining Primary and Secondary Intervention.   Lacking in the current body of intervention research are studies in which both primary and secondary levels of intervention have been provided to children at-risk for reading disabilities. A recent study conducted

Table II. Impact of high quality secondary level instruction on the percentage of children who require tertiary reading services defined as reading below the 30th percentile after intervention

Study	Hours of Instruction	Student/ Teacher Ratio	Reading %ile for Initial Identification of Risk Status	% of Lowest Readers Reading Below 30th %ile After Intervention	% of Students Reading Below 30th %ile after Intervention Extrapolated to The Total Population
Felton, 1993	340	1:8	16	24%	3.8%
Vellutino et al., 1996	35-65	1:1	15	30%	4.5%
Torgesen et al., 1999	88	1:1	12	23%	4.0%
Torgesen et al., in press	92	1:3	18	8%	1.0%
Torgesen et al., 2002	80	1:3	18	4%	.7%

by our research group at the University of Texas Health Science Center Houston, under funding from the Interagency Educational Research Initiative (J. M. Fletcher; P. G. Mathes; C. A. Denton and others) has examined the impact of primary and secondary intervention in tandem, providing an indication of what might be possible if the three-tier model were enacted as proposed (see Mathes et al. 2003).

This study of early literacy intervention took place in six elementary schools located in a large urban center. The schools served populations that were ethnically and economically diverse. During each of two years, we identified within these schools a sample of first-graders who showed significant risk for reading difficulties. Once identified, all children designated as at-risk within a school were randomly assigned to one of three conditions: Proactive Reading (*n* = 82), Responsive Reading (*n* = 83), or Quality Classroom only (*n* = 92).

As described above, in the Quality Classroom primary-tier intervention, teachers received professional development on accommodating academic diversity and linking assessment data to instructional planning. We then provided graphs reflecting frequent progress-monitoring of oral reading fluency for each child who participated in the study. Teachers were also offered consultation on individual children upon demand. On-the-minute time sampling observations of instruction in these classrooms confirmed that teachers allocated instructional time to critical elements of early literacy, using time in a manner similar to teachers in other studies with demonstrable effects for primary level instruction (e.g., Foorman and Schatschneider in press).

At the second tier, we provided one of two supplemental interventions, Proactive or Responsive Reading. Both Proactive Reading and Responsive Reading were delivered by highly trained certified teachers working with small groups of three children at a time. This instruction occurred daily for 40 minutes from October to May in addition to the regular classroom reading instruction. Thus, intervention children received a "double dose" of reading each day.

The first of the two secondary interventions, Proactive Reading, consists of a structured approach to instruction that provides carefully sequenced direct instruction and guided practice in phonemic awareness and alphabetic knowledge and skills, integrated with the application of the alphabetic principle and comprehension strategies in decodable text. The second intervention, Responsive Reading, also provides explicit alphabetic code instruction and comprehension strategy instruction with guided practice (although less time is spent practicing phonological elements and skills in isolation than in the Proactive format), and supports children in their application of phonemic decoding and comprehension strategies through extensive contextual reading and writing experiences, using books leveled for difficulty but not phonetically decodable. The essential difference in the design of the Proactive and Responsive Reading interventions is that the former follows a prescribed scope and sequence designed to reduce errors, separate confusing elements, and apply newly learned skills to highly decodable text, while the later provides no specified scope and sequence, and instead uses student responses as the source for planning and delivering instruction. Both interventions are comprehensive, integrated approaches to reading instruction that incorporate the principles from research outlined in recent consensus documents (i.e., Langenberg et al. 2000; Snow et al.1998), but reflect the differences in philosophy characteristic of reading education.

Full results of this study are not yet available, but early data analysis provides support for the implementation of a combination of primary and secondary intervention. Initial results indicate that many at-risk students were able to attain average reading performance with the provision of primary intervention alone. Only 16% of the at-risk students who received only enhanced classroom instruction performed below the 30th percentile on the year-end test of basic reading skills. However, students who received secondary intervention in addition to enhanced classroom instruction demonstrated significantly higher outcomes than those who received the primary intervention alone on several measures of reading and reading-related skills, including word identification, phonemic awareness, and oral reading fluency. Outcomes for the two secondary intervention groups did not differ significantly. Likewise, the numbers of children in the Proactive and Responsive groups who did not achieve normal performance on measures of word reading were very small. Only one child out of 80 who received the Proactive intervention and 8 out of 83 Responsive students failed to reach the average range on the Woodcock-Johnson III (W-J III, Woodcock, McGrew and Mather 2001) Basic Skills cluster at the end of first grade.

In sum, the evidence from our research and that of others we have cited suggests that, if high-quality primary and secondary instruction were regularly provided in our public schools, less than 2% of our children would require tertiary intervention. Currently, 5% to 17% of persons are identified as having reading disabilities, depending on how the category is defined (Shaywitz 1996).

Tertiary Intervention.   The potential power of effective tertiary intervention for eradicating reading failure is largely unknown. Traditional approaches to special education instruction for students with reading disabilities have produced lackluster gains, characterized by Torgesen and his colleagues (2001) as "stabilizing their degree of reading failure rather than remediating, or normalizing, their reading skills" (p. 34). Vaughn, Moody, and Schumm (1998) observed that many students identified as having learning disabilities do not receive small group differentiated instruction in the resource room. Likewise, many teachers in their study did not provide explicit instruction in phonological recoding, the construct most closely identified with severe reading disability (see Lyon 1995). However, in each of these studies, special education was not linked to high quality primary and secondary intervention, so they do not reflect the potential of tertiary instruction, but rather the limitations of our current model.

Insight into the potential of well-executed Tier 3 intervention comes from Torgesen and others (2001), in their study of intensive intervention with severely impaired readers, ages 8 to 10, who had previously been identified as having learning disabilities. Students in the interventions received instruction in one of two models, the Auditory Discrimination in Depth Program (now known as the

Lindamood Phoneme Sequencing Program for Reading, Spelling and Speech, Lindamood and Lindamood 1998), or an embedded phonics approach. Both interventions included explicit, systematic instruction in word-reading skills, but had different approaches to delivering this instruction. The most striking characteristics of the interventions offered in this study were their intensity and duration. Students received 1:1 intervention daily in two 50-minute sessions separated by a short break for a period of 8 to 9 weeks, for a total of 67.5 hours of instruction. Outcomes for students in the two groups were not significantly different; both made dramatic gains in standard score points in measures of both decoding and comprehension that persisted two years after the conclusion of intervention. Their reading rate, however, remained impaired. A particularly encouraging outcome of this study was the fact that about 40% of the students who were tutored because of severe reading problems were able to return full-time to the general education classroom in the year following the intervention, no longer in need of special education services.

From this important research, we can deduce that a relatively brief, but highly intense, tertiary intervention has the potential to "normalize" the decoding and comprehension skills of many students with severe reading difficulties, and that these effects may be maintained over time. The limited progress of these students in reading rate is of concern, and implies that they may need continued support, especially if they receive reading instruction in the regular education classroom. Further, the Torgesen et al. (2001) study demonstrates that even highly diverse intervention formats can be equally effective as tertiary interventions, if they include explicit, systematic instruction in word-identification strategies and are delivered with sufficient intensity.

What criteria should be used to indicate that students have made sufficient progress and no longer require secondary intervention?

Although examples from research at each level of intervention indicate that high quality instruction has the potential to substantially reduce reading failure within our schools, they provide little guidance about how to determine when children have responded adequately to intervention. Yet, in order to implement a "response to intervention" model for the identification of students with reading disabilities, criteria must be established that denote success in quality primary and secondary intervention. In order to explore this question, we examine the responses of students in our study to the Proactive Reading and Responsive Reading interventions.

Basic Reading Subskill Criteria

In our intervention study, we first evaluated response to intervention using the W-J III Basic Skills cluster, with scores at or above the 30th percentile indicating successful performance in the normal range. The Basic Skills cluster, a composite of Letter-Word Identification and Word Attack, was chosen because it is a norm-referenced evaluation of the ability to read words in lists, a construct closely linked to the presence of reading disability (see Lyon 1995). We selected the 30th percentile as the benchmark because it represents the lower boundary of the average range on the test.

In our study, 99% of the Proactive Intervention group in the two cohorts combined (*n* = 80) were able to perform at or above the 30th percentile on the Basic Skills cluster at the end of grade 1, with only one child out of the group not achieving this goal. Ninety percent of the students in the Responsive Intervention (n = 83) met this minimal benchmark, with 8 students scoring below the 30th percentile. Furthermore, 88% of the Proactive students and 81% of the Responsive students attained the 50th percentile on the same measure (Mathes et al. 2003). Thus, applying the criteria of performance in the low-average to average range on the tests of word identification and word attack suggests that few of the at-risk students in our study remained severely impaired in basic reading skills at the end of grade 1.

Oral Reading Fluency Criteria. Another criteria that could be used to evaluate response to intervention is oral reading fluency rate, usually measured in terms of the number of words read correctly per minute (WPM). Fluency (when it includes the component of reading accuracy) is a more stringent measure of reading competence than evaluation of reading subskills, as it requires the integration and automatization of decoding skills (LaBerge and Samuels 1974; Langenberg et al. 2000). Rayner and his colleagues (2001), in their analysis of the psychological aspects of reading acquisition, emphasize the importance of practice. As children gain facility with reading and practice in text, the child's lexicon, or number of words known in detail and recognized at sight, is built up. This practice effect, the authors state, "promotes many words to a functionally high-frequency status," adding that "Texts that contain a high proportion of familiar words will be read well, and the occasional low-frequency word provides an opportunity for phonological self-teaching" (p. 40). Further, reading practice facilitates the development of reading comprehension, vocabulary growth, and spelling (Rayner et al. 2001). With the development of so many literacy processes and skills dependent on efficient, fluent reading that comes with repeated practice, students who can read fluently in first grade are better positioned for overall success than their less fluent peers.

In application, reading rate has potentially large effects on a student's day-to-day classroom performance. Completion of assignments by students whose reading is labored requires increased task persistence that may be difficult to maintain. As reading accuracy is a component of oral reading fluency, it is likely that students whose fluency is not following normal patterns of development are unable to read accurately some assigned work without support. Thus, oral reading fluency may be an important marker for success in intervention programs.

Good and his colleagues (2002) analyzed the oral reading fluency scores of more than 36,000 first graders on passages contained in the Dynamic Indicators of Basic Early Literacy Skills (DIBELS). They determined that, in the spring of first grade, the 30th percentile (or the floor of the low-average range) for this group was equal to a raw score of 35 WPM, while the 50th percentile was equal to a raw score of 54 WPM. Using these benchmarks as criterion for adequate treatment response for children in our study, we found that 82% of the Proactive Group and 77% of the Responsive Group were able to read at least 35 WPM by the end of first grade, meeting the goal of low-average performance. This is in contrast to the 99% and 90% of each group, respectively, that attained the same percentile rank on the W-J III Basic Skills cluster administered in the same period. Using fluency goals, 47% of the Proactive students and 55% of the Responsive met the benchmark of 54 WPM, associated with the 50th percentile, while 88% and 81% of each group, respectively, performed at the mean on the word reading measure (Mathes et al. 2003).

We were also interested in the role that the end-of-first-grade fluency rate of students in our study might play in (a) their teachers' perception of their competence in first grade, reflected by retention status, and (b) the success experienced by these students in the following year. In order to explore these questions, we analyzed longitudinal data collected at the end of year 2 for all students who had participated in the first year of our study, in relation to the same students' oral reading fluency scores at the end of year 1. This full year 1 cohort (n = 169) represents students in each of the three at-risk conditions, along with a group of randomly-selected students who did not display risk characteristics.

Fluency and Retention in Grade.   Of the students in this cohort who never attained the fluency goal of 35 WPM, 42% were retained in first grade, while only 4% of the students who did meet this benchmark were retained. Comparing the performance levels of the 20 retainees in W-J III Basic Skills and in oral reading fluency, we found that 95% (all but one) had end-of-year-one Basic Skills scores at or above the 30th percentile, and 60% had performed at the mean. Their fluency was more impaired, with 75% of the group failing to meet the 35 WPM benchmark, and 85% failing to read at or above 54 WPM by the end of year 1. Interestingly, two of the retainees had oral fluency rates at or above 83 WPM. For the most part, teacher perceptions of the relative competence of students in our study may have been related to their oral fluency rate, and to their performance in the processes associated with the development of fluency.

Fluency and Future Performance in Basic Reading Skills. Students from our first cohort were given the W-J III subtests at the end of year 2, in order to monitor the maintenance of gains of students who had received intervention in year 1. We analyzed the relationship between these students' oral reading fluency at the end of year 1 and their year 2 W-J III Basic Skills cluster scores. This analysis indicated that, in our study, reading rate at the end of first grade had a significant relationship to students' word identification and word attack skills one year later.

Although the results of the research cited in this chapter strengthen the indication that the percentage of students with serious reading difficulties could be substantially reduced through the provision of quality second-tier intervention, it is critical that researchers continue to examine exit criteria for secondary intervention that are realistic, but also indicative of a high probability of continued progress in reading. Fluency may be the criteria with the most practical utility, as it has been linked to multiple literacy processes, including reading comprehension (see Rayner et al. 2001).

How long should students be provided with secondary intervention before the determination is made that tertiary intervention is warranted?

Closely related to the question of appropriate criteria for exit from second tier intervention is consideration of the length of time that this intervention should be offered to students before the determination is made that tertiary intervention is warranted. In other words, how do we know that our interventions have succeeded, and when do we determine that more intensive intervention is necessary?

Vaughn and Linan-Thompson (this volume) present a thorough discussion of the question of duration of intervention. These researchers explicitly studied the number of weeks of supplemental instruction required by a cohort of second graders who had persistent reading difficulties to reach pre-established reading performance criteria and exit intervention. These criteria were based primarily on oral reading fluency, with a score of 55 WPM set as the goal for exit from the intervention. The researchers provided secondary intervention to these students and assessed their progress at ten-week intervals. They found that approximately one fourth of the students met exit criteria after 10 weeks, one fourth after 20 weeks, and one fourth after 30 weeks. The last group did not meet exit criteria by the end of the 30-week period. Of the students who exited after 10 to 20 weeks of intervention, about 40% failed to show sufficient continued growth in their classroom reading programs (defined by the authors as a gain of at least 1 WPM per week) through the rest of the school year, and appeared to need further support. This indicates that they may have benefitted from a more extensive secondary intervention or a "maintenance" intervention of lower intensity.

In our current research, each child in the secondary intervention groups received this intervention from October through May of their first grade year, as we did not employ exit criteria. During this time their progress in oral reading fluency was monitored, as described above. As an indication of the length of time in intervention that might be required for students in each group to attain exit criteria based on reading rate, we analyzed the number of weeks in intervention that were required for each of these students to reach the benchmarks of 35 and 54 WPM. The fluency probes were administered in three-week intervals, so we computed the percentage of students in each group that achieved each benchmark at the end of 9 weeks, 21 weeks, and 30 weeks, along with the percentage that never achieved the designated fluency levels. The results of this analysis are reported in table III.

Table III. Cumulative percentage of students in Proactive Reading and Responsive Reading who met oral reading fluency benchmarks with varying lengths of time in intervention and the percentage who never attained the benchmarks

Fluency Goal	35 WPM		54 WPM	
Intervention	Proactive	Responsive	Proactive	Responsive
9 Weeks	2%	0%	1%	0%
21 Weeks	37%	46%	16%	20%
30 Weeks	82%	77%	47%	55%
Never	18%	23%	53%	45%

Note. WPM = Words read correctly per minute

Although from 37% to 46% of the first grade students in our secondary interventions attained the minimum fluency benchmark of 35 WPM after 21 weeks in intervention, about the same number of students required the entire 30-week period to reach this goal. If exit criteria were based on a stringent fluency criteria of 54 WPM (the 50th percentile), most students in this study would have required the full 30 weeks to meet the benchmark, and about half of the children would never have met it. Moreover, our analysis indicated that the rate at which first graders in our study achieved the 35 WPM goal (within 9 weeks, 21 weeks, 30 weeks, or not at all), and the rate at which they achieved the goal of 54 WPM, were significantly related to the trajectory of their future progress in reading.

Taken together, evidence from the Vaughn and Linan-Thompson (this volume) second-grade intervention study and our current research indicates that there exists a percentage of struggling primary-grade readers who can meet established literacy goals fairly rapidly when provided with secondary-level intervention, another group who eventually meet the goals if provided intervention over an extended length of time, and a third group who require more intensive intervention to develop oral reading fluency. The rate of student learning from quality intervention likely has implications for their level of need for subsequent support. In the Vaughn and Linan-Thompson study cited above, students who met the benchmark for success after the first 10 weeks continued to make adequate progress in their classroom reading programs for the next 10 weeks, although most of them lost this momentum in the third 10-week period. Students who met the exit criteria after 20 weeks were much less likely to sustain their rate of growth without subsequent support.

Support for this effect of learning rate comes from research described by Byrne, Fielding-Barnsley, and Ashley (2000). In their longitudinal analysis of effects of a preschool training program in phonological awareness, they found that some effects of preschool training persisted through grade 5. Within the experimental group, however, some students who had been successful in the intervention as young children were very poor readers in fifth grade. Further analysis of their data indicated that students who made slower progress in the preschool intervention, although they eventually reached criterion levels, tended to have more reading difficulties later in their school careers. They concluded that "children who are slow to grasp ideas early in reading development, even though they do finally grasp them, are liable to remain slow to acquire other principles or episodic traces that contribute to accurate word identification" (p. 666).

Thus, rate of response to instruction has strong potential for determining student needs for intervention of increasing intensity and duration. Consequently, the length of time in secondary intervention may be decreased, with the assumption that students who require long periods of time to reach exit goals may not sustain their gains after intervention has ceased, and therefore require tertiary intervention. Conversely, some students may avoid tertiary intervention through the provision of long-term maintenance intervention to support their continued progress. More longitudinal research is necessary to evaluate these hypotheses.

A RESEARCH AGENDA

Although we have research evidence as to effective models of reading intervention at the primary and secondary levels, and more limited knowledge of potentially effective tertiary intervention, we do not as yet know whether a three-tier reading intervention model can be consistently implemented to identify students in need of more intense special services reliably. This suggests a research agenda that addresses salient features of a model based on student response to "high quality" intervention as it would be implemented in diverse school settings.

A primary research question regarding this approach relates to the intervention formats that would be considered appropriate primary, secondary, and tertiary interventions in a wide-scale implementation. Our current study, and the work of Torgesen et al. (2001), suggest that effective intervention may take place in formats that originate from different theoretical perspectives. In the study conducted by Torgesen and his colleagues, severely impaired students tutored with an embedded phonics approach made comparable dramatic gains in basic reading skills to those of students receiving tutoring using a highly structured phonologically based intervention. In our study, students in two secondary interventions demonstrated comparable positive outcomes, although the interventions originated from opposing conceptualizations of effective early reading instruction. The common elements in these studies that appear critical for effective secondary and tertiary intervention are explicit instruction in phonological recoding and high treatment intensity. This proposition should be further validated, as a guide for policymakers who must decide the nature of "high quality" intervention in a three-tier model.

As we have demonstrated in this chapter, adequate response to this quality intervention might be determined using various measures of reading or reading-related skills. Our work suggests that oral reading fluency may be a more valid indicator of response to instruction than standardized tests of basic reading skills. The question of markers of adequate response can only be answered through longitudinal research that evaluates maintenance of intervention effects using diverse types of measures.

Similarly, only longitudinal studies can inform the determination of the optimum duration of secondary intervention prior to the onset of tertiary. The trajectories of oral reading fluency development of students in our current study suggest that some first grade students seem to integrate reading subskills sufficiently for the efficient reading of text only after substantial time in secondary intervention. Students who display a slower rate of acquisition of efficient reading may, in fact, require ongoing intervention in order to continue to make sufficient progress. This question is an important component of a research agenda related to response to intervention.

An additional primary question regarding the wide-scale implementation of a model such as the one we have described focuses on how such a model based on instructional practices that have been validated in research projects can be implemented well across multiple and diverse school contexts. Denton and Fletcher (this volume) suggest that many factors influence the successful large-scale replication of educational innovations, including qualities of the innovations themselves, the perceived rewards and costs of implementation, the existence of support networks for educators who are instigating change, and the model employed for disseminating and sustaining the innovation. The research agenda for implementation of a response-to-instruction model must address these questions regarding large-scale replication of research-based practices.

We propose that the implementation of such a model is worth the effort it would require. Overall, educators' conceptualization of reading ability and disability as a continuum of needs, and the implementation of a response to instruction model for the provision of intervention to children who need it, have the potential to: (a) dramatically reduce the numbers of students who persist in severe reading difficulties; (b) allocate resources to students who need them in ways that would be beneficial to those students, regardless of the source of their difficulties; and (c) make educators sensitive to the instructional needs of all children, rather than using a categorical label as an excuse for lowered expectations of success.

CONCLUSION

Our understanding of reading disability is evolving. It is clear that many students struggle to develop reading competence. Although most of these students exhibit common characteristics related to difficulties in processing the sounds of language, we have yet to satisfactorily answer the question, "When is a reading difficulty a serious reading disability?" The current practice of identifying reading disability according to a discrepancy between IQ and achievement scores, although relatively easy to implement, has been shown to be invalid. A more useful way to identify reading disability may be through the evaluation of a student's response to well-implemented, quality intervention.

The practical implementation of such a re-conception of reading disability presents great challenges for researchers, policy makers, and practitioners. Even so, what is clear from repeated studies is that the need to label any child as reading disabled can be substantially reduced through high quality instruction provided early in a child's school career. If this model can be implemented, resource rooms will serve a smaller percentage of the school population, enabling them to focus personnel and time on the delivery of long-term, intensive, highly explicit literacy instruction for those students who require it. A model that conceptualizes reading ability and disability as a continuum of needs has the potential to bring us closer to the elusive goal of universal literacy.

ACKNOWLEDMENTS

This research was supported by a grant from the National Science Foundation, National Institute of Child Health and Human Development, and the U.S. Office of Education-Office of Educational Research and Innovation under the Interagency Educational Research Initiative, NSF 9979968.

REFERENCES

Allor, J. H., Mathes, P. G., Torgesen, J. K., and Grek, M. 2002. Using adult volunteers to enhance the effects of peer-assisted literacy strategies with first-grade struggling readers: Research to practice issues. Manuscript in preparation.

Byrne, B., Fielding-Barnsley, R., and Ashley, L. 2000. Effects of preschool phoneme identity training after six years: Outcome level distinguished from rate of response. *Journal of Educational Psychology* 92:659–67.

Commission on Excellence in Special Education 2002. A new era: Revitalizing special education for children and their families. Retrieved on August 6, 2002, from http://www.ed.gov/inits/commissionsboards/whspecialeducation/

Felton, R. 1993. Effects of instruction on the decoding skills of children with phonological-processing problems. *Journal of Learning Disabilities* 26:583–89.

Fletcher, J. M., Francis, D. J., Rourke, B. P., Shaywitz, S. E., and Shaywitz, B. A.1992. The validity of discrepancy-based definition of reading disabilities. *Journal of Learning Disabilities* 25:555–61, 73.

Foorman, B. R., Francis, D. J., Winikates, D., Mehta, P., Schatschneider, C., and Fletcher, J. M. 1997. Early interventions for children with reading disabilities. *Scientific Studies of Reading* 3:255–76.

Foorman, B. R., and Schatschneider, C. in press. Measuring teaching practice during reading/language arts instruction and its relation to student achievement. In *Reading in the Classroom: Systems for Observing Teaching and Learning*, eds. S. Vaughn and K. Briggs. Baltimore, MD: Brookes Publishing.

Foorman, B. R., and Torgesen, J. 2001. Critical elements of classroom and small-group instruction promote reading success in all children. *Learning Disabilities Research and Practice* 16:203–12.

Francis, D. J., Shaywitz, S. E., Stuebing, K. K., Shaywitz, B. A., and Fletcher, J. M. 1996. Developmental lag versus deficit models of reading disability: A longitudinal individual growth curves analysis. *Journal of Educational Psychology* 88:3–17.

Good, R. H., Wallin, J., Simmons, D. C., Kame'enui, E. J., and Kaminski, R. A. 2002. *System-wide Percentile Ranks for DIBELS Benchmark Assessment* (Technical Report 9). Eugene, OR: University of Oregon.

Gresham, F. 2001. Responsiveness to intervention: An alternative approach to the identification of learning disabilities. Paper presented at The Learning Disabilities Summit, Washington DC, August.

Grigorenko, E. L. 2001. Developmental dyslexia: An Update on genes, brains, and environments. *Journal of Child Psychology and Psychiatry* 42:91–125.

Hatcher, P., and Hulme, C. 1999. Phonemes, rhymes, and intelligence as predictors of children's responsiveness to reading remediation. *Journal of Experimental Child Psychology* 72:130–55.

Hoskyn, M., and Swanson, H. L 2000. Cognitive processing of low achievers and children with reading disabilities: A selective meta-analytic review of the published literature. *The School Psychology Review* 29:102–19.

Jenkins, J., and O'Connor, R. E. 2001. Early identification for young children with reading/learning disabilities. Paper presented at The Learning Disabilities Summit, Washington DC, August.

Juel, C. 1988. Learning to read and write: A longitudinal study of children in first and second grade. *Journal of Educational Psychology* 80: 437–47.

Juel, C., and Minden-Cupp, C. 2000. Learning to read words: Linguistic units and instructional strategies. *Reading Research Quarterly* 35:458–92.

LaBerge, D., and Samuels, S. J. 1974. Toward a theory of automatic information processing in reading. *Cognitive Psychology* 6:293–23.

Langenberg, D. N. and associates 2000. Report of the national reading panel: Teaching students to read: An evidence-based assessment of the scientific research literature on reading and its implications for reading instruction: Reports of the subgroups. Bethesda, MD: National Institute of Child Health and Human Development, National Institutes of Health.

Lyon, G. R.1995. Toward a definition of dyslexia. *Annals of Dyslexia*, 45:–27.

Lyon, G. R., Fletcher, J. M., Shaywitz, S. E., Shaywitz, B. A., Torgesen, J. K., Wood, F. B., Schulte, A., and Olson, R. 2001. Rethinking learning disabilities. In *Rethinking Special Education for a New Century*, eds. C. E.

Finn, A. J. Rotherham, and C. R Hokanson, Jr. Washinton, D.C.: The Fordham Foundation.

Mathes, P. G., Denton, C. A., Fletcher, J. M., Anthony, J. L., Francis, D. J., and Schatschneider, C. 2003. An evaluation of two reading interventions derived from diverse models. Manuscript in preparation.

Mathes, P. G., and Denton, C. A. 2002. The prevention and identification of reading disability. *Seminars in Pediatric Neurology* 9:185–91.

Mathes, Howard, Allen, and Fuchs 1998. Peer-assisted learning strategies for first-grade readers: Responding to the needs of diverse learners. *Reading Research Quarterly* 33:62–94.

Mathes, P. G., Torgesen, J. K., and Allor, J. H. 2001. The effects of peer-assisted literacy strategies for first-grade readers with and without additional computer assisted instruction in phonological awareness. *American Educational Research Journal* 38:371–410.

Mathes P. G. Torgesen, J. K, Clancy-Menchetti, J. C., Santi, K. L, Nicholas, K., and Robinson, C. in press. A comparison of teacher-directed versus peer-assisted instruction with struggling first-grade readers. *Elementary School Journal*.

Mathes, P. G. and Torgesen, J. K., 1998. All children can learn to read: Critical care for student with special needs. *Peabody Journal of Education* 73:317–40.

Rayner, K., Foorman, B. R., Perfetti, C. A., Pesetsky, D., and Seidenberg, M. S. 2001. How psychological science informs the teaching of reading. *Psychological Science in the Public Interest* 2(2):31–74.

Shaywitz, S. E. 1996. Dyslexia. *Scientific American* November:98–104.

Simos, P. G., Fletcher, J. M., Bergman, E., Breier, J. I, Foorman, B. R., Castillo, E. M., Davis, R. N., Fitzgerald, M, and Papanicolaou, A. C. 2002a. Dylexia: Specific brain activation profile becomes normal following successful remedial training. *Neurology* 1–10.

Simos, P. G., Fletcher, J. M., Foorman, B. R., Francis, D. J., Castillo, E. M., Davis, R. N., Fitzgerald, M., Mathes, P .G., Denton, C., and Papanicolaou, A. C. 2002b. Brain activation profiles during the early stages of reading acquisition. *Journal of Child Neurology* 17:159–63.

Snow, C. E., Burns, M. S., and Griffin, P. eds. 1998. *Preventing Reading Difficulties in Young Children*. Washington, DC: National Academy Press.

Stanovich, K. E. 1991. Discrepancy definitions of reading ability: Has intelligence led us astray? *Reading Research Quarterly* 26:7–29.

Stuebing, K. K., Fletcher, J. M., LeDoux, J. M., Lyon, G. R., Shaywitz, S. E., and Shaywitz, B. A. in press. Validity of IQ-discrepancy classifications of reading disabilities: A meta-analysis. *American Educational Research Journal*.

Torgesen, J. K., and Burgess, S. R. 1998. Consistency of reading-related phonological processes throughout early childhood: Evidence from longitudinal-correlational and instructional studies. In *Word Recognition in Beginning Reading*, eds. J. Metsala and L. Ehri. Hillsdale, NJ: Lawrence Erlbaum Associates.

Torgesen, J. K., Alexander, A. W., Wagner, R. K., Rashotte, C. A., Voeller, K. K. S., and Conway, T. 2001. Intensive remedial instruction for children with severe reading disabilities: Immediate and long-term outcomes from two instructional approaches. *Journal of Learning Disabilities* 34:33–58.

Torgesen, J. K., Mathes, P. M., and Grek, M. L. 2002. Effectiveness of an early intervention curriculum that is closely coordinated with the regular classroom reading curriculum. Paper presented at the Pacific Coast Research Conference, San Diego, CA, February.

Torgesen, J. K., Wagner, R. K., Rashotte, C. A., Alexander, A. W. and Conway, T. 1997. Preventive and remedial interventions for children with severe disabilities. *Learning Disabilities: A Multidisciplinary Journal* 8:1–61.

Torgesen, J. K., Wagner, R. K., Rashotte, C.A. and Herron, J. 2002. A comparison of two computer assisted approaches to the prevention of reading disabilities in young children. Manuscript in preparation.

Torgesen, J. K., Wagner, R. K., Rashotte, C. A., Rose, E., Lindamood, P., Conway, J., and Garvan, C. 1999. Preventing reading failure in young children with phonological processing disabilities: Group and individual responses to instruction. *Journal of Educational Psychology* 91:579–94.

U.S. Department of Education, 2001. *The Nation's Report Card: Fourth-Grade Reading* 2000. Washington, DC: National Center for Education Statistics.

Vaughn, S., Gersten, R., and Chard, D. J. 2000. The underlying message in LD intervention research: Findings from research syntheses. *Exceptional Children* 67:99–114.

Vaughn, S. R., Moody, S. W., and Schumm, J. S. 1998. Broken promises: Reading instruction in the resource room. *Exceptional Children*, 64, 211–25.

Vaughn, S. R., and Linan-Thompson, S. 2002. A three-tiered intervention model for reducing reading disabilities. Paper presented at the Council for Exceptional Children Annual Convention, New York, April.

Vellutino, F. R., Scanlon, D. M., and Lyon, G. R. 2000. Differentiating between difficult-to-remediate and readily remediated poor readers: More evidence against the IQ-achievement discrepancy definition for reading disability. *Journal of Learning Disabilities* 33:223–38.

Vellutino, F. R., Scanlon, D. M., Sipay, E. R., Small, S. G., Pratt, A., Chen, R., and Denckla, M. B. 1996. Cognitive profiles of difficult-to-remediate and readily remediated poor readers: Early intervention as a vehicle for distinguishing between cognitive and experiential deficits as basic causes of specific reading disability. *Journal of Educational Psychology* 88:601–38.

Woodcock, R. W., McGrew, K. S., and Mather, N. 2001. *Woodcock-Johnson III Tests of Achievement.* Itasca, IL: Riverside.

Chapter • 9

Early Reading Intervention:
A Classroom Prevention Study and a Remediation Study

Benita A. Blachman, Christopher
Schatschneider, Jack M. Fletcher, and
Sheila M. Clonan

The purpose of this chapter is to describe the effects of an early reading intervention that was first used with small groups of low-income kindergarten and first grade children in a classroom prevention study (Blachman et al. 1999) and recently adapted for a remedial study with second and third grade reading disabled children who received one-to-one tutoring (Blachman et al. 2003). This instructional model includes an explicit emphasis on the phonologic and orthographic connections between words and focuses on building the word level skills that are critical to reading success. The model incorporates both explicit skill-based instruction and text-based reading in an integrated approach for struggling readers. Although the focus in this chapter will be on what we learned at the end of kindergarten, first grade, and second grade in our prevention study and what we learned post treatment and from a one-year follow-up of the reading disabled students in our recent tutoring study, we will also describe the evolution of our instructional model, as we moved from a classroom prevention model to a remedial study with children who had already exhibited reading difficulties.

Despite what we have learned from research about preventing early reading failure (see, for example, the report commissioned by the National Research Council [Snow, Burns, and Griffin 1998] and the Report of the National Reading Panel [NRP 2000] commissioned by Congress), the evidence suggests that prevention studies have been more successful and have had a more pervasive effect on different reading skills than studies focused on children who have already evidenced failure (Lyon et al. 2001; Torgesen 2000). Consequently, we were particularly interested in how adaptable a classroom-based prevention model that had been shown to improve reading skills might be for second and third grade children with reading disabilities.

CLASSROOM PREVENTION MODEL

The goals of our classroom prevention model (Blachman et al. 1999)[1] were two-fold: (1) to evaluate the influence on reading of a phoneme awareness (PA) program carried out by kindergarten teachers and their teaching assistants, and (2) to build on this kindergarten program with a first-grade reading program that provided explicit and systematic instruction in the alphabetic principle and in the word-level skills known to be important for building accuracy, fluency, and comprehension.

In this study, kindergarten children were drawn from four, demographically comparable low achieving and low-income, inner-city schools in upstate New York. We specifically selected children who attended 4 of the 5 lowest achieving schools (out of 21 elementary schools) in this urban district, with 85% of the children receiving free or supported lunch. Prior to the intervention, the 84 treatment children and 75 control children, all of whom were nonreaders, attended different schools, but did not differ on age, sex, race, socioeconomic status (SES), *Peabody Picture Vocabulary Test-Revised* (PPVT-R, Dunn and Dunn 1981) scores, phoneme awareness, letter name and letter sound knowledge, or word recognition. The children, as a whole, were in the low average range in receptive vocabulary on the PPVT-R. Although the district's kindergarten program included letter name and letter sound instruction, these children had limited knowledge of the alphabet as indicated by the fact that they knew, on average, only two letter sounds in January of kindergarten (prior to the beginning of the

[1]This study was funded by a grant to the first author from the National Center for Learning Disabilities.

intervention) and most were reported by their classroom teachers to be unable to write their names. Knowledge of alphabetic sounds is one of the strongest predictors of subsequent reading achievement in kindergarten (Schatschneider et al. 2002).

In the spring of the kindergarten year, the treatment children participated in small group (four or five children) phonological awareness lessons (adapted from the shorter, 28 lesson program used in Ball and Blachman 1991) conducted by classroom teachers and their teaching assistants. There were a total of 41 lessons, each lasting 15 to 20 minutes, and conducted during an 11-week period. Each lesson included three activities: (1) "say-it-and-move-it," a phoneme awareness activity in which children move disks to represent the spoken sounds in one-, two-, or three-phoneme words, first segmenting the word with the disks and then pronouncing the word naturally (blending the word), (2) a phoneme awareness practice activity, such as grouping pictures on the basis of shared sounds, (3) and one of a variety of games to teach the names and sounds of eight letters.

At the end of 11 weeks of instruction, treatment children significantly outperformed the control children on measures of phoneme segmentation, letter name and letter sound knowledge, reading phonetically regular real words and pseudowords, and developmental spelling. It is interesting to note that the children received only 10 to 13 hours of instruction in phonological awareness and the connections between the sound segments and letters. This time frame is consistent with the 5 to 20 hours of phoneme awareness instruction found in the NRP (2000) meta-analysis (see also Ehri et al. 2001b) to yield the strongest effect sizes and the greatest transfer to reading. Thus, although the treatment children entered the study with the same low literacy skills as the control children, at the end of the intervention, the treatment children demonstrated superior knowledge of the internal structure of words. They demonstrated this knowledge not only on measures of phonological segmentation and letter sounds, but also in their ability to begin to read words with phonetically regular patterns and to produce more sophisticated invented spellings. These early invented spellings provide insight into how young children perceive the sound system of their language (see Read 1986; Templeton and Morris 2000). In our study, invented spellings were enhanced by instruction that emphasized phonological awareness and sound-to-print connections.

The children were followed during first and second grade (Blachman et al. 1999). During first grade (and continuing to second grade for some children), the program included 30 minutes of daily group reading instruction that built on the kindergarten phoneme awareness instruction and emphasized explicit, systematic instruction in the alphabetic code. Lessons were built around a five-step core described below:

1. At the beginning of each lesson, the teacher quickly reviewed sound-symbol associations that had been learned previously and introduced new sound-symbol correspondences. A sound pack (set of cards) showing one grapheme (i.e., letters and letter clusters) per card was used. Children were expected to give the name and sound of the letter, as well as a key word for consonants and short vowels.

2. Instruction in phoneme analysis and blending skills was introduced next. Instead of teaching children to sound out an unknown word letter by letter (e.g., *buh-a-tuh*), as is done in many classrooms, the teachers used a procedure adapted from Engelmann (1969) to teach children to pronounce as a single unit a consonant (continuant) followed by a vowel. This avoids much of the distortion that comes from trying to produce sounds (e.g., stop consonants) in isolation. As I. Y. Liberman and Shankweiler (1979) pointed out (see also A. Liberman et al. 1967 and I. Y. Liberman 1971), sounding out a word letter by letter makes it impossible to recover the original word (e.g., *bat*), regardless of how quickly the child tries to blend the sounds together. To teach children to pronounce as a single unit a consonant followed by a vowel, a small white board was used. Teachers began with a pattern like the following:

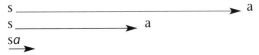

The child was taught to hold (or stretch out) the sound made by the first letter until the teacher pointed to the second letter, at which time the child would stretch out that sound. As the teacher pointed first to a consonant and then to a vowel, and as the letters were placed closer together, the length of time between sounds decreased until the two sounds were pronounced as a single unit. The teacher then added final consonants (initially, stop consonants) and the children learned to pronounce the whole word (e.g., *sat*). New short vowels were also introduced using this procedure. Most often, this activity was used only for a short time and then, depending on the needs of the children, eliminated from the lessons.

A second phoneme analysis and blending technique was used with all treatment children throughout the year. Adapted from a technique suggested by Slingerland (1971), the objective of this activity was also to help children learn to synthesize sounds without trying to blend the words letter by letter. Each child had a small pocket-chart (referred to as a "sound board") with consonants and vowels written on individual letter cards that were placed in the top pocket. Children were taught to manipulate the letters to form words. The teacher began by pronouncing a word, such as *fat*, emphasizing the vowel sound, and instructing the children to repeat the word, listen for the vowel sound, select the vowel grapheme that represented that sound, and move the vowel grapheme card from the top pocket to the lower pocket of the sound board. Next, the teacher repeated the word and instructed the children to identify the letter that represented the first sound in the word. The children then placed that letter in front of the vowel in the lower pocket. The teacher might then say, "Now we have *fa*. Our word is *fat*. What is the last sound we hear in *fat*?" After the children selected the *t* and put it at the end of the word, the children read the whole word naturally (i.e., they read the word as we would say it in normal speech). The teacher would then work through a series of preselected words, instructing the children to change *fat* to *fan*, for example, and, when new vowels were mastered, *fan* to *fin*. In a later lesson the children might change *fin* to *shin* and, eventually, as new syllable types were introduced on the sound board, change *shin* to *shine*.

3. The purpose of the third activity was to give children practice developing fluency reading words that they had practiced previously on the sound board. Specifically, phonetically regular words that the children had learned to construct and read accurately on the sound board (and new words with similar patterns) were put on flash cards and the children practiced reading them quickly. High frequency, irregular words were selected from the classroom basal reader and also introduced at this time. These words were written in a different color.

4. Next, children read connected text. Teachers selected stories from both phonetically controlled readers, such as the *Primary Phonics* series published by Educator's Publishing Service, and uncontrolled text from the Scott Foresman basal reading series used throughout the school district. (No other materials from the Scott Foresman series, such as workbooks, were used). All children went to the school library for additional reading material and also used trade books from their classroom libraries for independent reading at other times during the day. (It should be noted that although the sequence of activities and the materials used during the 30-minute reading lesson were the same in all the treatment classrooms, treatment teachers were free to use whatever books they thought appropriate for the rest of the day.)

5. The last step in each lesson was a short dictation activity. The teacher usually dictated four to six words and a sentence. The dictated words were selected from word lists practiced on the sound boards earlier in the lesson or words from the phonetically controlled readers. Children printed vowel headings at the top of each dictation page (e.g., *a* and *i*, or later, *ai, oa, ea*). These headings represented the particular vowel sounds that were the target sounds for that day's lesson. The dictation notebooks served as a record of student progress, as the children went from writing and reading simple closed syllable words (e.g., *ham*) to more complex syllable patterns (e.g., *lake, goat, bark*).

The goal of many of the early activities for the treatment children was to help the children develop accurate and fluent word recognition. At the same time, teachers were instructed to make sure that children were familiar with the meanings of all the words used in reading and spelling activities and a variety of strategies, such as retellings, were used to support story comprehension. As word recognition increased, time devoted to rereading stories and reading new stories increased. The control children, in contrast, spent 30 minutes of group reading instruction each day using a traditional basal reader and workbook and, at another time during the day, used a phonics workbook. Just as in the treatment classrooms, control children used trade books from school and classroom libraries at other times during the day. Both the treatment and control groups used the identical phonetically based spelling program required in all elementary schools in the district.

An assessment at the end of first grade revealed that the treatment children were significantly ahead of the control children on measures of phoneme awareness, letter name and letter sound knowledge, and three of four measures of word recognition. By the end of second grade, the treatment children significantly outperformed the control children on all four measures of word recognition, including a standardized measure of phonetically regular word and nonword reading and a standardized measure of word identification. The pattern in spelling was somewhat different. At the end of first grade, the treatment children significantly outperformed the control children on both a standardized spelling measure and an experimenter-devised measure of developmental spelling (for a detailed analysis of grade 1 spelling see Tangel and Blachman 1995). When the children were assessed again at the end of grade 2, there were no differences between the groups on the standardized measure of spelling (the only spelling measure administered at follow-up). A subsequent analysis, however, of spelling skill at the end of grade 2 that included only children in the lowest quartile in spelling found reliable differences between groups favoring the treatment children when partial credit was given for phonetically correct spelling, such as writing *lite* for *light*, on our standardized measure. In addition, the treatment children in the lowest quartile in spelling significantly outperformed the control children from the same quartile on all four measures of word identification. One possible explanation for the lack of spelling differences between the groups as a whole at the end of second grade was the fact that during both the first and second grade all children used the same phonetically based spelling program mandated by the school district. By the end of second grade, the level of spelling of the control children was comparable on a standardized measure to the level of spelling of the treatment children. However, their improved spelling did not appear to transfer to reading words. That is, at the end of second grade, we found that the children who had participated in phonological awareness instruction in kindergarten, followed in first grade by a phonetic approach for both reading and spelling, remained significantly ahead of the control children in reading words and nonwords.

Additional information from teachers reinforced our data regarding the superior reading of the treatment children. This school district used end-of-year performance on a reading test created by the district to determine recommendations for retention. At the end of second grade, teachers reported recommending 10 of the children in the control group for retention, while none of the children who had participated in our intervention were recommended for retention. In addition, teacher interviews at the end of second grade revealed that 31% of the control children were still reading in a first grade reader, while only 5% of the treatment children were still reading in a first grade reader. It is possible, of course, that these differences in book placement and retention were influenced by individual school factors (the treatment and control children began the study in different schools) and by the training provided to the treatment teachers. These factors were lessened somewhat by the fact that although the children attended only 4 of the 21 elementary schools in this district when the study began, when we completed our follow-up testing at the end of the second grade, the children were scattered among 14 of the 21 schools.

Finally, we think it is important to point out that the regular classroom teachers and the teaching assistants provided to all kindergarten teachers by the school district provided all instruction for this study. That is, we provided no additional teaching personnel to the schools. In addition, although the treatment children did have 10 to 13 hours of phonological awareness instruction in kindergarten, the intervention provided in first grade (and continuing to second grade for some children) did not increase the time spent on reading for the treatment children. Our 30-minute intervention, consisting of explicit alphabetic coding instruction and text reading using both decodable text and stories from the basal reading series, was merely a substitute for 30 minutes of basal reading instruction provided to control children. The remainder of the 90 minute language arts block was the same for both groups of children. *Thus, we changed very little in the overall scheme of the child's school day and yet saw marked differences in groups in terms of reading words at the end of second grade.*

Although a more extensive intervention might have increased differences between groups, it is important to recognize that much can be accomplished by changing relatively little and by working within the regular classroom constraints of a large, urban district. Professional development for teachers was also an important factor. We provided teachers with a theoretical framework for teaching phonological awareness and explicit teaching of the alphabetic code, aspects of instruction often lacking in teacher training programs (Liberman 1987; Moats 1995). We think this study provides evidence that when teachers are provided with an understanding of scientifically based principles of reading instruction, transferring this research to classroom practice is both possible and beneficial.

REMEDIAL TUTORING MODEL FOR SECOND AND THIRD GRADERS

In a recently completed study (Blachman et al. 2003)[2], we had the opportunity to adapt the classroom prevention model described above and evaluate its effectiveness with second and third grade poor readers who were selected on the basis of poor word-level skills. Children in our new study were tutored daily during either the second or third grade. Their progress was monitored for a year after the intervention ended—until the end of third grade for some children and the end of fourth grade for other children, depending on when they were tutored. In the remainder of this chapter, we will address the question—what did we learn about their reading and spelling post treatment and one year later?

We recruited the children for this study from 11 elementary schools representing four different school districts in upstate New York. To identify the children, we asked first and second grade teachers in May to identify right-handed children who were among the lowest 20% of readers in their classrooms. Children considered appropriate candidates for the study by their teachers were invited to participate in an initial screening. We screened a total of 295 children, administering the Word Attack and Word Identification subtests of the *Woodcock Reading Mastery Tests-Revised* (Woodcock 1987) and, when reading scores met our criteria, administering the WISC-III IQ (Wechsler 1991) test. Children were eligible for the study if they had a standard score below 90 (which put them below the 25th percentile) on either the Word Identification or the Word Attack subtest of the Woodcock and also if they had a standard score below 90 on the Basic Skills Cluster of the Woodcock. Children also had to have a Verbal IQ of at least 80. Eligible children were randomly assigned to either a treatment or control group. Our sample included 37 treatment and 32 control children who did not differ prior to intervention on age, IQ, mother's educational level, or Woodcock Word Attack, Word Identification, or Basic Skill Cluster scores.

---

[2]This research is part of a larger project that those of us in Syracuse and Houston are working on with Bennett Shaywitz and Sally Shaywitz at Yale Medical School and Ken Pugh and other colleagues at Haskins Laboratories. The major objective for the project is to evaluate the influence of an intensive reading intervention on the functional organization of the brain in children with reading disabilities. The research is one of several projects funded by a Center grant from the National Institute of Child Health and Human Development to the Yale Center for the Study of Learning and Attention. Bennett Shaywitz is the Principal Investigator for the Center grant. The research reported here is from a subcontract to Syracuse University, directed by the first author.

During the following school year, when the children were in second or third grade, the treatment children were given 50 minutes of one-to-one tutoring, five days per week. During the treatment year only, tutoring replaced any remedial reading help or resource instruction in reading that might otherwise have taken place outside of the regular classroom. Each child continued to get regular classroom reading instruction, but our project tutors served as their only out of class reading instruction for the year. Control children continued to get whatever services the school district provided, typically small group reading instruction provided by either a reading teacher or a special education resource teacher.

The tutors were all certified in reading or special education and all participated in an intensive 45-hour training program that the first author directed with a colleague, Darlene Tangel. Training was ongoing during the year, with approximately one, two-hour training meeting per month. To monitor treatment fidelity, each child was observed, on average, nine times during the course of the treatment year by either our tutoring coordinator, Rachel Karchmer, or one of the authors (Blachman or Clonan). In addition, tutors taped one lesson per week per child and these tapes were also used by two independent raters to monitor treatment fidelity. Two tapes for each child were rated (one from a three week period in the fall and one from a three week period in the spring), indicating that 90% of the lessons included all required elements. There was 100% inter-rater agreement.

Our tutoring program was structured to help children gain phonological knowledge and, at the same time, develop their understanding of how orthography represents phonology. Instruction was explicit, systematic, and focused on helping children understand the alphabetic principle. As in the first grade classroom prevention program described earlier, the core of the program was based on five steps: (1) a review of sound/symbol associations (e.g., showing a child a letter and asking the child to give the name, sound, and key word for the letter, as in "*a* says /a/ as in apple"), (2) practice making words by manipulating letter cards on a sound board (a pocket chart that holds the cards) or using scrabble tiles to develop specific decoding skills (e.g., making words with the closed syllable pattern, as in changing *lap* to *lip* to *flip*), (3) timed review of previously learned decodable words and high frequency sight words with the emphasis on building fluency, (4) oral reading of stories, and (5) dictation of words from earlier steps in the lesson. Accuracy and fluency were developed by learning the six basic syllable patterns in English. These include: closed syllables, as in *bat* and *stop*; silent "e" syllables, as in *same* and *plate*; open syllables, as in *go*, *she*, and the *si* in *si*lent; vowel + r syllables as in *car* and *torn*; vowel team syllables, as in *eat* and *pound*; and consonant + le syllables, as in can*dle* and sta*ple*. Children practiced reading these patterns in decodable texts, as well as in a wide variety of popular trade books. As children became more proficient readers, they progressed from reading single syllable words to multisyllable words made up of the previously learned syllable types (e.g., *Wisconsin*, a word many children might see as long and complicated, is made up of three, simple closed syllables). As the children progressed in reading, there was less need for their stories to be phonetically controlled (or decodable); thus, a wider array of reading material became available to them. For example, in addition to phonetically regular texts (such as *Primary Phonics*, Educator's Publishing Service 1995, and *Steck-Vaughn Phonics Readers*, Steck-Vaughn 1991), children read trade books that were not controlled (e.g., *Amelia Bedelia* series by Peggy Parish; *Arthur* series by Marc Brown) and expository texts reflecting, most often, science themes (e.g., *Curious Creatures* series, Curriculum Associates 1997). The selection of books varied according to the child's reading level and interest, but an important goal for all children was to get them "hooked on books" through reading a wide variety of trade books.

Although the five steps outlined in our first grade program remained the core of our remedial program, we made several specific changes to adapt our program for our second and third grade students. Throughout the lesson, there was a strong emphasis on more complex word structure (i.e., more work on multisyllable words) as soon as students showed some facility with closed syllables. We also placed a greater emphasis on fluency by including daily timed readings of isolated phonetically regular words and high frequency irregular words and included more text-based reading of both narrative and expository texts. Finally, tutors placed a greater emphasis on spelling dictation than had been the case in our earlier classroom-based prevention study. In our tutoring study, dictation was included daily, whereas in our prevention model described previously, teachers did not always get to dictation or alternated it with the sound board in order to complete the lesson in their allotted 30-minute time slot.

Figures 1 through 4 include sample pages from the dictation notebooks kept by each child. These notebooks, used throughout the intervention, documented the progress being made in spelling. Figures 1 and 2 show the spelling dictation of Mark, a second grader who began the year with problems in letter formation and little knowledge of the alphabetic principle and who, by the end

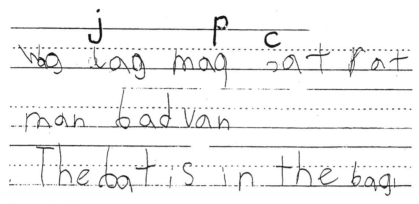

Figure 1.   Dictation produced by Mark, a second grader, at the beginning of the intervention in early October. Mark was still having difficulty with letter formation and was just beginning to spell simple closed syllable words.

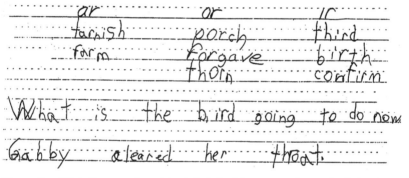

Figure 2.   Dictation produced by Mark in May, near the end of the intervention, showing improved letter formation and ability to spell words with the vowel + r pattern (the fifth syllable pattern introduced to the children).

of the year, was able to write words with five of the six syllable patterns. A sample of practice writing words with the vowel + r pattern is shown in figure 2. Figures 3 and 4 (see page 265) provide examples of dictation of a third grader, Jason, who had already started to build compound words (e.g., *backpack*) after learning the closed syllable pattern during the first few weeks of tutoring. In April, he was no longer using vowel headings and was learning the last of the six syllable types—the consonant +le pattern.

   In addition to the components listed above that were added to the second and third grade program, we also chose *not* to include oral phonological awareness instruction that *only* involved oral language activities. We, like others (see, for example, Blachman 1997

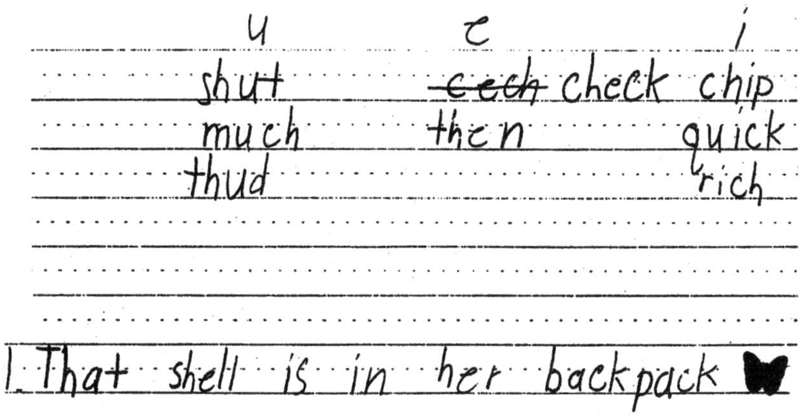

u   c   i

shut   ~~cech~~ check chip
much   then   quick
thud   rich

I. That shell is in her backpack 🦋

Figure 3. Dictation produced by Jason, a third grader, during the second half of October. He was able to spell simple closed syllable words with digraphs using all the short vowels.

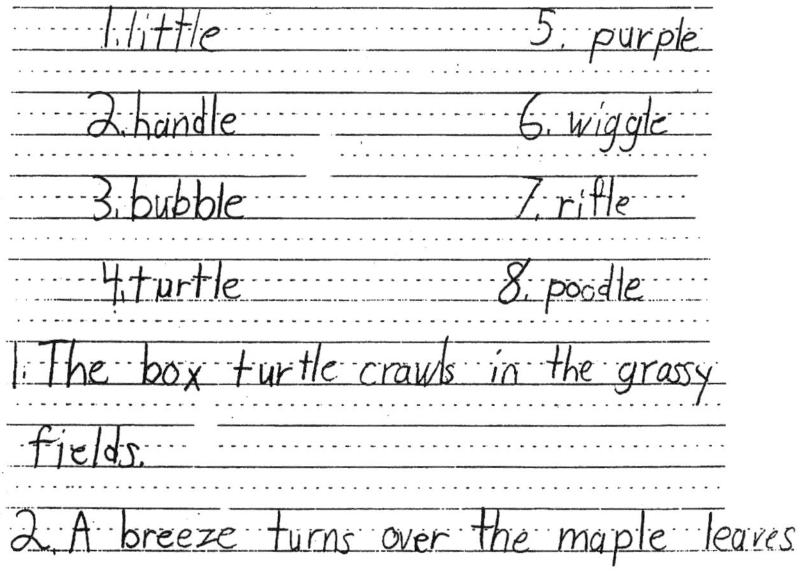

1. little   5. purple

2. handle   6. wiggle

3. bubble   7. rifle

4. turtle   8. poodle

I. The box turtle crawls in the grassy

fields.

2. A breeze turns over the maple leaves

Figure 4. Dictation produced by Jason in April, illustrating the ability to spell words with the consonant + le syllable pattern (the sixth and final pattern introduced to the children) and the ability to use previously learned syllable types when writing sentences from dictation.

and Wagner et al. 1997), consider these activities more appropriate for younger children and there is not strong evidence that these activities generalize to reading in the absence of a print component, especially in older children. Awareness of phonological structure was reinforced instead by focusing the child's attention on how phonology is represented in print. For example, on the sound board, after a child constructed the word *ship*, he might be asked "how many sounds?" and then "how many letters?" to reinforce the concept that phonemes are represented by letters and letter combinations. Phonological awareness was further reinforced during dictation by encouraging the child to say slowly, or stretch out, the word dictated by the tutor and, if necessary, tap out the individual sounds on his or her fingers (a technique borrowed from Wilson 1996) before writing the word. In addition to the five core steps, each lesson included a few final minutes of what we called "extended activities," specifically additional writing activities and games, as well as more reading of both narrative and expository texts, using a wide range of trade books to enhance fluency, comprehension, and a sense of enjoyment.

At the end of the intervention, the treatment children significantly outperformed the control children on standardized measures of word reading, spelling, and passage reading, including a measure of reading rate. When the children were tested one year later, the performance of the treatment children remained significantly superior on these measures (Blachman et al. 2003). We were also interested in the experiences of the treatment children who began the study with the highest word reading skills and those who began the study with less skill in word reading. Although all children started below the 25th percentile on the Woodcock Basic Skills Cluster (BSC), we regrouped the children into those who started above the 15th percentile (n = 19, with an average BSC score at the 19th percentile) and those who started at or below the 15th percentile (n = 18, with an average BSC score at the 7th percentile). At the end of the treatment year, we found that although the treatment children who started with higher word reading skills and those who started with less skill in word reading made relatively equivalent gains on our standardized measures, our tutoring program did not close the gap between the two groups.

It is interesting to note that the lower skilled children in the treatment group, on average, were less likely to be exposed to all six syllable patterns during the treatment year because they spent more time than the higher skilled children on earlier lessons (i.e., lessons related to learning to read closed syllables). In contrast, the higher skilled treatment children were, on average, more likely to be exposed to all patterns. As expected, both initial word reading score and the level of the program reached by the child at the end of the year were significantly related to end of year scores on our reading measures and spelling measures. This suggests that lower skilled treatment children may need a longer program (continuing to the following year), a more intense program (more minutes per day during the treatment year), and/or a program reinforced by classroom teachers. In our classroom prevention model, described earlier in the chapter, we continued our reading program into second grade for the children who were not exposed to all syllable patterns by the end of first grade and a similar model might benefit the lowest skilled children, like those in our tutoring study, who started the year, on average, at the 7th percentile in word reading.

We think this study reinforces the value of an intervention that emphasizes the phonologic and orthographic connections in words, while also emphasizing fluency and text reading practice. At the end of the treatment year, we saw significant differences on standardized measures of word reading, spelling, and paragraph reading, including a measure of reading rate. One year later, without receiving any additional input from our research team and participating only in whatever remediation the school provided, our treatment group continued to significantly outperform the control group on these same standardized measures. In general, the follow-up year data indicated that, for our groups as a whole, the children who received treatment demonstrated relative stability from one year to the next and maintained their gains.

Among the modifications we made to our program when we adapted our prevention model for use in our tutoring study was a greater emphasis on reading fluency and spelling. It is worth noting that the treatment children significantly outperformed the control children in both areas—although we do not know if these particular program modifications were responsible for the improvement. Specifically, on our passage reading measure, there were significant differences between treatment and control children not only in overall score on the test but also in reading rate at the end of the treatment year. These gains persisted in the evaluation at the end of the follow-up year (end of grade 3 or grade 4)– an important finding given the fact that *fluency* has been shown to be difficult to modify, even when a remediation program is highly successful in improving reading *accuracy* (Torgesen et al. 2001). Changes in spelling were also relatively stable over time, with the treatment children continuing to significantly outperform the control children in spelling at the end of the follow-up year. This is in contrast to our prevention study where spelling gains were not maintained at follow-up. We can only speculate that spelling appears to have been strengthened by the greater emphasis placed on this activity in our tutoring study compared to a more limited emphasis on spelling in our classroom prevention study.

These findings are important in light of the recent meta-analysis reported by the National Reading Panel (2000) (see also Ehri et al. 2001a) which indicates that, in general, it is more difficult to have an impact on the reading and spelling of reading disabled children who are introduced to phonics instruction after kindergarten and first grade. Our study and those of others (see, for example, Lovett and Steinback 1997; Torgesen et al. 2001; Wise, Ring, and Olson 1999) indicate that intensive and explicit instruction can make a substantial difference with children in grade 2 and above, although the intervention may need to be more systematic and of longer duration than with younger children.

An unfortunate, although not surprising, finding in our research came from children in the control group, most of whom received reading services from a reading teacher or a resource teacher during the two years that the children were monitored. Consistent with numerous studies that have found that there are limited benefits to be gained from school-based remedial reading services (Birman et al. 1987; Kennedy, Birman, and Demaline 1986; Moody et al. 2000; Snow, Burns, and Griffin 1998; Vaughn et al. 1998), our results indicated that the services provided to our control children were, for the most part, as Torgesen et al. (2001) put it, "stabilizing their degree of reading failure" (p. 34). The principles of instruction that are embedded in our intervention model and in models shown to be effective by numerous researchers, including Foorman et al. (1998), Torgesen et al. (1999), Vellutino et al. (1996) and others, are consistent with practices that have been supported recently by two independent and influential reading panels (Snow, Burns, and Griffin 1998; National Reading Panel 2000). We would hope that intensive and explicit instruction to develop the alphabetic principle, accurate and fluent word identification, and fluency, as well as frequent opportunities to engage in text-based reading, would be available in more schools to more children, so that our school-based programs could get beyond "stabilizing reading failure."

REFERENCES

Ball, E. W., and Blachman, B. A. 1991. Does phoneme awareness training in kindergarten make a difference in early word recognition and developmental spelling? *Reading Research Quarterly* 26:49–66.

Birman, B. F., Orland, M. E., Jung, R. K., Anson, R. J., Garcia, G. N., Moore, M. T., et al. 1987. *The Current Operation of the Chapter 1 Program.* Washington, DC: U.S. Government Printing Office.

Blachman, B. A. 1997. Early intervention and phonological awareness: A cautionary tale. In *Foundations of Reading Acquisition and Dyslexia: Implications for Early Intervention*, ed. B. A. Blachman. Mahwah, NJ: Lawrence Erlbaum Associates.

Blachman, B. A., Tangel, D. M., Ball, E. W., Black, R., and McGraw, C. K. 1999. Developing phonological awareness and word recognition skills: A two-year intervention with low-income, inner-city children. *Reading and Writing: An Interdisciplinary Journal* 11:239–73.

Blachman, B. A., Schatschneider, C., Fletcher, J. M., Francis, D. J., Clonan, S., Shaywitz, B. E., and Shaywitz, S. E. 2003. Effects of intensive reading remediation for second and third graders and a one year follow-up. Manuscript under review.

Dunn, L. M., and Dunn, L. M. 1981. *Peabody Picture Vocabulary Test-Revised* (PPVT-R). Circle Pines, MN: American Guidance Service.

Ehri, L. C., Nunes, S. R., Stahl, S. A., and Willows, D. M. 2001a. Systematic phonics instruction helps students learn to read: Evidence from the National Reading Panel's meta-analysis. *Review of Educational Research* 71:393–447.

Ehri, L. C., Nunes, S. R., Willows, D. M., Schuster, B. V., Yaghoub-Zadeh, Z., and Shanahan, T. 2001b. Phonemic awareness instruction helps children learn to read: Evidence from the National Reading Panel's meta-analysis. *Reading Research Quarterly* 36:250–87.

Engelmann, S. 1969. *Preventing Failure in the Primary Grades.* Chicago, IL: Science Research Associates.

Foorman, B. R., Francis, D. J., Fletcher, J. M., Schatschneider, C., and Mehta, P. 1998. The role of instruction in learning to read: Preventing reading failure in at-risk children. *Journal of Educational Psychology* 90(1):37–55.

Kennedy, M. M., Birman, B. F., and Demaline, R. E. 1986. *The Effectiveness of Chapter 1 Services: An Interim Report from the National Assessment of Chapter 1.* Washington, DC: U.S. Department of Education.

Liberman, A. M., Cooper, F. S., Shankweiler, D., and Studdert-Kennedy, M. 1967. Perception of the speech code. *Psychological Review* 74:731–61.

Liberman, I. Y. 1971. Basic research in speech and lateralization of language: Some implications for reading disability. *Bulletin of The Orton Society* 21:72–87.

Liberman, I. Y. 1987. Language and literacy: The obligation of the schools of education. In *Intimacy with Language: A Forgotten Basic in Teacher Education*, ed. W. Ellis. Baltimore: The Orton Dyslexia Society.

Liberman, I. Y., and Shankweiler, D. 1979. Speech, the alphabet, and teaching to read. In *Theory and Practice of Early Reading Vol. 2*, eds. L. B. Resnick and P. A. Weaver. Hillsdale, NJ: Lawrence Erlbaum Associates.

Lovett, M. W., and Steinbach, K. A. 1997. The effectiveness of remedial programs for reading disabled children of different ages: Does the benefit decrease for older children? *Learning Disability Quarterly* 20: 189–210.

Lyon, G. R., Fletcher, J. M., Shaywitz, S. E., Shaywitz, B. A., Torgesen, J. K., Wood, F. B., Schulte, A., and Olson, R. 2001. Rethinking learning disabilities. In *Rethinking Special Education for a New Century*, eds. C. E.

Finn, Jr., R. A. J. Rotherham, and C. R. Hokanson, Jr. Washington, DC: Thomas B. Fordham Foundation and Progressive Policy Institute.

Moats, L. C. 1995. The missing foundation in teacher education. *American Educator* 19(2):9, 43–51.

Moody, S. W., Vaughn, S., Hughes, M. T., and Fischer, M. 2000. Reading instruction in the resource room: Set up for failure. *Exceptional Children* 66(3):305–16.

Read, C. 1986. *Children's Creative Spellings*. London: Routledge & Kegan Paul.

Report of the National Reading Panel [NRP]. 2000. *Teaching Children to Read: An Evidence-based Assessment of the Scientific Research Literature on Reading and its Implication for Reading Instruction*. Washington, DC: National Institute of Child Health and Human Development.

Schatschneider, C., Fletcher, J. M., Francis, D. J., Carlson, C., and Foorman, B. R. 2002. Kindergarten prediction of reading skills: A longitudinal comparative analysis. Manuscript under review.

Slingerland, B. H. 1971. *A Multi-sensory Approach to Language Arts for Specific Language Disability Children: A Guide for Primary Teachers*. Cambridge, MA: Educators Publishing Service.

Snow, C. E., Burns, M. S., and Griffin, P. 1998. *Preventing Reading Difficulties in Young Children*. Washington, DC: National Academy Press.

Tangel, D. M., and Blachman, B. A. 1995. Effect of phoneme awareness instruction on the invented spelling of first grade children: A one year follow-up. *Journal of Reading Behavior* 27:153–85.

Templeton, S., and Morris, D. 2000. Spelling. In *Handbook of Reading Research. Vol. 2*, eds. M. L. Kamil, P. B. Mosenthal, P. D. Pearson, and R. Barr. Mahwah, NJ: Lawrence Erlbaum Associates.

Torgesen, J. K. 2000. Individual differences in response to early interventions in reading: The lingering problem of treatment resisters. *Learning Disabilities Research and Practice* 15:55–64.

Torgesen, J. K., Alexander, A. W., Wagner, R. K., Rashotte, C. A., Voeller, K. K. S., and Conway, T. 2001. Intensive remedial instruction for children with severe reading disabilities: Immediate and long-term outcomes from two instructional approaches. *Journal of Learning Disabilities* 34(1):33–58, 78.

Torgesen, J. K., Wagner, R. K., Rashotte, C. A., Rose, E., Lindamood, P., Conway, T., et al. 1999. Preventing reading failure in young children with phonological processing disabilities: Group and individual responses to instruction. *Journal of Educational Psychology* 91(4):579–93.

Vaughn, S., Moody, S. W., and Schumm, J. S. 1998. Broken promises: Reading instruction in the resource room. *Exceptional Children* 64(2): 211–25.

Vellutino, F. R., Scanlon, D. M., Sipay, E. R., Small, S. G., Pratt, A., Chen, R. S., et al. 1996. Cognitive profiles of difficult to remediate and readily remediated poor readers: Early intervention as a vehicle for distinguishing between cognitive and experiential deficits as basic causes of specific reading disability. *Journal of Educational Psychology* 88:607–38.

Wagner, R. K., Torgesen, J. K., Rashotte, C. A., Hecht, S. A., Barker, T. A., Burgess, S., et al. 1997. Changing relations between phonological processing abilities and word-level reading as children develop from beginning to skilled readers: A 5-year longitudinal study. *Developmental Psychology* 33:468–79.

Wechsler, D. 1991. *Wechsler Intelligence Scale for Children-Third Edition* (WISC-III). San Antonio, TX: The Psychological Corporation.

Wiederholt, J. L., and Bryant, B. R. 1992. *Gray Oral Reading Tests-Third Edition* (GORT-3). Austin, TX: PRO-ED.

Wilkinson, G. S. 1993. *The Wide Range Achievement Test 3* (WRAT3). Wilmington, DE: Wide Range.

Wilson, B. A. 1996. *Wilson Reading System.* Millbury, MA: Wilson Language Training.

Wise, B. W., Ring, J., and Olson, R. K. 1999. Training phonological awareness with and without explicit attention to articulation. *Journal of Experimental Child Psychology* 72: 271–304.

Woodcock, R. W. 1987. *Woodcock Reading Mastery Tests-Revised* (WRMT-R). Circle Pines, MN: American Guidance Service.

Section •IV

Instructional Conditions Necessary for Remediating Reading Difficulties in Older Children

Chapter • 10

Progress Toward Understanding the Instructional Conditions Necessary for Remediating Reading Difficulties in Older Children

*Joseph Torgesen, Carol Rashotte,
Ann Alexander, Jane Alexander, and,
Kay MacPhee*

The question of how to accelerate the reading growth of older children with serious reading difficulties sufficiently so they become capable of performing grade level work in reading has been with us for a long time (Clark and Uhry 1995). It is also a question that many parents, professionals, and researchers are actively seeking to answer. Phrased a little more broadly, it is also one of the questions that has motivated the research agenda on reading sponsored by governmental agencies and private foundations over the last 20 years. As defined by the National Institute of Child Health and Human Development (Lyon, Alexander, and Yaffee 1997), the goal has been to investigate the conditions that need to be in place for *all* children to acquire *adequate reading skills* in school. Because of the well publicized success of programmatic research on reading over the last two or three decades, the U.S. government recently passed a major educational bill called the No Child Left Behind Act. This law actively promotes the use of the "new research on reading" as a means to leave no child behind in the area of literacy skills. However, we still do not have consensus on the question that began this introductory paragraph. We, in fact, do not even know if it is possible to teach all children to read and understand material that is appropriate for their age or grade

In building a science of intervention for children with reading disabilities, a number of very different types of questions need to be answered. Historically, the questions most usually addressed in intervention research have concerned differences in the efficacy of one method versus another, or the efficacy of a particular method in contrast with a control group that did not receive the intervention. Sometimes these studies have involved careful contrasts in which specific components of instruction are varied systematically in order to isolate their effects singly or in combination with one another (Wise, Ring, and Olson 1999). Swanson (1999) reported a comprehensive meta-analysis of this type of intervention research with learning disabled children that found substantial effect sizes for a number of different types of interventions. These data are useful because they show that we understand many of the elements of effective instruction for children with reading disabilities, but they are limited in another way. They provide information about which instructional approaches are more effective than others, but they typically do not address questions about whether the most effective instructional techniques are sufficiently powerful to normalize the reading skills of children with reading disabilities.

For example, one excellent and widely cited study (Lovett et al. 1994) examined the relative effectiveness of several carefully contrasted interventions. This study produced useful information about critical elements of instruction for children with reading disabilities, and it showed that their core disabilities could be improved through direct instruction. However, at the conclusion of the study, the children's reading skills still fell in the severely disabled range. The children in the two strongest interventions began the study with an average standard score on a measure of word reading ability of 64.0 (which is below the 1st percentile), and at the conclusion of the study, their score was 69.5 (which is still below the 2nd percentile), with pre- and post-test scores on a measure of reading comprehension being 66.4 and 70.8. Although one could argue that continued application of the successful instructional techniques from this study would eventually bring the student's reading skills into the average range, in the absence of direct evidence we simply do not know if this assumption is correct.

Another interesting question that has been addressed in several recent intervention studies concerns changes in the localization and timing of brain functions that occur as a result of effective interventions. The central question addressed in this type of research is whether the localization and timing of brain processes that support reading are "normalized" in reading disabled individuals after effective interventions. Other chapters in this volume report studies of this nature, and it is interesting to observe a discrepancy in current findings from different laboratories conducting this type of research.

Papanicolaou and his colleagues from the University of Texas Health Sciences Center at Houston have reported (Fletcher et al. 2002; Papanicolaou, this volume) that the localization of reading related processes in the brain becomes much more normal in young children following successful reading interventions, while Guinevere Eden from Georgetown University, who worked with adults, has found a very different pattern (Eden 2002). In young children, effective intervention was accompanied by increased activity in the regions of the left hemisphere that are associated with reading in normal children, while in the adults, whose reading was also improved through the intervention, the effect seemed to be to increase activity in analogous regions of the right hemisphere. If these differences in outcomes for localization of function between children and adults are borne out in subsequent research, it will give rise to a set of interesting questions. For example, one question would concern relationships between severity of the reading disability and plasticity of brain function (the older subjects may have had more severe disabilities than the younger ones). Another set of questions would focus on whether there was a specific age range in which plasticity of brain function for reading actually begins to decline. This research also gives rise to questions about whether early responsiveness of the brain to intervention (in terms of changing patterns of activation) might signal stronger ultimate outcomes from the intervention.

A science of intervention for children with reading disabilities also requires research that focuses on the conditions that must be in place to actually bring the reading skills of reading disabled children into the normal range. Before we go further in discussing research focused on these questions, a brief discussion of the goals of reading instruction is needed. Although there are many issues about reading instruction itself that remain controversial, there is little controversy about the ultimate goal of reading instruction. Regardless of the position one takes on instructional issues, the ultimate goal of literacy instruction is to help children acquire the skills and knowledge that enable learning from, understanding, and enjoyment of written language. In even simpler terms, the most salient long-term goal for reading instruction is to help children acquire the ability to comprehend the meaning intended by the author in written text.

An important fact that must be considered when we set goals for reading attainment in all children is that reading comprehension is the joint product of language comprehension ability and word identification skills (Gough 1996; Hoover and Gough 1990). In other words, we must recognize the fact that general cognitive ability (specifically verbal ability and knowledge) strongly influences reading comprehension at the higher-grade levels in elementary school (Adams 1990), and in middle and high school. For this reason, we usually qualify the goal for reading instruction in the following way: the ultimate goal of reading instruction is to help children acquire the knowledge and skills necessary to comprehend printed material *at a level that is consistent with their general verbal ability or language comprehension skills*. If we were to adopt a strict grade level reading comprehension criteria (i.e., every child will be able to comprehend material written at grade level in 4th grade), this would imply an expectation for all children to have at least average verbal ability. Decades of cognitive intervention research suggest that it is unrealistic to expect all children to attain verbal ability estimates within the average range as a result of special instruction (Lee et al. 1990). Thus, it seems unrealistic to expect intervention specialists to accomplish this goal for children with very low verbal ability, particularly since they do not usually begin teaching these children until they have failed in learning to read for the first several years of elementary school. This statement does not ignore the fact that the verbal ability of many children can be dramatically increased by effective reading instruction (Torgesen 2001), it is just meant to acknowledge the fact that this may not be possible for all children.

In the remainder of this chapter, we will focus on research that provides information about the conditions that must be in place to "normalize" the reading skills of children who have struggled in learning to read for several years in elementary school. We will begin first with a brief outline of results that are typically achieved in public school special education programs, and then will consider in some detail outcomes from five intervention samples of children between nine and twelve years of age.

TYPICAL OUTCOMES FROM INTERVENTIONS PROVIDED
IN SPECIAL EDUCATION SETTINGS

We know from a variety of sources that typical public school interventions for children with reading disabilities can most accurately be described as stabilizing their degree of reading failure rather than remediating, or normalizing, their reading skills (Kavale 1988; Schumaker, Deshler, and Ellis 1986). That is, children do not fall farther behind in their reading skills once they are placed in special education, but neither do they "close the gap" in reading ability with average children of their same age level.

Recently, Hanushek, Kain, and Rivkin (1998) used a very large sample from the Texas Schools Microdata Panel to show that typical special education placements during the fourth and fifth grade years of elementary school accelerated reading growth by only .04 standard deviations over the rate the children had been achieving in their regular classroom placements. Although this represents a positive accomplishment for special education, it is hardly sufficient to normalize the reading skills of children with severe reading disabilities in any reasonable period of time. For example, if we assumed that a child with reading disabilities had been learning at a normal rate (an assumption that is clearly too generous) in the regular classroom, and that special education accelerated growth by .04 standard deviations a year, it would take 8.3 years for the child to move from a standard score of 75 to a standard score of 80! Said differently, it would take more than 8 years for special education to lift a child's reading scores from the 5th percentile to the 9th percentile.

The results from Hanushek, Kain, and Rivkin (1998) applied specifically to resource room, or pullout methods of instruction, but nearly identical results have been reported for "inclusion" interventions with older children. For example, across three different intervention sites, Zigmond and her colleagues (Zigmond et al. 1995), found that children with learning disabilities, as a group, experienced little movement in reading ability relative to normal children in their classrooms. Although, on average, they kept pace with normal reading growth during the interventions, they did not significantly close the reading gap that got them identified as learning disabled in the first place. When summarizing the results from several studies of effectiveness for instructional models requiring that children with reading disabilities be instructed in the regular classroom environment, Zigmond (1996) concluded that we have not yet determined how to incorporate effective instruction for children with reading disabilities "into the organization and management framework of a general education setting" (p. 187).

Observational studies of instruction in many special education classrooms (Vaughn, Moody, and Shuman 1998) have identified several reasons most placements are not more effective in bringing the reading skills of older children into the average range within a reasonable period of time. First, the interventions are offered with insufficient intensity. The teachers they observed were simply responsible for too many students; they were not able to offer them the individualized instruction required by older children who have struggled for several years in learning to read. Further, there was little direct instruction or guided practice in such critical components as phonemic decoding and phonemic awareness. Most instruction on word level skills involved "phonics" worksheets that the children completed independently. A final important element that was missing in the instruction observed by Vaughn and her colleagues was direct instruction in comprehension strategies, which has been shown to be a very effective form of instruction for older children with reading disabilities (Mastropieri and Scruggs 1997).

Given that current methods of instruction and implementation are generally less effective than is desirable, what do we know that can lead to improvement in this situation? We actually know a number of important things. First, recent studies of intensive interventions using older children with reading disabilities have demonstrated that it is possible to accelerate their reading growth to a much greater extent than is typically achieved in special education classrooms (Alexander et al. 1991; McGuinnes, McGuiness and McGuiness 1996; Rashotte, MacPhee, and Torgesen 2001; Torgesen et al. 2001; Truch 1994; Truch 2002; Wise, Ring, and Olson 1999). Second, all the methods that have been shown to produce strong growth in the reading skills of children with reading disabilities teach phonemic decoding skills very explicitly, and they provide many opportunities for supervised practice in the application of these skills during reading. Third, all the studies that have shown powerful instructional effects have provided instruction that is much more intensive than that typically provided in public school special education settings. Instruction has been successfully provided in a variety of teacher-student ratios, varying from 1:1 to about 1:4. None of the studies reporting strongly accelerated reading growth has employed instructional groups larger than about four children.

Differences across studies in the overall growth of reading skills in children with reading disabilities are strongly related to the level of reading skill the children have achieved before intervention begins. Children who begin intensive reading interventions with stronger reading skills tend to attain significantly higher reading skills than those who begin with weaker reading ability (Torgesen et al. 2001). As we accumulate more studies of intensive and appropriate interventions with older children, we will develop a much better sense of the amount of instruction required for children who begin at different levels of ability. We will also develop better knowledge of the ease or difficulty of remediation across different kinds of reading skills. For example, phonemic decoding skills appear to be relatively easy to "normalize" in older children, while reading fluency is much more difficult to remediate. (Torgesen, Rashotte, and Alexander 2001). Several of these issues are addressed in the following discussion of outcomes for five samples of children who began remediation at different levels of impairment and received differing amounts of intervention.

INTERVENTION OUTCOMES ACROSS FIVE SAMPLES OF CHILDREN IN LATE ELEMENTARY AND MIDDLE SCHOOL

We will present remedial outcomes for two samples of severely disabled children that began instruction with word level skills around the 2nd percentile, two other samples of moderately disabled readers with word level reading skills at approximately the 10th percentile, and a single sample of mildly impaired readers with beginning word level skills averaging close to the 30th percentile. Across all these samples, four common measures of reading skill were administered before and after the intervention. Phonemic decoding skills were measured by the Word Attack subtest of the *Woodcock Reading Mastery Test-Revised* (Woodcock 1987). Text reading accuracy, reading fluency, and reading comprehension were all measured by the *Gray Oral Reading Test-III* (Wiederholt and Bryant 1992). In these analyses, reading fluency is measured by the rate of oral reading of text. Outcomes for all samples will be reported in standard scores on a scale with mean of 100 and standard deviation of 15. Standard scores are a very useful metric for intervention studies, because they provide a precise estimate of the child's reading skills in relation to a large normative sample. Thus, if a child's standard score on a given reading skill improves substantially from pretest to post-test, it means that the instruction was effective in "closing the gap" with average readers. It is much more difficult to obtain improvements on standard scores than it is to improve raw scores, because an improvement in standard score means that the child is growing at a rate faster than average. Of course, if children with reading disabilities begin intervention two years below grade level, and they do not improve at a rate faster than average, they will always remain two grade levels below their peers in reading ability.

The first set of outcomes to be considered here comes from a study that was reported previously in the *Journal of Learning Disabilities* (Torgesen et al. 2001). The subjects were children in third through fifth grade with an average age of 9 years, 9 months at the start of intervention. The children had been in special education for an average of 16 months prior to the beginning of the study, and they all had word level reading skills more than 1.5 standard deviations below average. In fact, the average standard score at the beginning of remediation for the word identification subtest from the *Woodcock Reading Mastery Test-Revised* was 69, which is at the 2nd percentile. The children had an average verbal IQ of 93 and came from homes in the middle to lower-middle class range.

The children were randomly assigned to two instructional conditions that both taught phonemic awareness and phonemic decoding explicitly, but placed a very different emphasis on time spent reading connected text. One of the methods spent only 5% of the total instructional time reading meaningful text, while the other method allocated 50% of the instructional time to this activity. The children received 67.5 hours of individual instruction two hours a day for eight weeks. Their reading skills were measured before and immediately following instruction, and at one- and two-year follow-up intervals. The outcomes for both of the conditions were very similar, and in this report, we will focus on outcomes for the 30 children receiving one of the methods, the The Lindamood Phoneme Sequencing Program for Reading, Spelling, and Speech, (Lindamood and Lindamood 1998).

Pre- and posttest scores for the four reading measures mentioned earlier are presented in figure 1. Another measure of comprehension was available for this sample (Passage Comprehension from the WRMT-R), and it is included here because it provides an additional source of information about growth in this area. As can be seen from figure 1, this intervention produced very strong growth in phonemic decoding skills, substantial growth in text reading accuracy and comprehension, and only a small change in reading fluency when compared to children in the standardization samples for the tests. Phonemic decoding skills ended up solidly in the average range (the average range is defined as extending above the 30th percentile), while those for comprehension and accuracy approached the average range. In contrast, the relative reading fluency of the children in this sample remained severely impaired following the intervention, and it did not substantially change relative to average readers over the two year follow up period (Torgesen et al. 2001).

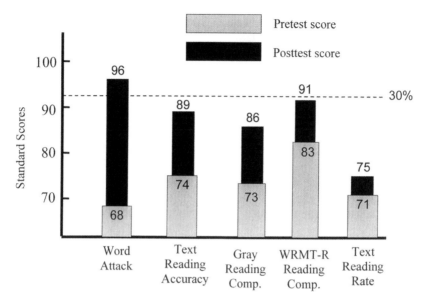

Figure 1.   Outcomes from 67.5 hours of 1:1 intervention using the Lindamood Phoneme Sequencing Program for Reading, Spelling, and Speech. From Torgesen et al., (2002). Intensive remedial instruction for children with severe reading disabilities: Immediate and long-term outcomes from two instructional approaches. *Journal of Learning Disabilities* 34: 33–58.

It is important to note that the lack of change in the standard score for reading fluency does not mean that the children in this study did not become more fluent readers in an absolute sense. In fact, as long as the difficulty level of passages remained constant, they became substantially more fluent. For example, at the pretest, the most difficult passage the children read on the *Gray Oral Reading Test* was read at 38 words per minute with 10 errors. At the two-year follow-up point, a passage of equivalent difficulty was read at 101 words per minute with 2 errors. The same pattern was observed on the next most difficult passage which was read at pretest at 42 words per minute with 6 errors, while at post-test an equivalent passage was read at 104 words per minute with one error. Thus, the children did show marked improvement in the fluency with which they could read relatively simple passages; it was only when they were compared to their peers on passages closer to their grade level that they continued to show a striking lack of fluency in their reading of text.

Although the children in this study did not "close the gap" with normal readers in reading fluency, they came very close to achieving average levels of reading skill in text reading accuracy and comprehension. Figure 2, for example, shows the reading growth of the children during the two-year period following the intervention. It also describes their growth during the 16 month period they were in special education prior to the start of intensive instruction, as well as their growth during the intervention period. The measure here is the broad reading scale (a combination of word reading accuracy and passage comprehension) from the *Woodcock-Johnson Psycho-Educational Battery-Revised* (Woodcock and Johnson 1989). At the conclusion of the two-year follow-up period, the children were reading on this measure at the bottom edge of the average range.

We are currently conducting a follow-up to this study that employs identical procedures for identifying subjects. That is, the children are currently in 3rd through 5th grade, are receiving or have been identified to receive special education services for reading disabilities, and achieve word level reading scores more than 1.5 standard deviations below the mean for their age. The study is being done in the same school district and in many of the same schools as the previous study, but it has been much more difficult to find subjects who meet the criteria of extreme deficits in word level reading skills. During the time between the two studies, and

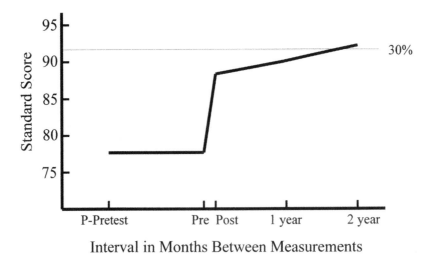

Interval in Months Between Measurements

Figure 2. *Growth* in broad reading skills before, during,and following intensive intervention using the Lindamood Phoneme Sequencing Program for Reading, Spelling, and Speech. From Torgesen et al., (2002). Intensive remedial instruction for children with severe reading disabilities: Immediate and long-term outcomes from two instructional approaches. *Journal of Learning Disabilities* 34: 33-58.

partly as a result of the first study, the school district has strengthened both its classroom reading programs and particularly its special education programs. In screening students for participation in the study, we found many children with word level skills that were relatively impaired (around one standard deviation below the mean), but we had to search much more extensively for students who met the more restrictive criteria we had used in the earlier study. The students in the new study are roughly similar in their beginning scores on the word identification subtest of the WRMT-R (mean standard score = 72) to students in the previous study, but the teachers who have worked in both studies indicated almost from the beginning of instruction that the second group has been much more difficult to teach than the students in the first study.

The instructional improvements within the schools from which we selected our subjects have introduced us directly to a potentially important moderating variable in intervention research with older children. If students are selected for a remedial study from within a relatively powerful instructional environment, they will likely be much more resistant to any new intervention than if they are selected by the same criteria after having been exposed to previous reading instruction that was relatively weak. Although we do not yet have direct measures of the changes in the instructional environment from which our students are being selected, we hope to obtain these data before the study is ready to report in its final form. Thus far, the children selected for participation in the present study have an average Verbal Intelligence score of 87, as compared to a score of 93 in the previous study.

The primary variable manipulated between the two instructional conditions in the present study is amount of fluency oriented repeated reading practice. Children in both conditions are receiving the The Lindamood Phoneme Sequencing Program for Reading, Spelling, and Speech as the core of their instructional program, but children in the accuracy plus fluency condition are receiving substantially greater amounts of instructional time devoted to fluency oriented practice at the individual phoneme, phonogram, word, phrase, and passage level than children in the other condition. Those assigned to the accuracy only condition are receiving an equivalent amount of instructional time, but their instruction is focused on extending their word analyses and text reading accuracy skills to as high a level as possible within the instructional time allotted. In addition, both groups are receiving 25 hours of instruction focused on reading comprehension strategies. Altogether, the children in this study are receiving 133 hours of instruction, which is twice that of the previous study. Eighty-three of the instructional hours are provided in a 1:1 format, while the remaining 50 hours are provided in small groups of 2 children each. Thus far, there have been no significant differences in outcomes for the two groups, so their outcomes are presented in figure 3 as a combined group of 45 children.

The results from this figure indicate that, despite the extra amount of instruction and the additional fluency oriented practice in one of the conditions, the results are very similar to our previous study. The biggest anomaly in these results, when compared to the last study, is the high score the children received on the measure of reading comprehension provided by the *Gray Oral Reading Test-Revised* at the pre-test. Our assumption at this point is that these high initial scores reflect some specific aspect of the reading instruction the children received in their previous special education placement. In contrast to the results from the GORT-3, the results for the passage comprehension test from the WRMT-R are very similar to the previous study. In other words, the additional 25 hours of instruction in the use of visualizing strategies for reading comprehension has thus far not produced stronger gains in reading comprehension than were obtained in the previ-

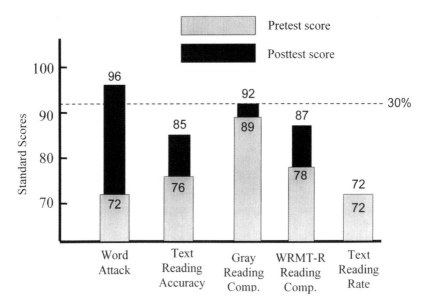

Figure 3.   Outcomes from 133 hours of intensive intervention using the Lindamood Phoneme Sequencing Program for Reading, Spelling, and Speech plus comprehension instruction and fluency practice.

ous study. Again, there was no impact of the intervention on the standard score for reading fluency in either of the groups.

We turn now to three samples of children who have all received as their intervention the *Spell Read P.A.T.*® (Phonological Auditory Training) program developed by Kay MacPhee (MacPhee 1998). This program, which is typically taught in small groups of 3 to 5 children, provides systematic instruction in phonemic decoding and phonemic awareness combined with fluency-oriented practice from the beginning of instruction. It also requires children to write and discuss responses to passages that are read together as a group. In a typical 70 minute session, the instructional activities are distributed as follows: 40 minutes—phonemic awareness/ phonemic decoding; 20 minutes—shared reading of text; 7 minutes —writing about what was read; 3 minutes—wrap up. The method has been evaluated in a previous published study (Rashotte, MacPhee, and Torgesen 2001) with very positive results.

The first sample for which we have current results was seen in a reading clinic over a period of about one year. The intervention was provided twice a week to groups of from 2 to 4 children, and the average number of hours of instruction was 60. The 48 children in the sample came from homes in the middle to upper-middle socio-economic range, and they averaged 11 years of age at the start of the intervention. Seventy-nine percent of the students were Caucasian, and 67% were male. The average score on the word identification subtest for this group at the beginning of the intervention was 92, which places them at the 30th percentile. The outcomes from their intervention are presented in figure 4.

There are three aspects of these data that are worthy of special comment. First, in spite of their relatively strong skills in phonemic decoding and reading accuracy (close to the bottom of the average range), the children began the intervention very impaired in reading fluency, with a score almost 2 standard deviations below the mean. Second, in this sample, standard scores on the fluency measure showed almost two standard deviations of improvement, and the children ended up with fluency scores solidly in the average range. Third, although fluency improved to the middle of the average range, it was still almost a standard deviation weaker than text reading accuracy, which was almost a standard deviation above average at the end of the intervention.

The next sample of children that received the Spell-Read intervention was seen in a public school setting. These were students from working class homes; 39% were Caucasian and 64% were male. The 14 children in this group averaged 12 years of age, and they received an average of 51 hours of instruction in groups

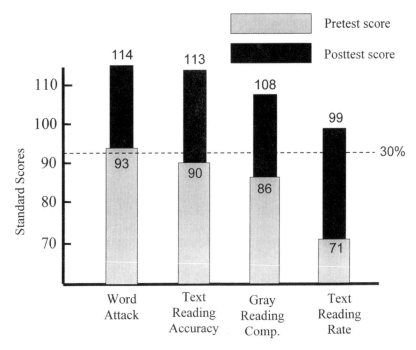

Figure 4.   Outcomes from 60 hours of small group instruction using the *Spell Read P.A.T.* intervention method.

varying from two to four children. Instruction was provided over a four month period. They began the intervention with a mean score on the word identification subtest from the WRMT-R test of 80, which places them at about the 10th percentile. Their results are presented in figure 5.

These data follow a pattern similar to the one just reported for the students that began the intervention with stronger word level skills, although both the magnitude of the growth and the level of reading skill at the conclusion of the intervention are substantially reduced. Again, there is growth in the children's standard score for fluency of 2/3 of a standard deviation, but it remains relatively impaired compared to the children's skills in phonemic decoding, text reading accuracy, and comprehension.

The final sample for which results are available was very similar to the public school, working class sample just reported; the major difference is that the amount of instruction was doubled. In this sample, 60% of the students qualified for free and reduced lunch, 45% were Caucasion, 45% African-American, and 10% were other minorities. The mean age was 12 years, and 53% were receiving special education services. The children received an average of

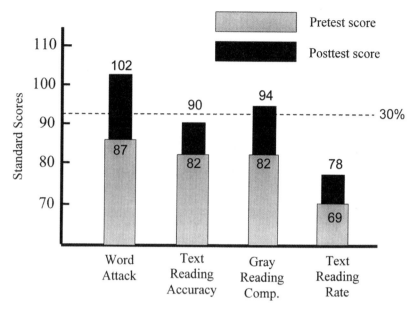

Figure 5.   Outcomes from 50 hours of small group instruction using the *Spell Read P.A.T.* intervention method

100 hours of *Spell Read* intervention in groups of 4 to 5 children, and they began the intervention with an average standard score on the word identification subtest of 83. Instruction was provided daily over a five-month period from late September through February. This study also involved a control group of children who were randomly assigned to receive an intervention that did not involve explicit instruction in phonemic awareness and phonemic decoding, but instead emphasized silent reading and focused on development of comprehension strategies. There were 20 children in each of the instructional conditions.

The outcomes for children in the *Spell Read* condition are presented in figure 6. The children in the other condition showed no significant change in their standard scores from pre- to post-test. This study cannot be used to directly compare the effectiveness of the two instructional methods, because the comprehension oriented condition was provided in much larger groups than the *Spell Read* intervention. Nevertheless, it is instructive to consider the effect sizes between the two conditions as a description of the potential value of the *Spell Read* intervention compared to instruction that might be typically provided to many students in special education classes. The effect sizes for the *Spell Read* condition were: phonemic decoding = 3.8, reading accuracy = 1.9, reading comprehension = 1.3, and

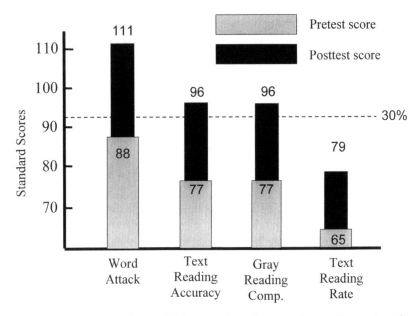

Figure 6.   Outcomes from 100 hours of small group instruction using the *Spell Read P.A.T.* intervention method

fluency = 1.7. The outcomes for the children in the *Spell Read* condition show a pattern similar to others that have already been reported. These children, who began the intervention with word level skills around the 10th percentile, attained scores for phonemic decoding, text reading accuracy and comprehension that were solidly within the average range, while reading fluency remained an area of relative impairment. However, it should be noted that very substantial gains (at least one standard deviation) were made in all areas of reading skill, and that, with the exception of reading fluency, these children had essentially "closed the gap" in reading ability with their same-age classmates.

GENERALIZATIONS ACROSS INTERVENTION SAMPLES

There were a number of important similarities, as well as differences, in the outcomes across these five intervention samples. First, all five studies reported substantial improvement in the reading skills of the children in the study relative to average children. In general, the interventions used were most successful at "closing the gap" with average readers in the area of phonemic decoding ability, and least successful in the area of text reading fluency. In all cases, as far as we can tell (we did not have direct verbal IQ measures for three of the samples), the interventions were successful in bringing reading comprehension skills to a level very close to the general verbal ability of the students. Finally, the amount of improvement in reading fluency appeared to be strongly related to the student's level of word reading accuracy at the beginning of the study. Table I reports a summary of the data showing the relationship between gains in reading fluency and initial status on the word identification subtest from the *Woodcock Reading Mastery Test-Revised*.

This table shows that improvements in reading fluency, as measured by changes in standard score, are related to both amounts of instruction and initial scores on the measure of word identification ability. The first two samples received roughly the same amount and type of instruction but began with substantially different word level skills. The sample with the higher word reading ability at the start of treatment made more than three times the overall gain in fluency. It is almost as though this sample was "poised" in some sense to accelerate in the development of fluency as a result of the intervention (Mercer 2002).

The second two samples began with similar levels of word reading ability, but received different amounts of intervention. The extra intervention was very helpful to students who began instruction with word level skills around the tenth percentile.Not only were their skills in phonemic decoding, text reading accuracy, and text comprehension completely normalized, but also the extra instruction produced greater gains in fluency (14 vs. 9 standard score points improvement). It was only the two samples with beginning word level skills at around the 2nd percentile that showed almost no relative gains in reading fluency from a substantial amount of intervention. Further, the focused fluency

Table I. A comparison of outcomes for reading rate across varying levels of initial word reading ability and amount of intervention.

Hours of Intervention	N	Instructional Method	Initial WID	Initial Rate	Post Rate	Rate Gain
60 (1:2–4)	48	Spell Read	92	71	99	28
50 (1:2–4)	14	Spell Read	80	69	78	9
100 (1;2–4)	20	Spell Read	83	65	79	14
68 (1:1)	29	Lindamood	69	71	75	4
133 (1:1, 1:2)	4	Lindamood + fluency	72	72	72	0

Note: All scores are standard scores with a mean of 100 and a standard deviation of 15

interventions provided in the second study, as well as the two-fold increase in instructional time, produced no noticeable improvement in fluency outcomes.

Of course, any conclusions resulting from a comparison of results across these five samples, such as attributing differences in outcome to a specific set of factors (amount or type of instruction or beginning word level skills) must be very tentative. The samples and instructional conditions differed in a number of important ways, not all of which were identified here. Thus, it is of interest to see whether the relationship between beginning status on the word identification measure and growth in text reading fluency can be found within each study as well as across the studies. In fact, this relationship was found consistently across the five samples. When we correlated initial score on the word identification measure with each student's standard score gain in reading fluency (controlling for initial level of fluency), the average correlation for all studies was .42, and the range of the correlations across samples was .33 to .55. In contrast, the average correlation between beginning scores on the Word Attack measure and gains in fluency was only .14. Thus, independent of the student's initial level of reading fluency, level of word reading accuracy at the beginning of the study predicted a substantial amount of variance in the extent to which fluency scores improved relative to average readers.

With these remarks as introduction, we would offer the following general conclusions from outcomes across these five intervention samples.

1. For many older children with word level reading skills around the 30th percentile, a relatively brief (60 hrs) dose of appropriate small group instruction can bring their skills in phonemic decoding, text reading accuracy and fluency, and comprehension solidly into the average range.

2. For many older children with word level reading skills around the 10th percentile, a more substantial dose (100 hrs) of appropriate small group instruction can bring their skills in phonemic decoding, text reading accuracy, and reading comprehension solidly into the average range. Although the gap in reading fluency can be closed somewhat, reading fluency is likely to remain substantially impaired.

3. For older children with word level reading skills around the 2nd percentile, intensive interventions can bring

phonemic decoding skills solidly into the average range and produce strong gains in text reading accuracy and reading comprehension. However, they are likely to leave the fluency gap essentially unaffected.

CONCLUDING THOUGHTS ABOUT THE FLUENCY GAP

We have earlier provided evidence that the most important single factor limiting the reading fluency of children with reading difficulties is the relatively limited size of their sight vocabulary (Torgesen, Rashotte, and Alexander 2001). When they are asked to read material that is close to their grade level in difficulty, these children recognize far fewer words in the passage at a single glance than do children who read in the average range. It is the necessity of slowing down to phonemically decode or guess at words that is the most critical factor in limiting the reading fluency of children with severe reading difficulties. As many others have also observed (Adams, 1990; Rayner et al., 2001), the most important key to fluent reading of any text is the ability to automatically recognize almost all the words in the text.

As we have also shown in an earlier analysis (Torgesen et al. 2002), other factors, such as the size of one's vocabulary, may contribute more to individual differences in reading fluency as word reading ability improves. In addition, other factors, such as trade-offs between speed and accuracy or a simple lack of awareness of what it means to push oneself toward more fluent reading, may exercise more of an influence on individual differences in reading fluency when limited sight word vocabulary does not play too great a role. Adjustments in this latter area, for example, may have been involved in the very large increases in reading fluency experienced by children who began the intervention with word level reading skills at roughly the 30th percentile.

These children improved almost two standard deviations in reading fluency after only 60 hours of small group intervention. It is difficult to believe that this large increase in relative reading fluency occurred solely as a result of an increase in the size of their sight word vocabulary during the relatively brief interval in which the intervention was provided. Further support for this idea comes from the large difference between their reading accuracy and reading fluency scores at the beginning of the intervention. Both children at the 30th percentile in word reading accuracy and those at the 10th percentile showed a relatively larger gap between text reading accuracy and text reading rate at the beginning of the intervention than those who began at the 2nd percentile. Although this may have resulted from a floor effect in the measurement of fluency, it is interesting to consider the possibility that the children with the higher scores on the word identification test had more words in their lexicon that were "on the verge" of becoming automatically recognizable. Another possibility is that these children were simply hesitant readers who had not been prodded sufficiently, or practiced sufficiently, in order to assemble all the skills required for coordinated, fluent reading of text. Both of these factors might produce a readiness for acceleration in reading fluency that is not present in children whose sight word vocabularies are so extremely limited that they perform at the 2nd percentile on measures of word identification accuracy at the beginning of intervention.

These latter children start with such a deficit in word reading ability that is impossible for them to add words to their sight word vocabulary at a rate sufficient to close the gap with average readers. Thus part of the remaining fluency gap for both children who begin at the 2nd, as well as the 10th percentile in word reading ability, may result from the fact that average readers are also adding words to their sight word vocabularies at a rapid rate at the ages of these children. Another way to say this is that reading fluency for grade level text is a rapidly moving target during the late elementary and middle school years. Each year, grade level text contains a richer, broader selection of words. To maintain grade level fluency, one must continue to add these new words to one's sight word vocabulary at the pace of a normal reader. Children who have very limited sight word vocabularies in grade 5 must add words to their sight word vocabularies at a much faster rate than normal if they expect to close the gap in reading fluency for grade level text. To do this, they would either have to engage in considerably more reading practice than normal, or add words to their sight word vocabulary more easily than average readers. Neither of these possibilities is likely to be the case.

One final factor may be operating to limit fluency increases in children with the most serious reading impairments. Many of these children may have an additional deficit in the ability to form the orthographic representations that are the basis for automatic word recognition (Wolf and Bowers 1999). That is, their extremely low scores on word identification measures at the beginning of the intervention may result from factors that are independent from their inability to decode words using phonemic strategies (Ehri 1998; Share and Stanovich 1995). This additional cognitive deficit may continue to place limits on the development of reading fluency even after reading accuracy problems are cor-

rected. Although this independent difficulty in forming orthographic representations is not adequately understood at present, if
it is real, it could help to explain the enduring, and extremely difficult to remediate, problems in reading fluency that remain for
many children following intensive reading interventions.

ACKNOWLEDGMENTS

The research reported in this chapter was supported by grant
HD30988 "Prevention and Remediation of Reading Disabilities" from
the National Institute of Child Health and Human Development.

REFERENCES

Adams, M. J. 1990. *Beginning to Read.* Cambridge, MA: MIT Press.

Alexander, A., Anderson, H., Heilman, P. C., Voeller, K. S., and Torgesen,
J. K. 1991. Phonological awareness training and remediation of analytic decoding deficits in a group of severe dyslexics. Annals of Dyslexia
41:193–206.

Clark, D. B., and Uhry, J. K. 1995. *Dyslexia: Theory and Practice of Remedial
Instruction, 2nd Edition.* Baltimore, MD: York Press.

Eden, G. 2002. Physiological correlates of reading intervention fMRI studies in children and adults. Paper presented at semi-annual conference
of the International Dyslexia Research Foundation (The Dyslexia Foundation), June 11–15, at Kona, Hawaii.

Ehri, L. C. 1998. Grapheme-phoneme knowledge is essential for learning
to read words in English. In *Word Recognition in Beginning Reading*, eds.
J. Metsala and L. Ehri. Hillsdale, NJ: Lawrence Erlbaum Associates.

Fletcher, J. et al. 2002. (article in neuroscience journal)

Gough, P. B. 1996. How children learn to read and why they fail. *Annals
of Dyslexia* 46:3–20.

Hanushek, E. A., Kain, J. F., and Rivkin, S. G. 1998. Does special education
raise academic achievement for students with disabilities? National Bureau of Economic Research, Working Paper No. 6690, Cambridge, MA.

Hoover, W. A., and Gough, P. B. 1990. The simple view of reading. *Reading and Writing*, 2: 127–60.

Kavale, K. A., 1988. The long-term consequences of learning disabilities.
In *The Handbook of Special Education: Research and Practice*, eds. M. C.
Wang, H. J. Walburg, and M. C. Reynolds. New York: Pergamon.

Lee, V., Brooks-Gunn, J., Schnur, E., and Liaw, F. 1990. Are Head Start effects sustained? A longitudinal follow-up comparison of disadvantaged
children attending Head Start, no preschool, and other pre-school programs. (Publication info?)

Lindamood, P., and Lindamood, P. 1998. *The Lindamood Phoneme Sequencing Program for Reading, Spelling, and Speech.* Austin, TX: PRO-ED, Inc.

Lovett, M. W., Borden, S. L., Lacerenza, L., Benson, N. J., and Brackstone,
D. 1994. Treating the core deficits of developmental dyslexia: Evidence
of transfer of learning after phonologically-and strategy-based reading
training programs. *Journal of Educational Psychology* 30:805–22.

Lyon, G. R., Alexander, D. and Yaffee, S. 1997. Progress and promise in research in learning disabilities. *Learning Disabilities: A Multidisciplinary Journal* 8:1–6.

MacPhee, K. 1998. *Spell Read P.A.T.* Spell Read P.A.T. Learning Systems, Inc.: Charlottetown, Canada.

Mastropieri, M. A., and Scruggs, T. E. 1997. Best practices in promoting reading comprehension in students with learning disabilities: 1976–1996. *Remedial and Special Education* 18:197–213.

McGuinnes, C., McGuiness, D., and McGuiness, G. 1996. Phono-Graphix: A new method for remediating reading difficulties. *Annals of Dyslexia* 46:73–96.

Mercer, C. 2002. Reading Fluency: Definition, research, and implications. Invited address to the Just Read, Florida! Leadership Conference, Tampa, FL, July.

Rashotte, C. A., MacPhee, K., and Torgesen, J. K. 2001. The effectiveness of a group reading instruction program with poor readers in multiple grades. *Learning Disability Quarterly* 24:119–34.

Raynor, K., Foorman, B. R., Perfetti, C. A., Pesetsky, D., and Seidenberg, M. S. 2001. How psychological science informs the teaching of reading. *Psychological Science in the Public Interest* 2:31–73.

Schumaker,J. B., Deshler,D. D., and Ellis,E. S. 1986. Intervention issues related to the education of learning disabled adolescents. In *Psychological and Educational Perspectives on Learning Disabilities*, eds. J. K. Torgesen and B. Y. L. Wong. New York: Academic Press.

Share, D. L., and Stanovich, K. E. 1995. Cognitive processes in early reading development: A model of acquisition and individual differences. *Issues in Education: Contributions from Educational Psychology* 1:1–57.

Swanson, H. L. 1999. Reading research for students with LD: A meta-analysis of intervention outcomes. *Journal of Learning Disabilities* 32:504–32.

Torgesen, J. K., Alexander, A. W., Wagner, R. K., Rashotte, C. A., Voeller, K., Conway, T. and Rose, E. 2001. Intensive remedial instruction for children with severe reading disabilities: Immediate and long-term outcomes from two instructional approaches. *Journal of Learning Disabilities* 34: 33–58.

Torgesen, J. K., Rashotte, C. A., Alexander, A. 2001. Principles of fluency instruction in reading: Relationships with established empirical outcomes. In *Dyslexia, Fluency, and the Brain*, ed. M. Wolf. Baltimore, MD: York Press.

Truch, S. 1994. Stimulating basic reading processes using Auditory Discrimination in Depth. *Annals of Dyslexia* 44:60–80.

Truch, S. 2002. Outcomes from intensive remedial interventions using the Phono-Graphix method. Unpublished manuscript, The Reading Foundation: Calgary, Alberta, Canada.

Vaughn, S. R., Moody, S. W., and Shuman, J. S. 1998. Broken promises: Reading instruction in the resource room. *Exceptional Children* 64: 211–25.

Wiederholt, J. L. Y Bryant, B. R. l992. *Gray Oral Reading Tests—III.* Austin, TX: PRO-ED.

Wise, B. W., Ring, J., and Olson, R. K. 1999. Training phonological awareness with and without explicit attention to articulation. *Journal of Experimental Child Psychology* 72:271–304.

Wolf, M. A. and Bowers, P. G. 1999. The double-deficit hypothesis for the developmental dyslexias. *Journal of Educational Psychology* 91:415–38.

Woodcock, R. W. 1987. *Woodcock Reading Mastery Tests-Revised.* Circle Pines, Minn.: American Guidance Service.

Woodcock, R. W., and Johnson, M. B. 1989. *Woodcock-Johnson Psycho-Educational Battery-Revised.* Allen, TX: DLM/Teaching Resources

Zigmond, N. Jenkins, J., Fuchs, L., Deno, S., Fuchs, D., Baker, J. N., Jenkins, L., and Coutinho, M. 1995. Special education in restructured schools: Findings from three multi-year studies. *KAPPAN* 76:531-35.

Zigmond, N. 1996. Organization and management of general education classrooms. In *Research on Classroom Ecologies*, eds D. L. Speece and B. K. Keogh. Mahwah, NJ: Lawrence Erlbaum Publishers.

Chapter • 11

Group Size and Time Allotted to Intervention:
Effects for Students with Reading Difficulties

Sharon Vaughn and Sylvia Linan-Thompson

Mounting evidence suggests that most students with reading problems can make significant gains in reading if provided systematic, explicit and intensive reading instruction based on critical elements associated with improved reading such as phonemic awareness, phonics, fluency in word recognition and text reading, and comprehension (Foorman et al. 1998; Foorman and Torgesen 2001; Iversen and Tunmer 1993; Torgesen et al. 2001; Vellutino et al. 1996). Theory and research-based evidence have converged to define the critical elements of reading intervention associated with improved outcomes for struggling readers. This has been one of the most significant findings in education in the past 50 years (Foorman and Torgesen 2001; Stanovich 2000).

A consistent finding in meta-analyses examining effective instructional practices for students with reading and learning disabilities is that a combination of explicit and systematic instruction with carefully scaffolded instruction that provides modeling and feedback is associated with improved academic outcomes (Elbaum et al. 2000; Swanson, Hoskyn, and Lee 1999; Vaughn, Gersten, and Chard 2000). Other features of instruction for reading that are associated with effective outcomes are grouping for reading instruction and the duration of supplemental reading instruction. In this chapter, we discuss the implications of two critical features of supplemental reading instruction for students with reading problems: group size and intensity of instruction as measured by duration of instruction. Findings from two intervention studies conducted in subsequent years with two different cohorts of second-grade students at-risk for reading problems are presented. The studies were designed to address questions regarding the features of instruction (i.e., grouping and intensity of instruction) that are associated with improved outcomes for students with reading problems.

GROUP SIZE AND READING OUTCOMES

Grouping practices, like many other practices in reading instruction, have been on a swinging pendulum (Chall 2000). Until the early 1980s, reading instruction in the elementary grades consisted of small, same-ability group instruction provided most frequently by the classroom teacher. For the last two decades, grouping instruction has shifted so that small-group instruction occurred infrequently and students were most often provided whole-class instruction followed by independent work (Schumm, Moody, and Vaughn 2000). Flexible grouping has been advocated (Radencich and McKay 1995) though not usually implemented (Schumm, Moody and Vaughn 2000).

The shift away from small, same-ability groups was grounded in two prevailing positions. First, ability grouping was associated with differential treatment for low and high achieving groups, reduced self-concept on the part of low achieving students, and reduced instructional time for low achievers (e.g., Allington 1980; Barr 1989; Calfee and Brown 1979; Hiebert 1983; Hunter 1978). The second position was that learning to read was a natural process and that as long as students were provided with ample opportunity to interact with a range of authentic texts they would acquire the skills needed to be proficient readers (Goodman 1996). These two prevailing positions provided the support educators needed to shift from small same-ability groups to whole-class instruction for reading.

Increasing research on the effectiveness of small-groups and pairs on improved outcomes in reading (Elbaum et al. 1999; Lou et al. 1996; Mathes and Fuch 1994; Swanson, Hoskyn, and Lee 1999), has yielded considerable evidence that same-ability, small-group reading instruction, particularly for students with significant reading problems, is warranted. Furthermore, recent research has documented the effectiveness of supplemental small-group reading intervention on low-performing students in the primary grades (e.g., Haager and Windmueller 2001).

Over the past few years, my colleagues and I have investigated grouping practices for reading in both general and special education settings. Initially, we conducted individual interviews with 29 third-grade teachers and 20 special education teachers (Moody, Vaughn, and Schumm 1997) to obtain their report on how they grouped students for reading instruction and why they grouped students that way. A subset of 29 of these teachers agreed to participate in follow-up focus group interviews. General education teachers perceived that they had less control than did special education teachers over issues related to grouping for reading instruction. Although special education teachers perceived that they could group students in whatever ways they determined were productive, general education teachers perceived that there were curriculum issues decided at the school and district level that significantly influenced how they grouped students for reading. General education teachers reported that they primarily used whole-class instruction and mixed-ability groups as a follow-up to their whole-class instruction for reading. Special education teachers reported that they were far less likely to use whole-class instruction and revealed that they grouped students based on academic and social needs.

Subsequent to teacher interviews, we conducted interviews with students ($n = 549$), from 3rd, 4th, and 5th grade, to determine their perceptions of how they were grouped for reading instruction and their preferences about grouping practices (Elbaum, Schumm, and Vaughn 1997). Overall, these students reported that working in a small group or with one other student was more beneficial when students participated who represented a range of abilities. However, students also reported that whole-class instruction and working alone were the formats for reading instruction that were most often provided by their teacher. This report by students is consistent with classroom observations during reading (Fisher and Hiebert 1990; Schumm, Moody, and Vaughn 2000). Students also frequently referred to getting help from classmates but never mentioned getting help from the teacher.

Our third study (Schumm, Moody, and Vaughn 2000) was a year-long investigation with 29 third-grade teachers—all of whom had at least one student with significant reading disabilities in their class for reading instruction. Consistent with previous findings, observations during reading instruction indicated that teachers used primarily whole-class activities and independent activities. Teachers infrequently used small groups and student pairing. Of the 29 third grade teachers, only 3 implemented same-ability groups and that was primarily for the low-achieving students. Four other teachers regularly used mixed-ability groups. Despite the fact that all 29 teachers taught in a highly urban setting where many of their children were reading significantly below grade level, fewer than 25% used any grouping procedure other than whole-class instruction with independent activities. Student outcomes for all achievement groups for word recognition and comprehension were low compared with previous yearly gains. Overall, high-achieving students (based on above average grade level reading at the beginning of the school year) made only 0.7 of one-year gain in word recognition and one-year gain in comprehension. Average-achieving students faired much worse with 0.5 of a year gain in word recognition and 0.2 in comprehension. Low-achieving students (reading at second grade level) made only 0.4 of a year gain in word recognition and 0.3 in comprehension. The lowest gains of all were made by the students identified as reading disabled who acquired only 0.1 of a year gain in word recognition and 0.2 in comprehension.

These lackluster achievement scores might be better tolerated if students' attitudes and interest in reading were positively affected. In this same study, students' attitudes toward reading were examined on recreational reading and school reading. Students' attitudes toward reading in school and at home declined significantly from fall to spring. Thus, we concluded that this "one size fits all" method of whole-class instruction in reading followed by independent activities "fits" none of these students very well. Average-to-high achieving students made very modest academic gains and lower scores on reading attitude over the school year, and students who were low-achieving or with reading disabilities demonstrated minimal or no gains and also reported lower attitudes toward reading over the school year.

Our next step was to conduct two meta-analyses on grouping practices for reading. The first meta-analysis examined the effectiveness of grouping practices on reading outcomes for students with disabilities (Elbaum et al. 1999). A complete search of all studies that included a comparison group and took place between 1975 and 1995 was conducted (dissertations and other unpublished sources such as ERIC were included in the search). Results yielded 19 studies that contrasted different grouping formats and one study that contrasted different roles in student pairing.

Results for reading outcomes by three different grouping patterns were reported. The overall effect size for alternative grouping formats (small group, student pairs) when compared with very large group or whole class was 0.43. Reducing the group size improved the outcomes for students with disabilities by nearly 1/2 of a standard deviation not controlling for the instructional program. Student pairing, which requires minimal time from the teacher, was associated with an overall effect size of 0.40. Small group instruction yielded a high effect size (1.61), however, it reflected the findings from one study only. Overall, the findings provided strong support for the use of alternative grouping practices for reading instruction. "Ultimately, the design and implementation of more effective grouping practices is likely to have a direct impact not only on students' reading achievement but also on the extent to which students with disabilities can be successfully integrated in general education classrooms for reading instruction" (p.411, Elbaum et al. 1999).

A second meta-analysis examined the effects of one-to-one instruction in reading for students with reading problems (Elbaum et al. 2000). A complete search of all studies that included a comparison group and were published between 1975 and 1998 was conducted (dissertations and other unpublished sources such as ERIC were included in the search). Results yielded 29 studies and 42 samples that contrasted one-to-one instruction with an alternative grouping format (almost always whole-class instruction).

The overall effect size for one-to-one tutoring (one adult with one child) was 0.41. Trained college students (1.65) and trained volunteers (0.59) were particularly effective as tutors. Studies within the meta-analysis that compared one-to-one instruction with one-to-three instruction resulted in no significant gains in favor of one-to-one instruction.

In summary, multiple data sources including student and teacher interviews and surveys, as well as classroom observations have revealed that the norm for reading instruction over the last 10 years has been whole-class, undifferentiated instruction. Furthermore, this one size fits all approach to grouping for reading has yielded minimal gains particularly for the poorest readers. It is not difficult to explain why teachers might prefer teaching all students to read at the same time. Teachers perceive that they are better able to: (a) maintain classroom "control," (b) prepare one lesson rather than the multiple lessons needed with small group instruction, and (c) reduce the number of materials and preparations required. Thus, teaching the class as a whole is less effortful and reduces many classroom management problems that may arise when some students work independently or with other students while the teacher is providing instruction to a small group.

Unfortunately, many students' progress in reading is inadequate unless they are provided the intensive and systematic instruction available through small-group instruction.

Study 1: Varying Group Size and Reading Outcomes for Struggling Readers

We have been interested in the features of instruction (e.g., grouping, duration) that are associated with effective outcomes for struggling readers. As a result of the two previously reported meta-analyses (Elbaum et al. 1999, 2000), we realized that there was an inadequate research base for determining the effectiveness of various group sizes on reading outcomes for struggling readers. Studies that held intervention constant and compared group size were not available (Elbaum et al. 2000). The two studies that compared one-to-one instruction with small group instruction (one-to-three, Acalin 1995; and one-to-four, Evan, 1996) revealed that outcomes were not differentiated in favor of one-to-one instruction. However, in both of these studies the one-to-one instruction was Reading Recovery and the small group instruction was a different intervention. Thus, it is difficult to discern if group size or intervention type or both influenced outcomes. The following study attempted to address the question about "how small" does small group instruction need to be to improve reading outcomes significantly for struggling readers.

In this study, 2nd grade monolingual English students and English language learners (all students were learning to read in English) were assigned to the same treatment condition (30 minutes of daily supplemental reading instruction for 58 sessions) and the group size varied (one teacher with 10 students 1:10, one teacher with 3 students 1:3, and one teacher with one student—1:1). This study allowed us to determine the effectiveness of 3 different grouping formats on student performance. All students (n = 77) were learning to read in English.

Participants.   The 77 second-graders who participated in this study were drawn from 10 Title I schools in two neighboring school districts. All students were identified as struggling readers by their teachers and failed the second-grade benchmark test in reading (Texas Primary Reading Inventory).

Measures and Procedures.   All measures were administered on three occasions over the course of about 20 weeks. All students were administered measures immediately prior to the intervention, after the intervention (approximately 58 daily sessions), and then between four to six weeks after supplemental intervention stopped.

Measures administered on each occasion included: (a) Woodcock Reading Mastery Test Revised (WRMTR; American Guidance Services 1987) subtests for word attack and passage comprehension, (b) the Test of Oral Reading Fluency (TORF; Children's Educational Services, Inc., 1987), and (c) Dynamic Indicators of Basic Early Literacy Skills (DIBELS): Segmentation Fluency (Good and Kaminski 1996). Raw scores were reported for the WRMTR-Word Attack and Passage Comprehension. Words correct per minute were calculated for the TORF, and for the DIBELS segmentation fluency the number of sound segments produced in one minute in response to words provided orally (see tables I, II, and III).

Students were assigned within school to one of three groups: (a) one-to-one reading instruction (1:1), (b) one-to-three reading instruction (1:3), or (c) one-to-ten reading instruction (1:10). All students received the same number of sessions of supplemental reading ($n = 58$) for approximately 30 minutes each session and addressed the same critical elements of reading described in the intervention. To assure that the elements of reading remained relatively constant across all groups an Implementation Validity Checklist was used to assure adherence to the treatment protocol. Tutors were observed nine times to assure implementation was conducted with fidelity

Intervention.   The intervention was provided by five female tutors experienced in teaching reading to students with reading difficulties (four were certified teachers). All tutors were provided extensive training prior to the initiation of the study (more than 20 hours) and met with the research team leaders each week to obtain further information on how to address specific issues related to teaching and intervention—particularly for students who were making inadequate progress.

The intervention focused on the elements of reading development that have been identified as essential for struggling readers (Adams 1990; Foorman and Torgesen 2001; National Reading Panel Report 2000; Pressley 1998; Snow, Burns, and Griffin 1998). These included: phonemic awareness, phonics with special attention to systematic mastery of sound-letter relationships as well as word families, fluency (word and text), instructional level reading and comprehension, and spelling with writing.

Effect size findings.   Results from this study indicated that second-grade students with reading problems who were provided explicit instruction in the critical elements of reading in groups of 1:1, 1:3,

Table I. Means, Standard Deviations, and Pre to Post Effect Sizes for Outcome Measures: 1 on 1, n = 27

Outcome Measure	Pre-test		Post-test		Follow-up		Pre to Post Effect Size
	M	SD	M	SD	M	SD	d
Word Attack	7.44	7.32	14.85	8.16	14.92	7.88	.82
Passage Comprehension	10.63	6.74	17.78	7.37	19.30	7.62	1.53
Segmentation Fluency	36.92	18.31	54.74	8.72	52.52	12.46	.95
TORF	25.48	20.28	50.37	34.54	54.37	34.11	1.41

Note. TORF = Test of Oral Reading Fluency

Table II. Means, Standard Deviations, and Pre to Post Effect Sizes for Outcome Measures: 1 on 3, n = 29

Outcome Measure	Pre-test		Post-test		Follow-up		Pre to Post Effect Size
	M	SD	M	SD	M	SD	d
Word Attack	8.14	6.79	12.86	7.59	13.72	6.62	.72
Passage Comprehension	10.72	6.17	17.14	6.21	19.55	6.29	1.42
Segmentation Fluency	37.66	14.64	50.69	10.33	51.66	12.24	.81
TORF	23.76	16.00	45.31	25.32	48.72	27.37	1.72

Note. TORF = Test of Oral Reading Fluency

Table III. Means, Standard Deviations, and Pre to Post Effect Sizes for Outcome Measures: 1 on 10, *n* = 21

Outcome Measure	Pre-test		Post-test		Follow-up		Pre to Post Effect Size
	M	*SD*	*M*	*SD*	*M*	*SD*	*d*
Word Attack	2.90	3.45	8.86	5.27	8.14	5.14	1.46
Passage Comprehension	7.90	5.01	12.48	5.69	14.43	6.04	1.07
Segmentation Fluency	33.10	13.20	45.57	10.84	45.52	10.60	.90
TORF	17.38	9.36	31.05	15.34	32.67	14.78	1.43

Note. TORF = Test of Oral Reading Fluency

and 1:10 made progress in reading. Regardless of group size, gains in comprehension, phoneme segmentation and fluency yielded high effect sizes (see tables I, II, and III). Only for group size of 1:3 for word attack were the effect sizes smaller than .80. In second grade, the number of words read correctly in a minute may be the best indicator of overall performance (Hasbrouck and Tindal 1992). In 12 weeks, students in the 1:10 group gained 14 words on average, in the 1:3 group they averaged 21 words per minute gains, and in the 1:1 group almost 25 words per minute gains. For a complete report on the findings from this study, see Vaughn et al. (in review).

DURATION OF INSTRUCTION AND RESPONSE TO TREATMENT

Despite the general acceptance that intensity of instruction can have a significant effect on outcomes for struggling readers (Brown and Felton 1990; Foorman and Torgesen 2001; Kavale 1988), minimal attention in the research literature on reading interventions has been directed toward determining the amount of supplemental instruction required to assure students meet minimal criteria for success in reading. Lack of sufficient time for supplemental reading instruction has been cited as a reason for not better understanding issues related to duration of reading interventions and outcomes (Brown and Felton 1990; Simmons and Kameenui 1998). For the purpose of this study, we considered intensity of instruction to include the amount of time (both each day and then over time) that an instructional program is provided to students.

Torgesen and colleagues (2001) conducted an extensive examination into the long-term effects of an intensive intervention designed to improve reading outcomes for students who were identified as learning disabled and significantly low in reading. Three cohorts of 20 students (8–10 years old) received one of two instructional programs, Auditory Discrimination in Depth program (ADD) or Embedded Phonics (EP). Providing one-to-one instruction in 50-minute sessions twice a day until 67.5 hours were completed ensured intensity of instruction over a relatively short period of time (8–9 weeks). After completing the intensive intervention, students received generalization training once a week for 50 minutes for eight weeks in their classroom. Student growth was statistically significant from pre-test to post-test on all reading measures. During the follow-up period (post-test to 2 year follow-up), students' growth was stable on four reading measures and increased on three measures. On one measure, word attack, students' growth failed to keep pace with that of their peers. However, when students were grouped according to their standard scores on reading measures at pre-test (high, mid +, mid -, low) and their growth rates were compared over time, the strongest divergence among the groups occurred during the follow-up period. Therefore, intensive instruction provided over a short period of time (8–9 weeks), resulted in substantial gains that were maintained for up to 2 years with differential effects for students with varying levels of reading skills at pre-test.

In an examination of the effects of a one-year or two-year treatment on various outcomes including reading on youngsters with learning problems who were assessed after one and then two years of a multifaceted, neurocognitive treatment indicated that students made gains in reading after one year and continued gains after the second year with the greatest gains occurring from year 1 to year 2 (Lamminmaki et al. 1997). This study suggests that for many students with significant learning problems, an extensive intervention time is needed. Reynolds and colleagues have conducted considerable research with young children at-risk and have determined that an add-on intervention that is provided over time is associated with improved outcomes in reading (Reynolds 1994).

To provide an overview of current research on the effects of duration on student outcomes, we applied a procedure used by McGuiness, McGuiness, and McGuiness (1996) and Torgesen and colleagues (2001) in which the number of standard score points gained per hour of intervention can be calculated as a metric of the effectiveness of the intervention. Table IV summarizes the findings from research studies that: (a) provided early intervention in reading to young students with significant reading problems, and (b) used one or more of the subtests from the *Woodcock Reading Mastery Test* (American Guidance Services 1987). We calculated the number of standard score points gained per hour of intervention for each of the studies for those measures for which standard scores as a common metric were reported (subtests from WRMTR).

Considering the McGuiness, McGuiness, and McGuiness (1996) study as an outlier, there is considerable convergence in the findings. Word attack scores ranged from .26 to .76, word identification scores ranged from .07 to .34 and passage comprehension from .11 to .90. Group size did not appear to be associated with improved outcomes although most students were taught in groups of yhree or fewer children. The O'Shaughnessy and Swanson (2000) study demonstrated high effects per hour of intervention for word attack and passage comprehension and they had one of the larger group sizes, one adult with five students.

Table IV.   Gains in Standard Scores Per Hour of Instruction

Studies		Word Attack	Word Identi-fication	Passage Compre-hension
Alexander et al. (1991) 7.8 to 12. 8 years old (mean CA = 10.8) 65.2 hours, 1 : 1 No control group		.32	.19	–
Lovett et al. (1994) 7 to 13 years old (Mean CA = 9.6) 35 hours, 1 : 2 Control group	PHAB/DI method	–	.13	.14
	WIST method	–	.11	.11
Lovett and Steinbach (1997) 7 to 12 years old 35 hours, 1 : 2 or 3 Control group	PHAB/DI method	.31	.10	–
	WIST method	.29	.11	–
McGuinness, McGuinness, and McGuinness (1996) 6.2 to 15.11 years old 8 hours, 1 : 1 No control group		2.57	1.7	–
O'Shaughnessy and Swanson (2000) 2nd graders (Mean CA = 7.8 years old) 9 hours, 1 : 5 Control group	PAT method	.76	.21	.70
	WAT method	.49	.07	.90
Rashotte, MacPhee, and Torgesen (2001) 6.1 to 12.8 years old (Mean CA = 8.9) 35 hours, 1 : 3 to 5 Control group		.47	.17	.35
Torgesen et al. (2001) 8 to 10 years old 67.5 hours, 1:1 No control group	ADD method	.41	.20	.12
	EP method	.30	.21	.15
Truch (1994) 6 to 12 years old (60%), 13 to 17 (25%), 18 and over (15%) 80 hours, 1 : 1 No control group		–	.21	–

Table IV.   continued

Studies		Word Attack	Word Identi- fication	Passage Compre- hension
Vadasy et al. (1997) 1st graders 54 hours, 1:1 Control group		–	.34	–
Vaughn et al. (2002) 6.9 to 9.2 years old (mean CA = 7.7) 29 hours, 1 : 1, 1 : 3,	1:1	.41	.14	.25
or 1 : 10	1:3	.25	.12	.21
No control group	1:10	.23	.07	.16
Wise, Ring, and Olson (1999)	Combination	.31	.22	.14
7 to 11 years old 40 hours, 1: 3 + 1:1	Sound manipulation	.31	.24	.05
computer practice Control group	Articulation only	.26	.28	.07

Note. CA = Chronological Age. ADD method = The Auditory Discrimination in Depth. EP method = Embedded Phonics. PHAB/DI method = Phonological analysis and blending/direct instruction program. WIST method = Word identification strategy training program. PAT method = Phonological Awareness Training. WAI method = Word Analogy Training. 1 : 1 = One on one grouping instruction. 1 : 3 = 1 : 3 grouping instruction. 1 : 10 = 1 : 10 grouping instruction.

Study 2: Duration and Reading Outcomes for Struggling Readers

In our second study, we addressed intensity (number of hours supplemental instruction was provided) by providing a similar intervention to all students (Vaughn, Linan-Thompson, and Hickman-Davis, in review) and exiting students from supplemental intervention at the end of 10-week intervals based on meeting a prior established criteria for exit. Thus, a cohort of second-grade students was assigned to supplemental reading instruction in group sizes of 1:3 (the most effective and efficient group size) and the duration of their reading instruction varied based on their response to treatment. Criteria for exit-from-treatment were established and students were tested after each 10 weeks of instruction (approximately 50 sessions) for 3 10-week segments (30 weeks total). In this study, the time or duration a student participated in supplemental reading instruction varied based on student progress. The core reading instruction in the classroom was maintained throughout the provision of supplemental reading instruction. We were interested in the variation of time required for struggling second-grade readers to acquire proficiency in reading so that they might be discontinued from supplemental reading instruction and able to learn from the core reading instruction in the classroom. In essence, considering time as one of the most critical components of intensity, we were interested in variation in the amount of time required to meet pre-established criteria for exit within a relatively homogenous group of struggling readers.

Thus, the purpose of this study was to determine: (a) treatment effectiveness, (b) the number of students who would meet exit criteria after 10, 20, and 30 weeks of supplemental instruction, (c) the number of students who would not meet exit criteria, and (d) the variables that would predict membership in the group of students who did not meet exit criteria.

Participants. Forty-five second-grade students participated (25 females, 20 males). The majority of the students were Hispanic/Latino (largely Mexican-American; $n = 35$), 6 were white and 4 African American. Fifteen students were English language learners. Nine were enrolled in bilingual education classrooms and 6 received English as a Second Language (ESL) services. All students were learning to read in English.

Measures and Procedures. Reading fluency was used as the primary criteria for exit from supplemental reading instruction and was administered at 4 data points: prior to intervention and after 10, 20, and 30 weeks of intervention. All students were administered the fluency measure (TORF; Children's Educational Services, Inc. 1987) at all data points even after they met exit criteria. Measures administered prior to intervention and then after 30 weeks later were the *Woodcock Reading Mastery Test Revised* (WRMTR; American Guidance Services 1987) subtests for word attack and passage comprehension, and the *Comprehensive Test of Phonological Processing* (Wagner, Torgesen, and Rashotte 1999), blending, elision, rapid letter naming and rapid digit naming subtests.

Students who met exit criteria at each testing period discontinued participation in the subsequent 10 weeks of intervention. Criteria for exit from the intervention were pre-established as: (1) performance on the TORF above 55 CWPM on a 2nd grade level passage, (2) mastery level on TPRI second grade screening, and (3) performance of at least 50 CWPM on second grade passages for 3 consecutive weeks during weekly progress monitoring.

Intervention. The intervention was provided by four female tutors experienced in teaching reading to students with reading difficulties. All tutors were provided extensive training prior to the initiation of the study (more than 20 hours) and met with the research team leaders each week to obtain further information on how to address specific issues related to teaching and intervention—particularly for students who were making inadequate progress. Additionally, all tutors were observed and coached by researchers to assure quality implementation. Tutors taught students in groups of three and to the extent possible, students were placed with other students who had similar reading skills and needs.

The intervention focused on five elements of reading development that have been identified as essential for beginning readers (National Reading Panel Report 2000; Snow, Burns, and Griffin 1998): phonemic awareness, phonics with special attention to systematic mastery of sound-letter relationships as well as word families, fluency (word and text), instructional level reading and comprehension, and spelling with writing

Findings. The first research question asked, *"How many struggling readers will exit at each of the three testing periods?"* Upon completion of the study students were assigned to one of the four categories based on their performance: (a) *early exit*—students whose progress in reading allowed them to exit supplemental reading instruction after 10 weeks of intervention ($n = 6$ boys, 4 girls; 9 Hispanic/Latino and 1 African-American), (b) *mid-term exit*—students whose progress allowed them to exit supplemental reading instruction after 20 weeks of intervention ($n = 5$ boys, 9 girls; 10 Hispanic/Latino, 2 African American, 2 white), (c) *late exit*—students whose progress in reading allowed them to exit supplemental reading instruction after 30 weeks of intervention ($n = 5$ boys, 5 girls; 9 Hispanic/Latino, 1 white), and (d) *no exit*—students whose progress was never adequate for exiting instruction even after 30 weeks of supplemental reading instruction ($n = 4$ boys, 7 girls; 7 Hispanic/Latino, 1 African American, 3 white). Interestingly, approximately equal numbers of students were in each of the four groups, with slightly more students who exited after 20 weeks (14 students exited after 20 weeks and 10 exited after 10 and 30 weeks). Eleven students did not meet exit criteria even after 30 weeks of supplemental instruction. The students who never met criteria to exit from supplemental instruction represented fewer than 25% of the struggling readers in this study. The sample of struggling readers in this study represented the lowest 20% of second-grade students in these schools, thus the students who did not profit substantially from supplemental instruction represented less than 5% of the school population.

The second research question asked, *"What number of students who met exit criteria after 10 and 20 weeks of supplemental reading instruction will continue to meet criteria?"* Twenty-three of the 24 students who met exit criteria after 10 and 20 weeks continued to make gains without supplemental reading instruction. All of the students who exited after 10 weeks of supplemental reading instruction, and all but one student who exited after 20 weeks of supplemental reading instruction, continued to meet criteria for exit at subsequent testing periods.

A related question addressed was, *"How many of the students who met exit criteria after 10 and 20 weeks of supplemental reading instruction made minimal progress in the classroom—defined as averaging 1 correct word per week on the TORF?"* Using the gains on the TORF over time for each group as an indicator of progress, we can determine those students in each group who continued to make progress in reading with only the reading instruction provided by the general education classroom. Of the 10 students who met exit criteria after 10 weeks, all of them continued to make at least one word per week progress on the TORF for the next 10 weeks. However, after 20 weeks without supplemental reading instruction, 3 of the 10 students made less than minimal progress on the TORF. In all three cases, these students made little or no progress from week 20 to week 30. One student gained 3 words during that 10-week period, another student 4 words and a third student's performance was reduced by 4 words. The long-term performance of students who met exit criteria after 20 weeks of reading instruction is not as positive as the early exit group (after 10 weeks). Although all of the students who exited after 10 weeks continued to make progress without supplemental reading, only 9 of the 15 students who exited after 20 weeks continued on an acceptable trajectory for reading fluency. Three of the 5 students lost ground by having their fluency decrease slightly over the 10-week period and the two who increased made very minimal gains.

The overall implications from these data suggest that many but not all of the students who made very good gains in supplemental reading instruction continued to make progress in the general education classroom after supplemental reading instruction was no longer provided. Students who failed to thrive (did not make minimal gains on the TORF) in the general education classroom following supplemental reading instruction can not be identified by pre-intervention scores on the TORF since "thrivers" (those who made adequate progress post supplemental intervention) and those who did not, covered the range of early TORF scores. It may be that some of the learning problems demonstrated by students who are at-risk for reading problems are that they have difficulties associated with learning through large class instruction and their learning needs can really only be met by small-group instruction.

These findings can be illustrated by highlighting the progress of two students who participated in the supplemental reading instruction: Austin and Eduardo. Both of these students performed similarly during the first 10 weeks of supplemental reading instruction and made substantial gains. However, they differ in that Austin failed to continue gains in fluency after he exited supplemental instruction whereas Eduardo's fluency scores continued to increase. See figure 1 for a graphic illustration.

As can be seen in figure 1, Austin's pre-intervention scores on the TORF were 24 Correct Words Per Minute (CWPM) and after 10 weeks of supplemental instruction his scores increased substantially to 73 CWPM. Both passages represented 2nd grade reading

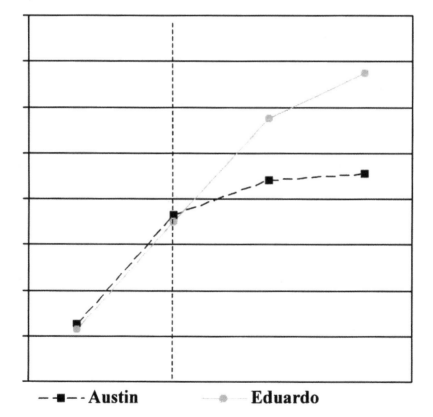

— ■ — **Austin**   ● **Eduardo**

Figure 1.   Austin and Eduardo's progress on the 2nd grade passages of the TORF over time (exited after 10 weeks of supplemental instruction).
Note: Dotted vertical line is where each student met exit criteria and supplemental reading instruction was terminated.

levels. Austin averaged an increase of 4.9 CWPM per week during supplemental reading instruction, which reflects a highly accelerated growth rate in reading. Ten weeks after exit from supplemental reading instruction, his TORF performance was 88 CWPM suggesting that he was continuing to profit from the general education classroom, but not at anywhere near the rate he profited when provided supplemental reading instruction. As compared with his rate of growth of 4.9 CWPM, now he was improving at an average rate of 1.5 CWPM per week. His benefit from the general education classroom without supplemental reading decreased even more over the subsequent 10-week period. His CWPM of 91 indicated a gain of only 3 words in 10 weeks. Thus, this student went from almost 5 CWPM gain per week during supplemental instruction to less than .4 CWPM in less than 20 weeks following exit from supplemental reading instruction. This provides significant evidence that this student's performance in the classroom did not adequately support his growth in reading.

In contrast, Eduardo began supplemental reading instruction with a similar though slightly lower performance on the TORF (23 CWPM) (see figure 1). After 10 weeks of supplemental instruction he continued to mirror the performance of Austin on the TORF by improving the same number of words per week and scoring 70 CWPM. However, the comparison stops there as Eduardo continued to profit considerably from the reading instruction in the general education classroom by testing 115 CWPM on the TORF ten weeks after supplemental reading instruction was discontinued and 135 CWPM twenty weeks after supplemental reading instruction. The cases of Austin and Eduardo illustrate that students' progress in reading following supplemental reading instruction will not progress at the same rate and thus students that meet exit criteria may still need to be monitored recognizing that some may need additional supplemental instruction later. We believe that there is sufficient evidence to support the position that students who are at-risk for reading problems require ongoing progress monitoring with supplemental support as needed to assure they maintain progress.

Students who required 20 weeks of supplemental reading instruction were more likely to return to low levels of performance when supplemental reading instruction was terminated. Ten weeks after supplement instruction was discontinued, 5 of 14 of these students made less than minimal gains in the general education classroom. Armando illustrates a student who failed to continue to profit from reading instruction when the general reading program was all that was provided, whereas Patricia represents a "thriver" who continued to profit from the general reading program alone. These students make an interesting contrast since both of them are English language learners and both demonstrated similar scores at pre-intervention, after 10 weeks of intervention, again after 20 weeks of intervention. They contrast markedly when followed 10 weeks after supplemental instruction was discontinued (see figure 2). Patricia was able to profit from the general reading program provided in the classroom whereas Armando was not. This again illustrates the value of continuous progress monitoring of at-risk students because all do not profit from reading instruction provided as part of the general education program.

Did the four groups of students (early exit, mid-term exit, late exit, and no exit) benefit differentially from the supplemental reading instruction? All four groups of students (early exit, mid-term exit, late exit, and no exit) more than doubled their performance on the TORF

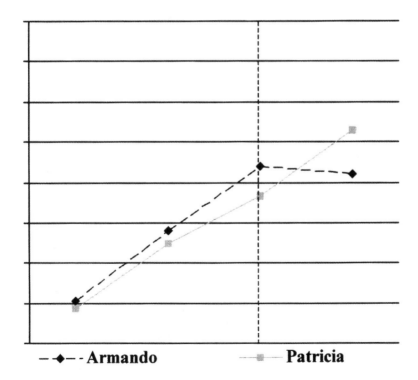

—◆— Armando   **—■— Patricia**

Figure 2.   Armando and Patricia's progress on the 2nd grade passages of the TORF over time (exited after 20 weeks of supplemental instruction). Note: Dotted vertical line is where each student met exit criteria and supplemental reading instruction was terminated.

from pre-test scores to scores 10 weeks after supplemental instruction. This suggests that all four groups of students profited considerably even from just 10 weeks of supplemental reading instruction. However, students in each group did not benefit equally. Standardized mean difference effect sizes on the TORF after 10 weeks were: 2.75 (10 week exit), 2.32 (20 week exit), 2.57 (30 week exit), 1.45 (no exit). These rates were pretty consistent over time as long as students remained in supplemental reading instruction. The ten students who met early exit criteria demonstrated fluency scores prior to supplemental instruction that were, relative to the other at-risk students, on the high end of the distribution.

All four groups made their largest gains on the TORF during the first 10 weeks of instruction. This corresponds with other research that indicates that students often make the largest gains initially from the intervention in reading and though their gains are adequate as the instruction continues over time, they are less substantial. Refer again to table IV, which provides an overview of the standard score points per hour of intervention as a metric of effectiveness. You can see from this table that all but two (McGuinness, McGuinness, and McGuinness 1996—8 hours; O'Shaughnessy and Swanson 2000—9 hours) of the 12 studies reported provided interventions for 29 hours or longer. Both of the studies that provided relatively brief interventions were associated with the highest gains per hour providing some support for the high impact of early, intensive supplemental instruction.

Elbaum et al. (2000) conducted a meta-analysis on the effectiveness of one-to-one instruction for reading. They examined the extent to which duration of the study was associated with positive outcomes in reading. Results from 30 samples revealed that intervention was reliably associated with variation in effect sizes with those interventions that lasted up to 20 week yielding a significantly higher effect size (.65) compared with those that were longer than 20 weeks (.37). Thus, there seems to be compelling evidence that students with reading difficulties who are provided supplemental reading instruction realize the largest gains early, though they continue to make gains throughout the intervention.

We were also interested in determining *which measures prior to intervention would differentiate groups?* To address this question, scores from students who met exit criteria (10, 20, and 30 week exit students) were compared with those students never met exit criteria (see figure 3 for overall results). A series of a priori contrasts were performed coding early, mid, and late exit group participants as 1 with the no exit group coded as –3. Contrast coefficients were 1 1 1 –3. Word attack (WRMTR) and phonological processing com-

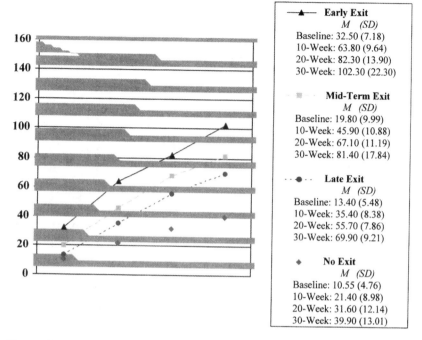

Figure 3. Mean TORF scores (Words correct per minute) over time for early exit, mid-term exit, late exit, and no exit students.

posite score (CTOPP) did not significantly differentiate these four groups of students at pre-test ($t = 1.57$, $p = .12$ for word attack; $t = .61$, $p = .54$ for phonological processing). The measures that seemed to predict student's ability to benefit from supplemental instruction were speed of processing as determined by rapid automatic naming tasks ($t = 3.70$, $p < .01$) as well as word-level reading ($t = 4.40$, $p < .01$) and comprehension ($t = 2.73$, $p < .01$). This would seem to indicate that while all the students lacked phonological awareness skills, those students who also lacked rapid automatic naming were less likely to benefit from instruction. This is in line with findings that differences in phonological awareness and rapid automatic naming influence the acquisition of early word reading skills (Wagner et al. 1997). Slower processing combined with lack of phonological awareness and phonics skills could account for the students' difficulty with word-level reading, which would in turn have an impact on oral reading fluency and comprehension.

SUMMARY

Through converging findings, the critical elements of reading instruction associated with improved outcomes for struggling readers have been identified (National Reading Panel Report 2000; Stanovich 2000). However, we know considerably less about how such critical features of reading instruction such as grouping and intensity of intervention influence outcomes for students as a whole and differentially for subgroups of students (Foorman and Torgesen 2001). This chapter summarized research on grouping and intensity of instruction and described two studies that addressed each of these issues.

The two studies highlighted in this chapter have contributed to our understanding of how the features of instruction influence reading outcomes. The first study examined the effects of group size (1:1, 1:3, 1:10) on the reading outcomes of students. By providing a similar treatment to all struggling readers, we were able to determine the effect of group size on student outcomes. Overall, we were impressed with the gains that students across groups made during the 11 weeks of daily supplemental reading instruction. There were no statistically significant differences between students in 1:1 and 1:3 groups though both groups outperformed students in 1:10.

The second study, on duration of intervention, provided all 2nd grade participants (struggling readers) with supplemental instruction until they achieved a priori established criteria for exit. Thus, student progress determined the length of intervention.

Results of these studies provide guidelines about the efficacy of varying group sizes and the intensity of supplemental instruction needed by struggling readers. This information can aid teachers and school administrators in planning for and allocating resources. For example, an administrator who knows that students who are provided supplemental reading instruction in small groups perform as well as students instructed one-to-one can provide supplemental instruction to more students. Likewise, determining the amount of instruction needed by students and providing supplemental instruction based on need allows administrators to assign supplemental teaching personnel more effectively.

Although we are making headway in identifying the intensity of instruction needed by students, we still need to determine how to meet the instructional needs of the students who do not thrive in general education classrooms even with good core reading instruction. Even when provided supplemental instruction, some students have difficulty maintaining those gains without ongoing support. Perhaps the clear and valued role of special education is to provide ongoing supplemental instruction to those students whose progress in the general education classroom is lower than expected.

ACKNOWLEDGMENTS

This work was supported in part by OSEP Grant #324D990023, Project IMPROVE: Improving Word Recognition of English Language Learners with Learning Disabilities. Special thanks to Ae-Hwa Kim whose expert assistance improved the chapter.

REFERENCES

Acalin, T. A. 1995. A comparison of Reading Recovery to Project Read. Unpublished master's thesis. California State University, Fullerton.

Adams, M. J. 1990. *Beginning to Read: Thinking and Learning about Print.* Cambridge, MA: MIT Press.

Alexander, A., Andersen, H. G., Heilman, P. C., Voeller, K. K. S., and Torgesen, J. K 1991. Phonological awareness training and remediation of analytic decoding deficits in a group of severe dyslexics. *Annals of Dyslexia* 41:193–206.

Allington, R. 1980. Teacher interruption behaviors during primary-grade oral reading. *Journal of Educational Psychology* 72:371–77.

American Guidance Services. 1987. *Woodcock Reading Manual.* Circle Pines, MN: American Guidance Services.

Barr, R. 1989. The social organization of literacy instruction. In *Cognitive and Social Perspectives for Literacy Research and Instruction*, eds. S. McCormick and J. Zutell. Chicago: National Reading Conference.

Brown, I. S., and Felton, R. H. 1990. Effects of instruction on beginning reading skills in children at risk for reading disability. *Reading and Writing: An Interdisciplinary Journal*, 2(3):223–41.

Calfee, R., and Brown, R. 1979. Grouping students for instruction. In *Classroom Management: Seventy-eighth Yearbook of the National Society of the Study of Education*, ed. D. L. Duke. Chicago: University of Chicago Press.

Chall, J. 2000. *The Academic Achievement Challenge: What Really Works in the Classroom?* New York, NY: Guilford.

Children's Educational Services, Inc. 1987. *Test of Oral Reading Fluency.* Minneapolis, MN: Author.

Elbaum, B. E., Schumm, J. S., and Vaughn, S. 1997. Urban middle-elementary students' perceptions of grouping formats for reading instruction. *Elementary School Journal* 97(5):475–500.

Elbaum, B. E., Vaughn, S., Hughes, M. T., and Moody, S. W. 2000. How effective are one-to-one tutoring programs in reading for elementary students at risk for reading failure? *Journal of Educational Psychology* 92(4):605–19.

Elbaum, B. E., Vaughn, S., Hughes, M. T., and Moody, S. W. 1999. Grouping practices and reading outcomes for students with disabilities. *Exceptional Children* 65(3):399–415.

Evans, T. L. P. 1996. I can read deze books: A quantitative comparison of the reading recovery program and a small- group instruction. Unpublished doctoral dissertation, Auburn University, Auburn, Alabama.

Fisher, C. W., and Hiebert, E. H. 1990. Characteristics of tasks in two approaches to literacy instruction. *Elementary School Journal* 91(1):3–18.

Foorman, B. R., Francis, D. J., Fletcher, J. M., Mehta, P., and Schatschneider, C. 1998. The role of instruction in learning to read: Preventing reading failure in at-risk children. *Journal of Educational Psychology* 90(1):37–55.

Foorman, B. R., and Torgesen, J. 2001. Critical elements of classroom and small-group instruction promote reading success for all children. *Learning Disabilities Research and Practice* 16(4):203–12.

Good, R. H., and Kaminski, R. A. 1996. Assessment for instructional decisions: Toward a proactive/prevention model of decision-making for early literacy skills. *School Psychology Quarterly* 11(4):326–36.

Goodman, K. S. 1996. On Reading. Portsmouth, NH: Heineman.

Haager, D., and Windmueller, M. P. 2001. Early reading intervention for English language learners at-risk for learning disabilities: Student and teacher outcomes in an urban school. *Learning Disability Quarterly* 24:235–50.

Hasbrouck, J. E., and Tindal, G. 1992. Curriculum-based oral reading fluency norms for students in grades 2 through 5. *Teaching Exceptional Children* 24:41–44.

Hiebert, E. H. 1983. An examination of ability grouping for reading instruction. *Reading Research Quarterly* 18:231–55.

Hunter, D. 1978. Student on-task behavior during second grade reading group meetings (Doctoral dissertation, University of Missouri-Columbia). Dissertation Abstracts International, 39, 4838A.

Iversen, S., and Tunmer, W. E. 1993. Phonological processing skills and the Reading Recovery program. *Journal of Educational Psychology* 85(1):112–26.

Kaminski, R. A., and Good, R. H. 1996. Toward a technology for assessing basic early literacy skills. *School Psychology Review* 25(2):215–27.

Kavale, K. A. 1988. The long-term consequences of learning disabilities. In *The Handbook of Special Education: Research and Practice*, eds. M. C. Wang, H. J. Walburg, and M. C. Reynolds. New York: Pergamon.

Lamminmaeki, T., Ahonen, T., Todd de Barra, H., Tolvanen, A., Michelsoon, K., and Lyytinen, H. 1997. Comparing efficacies of neurocognitive treatment and homework assistance programs for children with learning difficulties. *Journal of Learning Disabilities* 30(3):333–45.

Lou, Y., Abrami, P. C., Spence, J. C., Poulsen, C., Chambers, B., and d'Appolonia, S. 1996. Within-class grouping: A meta-analysis. *Review of Educational Research* 66(4):423–58.

Lovett, M. W., Borden, S. L., DeLuca, T., Lacerenza, L., Benson, N. J., and Brackstone, D. 1994. Treating the core deficits of developmental dyslexia: Evidence of transfer of learning after phonologically- and strategy-based reading training program. *Developmental Psychology* 30(6): 805–22.

Lovett, M. W., and Steinbach, K. A. 1997. The effectiveness of remedial programs for reading disabled children of different ages: Does the benefit decrease for older children? *Learning Disability Quarterly* 20: 189–210.

Mathes, P. G., and Fuchs, L. S. 1994. The efficacy of peer tutoring in reading for students with mild disabilities: A best-evidence synthesis. *School Psychology Review* 23(1):59–80.

McGuiness, C., McGuiness, D., and McGuiness, G. 1996. Phono-Graphix: A new method for remediating reading difficulties. *Annals of Dyslexia* 46:73–96.

Moody, S. W., Vaughn, S., and Schumm, J. S. 1997. Instructional grouping for reading: Teachers' views. *Remedial and Special Education* 18(6):347–56.

National Reading Panel 2000. Report of the national reading panel. Teaching children to read: An evidence-based assessment of the scientific research literature on reading and its implications for reading instructions (NIH Publication No. 00-4769). Washington, DC: U.S. Government Printing Office.

O'Shaughnessy, T. E., and Swanson, H. L. 2000. A comparison of two reading interventions for children with reading disabilities. *Journal of Learning Disabilities* 33(3):257–77.

Pressley, M. 1998. *Reading Instruction that Works: The Case for Balanced Teaching.* New York, NY: Guilford.

Radencich, M. C., and McKay, L. J. 1995. *Flexible Grouping for Literacy in the Elementary Grades* (ERIC Document Reproduction Service No. ED 382936).

Rashotte, C. A., MacPhee, K., and Torgesen 2001. The effectiveness of a group reading instruction program with poor readers in multiple graders. *Learning Disability Quarterly* 24:119–34.

Reynolds, A. J. 1994. Effects of a preschool plus follow-on intervention for children at risk. *Developmental Psychology* 30(6):787–804.

Schumm, J. S., Moody, S. W., and Vaughn, S. R. 2000. Grouping for reading instruction: Does one size fit all? *Journal of Learning Disabilities* 33(5):477–88.

Simmons, D. C., and Kameenui, E. ed. 1998. *What Reading Research Tells Us about Children with Diverse Learning Needs: Bases and Basics.* Mahwah, NJ: Lawrence Erlbaum Associates.

Snow, C. E., Burns, S., and Griffin, P. 1998. *Preventing Reading Difficulties in Young Children.* Washington, DC: National Academy Press.

Stanovich, K. E., 2000. *Progress in Understanding Reading: Scientific Foundations and New Frontiers.* New York: Guilford.

Swanson, H. L., Hoskyn, M., and Lee, C. 1999. *Interventions for Students with Learning Disabilities.* New York, NY: Guilford.

Texas Education Agency 1998. *Texas Primary Reading Inventory* (TPRI). Austin, TX: Texas Education Agency.

Torgesen, J. K., Alexander, A. W., Wagner, R. K., Rashotte, C. A., and Voeller, K. S., and Conway, T. 2001. Intensive remedial instruction for children with severe reading disabilities: Immediate and long-term outcomes from two instructional approaches. *Journal of Learning Disabilities* 34(1): 33–58,78.

Truch, S. 1994. Stimulating basic reading processes using auditory discrimination in depth. *Annals of Dyslexia* 44:60–80.

Vadasy, P. G., Jenkins, J. R., Antil, L. R., Wayne, S. K., and O'Connor, R. E. 1997. Community-based early reading intervention for at-risk first graders. *Learning Disabilities Research and Practice* 12(1):29–39.

Vaughn, S., Gersten, R., and Chard, D. J. 2000. The underlying message in LD intervention research: Findings from research syntheses. *Exceptional Children* 67(1):99–114.

Vaughn, S., Linan-Thompson, S., and Hickman-Davis, P. in press. Response to treatment as a means of identifying students with reading/ learning disabilities. *Exceptional Children.*

Vaughn, S., Linan-Thompson, S., Kouzekanani, K., Bryant, D., Dickson, S., and Blozis, S. A. in review. Grouping for reading instruction: Students with reading difficulties who are monolingual English or English language learners. *Remedial and Special Education.*

Vellutino, F. R., Scanlon, D. M., Sipay, E. R., Small, S. G., Pratt, A., Chen, R., and Denckla, M. B. 1996. Cognitive profiles of difficult-to-remediate and readily remediated poor readers: Early intervention as a vehicle for distinguishing between cognitive and experiential deficits as basic causes of specific reading disability. *Journal of Educational Psychology* 88(4):601–38.

Wagner, R., Torgesen, J., and Rashotte, C. 1999. *Comprehensive Test of Phonological Processing.* Austin, TX: PRO-ED.

Wagner, R. T., Torgesen, J. K., Rashotte, C. A., Hecht, S. A., Baker, T. A., Burgess, S. R., Donahue, J., and Garon, T. 1997. Changing relations between phonological processing abilities and word-level reading as children develop from beginning to skilled readers: A 5-year longitudinal study. *Developmental Psychology* 33:468–79.

Wise, B. W., Ring, J., and Olson, R. K. 1999. Training phonological awareness with and without explicit attention to articulation. *Journal of Experimental Child Psychology* 72:271–304.

Chapter • **12**

Can Diagnostic Reading Assessment Enhance General Educators' Instructional Differentiation and Student Learning?

Lynn S. Fuchs and Douglas Fuchs

In the United States today, one-quarter of all adults are functionally illiterate: They cannot read a note sent home from school or the information on a medicine bottle (Riley 1996). The problems associated with failing to learn to read are serious. Illiteracy is related to high-school drop out (Juel 1995), incarceration, lack of civic awareness and involvement, poor health maintenance, and poverty (Sarkees-Wircenski and Wircenski 1994). So, a heavy burden exists on schools to reduce the prevalence of reading failure.

In addressing this problem, important work has been accomplished over the past decade to identify instructional methods that reduce reading failure in general education. Foorman et al. (1998), for example, documented how explicit instruction on the alphabetic code reduced the percentage of failing first-grade students from approximately 45 to 16—an impressive accomplishment. Of course, a 16% failure rate still leaves an unacceptably high proportion of students with reading problems. A subset, perhaps one-third, of these nonresponders will require intensive forms of reading instruction, which necessitate resources beyond what can be expected of general education. Yet, schools continue to struggle to identify classroom methods that can enhance the reading development of the remaining two-thirds (i.e., 10% of the population or higher, depending on the nature of classroom reading instruction).

One aspect of general education that increases the challenge of meeting student needs is the diversity of skill found in any given classroom. To illustrate this diversity, we provide figure 1, where each vertical array displays the reading curriculum-based measurement (CBM) scores of a single class of second graders. On average, the difference between the lowest- and highest-performing student in the same class is 138 words read correctly from text in 1 minute; this constitutes the difference, for example, between a nonreader and one performing at a third-grade level. Moreover, in Class 10, where scores are most homogeneous, the range remains a disturbing 102 words and, even if we omit scores more than 1 standard deviation above the class mean, the average range is an impressive 93 words. At the same time, students' responsiveness to the same teacher's instructional environment also reveals dramatic heterogeneity. Within the same class, the difference between the lowest and highest CBM slopes averages 3.31 words of improvement per week (see figure 2). For example, in the most

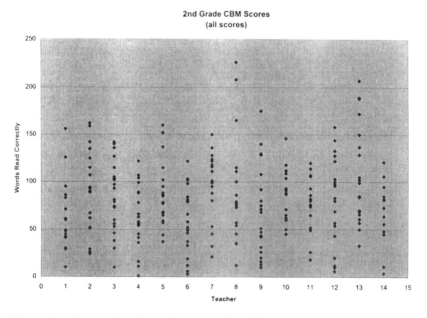

Figure 1.   Arrays of within-class curriculum-based measurement scores.

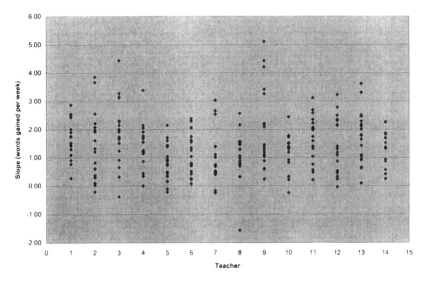

Figure 2.   Arrays of within-class curriculum-based measurement slopes.

representative class, slopes run from zero (i.e., no improvement per week) to a weekly increase of 3.39 words read correctly. Such heterogeneity, in both performance level and responsiveness to instruction, dictates that general education instruction be differentiated. Unfortunately, research indicates that classroom teachers rarely engage in instructional adaptation.

Instructional adaptation can be conceptualized in two categories (Fuchs, Fuchs, and Bishop 1992). *Routine adaptation* reflects the extent to which teachers establish beginning-of-school-year routines, in which all students participate, to incorporate varied goals and instructional methods systematically. Examples of routine adaptation are reading groups, which operate on different levels of text, and learning centers, which provide students with varied instructional experiences. Unfortunately, as Baker and Zigmond (1990) documented with teacher interviews and classroom observations, teachers typically teach reading in single, large groups with little in the way of routine adaptation.

Research also suggests that, when faced with specific student difficulties, general educators fail to introduce *specialized adaptation*. Kagan and Tippins (1991) found that when reflecting on videotapes of their teaching, student teachers did not generate instructional adaptations to address inadequate academic response. Experienced teachers also demonstrate few instances of only minor types of specialized adaptation (Baker and Zigmond 1990). Fuchs, Fuchs, and Bishop (1992) corroborated these findings, showing that only 25% of general educators made any revision to six-week instructional plans and that, of the adaptations introduced, few revealed alternative instructional approaches or varied goals. Of 57 teachers who had engaged in specialized adaptation, 13 moved students into supplementary services, 6 extended time lines for achieving objectives, and 2 reduced expectations for end-of-year performance. So, general educators tend to avoid specialized adaptation and, when they do adapt instruction, they do so in ways that lower expectations.

In light of this literature, we (Fuchs, Fuchs, and Bishop 1992) examined differences and similarities in adaptation as a function of classroom setting (general education classrooms vs. resource rooms), teacher type (general vs. special educator), and the assessment methods teachers use to prompt adaptation. Ongoing classroom assessment, operationalized as CBM, was important to instructional adaptation. Compared to general and special educators who did not use CBM, special educators using CBM modified goals more frequently, adjusted student-teacher ratios and instructional methods more often, and depended more heavily on objective methods for judging the success of new instructional activities and for gauging student progress. This illustrates the potential for classroom assessment to prompt instructional adaptation. And, in fact, a longstanding literature within special education documents how systematic, ongoing assessment can increase teachers' instructional adaptation and enhance student learning (see Fuchs and Fuchs 1998) for a summary of some of that work). The question nevertheless remains whether assessment can prompt *general educators* to differentiate their reading instruction to address the wide range of skills represented in their classrooms.

In this chapter, we explore this question. We begin by providing background information on CBM and explaining how, in reading, CBM is stronger for the purpose of identifying at-risk students, who require additional or alternative forms of instruction, than for providing teachers with diagnostic information about how to differentiate instruction to meet student needs. After presenting this CBM overview, we rely on work conducted in spelling to discuss the potential for diagnostic analysis for informing instructional planning. We then provide an overview of recent work exploring the utility of diagnostic reading analysis, incorporated within CBM, to enhance planning. We describe the nature of the diagnostic assessment and report on a study testing its contribution to general educators' reading instruction.

BACKGROUND INFORMATION ON CBM

Curriculum Based Measurement was designed to provide teachers with reliable, valid, and efficient indicators of academic competence with which to gauge individual student standing at a given point in time or to index student progress over time. Three features distinguish CBM from most forms of classroom assessment. First, CBM is standardized: The behaviors to be measured and the procedures for measuring those behaviors are specified. Second, CBM's focus is long term: Testing methods and content remain constant, with equivalent weekly tests spanning the school year. Third, each week's test content reflects the performance desired at the end of the year and therefore samples the many dimensions of the year's curriculum. So, standardized procedures, long-range consistency, and an integrated focus on the many skills cumulatively addressed in the annual curriculum are CBM's distinguishing features.

To use CBM in reading, a teacher establishes a broad, long-term outcome such as competent second-grade performance. Then, relying on established methods, the teacher identifies 30 passages of equivalent, second-grade difficulty. Each week, the teacher administers one test by having the student read aloud from a passage for 1 minute; the score is the number of words read correctly. Scores are graphed against time. Each simple, brief assessment produces an indicator of reading competence because it requires a multifaceted performance. This performance entails, for example, a reader's skill at automatically translating letters into coherent sound representations, unitizing those sound components into recognizable wholes and automatically accessing lexical representations, processing meaningful connections within and between sentences, relating text meaning to prior information, and making inferences to supply missing information. As competent readers translate text into spoken language, they coordinate these skills in an obligatory, seemingly effortless manner.

Because oral reading fluency reflects this complex performance, it can be used to characterize reading expertise and to track its development in the primary grades (e.g., Biemiller 1977–1978; Fuchs and Deno 1991). Performance levels at a given time are compared between individuals to designate risk status, and performance slopes are used to track individuals' reading development. These strategies for characterizing reading competence and improvement have been shown to be more sensitive to inter- and intra-individual differences than those offered by other reading measures (e.g., Marston, Fuchs, and Deno 1985). Frederiksen (1981), for example, demonstrated that the number of reading errors in context did not distinguish high- and low-ability readers as well as the chronometric aspect of processing, such as oral reading rate.

As might be expected, therefore, CBM demonstrates traditional reliability and validity. Strong concurrent validity has been demonstrated with respect to commercial reading tests (Fuchs and Fuchs 1992; Marston 1989), question answering, cloze completion, recall of passages (Fuchs and Fuchs 1992; Fuchs, Fuchs, and Maxwell 1988), and teacher judgments of reading competence (Fuchs and Fuchs 1992; Fuchs, Fuchs, and Deno 1982). Other technical features include predictive validity (Fuchs and Hamlett 1997), construct validity (Kranzler, Brownwell, and Miller 1996; Shinn et al. 1992), discriminative validity with respect to special education status (Deno, Mirkin, and Chiang 1982; Shinn et al. 1987) and grade (Deno 1985; Fuchs and Deno 1992; Fuchs et al. 1993), and stability (Fuchs, Deno, and Marston 1983; Fuchs and Fuchs 1992).

Of course, traditional reliability and validity are insufficient for the modeling of growth. Curriculum Based Measurement does, however, also demonstrate properties relevant for the depiction of change. For example, CBM provides a common test framework for children within a fixed age range; so, it is possible to judge performance over an academic year on the same raw score metric, which appears to tap a qualitatively constant construct within a given year. In addition, CBM provides alternate forms for repeatedly sampling performance over time, and produces acceptable standard errors of estimate relative to slope (Fuchs and Fuchs 1992). Research also provides the basis for an empirical approximation of the shape of CBM growth curves. Fuchs et al.. (1993), for example, examined reading growth rates when CBM was conducted for 1 school year. For most students, a linear relationship adequately modeled progress. (When significant quadratic terms occurred, growth was typically described by a negatively accelerating curve, in which student performance improves over a year, but the amount of that progress gradually declines. As suggested in cross-sectional data, a negatively accelerating pattern also characterizes growth across academic years.) These findings, in combination with corroborating evidence (Good, Deno, and Fuchs 1995; Good and Shinn 1990), support a tentative conceptualization of within-year CBM growth as a linear function, where slope is the primary parameter describing change.

In addition, CBM registers student improvement with code- or meaning-based approaches to reading instruction (Hintze and Shapiro 1997; Hintze, Shapiro, and Lutz 1994) and is sensitive to growth made under a range of treatments (Fuchs, Fuchs, and Hamlett 1989b; Marston, Fuchs, and Deno 1986). In a related way, teachers' instructional plans, developed in response to CBM, incorporate a wide range of reading methods including, for example, decoding instruction, repeated readings, vocabulary instruction, story grammar exercises, and semantic mapping activities (Fuchs et al. 1992). So, CBM is not tied to a particular reading instructional method and can be used to index response to alternative approaches to teaching reading.

Perhaps most importantly, however, studies indicate that CBM enhances special educators' capacity to plan programs for and effect achievement among students with serious reading problems. The methods by which CBM informs reading instruction rely on the graphed performance indicator. That is, decisions are tied to the rate of growth on the number of words read correctly in 1 minute: If a student's growth trajectory is judged to be adequate, the teacher increases the student's goal for year-end performance; if not, the teacher revises instruction. Research shows that these decision rules produce more varied instructional programs, which are more responsive to individual needs (Fuchs, Fuchs, and Hamlett 1989b), with more ambitious student goals (Fuchs, Fuchs, and Hamlett 1989a) and stronger end-of-year scores on commercial reading tests (e.g., Fuchs, Deno, and Mirkin 1984).

Nevertheless, the utility of CBM for the purpose of informing the nature of instructional plans is limited. Although reading text aloud with fluency may require simultaneous coordination across component skills, it is difficult to extract from the CBM score reliable descriptions of those component skills to describe a student's strengths and weaknesses. Moreover, although special educators, for whom the individual student is the decision-making unit, can use the graphed performance indicator to derive treatments inductively that produce growth, such a framework is not only logistically impossible for, but also conceptually unfamiliar to general educators (cf. Clark and Elmore 1981). For these reasons, we recently designed a reading diagnostic framework for use with CBM. To illustrate the potential of diagnostic analysis, we describe prior work on CBM diagnostic analysis in spelling.

CBM DIAGNOSTIC ANALYSIS IN SPELLING

With spelling CBM, teachers identify the pool of words constituting the annual curriculum. Each test is a random sample of 20 words (with replacement across tests); teachers dictate words at 7-second intervals for 2 minutes while students write words. The performance indicator of spelling competence at that grade level is the number of correctly spelled pairs of letters, or letter sequences (LS). To facilitate data management and diagnostic analysis, software structures test administration: Students enter responses via keyboard, and the computer scores and saves responses (Fuchs et al. 1991b). This permits item-by-item diagnostic analysis to supplement graphed analyses of the performance indicator.

The computer conducts a diagnostic analysis on the most recent 50 items the student has attempted across tests. The computer sorts the words from most to least correctly spelled, in terms of the percentage of correct LS, and categorizes the spellings as corrects, near misses (60–99% LS), moderate misses (20–59% LS), and far misses (0–19% LS). The computer also searches for 24 types of errors and does a frequency count of opportunities for and occurrences of each error type. It also makes recommendations about "Key Errors" on which to focus instruction, based on the relative frequency of the student's error types and on the likelihood (according to our judgment) that instruction on those error types will yield improvement. A sample diagnostic analysis is shown in figure 3.

Reliability and validity of this analysis was assessed for pupils with and without identified reading disability in Grades 1 to 6, who had been monitored with CBM over 3 to 9 months (Fuchs et al. 1990). Reliability was indexed via agreement between two profiles derived one week apart, which added 1 to 3 new assessments. Agreement, calculated for each skill, ranged between 82% and 91% at the different grades and for the samples of students with and without disability. For the 24 error types, agreement ranged between 95% and 100%. Validity, indexed by correlating the average percentage correct across the 24 error types with the median letter sequences correct score for the same time frame, was .87.

We conducted a series of studies examining the instructional utility of this diagnostic analysis. Fuchs et al. (1991b), for example, investigated how diagnostic analysis affected teachers' instructional adaptation and student achievement. Thirty special educators, who taught self-contained or resource programs, were assigned randomly to four treatments: CBM with graphed and diagnostic analysis, CBM with graphed analysis plus ordered lists of misspelled words, CBM with graphed analysis only, and no CBM (i.e., control). Each teacher identified for participation four students who had been identified as having a learning disability or behavior disorder (according to state identification procedures) and had reading and spelling IEP goals. Teacher and student demographics across treatment groups were comparable. Curriculum Based Measurement teachers tracked pupil progress toward spelling goals for

Name: John Smith   Spelling 4   Date: 3/12   Page 1

Corrects (100% LS)	14 word(s)
Near Misses (60-99% LS)	19 word(s)
Moderate Misses (20-59% LS)	16 word(s)
Far Misses (0-19% LS)	1 word(s)

Type	Correct	Possible	Pct		Type	Correct	Possible	Pct
Sing cons	48	50	96		Final vow	3	7	42
Blend	7	10	70		Double	3	4	75
FSLZ	0	0	--		c/s	0	1	0
Single vow	21	31	67		c/ck	0	2	0
Digraph	6	8	75		-le	4	7	57
Vowel + N	6	8	75		ch/tch	2	2	100
Dual cons	13	25	52		-dge	0	1	0
Final e	1	5	20		Vowel team	4	12	33
igh/ign	0	0	--		Suffix	5	6	83
ild/old	0	0	--		tion/sion	0	1	0
a+l+cons	0	0	--		ance/ence	0	0	--
Vowel + R	9	14	64		sure/ture	0	0	--

KEY ERRORS

Dual cons	Final e	Final vow
learner-leaner	alone-alon	taste-tast
sample-samble	knife-knif	hero-hearow
chart-chard	rare-rar	lazy-lazz
mumble-mobble	cube-cub	unlucky-unluke
tractor-trater		
apart-apeot		

Name: John Smith   Spelling 4   Date: 3/12   Page 1

————————Corrects (100% LS)————————

100	March	March
100	death	death
100	sometimes	sometimes
100	thankful	thankful
100	baker	baker
100	uncover	uncover
100	shy	shy
100	weakness	weakness
100	forgot	forgot
100	eyes	eyes
100	army	army
100	powerless	powerless
100	wife	wife
100	mix	mix

————————Near Misses (60-99% LS)————————

77	shipment	shapment	Single vow	
75	instead	insted	Vowel team	
75	patches	patces	Digraph	
75	moisten	mosten	Vowel team	
75	quieter	quiter	Vowel team	
75	learner	leaner	Dual cons	
75	trouble	trubble	Vowel team	
71	sample	samble	Dual cons	
71	listen	lesten	Single vow	
66	badge	bage	-dge	
66	taste	tast	Final vow	
66	chart	chard	Dual cons	
66	alone	alon	Final e	
66	restless	reasless	Blend	
66	knife	knif	Final e	
60	hero	hearow	Final vow	Vowel + R
60	rare	rar	Final e	
60	cube	cub	Final e	
60	lazy	lazz	Final vow	

————————Moderate Misses (20-59% LS)————————

57	tickle	teakle	c/ck	Single vow
57	French	fanch	Vowel + N	Blend
57	mumble	mobble	Dual cons	Single vow
50	unlucky	unluke	Final vow	c/ck
50	tractor	trater	Vowel + R	Dual cons
50	apart	apeot	Vowel + R	Dual cons
44	calendar	cander	Vowel + R	Vowel + N	Sing Cons
42	mumble	mommbe	-le	Single vow
40	rail	real	Vowel team	
37	station	stanch	tion/sion	
28	sample	scembe	-le	Dual cons	Single vow
25	certain	chanten	Vowel team	Vowel + R	c/s
25	squeeze	scease	Vowel team	Digraph	Sing cons
20	limb	lem	Single vow	Dual cons
20	treatment	tempemt	Suffix	Vowel team	Blend
20	limb	leam	Dual cons	Single vow

————————Far Misses (0-19% LS)————————

| 14 | giggle | gelly | -le | Double | Single vow |

Figure 3.   Curriculum-based measurement diagnostic profile for an individual student in spelling.

15 weeks by assessing CBM performance twice weekly. Each week, teachers evaluated the database using software that automatically applied decision rules to graphs of the performance indicators. In addition, depending on treatment group, teachers received diagnostic analysis or ordered lists of errors.

Results indicated that teachers who received diagnostic analysis cited skills for instruction most specifically and introduced more adaptations than any other group. In terms of achievement, effect sizes increased as the CBM information became more descriptive, and the achievement of the graphed plus diagnostic analysis group was reliably better than that of the control and graph-only groups; the achievement of the ordered word lists group was reliably better than that of controls, but not significantly different from that of diagnostic analysis. Together, the adaptation and achievement data indicated that increasingly rich supplementary analyses of student responses may help special educators design better spelling programs.

EXTENDING DIAGNOSTIC ANALYSIS TO READING

As these findings illustrate, and as related studies in spelling (Fuchs et al. 1991a) and math (Fuchs et al. 1990) corroborate, diagnostic assessment has the potential to help teachers plan instruction that is more varied, is more responsive to individual needs, and promotes stronger outcomes. It is unfortunate, therefore, that few related studies have been conducted in reading. Some work has focused on special educators' diagnostic reading comprehension assessment. Fuchs, Fuchs, and Hamlett (1989c), for example, showed that student learning increased when special educators diagnostically assessed students' weekly retells in structured ways. Effects were, however, limited to outcome measures aligned with the weekly retells; effect sizes diminished as the dependent variables become more distal, general measures of reading achievement. Moreover, related work is noticeably absent with respect to general education and in terms of providing diagnostic assessment beyond comprehension.

In contrast to previous work, our current focus on diagnostic reading assessment addressed skills pertinent to developing readers, and the goal was to provide a useful assessment for general and special educators serving classrooms of primary-grade children with diverse reading profiles. The challenge was to identify an assessment that not only is adequate technically, but also is feasible for routine administration with many children and provides enough detail to inform instruction without overwhelming teachers with more information than they can handle. Of course, the ultimate value of any diagnostic system must be judged by its capacity to enhance teacher planning and increase student learning.

Our diagnostic system was designed to be used in conjunction with reading CBM where, as already described, competence is assessed via weekly 1-minute oral text reading and where graphed analysis of performance indicators signals teachers when a student's rate of development is inadequate and that alternative instruction is required. Our goal was to extend this framework in two ways. First, we sought to identify CBM cut-points corresponding with the need for instructional work in decoding, fluency, and comprehension. Second, we sought to develop brief follow-up assessments that would provide diagnostic analyses of decoding and comprehension strengths and weaknesses. Our notion was that the CBM performance indicator could be used efficiently to form instructional groups requiring decoding, fluency, or comprehension work; then, relatively brief follow-up assessment could be used to divide the decoding and comprehension groups further into clusters focusing on different skills matched to student needs.

Development

In two sittings, Hosp and Fuchs (2002) administered the following measures to 74, 81, 79, and 75 children at grades 1 to 4, respectively: (1) two CBM passages at the level corresponding to students' grade placement; (2) for each passage, five open-ended comprehension questions (see Comprehension Skills Inventory description); (3) a decoding skills test comprising 60 pseudo words (see Decoding Skills Battery description)[1]; and (4) the Woodcock Reading Mastery

---

[1]We considered incorporating the Decoding Skills Test (DST; Richardson and DiBenedetto 1985), but rejected its use for the following reasons. First, the scope of the DST is broader than decoding, providing an index of word identification (with a corresponding basal level placement) and contextualized word identification and decoding skill, reading fluency, and comprehension. As might be expected, therefore, administration time (30 minutes per student) is longer than we could expect teachers to devote to diagnostic assessment on a routine basis. Even the decoding portion of the DST takes longer (10-15 minutes) than we deemed feasible.

Second, the DST decoding skills framework is relatively narrow. For monosyllabic words, it addressed closed vowel, finale e, and vowel teams. Within polysyllabic decoding, the DST does not categorize strengths and weaknesses. In addition, to derive one estimate of competence with consonant blends, the DST assesses consonant blends for each monosyllabic word type; we judged it more efficient to incorporate one, separate CVCC category.

Third, the DST assesses decoding skills using real and nonsense words. Our preliminary analyses indicated that conclusions about decoding skills were stronger when based completely on nonsense words. Moreover, nonsense words on the DST are orthographically related to real words (i.e., nonsense words were created by

Test-Word Identification, Word Attack, and Passage Comprehension subtests (Woodcock 1998). Also, within three weeks, during a third sitting, we re-administered CBM, the Comprehension Skills Inventory, and the Decoding Skills Battery to a subset of students (n = 29, 30, 30, and 30 at grades 1–4, respectively).

Comprehension Skills Inventory.   The Comprehension Skills Inventory comprised five questions per CBM passage. These questions corresponded to five skills for which we identified research-validated teaching methods: predicting the next event in a story, sequencing the events of a story, identifying a paragraph's main idea, using context to infer the meaning of difficult vocabulary words, and identifying a story's theme. Our notion was that if we could pinpoint comprehension skill deficits, we could target instruction designed to meet the student's need.

To develop the inventory, special education graduate students framed an initial set of questions, with one question for each comprehension skill for each CBM passage. Next, an individual experienced in developing comprehension questions revised these questions to insure alignment with the instructional taxonomy. Then, five graduate students answered questions without reading passages to eliminate questions for which answers could be inferred on the basis of the questions alone. Finally, two experienced judges again revised questions to insure alignment with the instructional taxonomy. Following data collection, we developed a scoring key for each question to address the range of responses; then, one graduate student scored responses, with strong agreement with an independent scorer.

Unfortunately, reliability and validity data were disappointing. For the total number of questions answered correctly, stability and correlations with other measures of reading performance were strong. However, stability and correlations were low for the individual questions—the unit of analysis required for diagnostic analysis. We speculated that, for reliable and meaningful assessment of the individual skills, an inventory that aggregated perfor-

---

changing 1–2 consonants in real words used on the real-word decoding subtest). We instead wished to make nonsense words as dissimilar to real words as possible (i.e., rhyming words were avoided as possible).

Fourth, the DST does not provide mastery status by phonic skill. Rather, the tester analyzes intraindividual patterns. Our goal, by contrast, was to designate mastery status by phonic skill.

Fifth, the DST does not report reliability and validity separately by phonic skills (only for real vs. nonsense word total scores). Our goal was to provide technical data by phonic skill (total score per phonic skill as well as mastery/nonmastery status). And, relatedly, DST technical data were provided across grades 2–6; we were interested in psychometric estimates for each grade, 1–4.

mance on multiple questions for each of the five comprehension skills would be required. Administration time for such an assessment, which would require the reading of multiple passages, would be longer than we might expect of teachers. On the basis of poor technical properties for the inventory we had created, we eliminated it from the diagnostic system. Consequently, our diagnostic system only provided a broad recommendation for comprehension work, without distinctions about the nature of that instruction.

Decoding Skills Battery.   We enjoyed better success with the Decoding Skills Battery. Across one fall semester, we used an iterative process with 43 second-grade and 37 fifth-grade students to identify six pseudo words for each of 10 decoding skills. Then, using the sample of 309 first through fourth graders, we examined issues of task difficulty and discrimination using models from item response theory (for those results, see Hosp and Fuchs 2001). We ordered the 60 items and identified basal and ceiling rules that minimized false negatives for nonmastery of decoding skills. In addition, for each skill at each grade level, we considered alternative mastery criteria, selecting the criterion that maximized the correlation with the Woodcock Word Attack. Based on the complete set of analyses, we decided, for designating mastery within the diagnostic analysis, to merge CVC and CVCC and to eliminate two skills (multisyllabic decoding skills with long vowels in the first syllable). Using Cronbach's alpha to index stability and internal consistency across the six items for each of the remaining skills (for each skill, three items administered in one sitting; three in another sitting), coefficients ranged between .71 and .86 at grade 1; between .71 and .82 at grade 2; between .68 and .84 at grade 3; and between .70 and .78 at grade 4.

We also designed software to support administration (and insure accurate identification of basals and ceilings). The software prompts teachers where to begin testing, which page of items to administer next, and when to terminate testing. Administration takes 1 to 5 minutes. At the end of testing, the computer assigns each item a correct or incorrect code, determines mastery status for each skill, and identifies for instruction two skills (the next harder skills as introduced in the curriculum, which are nonmastered as indicated with the Decoding Skills Battery).

Curriculum Based Measurement cut-points for decoding, fluency, and comprehension.   Curriculum Based Measurement cut-points for recommending decoding instruction were formulated using categorical and regression tree (CART) analysis (Lewis 2000). CART is an atheoretical tree-building technique for generating clinical decision rules. It relies on binary recursive partitioning and requires no assumptions about the underlying distribution of the predictor variables. The analysis comprises four steps, the first of which involves tree building via recursive splitting of nodes. Step two terminates tree building when a maximal tree (typically overfitting the data) is identified. The third step involves pruning, which results in a sequence of increasingly simpler trees and, in the final step, an optimal tree is selected to fit (without overfitting) the data. We also engaged in cross validation analysis. In addition to CBM, we entered into the CART analysis predictors that routinely would be available to teachers: student demographics and teacher ratings. The predicted status was adequate versus inadequate decoding (adequate decoding was set at a standard score of 90 or higher on the Word Attack subtest of the *Woodcock Reading Mastery Tests*). Useful predictors incorporated within the decision tree were IEP reading status, teachers' rating of reading competence (high, average, low), subsidized lunch status, grade, sex, teachers' rating of mathematics competence, and teachers' rating of classroom behavior problems (none, occasional, frequent). Curriculum Based Measurement was used at six decision nodes, the first occurring at the second-level node (IEP reading status was entered first). The hit rate ([TP + TN]/n) was 87% (cross validation: 84%); sensitivity (TP/[TP + FN]) was 98% (cross validation: 86%), and specificity (TN/[TN + FP]) was 88% (cross validation: 84%).

Continued work on larger sample sizes is warranted to explore appropriate CBM cut-points for recommending decoding instruction. In the study described below, however, we used this decision tree to identify students for decoding instruction. In addition, students were recommended for fluency practice if they were predicted to have adequate decoding status, but their CBM score placed them lower than .5 standard deviations above the mean on a regional sample. The remaining set of students, who were predicted to achieve adequate decoding status and whose CBM score placed them more than .5 standard deviations above the mean, were identified for comprehension instruction.

Teachers administered CBM with the assistance of a computer program. As the student read aloud from a printed copy of the passage, the teacher used the cursor to mark errors on the screen. The computer terminated testing at one minute and calculated the number of words read correctly. Using the decision tree formulated via the CART analysis, the software considered the student's CBM score, demographics, and teachers' initial ratings. For students predicted to fall into the inadequate decoding group, the computer initiated administration of the Decoding Skills Battery. Every three weeks, the computer generated individual student reports and a class report. See figure 4 for a sample class report.

THE EFFECTS OF DIAGNOSTIC CBM ANALYSIS ON GENERAL EDUCATORS' INSTRUCTIONAL ADAPTATION AND STUDENT LEARNING

To explore the potential for diagnostic CBM analysis to prompt general educators' instructional adaptation and, thereby, enhance student learning, we conducted a 15-week study in four high-poverty and three middle-class schools. Below, we describe our study methods and summarize our findings.

What We Did

Participants were 28 second-grade teachers who volunteered to participate in any of the study conditions. All teachers used the same Scott-Foresman reading series in the same district, which mandated a 2-hour reading/language arts instructional block. Stratifying within school, we randomly assigned teachers to four conditions: (1) no instructional consultation and no CBM (i.e., control), (2) instructional consultation (i.e., consultation-only), (3) instructional consultation with CBM (i.e., CBM), and (4) instructional consultation with CBM with diagnostic analysis (i.e., CBM+diagnostic analysis). We incorporated instructional consultation into treatment because prior work shows the importance of consultation in helping special education teachers use CBM productively (e.g., Fuchs et al. 1991, Wesson 1991). Teacher demographics were comparable across treatment groups.

All children (97%) for whom we obtained consent were included. Students were pretested on the *Comprehensive Reading Assessment Battery* (CRAB; Fuchs, Fuchs, and Hamlett 1989c) and the Word Identification and Word Attack subtests of the *Woodcock Reading Mastery Test* (Woodcock 1998). Student demographics and initial achievement scores were comparable across conditions.

Teachers attended an after-school workshop, where they learned how to complete an Instructional Plan Sheet, on which teachers recorded the basic features of their reading program: arrangement (e.g., whole class), skills (e.g., compare/contrast, inflected endings), materials (e.g., Scott-Foresman worksheets), and activities (e.g., fill in letters to make words). On these Instructional Plan Sheets, teachers also used the same features to describe "other reading activities" designed to meet specific student needs. Teachers completed their first Instructional Plan Sheets at the workshop.

Also at the workshop, Curriculum Based Measurement teachers learned about CBM and practiced using the administration software; CBM+diagnostic analysis teachers did the same with the Decoding Skills Battery. In their classrooms, CBM teachers then administered one round of testings, during which research assistants observed at least two administrations and provided corrective feedback.

Study activities recurred in 3-week cycles. Each cycle incorporated the following activities. Each week, CBM and CBM+diagnostic analysis teachers collected one CBM on each student in their classes; at the end of each testing, they shared with the student a computer-generated graph showing CBM scores over time. At the end of the Week 3 administration, the CART analysis tree rules were applied to identify students (in the CBM+diagnostic analysis group) in need of decoding instruction. For those students, the computer looped into administration of the Decoding Skills Battery. At the end of Week 3, research assistants printed computer-generated individual and class reports (see figure 4) for teachers in both CBM groups; only those with diagnostic analysis received recommendations about comprehension, fluency, and decoding instruction and information about specific decoding skills deficits.

Also during Week 3, research assistants conducted 30-minute instructional consultations with teachers in both CBM groups and in the instructional consultation-only group. These consultations

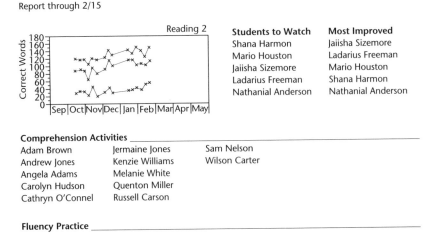

Figure 4.   Curriculum-based measurement report for a second-grade class, which includes diagnostic analysis.

Name	Comprehension	Fluency	MAT/LAST	TIME	CAR	BEAT	HAPPY	PUBLIC	RUNNING
Adam Brown	C								
Andrew Jones	C								
Angela Adams	C								
Carolyn Hudson	C								
Cathryn O'Connel	C								
Jaiisha Sizemore			Hot	Hot	Hot	Hot	Warm	Warm	Hot
Jermaine Jones	C								
Kenzie Williams	C								
Ladarius Freeman			Warm	Cold	Hot	Cold	Hot	Warm	Warm
Mario Houston			Warm	Cold	Hot	Cold	Warm	Cold	Warm
Melanie White	C								
Nathanial Anderson			Cold	Cold	Cold	Cold	Cold	Cold	Cold
Quenton Miller	C								
Russell Carson	C								
Sam Nelson	C								
Shana Harmon			Hot	Hot	Hot	Hot	Warm	Warm	Hot
Wilson Carter	C								

▯▯▯   Cold. Missing most of these words

▦   Warm. Getting some of these words right.

■   Hot. Getting most of these words right.

MAT/LAST: closed syllable, short vowel, e.g., bed, top, hat, cat, bump, mast, damp
TIME: final e, long vowel, e.g., cake, poke, same, woke, mine, rose, gate
CAR: vowel r controlled, e.g., fur, nor, per, sir, her, tar
BEAT: two vowels together, e.g., soap, maid, jean, loaf, paid, meal
HAPPY: divide between two like consonants, e.g., lesson, bubble, battle, giggle
PUBLIC: divide between unlike consonants, e.g., elbow, walrun, doctor, victim, admit
RUNNING: divide between double consonant with suffix, e.g., batter, sipped, hitting, tanned, bitten

Name	Score	Growl
Jermaine Jones	146	*1.17
Kenzie Williams	133	*1.32
Wilson Carter	132	*3.05
Carolyn Hudson	132	*2.37
Cathryn O'Connel	123	*0.80
Angela Adams	122	*0.30
Sam Nelson	120	*0.31
Andrew Jones	115	*0.49
Russell Carson	106	*1.40
Adam Brown	105	*1.61
Quenton Miller	104	*2.61
Melanie White	93	*1.55
Shana Harmon	77	*0.69
Mario Houston	58	*0.95
Jaiisha Sizemore	54	*1.21
Ladarius Freeman	38	*0.90
Nathanial Anderson	17	*0.45

Score
    Average score   99.0
    Standard deviation   37.3
    Discrepancy criterion   01.7

Slope
    average slope   +1.21
    Standard deviation   0.69
    Discrepancy criterion   +0.32

Students identified with dual discrepancy criterion
                    Score   Slope

Figure 4. *continued*

were guided by scripts, which prompted teachers to consider the needs of their students; for CBM teachers, the scripts guided teachers to examine features of the CBM class reports. During these consultations, research assistants used a notebook of instructional procedures, sorted into decoding, fluency, and comprehension activities. When teachers expressed the need to address student difficulties in one or more of these areas, research assistants invited teachers to consider the relevant notebook activities; when teachers committed to the use of a notebook activity, they received all materials necessary for implementation. At the end of the consultation sessions, teachers made revisions to their Instructional Plan Sheets to reflect changes they had decided to incorporate. These changes sometimes were based on notebook activities; other times, teachers identified revisions independent of the notebook. During the subsequent 3-week cycle, research assistants observed a reading instruction session. Research assistants later coded the observational data to estimate the alignment between the Instructional Plan Sheets and actual instruction.

This 3-week cycle recurred five times, with a study duration of 15 weeks running from October to March. The reliability of teachers' testing was assessed with five administrations, selected randomly, during each 3-week cycle; the percentage of agreement exceeded 99 over the 14 teachers and the five cycles; agreement on the Decoding Skills Battery was similarly high. Teachers conducted testing according to the required schedule, with the exception of one teacher who, three weeks after winter break, had only one, rather than the three required January test scores on each student in her class. Consultations occurred as required within each 3-week cycle (although rescheduling occurred frequently due to teacher absences, unexpected assemblies, etc.), and audiotapes of the consultation sessions revealed compliance with questions on the scripts. Using the observational data, we estimated overlap between Instructional Plan Sheets and actual instruction on the instructional adaptation variables to be 82%.

Students were post-tested on the same measures, and teachers in all four groups again completed Instructional Plan Sheets. Each consultation session was audio taped and transcribed. Transcriptions of the fourth instructional consultation sessions were coded, blind to study condition, with 95% agreement on 20% of protocols.

What We Found

In this chapter, we report findings based on the first- and fourth-round Instructional Plan Sheets, the fourth-round instructional consultation sessions, the fifth-round CBM data, and a post-treatment teacher questionnaire. The first-round Instructional Plan Sheet data were available on all teachers; the fourth-round Instructional Plan Sheet and instructional consultation session data were available on teachers in the three experimental groups; the CBM data were available for teachers in the two CBM groups; and the post-treatment teacher questionnaire, which assessed the utility and feasibility of CBM, was available for teachers in both CBM groups. In statistical analyses, we used teacher as the unit of analysis. In light of the low power associated with the statistical tests, we report effect sizes (ESs) for nonsignificant differences to help researchers estimate effects for planning subsequent studies.

Initial levels of routine and specialized adaptation. Our first goal was to describe teachers' initial levels of adaptation so we could examine the representativeness of our sample and determine whether the treatment groups were comparable on a variable we were hoping to effect. From the first-round Instructional Plan Sheets (collected six weeks after the first day of the school year), we counted the number of times teachers described activities that could be classified as routine adaptation: beginning-of-the-year routines, in which all students participate, which systematically provide for varied goals and instructional methods. We also coded instances of specialized adaptation by which teachers address specific student difficulties; we defined specialized adaptation liberally, as any reading instructional activity designated for a subset of (not all) students in a class.

Among our sample of teachers, instances of routine adaptation were limited to Accelerated Reader, partner reading, computer-assisted instruction, and SRA Kits. On average, teachers cited 1.00 instance ($SD = .58$) of routine adaptation in the control group; .86 ($SD = .69$) in the consultation-only group; 1.00 ($SD = .82$) in the CBM group; and .57 ($SD = .53$) in the CBM+diagnostic analysis group, $F(3,24) = .65$, $p = .591$. So, we found relatively few instances of beginning-of-school-year routines designed to incorporate varied goals and instructional methods, and the routine adaptation mechanisms used by the teachers differentiated learning activities via independent, self-paced activities (*Accelerated Reader*, computer-assisted instruction, SRA Kits) or student mediation (partner reading). Teacher-led instruction was, by contrast, reserved for whole-class, undifferentiated instruction. The low level of differentiation in these 28 classes was also reflected in the fact that every teacher addressed the exact same set of reading skills on the first-round Instructional Plan Sheets—a skill set borrowed entirely from the relevant unit of the Scott-Foresman reading manual. The level of routine adaptation was, therefore, similar to those documented in previous work (e.g., Baker and Zigmond 1990; McIntosh et al. 1993). The same was true for specialized adaptation. On average, teachers cited .71 instances ($SD = 1.11$) of specialized adaptation in the control group; .43 ($SD = .53$) in the consultation-only group; .29 ($SD = .76$) in the CBM group; and .57 ($SD = .79$) in the CBM+diagnostic analysis group, $F (2,18) = .290$, $p = .751$. Our teachers relied heavily on seat work to accomplish specialized adaptation; two teachers (one in the control group and one in the instructional consultation group) did incorporate teacher-directed instruction on specific decoding skills to address student difficulties. For the most part, however, as reflected both in routine and specialized adaptation, our sample of teachers, like others in the literature, began the study with low levels of instructional differentiation.

Teacher concern about student progress.   Our hope was that the use of ongoing, systematic assessment might prompt teacher concern about individual students and thereby lead to increasing levels of specialized adaptation. So, within the context of the instructional consultation sessions, a standard series of questions was posed to assess teacher concern about individual student progress: "Do you have children whose progress seems problematic? Which children are you concerned about?, and [For each child identified as demonstrating inadequate progress,] Why are you concerned about ___ ?"

As expected, based on previous CBM research conducted with special educators (e.g., Fuchs, Deno, and Mirkin 1984), the number of students for whom our general education teachers judged progress to be problematic differed as a function of treatment condition: a mean of 1.86 students in the consultation-only group ($SD = 1.57$), 3.57 students in the CBM group ($SD = 1.81$), and 5.29 students in the CBM+diagnostic feedback group ($SD = 1.57$), $F (2,18) = 4.21$, $p = .032$. Follow-ups, using the Bonferroni alpha adjustment, showed that the difference between the consultation-only and CBM+diagnostic feedback groups was statistically significant, with an ES of 1.51; the ES between the two CBM groups, although not significantly different, was 0.72. So, it seems that assessment can be used to raise teacher concern about students' reading progress and that, with increasing levels of diagnostic information, concern may increase.

When probed about the reason for student difficulties, teacher responses also varied as a function of treatment condition. That is, we found a significant relation between treatment and reason for concern, $X^2 (2, N = 21) = 8.14$, $p = .017$. Of instructional consultation teachers, 71% described their concerns without reference to or description of students' reading problems; instead, they cited reasons beyond teacher control to explain student failure (e.g., ELL status, special education status, attention or motivation problems, inadequate parental involvement). A smaller proportion of CBM teachers took this approach (29% for CBM; 0% for CBM+diagnostic analysis): In response to the same question, they tended to describe students' reading progress or performance.

Subsequent specialized adaptation. Teachers' specialized adaptation did increase as a function of treatment condition. Among instructional consultation teachers, we saw no increase from the first- to the fourth-round Instructional Plan Sheets. By contrast, the instances of specialized adaptation increased .43 for CBM teachers (SD = .53) and .86 for CBM+diagnostic analysis teachers (SD = .90). The analysis of variance approached statistical significance, F (2,18) = 3.52, p = .051. Follow-ups, using the Bonferroni alpha adjustment, revealed that the increase in specialized adaptation for the CBM+diagnostic analysis teachers exceeded the increase for the consultation-only teachers. The ES comparing these groups was 1.53; the ES comparing the CBM groups, .52; the ES comparing the consultation-only with CBM groups, .92. The specialized adaptation activities included decoding portions of peer-assisted learning strategies (D. Fuchs et al.. 2001), small-group teacher-directed decoding instruction, comprehension small-group instruction, one-to-one tutoring with a volunteer, and homework assignments requiring one-to-one work with a parent. Consequently, it appears that CBM prompted greater specialized adaptation among general educators and that the diagnostic analysis had a value added in increasing instructional differentiation.

We were, nevertheless, disappointed that the levels of fourth-round instructional adaptation remained low. The instances of specialized adaptation, after treatment had been in place for 12 weeks, averaged .43 (SD = .53) among consultation-only teachers, .71 (SD = 1.11) among CBM teachers, and 1.41 (SD = 1.27) among CBM+diagnostic analysis teachers. So, even the highest-performing CBM+diagnostic analysis teachers typically manifested one instance of instructional adaptation even though they typically were identifying four or five students with reading difficulty. They often addressed all of these students' difficulties with one, simultaneous instructional action. Student performance data sometimes indicated the appropriateness of that decision; other times, not.

Reading achievement. In light of the relatively low levels of instructional adaptation, even among the highest performing group of teachers, we were not surprised to find disappointing achievement results. Curriculum Based Measurement teachers effected a mean slope of 1.37 (SD = .39) among their students; CBM+diagnostic analysis, 1.57 (SD = .21), F (1,12) = 1.24, p = .29. The effect size comparing the two groups was a moderate .67.

Teacher judgments of the utility and feasibility of CBM. As revealed on a post-treatment questionnaire, CBM teachers, with and without diagnostic analysis, reported that they found CBM helpful in planning instruction (a mean of approximately 80 on a 100-point scale); they found weekly CBM relatively easy to collect (a mean of approximately 80 on a 100-point scale); they found the computer easy to use for collecting the assessment data (a mean of 93 on a 100-point scale for CBM teachers; 84 for CBM+diagnostic analysis teachers); and they planned to continue using CBM throughout the remaining of the school year and during the upcoming year (mean probability of .88).

CONCLUSIONS AND NEXT STEPS

Results provide only modest evidence that classroom reading assessment, even with a diagnostic component designed to prompt instructional differentiation, can reduce the prevalence of reading failure. Below, we summarize study findings and then consider the appropriate role for assessment within the context of general education.

Before teachers engage in instructional differentiation, they must recognize student difficulty, and results clearly indicated that the use of objective, ongoing classroom-based assessment prompted greater levels of teacher concern about students' reading progress. Moreover, with increasing levels of diagnostic information, concern may increase. The corresponding ESs were large: 1.51 comparing the CBM+diagnostic analysis group with consultation-only teachers and .72 comparing the two CBM groups. In a related way, CBM teachers (with and without diagnostic analysis) were more likely to describe student difficulties in terms of reading performance; by contrast, without ongoing assessment feedback, consultation-only teachers tended to cite reasons beyond their control to explain students' lack of progress. This pattern suggests the possibility that assessment information may enhance teachers' understanding and feelings of responsibility for their students' reading difficulties.

In fact, findings more clearly revealed that CBM prompted general educators' specialized adaptation, with diagnostic analysis adding a practically important value: ESs were 1.53 comparing the CBM+diagnostic analysis and the consultation-only groups, .92 comparing the CBM and consultation-only groups, and .52 comparing the two CBM groups. Despite these sizeable effect sizes, outcome levels of specialized adaptation designed to address teacher concern remained low. In a corresponding way, student achievement effects were not reliable, but the effect size of .67 comparing the CBM and CBM+diagnostic analysis groups was similar to the moderate effect on specialized adaptation and suggests some potential value of CBM to help general educators plan more effectively for their students.

In light of these findings, it is interesting to consider the appropriate role for and potential of classroom reading assessment within general education. On the one hand, to plan instruction, general educators tend to think about the flow of classroom activities rather than individual responsiveness to instruction (Clark and Elmore 1981). In such a context, prompting teachers to tailor instruction to meet individual needs, even when presented with assessment information revealing such need, represents a significant challenge. In fact, nearing the end of the study, specialized adaptation remained disappointingly low. Even the highest-performing CBM+diagnostic analysis teachers typically manifested only one instance of instructional adaptation, even as they typically identified four or five students with reading difficulty. Such findings raise the possibility that the appropriate role for assessment within the context of general education may be limited to signaling the need for some type of secondary or tertiary level of intervention, which others are responsible for implementing. Our data suggest that CBM, which incorporates diagnostic analysis, may serve this role better than reliance on the CBM performance indicator alone.

At the same time, giving up on general educators' capacity to effect instructionally differentiated reading instruction may be premature. Analogous work conducted in the area of math suggests a potential strategy for helping general educators address individual student needs, as revealed via assessment, through routine adaptation. In 1990 we initiated a research program in math examining the role of CBM in prompting general educators' instructional differentiation. Early studies showed that CBM, with diagnostic analysis of students' math skill strengths and deficits, raised teacher concern but failed to prompt teachers to modify their instruction to address student difficulties (Fuchs et al. 1994). Those findings echo current results. In response to teachers' reluctance to modify their instructional programs to address students' math needs, we introduced peer-assisted learning strategies as a form of routine adaptation, established at the beginning of the year, by which teachers could assign pairs of students to work simultaneously on different skills, in different ways. The combination of ongoing classroom assessment with a routine structure for incorporating instructional differentiation in fact dramatically increased instructional adaptation as well as student learning (e.g., Fuchs et al. 1997, Fuchs et al. 1995). In a similar way, classroom-based reading assessment may exert stronger effects on instructional adaptation and student learning if it is used in combination with a classroom routine by which instructional adaptation can be easily incorporated. We are now designing a study to test this possibility.

Of course, it is instructive to note that even when classroom-based assessment is blended with a classroom routine to permit instructional adaptation, not all students demonstrate adequate rates of growth (e.g., Fuchs et al. 1997). As this documents, some portion of the population will require intensive forms of reading instruction beyond what can be expected of general education. Nevertheless, schools continue to struggle to identify classroom methods that can enhance the reading development of a greater portion of the general population, without the need for expensive tutoring. Continued work exploring the contribution of classroom-based assessment, therefore, seems appropriate.

ACKNOWLEDGMENTS

The research described in this paper was supported in part by Grant #H324C000022 from the U.S. Department of Education, Office of Special Education Programs, and Grant HD 15052 from the National Institute of Child Health and Human Development to Vanderbilt University. Statements do not reflect the position or policy of these agencies, and no official endorsement by them should be inferred.

REFERENCES

Baker, J., and Zigmond, N. 1990. Are regular education classes equipped to accommodate students with learning disabilities? *Exceptional Children* 56:515–26.

Biemiller, A. 1977-1978. Relationship between oral reading rates for letters, words, and simple text in the development of reading achievement. *Reading Research Quarterly* 13:223–53.

Clark, C. M., and Elmore, J. L. 1981. Transforming curriculum in mathematics, science, and writing: A case study of teacher yearly planning (Research Series No. 99). East Lansing: Michigan State University, Institute for Research on Teaching.

Deno, S. L. 1985. Curriculum-based measurement: The emerging alternative. *Exceptional Children* 52:219–32.

Deno, S. L., Mirkin, P., and Chiang, B. 1982. Identifying valid measures of reading. *Exceptional Children* 49:36–45.

Foorman, B. R., Francis, D. J., Fletcher, J. M., Schatschneider, C., and Mehta, P. 1998. The role of instruction in learning to read: Preventing reading failure in at-risk children. *Journal of Educational Psychology* 90:37–55.

Fredericksen, J. R. 1981. Sources of process interactions in reading. In *Interactive Processes in Reading*, eds. A. M. Lesgold and C. A. Perfetti. Hillsdale, NJ: Lawrence Erlbaum Associates.

Fuchs, L. S., and Hamlett, C. L. In preparation. The predictive ability of curriculum-based measurement from kindergarten through third grade.

Fuchs, L. S., and Deno, S. L. 1992. Effects of curriculum within curriculum-based measurement. *Exceptional Children* 58:232–43.

Fuchs, D., Fuchs, L. S., Mathes, P., and Simmons, D. C. 1997. Peer-Assisted Learning Strategies: Making classrooms more responsive to student diversity. *American Educational Research Journal* 34:513–44.

Fuchs, L. S., and Deno, S. L. 1991. Paradigmatic distinctions between instructionally relevant measurement models. *Exceptional Children* 57:488–501.

Fuchs, L. S., Deno, S. L., and Marston, D. 1983. Improving the reliability of curriculum-based measures of academic skills for psychoeducational decision making. *Diagnostique* 8:135–49.

Fuchs, L. S., Deno, S. L., and Mirkin, P. K. 1984. Effects of frequent curriculum-based measurement on pedagogy, student achievement, and student awareness of learning. *American Educational Research Journal* 21:449–60.

Fuchs, L. S., and Fuchs, D. 1992. Identifying a measure for monitoring student reading progress. *School Psychology Review* 21:45–58.

Fuchs, L. S., Fuchs, D., and Bishop, N. 1992. Instructional adaptation for students at risk. *Journal of Educational Research* 86:70–84.

Fuchs, L. S., Fuchs, D., and Deno, S. L. 1982. Reliability and validity of curriculum-based informal reading inventories. *Reading Research Quarterly* 18:6–26.

Fuchs, L .S., Fuchs, D., and Hamlett, C. L. 1989a. Effects of alternative goal structures within curriculum-based measurement. *Exceptional Children* 55:429–38.

Fuchs, L. S., Fuchs, D., and Hamlett, C. L. 1989b. Effects of instrumental use of curriculum-based measurement to enhance instructional programs. *Remedial and Special Education* 10(2):43–52.

Fuchs, L. S., Fuchs, D., and Hamlett, C. L. 1989c. Monitoring reading growth using student recalls: Effects of two teacher feedback systems. *Journal of Educational Research* 83:103–11.

Fuchs, L. S., Fuchs, D., Hamlett, C. L., and Allinder, R. M. 1990. The reliability and validity of skills analysis curriculum-based measurement. *Diagnostique* 14:203–21.

Fuchs, L. S., Fuchs, D., Hamlett, C. L., and Allinder, R. M. 1991a. Effects of expert system advice within curriculum-based measurement on teacher planning and student achievement in spelling. *School Psychology Review* 20:49–66.

Fuchs, L. S., Fuchs, D., Hamlett, C. L., and Allinder, R .M. 1991b. The contribution of skills analysis to curriculum-based measurement in spelling. *Exceptional Children* 57:443–52.

Fuchs, L. S., Fuchs, D., Hamlett, C. L., Phillips, N., and Benz, J. 1994. Class-wide curriculum-based measurement: Helping general educators meet the challenge of student diversity. *Exceptional Children* 60:518–37.

Fuchs, L. S., Fuchs, D., Hamlett, C. L., Phillips, N. B., Karns, K., and Dutka, S. 1997. Enhancing students' helping behavior during peer-mediated instruction with conceptual mathematical explanations. *Elementary School Journal* 97:223–50.

Fuchs, L. S., Fuchs, D., Phillips, N. B., Hamlett, C. L., and Karns, K. 1995. Acquisition and transfer effects of classwide peer-tutoring learning strategies in mathematics for students with varying learning histories. *School Psychology Review* 24:604–20.

Fuchs, L. S., Fuchs, D., Hamlett, C. L., and Ferguson, C. 1992. Effects of expert system consultation within curriculum-based measurement using a reading maze task. *Exceptional Children* 58:436–50.

Fuchs, L. S., Fuchs, D., Hamlett, C. L., and Stecker, P. M. 1990. The role of skills analysis to curriculum-based measurement in math. *School Psychology Review* 19:6–22.

Fuchs, L. S., Fuchs, D., Hamlett, C. L., and Stecker, P. M. 1991. Effects of curriculum-based measurement and consultation on teacher planning and studen achievement. *American Educational Research Journal* 28:617–41.

Fuchs, L. S., Fuchs, D., Hamlett, C. L., Walz, L., and Germann, G. 1993. Formative evaluation of academic progress: How much growth can we expect? *School Psychology Review* 22:27–48.

Fuchs, L. S., Fuchs, D., and Maxwell, L. 1988. The validity of informal reading comprehension measures. Remedial and Special Education 9(2):20–28.

Good, R. H., Deno, S. L., and Fuchs, L. S. 1995. Modeling academic growth for students with and without disabilities. Paper presented at the third annual Pacific Coast Research Conference, Laguna Beach, CA, February.

Good, R. H., and Shinn, M. R. 1990. Forecasting accuracy of slope estimates for reading curriculum-based measurement: Empirical evidence. *Behavioral Assessment* 12:179–94.

Hintze, J. M., and Shapiro, E. S. 1997. Curriculum-based measurement and literature-based reading: Is curriculum-based measurement meeting the needs of changing reading curricula? *Journal of School Psychology* 35:351–75.

Hintze, J. M., Shapiro, E. S., and Lutz, G. 1994. The effects of curriculum on the sensitivity of curriculum-based measurement in reading. *The Journal of Special Education* 28:188–202.

Hosp, M. K., and Fuchs, L. S. 2001. The relation between curriculum-based measurement and decoding skill. Unpublished doctoral dissertation, Vanderbilt University.

Hosp, M. K., and Fuchs, L. S. 2002. Dimensionality of decoding skill: An application of item response theory. Manuscript in preparation.

Juel, C. 1995. What makes literacy tutoring effective? *Reading Research Quarterly* 31:268–89.

Kagan, D. M., and Tippins, D. J. 1991. Helping student teachers attend to student cues. *The Elementary School Journal* 91:343–56.

Kranzler, J. H., Brownell, M. T., and Miller, M. D. 1996. The construct validity of curriculum-based measurement of reading: An empirical test of a plausible rival hypothesis. Paper presented at the annual meeting of the American Educational Research Association, New York, April.

Lewis, R. J. 2000. An introduction to classification and regression tree (CART) analysis. Paper presented at the annual meeting of the Society for Academic Emergency Medicine, San Francisco, June.

Marston, D. 1989. Curriculum-based measurement: What is it and why do it? In *Curriculum-Based Measurement: Assessing Special Children*, ed. M. R. Shinn. New York: Guilford.

Marston, D. , Fuchs, L. S., and Deno, S. L. 1985. Measuring pupil progress: A comparison of standardized achievement tests and curriculum-related measures. *Diagnostique* 11:77–90.

McIntosh, R., Vaughn, S. R., Schuum, J. S., Haager, D., and Lee, O. 1993. Observations of students with learning disabilities in general education classrooms. *Exceptional Children* 60:249–61.

Richardson, E., and DiBenedetto, B. 1985. *Decoding Skills Test*. Los Angeles: Western Psychological Services.

Riley, R. W. 1996. Improving the reading and writing skills of America's students. *Learning Disability Quarterly* 19:67–69.

Sarkees-Wircenski, M, and Wircenski, J. L. 1994. Transition programming for individuals from special populations. In *High School to Employment Transition: Contemporary Issues*, ed. A. J. Paulter, Jr. New York: Guilford.

Shinn, M. R., Good, R. H., Knutson, N., Tilly, W. D., and Collins, V. 1992. Curriculum-based reading fluency: A confirmatory analysis of its relation to reading. *School Psychology Review* 21:458–78.

Shinn, M. R., Tindal, G., Spira, D., and Marston, D. 1987. Practice of learning disabilities as social policy. *Learning Disability Quarterly* 10:17–28.

Wesson, C. L. 1991. Curriculum-based measurement and two models of follow-up consultation. *Exceptional Children* 57:246–57.

Woodcock, R. W. 1998. *Woodcock Reading Mastery Tests - revised*. Circle Pines, MN: American Guidance.

Section • V

Remediating Oral and Written Language Understanding

Chapter • 13

Working for Time:
Reflections on Naming Speed, Reading Fluency, and Intervention

*Maryanne Wolf, Beth O'Brien,
Katharine Donnelly Adams, Terry Joffe,
Julie Jeffery, Maureen Lovett, and
Robin Morris*

Pascal once wrote that there are few new thoughts on this earth, but that there is rearrangement. Pascal's characterization will be the conceptual denominator of this chapter, as we discuss what we mean by reading fluency, what we include in an evolving fluency intervention program, and how we conceptualize reading itself. For indeed we view reading as a three-ring cortical, subcortical, and cerebellar parallel-processing act, which makes a unique *rearrangement* of perceptual, cognitive, linguistic, and motoric regions in the brain never intended for reading at all! In this chapter we wish to reflect on how all of these regions, originally devoted to "other things," become one fluid, almost-automatic operation that we unceremoniously call fluent reading. We wish to examine the underlying skills that contribute to the development of fluency, and to look hard at some of the reasons that fluent reading fails to develop in many children with reading disabilities. It is our view that the deceptively complex naming speed task is one of our best predictors of the efficiency of the underlying processes involved in later fluency (Wolf 1991; Wolf and Bowers 1999).

Within that context we will examine some of the historical studies that bear on an understanding of fluency and some recent studies in English and several other language systems that indicate discrete subtypes of children with naming speed and fluency problems. Next we describe the RAVE-O (Retrieval, Automaticity, Vocabulary, Engagement with Language, Orthography) intervention program (Wolf, Miller, and Donnelly 2000). This program was created for children with rate-related deficits and was designed to address, as systematically as we know how, the component skills that underlie fluency's development. Finally, we will briefly summarize a first set of results on the efficacy of this program for several aspects of reading, fluency, and comprehension.

BACKGROUND

The history of the research program in this chapter begins with a set of principles and hypotheses stemming from early work both in neurology and physiology by Donald Hebb (1949), Norman Geschwind (1974), Martha Denckla (1972) and Rita Rudel (Denckla and Rudel 1976a, 1976b; Rudel 1985), and also in cognitive psychology by LaBerge and Samuels (1974), Doehring (1976), and Perfetti (1985, 1992). Today these fields comprise parallel directions in the cognitive neurosciences. For our purposes, we will divide background material into each of these earlier areas of contributions and then show their convergence in a new intervention on fluency and comprehension.

Physiology and Neurology

One of the pioneer physiological scientists in the mid-twentieth century, Hebb contributed some of the most basic principles that undergird the work presented here on fluency. More specifically, Hebb modeled, at the neuronal level, how individual cells come to learn to work together to increase the rapidity and process-efficiency of various functions. For example, in the visual system when an unknown stimulus is first detected by the retina, there is an activation in the visual cortex of multiple, highly programmed, highly specific individual cells. After repeated exposures to the same stimulus, the individual cells become a working unit, or cell assembly. These units learn to work together in precise synchrony, so that recognition of frequently viewed stimuli (like letters) becomes so efficient, it is virtually "*automatic.*" Hebb posited that one powerful result of cell assemblies in perceptual areas is a reservoir of *mental representations* of frequently perceived stimuli. In terms of the reading process and the development of fluency, cell assemblies in the visual regions are the physiological basis of *orthographic representations* of frequently viewed letters, letter patterns, and words.

The second principle derives from theory in behavioral neurology by Geschwind, Denckla, and Rudel. To our knowledge, Geschwind was the first scientist to highlight the potential importance of the naming or word-retrieval system as a predictor of reading. Based in part on the first case of classic alexia (i.e., acquired reading loss resulting from brain lesion) in 1892 by Dejerine, Geschwind hypothesized that the best predictor of later reading would be a child's early capacity at color-naming. An autopsy of Dejerine's patient revealed two sets of older lesions: one set[1] included the left visual or occipital area, and a lesion in the splenium or posterior portion of the corpus callosum (those fiber tracts connecting the two hemispheres). This set of lesions caused the French businessman-patient to lose his ability to read words and name colors. Geschwind conjectured that because both color naming and reading were lost through these discrete lesions, both functions must use similar structures and require many of the same cognitive, linguistic, and perceptual processes involved in retrieving a verbal match for a visual stimulus. Color-naming, therefore, Geschwind reasoned, should be a good early predictor of later reading.

Geschwind's color-naming hypothesis led to an unusual discovery by pediatric neurologist Denckla who tested the color-naming abilities of a small group of dyslexic and average reading children. What she discovered was the beginning of what is called "naming-speed research," and it begins with the fact that dyslexic readers can name colors perfectly well! What they can not do is name them *rapidly* in comparison to their peers. Denckla went on to construct the Rapid Automatized Naming (RAN) tasks, in which the child names 50 stimuli as rapidly as possible (e.g., 5 common letters, or 5 digits, or 5 colors, or 5 pictured objects, repeated randomly 10 times on a board). In a series of studies, Denckla and Rudel (1974, 1976a, 1976b) found that performance on the RAN differentiated dyslexic children from average readers, as well as other learning-disabled children, a conclusion also reached early on by Spring and Capps (1974).

The question ever since has been **why**. Although there has been considerable progress in understanding the relationship between the processes underlying naming speed and reading, a

---

[1]The second set of lesions impacted the angular gyrus region and caused a complete loss of all reading and writing.

consensual view still eludes the field, in part because of a long-held assumption that naming speed is a form of phonological skill, rather than an independent set of processes that include phonological ones. (See reviews of this extensive body of literature in Wolf and Bowers 1999; Wolf et al. 2002). The search for answers to these issues became the unexpected driving force for exploring aspects of reading disabilities heretofore unexplained in the reading field's previous emphasis on the phonological system. The range of studies and methodologies involved in naming-speed research now include (1) cross-sectional behavioral studies; (2) longitudinal studies; (3) cross-linguistic predictive and longitudinal studies in German, Spanish, Dutch, Finnish, Hebrew, and Chinese; (4) computerized speech data; (5) brain imaging studies of activation patterns during naming-speed tasks; and (6) subtype classifications (see review in Wolf and Bowers 1999). In the rest of this section we will very briefly summarize major findings in these six categories of research and then return to the second area of contribution to fluency in cognitive research.

Cross-sectional Studies.   Data from two and a half decades of studies indicate that processes underlying naming speed differentiate most children with dyslexia from other readers at every age tested from kindergarten through adulthood (Wolf et al. 2002). It is not the case, however, that every child with severe reading impairments has naming-speed deficits, as will be discussed in the subtype discussion. What is most important for research in this chapter is that early naming-speed performance is predictive of later word-reading fluency. In other words, as we shall indicate a bit later in models of the two processes, there appears considerable overlap between the processes underlying naming speed and word-reading speed (see Bowers et al. 1994).

In addition, there are several studies which indicate that poor readers whose reading level is commensurate with their achievement or IQ scores (sometimes called *non-discrepant* or *garden variety* readers) do not necessarily exhibit slowed naming speed (Badian 1996; Biddle 1996; Wolf and Obregon 1992). This finding needs exploration and further replication, but suggests that unlike phoneme awareness tasks, RAN tasks differentiate the putative discrepant readers from both non-discrepant and average readers. This finding also suggests that the more non-discrepant readers there are in any sample, the less strongly naming speed will predict reading.

A fascinating, ongoing area of comparison involves African-American children who speak African-American Vernacular English (AAVE). Most impaired AAVE readers have naming-speed deficits, but no difference is found between them and non AAVE-speaking dyslexic peers. What is more interesting is that there are significant phoneme awareness differences that distinguish these groups (see Gidney et al. 1998). Our research group is working to tease apart some of the potentially linguistic-based factors contributing to this finding.

Longitudinal Studies. Results from a five-year longitudinal study by Wolf, Bally, and Morris (1986) indicated differences in naming speed for children with reading disabilities from the first day of kindergarten with differences most dramatic for letters. Many children with dyslexia, therefore, began school with both a general retrieval-speed problem, and a particular difficulty with letter-naming's retrieval rate. These differences were maintained through Grade 4 for all categories, but especially for the more automatized categories of letters and numbers. Meyer et al. (1999) showed these differences continue through Grade 8 into adulthood (see also Scarborough and Domgaard 1998; Wolff 1993), even for compensated adults. Similar results are found in Dutch (van den Bos 2002) and Finnish (Korhonen 1995).

Cross-linguistic Studies: We now know from studies conducted among many regular orthographies—German (Naslund and Schneider 1991; Wimmer and Hummer 1990; Wimmer 1993, 2001; Landerl and Wimmer 2000; Wolf et al. 1994), Dutch (van den Bos 1998, 2002; Yap and Van der Leij 1993, 1994), Finnish (Korhonen 1995; Lyttinen et al. 1995), and Spanish (Novoa and Wolf 1984; Novoa 1988)—that serial naming speed is a powerful predictor in these more transparent languages. Further, it appears naming-speed performance becomes an even stronger, more important diagnostic indicator and predictor of reading performance in the more transparent orthographies. Naming speed is an equally strong predictor in Hebrew orthography (Breznitz 2001). Perhaps most unexpected are the findings in the Chinese language with its morpho-syllabic orthography (Ho in press). Despite our initial surprise, the Chinese findings are in some ways quite understandable from a linguistic perspective. First, although Chinese involves some phonological processing, particularly through the use of determinatives or phonetic markers for highly used words, phonology is secondary to morphology and semantics. Second, the Chinese system's use of a more morphemic-based orthography would tend to emphasize the direct connection between a visual symbol and a verbal referent, just as naming speed tasks require (see, however, a differing perspective, McBride-Chang and Kail 2002).

The importance of the cumulative cross-linguistic findings is that they indicate a more universal predictive capacity than originally understood for the processes underlying naming speed. It is of particular interest that across these cross-linguistic comparisons, including Chinese, the tasks believed to be most predictive in English—phoneme-awareness—are usually less predictive than the naming-speed measure in those languages. Such a finding underscores the need not to assume that findings in our morphophonemic English orthography can be exported whole-cloth to explain phenomena in other orthographies, a point eloquently and often stressed by Wimmer (2002).

Computerized Analyses. Using computer programs to digitize the speech stream of children performing the RAN task, three labs (Wolf and Obregon 1992; Neuhaus et al. 2001; Wagner et al., this volume) have converging evidence concerning where in the speech stream dyslexic readers differ. Results indicate no group differences for articulation (see, however, Snyder and Downey 1995), end-of-line scanning, or fatigue-related effects; but rather, significant group differences for the interstimulus intervals (ISIs) or pause-time between stimuli. The latter represents the "gap of time" between the response to one stimulus and the response to the next. Within this interstimulus gap occur multiple processes that include in-hibiting the response to the previous stimulus (*attentional systems* within *executive functions*); shifting the system to anticipate and respond to the current stimulus (e.g., *anticipatory facilitation*, Wood, Flowers, and Grigorenko 2001); perceiving the current stimulus (*perceptual system*); and accessing and retrieving a verbal label (*semantic, phonological*, and *lexical retrieval systems*). Thus, this research does not so much locate the exact source of differences, as it does focus our attention on a smaller set of relevant variables that include phonological contributions along with others.

Brain Imaging Analyses. One of the challenges in naming-speed research is to give a more exact accounting of components that underlie rapid naming. Brain images of areas activated during a naming task provide one type of converging evidence that can be used to specify which regions of the brain are involved. Misra et al. (2002) are conducting ongoing functional magnetic resonance imaging (fMRI) studies of average adult readers during a covert simulation of the RAN task for Letters and Objects. Later studies will compare these data with developmental populations and readers with a history of dyslexia. Preliminary findings show widespread activation in frontal, temporal, occipital, parietal, and cerebellar areas with particularly strong activation in middle, frontal, and angular gyrus regions. Important to earlier researcher's discussions of whether naming speed should be classified as a phonological task, there were strikingly different activation patterns, as well as discrete areas of overlap, with a phoneme elision task.

The brain-imaging results together with the behavioral and computerized investigations reinforce the following: (a) the multiple-componential nature of letter-naming speed; (b) the conceptualization that phonological processes represent one set of processes among many that are involved in naming speed; and (c) the notion that with multiple component parts, there can be different possible sources of breakdown (for an elaborated discussion of models, see Wolf and Bowers 1999). Such a broader perspective leads us to two other conclusions: first, the components of naming speed represent a mini-version or subset of the components of reading. Within this view, both naming and reading can be considered ensembles of multiple perceptual, lexical, and motoric processes. A model of letter-naming fluency is provided in figure 1 that illustrates the many components involved. A model of word-level fluency in figure 2 shows both the substantial overlap of

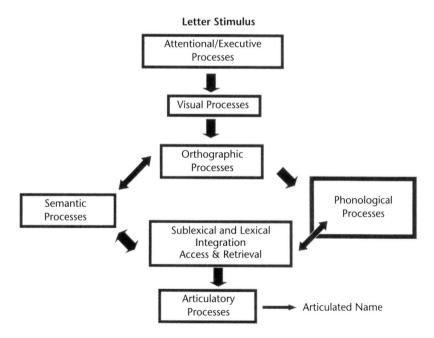

Figure 1.   Model of Letter Naming Fluency

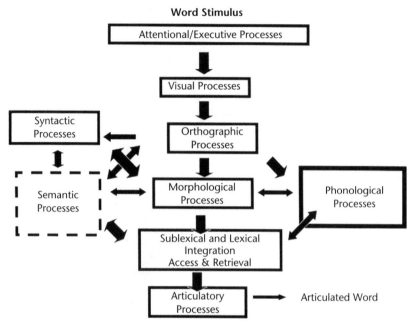

Figure 2.   Model of Word Level Fluency

components at the letter and word levels, and also several components with less or no overlap at the lexical level. All of these sub-processes must function smoothly and rapidly if the child is to produce a verbal match for an abstract, visually presented letter or word. Both the overlap of processes and the requirement for rapidity across them form the basis, we believe, for the broad prediction strength of naming-speed tasks for reading across all languages tested to date. Naming speed for letters is an early approximation of reading speed for words, and it can be done at least a year before reading is ever taught.

The second conclusion is that if there are multiple components involved in intact letter or word naming, there can be multiple sources of breakdown. And if that is the case, there should be children with different subtypes of reading failure, the topic of our next subsection.

SUBTYPE CLASSIFICATION: THE DOUBLE-DEFICIT HYPOTHESIS

One of the most powerful forms of data demonstrating naming speed's relative independence from phonological deficits involves work begun a decade ago on potential subtypes in our reading impaired populations. Originally conceptualized by Bowers and Wolf (1993), what has come to be called the Double Deficit Hypothesis (DDH) contains three basic tenets. First, within the well-known heterogeneity of dyslexic readers there are at least three major subtypes of dyslexic readers, characterized by the presence, absence, or combination of two core deficits in phonology and naming speed. Thus, there are (a) poor readers who have phonological deficits without problems in naming speed; (b) readers who have adequate phonological and word attack skills, but early naming-speed deficits and later reading fluency and comprehension deficits (Note: these children would be missed by most diagnostic batteries, because decoding is accurate.); and (c) children with both or "double deficits."

The second tenet of the DDH is that children with both core deficits represent the most severely impaired subtype in all aspects of reading—particularly in reading fluency and comprehension—because there are fewer areas of compensation available. Lovett and her colleagues (Lovett, Steinback, and Frijters 2000a) and Manis and his colleagues (Manis, Doi, and Bhadha 2000) confirmed the presence of similar subtypes in their differing types of data bases. In the most comprehensive subtype classifications to date, Morris and his colleagues (1998) found a range of subtypes, which included a rate without phonological deficit group, and importantly a profoundly impaired group with both deficits (the latter subgroup also had memory involvement). Badian (1996) and Ho, Chan Tsang, and Lee (in press) indicate the presence of a third distinct subtype in their English-speaking and Chinese-speaking populations, which they call orthographic. Berninger has long speculated about such a group (1994).

Wolf and Bowers (1999, 2000) called their classification of subtypes the Double-Deficit Hypothesis, as an acknowledged transitional vehicle to underscore the need to go beyond an emphasis too exclusively placed on phonological deficits. By no means do they or we believe there are only these types of deficit patterns. In every analysis by us and in other colleagues' re-analyses, there are small groups of children who can be characterized by neither deficit, and yet still have severe reading disability (see Lovett, Steinbach, and Frijters 2000). What the Double-Deficit Hypothesis was meant to underscore is the need to understand how independent these two major types of deficits can be in our samples and in our classrooms, with all the implications this has for expanding the foci of existing interventions. The single most important implication is that for children with fluency problems most existing programs, which focus largely on phonological skills, are necessary but insufficient. These children need, in addition to existing programs, daily, early emphases on automaticity and fluency.

Extensive data now replicate the existence of these three subtypes of impaired readers in several language systems (e.g., German, Dutch, Finnish, and Hebrew). But, there are linguistic surprises that are emerging along with these new analyses in different languages and dialects within languages. For example, in English, Lovett, Steinbach, and Frijters (2000) studied a large sample of the most severely impaired, clinically referred readers and found that more than half are the double-deficit type, with the remainder divided across the single deficit subtypes with about 10% unspecifiable deficits. By contrast, Breznitz (personal correspondence, 2000) reports that out of 375 dyslexic children studied in Hebrew, the overwhelming majority would be double-deficit readers with 56 readers classified as naming-speed deficit, and only 15 readers classified with solely phonological deficits.

The third, evolving tenet of the Double-Deficit Hypothesis is that these collective data underscore the need to understand the role of rate of processing and fluency in reading development and to create fluency intervention that addresses these issues. Until recently, children with single, phonological-deficits were adequately treated with current programs emphasizing phonological awareness and decoding. However, the other two subtypes with their explicit problems in naming speed and reading fluency were never sufficiently remediated and may have contributed to the numbers of children called "treatment resisters" (Torgesen, Wagner, and Rashotte 1994) or "nonresponders" (al Otaiba, Fuchs, and Fuchs, in press). In the next section of this chapter we describe both an historically based, developmental-componential view of fluency and an intervention program constructed on its principles.

TOWARD A DEVELOPMENTAL, COMPONENT-BASED VIEW OF FLUENCY IN READING DEVELOPMENT AND READING INTERVENTION

Other Historical Contributions to Fluency in Cognitive Psychology

In addition to work stemming from the neurosciences, there is a strong line of earlier research contributing to fluency in cognitive psychology (see Wolf and Katzir-Cohen 2001). We will highlight here several major theorists and the pertinent principles derived from them. LaBerge and Samuels (1974) used information-processing theory in cognitive psychology to present a model of *automaticity* in reading. According to their view, reading becomes progressively

more automatic as the underlying subskills of reading achieve automaticity: "When one describes a skill at the macro level as being
automatic, it follows that the subskills at the micro level and their
interrelations must also be automatic" (p. 295). The first stage of
these subskills in their model involves the visual code and the uni-
tization of visual stimuli. As visually coded information achieves
rapidity, attentional resources can be allocated to other areas like
semantic codes and ultimately comprehension.

Two major principles for fluency can be derived from LaBerge
and Samuel's work: (1) the concept of automaticity for underlying
subskills; and (2) the important notion that as lower-level subskills
achieve automatic rates, attention can be allocated to higher-level
comprehension related skills. A central premise in our later discussion of intervention is that *macro-level reading fluency is based on
the automaticity of micro-level subskills and their connections.*

A second major theorist in this earlier period is Doehring
(1976) who provided the first systematic study of the development
of fluency in reading subskills from kindergarten to the end of
high school. His seminal Society for Research in Child Development (SRCD) monograph charted children's developing rate
changes from the level of symbols (e.g., colors), letters, letter patterns, word, phrases, to sentences. Doehring's goal was to chart:

> . . . the relative course of acquisition of skills for processing the
> graphological features of letters, the orthographic regularities of let-
> ter combinations, the semantic features of words, and the semantic-
> syntactic constraints of word sequences. These are the skills that
> must be mastered beyond the level of simple accuracy to the point
> where accurate processing becomes rapid enough to be classified as
> fluent reading. (p. 2).

In essence, our work incorporates Doehring's pioneering developmental, level-based, component-based approach to reading fluency both in our evolving definition of fluency and in our
intervention.

The third theorist, Perfetti (1977, 1985, 1992) represents an
integration of past and present work in the cognitive sciences.
Like others, he employed key information processing principles.
Using the earlier term "verbal efficiency," Perfetti presented a
comprehensive account of most of the components and variables
necessary for "effective reading speed," e.g., general symbol activation and retrieval; various recognition processes; lexical access
and retrieval; working memory; learning and practice. Particularly
emphasized in Perfetti's view of efficiency is the quality of orthographic, phonological, and semantic representations—"to the extent that these codes are retrieved rapidly and are high in quality,

the system is efficient" (Perfetti 1985, p. 118). The implications of this view are important to delineate. First, the child who has *not* formed high-quality representations in any of these representational codes will have a less efficient system. Second, the child who is unable to retrieve these representations rapidly will also be less efficient. Both pathways will result in a system unable to allocate attentional resources to comprehension.

Carver's work on "rauding theory" (1990, 1991, 1997) (where rauding denotes the fastest rate in which good comprehension can occur) adds several additional variables of importance to this view: age, teaching, or instructional factors; decoding processes, and three "speed variables"—cognitive speed, decoding speed, and naming speed. Like Carver there are an increasing number of researchers, among them Kail (Kail and Park 1994; McBride-Chang and Kail 2002) and Breznitz (2001), who assert the importance of understanding the influence of a more systemic, cognitive speed (see Farmer and Klein 1995; Marcus 1997).

What are the conclusions that can be drawn about fluency from Hebb, Geschwind, Denckla and Rudel on the one hand, and Laberge and Samuels, Doehring, and Perfetti on the other? We suggest that any current view of fluency development should incorporate the following elements from past research: first, there should be attention to the development of high-quality orthographic, phonological, semantic, and syntactic representational systems. Second, attention should be given to the connections between and among these systems. Third, there should be an emphasis on the rapid retrieval of information from each system through learning and practice.

What is curious about the field's current view of fluency is that it reflects very few of these historical principles. The reality is that current perspectives on fluency incorporate very little from past research, with most definitions approaching fluency as basically an **outcome** of accuracy in processes like decoding. In two excellent recent reviews of the fluency literature, Meyer and Felton (1999) and Meyer (2002) summarize most consensual views of fluency as "the ability to read connected text rapidly, smoothly, effortlessly, and automatically with little conscious attention to the mechanics of reading such as decoding." Such a view of fluency reflects little of the teeming subprocesses that contribute to it. In an effort to avoid the validation issues in such a definition, Torgesen and his colleagues (2001) opted for the minimalist definition of "rate and accuracy in oral reading" (p. 4), used in curriculum-based assessment research (Shinn et al. 1992). Similarly, the National Reading Panel's definition of fluency as "the immediate result of word recognition proficiency" (2000, pp.3-5) permits the simple procedure of testing for proficiency in word recognition, just as Torgesen et al.'s view can be assessed by performance on an oral reading measure that incorporates rate and accuracy.

We concur with these methodological concerns, but believe that there are still thornier and indeed fundamental issues to confront about the complex nature of fluency development. Just as emphasized by LaBerge and Samuels (1974), Doehring (1976), and Perfetti (1985), we believe it is essential to define fluency in terms of its component parts and various levels of reading subskills— letter, letter pattern, word, sentence, and passage. Together with Kame'enui et al. (2001), we suggest a figure-ground shift for the conceptualization of fluency: that is, as a developmental process, as well as an outcome. In a broad-ranging paper, Kame'enui and his colleagues conceptualized fluency in a more developmental manner as both the <u>development</u> of "proficiency" in underlying lower-level and component skills of reading (e.g., phoneme awareness), and also as the <u>outcome</u> of proficiency in higher-level processes and component skills (e.g., accuracy in comprehension).

Berninger and her colleagues (Berninger et al. 2001) take a still broader view, with a systems-approach to fluency. Fluency in this approach is influenced by (a) the characteristics of stimulus input (e.g., rate and persistence of a visual signal or speech signal); (b) the efficiency and automaticity of internal processes (e.g., the development of phonological, orthographic, and morphological systems); and (c) the coordination of responses by the executive functions system. Berninger is one of the few researchers to place special importance on the role of morphological knowledge (see this volume) about words in facilitating the development of orthographic rate and overall fluency.

In an effort to integrate historical and current research on fluency, Wolf and Katzir-Cohen (2001) put forth the following developmental definition:

> In its beginnings, reading fluency is the product of the initial development of accuracy and the subsequent development of automaticity in underlying sublexical processes, lexical processes, and their integration in single-word reading and connected text. These include perceptual, phonological, orthographic, and morphological processes at the letter-, letter-pattern, and word-level; as well as semantic and syntactic processes at the word-level and connected-text level. After it is fully developed, reading fluency refers to a level of accuracy and rate, where decoding is relatively effortless; where oral reading is smooth and accurate with correct prosody; and where attention can be allocated to comprehension (p. 219).

Such a developmental, more encompassing view of reading fluency has, we believe, profound implications for prevention, intervention, and assessment. For, within a developmental perspective, efforts to address fluency must start at the beginning of the reading acquisition process, not after reading is already acquired. Most current fluency instruction tends to work on the connected text levels after reading is acquired.

More specifically, most current efforts in fluency do not work within a prevention framework, but as Stahl described (Stahl, Heubach, and Crammond 1997), are based largely on the Repeated Reading technique (Dahl 1974; Dowhower 1994; Samuels 1985; Young, Bowers, and MacKinnon 1996). In this approach, the already "reading" child is asked to reread a passage at an appropriate level several times until fluent on that passage. Repeated reading methods were designed to increase reading rate for the particular materials being used and also for similar materials. Based on previously discussed information processing principles (LaBerge and Samuels 1974; Perfetti 1985), the conceptual principle is that more time can be allocated to comprehension skills when the rate of decoding is increased. From a developmental context, such a treatment is an important and efficacious tool when used at a particular phase of fluency development.

Repeated reading by itself, however, would be insufficient to address the development of rapid processing in the multiple, sublexical systems, as well as the development of semantic (vocabulary) and syntactic systems. The importance of working preventively before difficult fluency problems ever begin is an explicit theme in the recent studies by Torgesen, Rashotte, and Alexander (2001) and by Kame'enui et al. (2001). It is an implicit theme in Lyon and Moats (1997), who articulated some of the major concerns in current reading intervention research:

> Improvements in decoding and word-reading accuracy have been far easier to obtain than improvements in reading fluency and automaticity. This persistent finding indicated there is much we have to learn about the *development of componential reading skills* and how such skills mediate reading rate and reading comprehension. (p. 570, our italics)

In this passage Lyon and Moats (1997) pinpointed not only the field's difficulty in ameliorating the problem of fluency, but also a potential method for solving it: that is, specifying the subcomponents involved in fluency over development. As summarized briefly earlier, we believe some of the historical research—from Hebb to Perfetti—when complemented by current work (e.g., models of naming speed) provides a reasonable foundation for a first specification of the multiple processes and components involved. These include the following fluency-related processes: letter perception; orthographic representation; phonological representation; semantic representation; lexical access and retrieval; decoding and word-identification skills; morphological, syntactic, and prosodic knowledge; and finally, inference and comprehension skills. In other words, the difficult implication of past and present work on automaticity and efficiency is that reading fluency calls upon all the major processes and subskills involved in reading itself. Such a conclusion is actually problematic because it can lend itself to the facile interpretation that one need not do anything more than what is already being done in present reading instruction and intervention. Indeed for most children, reading fluency follows exactly that straightforward formula. But what of children who cannot learn to read or who have learned to read, but have never attained fluency? It is for these children that we have gone below the surface of our theoretical definitions and specifications to apply what we know about the structure of reading fluency to what we teach.

FLUENCY INTERVENTION: RAVE-O

Over the last five years under the auspices of funding from the National Institute of Child Health and Human Development, we have designed and tested an experimental, multi-componential approach to fluency instruction. The program emerged as the result of a collaboration by Morris, Lovett, and Wolf (1995) to investigate a multi-dimensional view of reading disabilities and the efficacy of different theory-based treatments for children with specific forms of dyslexia. Lovett and her colleagues (1994, 2000a and b; in press) pioneered the *"differential treatment outcome"* approach in their long history of work testing the effects of phonological and metacognitive strategy approaches for the teaching of reading.

Described in detail in Wolf, Miller, and Donnelly (2000), the RAVE-O program (Retrieval, Automaticity, Vocabulary-Elaboration, Enrichment with Language, and Orthography) has three key aims for each child: first, the development of accuracy and automaticity in sublexical and lexical levels; second, increased rate in word attack, word identification, and comprehension; and third, a transformed attitude toward language. The program simultaneously addresses both the need for automaticity in phonological, orthographic, semantic, syntactic, and morphological systems and the importance of teaching <u>explicit connections</u> among these linguistic systems. This latter feature is based in part on research that stresses the explicit linkages or connections among the ortho-graphic, semantic, and phonological processes (Adams 1990; Foor-man 1994; Seidenberg and McCelland 1989). Berninger et al. (2001; Berninger, this volume), Adams (1990), and Moats (2000) add the connections between morphosyntactic knowledge and these other processes.

The RAVE-O program is taught only in combination with a program that teaches systematic, phonological analysis and blend-ing (see Lovett et al. 2000a and b). Children are taught a group of core words each week that exemplifies critical phonological, or-thographic, and semantic principles. Syntactic and morphological principles are gradually added after initial work has begun in the program. Each core word is chosen on the basis of: (a) shared phonemes with the phonological-treatment program; (b) se-quenced orthographic patterns; and (c) semantic richness (e.g., each core word has at least three different meanings). First, the multiple meanings of core words are introduced in varied seman-tic contexts. Second, children are taught to connect the phonemes in the core words with the trained orthographic patterns in RAVE-O. For example, children are taught individual phonemes in the phonological program (like "a," "t," and "m") and orthographic chunks with the same phonemes in RAVE-O (e.g., "at" and "am" along with their word families; see work of Goswami 1999).

There is daily emphasis on practice and rapid recognition of the most frequent orthographic letter patterns in English. Com-puterized games (see Speed Wizards, Wolf and Goodman 1996) and a new set of manipulative materials (e.g., letter dice, sound sliders, cards, etc.) were designed to allow for maximal practice and to increase the speed of orthographic pattern recognition (i.e., onset and rime) in a fun fashion.

There is a simultaneous emphasis on vocabulary and re-trieval, based on earlier work in vocabulary development that sug-gests that one retrieves fastest what one knows best (see Beck, Perfetti, and McKeown 1982; German 1992; Kame'enui, Dixon, and Carnine 1987; Wolf and Segal 1999). Vocabulary growth is conceptualized as essential to both rapid retrieval (in oral and written language) and to improved comprehension, an ultimate goal in the program. Retrieval skills are taught through a variety of ways including a set of metacognitive strategies called the "Sam Spade Strategies."

Sam Spade also appears as a character in the series of compre-hension stories (e.g., *Minute Mysteries* and *Minute Adventures*). These stories accompany each week of RAVE-O and directly ad-dress fluency in comprehension in several ways. The controlled vocabulary in the timed and untimed stories both incorporates the week's particular orthographic and morphological patterns, and emphasizes the multiple meanings of the week's core words. The stories provide a superb vehicle for repeated reading practice, which, in turn, helps fluency in connected text. Thus, the Minute Stories are multi-purpose vehicles for facilitating fluency in phonological, orthographic, and semantic systems at the same time that they build comprehension skills. In this way, all knowledge systems that were taught explicitly earlier in the week in separate domains are called upon to work together in order to comprehend a story. In conjunction with the other activities, Minute Stories encapsulate our goal to facilitate fluency at every level, and as a result contribute to comprehension skills. For, the end of all our work on fluency is for nought if it is not connected to comprehension. Fluency is our best known bridge to ease in comprehension. The end of all our labors on RAVE-O, therefore, is not about how rapidly children read, but how well they understand (and enjoy) what they read.

Connected to this ultimate goal in every daily lesson in RAVE-O is an additional system too little discussed by many of us—that is, the affective-motivational one. The secret weapon of this program is the deceptive cover of *whimsy* over the program's systematicity. There is a daily emphasis for the teacher and the student on having fun with and ultimately owning these words and all the words and concepts they include. We seek in as many ways as we can to employ teachers' love of language to empower children who come to us all too often as "strangers in their own language" (Chukovsky 1963, p.9). In the process we seek engaged teachers and engaged learners.

Are there example results to date of RAVE-O's ability to advance children's accuracy and rate of processing at the letter, word, and connected text levels? Figure 3 provides a glimpse at some of the first results on the *Gray Oral Reading Test* (Wiederholt and Bryant 1992) from our study of RAVE-O for a group of severely impaired second and third grade readers, who also have low average WISC-3 (Wechsler 1991) vocabulary results. The GORT-3 required the children to read connected text orally, and assessed their accuracy, speed, and comprehension. RAVE-O builds on the direct instruction phonologically based program called PHAB (Phonological and Strategy Training; Lovett, Lacerenza and Borden 2000b) and is contrasted with PHAB plus WIST (Phonological Analysis and Blending/Direct Instruction plus Word Identification Strategy Training) and PHAB plus CSS (Phonological Analysis and Blending/Direct Instruction plus Classroom Survival Skills), also

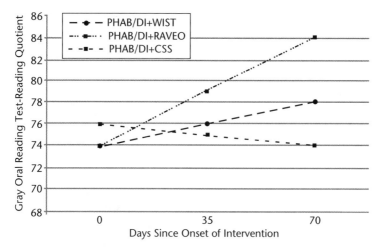

Figure 3. Response to Reading Programs by Children with Low Average WISC-3 Vocabulary Scores

used by Lovett et al. (2000b). These preliminary results, and those to be presented in the summary from this study, strongly support RAVE-O's potential for advancing children's reading performance at the letter, word, and text levels.

SUMMARY

The leitmotiv of this chapter is Pascal's powerful notion of *re-arrangement*. We have applied this concept to a conceptualization of the reading brain, whereby in order to read, the human brain calls upon an array of regions originally devoted to other things: perceiving tiny, visual features; hearing and segmenting the small-est units of sounds in spoken language; understanding a symbol; retrieving a word and its meaning(s); and integrating all these regions in lightning, almost-automatic speeds. It is this last function—with its explicit requirements of time—that has occu-pied our theoretical goals in this chapter. We have traced some of the major contributors in the twentieth century to theories of reading fluency, and we have connected some of the research on naming speed, particularly letter naming, to an understanding of the speed with which we read a word or a paragraph.

In the process of connecting these contributions to fluency, we discussed a new definition and approach to fluency, based upon the development of reading fluency's component parts. Such an approach, we suggested, represents a figure-ground shift in the field of reading research—from an emphasis on fluency as outcome, to a dual emphases on development and on individual processes. Within such an approach, we described an innovative, still evolving reading fluency intervention, the RAVE-O program. The program itself represents our first efforts to apply a *rearrangement* of best teaching practices and novel metacognitive strategies to a systematic rendering of fluency's component structure.

Preliminary results were presented that point to the potential efficacy of such a comprehensive, developmental approach for reading impaired students who have fluency and comprehension difficulties. We are especially hopeful about the effects of the RAVE-O program in changing comprehension (e.g., on the Gray Reading Quotient with its combination of fluency and comprehension scores). Future analyses are already underway to analyze the differential treatment effects of this program for particular subtypes of children with reading disabilities (for example, children with primarily phonological deficits, or naming-speed/fluency deficits, or both). It is imperative to understand whether the general efficacy of RAVE-O or any other intervention is based on the gains (or lack of gains) made by specific profiles of children. Do some subtypes require far more of such a treatment or a different one entirely?

Finally, we wish to end on an admittedly provocative note. The goal of working toward reading fluency has only a little to do with fluency itself. Just like decoding accuracy, fluency is a bridge toward comprehension and the desire to read more, which will ultimately enable deeper comprehension. Fluency, therefore, is a means—just like decoding—to a higher end than itself. For the end of all our efforts is a child who reads accurately enough and fluently enough to understand what she reads and to reach for more. In our interventions, we would like to rearrange this child's world early in the acquisition process to make that happen before later curricular requirements overwhelm the system. It is in this very real sense that both we and the child are "working for time."

The end of this story of naming speed, fluency, and its intervention is not available to anyone; we are, to be sure, in the very middle of it. It is a story that began improbably but one that has the capacity, we now believe, of illuminating some of the perplexing reasons particular children have failed our best past efforts at remediation.

REFERENCES

Adams, M. J. 1990. *Beginning to Read: Thinking and Learning about Print.* Cambridge, MA: MIT Press.

Al Otaiba, S., Fuchs, D., and Fuchs, L. in press. Characteristics of children who are unresponsive to early literacy intervention.

Badian, N. 1996.Dyslexia: A validation of the concept at two age levels. *Journal of Learning Disabilities* 29(1):102–12.

Beck, I. L., Perfetti, C. A., and McKeown, M. G. 1982. Effects of long-term vocabulary instruction on lexical access and reading comprehension. *Journal of Educational Psychology* 74: 506–21.

Berninger, V. W., ed. 1994. *The Varieties of Orthographic Knowledge.* Boston: Kluwer Press.

Berninger, V. W., Abbott, R. D., Billingsley, F., and Nagy, W. 2001. Processes underlying timing and fluency of reading: Efficiency, automaticity, coordination, and morphological awareness. In *Dyslexia, Fluency, and the Brain,* ed. M. Wolf. Baltimore, MD: York Press.

Biddle, K. R. 1996. The development of visual naming speed and verbal fluency in average and impaired readers: The implications for assessment, intervention, and theory. Unpublished doctoral dissertation, Tufts University, Boston, MA.

Bowers, P. G., and Wolf, M. 1993. Theoretical links between naming speed, precise timing mechanisms and orthographic skill in dyslexia. *Reading and Writing: An Interdisciplinary Journal* 5:69–85.

Bowers, P. G., Golden, J. O., Kennedy, A., and Young, A. 1994. Limits upon orthographic knowledge due to processes indexed by naming speed. In *The Varieties of Orthographic Knowledge: Theoretical and Developmental Issues,* ed. V. Berninger. The Netherlands: Kluwer Academic Publishers.

Breznitz, Z. December 13, 2000. Personal Correspondence.

Breznitz, Z. 2001. The role of inter-modality temporal features of speed of information processing in asynchrony between visual-orthographic and auditory-phonological processing. In *Dyslexia, Fluency, and the Brain,* ed. M. Wolf. Baltimore, MD: York Press.

Carver, R. P. 1990. *Reading Rate: A review of Research and Theory.* Boston: Academic Press, Inc.

Carver, R. P. 1991. Using letter naming speed to diagnose reading disability. *RASE-Remedial and Special Education* 12(5):33–43.

Carver, R. P. 1997. Reading for one second, one minute, or one year from the perspective of rauding theory. *Scientific Studies of Reading* 1:3–43.

Chukovsky, K. 1963. *From Two to Five.* Berkeley and Los Angeles, CA: University of California Press.

Dahl, P. 1974. An experimental program for teaching high speed word recognition and comprehension skills (Rep. No. Final report project #3-1154). Washington, DC: National Institute of Education.

Deeney, T., Gidney, C., Wolf, M., and Morris, R. 1999. Phonological skills of African-American reading-disabled children. Paper presented at 6th Annual Meeting of the Society for the Scientific Study of Reading. Montreal, Canada.

Dejerine 1892. Contribution a letude anatomo-pathologique et cliniquedes differents varieties de cecite verbale. *Comp. Rend. Scean. Soc. Biol.* 4:61–90.

Denckla, M. B. 1972. Color-naming defects in dyslexic boys. *Cortex* 8:164–76.

Denckla, M. B., and Rudel, R. G. 1974. Rapid automatized naming of pictured objects, colors, letters, and numbers by normal children. *Cortex* 10:186–202.

Denckla, M. B., and Rudel, R. G. 1976a. Naming of objects by dyslexic and other learning-disabled children. *Brain and Language* 3:1–15.

Denckla, M. B., and Rudel, R. G. 1976b. Rapid automatized naming (R.A.N.): Dyslexia differentiated from other learning disabilities. *Neuropsychologia* 14:471–79.

Doehring, D. G. 1976. Acquisition of rapid reading responses. *Monograph of the Society for Research in Child Development* 165 (2).

Dowhower, S. L. 1994. Repeated reading revisited: Research into practice. *Reading and Writing Quarterly: Overcoming Learning Difficulties* 10:343–58.

Ellis, A. W. 1985. The production of spoken words: A cognitive neuropsychological perspective. In *Progress in the Psychology of Language, Vol. 2.*, ed. A. W. Ellis. Hillsdale, NJ: Lawrence Erlbaum Associates.

Farmer, M., and Klein, R. 1995. The evidence for a temporal processing deficit linked to dyslexia: A review. *Psychonomic Society* 2:460–93.

Foorman, B. R. 1994. Phonological and orthographic processing: Separate but equal? In *The Varieties of Orthographic Knowledge: Theoretical and Developmental Issues*, ed. V. W. Berninger. Boston: Kluwer Academic Publishers.

German, D. J. 1992. Word-finding intervention for children and adolescents. *Topics in Learning Disorders* 13:33–50.

Geschwind, N. 1974. *Selected Papers on Language and the Brain.* D. Reidel: Dordrecht, Holland.

Gidney, C., Deeney, T., Wolf, M., Holmes, J., Cirino, P. and Morris, R. 1998. The presence of phonological and naming-speed deficits in African-American children. Poster presented at the Conference on Language Development in African-American Children. Memphis, TN.

Gough, P., and Tunmer, W. 1986. Decoding, reading, and reading ability. *Remedial and Special Education* 7:6–10.

Goswami, U. 1999. Integrating orthographic and phonological knowledge as reading develops: Onsets, rimes, and analogies in children's reading. In *Converging Methods for Understanding Reading and Dyslexia. Language, Speech, and Communication*, eds. R. Klein and P. McMullen

Goswami, U. 1993. Toward an interactive analogy model of reading development: Decoding vowel graphemes in beginning reading. *Journal of Experimental Child Psychology* 56:443–75.

Hebb, D. O. 1949. *The Organization of Behaviour.* New York: John-Wiley.

Ho C., Chan, D., Tsang, S-M, and Lee, S-H. In press. The Cognitive Profile and Multiple-Deficit Hypothesis in Chinese Developmental Psychology. To appear in *Developmental Psychology.*

Huey, E. 1908. *The Psychology and Pedagogy of Reading.* Cambridge: MIT Press.

Kail, R. 1991. Developmental change in speed of processing during childhood and adolescence. *Psychological Bulletin* 109(3):490–501.

Kail, R. and Park Y. 1994. Processing time, articulation time, and memory span. *Journal of Experimental Child Psychology.* 57(2): 281–291.

Kame'enui, E. J., Dixon, R. C., and Carnine, D. W. 1987. Issues in the design of vocabulary instruction. In *The Nature of Vocabulary Acquisition*, eds. M. G. McKeown and M. E. Curtis. Hillsdale, NJ: Lawrence Erlbaum Associates.

Kame'enui, E. J., Simmons, D. C., Good, R. H., and Harn, B. A. 2001. The use of fluency-based measures in early identification and evaluation of intervention efficacy in schools. In *Dyslexia, Fluency, and the Brain*, ed. M. Wolf. Baltimore, MD: York Press.

Korhonen, T. 1995. The persistence of rapid naming problems in children with reading disabilities: A nine-year follow-up. *Journal of Learning Disabilities* 28:232–39.

LaBerge, D., and Samuels, S. J. 1974. Toward a theory of automatic information processing in reading. *Cognitive Psychology* 6:293–323.

Landerl, K., and Wimmer, H. 2000. Deficits in phoneme segmentation are not the core problem of dyslexia: Evidence from German and English children. *Applied Psycholinguistics* 21:243–62.

Lovett, M. W., Borden, S., DeLuca, T., Lacerenza, L., Benson, N., and Brackstone, D. 1994. Treating the core deficits of developmental dyslexia: Evidence of transfer of learning after phonologically and strategy based reading training programs. *Developmental Psychology* 30: 805–22.

Lovett, M. W., Lacerenza, L., and Borden, S. L. 2000b. Putting struggling readers on the PHAST track: A program to integrate phonological and strategy-based remedial reading instruction and maximize outcomes. *Journal of Learning Disabilities* 33 (5):458–76.

Lovett, M. W., Lacerenza, L., Borden, S., Frijters, J., Steinbach, K., and DePalma, M. (in press). Components of effective remediation for developmental reading disabilities: Continuing phonological and strategy-based instruction to improve outcomes. *Journal of Educational Psychology.*

Lovett, M. W., Steinbach, K. A., and Frijters, J. C. 2000a. Remediating the core deficits of developmental reading disability: A double-deficit perspective. *Journal of Learning Disabilities* 33(4):334–58.

Lyons, G. R., and Moats, L. 1997. Critical conceptual and methodological considerations and reading intervention research. *Journal of Learning Disabilities* 30:579–88.

Lyttinen, H., Leinonen, S., Nikula, M., Richardson, V., Aro, M., and Leiwo, M. 1995. In search of core features of dyslexia: Observations concerning highly orthographically regular Finnish language. In *The Varieties of Orthographic Knowledge: Theoretical and Developmental Issues*, ed. V. W. Berninger. The Netherlands: Kluwer Academic Publishers

Manis, F. R., Doi, L. M., and Bhada, B. 2000. Naming speed, phonological awareness, and orthographic knowledge in second graders. *Journal of Learning Disabilities* 33:325–33.

Marcus, D. 1997. An investigation of the relationship of naming speed, processing speed, and reading in young, reading-impaired children. Unpublished master's thesis, Tufts University.

McBride-Chang, K., and Kail, F. 2002. Cross-cultural similarities in the predictors of reading acquisition. *Child Development* 73(5):1392–407.

Meyer, M. S. 2002. Repeated reading: An old standard is revisited and renovated. *Perspectives,* 28(1):15–18.

Meyer, M. S., and Felton, R. H. 1999. Evolution of fluency training: Old approaches and new directions. *Annals of Dyslexia* 49:283–306.

Meyer, M. S., Wood, F. B., Hart, L. A., and Felton, R. H. 1998. Longitudinal course of rapid naming in disabled and nondisabled readers. *Annals of Dyslexia.* 48:91–114.

Misra, M., Katzir, T., Wolf, M., and Poldrack, R. 2002. Neural systems for Rapid Automatized Naming (RAN) using fMRI: Effects of automaticity in skilled readers. Unpublished paper.

Moats, L. C. 2000. *Speech to Print.* Baltimore, MD: Brookes Publishing Co.

Morris, R., Stuebing, K., Fletcher, J., Shaywitz, S., Lyon, R., Shankweiler, D., Katz, L., Francis, D., and Shaywitz, B. 1998. Subtypes of reading disability: A phonological core with cognitive variability. *Journal of Educational Psychology* 90:1–27.

Naslund, J. C., and Schneider, W. 1991. Longitudinal effects of verbal ability, memory capacity, and phonological awareness on reading performance. *European Journal of Psychology of Education* 4:375–92.

National Reading Panel 2000. *Teaching Children to Read: An Evidence-based Assessment of the Scientific Research Literature on Reading and Its Implications for Reading Instruction.* Washington, DC: National Institute of Child Health and Human Development.

Neuhaus, G., Foorman, B., Francis, D., and Carlson, F. 2001. Measures of information processing in Rapid Automatized Naming (RAN) and their relation to reading. *Journal of Experimental Child Psychology* 78(4):359–73.

Novoa, L. 1988. Word-retrieval process and reading acquisition and development in bilingual and monolingual children. Unpublished doctoral dissertation. Harvard University, Cambridge, MA.

Novoa, L., and Wolf, M. 1984. Word-retrieval and reading in bilingual children. Paper presented at Boston University Language Conference, Boston, MA.

Obregon, M. 1994. Exploring naming timing patterns by dyslexic and normal readers on the serial RAN task. Unpublished Master's thesis. Tufts University, Boston, MA.

Perfetti, C. 1977. Language comprehension and fast decoding: Some psycholinguistic prerequisites for skilled reading comprehension. In *Cognition, Curriculum, and Comprehension*, ed. J. T Guthrie. Newark, DE: International Reading Association.

Perfetti, C. A. 1985. *Reading Ability*. New York: Oxford University Press.

Perfetti, C. A. 1992. *Reading Acquisition*. Hillsdale, NJ: Lawrence Erlbaum Associates.

Rudel, R. 1985. Definition of dyslexia: Language and motor deficits. In *Dyslexia: Current Status and Future Directions*, eds. F. Duffy and N. Geschwind. Boston: Little Brown.

Samuels, S. J. 1985. Automaticity and repeated reading. In *Reading Education: Foundations for a Literate America*, eds. J. Osborn, P. T. Wilson, and R. C. Anderson. Lexington, MA: Lexington Books.

Scarborough, H. S., and Domgaard, R. M. 1998. An exploration of the relationship between reading and rapid serial naming. Poster presented at meeting of Society for Scientific Study of Reading. San Diego, CA.

Seidenberg, M., and McCelland, J. 1989. A distributed developmental model of word recognition and naming. *Psychological Review* 96:35–49.

Shaywitz, S., Shaywitz, B., Pugh, K., Fulbright, R., Constable, R. T., Mencl, W. E., Shankweiler, D., Liberman, A., Skudlarski, P., Fletcher, J., Katz, L., Marchione, K., Lacadie, C., Gatenby, C., and Gore, J. 1998. Functional disruption in the organization of the brain for reading in dyslexia. *Neurobiology* 95:2636–41.

Shinn, M. R., Good, R. H., Knutson, N., Tilly, W. D., and Collins, V. L. 1992. Curriculum based measurement of oral reading fluency: A confirmatory analysis of its relation to reading. *School Psychology Review* 21:45–79.

Snyder, L., and Downey, D. 1995. Serial rapid naming skills in children with reading disabilities. *Annals of Dyslexia* 45:31–50.

Spring, C., and Capps, C. 1974. Encoding speed, rehearsal, and probed recall of dyslexic boys. *Journal of Educational Psychology* 66:780–86.

Stahl, S., Heubach, K., and Crammond, B. 1997. Fluency-oriented reading instruction. *Reading Research Report* 79:1–38.

Stanovich, K. E. 1986. "Matthew effects" in reading: Some consequences of individual differences in acquisition of literacy. *Reading Research Quarterly* 4:360–407.

Stanovich, K. E. 1992. Speculations on the causes and consequences of individual differences in early reading acquisition. In *Reading Acquisition*, eds. P. B. Gough, L. C. Ehri, and R. Treiman. Hillsdale, NJ: Lawrence Erlbaum Associates.

Torgesen, J., Rashotte, C., and Alexander, A. 2001. The prevention and remediation of reading fluency problems. In *Dyslexia, Fluency, and the Brain*, ed. M. Wolf. Baltimore, MD: York Press.

Torgesen, J. K., Wagner, R. K., and Rashotte, C. A. 1994. Longitudinal studies of phonological processing and reading. *Journal of Learning Disabilities* 27:276–86.

van den Bos, K. 1998. IQ, phonological awareness, and continuous-naming speed related to Dutch children's poor decoding performance on two word identification tests. *Dyslexia* 4:73–89.

van den Bos, K., Zijlstra, B., lutje Spelberg, H. 2002. Life-span data on continuous-naming speeds of numbers, letters, colors, and pictured objects, and word-reading speed. *Scientific Studies of Reading* 6 (1):25–49.

Wechsler, D. 1991. *Manual for the Wechsler Intelligence Scale for Children - Third Edition.*: The Psychological Corp., San Antonio.

Wiederholt, J. L., and Bryant, B. 1992. *Gray Oral Reading Test, (GORT-3)*. PRO-ED: Austin, Texas.

Wimmer, H. 1993. Characteristics of developmental dyslexia in a regular writing system. *Applied Psycholinguistics* 14:1–34.

Wimmer, H. 2002. Dysfluent reading in the absence of spelling difficulties: A specific disability in regular orthographies. *Journal of Educational Psychology* 94(2):272–77.

Wimmer, H., and Hummer, P. 1990. How German-speaking first graders read and spell: Doubts on the importance of the logographic stage. *Applied Psycholinguistics* 11:349–68.

Wolf, M. 1991. Naming speed and reading: The contribution of the cognitive neurosciences. *Reading Research Quarterly* 26:123–41.

Wolf, M., and Bowers, P. 1999. The "double-deficit hypothesis" for the developmental dyslexias. *Journal of Educational Psychology* 91:1–24.

Wolf, M. and Bowers, P. 2000. The question of naming-speed deficits in developmental reading disabilities: An introduction to the Double-Deficit Hypothesis. *Journal of Learning Disabilities* 33:322–24.

Wolf, M., Bowers, P., and Biddle, K. R. 2000. Naming-speed processes, timing, and reading: A conceptual review. *Journal of Learning Disabilities* 33:387–-407.

Wolf, M., Bally, H., and Morris, R. 1986. Automaticity, retrieval processes, and reading: A longitudinal study in average and impaired readers. *Child Development* 57:988–1000.

Wolf, M., and Goodman, G. 1996. *Speed Wizards*. Computerized reading program. Tufts University and Rochester Institute of Technology.

Wolf, M., Miller, L., and Donnelly, K. 2000. Retrieval, Automaticity, Vocabulary Elaboration, Orthography (RAVE-O): A comprehensive, fluency-based reading intervention program. *Journal of Learning Disabilities* 33:322–24.

Wolf, M., Goldberg, A., Gidney, C., Cirino, P., Morris, R., and Lovett, M. 2002. The second deficit: An investigation of the independence of phonological and naming-speed deficits in developmental dyslexia. *Reading and Writing* 15:43–72.

Wolf, M., and Katzir-Cohen, T. 2001. Reading fluency and its intervention. *Scientific Studies of Reading*. (Special Issue on Fluency), eds. E. Kameenui and D. Simmons 5:211–38.

Wolf, M., and Obregon, M. 1992. Early naming deficits, developmental dyslexia, and a specific deficit hypothesis. *Brain and Language* 42:219–47.

Wolf, M., and Segal, D. 1999. Retrieval-rate, accuracy, and vocabulary elaboration (RAVE) in reading impaired children: A pilot intervention program. *Dyslexia: An International Journal of Theory and Practice* 5:1–27.

Wolf, M., Pfeil, C., Lotz, R., and Biddle, K. 1994. Towards a more universal understanding of the developmental dyslexias: The contribution of orthographic factors. In *The Varieties of Orthographic Knowledge I: Theoretical and Developmental Issues*, ed. V. W. Berninger. Dordrecht, The Netherlands: Kluwer.

Wolff, P. 1993. Impaired temporal resolution in developmental dyslexia: Temporal information processing in the nervous system. In *Annals of the New York Academy of Sciences*, eds. P. Tallal, A. Galaburda, R. Llinas, and C. von Euler 682:87–103.

Wood, F., Flowers, L., and Grigorenko, E. 2001. On the functional neuroanatomy of fluency or why walking is just as important to reading as talking is. In *Dyslexia, Fluency, and the Brain*, ed. M. Wolf. Baltimore, MD: York Press.

Yap, R., and van der Leij, A. 1993. Word processing in dyslexics: An automatic decoding deficit? *Reading and Writing: An Interdisciplinary Journal* 5(3):261–79.

Yap, R., and van der Leij, A. 1994. Testing the automatization deficit hypothesis of dyslexia via a dual-task paradigm. *Journal of Learning Disabilities* 27(10):660–65.

Young, A., Bowers, P., and MacKinnon, G. 1996. Effects of prosodic modeling and repeated reading on poor readers' fluency and comprehension. *Applied Psycholinguistics* 17:59–84.

Chapter • **14**

Effective Treatment for Children with Dyslexia in Grades 4–6:
Behavioral and Brain Evidence

Virginia W. Berninger, William E. Nagy, Joanne Carlisle, Jennifer Thomson, Diana Hoffer, Sylvia Abbott, Robert Abbott, Todd Richards, and Elizabeth Aylward

FRAMING THE RESEARCH QUESTION

A rapidly expanding research literature provides scientific support for the effectiveness of early intervention in reading (e.g., Blachman et al. 1999; Felton 1993; Foorman et al. 1998; Jenkins et al. 2000; Torgesen et al., 1999; Uhry and Shepherd, 1997; Vellutino et al., 1996; Wasik and Slavin, 1993). This research provides strong evidence for the effectiveness of training in phonological awareness and alphabetic principle for beginning readers, in general, and especially for those most at-risk for learning to read (e.g., Ehri et al. 2002; Rayner et al. 2001). Phonological awareness is perceiving and analyzing the sound units in spoken words. Sound units that correspond to graphemes (one or two alphabet letters) are phonemes. Alphabetic principle refers to mapping graphemes onto phonemes and may be used in phonological decoding—translating a written word into a spoken word.

Even when early intervention is implemented, it is clear that it does not eliminate all reading problems. In addition, some at-risk children do not receive early intervention. Numerous investigators have identified children who failed to respond to early intervention or who responded slowly compared to peers. This study was conducted, therefore, to identify effective components of instructional intervention for students in the upper elementary grades with persisting reading problems. In designing the study we drew on the work of other investigators and some of our own preliminary studies.

In a series of studies, Lovett, who has the longest standing systematic research program on treatment of persisting reading problems, compared two instructional approaches. The first approach, which was phonological, used direct instruction techniques from a commercially available program to teach phonological analysis, sound blending, and rules of letter-sound correspondences. The second, which was metacognitive, taught four strategies for identifying unknown words—analogy, search for the known part of the word, substitution of alternative vowel pronunciations, and removal of prefixes and affixes. These instructional approaches were compared to each other and to a contact control treatment (a treatment that gives the same amount of attention to participants as the experimental treatments but in a different domain from the one under investigation). Lovett et al. (1994) found that each of the contrasting instructional components exerted its greatest effects on different learning outcomes: Benefits of the phonological treatment were observed on the phonological measures, whereas benefits of the metacognitive components were observed on the measures of real word reading (learning specific words). Lovett, Steinbach, and Frijters (2000) replicated this pattern of findings.

Lovett et al. (2000) extended this work by comparing combinations of the phonological- and strategy-based treatments (varying which one came first and which came second) with each treatment alone and with a contact control treatment. In this study, they modified the strategy-based treatment used in previous studies to include a greater focus on subsyllabic rime units (word families), for the purpose of encouraging students to be word detectives and analyze words more fully (Gaskins 1997). In contrast, the phonological treatment focused on teaching the alphabetic principle using grapheme-phoneme correspondence. Lovett and colleagues found that, in general for most outcomes, the combined phonological and strategy treatments were more effective, regardless of order of implementation, than either treatment

alone. Although the recommended treatment for persisting reading disabilities typically includes intensive instruction in the alphabetic principle (e.g., Birsch 1999; Clark and Uhry 1995), some
research has shown that instructional feedback at the whole word
level is equally effective (e.g., Wise and Olson 1995). That result is
consistent with Lovett and colleagues' finding that instruction in
both grapheme-phoneme correspondences and strategies involving other units of analysis are effective in treating persisting reading difficulties.

Torgesen et al. (2001) compared two instructional programs
that differed in the breadth and depth of phonological awareness
and decoding instruction. The first, which included an articulatory
feedback component to develop phonological awareness through
articulatory awareness, provided the most phonological training,
whereas the second provided more work with words in context.
Both treatments were effective (effect sizes ranged from 4.4 to 3.9),
but were not differentially effective, demonstrating that there is
more than one effective way to teach upper elementary grade students with persisting reading problems. This result is consistent
with the findings of Wise, Ring, and Olson (1999) who found that
articulatory training is one way, but not the only way, for developing phonological awareness in students with persisting reading
problems; phoneme manipulation was as effective, and sometimes
more effective, for this purpose.

The research studies discussed so far have directed instruction
to different units of orthographic-phonological correspondence,
for example, grapheme-phoneme correspondence, syllable, and
whole word, and typically also included activities for developing
phonological awareness. A research literature has also emerged on
linguistic awareness that emphasizes orthographic awareness and
morphological awareness as well as phonological awareness in
word learning. Orthographic awareness is the ability to perceive
and analyze letter units in words. Morphological awareness is the
ability to perceive and analyze word parts corresponding to prefixes and affixes and the word base or stem that already has a suffix. Henry (1989, 1990) played an important role in stimulating
treatment research grounded in this broad view of linguistic
awareness. For example, Henry (1989) showed that third and fifth
graders benefitted more from instruction that included explicit
training in syllable, morphological, word, and sentence patterns
and the alphabetic principle in addition to traditional basal instruction in reading and spelling than from instruction that included all those components except the alphabetic principle or
that included only the basal instruction. Henry (1990) developed

an instructional program that explicitly teaches morphemes and their spelling for words of different origin (Anglo Saxon, Latin, and Greek).

An emerging research literature is adding to our understanding of orthographic and morphological awareness. Beyond the initial stage of learning to read, teaching students to decode words in a left-to-right manner letter-by-letter may be insufficient for learning to read words that become increasingly complex in terms of orthographic, syllabic, morphological, and morphophonemic patterns. They need to develop *orthographic awareness* of how each letter position influences the word identity, of how two-letter units may correspond to phonemes, and of how even larger sub-syllabic, multi-letter units may have predictable pronunciations. Minimal pairing of words that differ by just one grapheme directs attention to letter positions throughout a word and improved word decoding at all letter positions in a word for students with persisting reading difficulty (McCandliss et al. 2003). Ability to attend to and remember two-letter spelling units in words coded in short-term memory predicted faster versus slower responding in a first grade intervention for at-risk readers. For those who had been the slower responders during first grade, their ability to learn correspondences between two-letter spelling units and phonemes predicted reading achievement during second grade (Berninger et al. 2002). Highlighting common multi-letter units in word families by blocking them on lists transferred to improved word learning for struggling readers (Levy 2001).

A growing body of research is (a) pointing to the importance of morphological awareness in learning to read and spell polysyllabic words, (b) describing the normal development of morphological awareness, and (c) pinpointing differences between good and poor readers and spellers in coordinating morphological, phonological, and orthographic information in words (Carlisle 2000; Carlisle and Nomanbhoy 1993; Carlisle and Stone in press; Fowler and Liberman 1995; Leong 1989, 2000; Mahoney, Singson, and Mann 2000; Nagy, Diakidoy, and Anderson 1993; Nagy et al. 1994; Singson, Mahony, and Mann 2000; Tyler and Nagy 1989, 1990). Based on group means, children who received training in syllable and morphological awareness in addition to orthographic and phonological awareness did not improve significantly more in their reading than children who received only training in orthographic and phonological awareness; but growth curve analyses for individual children showed a tendency for more children to grow faster in reading if they received the additional syllable and morphological awareness training than if they did not (Abbott and Berninger, 1999).

Other treatment research demonstrates the importance of automatizing subskills of reading so that reading of text is fluent—effortless, fast, smooth, and coordinated (Kame'enui and Simmons 2001; Stahl, Heubach, and Crammond 1997; Wolf 2001; Wolf and Katzir-Cohen 2001). A variety of instructional techniques have been found to be effective in achieving fluency, ranging from repeated readings (e.g., Bowers 1993; Young, Bowers, and MacKinnon 1996), pretraining words to time criteria or setting time limits (e.g., Levy, Abello, and Lysynchuk 1997), computer-regulated accelerated reading based on one's fastest self-paced reading (Breznitz 1997), and wide reading, which is independent reading of a variety of literature selections (Stahl, Heubach, and Crammond 1997). RAVO (Wolf et al. this volume) is a research-supported curriculum for developing reading fluency.

The main purpose of our treatment research was to examine the effects of the treatment on brain substrates in an image-teach-image design in which participants were randomly assigned to one of two treatments that contrasted in the kind of linguistic awareness training. Because such designs are expensive to conduct, sample size was necessarily relatively small. In planning our treatment study, we took into account findings of the National Reading Panel (2000) regarding scientifically supported, balanced reading instruction, the research on automaticity and fluency, the research on orthographic, phonological, and morphological awareness in word learning, and the work of Lovett and colleagues, Torgesen and colleagues, Gaskin and colleagues, and Wise and colleagues in working with students with persisting reading problems. Table I summarizes the unique and common components of each of the treatments that we compared. The unique components consisted of seven comparable kinds of activities for developing each of the kinds of linguistic awareness. The common components consisted of the instructional activities recommended by the National Reading Panel.

METHOD

Participants

Twenty children (4 girls and 16 boys) who had just completed fourth, fifth, or sixth grade participated in our instructional study during the summer of 2001 when they were not attending school or enrolled in other instructional programs. All were probands, that is, children who met the inclusion criteria to qualify their families for participation in a family genetics study (Berninger, Abbott, Thomson et al. 2001). To qualify, children had to fall below the population mean and achieve at least one standard deviation below their pro-rated Verbal IQ (Verbal Comprehension factor) in one or more of the following skills: *Woodcock Reading Mastery Test-Revised* (WRMT-R) (Woodcock 1987) Word Identification or Word Attack accuracy, *Test of Real Word or Pseudoword Reading Efficiency* (TOWRE) (Torgesen, Wagner, and Rashotte 2000), *Gray Oral Reading Test—Third Edition* (GORT-3) (Widerholt and Bryant 1992) accuracy or rate, or *Wide Range Achievement Test—Third Edition* (WRAT3) Spelling (Wilkinson 1993). Typically, children who are referred to and qualify for this family genetics study are impaired in all or almost all of these measures of single word or pseudoword reading, oral reading, and spelling. In addition, children identified in this manner have a history of failing to be brought up to grade level with supplementary instruction or special education services and tend to be impaired in language phenotype markers (orthographic, phonological, and rapid automatic naming) (Berninger, Abbott, Thomson et al. 2001); 87% had a double deficit in phonological and rapid automatic naming skills. The children in this intervention study did not have primary language disability based on history or standardized test results; as a group, they scored slightly above the population mean on *Clinical Evaluation of Language Function—Third Edition* (CELF3) (Semel, Wiig, and Secord 1995) Formulated Sentences ($M = 10.6$, $SD = 2.3$). Only one had attention deficit disorder; the rest varied along a continuum on indicators of inattention (self-regulation of attentional processes) as distinct from hyperactivity (problems in regulating appropriate activity levels). None had conduct disorder.

We point out differences between our sample and other samples used in treatment research for persisting reading problems because differences in verbal reasoning, receptive and expressive language, and attentional difficulties may affect generalizability of treatment results. The Verbal IQ of our sample was substantially higher on average ($M = 110.6$, $SD = 11.0$) than in the Lovett et al. (1994) study ($M = 91.5$, $SD = 14.4$), the Lovett, Steinbach, and Frijters (2000) study ($M = 91.1$, $SD = 10.6$), or the Torgesen, Alexander et al. (2001) study ($M = 92.2$ or 93.0, $SD = 8.5$ or 12.3, depending on treatment) and showed less range in our study (94 to 128) than in the Lovett studies (58–133, Lovett, Steinbach, and Fritjers 2000; 60–122, Lovett et al. 2000). The age range in our sample (10.6 to 12.5 years), like that of Torgesen et al.'s sample (8 to 10 years), was more narrow than that of Lovett and colleagues who enrolled children from 7 to 13 in their studies. In contrast to our sample, which was not impaired in expressive or receptive language and did not have major attentional difficulties, the Torgesen et al. sample, prior to treatment, had markedly impaired CELF Expressive Language (76.2, *SD* = 9.1) and Receptive Language (*M* = 79.7, *SD* = 11.0); most of their sample had attention deficit disorder (71%–81%, depending on treatment group, half of whom were on medication at various times). Thus, the Torgesen et al. treatment may be the treatment of choice for students with comorbid language disability, reading disability, and attention deficit disorder.

Motivational Theme

A two-part theme was used to motivate older students with chronic reading problems to come to the university during the summer for yet more reading instruction. Typically these students have received considerable prior help in and outside of school and are discouraged and sometimes depressed and angry. We use motivational themes to engage them in the treatment. The theme of **Third-Rocker's R-Files** builds upon the concept of aliens who come to earth to observe and decipher earth's (Third Rock from the Sun) culture and of humans who try to decipher alien intelligence to find the truth that is out there (X-Files). Our goal was to show the students the secrets to unlocking the code in written English words, which may seem like an alien language to them, but the key is out there. We emphasized that the strategies we were teaching them would help them unlock the code. Students were, therefore, encouraged to be **Word Detectives**, like Sherlock Holmes and Watson, in using as many clues as possible to decipher the code and create their own R-Files in their mind. To explain the value of codes, we also discussed the Navaho code talkers who received a presidential award for their contribution to winning World War II. We also discussed code writing in developing computer programs. We read them a short story from *Read Naturally* about Albert Einstein who started doing better at school after his uncle told him to be a **detective**.

Each student had a Work Folder to use during the intervention. Each Work Folder had Web cartoons of Sherlock Holmes and Watson with magnifying glasses aimed at the words Word Detectives. The cover had this statement: This R-File belongs to 3rd Rocker (*name of child*). The Work Folder contained the R-file for recording earned points during instruction. It also contained response forms for each of the seven activities that were unique to each treatment (as explained later). On the last day, each child wrote a message to Dr. Lingo, the Grand PoohBah of Linguists in the Universe, about the conclusion of their mission—what they learned about decoding Earth's English.

Each student also participated in three virtual reality activities that involved children in collaborative, problem solving activities in science and visual-spatial reasoning: virtual reality modeling, a virtual tour of the Puget Sound under water, and a building layout activity. For the first activity, children built animations or stories using Alice Modeling Software. For the second activity, children swam or flew anywhere they wished while performing scientific investigation, for example, watching the effect of releasing particles into the water and making predictions about their movements. For the third activity, they created a layout for a building by placing, moving, and replacing virtual objects. We hoped that the high level of presence (focused attention) and engagement (active learning) that virtual reality is hypothesized to create (cf., Csikszentmihali 1990) would transfer to a high level of focused attention and cognitive engagement in word study as well. At the very least these children enjoyed their success with these activities, which served to counteract the frustration they had experienced with reading.

Experimental Design and Implementation

Children were randomly assigned to either the phonological awareness or morphological awareness treatment group. Two experienced, certified teachers worked as a team to deliver the warm-up and both experimental treatments. Two other experienced, certified teachers worked as a team to deliver the other common components of the curriculum that both treatment groups received. Instruction took place in groups of ten. Two teacher helpers, who were learning the procedures to use in their own teaching, assisted the first team in (a) monitoring on-task and organizational behaviors of students during instruction, (b) awarding R-file points, (c) individual progress monitoring (transferring activities and first- and second- oral readings), and (d) record keeping. R-file points were not traded in for other reinforcers, but children were given a choice of snacks in between the first and second one-hour segments of each session.

The learning environment had many features of the subsystems contributing to the functional system of the developing reading brain (Berninger and Richards 2002).

- To maintain arousal and attention, children were given R-file points for responding correctly and activities were designed for frequent responding in multiple modalities (oral, written, manipulating cards, etc.).

- To avoid habituation or off-task novelty-seeking, activities were of brief duration, changed frequently, and varied in nature.
- To avoid overload in working memory, activities followed a predictable routine for both the unique and common components of treatment even though the content (items) of those activities changed.
- To develop automaticity, a small part of each lesson was aimed at creating automatic grapheme-phoneme correspondences.
- To optimize engagement and active, strategic thinking, the instructional activities, goals, and materials were highly preplanned in advance, but during the sessions, teachers relinquished control and encouraged children to respond freely to questions teachers posed, to question the teacher and each other, to debate, and to reflect about strategy application. Nothing in the lessons was scripted. Neither was instruction left to chance or incidental instruction during a "teachable moment." Each lesson had explicit instructional goals, and teachers used explicit, but flexible, means to achieve those goals.
- To provide feedback needed for executive management, teachers provided other-regulation cues for goal-setting, self-monitoring, self-regulating, and staying on task. For example, the instructions provided by the teacher made the goals explicit, the R-file points children earned and the daily graphs during transferring and fluency activities provided immediate feedback about performance, and teacher prompts redirected off-task behaviors to the task at-hand.

The lessons contained instructional components aimed at both automatization and strategy application because functional brain systems draw on both (Berninger and Richards 2002). Automatizing low-level skills frees up limited resources of working memory for high-level reflection and problem solving. Strategizing is an effective way to self-regulate the system in meeting goals. The feedback component was important because children whose performance is continually assessed and who are given feedback learn more (Fuchs and Fuchs 1999; Fuchs et al. 1994). Overall, this learning environment implemented a Direct Explanation approach rather than a Direct Instruction (scripted) approach (Duffy 2002). Direct explanations often took the form of leading children to generalizations they articulated for themselves on the basis of the teacher's preplanned activities and clear instructional goals.

The first treatment emphasized morphology, whereas the second one emphasized phonology. Because we had limited space and staff, the following schedule was used. The morphology group received the seven unique components of their treatment the first hour, followed by the common components the second half. The phonology group received the common components the first hour, followed by the seven unique components of their treatment the second hour. The unique and common components can be found in table I. Children left the group for virtual reality activities only during the common components treatment; the number of ses-

Table I.   Overview of the Experimental Treatments[a,b,c]

	Morphological Treatment	Phonological Treatment
Warm-Up to Automatize the Alphabetic Principle		
Spelling-Phoneme Units Anglo-Saxon and Latin and Greek correspondences)	Chant spelling-phoneme associations in and out of word context	Chant spelling-phoneme associations in and out of word context
Word Learning	**Word Building:** Written words are created from bases + affixes.	**Word Building** Syllables and phonemes in spoken words are analyzed and synthesized.
	Word Generating: New written words are generated using the same affixes as in Word Building.	**Word Generating:** New spoken words are generated using the same phonemes as in Word Building.
	Unit Finding: Bases are underlined and affixes circled in written words.	**Unit Finding:** Spelling units are underlined/ rewritten for the same words first practiced orally.
	Transferring: Reading new words with the same affixes.	**Transferring:** Reading new Jabberwocky words with the same spelling-phoneme units.
Insight into Writing System		
Students' responses on all three activities serve as basis for reflective group discussions.		
Relating Units	**Are they family relatives?** Does first word come from the second word?	**Are they twins?** Do color coded spelling units in Jabberwocky words stand for the same sound?
Sorts	**Sort on basis of affixes**	**Sort on basis of alternations**
Does It Fit?	**Sort words into sentence contexts**	**Sort spelling units into word contexts**

Table I.   continued

	Morphological Treatment	Phonological Treatment
Application of Strategies		
	Common Components across Treatments	
	Morphology Feedback	**Phonology Feedback**
Independent silent reading and highlighting of unknown words and discussing decoding strategies	Find the Fix Strategy	Find the Spelling Unit Strategy
Fluency and Comprehension		
Graph accuracy and time for first and second 1-minute oral readings		
Oral reading of entire passage	alphabetic principle and meaning units	alphabetic principle
Written summarization of the same passage		
Reflective discussion of the same passage		
Book Reading and/or Composing		
Children read from *Sherlock Mystery Reader* (Doyle, 1995), completed writing assignments about the stories, and illustrated what they had read and written.		

[a]Nagy proposed that the reading curriculum include instruction aimed at Word Learning, Insight into the Writing System, Application of Strategies, and Fluency and Comprehension.

[b]The four Word Learning Activities and the last two activities of Insight into the Writing System of the Morphological Treatment drew upon preliminary studies of Carlisle and colleagues. The authors designed comparable activities for the phonological treatment that had similar processing requirements but operate on a different level of language. Most of these are based on earlier intervention studies in the University of Washington Multidisciplinary Learning Disabilities Center.

[c]The Relating Activities of both treatments are based on the functional imaging tasks designed by the first two authors for concurrent brain imaging studies in which fourteen of the children also participated.

sions missed for virtual reality was equated across treatments. Fidelity of treatment implementation was monitored through daily team meetings after the sessions were complete to discuss any problems and to complete self-monitoring checklists. The team members cued each other during the instructional sessions if they thought the other teacher was departing from standard procedures.

Rationale for Instructional Treatments

Both the Morphology and Phonology Treatments had components focused on Word Learning, Insight into the Writing System

(Linguistic Awareness), Application of Strategies, and Fluency and Comprehension. To this four-part structure, we added common instructional components across the two treatments: an initial warm-up (to introduce/review key grapheme-phoneme correspondences), fluency training, comprehension instruction, and a culminating book reading and writing activity. See table I for this schema applied to each of 14 lessons in each treatment. Items used in each lesson for each of the seven components of each treatment are available from the first, second, or third author to any researcher or teacher who would like to investigate or implement the instructional treatments. In this chapter we provide the items used in the first lesson of each of the seven activities in each treatment as examples of the items used in all lessons.

MORPHOLOGY TREATMENT

The teacher read the following *introduction* at the beginning of each of the first five sessions and later directed children's attention to a copy of it in their student work folders for future reference. The purpose was to provide continual metalinguistic awareness of why students were engaging in the activities they were asked to perform. The teachers said,

> It is normal to come across words that you do not know. One way to figure out unknown words is to use their word parts that signal or "fix" their meaning. We will call these parts at the beginning of words prefixes because they come before the rest of the word, and those parts at the end of the word postfixes because they come after the rest of the word. (Others call the parts at the end of word suffixes.) Words also have base parts that signal their meaning. Some words only have bases, some have prefixes and bases, some have bases and postfixes, and some have prefixes, bases, and postfixes. We will do seven different kinds of activities in each session to teach you to be Word Detectives who use these word parts to decode words: Word Building, Word Generating, Unit Finding, Word Transferring, Deciding If Words Are Relatives, Sorting by Word Part Features, and Sorting by Sentence Context. These activities should give you lots of strategies for using word parts to figure out words. We will use our electronic timer for the second through fourth activities but not the others. Let's begin.

Word Learning—Word Building Instructional Procedures

Large cards with each *prefix*, *base*, and *suffix* in the following words were kept in large envelopes marked prefixes, bases, and suffixes and used as needed for a specific lesson. The second author identified 30 suffixes that occur most frequently and thus are of high utility for struggling readers. Given limited instructional time, these are the ones to focus on. Capitalized letters indicate these high-utility affixes, which were practiced in various lessons.

REmember UNclear INvisible DISlike IMpolite addiTION saltY completeLY importANT harmLESS reportER announceMENT mouthFUL sickNESS washABLE nervOUS brownISH scientIST expensIVE electrIC elementARY northERN leaderSHIP differENT amazING projectOR magicAL goldEN creativITY toWARD

> The teacher said,
>
> We will always start by building ten words from their parts. I will take one card from each of two piles and hold both up for all to see. The first person who says the word earns a point for his or her R-File (a record form to tally all earned points). However, all of you are to write the word in a box on the form in your folder. This form has a series of boxes, each with three sections—one for prefixes, which are at the beginning of words, one for bases, and one for suffixes, which we will call postfixes because they come at the end of words. Only use the sections of the box that you need for the word part in each word. Sometimes we will build words from a prefix and a base and sometimes we will build them from a base and a postfix.

Then for each lesson the teacher drew from the large envelopes the large cards with the word parts needed for each word in a lesson and held them up high for all students to see. After one student correctly synthesized the word parts to pronounce the word, each child wrote each word part in the correct box in the row on a work sheet. In Lesson 1, children constructed these words from their word parts: completely, washable, brownish, dislike, scientist, leadership, mouthful, different, amazing, northern.

Word Learning—Word Generating Instructional Procedures

The teacher explained that R-Files have a double meaning. Not only are they the files in our work folders in which we accumulate points for correct answers but also they are files in "OUR minds" in which we store the words we learn. Then the teacher said:

> Word Detectives sometimes get their clues from generating and reasoning about similar cases. Readers can do the same—use what they know about words to generate new words in their minds. For the next five minutes I would like you to think of a word that has each of the ten parts we just practiced. Each word just has to have one of the parts—not all ten! If you can think of more than one word for each part that is great. Write the words you think of on the record form. If you need help in spelling the word, just raise your hand and a teacher will help you. After five minutes, we will share with each

other all the words we thought of. Let's see how many words you can think of that have this part.

Children are given a written form with each of the ten affixes just practiced in Word Building and asked to generate a new word for each of the parts. At the end of five minutes, the teacher wrote on the chalkboard each contribution and left up for display those that contained the unit used as a morpheme. Children received one R-file point for each plausible word they shared in which the word part (e.g., er) was used as a morpheme (e.g., builder) but not for a word part with the same letters and sounds that did not function as a morpheme (e.g., corner). For Lesson 1 children generated words using these word parts: *ly, able, ish, dis, ist, ship, ful, ent, ing, ern.*

Word Learning—Unit Finding Instructional Procedures

Children were given work sheets with the lists of words (double-spaced) for the lesson and were asked to underline the base word and circle the affixes. The teacher said,

> Word Detectives solve their mysteries by paying attention to details. The details you need to pay attention to in decoding are the base and the beginning and end "fixes" if there are any. I want you to underline the base—main meaning part of the word—and circle any "fixes" at the beginning or end that might modify or qualify that meaning. I want to see how many of these word details you can find in two minutes. After time is called, we will share with each other the word clues we found.

Children received R-file points for sharing. For Lesson 1, children identified word parts in the following words: *submarine, impersonate, irresponsible, imbalance, cooperation, previewed, unbecoming, unturned, misjudgment, unhappiness.*

Word Learning—Transferring Instructional Procedures

For each lesson, children read a list with ten words containing the same affixes practiced under word building. They read the list to a teacher who timed them, recorded the time on their R-File record, and indicated whether (a) the affix part was pronounced correctly, (b) the whole word was pronounced correctly, and (c) the child needed to refer to the student card for spelling-phoneme correspondences. The teachers said,

> Once Word Detectives figure out the code they can apply it to new words or cases. Here are some words that have the same parts that we have practiced. I want to see how accurately and fast you can say

these words. We will record your accuracy and time on the reading rocket in your R-file. You may refer to the student card with spelling-phoneme correspondences if that helps you.

For Lesson 1 children were asked to pronounce these words: *lonely, huggable, warmish, disable, druggist, friendship, helpful, movement, melting, western.*

Insight—Relational Units Instructional Procedures

The teacher said,

> To solve puzzles, Word Detectives need to pay attention not only to clues in a single word but also to how the clues in a word are related to other words they know. Just as a child comes from her or his parents, some words come from, that is, they are made from, the meaning of other words and thus belong to the same family of word meanings, but other words are not from the same family of word meanings even though they may resemble other words in spelling or sound. I want you to listen carefully and after I say each pair of words, circle yes on your work sheet if you think the first word comes from the second one and circle no if you do not think it does.

If any child did not get an item correct, the teacher provided a sentence using the first word and asked if that word as used in the sentence might come from the second word. For Lesson 1 children made "comes from" decisions for these word pairs: *reporter/ report; respectfully/respect; mayor/may; transportation/transport; tenor/ ten; orange/or; specifically/specific; injection/inject; onion/on; pillow/ pill.*

Insight—Word Sorts based on Affix Features
Instructional Procedures

The generalization for each set is the conclusion the teacher helps children arrive at, through Socratic questioning, by the end of the sorting activity (Bear 2000). The teachers said,

> Once Word Detectives get clues they have to make sense of them. They have to do a special kind of thinking in which they draw conclusions from the evidence, just as Sherlock Holmes and Watson did. In this activity helpers will hold two to three large cards with labels. Then I will show you a smaller card with a word on it. The first person to classify the word on the smaller card correctly may take the card to the helper holding the larger card with the correct label. As a group, we will discuss what conclusion we can draw from the group sorting we just did.

Children earned R-file points for each correct classification. For Sort 1, which was designed to help children arrive at the generalization that a prefix cannot be identified just on the basis of spelling, the following words were sorted into these categories labeled with large cards labeled *Prefix* or *No Prefix*: *realize, rewind, recapture, ready, recall, renter, reach, redo, restaurant, retell, reorganize, reentry.*

Insight—Does it Fit? Word Sorts based on Sentence Context Instructional Procedures

The purpose of this activity was to help children see the importance of analyzing words fully. The teacher said,

> Another way that Word Detectives have to make sense of their clues is by examining them for the Context, that is the place in which they occur and all the surrounding clues. Each of the three sentences you will see has a blank. Each of the Word Pools you will see has one word in the box that fits sensibly into the blank but mostly words that would not fit into the blank. To figure out which words would or would not fit into the blank, that is, into the context of the sentence, you need to pay close attention to all the spelling, sound, and meaning clues of the words in the pool and in the words in the sentence. That is, you have to fully analyze all the evidence you have at hand! As soon as you think you know a word that would fit into the sentence, write it in the blank. As a Word Detective, it is important that you examine all the evidence—consider all the words—before you make your decision about which word fits. After everyone is finished, we will discuss whether everyone agrees on which word fits in each item.

The words in the Word Pool were in a box just below each sentence on the student worksheet. An example of this activity from Lesson 1 is as follows: *The melting popsicle turned into a _____ mess.*

Word Pool: *former, formless, forming, helpless*

PHONOLOGICAL TREATMENT

The teacher read the following introduction at the beginning of each of the first five sessions and called children's attention to it in the student work folders for future reference. The purpose was to provide continual metalinguistic awareness of why students were engaging in the activities they were asked to perform. The teacher said,

> It is normal to come across words you do not know. One way to figure out an unknown word is to find the spelling units and think about their associated sound. We will call these spelling-sound correspondences the alphabetic principle. Sometimes in English more than one sound is associated with the same spelling unit. We will

do seven different kinds of activities in each session to teach you to be a Word Detective who uses the alphabetic principle and sound patterns in words to decode unknown words: Word Building, Word Generating, Unit Finding, Word Transferring, Deciding If Spelling Units Are Relatives, and Sorting by Word Context. These activities should give you lots of strategies for using spelling units and their relationships to sounds to figure out words. We will use our electronic timer for the second through fourth activities but not the others. Let's begin.

Word Learning—Word Building Instructional Procedures

Each lesson had a mix of spoken monosyllabic and polysyllabic Jabberwocky words. The teacher said,

> We will always start by saying and analyzing the sounds in each word. We will not use real words, but rather Jabberwocky words, like from the poem in Alice in Wonderland."

The teacher then read an excerpt from this poem and then continued with instructions.

> First close your eyes and listen as I say a word. Then hold up the number of fingers for the number of syllables you hear in it. If we disagree, then we will discuss it. Then open your eyes and use these colored discs to count out the number of phonemes in each syllable. Altogether we will practice ten words each time.

In Lesson 1 the following words were first segmented and then synthesized: *smewbry, pluce, prite, knelph, trabe, hebtou, blesp, nimoin, haifraff, soatyaz.*

Word Learning—Word Generating Instructional Procedures

The teacher explained that R-files have a double meaning. Not only are they the files in our work folders where we record our points for correct answers but they are also the "files in OUR minds" in which we store the words we learn. The teacher said,

> Word Detectives sometimes get their clues from generating and reasoning about similar cases. Readers can do the same—use what they know about sounds in words to generate new words in their minds. For the next five minutes I would like you to think of words that have the same sounds as the ones I say. I will write the words you think of on the board to share with the others. Let's see how many different words you can think of in 30 seconds that have this sound.

The teacher provided the sound unit (phoneme) and asked children to generate real words or Jabberwocky words orally with that sound unit. The teacher recorded on chalkboard the words the *group* generated in 5 minutes (30 seconds per phoneme). She encouraged fast responding and a sense of excitement in word generation and accepted words with alternative, plausible spellings for the phoneme. Teacher helpers gave each child who contributed a word R-file points. For Lesson 1 children generated real or made up words for the phonemes associated with these spelling units: *ch, u, ng, le, w, m, s, wh, ul, er.*

Word Learning—Unit Finding Instructional Procedures

The same ten words practiced under word building were presented visually on work sheets. Originally children were asked to underline the spelling units in each word but when selective attention to individual letters or letter groups proved too difficult for many, they were asked to rewrite each word, spelling unit by spelling unit, leaving spaces between spelling units. This approach appeared to be more helpful in finding the spelling units. They were given two colored markers (one for each of the University of Washington Husky colors) and asked to write adjacent spelling units in different, alternating colors. Teachers said,

> Word Detectives solve their mysteries by paying attention to details. The details you need to pay attention to in decoding are the spelling units and the sounds to which they correspond. I want to see how many of these spelling units you can find in two minutes. After time is called, we will share with each other these word clues we found.

Initially students needed more than two minutes to parse all ten words into their spelling units, but eventually they reached this time criterion. Children who completed the activity correctly within the time limits received R-file points. Once everyone agreed on how to parse the words into spelling units, the group made the sound that went with each spelling unit and then synthesized the sounds into a recognizable whole word. For *Lesson 1* children rewrote words into their component spelling units as follows and then synthesized the sounds that go with them to pronounce the made-up word: *sm ew bry, pl u.e c, pr i.e t, kn el ph, tr a.e b, h e b t ou, bl e sp, n i m oi n, h ai fr a ff, s oa t y a z.*

Word Learning—Transferring Instructional Procedures

Children were given ten new words that were not practiced but contained target spelling units in the practiced words. They were evaluated as to whether they could decode phonologically these spelling units correctly in a different word context. The transfer words were constructed by altering one consonant, or one vowel, spelling unit in Jabberwocky words used in Word Building. The teacher said,

> Once Word Detectives figure out the code they can apply it to new words or cases. Here are some words that have the same spelling units that we have practiced. I want to see how accurately and fast you can use those spelling units to say these words. We will record your accuracy and time on the reading rockets in your R-file. You can refer to your card with spelling-sound correspondences if that helps you.

Teachers recorded accuracy for whole words and spelling units and noted whether children referred to the student card with spelling-phoneme correspondences. For Lesson 1, children pronounced these words: *snewbry, plute, stite, chelph, blabe, rebtou, stesp, ridmoin, saifraff, loatyaz.*

Insight—Relational Units Instructional Procedures

Children were asked to indicate by circling *YES* or *NO* on a worksheet whether the underlined spelling units in a pair of Jabberwocky words could stand for the same sound. If there were differences of opinion, those items were discussed in reference to the prior warm-up activities with spelling-phoneme correspondences. In contrast to the purpose of the warm-up that was to put this knowledge of grapheme-phoneme correspondences on automatic pilot, the purpose of this activity was to reflect consciously upon the system of spelling-sound correspondences. The teacher said,

> To solve puzzles, Word Detectives need to pay attention not only to clues in a single spelling-sound correspondence but also to how those clues are related to other spelling-sound correspondences they know. I want you to look carefully at each pair of words and circle YES on your work sheet if you think the underlined spelling units in each word stand for the same sound. Remember that sometimes the same spelling unit stands for different sounds, and that sometimes the same sound is spelled in different ways. Let's see how many decisions about spelling-phoneme correspondences you can make in two minutes.

Children received R-file points for completing the activity within the time limits. For Lesson 1, they made decisions about the underlined letters in these word pairs: magic/magnet; circus/circle; wrong/right; plumber/monkey; super/parties; knocks/foxes; photo/enough; bookends/noontime; yelling/fry; juggle/fudge.

Insight—Word Sorts based on Alternations Instructional Procedures

The teacher said,

> Once Word Detectives get clues they have to make sense of them. They have to do a special kind of thinking in which they draw

conclusions from the evidence, just as Sherlock Holmes and Watson did. In this activity I will put out two to three large cards with labels. Then I will show you a smaller card with a word on it. As a group, we will discuss where to place the smaller cards, according to the category to which these belong; the categories are labeled on the larger cards. At the end we will discuss what conclusion we can draw from the group sorting we just did.

The teacher continued,

Just as some people have more than one name (nicknames), some letters stand for more than one sound. This spelling unit (name letters in spelling unit for the lesson) has more than one sound. The nicknames for /name spelling unit/ are (make the phoneme sounds). I have written a symbol for each of these sounds at the top of a large card. Let's look at some words that have these nickname sounds and put them on the card for the right category.

The teacher presented word cards one at a time. As she presented the card, she named the word and pointed to the underlined spelling unit and produced the associated phoneme; then she asked children to place the small word card on the large card with the correct nickname sound for that spelling unit. She continued this procedure until all words were presented and sorted. Then she helped children articulate the generalization that a specific spelling unit may stand for a small set of sounds. Children received R-file points for each correct categorization of a spelling unit by its associated phoneme. For Lesson 1, children sorted the following words with the spelling unit c into categories labeled with the Nicknames /k/ and /s/: c̲ity, c̲andle, c̲eiling, c̲ake, c̲ent, bec̲ause, bec̲ome, penc̲il, danc̲e, c̲older.

Insight—Sorting by Word Context—Does It Fit?
Instructional Procedures

Children were given words with a blank and then a spelling pool with spelling units. The task was to choose the spelling unit that could fit into the blank because it spelled a real word in that word context. Five of the words in each lesson came from the reading passages from *Read Naturally* (Turman Publishing 1997) for that lesson. The teacher said,

Another way that Word Detectives have to make sense of their clues is by examining them for the Context, that is the place in which they occur and all the surrounding clues. Each of the words you will see has a blank. Each of the Spelling Pools you will see has one spelling unit that fits sensibly into the blank, but mostly spelling units that would not fit into the blank. To figure out which spelling unit would or would not fit into the blank, that is, into the context of the word, you need to pay close attention to all the spelling and sound clues of the word. That is, you have to fully analyze all the evidence you have at hand! As soon as you think you know a spelling unit that would fit and make a real word, circle it. As a Word Detective, it is important that you examine all the evidence— consider all the spelling units—before you make your decision about which spelling unit fits in the word.

An example of a Lesson 1 item is *spid__* (*ar, er, ir, or, ur*). These items contained spelling units that stand for the same sound but only one of the spelling units in a word-specific context spells a real word with meaning.

COMMON COMPONENTS ACROSS TREATMENTS

Warm-UP: Automatizing Spelling-Phoneme Correspondences

For the first week, the teacher named the letter or letter group on the student card, said the pictured word or spelled-out word containing a target phoneme, and produced the target phoneme; then the students took a turn and repeated what was named or produced. This approach developed orthographic awareness of spelling units, phonological awareness of corresponding phonemes in and out of word context, and automaticity of spelling-phoneme correspondence. Thereafter, the teacher just named the letter or letter group and produced the target phoneme, and then the students took a turn and repeated what the teacher said. Teachers monitored whether children were coordinating their looking at the relevant letters and pictured words with their naming of the letters and words and producing phonemes.

Applying Word Strategies

High interest selections from *Read Naturally* were selected at targeted grade levels for this sample. Children first read the short passage silently and used highlighters on transparent overlays to target words they could not identify while reading silently. The highlighted words were then used to model how to apply strategies to unlock the code. Each child shared an equal number of highlighted words for the group discussion. For the Morphology Treatment, teachers provided instructional cues using only the alphabetic principle and meaningful parts of words. They taught Carlisle's Find the Fix Strategy: Find the base and think about its meaning. Is there a prefix? If so, think about its meaning. Is there a postfix? If so, think about its meaning. Now say the word and figure out what it might mean in this context. For the Phonology Treatment, teachers provided only instructional cues involving the alphabetic principle.

Guided Oral Reading for Fluency and Comprehension

Individual children read orally to the teacher or teaching assistant who recorded on a graph the number of words read correctly in one-minute. Then children summarized in writing what they had read. After that, the group engaged in a teacher-led reflective discussion in which children were encouraged to summarize accurately the content, including the main idea and supporting details (text-based comprehension, Kintsch 1998), and to go beyond what was stated and engage in inferential thinking (situation-based comprehension, Kintsch 1998). While they waited their turn for timing of the second one-minute oral reading, students illustrated what they had read and discussed with colored pencils or markers. For the remainder of the session, the children read stories in a collection of Sherlock Holmes mysteries and discussed them and wrote about them.

RESULTS

Psychometric Measures of the Effects of Instruction

The treatment groups did not differ significantly in age in months. Prior to the instructional study, the treatment groups did not differ significantly in WRMT-R Word Attack, TOWRE Pseudoword Efficiency, or UW Morphological Decoding Fluency (accuracy or time). Table II summarizes scores on each measure at pretest and posttest for each treatment group.

Table II.   Before and After Treatment Means and Standard Deviations

| | Morphological Treatment | | | | Phonological Treatment | | | |
| | Pretest | | Posttest | | Pretest | | Posttest | |
Tests	M	SD	M	SD	M	SD	M	SD
WRMT-R[a]								
WA	82.1	7.4	88.4	9.0	87.2	12.6	93.7	11.4
TOWRE[b]								
Pseudo Eff	80.5	7.2	84.9	6.9	83.0	8.1	83.8	6.3
UW Morpholgical Decoding Test[c]								
Accuracy	28.5	7.6	32.5	5.9	27.8	10.8	30.5	11.2
Time	80.1	33.1	93.0	56.3	79.2	25.5	92.1	40.8

[a]*Woodcock Reading Mastery Test Revised* (WRMT-R) (Woodcock, 1987) Word Attack (WA); standard scores with $M = 100$; $SD = 15$.

[b]*Test of Word Reading Efficiency* (TOWRE) Pseudoword Reading Efficiency (Pseudo Eff); standard scores with $M = 100$; $SSD = 15$.

[c]unpublished University of Washington Decoding Fluency (pronouncing lists of words with suffixes); raw scores

The purpose of the analyses that follow was to evaluate whether children had begun to respond to a relatively brief, 28-hour, three-week intervention before they were reimaged. We targeted the decoding measures for these analyses because all the children were selected for the intervention because of low decoding skills. The two decoding measures used to evaluate response to intervention differ in that only on the UW Morphological Decoding Test do all stimuli have a stem and suffix; children might develop a set for using a morphemic strategy in addition to grapheme-phoneme correspondence in the decoding process on this measure, but could draw on morphological as well as orthographic and phonological knowledge in decoding on the other measures as well.

Mixed ANOVA, with sessions (pretest/posttest) as a within-subjects variable and groups as a between-subjects variable, were conducted. Both accuracy (WRMT-R Word Attack), $F (1,18) = 15.74$, $p = .001$, and rate (TOWRE Pseudoword Reading Efficiency), $F (1, 18) = 12.81$, $p = .002$, of phonological decoding improved significantly from pretest to posttest. The sessions variable did not interact significantly with group on the accuracy measure, thus indicating that both groups responded to the intervention in terms of improved accuracy of phonological decoding. The sessions variable did interact significantly with group, $F (1, 18) = 6.14$, $p = .023$, on the rate measure; the morphology treatment group improved significantly more than the phonology treatment group in efficiency of phonological decoding. A possible explanation for this finding is that the efficiency of phonological decoding depends on an interaction between phonological and morphological awareness. We discuss this preliminary finding further in the results for brain imaging and the general discussion for the chapter and emphasize the need for further research and replication. Both accuracy, $F (1, 18) = 12.24$, $p = .003$, and time, $F (1, 17) = 4.85$, $p = .042$, increased significantly on the UW Morphological Decoding Fluency Test from pretest to posttest. The session variable did not interact significantly with either the accuracy or time measure on this test, thus indicating that both treatment groups showed improved accuracy and slower times in decoding words with stems and suffixes. We speculate that the slower times indicate that the students are more fully analyzing the word clues for decoding as a result of the Word Detective curriculum. Also, the rate of decoding may have decreased on the TOWRE but increased on the UW Morphological Decoding Test because the latter has longer word items.

Taken together, the converging evidence that the children with dyslexia showed increased accuracy in decoding on two different measures of the construct indicates that even severe dyslexics with persisting reading problems in grades 4 to 6 can increase their reading achievement, and the effects can be detected early in the intervention. *Furthermore, phonological awareness and morphological awareness were equally effective in increasing accuracy of phonological decoding when the linguistic awareness component was embedded in a balanced reading program that had all the components recommended by the National Reading Panel (2000).*

Brain Imaging

Of the 20 children who participated in the instructional study, only 14 were able to participate in the brain imaging studies. That is because only right handed children who do not wear braces or nonremovable metal can be imaged. Seven of these children were in the phonological awareness treatment group and seven were in the morphological awareness group. All fourteen children were not included in every analysis because sometimes brain scans are not usable at both pretest and posttest because of motion artifact, strong lipid signal, or scanner/mechanical problems. The sample size is small because this kind of research is labor and time intensive as well as very expensive. However, the sample size is comparable to the majority of the studies in the functional imaging literature over the past fifteen years. We also carefully match on age and Verbal IQ of the participants in all of our studies.

Each of the fourteen children participated in two imaging studies before and after the treatment. One was a functional magnetic resonance spectroscopic imaging (fMRS) study that assesses activation of a specific chemical—lactate—in reference to a common standard—NAA, which is another chemical in brain cells. Lactate is known to be involved in the end state of metabolism during energy utilization and thus may be a neural substrate for efficiency of mental processes (Serafini et al., 2001). A decrease in lactate activation may reflect increased efficiency in mental processes. The other was a functional magnetic resonance imaging (fMRI) study that assesses blood oxygenation level dependent (BOLD) response, that is, energy utilization on the basis of blood flow to specific regions of the brain during mental processing. Our laboratory has shown convergence in brain location of effects across the different levels of neural substrate indexed by these two imaging modalities (Serafini et al. 2001).

Functional magnetic resonance imaging study (fMRS).   Richards et al. (in press) showed that, during a phonological (rhyme) judgment task, the students with dyslexia had significantly more lactate (chemical) activation in left frontal regions than good readers before, but not after, treatment, as we had found in prior studies. The phonological task requires judgments as to whether pairs of real and/or pseudowords do (e.g., wheel/treel, miss/kiss, zile/quile) or do not (e.g., mouse/zile, prite/quile, kiss/grape) rhyme. However, in contrast to the treatment used in the prior research that combined phonological and morphological strategies (Berninger 2000), in the study described in this chapter children were randomly assigned to a phonology or morphology treatment so that the treatments could be compared. Individual subject analyses showed that the decrease in lactate activation was significantly associated with the morphological rather than the phonological treatment. All but one child with dyslexia in the morphological treatment decreased in lactate activation during phonological judgment after treatment, whereas all the students with dyslexia in the phonological treatment stayed the same or increased in lactate activation during phonological judgment after treatment.

Because reduction in lactate activation may reflect increased efficiency of mental processing (related to improved metabolic efficiency as explained earlier), one interpretation of the fMRS results is that morphology treatment increases the efficiency of neural processes during phonological processing. This finding at the neural level meshes with the finding at the behavioral level— that efficiency, as indexed by decreased speed, tends to improve after morphological training when decoding can draw on morphological as well as orthographic and phonological knowledge. The explanation for this finding, with converging behavioral and brain evidence, is that word reading draws on orthographic word forms, phonological word forms, and morphological word forms and their interrelationships at the word and subword levels of analyses (Berninger, Abbott, Billingsley et al. 2001; Berninger and Richards 2002). Just as a six-cylinder car operates more efficiently when all cylinders are functional, so may the circuits of the brain underlying word-learning function operate more efficiently when all word forms and their parts are orchestrated—orthographic, phonological, and morphological. Orthographic, phonological, and morphological processes are distinct at one level (their underlying brain circuits are spatially separated) but not at another level (their associated processes may become functionally integrated in time) (Berninger and Richards 2002). At issue is whether morphological processing contributes in some way to the functional integration of different word and subword language codes in time. Further research is needed on this issue.

The finding that morphological treatment improved efficiency on a phonological judgment task also points to the importance of considering the interaction of phonological and morphological awareness in reading instruction. One of the brain regions in which many brain imaging researchers have reported differences between students with dyslexia and good readers is the inferior frontal gyrus, which may be involved in integrating phonological and morphological information about words (see Berninger and Richards 2002). Another puzzle we are trying to solve in our ongoing work is why people with dyslexia are able to orchestrate their circuits for word learning more efficiently when orthography, phonology, and morphology are activated, in contrast to good readers who are better able than people with dyslexia to orchestrate selectively just the orthography and phonology circuits when tasks require that only these circuits be activated.

Functional magnetic resonance imaging (fMRI) study. Aylward et al. (2003) administered two sets of tasks. In the first set, a letter-sound match/mismatch task alternated with a letter match/mismatch task. The first task used only pairs of pronounceable pseudowords. In each pseudoword, one or two letters were printed in pink, with the rest of the letters printed in black. The letter-sound match/mismatch task required the child to determine whether the letters in pink could stand for the same sound in the two words, and thus involved both orthographic and phonological processing. The second task used pairs of unpronounceable letter strings and required the child to determine whether the letters in each string matched exactly, thus involving orthographic but not phonological processing. Comparison of the brain activation for the two tasks showed where brain activation is unique for *phoneme mapping*, which is, mapping phonemes onto letters. In the second set, a morphological judgment task (Does the top word come from the bottom word and is thus related in meaning?) alternated with a synonym judgment task (Do the two words mean the same?). The first task used polysyllabic words in which the end syllable was either a morpheme (builder) or an orthographic foil (corner) that was spelled the same, but did not function as a morpheme (word part with meaning). Children decided whether the polysyllabic words came from corresponding monosyllabic words that were (build) or were not (corn) related to them semantically. The second task used word pairs that were or were not synonyms and required a general semantic judgment based on non-affixed word stems (e.g. boy/girl, baby infant). Comparison of the brain activation for the two tasks showed where brain activation is unique for morpheme mapping, which is, mapping suffixes onto word stems.

A synopsis of the important findings follows. Controls showed different patterns of brain activation for phoneme mapping and morpheme mapping and these differences were generally stable across time from pretest to posttest. Students with dyslexia and controls differed in morpheme mapping and phoneme mapping before, but, for the most part, not after, treatment. Preliminary analyses based on group comparisons between the two dyslexic treatment groups also suggested some differential brain response to the two kinds of linguistic awareness treatment that was not detected in behavioral measures. However, any conclusions on this topic await additional, more refined analyses of individual subjects, which are now in progress and are theory-driven based on prior research in neurolinguistics relevant to the internal organization of the mental lexicon.

DISCUSSION

We begin the discussion with a reminder that the purpose of our instructional study was to integrate brain imaging and treatment research to study nature-nurture interactions in students with dyslexia. Our groups are small, the intervention lasted for only three weeks, the interpretation of results is preliminary, and further replications are necessary. Nevertheless, we think the preliminary findings suggest that (a) children with dyslexia and age- and Verbal IQ-matched good readers may differ in brain activation associated with morpheme mapping as well as phoneme mapping, and (b) even older students with dyslexia can respond and respond relatively quickly to systematic reading instruction that is balanced and contains all the recommended instructional components of the National Reading Panel (2000). It is encouraging that the early response to instruction can be detected at both the behavioral level (increased accuracy of phonological decoding on two different tests) and brain levels (decreased lactate activation and elimination of most differences between students with dyslexia and controls in fMRI BOLD response). Other investigators have also found that the brain is responsive to instructional intervention. The University of Texas at Houston group that uses a technique responsive to time-sensitive electrophysiological changes has shown positive brain and behavioral changes following phonological training in subjects with dyslexia spanning early to middle childhood to adolescence (e.g., Papanicolaou et al. this volume; Simos et al. 2002). The Georgetown University group that uses fMRI has shown positive brain and behavioral changes following the Lindamood articulatory awareness approach to training phonological skills in adults with severe dyslexia (Eden 2002).

Some wonder how developmental dyslexia, a genetic disorder, can be responsive to instructional treatment. Others wonder whether all reading problems are simply the result of a lack of systematic, intensive reading instruction. On the one hand, genetic constraints make it more difficult to learn to read—not impossible. Genes are not disease-causing agents and do not fully determine organisms (Ridley 1999). Our results show that older people with dyslexia are teachable and responsive to instruction. The challenge is to create sustainable learning environments in schools to maintain and support further literacy learning. Researchers have shown, however, that teachers do not know how to organize instruction to meet the vast learning differences in every classroom (Schumm, Moddy, and Vaughn 2000). Until educators are prepared to create the kinds of sustained learning environments that people who are dyslexic need, we will not know the extent to which dyslexia may be preventable. Treating dyslexia, therefore, requires instruction aimed at educators as well as students.

Some look to brain imaging research for identifying the cause of dyslexia—how dyslexic brains differ from brains of good readers. A sizable literature documents a number of such differences in different neural substrates, as assessed by different technologies, and on a number of different tasks (reviewed in Berninger and Richards 2002). There are reasons that it is harder for students with dyslexia to learn to read and spell. At the same time, a growing literature documents that the brains of people with dyslexia are responsive to instruction and that they can learn to read. That is, dyslexia is best understood in the context of nature-nurture interactions. We propose that future research on treatment of dyslexia build upon three guiding principles related to nature-nurture interactions.

First, the phenotypic expression of dyslexia is a moving target that changes across the developmental window (see Berninger 2000, 2001; Berninger, Abbott, Thomson et al., 2001, for review of evidence). For example, extreme difficulty in learning to name letters, often evident at the beginning of kindergarten, gives way to a severe problem in learning grapheme-phoneme correspondences and decoding, which gives way to a tough-to-remediate problem in automaticity of word recognition and oral reading fluency, which gives way to persisting spelling and written expression difficulties. Thus, one must be very cautious in assuming that response to a short-term intervention, even with follow-up a year or two later, is sufficient to evaluate whether a reading disorder with a genetic basis is fully cured. Dyslexia may be treatable even if the underlying brain basis is not fully normalized on all relevant neural variables, which are not yet fully understood. Brain changes in the direction of eliminating differences between people with dyslexia and good readers indicate that the disorder is responsive to instructional intervention—not that the student has reached full mastery of reading. Even for normal readers, reading mastery is a developmental process acquired over a large time span and requires twelve or more years of schooling.

Second, low reading achievement may have different implications for etiology, treatment, and prognosis when it occurs in profiles with different patterns across developmental domains (Berninger 2001). For example, within a sample of children selected for early intervention on the basis of low reading achievement alone and followed over two years, four reading profiles emerged (Berninger et al. 2002). These profiles were defined on the basis of the simple view of reading that the fundamental components of beginning reading are word reading and comprehension (Gough, Juel, and Griffith 1992). First, among the fastest responders, who quickly caught up to grade level or beyond, most had relative deficits in word reading only; with an early boost in word reading skills, their reading appeared to be on track. Second, a smaller number had relatively greater deficits in reading comprehension than in word reading even though their word reading was low initially; although they quickly improved to grade level or beyond in word reading, they might be at-risk for future reading comprehension problems. Third, among the slower responders who had substantial deficits in both word reading and reading comprehension, most had relatively greater deficits in reading comprehension. They required two years of intervention and did eventually reach the average range of word reading, but they required explicit instruction in reading comprehension and word reading to do so. Fourth, among the slower responders was a smaller group that had sizable problems in word reading but not necessarily in reading comprehension at this early stage of reading development; they, too, required two years of intervention to reach the average range of word reading. We suspect that this group is most likely the early emerging profile of dyslexia as we study it in our family genetics study.

As a field we aspire to serving all children with persisting reading needs along the language learning continuum (Wallach and Butler 1994). Therefore, we believe that researchers should define carefully the sample characteristics of students with persisting reading problems so that results of instructional intervention can be appropriately generalized to specific student populations in planning, implementing, and evaluating instructional programs. For example, the samples studied by Torgesen and colleagues and Lovett and colleagues may have a larger percentage of children with language processing problems that are not specific to reading disability, are specific to primary language disability, and involve attention deficit disorder than our sample does. Some of these children may have different instructional needs than those with dyslexia in our study and even instructional needs that transcend reading instruction alone. All children deserve reading instruction that is appropriate to their language learning profile. Reading ability is normally distributed in the general population, but some reading disability falls within the lower limits of the normal range and some falls outside it. To fully understand relationships between reading disability and effective instructional interventions, we may need to reconsider how we define persisting reading disability—not just on the basis of low achievement in the word reading domain but also on the basis of low achievement in word reading in the context of a profile that takes into account multiple domains of developmental, language, and academic skills (Berninger 2001; Berninger and Abbott 1994).

Third, the cause of a persisting reading disability should not be confused with the most effective treatment for it (Berninger et al. 1997; Stanovich 1998). At the *genotypic level* of analysis, the cause of persisting reading problems is errors in the sequencing of four chemicals—adenine, cytosine, guanine, and thymine (Ridley 1999)—that translate in complex ways to the multi-level, developing neural architecture of the reading brain. The chemical sequencing is so complex that geneticists differentiate between the smaller "spelling" units of very long sequences and the "syntactic" units of enormously long sequences (Ridley 1999). To add further complexity, there may be multiple genes, each associated with a different behavioral subphenotype, which no matter how refined the subphenotype is, still probably draws on multiple brain structures and processes. Alternatively, there may be a small set of major genes or a major master gene exerting effects on different aspects of the multi-level neural architecture, thereby affecting multiple circuits and subprocesses in possibly different ways at different stages of development. At the *neurological level of analysis*, the cause of persisting reading problems is anomalies in different levels and places of the neural substrates underlying the complex, multi-level neural architecture of the functional brain system (see Berninger and Richards 2002, for review of the evidence). At the *psychological level of analysis*, the cause appears to be a phonological core deficit and related language and possibly non-language processes affecting word reading that do appear to have a genetic basis (Hsu et al. 2002; Morris et al. 1998; Olson, Forsberg, and Wise 1994; Wijsman et al. 2000). However, at a behavioral level, many levels of language processing in the preschool years predict later reading disability (Scarborough 2001). At the *educational level of analysis*, the cause may be (a) instructional programs that are not tailored to the language learning needs of students with persisting reading difficulties and (b) the failure of colleges of education to prepare preservice teachers adequately for teaching literacy to students in their future classrooms who will undoubtedly have diverse language learning abilities.

Churchland (1989) cautioned psychologists embracing the cognitive neuroscience revolution that, however we define our constructs, brain research may cause our theories and mental constructs to unravel, and we may need to reinvent new ones. Given the complexities of genetically, neurologically, behaviorally, and educationally constrained reading systems, we should be very cautious in prematurely rejecting any of the various reported research findings, especially those that are replicated, or evidence-based theories about the nature of brain basis of developmental dyslexia. Ultimately, solving the puzzle will probably require a synthesis of a complex set of multidisciplinary findings.

Fortunately, the puzzle of how to teach people with dyslexia to read effectively through instructional research may be within closer grasp than the definitive theory of its etiology. As discussed in the introduction, the evidence is strong that one component of effective early treatment is explicit training in phonological awareness and the alphabetic principle. Mounting evidence supports the addition of morphological awareness training to orthographic and phonological training in working with older students with dyslexia (and probably all literacy-learning students). Morphology training is most effective as an add on—not a replacement for orthographic and phonological awareness training in older students with persistent reading problems (Henry 1990). For one thing, the words encountered in textbooks in grades 4 and above have an increasing number of polysyllabic words with word parts that convey meaning. Many of these come from the Latin and Greek layers of the language (Balmuth 1992; Beeler 1988; Henry 1990).

Furthermore, in keeping with Churchland's (1989) admonition that we may need to rethink our constructs, we acknowledge that there may be no pure morphological task! Six of the activities in the Phonology Treatment in table I required attending only to orthographic and phonological units—not meaning units. <u>All the activities in the Morphology Treatment required that children</u>

attend to orthographic units, access phonological units, and process meaning units (see activities in table I for Morphology Treatment). Consider the fifth activity under morphological training in table I in which children are asked to sort words like undemanding, unique, under into these categories: Prefix Meaning Not, Prefix Meaning One, and No Prefix. Clearly correct categorization of these words requires careful attention to and orchestration of the orthographic spelling patterns, phonology, and morphology. Children must think about whether spelling patterns function as word parts conveying meaning, and if they do involve morphemes, how that affects their pronunciation. Morphological awareness training may help children learn to coordinate all the language codes they need for word learning (figure 1, Berninger, Abbott, Nagy, and Billingsley 2001) when reading material contains an increasing proportion of polysyllabic words of diverse origin in the history of the English language. If this claim is supported by future research, it will suggest that morphology provides a built-in executive function within the language system for coordinating the other codes underlying polysyllabic word learning.

We end with the instructional relevance of this image-treat-image study and other instructional studies conducted in our research group for older students with dyslexia or other language-learning needs. Teachers need to design instruction aimed not only at orthographic, phonological, and morphological awareness but also at their *interrelationships*. These interrelationships yield the multi-level linguistic clues that word detectives use to learn accurate and efficient word decoding. Early in literacy learning, children need to learn to disregard meaning of free-standing morphemes (monosyllabic words) so that they can attend to the grapheme-phoneme correspondence underlying the alphabetic principle—that is, they need to attend to orthography and phonology and their interrelationships. Later in their development of word decoding skills, children need to learn to pay attention to meaning—not just at the word level but also at the subword level. Language learners who have morphological awareness can attend to those word parts that convey meaning and at the same time orchestrate the multiple codes and mapping operations involved in learning to read polysyllabic words.

ACKNOWLEDGMENTS

A Multidisciplinary Learning Disabilities Center Grant from the National Institute of Child Health and Human Development, P50 33812-07, supported the research reported in this chapter.

Special thanks to William Winn who provided the Virtual Reality activities for the children in the instructional study and to Suzie Dickens and Sandra Hiramatsu who served as teaching assistants.

REFERENCES

Abbott, S., and Berninger, V. 1999. It's never too late to remediate: A developmental approach to teaching word recognition. *Annals of Dyslexia* 49:223–50.

Aylward, E., Richards, T., Berninger, V., Nagy, W., Field, K., Grimme, A., Richards, A., Thomson, J., and Cramer, S. 2003, April. Instructional Treatment Associated with Changes in Brain Activation in Children with Dyslexia. *Neurology.*

Balmuth, M. 1992. *The Roots of Phonics.* A Historical Introduction. Baltimore: York Press.

Bear, D., Invernizzi, M., Templeton, S., and Johnston, F. 2000. *Words Their Way. Word Study for Phonics, Vocabulary, and Spelling Instruction (2nd ed.).* Upper Saddle River, NJ: Merrill (Prentice Hall).

Beeler, D. 1988. *Book of Roots. A Full Study of Our Families of Words.* Homewood, IL: Union Representative.

Berninger, V. 2000. Dyslexia an invisible, treatable disorder: The story of Einstein's Ninja Turtles. *Learning Disability Quarterly* 23:175–95.

Berninger, V. 2001. Understanding the lexia in dyslexia. *Annals of Dyslexia* 51:23–48.

Berninger, V., and Richards, T. 2002. *Brain Literacy for Educators and Psychologists.* New York: Academic Press.

Berninger, V., and Abbott, R. 1994. Redefining learning disabilities: Moving beyond aptitude-achievement discrepancies to failure to respond to validated treatment protocols. In *Frames of Reference for the Assessment of Learning Disabilities: New Views on Measurement Issues,* ed. G R Lyon. Baltimore: Paul H. Brookes Publishing Co.

Berninger, V., Abbott, R., Billingsley, F., and Nagy, W. 2001. Processes underlying timing and fluency: Efficiency, automaticity, coordination, and morphological awareness. In *Dyslexia, Fluency, and the Brain,* ed. M. Wolf. Baltimore: York Press.

Berninger, V., Abbott, S., Reed, L., Greep, K., Hooven, C., Sylvester, L., Taylor, J., Clinton, A., and Abbott, R. Directed reading and writing activities: Aiming intervention to working brain systems. In *Prevention and Intervention Issues across the Life Span,* eds. S. Dollinger and L. DiLalla. Hillsdale, NJ: Lawrence Erlbaum Associates.

Berninger, V., Abbott, R., Thomson, J., and Raskind, W. 2001. Language phenotype for reading and writing disability: A family approach. *Scientific Studies in Reading* 5:59–105.

Berninger, V., Abbott, R., Vermeulen, K., Ogier, S., Brooksher, R., Zook, D., and Lemos, Z. (2002). Comparison of faster and slower responders: Implications for the nature and duration of early reading intervention. *Learning Disability Quarterly* 25:59–76.

Birsh, J., ed. 1999. *Multisensory Teaching of Basic Language Skills.* Baltimore: Paul H. Brookes.

Blachman, B., Tangel, D., Ball, E., Black, R., and McGraw, C. 1999. Developing phonological awareness and word recognition skills: A two-year intervention with low-income, inner-city children. *Reading and Writing: An Interdisciplinary Journal* 11:239–73.

Bowers, P. 1993. Text reading and rereading: Predictors of fluency beyond word recognition. *Journal of Reading Behavior* 25:133–53.

Breznitz, Z. 1997. Enhancing the reading of dyslexic children by reading acceleration and auditory masking. *Journal of Educational Psychology* 89:103–13.

Carlisle, J. 2000. Awareness of the structure and meaning of morphologically complex words: Impact on reading. *Reading and Writing. An Interdisciplinary Journal* 12:169–90.

Carlisle, J., and Nomanbhoy, D. 1993. Phonological and morphological development. *Applied Psycholinguistics* 14:177–95.

Carlisle, J., and Stone, C. In press. The effects of morphological structure on children's reading of derived words. In *Reading Complex Words: Cross-language Studies*, eds. E. Assink and D. Santa. Dordrecht, The Netherlands: Kluwer.

Churchland, P. 1989. *Neurophilosophy*. Toward a Unified Science of the Mind/Brain. Cambridge, MA: The MIT Press.

Clark, D., and Uhry, J. 1995. *Dyslexia: Theory and Practice of Remedial Instruction (2nd ed.)*. Baltimore, York Press.

Csikszentmihalyi, M. 1990. *Flow: The Psychology of Optimal Performance.* New York: Harper and Row.

Doyle, A. C. 1995. *The Adventures of Sherlock Holmes.* New York: Barnes and Noble.

Duffy, G. 2002. The case for direct explanation of strategies. In *Comprehension Instruction: Research-based Best Practices*, eds. M. Pressley, and C. Block. New York: Guildford.

Eden, Guinevere. 2002. Physiological correlates of reading intervention fMRI studies in children and adults. Paper presented at semi-annual conference of the International Dyslexia Research Foundation (The Dyslexia Foundation), June 11–15, at Kona, Hawaii.

Ehri, L., Nunes, Stahl, S., and Willows, D. 2002. Systematic phonics instruction helps students learn to read: Evidence from the National Reading Panel's Meta-analysis. *Review of Educational Research* 71:393–447.

Felton, R. 1993. Effects of instruction on decoding skills in children with phonological processing problems. *Journal of Learning Disabilities* 26:583–89.

Foorman, B., Francis, D., Fletcher, J., Schatschneider, C., and Mehta, P. 1998. The role of instruction in learning to read: Preventing reading failure in at-risk children. *Journal of Educational Psychology* 90:37–55.

Fowler, A., and Liberman, I. 1995. The role of phonology and orthography in morphological awareness. In *Morphological Aspects of Language Processing*, ed. L. Feldman. Hillsdale, NJ: Lawrence Erlbaum Associates.

Fuchs, L., and Fuchs, D. 1999. Monitoring student progress toward the development of reading competence: A review of three forms of classroom-based assessment. *School Psychology Review* 28:659–71.

Fuchs, L., Fuchs, D., Hamlet, C., Phillips, N., and Bentz, J. 1994. Classwide curriculum-based measurement: Helping general educators meet the challenge of student diversity. *Exceptional Children* 60:518–37.

Gaskins, I., Ehri, L., Cress, C., O'Hara, C., and Donnelly, K. 1997. Procedures for word learning: Making discoveries about words. *The Reading Teacher* 50:312–27.

Gough, P., Juel, C., and Griffith, P. 1992. Reading, spelling, and the orthographic cipher. In *Reading Acquisition*, eds. P. Gough, L. Ehri, and R. Treiman. Hillsdale, NJ: Lawrence Erlbaum Associates.

Henry, M. 1989. Children's word structure knowledge: Implications for decoding and spelling instruction. *Reading and Writing* 1:135–52.

Henry, M. 1990. *Words. Integrated Decoding and Spelling Instruction Based on Word Origin and Word Structure*. Austin, TX: PRO-ED.

Hsu, L., Berninger, V., Thomson, J., Wijsman, E., and Raskind, W. 2002. Familial aggregation of dyslexia phenotypes: Paired correlated measures. *American Journal of Medical Genetics/Neuropsychiatric Section* 114:471–78.

Jenkins, J., Vadasy, P., Firebaugh, M., and Profilet, C. 2000. Tutoring first grade struggling readers in phonological reading skills. *Learning Disabilities: Research and Practice* 15:75–84.

Kame'enui, E., and Simmons, D. 2001. Introduction to this special issue: The DNA of reading fluency. *Scientific Studies of Reading* 5:203–10.

Kintsch, W. 1998. *Comprehension. A Paradigm for Cognition*. Cambridge, United Kingdom: Cambridge University Press.

Leong, C. K. 1989. Productive knowledge of derivational rules in poor readers. *Annals of Dyslexia* 39:94–115.

Leong, C. K. 2000. Rapid processing of base and derived forms of words and grades 4, 5, and 6 children's spelling. *Reading and Writing. An Interdisciplinary Journal* 12:277–302.

Levy, B. A. 2001. Moving the bottom. Improving reading fluency. In *Dyslexia, Fluency, and the Brain*, ed. M. Wolf . Balltimore, MD: York Press.

Levy, B. A., Abello, B., and Lysynchuk, L. 1997. Transfer from word training to reading in context: Gains in fluency and comprehension. *Learning Disabilities Quarterly* 20:173–88.

Lovett, M., Borden, S., De Luca, T., Bensen, N., and Brackstone, D. 1994. Treating the core deficits of developmental dyslexia: Evidence of transfer of learning after phonological- and strategy- based reading training programs. *Developmental Psychology* 30:805–22.

Lovett, M., Lacerenza, L., Borden, S., Frijters, J., Steinbach, A., and DePalma, M. 2000. Components of effective remediation for developmental reading disabilities: Combining phonological and strategy-based instruction to improve outcomes. *Journal of Educational Psychology* 92:263–83.

Lovett, M., Steinbach, K., and Frijters, J. 2000. Remediating the core deficits of developmental reading disability: A double-deficit perspective. *Journal of Learning Disabilities* 33:334–58.

Mahoney, D., Singson, M., and Mann, V. 2000. Reading ability and sensitivity to morphological relations. *Reading and Writing. An Interdisciplinary Journal* 12191–218.

McCandliss, B., Beck, I., Sandak, R., and Perfetti, C. 2003. Focusing attention on decoding for children with poor reading skills: Design and preliminary tests of the word building intervention. *Scientific Studies in Reading* 7:75–104.

Morris, R., Stuebing, K., Fletcher, J., Shaywitz, S., Lyon, G. R., Shankweiler, D., Katz, L., Francis, D., and Shaywitz, B. 1998. Subtypes of reading disability: Variability around a phonological core. *Journal of Educational Psychology* 90:347–73.

Nagy, W., Diakidoy, I., and Anderson, R. 1993. The acquisition of morphology: Learning the contribution of suffixes to the meaning of derivatives. *Journal of Reading Behavior* 25:15–170.

Nagy, W., Osborn, J., Winsor, P., and O'Flahavan, J. 1994. Structural analysis: Some guidelines for instruction. In *Reading, Language, and Literacy*, eds. F. Lehr and J. Osborn. Hillsdale, NJ: Lawrence Erlbaum Associates.

National Reading Panel 2000. *Teaching Children to Read: An Evidence-based Assessment of the Scientific Research Literature on Reading and Its Applications for Reading Instruction*. Washington D C: National Institute of Child Health and Human Development (NICHD).

Olson, R., Forsberg, H., and Wise, B. 1994. Genes, environment, and the development of orthographic skills. In *The Varieties of Orthographic Knowledge I.: Theoretical and Developmental Issues*, ed. V. W Berninger. Dordrecht, the Netherlands: Kluwer Academic.

Rayner, K., Foorman, B., Perfetti, C., Pesetsky, D., and Seidenberg, M. 2001. How psychological science informs the teaching of reading. *Psychological Science in the Public Interest* 2:31–74.

Richards, T., Berninger, V., Aylward, E., Richards, A., Thomson, J., Nagy, W., Carlisle, J., Dager, S., and Abbott, R. 2002. Reproducibility of proton MR spectroscopic imaging (PEPSI): Comparison of dyslexic and normal reading children and effects of treatment on brain lactate levels during language tasks. *American Journal of Neuroradiology* 23:1678–85.

Ridley, M. 1999. Genome. The Autobiography of a Species in 23 Chapters. New York: Harper Collins Publishers, Inc.

Scarborough, H. 2001. Connecting early language and literacy to later reading dis(abilities): Evidence, theory, and practice. In *Handbook for Research in Early Literacy*, eds. S. Neuman and D. Dickson. New York: Guilford Press.

Schumm, J., Moody, S., and Vaughn, S. 2000. Grouping for reading instruction: Does one size fit all? *Journal of Learning Disabilities* 33:477–88.

Semel, E., Wiig, E., and Secord, W. 1995. *Clinical Evaluation of Language Fundamentals: Third Edition*. San Antonio, TX: Psychological Corporation.

Serafini, S., Steury, K., Richards, T., Corina, D., Abbott, R., and Berninger, V. 2001. Comparison of fMRI and PEPSI during language processing in children. *Magnetic Resonance in Medicine* 45:217–25.

Simos, P. G., Fletcher, J., Foorman, B., Francis, D., Castillo, E., Davis, R., Fitzgerald, M., Mathes, P., Denton, C., and Papanicolaou, A. 2002. Dyslexia-specific brain activation profile becomes normal following successful remedial remedial training. *Neurology* 58:1203–13.

Singson, M., Mahony, D., and Mann, V. 2000. The relation between reading ability and morphological skills: Evidence from derivational suffixes. *Reading and Writing. An Interdisciplinary Journal* 12:219–52.

Stahl, S., Heubach, K., and Crammond, B. 1997. *Fluency-oriented Reading Instruction* (Reading Research 79). Athens, GA. National Reading Center.

Stanovich, K. 1988. Twenty-five years of research on the reading process: The grand synthesis and what it means for our field. *National Reading Conference Yearbook* 47:44–58.

Torgesen, J., Alexander, A., Wagner, R., Rashotte, C., Voeller, K., Conway, T., and Rose, E. 2001. Intensive remedial instruction for children with severe reading disabilities: Immediate and long-term outcomes from two instructional approaches. *Journal of Learning Disabilities* 34:33–58.

Torgesen, J., Wagner, R., and Rashotte, C. 2000. *Test of Word Reading Efficiency* (TOWRE). Austin, TX: PRO-ED.

Torgesen, J., Wagner, R., Rashotte, C., Rose, E., Lindamood, P., Conway, T., and Garwan, C. 1999. Preventing reading failure in young children with phonological processing disabilities: Group and individual responses to instruction. *Journal of Educational Psychology* 91:579–93.

Turman Publishing. 1997. *Read Naturally*. St. Paul, MN: Turman Publishing.

Tyler, A., and Nagy, W. 1989. The acquisition of English derivational morphology. *Journal of Memory and Language* 28:649–67.

Tyler, A., and Nagy, W. 1990. Use of derivational morphology during reading. *Cognition* 36:17–34.

Uhry, J., and Shepherd, J. 1997. Teaching phonological recoding to young children with phonological processing deficits: The effect on sight vocabulary acquisition. *Learning Disabilities Quarterly* 20:104–25.

Vellutino, F., Scanlon, D., Sipey, E., Small, S., Pratt, A., Chen, R., and Denckla, M. 1996. Cognitive profiles of difficult-to-remediate and readily remediated poor readers. Early intervention as a vehicle for distinguishing between cognitive and experiential deficits as basic causes of specific reading disability. *Journal of Educational Psychology* 88:601–38.

Wallach, G., and Butler, K. eds. 1994. *Language Learning Disabilities in School-age Children and Adolescents: Some Principles and Applications (2nd ed.)*. New York: Maxwell Macmillan International.

Wasik, B., and Slavin, R. 1993. Preventing early reading failure with one-to-one tutoring: A review of five programs. *Reading Research Quarterly* 28:179–200.

Wiederholt, J., and Bryant, B. 1992. *Gray Oral Reading Test, Third Edition* (GORT-3). Psychological Assessment Resources. Odessa, FL.

Wijsman, E., Peterson, D., Leutennegger, A., Thomson, J., Goddard, K., Hsu, L., Berninger, V., and Raskind, W. 2000. Segregation analysis of phenotypic components of learning disabilities I. Nonword memory and digit span. *American Journal of Human Genetics* 67:631–46.

Wilkinson, G. 1993. *Wide Range Achievement Test, Third Edition* (WRAT3). Wilmington, DE: Wide Range, Inc.

Wise, B., and Olson, R. 1995. Computer-based phonological awareness and reading instruction. *Annals of Dyslexia* 45:99–122.

Wise, B., Ring, J., and Olson, R. 1999. Training phonological awareness with and without explicit attention to articulation. *Journal of Experimental Child Psychology* 72:271–304.

Wolf, M. ed. 2001. *Dyslexia, Fluency, and the Brain*. Baltimore, MD: York Press.

Wolf, M., and Katzir-Cohen, T. 2001. Reading fluency and its intervention. *Scientific Studies of Reading* 5:211–38.

Woodcock, R. 1987. *Woodcock Reading Mastery Test Revised* (WRMT-R). Circle Pines, MN: American Guidance.

Young, A., Bowers, P., and MacKinnon, G. 1996. Effects of prosodic modeling and repeated reading on poor readers' fluency and comprehension. *Applied Psycholinguistics* 17:59–84.

Chapter • 15

A Vocabulary Enrichment Program for Third and Fourth Grade African-American Students:
Description, Implementation, and Impact

Barbara R. Foorman, Latrice M. Seals, Jason Anthony, and Sharolyn Pollard-Durodola

The demographics of the school age population are shifting rapidly in the United States. The percentage of minority students is increasing, especially the percentage of school-age Hispanics. Hispanic enrollment jumped from 9.9% in 1986 to 16.3% in 2001 (National Center for Education Statistics 2001a). With this large increase comes an increase in the percentage of English language learners. Results from the National Assessment of Educational Progress (NAEP) show that 37% of fourth graders read below the basic proficiency level for Grade 4, but among minority students this percentage is an alarming 63% for African-American fourth graders and 58% for Hispanic fourth graders (National Center for Education Statistics 2001b). An important part of being a reader is understanding what is read. It is not enough to pronounce words correctly; we must develop students' oral language so that they can access the meanings of the words they read. The objective of this chapter is to review research on vocabulary instruction in the early grades, with particular attention to a vocabulary enrichment program developed for African American third and fourth graders.

VOCABULARY ACQUISITION

A nativist view stresses the hardwired nature of language, the autonomy of syntax, and emerging phonological structures (Chomsky 1965, 1995). But even this view admits to the interactive influence of social and cognitive factors as the infant develops in a particular speech/hearing community (Pinker 1994). The infant acquires the phonological features, grammar, and vocabulary of that community. To the extent that the community is literate and economically advantaged, children will be exposed at home to decontextualized, literate forms of language that they will encounter at school. However, children who are minimally exposed to literacy and decontextualized language at home are behind their peers on the first day of school (Snow, Burns, and Griffin 1998). Researchers found that children from higher socioeconomic status (SES) homes knew twice as many words as lower SES children (Graves 1987; Graves and Slater 1987). The gaps are apparent in preschool, where Hart and Risley (1995) estimate it would take 41 hours a week of intensive vocabulary instruction to close the vocabulary differences between advantaged and disadvantaged children. Hart and Risley (1995) traced the origin of the gaps to the infancy and toddler periods. They followed 40 families that varied in SES from the child's first birthday until 36 months. They found that by 36 months of age children in middle class families had three times as much language directed at them as children in lower-class families. Additionally, the children of the middle-class families produced twice as much language as their economically disadvantaged peers.

In addition to the sheer *quantity* of language preschoolers are exposed to, the *quality* matters as well. Hart and Risley (1995) found that the children from low SES backgrounds were more likely to have (a) exposure to fewer novel words during parental interactions, (b) more commands rather than prompts and questions from parents, and (c) they were less likely to receive affirmative feedback from their parents than children from middle-class backgrounds. Dickinson and his colleagues (Dickinson and Sprague 2001; Dickinson and Tabors 2001) have studied oral language characteristics of Head Start classrooms. They found that kindergarten vocabulary and literacy scores were influenced by home literacy support, vocabulary environment, curriculum quality, and teacher talk. The aspects of teacher talk most predictive of end-of-kindergarten literacy-related success were (a) use of novel words, (b) ability to listen to children and to extend their comments, and (c) tendency to engage children in intellectually challenging conversations about non-present topics. Kindergarten literacy outcomes, in turn, predicted vocabulary and reading comprehension outcomes in middle school. In the intervening years the influence of oral language on decoding skills is indirect. Specifically, the impact of vocabulary on decoding is mediated by the impact of phonological processing and print knowledge on decoding (Storch and Whitehurst 2002).

VOCABULARY AND READING DEVELOPMENT

The fact that vocabulary size in first grade has only an indirect influence on word reading skills is not an excuse to ignore vocabulary instruction in the early grades. As soon as reading assessments go beyond accuracy to tap understanding of what is read, vocabulary knowledge begins to have a direct effect on word recognition skill (Beck and McKeown 1991; Beck, McKeown, and Omanson 1987). Without systematic and effective intervention for children with limited vocabularies, differences in the rate and quantity of vocabulary growth will increase over time as compared to peers who meet or exceed age-appropriate vocabulary norms (Nagy 1988). Nagy and Anderson (1984) estimate that there are 88,700 word types in English and that students typically learn about half of them. This suggests that the average child learns about 3,000 new words each year (Stahl 1999; White, Graves, and Slater 1990). Direct teaching cannot cover 3,000 words a year. If 15 words are taught per week for 35 weeks in the school year and five weeks in the summer, then 600 words (40 weeks x 15 words) could maximally be taught directly. Clearly the majority of the 3,000 words must come from context (Sternberg 1987). One important context is reading itself. The more students read, the more words they are exposed to and the more likely their vocabularies will grow (Cunningham and Stanovich 1991). There are, however, much lower estimates of the number of words students learn, such as D'Anna, Zechmeister, and Hall's (1991) estimate of 17,000, or approximately 1,000 words a year. This much lower estimate makes the possibility of direct instruction in vocabulary more plausible.

Exacerbating the SES gaps in vocabulary size is the nature of vocabulary instruction promoted by basal reading programs. Teachers highlight a few words for instruction before reading a text selection. Instruction consists mostly of providing definitions either solely in the context of the text selection or by using dictionary definitions. Dictionary definitions are usually too short and too divorced from children's language to be meaningful to children. Our analysis of the vocabulary demands of six widely used first-grade basals revealed surprising findings (Foorman et al. 2003). Using an electronic version of the *Living Word Vocabulary* (LWV; Dale and O'Rourke 1981), we found that 80% of the words in four of the basals were above the fourth grade level. A level in the LWV is defined as the grade at which 67% to 80% of students know a word's meaning. The two basals with the vast majority of words at the first and second grade level were widely used in school reform efforts—Success for All (Slavin and Madden 2001) and Reading Mastery I (Englemann and Bruner 1995). In addition to the restriction on vocabulary range in these two first-grade basals, the corpora of words were much smaller. The four large basals contained from 2672 to 3871 unique words (types) and from 21,410 to 59,347 repetitions of words (tokens). In contrast, SFA had 1633 types and 14,016 tokens, while Reading Mastery I had 370 types and 5567 tokens. The corpora of words in these two basals may be appropriate to teach beginning reading, but they are limited in their appropriateness for expanding vocabulary size. In contrast, the size of the corpora and the difficulty level of the words in the four large basals make these reading programs a challenge for all students except those performing above grade level.

INSTRUCTIONAL TECHNIQUES FOR EXPANDING VOCABULARY SIZE

There is surprisingly little research on effective instructional methods for enhancing vocabulary knowledge, according to the report of the National Reading Panel (NRP; NICHD 2000). Members of this panel's subgroup on vocabulary were unable to conduct a meta-analysis because of the dearth of quality studies. In summarizing their findings, subpanel members advised that using a single instructional method in teaching new words would not yield optimal growth in vocabulary. In order to achieve optimal vocabulary growth, several instructional techniques should be combined, depending on the age, need, and ability of the students. The NRP report is highly critical of traditional vocabulary instruction found in classrooms and in basals in which students must rely on contextual information and on writing and memorizing definitions as the primary sources of vocabulary instruction. In spite of the disappointing findings of the NRP, there are four promising vocabulary approaches with some evidence of effectiveness for expanding elementary school children's vocabulary size. They are: (1) Text

Talk (Beck and McKeown 2001; Beck, McKeown, and Kucan 2002); (2) an upper-elementary vocabulary program (Beck, Perfetti, and McKeown 1982); (3) Vocabulary Improvement Project (VIP; McLaughlin, August, and Snow 2000); and (4) Vocabulary Enrichment Project (VEP; Seals, Foorman, and Anthony 2002). Text Talk was a research project in kindergarten, first, and second grade classrooms aimed at maximizing the benefits of reading aloud. The upper-elementary vocabulary program provided a 5-day lesson cycle over 12 weeks for fourth graders in an urban school. Vocabulary Improvement Project was a multi-site project in which a five-day lesson cycle was taught over a 20-week period to fourth and fifth grade English language learners, using trade books with an immigration theme. Vocabulary Enrichment Program also was a multi-site project with a five-day lesson cycle over a 20-week period. However, VEP was designed for third and fourth grade African American students, with trade books reflecting African American themes. Each of these programs will be described in more detail, with particular attention to our program, VEP.

Text Talk.   The goals of Text Talk are (a) to improve comprehension by asking children questions that encourage them to express and connect ideas in stories, and (b) to enhance vocabulary development (Beck and McKeown 2001). Three words per story in 80 trade books were targeted for direct instruction after a story had been read and discussed. Words targeted were deemed useful in multiple contexts, capable of being used in a variety of instructional activities, and within the intellectual understanding of the children. The basic instructional sequence includes the following steps (Beck, McKeown, and Kucan 2002, pp. 65–66):

1. Read the story.
2. Contextualize the word within the story.
3. Have the children say the word.
4. Provide a student-friendly explanation of the word.
5. Present examples of the word used in a context different from the story context.
6. Engage the children in activities that get them to interact with the words.
7. Have children say the word.

Maintenance of word meanings is a critical component of Text Talk. Examples of maintenance activities are: placing target words on a bulletin board and making tally marks each time they are used, applying previously targeted words to new stories, creating a dictionary with word meanings and sample sentences, and incorporating words into the daily message and into reading and writing activities. At this time no empirical evidence of Text Talk's effectiveness is available.

Upper elementary vocabulary program   To develop vocabulary in upper elementary grades, Beck, McKeown, and Kucan (2002) stress the importance of the frequency of exposure to target words, the richness of instruction, and the transfer of words beyond the classroom. In terms of frequency, Beck, McKeown, and Kucan (2002) recommend introducing about 10 words per week with 8 to 10 exposures to each word across the week. Rich instruction refers to instruction that goes beyond definitions, such as activities in which students use words, explore aspects of their meaning, and relate them to other words (Stahl 1999). For example, relationships among words can be explored by presenting questions that juxtapose two target words not obviously related: "Could a *virtuoso* be a *rival*?" (Beck, McKeown, and Kucan 2002, p. 75). Transfer beyond the classroom is facilitated through games such as Word Wizard (Beck, Perfetti, and McKeown 1982). In Word Wizard students win points by bringing evidence of encounters with target words from outside the classroom.

Beck, Perfetti, and McKeown (1982) created a 5-day lesson cycle for their 12-week vocabulary program for 27 fourth graders in an urban school. The teacher organized presentation of 104 target words around themes to help students remember the words and to help teachers create coherent activities. Words were introduced on Day 1 by having students develop definitions for target words represented with pictures. During Days 2 to 4, students engaged in activities such as completing a sentence, selecting the word that fit within a sentence, selecting between pairs of target words, or having partners time each other in matching words and definitions. A multiple-choice test was administered on Day 5. This test was challenging in that distractors were related to the week's theme and the wording of correct responses was not the verbatim definition with which the students had worked.

At the end of the 12-week program, the 27 students completed tasks requiring semantic processing: Single-word decision, sentence verification, and story recall. On all of these tasks, instructed students performed better than the 39 control students matched on pretests consisting of a standardized reading test and a multiple-choice vocabulary measure in which target words were the stem. Results suggest that not only can instructed fourth graders learn the meaning of the words taught, but that they also can process instructed words more efficiently in story retellings.

This is evidence of transfer of the word meaning in isolation to the word meaning in orally presented connected text.

The Vocabulary Improvement Project (VIP). The VIP was a three-year longitudinal study by McLaughlin, August, and Snow (2000; see Lively et al. 2003) that examined the effects of a vocabulary curriculum on the reading ability of 317 fourth- and fifth-grade students in California, Massachusetts, and Virginia. Of these participating students, 109 were Spanish-speaking English-language learners and 208 were English-only students. During the first year of the study, the authors documented the gap in vocabulary knowledge in the two groups of students and piloted vocabulary lessons based on target words located in Arnold Lobel's book of classic fables that were central to the story meaning and were likely to be encountered in curriculum in the upper-elementary grades. In the second year of the study, the curriculum was revised to include trade books, diaries, and newspaper stories with an immigration theme. The core vocabulary was selected as before but activities required more in-depth processing in line with the literature on vocabulary acquisition (e.g., Beck, McKeown, and Omanson 1987). For four days each week, twelve target words were studied in 20 to 40 minute semi-scripted lessons. After 12 weeks of instruction with fourth graders, McLaughlin, August, and Snow (2000) found that vocabulary knowledge improved, especially among English-language learners. However, there were no generalized improvements in vocabulary or in reading comprehension when instructed students were compared to similar students in the same school.

During the third year of the study the intervention was continued with two groups of fifth graders—the previous fourth grade cohort and a new group of fifth graders. The vocabulary program significantly improved vocabulary and reading comprehension scores for both English-language learners and English-only students relative to control students. However, for students who had been in the program for two years, the additional year produced significant gains in vocabulary but not in reading comprehension. Thus, as we saw in Beck, Perfetti, and McKeown (1982), vocabulary instruction has an impact on knowledge of word meanings but rarely generalizes to comprehension of connected text. An additional result from McLaughlin, August, and Snow (2000) was that VIP reduced the gap between English-language learners and native speakers by approximately 50%, from about one standard deviation on vocabulary and reading comprehension measures to .5 standard deviations.

Vocabulary Enrichment Program (VEP). The Vocabulary Enrichment Program (VEP) was part of a longitudinal study conducted by the first author in 17 inner city schools in Houston, Texas and in the District of Columbia. Approximately 1300 children were followed from kindergarten through Grade 4, and each year the approximately 112 teachers of these students participated in ongoing professional development concerning research-based reading practices (Foorman and Moats in press). During the primary grades these at-risk students developed reading skills that were solidly at national average, although there was considerable teacher-level variability (Foorman et al. in press; Foorman et al. 2003). In spite of this general reading improvement, vocabulary scores, as measured by the *Peabody Picture Vocabulary Test-Revised* (Dunn and Dunn 1981), remained in the lower quartile (i.e., at the 15th percentile, on average). Moreover, our observations of reading/language arts instruction when the students were in first and second grades revealed that only 3.5% of instruction was devoted to vocabulary instruction in Grade 1 and 6% in Grade 2 (Foorman and Schatschneider in press). Concerned that our students would be decoding words they could not understand when they began to read across the curriculum in Grade 4—what Chall (1983) called the 4th grade slump—we decided to develop a vocabulary program for Grades 3 and 4. We drew upon the work of Beck and her colleagues and the McLaughlin et al. (2000) Vocabulary Improvement Project (VIP) in designing our Vocabulary Enrichment Project (VEP).

Because 95% of our students were African American, we organized VEP around biographies and realistic and historical fiction depicting African-American heroes and heroines. Recent research on African American students' reading development suggests that presenting students with literature containing heroes and heroines that share physical characteristics with students may enliven the reading lesson, making the reading experiences more meaningful and interesting (Hefflin and Barksdale-Ladd 2001). Additionally, one of us had documented the features of African American Vernacular English exhibited by students participating in the study (Seals 2001). One of the goals of VEP, therefore, was to build vocabulary knowledge by increasing students' sensitivity to differences between African American Vernacular English (AAVE) and Standard American English (SAE).

Labov (1972, p. xiii) defines AAVE as "the relatively uniform dialect spoken by the majority of black youth in most parts of the United States today, especially in the inner city." Labov also points out that AAVE is spoken in rural areas and is used by black adults in informal speech. SAE refers to speech that is socially desirable, such as the Midwestern accent of the voice of directory assistance or the speech of most national newscasters. The sound-spelling mappings of basal readers typically reflect Midwestern (i.e., SAE) pronunciations (Foorman, Breier, and Fletcher in press). Given that both English-language learners and AAVE speakers may face similar challenges in acquiring SAE, it is possible that gains experienced by English-language learners when given systematic vocabulary instruction in thematically relevant literature (such as the immigration theme in VIP) may also occur for AAVE-speaking students who are presented with a vocabulary curriculum that addresses differences between AAVE and SAE. Thus, programs such as VIP and VEP, which expose differences between students' native speech and SAE, may empower children by removing the stigma that is associated with their home language, as well as by clearing up confusion in communication with students and teachers who are not native speakers of the students' home language. In the following sections, we will describe the VEP curriculum in greater detail and then present empirical results of the program's effectiveness with third and fourth graders.

VOCABULARY ENRICHMENT PROGRAM: CURRICULUM

Vocabulary Enrichment Program is a twenty-week vocabulary curriculum that is taught by the classroom teachers on a five-day cycle for 30-minutes each day. The curriculum affords multiple exposures of the weekly target words through the use of vocabulary instructional methods that research described above suggests are effective for children in elementary school. The instructional techniques for VEP include: (a) context activities, (b) morphological elements, (c) word roots, (d) synonyms/antonyms, (e) inferencing skills, (f) summarizing skills, (g) multiple meanings, (h) dictionary skills, (i) word games, (j) semantic feature analysis, (k) prefixes/suffixes, (l) figurative language, (m) paraphrasing, and (n) deep processing activities. Deep processing activities consist of open-ended questions which lead to discussions that encourage students to relate what they have learned about target words to prior knowledge brought from home and personal experiences.

Word Selection. Criteria for selection of words for the vocabulary curriculum consisted of appearance on Dale and O'Rourke's *Living Word Vocabulary* (LWV; Dale and O'Rourke 1981) and in one of the reading selections. Reading selections were drawn from classroom sets of six, age-appropriate books from the African American thematic literature described above. The LWV consists of 44,000 word meanings grouped according to the level at which 67% to 80% of students from grades 4 through college knew the meanings. To ensure that target VEP words were at the third and fourth grade instructional level, we selected words from level 4 of the LWV. Level 4 represents the level at which 67% to 80% of third and fourth graders knew the word meanings. Level 6 represents the level at which 67% to 80% of fifth and sixth graders knew the word meanings.

The first step in word selection was to examine the reading selection for words essential to understanding the text. Next, the list of words in level 4 LWV was examined to see if those words were on the list. Words that were found both in the reading selection and on the word list were selected as target words for the week. When less than 15 words for a one-week lesson could be found on both the level 4 LWV list and the words identified as essential to the understanding of the reading selection, additional words were taken from the words identified as essential in the reading selection.

Of the 300 vocabulary words presented over the twenty instructional weeks (15 words per week x 20 weeks of instruction = 300), 252 words were found in both the reading and on the Dale and O'Rourke word list for Grade 3, and 275 were found in both for Grade 4. The remaining words were not found on the word list, and only appeared in the reading selection.

Procedure.   On Day 1 of each week, new vocabulary words were presented. Using an overhead projector, the teacher assisted the class in sounding out the vocabulary words, syllable by syllable. Teachers were trained in the features of AAVE and in how to demonstrate SAE pronunciations of target words by hyper-enunciating word parts that are vulnerable to the influences of AAVE. Word parts that tend to be omitted or altered in AAVE appear in a red font on the Word List transparency. Teachers were told to listen closely as their students repeated vocabulary words. If a word was spoken in AAVE or not clearly enunciated by a student, the teacher was to say, "Let's say this word again. Listen to the sounds closely. Re-pre-sent." Next, the teacher defined each word with a sentence. Finally, directions for the at-home assignment were discussed. The Day 1 at-home assignment consisted of: reviewing the vocabulary words, writing the definitions of the words on flash cards, and a synonym and riddle activity.

On Day 2 of the cycle, the class reviewed the Day 1 at-home assignment. Next, the book containing the reading selection was presented. Teachers introduced the title, author, and asked students to predict the storyline. Students were instructed to listen and follow along as their teacher read the passage aloud. They were asked to give the teacher a "thumbs up" each time they heard a target vocabulary word. Next, the teacher asked the students to listen and follow along as she read selected paragraphs again. Students were then asked to paraphrase the paragraphs. Finally, directions for the at-home assignment were discussed. On Day 2, the at-home assignment consisted of a word substitution activity and an odd-word identification activity.

On Day 3, the class reviewed the Day 2 at-home assignment and completed an in-class contextual analysis assignment. Once all students had selected a word, the teacher called upon a student to tell the class which word they had selected and to explain why they chose that answer. On Day 3, the at-home assignment consisted of another contextual analysis activity. An example from Day 3, Week 8 of the Grade 4 VEP curriculum is provided in the text box below. Notice the emphasis on reviewing, contrasting, and extending word meanings within a highly motivating story, *Meet Addy* from the American Girls Collection.

On Day 4 of the cycle, the class reviewed the Day 3 at-home assignment and worked on expanding meanings through one of the following activities: (a) contextual analysis, (b) morphological elements, (c) word roots, (d) synonyms/antonyms, (e) inferencing skills, (f) summarizing skills, (g) multiple meanings, (h) word analysis, (i) dictionary skills, (j) word games, (k) semantic feature analysis, and (l) deep processing activities. On Day 4, the at-home assignment consisted of a crossword puzzle containing the vocabulary words, and reviewing the flash cards to prepare for the Day 5 assessment.

On Day 5, the class reviewed the Day 4 at-home assignment, played the Bingo game and completed an expanding meaning activity from one of the above listed areas. Finally, students took a fifteen-item in-class assessment that reviewed the students' understanding of the vocabulary words. The assessment was read to students item by item so that reading ability would not interfere with students being able to complete the test successfully.

VOCABULARY ENRICHMENT PROGRAM: GRADE 3 RESULTS

An evaluation of the vocabulary enrichment program (VEP) was conducted with 27 third grade teachers from five of the 17 schools participating in our project. Schools were matched on demographics and then assigned to either an intervention or comparison group. The 12 teachers in the comparison group taught vocabulary

Vignette of a Fourth Grade Class,
Ms. Danbury, Teacher
Rettick Elementary
Week 8, Day 3

At 8:05, the students are quickly reviewing vocabulary words (e.g., courage, disguise, streak, etc) silently from Day 1. Other students are eagerly rereading "Into the Night" of *Meet Addy* from the **American Girls** collection. When the teacher is ready, she enthusiastically has students chant the school's learning creed and goals that are encouraged on a daily basis. Ms. Danbury quickly walks in between rows of students, reminding everyone that they are *smart* and that they have a lot to accomplish this morning.

All students have by now located the *Vocabulary Review* and are ready when Ms. Danbury quickly has students chorally read each row of words. Using a technique that she refers to as *Rapid Word Drills*, the teacher gives word clues:

"Who can tell me which word is a synonym for *injury*?"
"Who can tell me which word is the opposite of *fear*?"
"Who can tell me which word means to *anticipate*?"

There is a flutter of student hands, as each child eagerly awaits to identify the correct word. The teacher concludes this three minute warm up by stating how well the children have studied and that they are all becoming real *word detectives*.

Ms. Danbury now moves on to the activity focusing on *Context Clues*. Briskly, the teacher reminds everyone to put on their thinking caps and calls on individual students to read a sentence. Each volunteer reads a sentence and identifies context clues that assist in selecting the most appropriate vocabulary word for each sentence. Correct answers are followed by lavish praise and encouragement to *think hard*. Five items are completed and discussed in class before moving on to the *Writer's Corner*.

With a serious expression, the teacher reads the words of Uncle Solomon, a character in the story they are reading:
"You hold on to that half dime. You gonna need it where you going. Freedom cost, you hear me? Freedom's got its cost."

Ms. Danbury, now with arms folded, asks students to imagine that they are Addy, the main character. What does it mean—freedom's got its cost? What might you give up in order to be free?

Excitedly, students raise their hands with ideas on what they would sacrifice in order to obtain personal freedom:
"My clothes. My friends. My house and where I live. My job. My name . . ."

Ms. Danbury asks, "Would you sacrifice a little or would you sacrifice *everything*?" They all respond chorally, "Everything!" The teacher then summarizes by saying the following. "Then, maybe what Uncle Solomon means is that freedom costs *everything*. In order to be truly free, you must be willing to give up *everything*!" There is silence as everyone ponders the meaning of Uncle Solomon's wise words.

Figure 1. Vignette of a Fourth Grade Lesson in the Vocabulary Enrichment Program

from the basal reading program. The 15 VEP teachers received two days of after-school training and follow-up coaching in the classroom. Fidelity of implementation was monitored and percentage of expected components exceeded the criterion of .80.

Demographic data are reported in table I for each group. Students in the VEP and control classrooms completed an IRT-based vocabulary test and the Word Identification subtest of the Woodcock-Johnson Psychoeducational Battery (WJ-R; Woodcock and Johnson 1989) at pre-test and post-test. Other language and literacy tests were administered only as post-tests: PPVT-R; WJ-R Word Attack; WJ-R Passage Comprehension; WISC-R Similarities (Wechsler 1974), and reading comprehension from the Comprehensive Reading Assessment Battery (CRAB; Fuchs, Fuchs, and Hamlett 1989).

The intervention and comparison groups had equivalent vocabularies at pretest, $F(1,134) = .63$, $p > .64$. However, students in the intervention group tended to have higher Word Identification scores at pretest ($Xs = 56.1$ and 49.7, $Sds = 26.0$ and 24.7, respectively), $F(1,134) = 3.6$, $p = .06$. Therefore, one-way ANCOVAs were performed on post-test scores from the PPVT-R, Similarities, Word Attack, Passage Comprehension, and CRAB, controlling for pretest differences in Word Identification. These analyses revealed no significant intervention effects. However, the covariate was significantly related to scores on the PPVT-R, Word Attack, Word Identification, Passage Comprehension, and CRAB, $F(1,121) = 38.97$–323.18, $ps < .001$. A repeated measures ANOVA examining growth in vocabulary revealed a significant main effect of Time, $F(1,145) = 256.55$, $p < .001$ and a significant Group by Time interaction, $F(1,129) = 35.7$, $p < .001$, such that students in the intervention group experienced more growth in vocabulary. This differential gain in vocabulary scores in the VEP group relative to

Table I. Sample Demographics by Group in Grade 3 Vocabulary Enrichment Program

Demographics	Group	
	VEP	Comparison
# of Classrooms	15	12
# of Children	176	130
Age in Months (SD)	106 (8)	106 (8)
Race		
African American	93%	98%
Hispanic	07%	02%
Caucasian		
Sex		
Female	57%	44%
Male	43%	56%

the comparison group is shown in figure 2. The eta-squared statistic indicated that 14% of the variance in vocabulary growth was attributable to the VEP intervention. Repeated measures ANOVA examining growth in Word Identification skills found only a main effect of Time, $F(1,131) = 139.80$, $p < .001$. In summary, we found that third grade students who participated in the Vocabulary Enrichment Program had significant gains in vocabulary. However, these gains did not generalize to improvements in verbal reasoning, reading comprehension, or decoding.

VOCABULARY ENRICHMENT PROGRAM: GRADE 4 RESULTS

We also conducted an evaluation of the vocabulary enrichment project (VEP) with fourth grade teachers from the eight Houston schools participating in our longitudinal project.[1] Schools were matched on demographics and then assigned to either an intervention group or a comparison group. Again, comparison teachers taught vocabulary from the basal readers and VEP teachers were trained by project staff after school on two days and then coached in the classroom, as needed. Fidelity of implementation was recorded.

Table II reports the sample's demographic information by group. The same measures of students' decoding abilities and knowledge of the vocabulary in the VEP curriculum were administered at

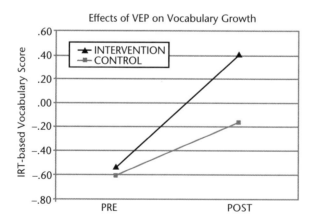

Figure 2. Effects of the Vocabulary Enrichment Program on Vocabulary Growth in Grade 3

[1]Because the project in Washington, DC ended in June, 2001, we did not follow the final cohort of third graders into Grade 4 in that site.

Table II.   Sample Demographics by Group in Grade 4 Vocabulary Enrichment Program

Demographics	Group	
	VEP	Comparison
# of Classrooms	11	10
# of Children	105	108
Age in Months (SD)	118 (7)	118 (8)
Race		
African American	92%	97%
Hispanic	07%	02%
Caucasian	01%	01%
Sex		
Female	47%	53%
Male	53%	47%

pre-intervention and post-intervention times. The two groups had equivalent word reading abilities and equivalent understanding of the VEP words at pre-test, $Fs(1,212) < .55$, $ps > .40$. Additional standardized measures of language (i.e., PPVT-Revised and Wechsler Intelligence Scale for Children- Similarities) and literary (i.e., Woodcock-Johnson Word Identification, Word Attack, and Passage Comprehension) were administered at post-intervention only.

We used multilevel modeling to account for the nested nature of the data while examining the impact of the VEP intervention on students' language and reading abilities. The first set of mixed models predicted post-test scores on vocabulary and language measures while controlling for classroom teacher effects and students' pre-test scores on the VEP vocabulary test. Intervention group and pre-test vocabulary scores were unrelated to post-intervention scores on the PPVT-R, VEP vocabulary, and WISC III Similarities, $Fs(1,192) < 1.20$, $ps > .25$. However, there were significant teacher effects on all three language outcomes, $zs > 2.15$, $ps < .01$.

A second set of mixed models predicted post-intervention literacy scores while controlling for classroom teacher and children's pre-intervention scores on the word reading test. Intervention group and pre-intervention word reading were unrelated to post-intervention scores on the standardized decoding and comprehension measures, $Fs (1,175) = 0.02$ to 0.90, $ps = .70$ to $.34$. However, there were significant teacher effects on Passage Comprehension and Word Identification scores, $zs = 2.23$ and 1.86, $ps = .01$ and $.03$. Also, teacher effects on Word Attack scores approached significance, $z = 1.45$, $p = .07$. In contrast to the results with the standardized reading outcomes, both intervention group and pre-intervention word reading were significant predictors of students' scores on the IRT-based word reading measure, $Fs(1,192) = 4.05$ and 61.05, $ps <$ .01 and .001, respectively. There were no teacher effects on this word reading outcome, $zs = 0.82$, $p > .20$.

The above findings suggested that, in general, the fourth grade VEP intervention had little impact on students' language and reading abilities. However, given the findings that indicated that the classroom teacher had reliable effects on language and reading outcomes along with our observations that the intervention teachers varied in how well they implemented the VEP program, we thought it potentially fruitful to determine if there were indeed significant differences in teachers' fidelity to the program and if such differences accounted for some of the teacher effects on the students' language and reading outcomes that were found within the intervention group.

Classroom teachers were observed during the classroom period that was devoted to VEP instruction, which was typically the language arts period. The 10 VEP teachers were observed an average of 10.5 times during the year. Observers were trained research assistants who exceeded a reliability criterion of .80. Observers recorded the number of implemented activities and the number of activities expected for the particular lesson that was observed. Observers also rated the quality of implementation of each activity that was observed and recorded whether or not each activity was properly sequenced. Proportion of implemented activities, proportion of properly sequenced activities, and average quality of implementation were calculated for each observation. These daily summary variables were then averaged across all observations to form three fidelity variables that quantified how closely teachers implemented the VEP program: average proportion of implementation, average quality of implementation, and average proportion of properly sequenced activities. Finally, observers' responded to four questions that assessed general teaching effectiveness. The questions were "Does teacher follow (VEP) manual closely?" "Does teacher appear comfortable with (VEP) materials?" "Does teacher extend lesson when appropriate?" and "Does teacher interact with students or groups?" We computed daily totals on these four items and then averaged them across observations to form a global teaching effectiveness variable.

Five of the six inter-correlations among the four fidelity variables were significant at the $p < .05$ level, $rs = .10$ to $.94$, $ps = .28$ to .001. These results support the validity of the fidelity ratings and suggest that teachers who implemented the VEP program more regularly also implemented the program better and were generally better teachers. There were reliable teacher differences in general teacher effectiveness and average proportion of properly sequenced VEP activities, $Fs(10, 115) = 2.49$ and 1.96, $ps = .01$ and $.05$, respectively. Teacher differences in average proportion of implementing VEP activities and average quality of that implementation were less reliable, $Fs(10, 115) = 1.60$ and 1.41, $ps = .11$ and $.19$, respectively. Nonetheless, we proceeded to examine the extent of the association between teachers' fidelity to the VEP program and classroom level outcomes.

In general, fidelity ratings were positively and substantially correlated with classroom averages on post-intervention language scores ($rs-.04$ to $.81$, see table 3). However, only the highest of these correlations was significant because of the small sample of only ten teachers. Fidelity ratings were less highly correlated with reading outcomes than with language outcomes. The four fidelity variables collectively accounted for approximately 58% of the variance in VEP scores, 45% of the variance in PPVT-R scores, and 78% of the variance in Similarities scores, after controlling for pre-intervention VEP scores. Because these regression analyses were based on only ten subjects, the findings, although substantial, are not reliable.

In summary, the fourth grade VEP intervention failed to benefit students' vocabulary development uniformly. However, our analyses of the fidelity data indicated that teachers who implemented the VEP program regularly and did so more closely to protocol had classrooms with higher language skills at the end of the year. A major reason for the uneven implementation of VEP in fourth grade Houston classrooms was competition for time from the curriculum designed to prepare students for the state accountability test. On average, one-third of the 90-minute reading/language arts block was devoted to this curriculum, which occurred daily from September until the writing assessment in February and the reading test in April. In conclusion, we view these results as providing partial support for our fourth grade VEP program. They also highlight the need for researchers and schools to provide teachers with much support during their transitions into new curricula.

CONCLUSION

In spite of the consensus regarding the importance of vocabulary development during the elementary school years (Snow et al. 1998), there is a surprising dearth of research on effective vocabulary instruction (NICHD 2000). This lack of research may be an artifact of vocabulary work being integrated into reading/language

Table III. Correlations of Fidelity Ratings with Language and Reading Outcomes in Grade 4 Vocabulary Enrichment Program

	Language Outcomes			Reading Outcomes		
Fidelity Ratings	VEP Vocabulary	PPTV-R Vocabulary	WISC Similarities	WJ-R Word Attack	WJ-R Word Identification	WJ-R Passage Comprehension
Proportion of Implementation	0.27	0.14	0.81**	0.03	0.11	0.03
Proportion of Properly Sequenced Implementation	0.14	0.41	0.66	0.32	0.21	0.24
Average Quality of Implementation	-0.00	0.27	0.58	0.07	-0.09	0.06
General Teacher Effectiveness	0.00	0.57	-0.04	0.36	0.05	0.29
Classroom Management	-0.10	0.43	-0.21	0.31	0.02	0.27

Note. $N = 10$; *$p < .05$; **$p < .01$.

arts instruction in the primary grades and limited to a "before reading" activity. But the vocabulary demands of the text selections in the current basal reading programs are high and assume above grade-level knowledge of word meanings. Hence, an emphasis on vocabulary instruction in the early grades is clearly warranted.

We reviewed four promising vocabulary programs: Text Talk (Beck and McKeown 2001), an upper-elementary vocabulary program (Beck, Perfetti, and McKeown 1982), Vocabulary Improvement Project (VIP; McLaughlin, August, and Snow 2000), and the authors' Vocabulary Enrichment Project (VEP). Text Talk builds on reading aloud from trade books for students in kindergarten, first, and second grades. All of these programs locate words in engaging text, define the targeted words in context, then involve the students in activities that extend word meanings to new contexts and to deeper levels of understanding. Effectiveness data are not yet available for Text Talk, but some promising data are available for VIP and VEP. The VIP reduced the gap between fifth grade English-language learners and English-only students by 50%—from one standard deviation to a half of a standard deviation. Clearly, direct instruction in vocabulary is a potent tool for boosting vocabulary for English-language learners. However, both VIP and VEP in third grade, as well as Beck, Perfetti, and McKeown's (1982) early work with fourth graders, found that vocabulary instruction improves knowledge of word meanings, but rarely generalizes to comprehension of connected text. Furthermore, the fidelity analyses of data from the fourth VEP classrooms provides a poignant reminder of how difficult it can be to achieve and maintain quality implementation in actual school settings.

We conclude that vocabulary instruction must begin at the very beginning of schooling—in preschool—if the SES gap is to be closed (Foorman et al. 2002). The variability in estimates of high school students' vocabulary size—from 17,000 to 44,000—make it difficult to gauge the exact number of words to target each day for vocabulary instruction, but the 8 to 10 words targeted each week in Text Talk in grades K-2 and the 15 words targeted weekly in VIP and VEP in grades 3 to 5 provide examples of plausible ranges. These programs agree on basic instructional points:

- Words to target: Those critical to story understanding, that are at or above grade-level, and that can be extended derivationally and conceptually.
- Number of words to target: Approximately 3 per day, or 15 per week.
- Source of target words: From engaging, motivating text.

- Instructional strategies: Move from contextualized definitions to deep understanding of word meanings found in multiple contexts that serve to maintain understanding.

In sum, it is not adequate to relegate vocabulary instruction to "before reading," contextualized definitions of words selected for beginning reading instruction. Such words are selected to maximize decoding instruction, not to enhance vocabulary development. Teachers need to allocate sufficient instructional time to develop word meanings beyond the story context. It is difficult to operationalize "sufficient" time, but clearly the 3.5% and 6% of time we observed allocated to vocabulary instruction in the Houston and Washington, D.C. classrooms in first and second grades was inadequate to have an impact on scores on a standardized vocabulary test. Vocabulary instruction needs to permeate the instructional day so that teachers have time to extend words encountered in specific contexts to a variety of contexts in order to build the decontextualized language that literate people use to discuss literacy products. Only by so doing can we begin to close the vocabulary gap evident in lower SES and minority children.

ACKNOWLEDGMENTS

This work was supported by a grant from the National Institute of Child Health and Human Development (NICHD), HD30995, "Early Interventions for Children with Reading Problems." We acknowledge the support of the teachers and principals who participated in this project and the help of Michele Hoffman in manuscript preparation.

REFERENCES

Beck, I. L., and McKeown, M. G. 1991. Social studies texts are hard to understand: Mediating some of the difficulties. *Language Arts* 68 (6):482–90.

Beck, I. L., and McKeown, M. G. 2001. Text talk: Capturing the benefits of read-alouds experiences for young children. *The Reading Teacher* 55:10–20.

Beck, I., McKeown, M., and Kucan, L. 2002. *Bringing Words to Life: Robust Vocabulary Instruction*. New York: Guilford Press.

Beck, I., McKeown, M., and Omanson, R. 1987. The effects and uses of diverse vocabulary instructional techniques. In *The Nature of Vocabulary Acquisition*. M. G. McKeown and M. E. Curtis, eds. Hillsdale, NJ: Lawrence Erlbaum Associates.

Beck, I. L, Perfetti, C. A., and McKeown, M. G. 1982. Effects of long-term vocabulary instruction on lexical access and reading comprehension. *Journal of Educational Psychology* 74: 506–21.

Chall, J. S. 1983. *Stages of Reading Development.* New York: McGraw-Hill.

Chomsky, N. 1965. *Aspects of the Theory of Syntax.* Cambridge, MA: MIT Press.

Chomsky, N 1995. The Minimalist Program. Cambridge, MA: MIT Press.

Cunningham, A. E., and Stanovich, K. E. 1991. Tracking the unique effects of print exposure in children: Associations with vocabulary, general knowledge, and spelling. *Journal of Educational Psychology* 83:264–74.

D'Anna, C. A., Zechmeister, E. B., and Hall, J. W. 1991. Toward a meaningful definition of vocabulary size. *Journal of Reading Behavior* 23:109–22.

Dale, E., and O'Rourke, J. 1981. *Living Word Vocabulary.* Chicago: World Book/Childcraft International.

Dickinson, D. K., and Sprague, K. E. 2001. The nature and impact of early childhood care environments on the language and early literacy development of children from low-income families. In *Handbook of Early Literacy Research*, eds. S. Neuman and D. Dickinson. New York, NY: Guilford Press.

Dickinson, D. K., and Tabors, P. O. 2001. *Beginning Literacy with Language.* Baltimore, MD: Brookes Publishing Co.

Dunn, L. M., and Dunn, L. M. 1981. *Peabody Picture Vocabulary Test-Revised.* Circle pines, MN: American Guidance Service.

Englemann, S., and Bruner, E. 1995. *Reading Mastery I.* Chicago, IL: SRA/McGraw-Hill.

Foorman, B. R., Anthony, J., Seals, L., and Mouzaki, A. 2002. Language development and emergent literacy in preschool. *Seminars in Pediatric Neurology* 9:172–83.

Foorman, B. R., Breier, J. I., and Fletcher, J. M. in press. Interventions aimed at improving reading success: An evidence-based approach. *Developmental Neuropsychology.*

Foorman, B. R., Francis, D. J., Carlson, C., Chen, D. T., Moats, L. C., and Fletcher, J. M. in press. The necessity of the alphabetic principle to phonemic awareness instruction. *Reading & Writing.*

Foorman, B. R., Francis, D. J., Davidson, K., Harm, M., and Griffin, J. 2003. Variability in text feature in six grade 1 basal reading programs. Manuscript submitted for publication.

Foorman, B. R., and Moats, L. C. in press. Conditions for sustaining research-based practices in early reading instruction. *Remedial and Special Education.*

Foorman, B. R., and Schatschneider, C. in press. Measuring teaching practice during reading/language arts instruction and its relation to student achievement. In *Reading in the Classroom: Systems for Observing Teaching and Learning*, eds. S. R. Vaughn and K.Briggs. Baltimore, MD: Brookes Publishing Co.

Foorman, B. R., Schatschneider, C., Fletcher, J. M., Francis, D. J., and Moats, L. C. 2003. The impact of instructional practices in grades 1 and 2 on reading and spelling achievement in high poverty schools. Submitted

Fuchs, L. S, Fuchs, D., and Hamlett, C. L. 1989. Monitoring reading growth using student recalls: Effects of two teacher feedback systems. *Journal of Educational Research* 83:103–10.

Graves, M. F. 1987. The relationship between word frequency and reading vocabulary using six metrics of frequency. *Journal of Educational Research* 81:81–90.

Graves, M. F., and Slater, W. H. 1987. The development of vocabularies in rural disadvantaged students, inner city disadvantaged students, and middle-class suburban students. Paper presented at the meeting of the American Educational Research Association meeting in Washington, D.C.

Hart, B., and Risley, T. R. 1995. *Meaningful Differences in the Everyday Experience of Young American Children.* Baltimore, MD: Brookes Publishing Company.

Hefflin, B. R., and Barksdale-Ladd, M. A. 2001. African American children's literature that helps students find themselves: Selection guidelines for grades K–3. *The Reading Teacher* 54:810–19.

Labov, W. 1972. *Language in the Inner City: Studies in the Black English Vernacular.* Pennsylvania: University of Pennsylvania Press Inc.

Lively, T., August, D., Snow, C., and Carlo, M. 2003. *Vocabulary Improvement Program for English Language Learners and Their Classmates.* Baltimore, Maryland: Brookes Publishing.

McLaughlin, B., August, D., and Snow, C. 2000. *Vocabulary Knowledge and Reading Comprehension in English Language Learners: Final Performance Report.* California: Office of Educational Research and Improvement.

Nagy, W. E. 1988. *Teaching Vocabulary to Improve Reading Comprehension.* Urbana, IL: National Council of Teachers of English; Newark, DE: International Reading Association.

Nagy, W. E., and Anderson, R. C. 1984. How many words are there in printed school English? *Reading Research Quarterly* 19:304–330.

National Center for Education Statistics. 2001a. *Common Core of Data (CDD): State Nonfiscal Survey of Public Elementary/Secondary Education.* Washington, D.C: U.S. Department of Education.

National Center for Education Statistics. 2001b. *Fourth Grade Reading Highlights 2000: The Nation's Report Card.* Washington, D.C: U.S. Department of Education.

National Institute of Child Health and Human Development. 2000. *National Reading Panel Report.* Washington, D.C.: National Institutes of Health.

Pinker, S. 1994. *The Language Instinct.* New York, NY: William Morrow and Co.

Seals, L. M. 2001. Does sensitivity to African-American vernacular English affect phonological awareness testing? Master's thesis, University of Houston.

Seals, L. M., Foorman, B. R., and Anthony, J. Evaluation of a vocabulary enrichment program for at-risk third graders. Poster presented at the Society for the Scientific Study of Reading in Chicago, June 29, 2002.

Slavin, R. E. and Madden, N. A. 2001. Success for all: An overview. In *Success for All: Research and Reform in Elementary Education*, eds. R. Slavin and N. Madden. Mahwah, NJ: Lawrence Erlbaum Associates.

Snow, C. E., Burns, M. S., and Griffin, P., eds. 1998. *Preventing Reading Difficulties in Young Children.* Washington, DC: National Academy Press.

Stahl, S. A. 1999. *Vocabulary Development.* Cambridge, MA. Brookline Books.

Sternberg, R. J. 1987. Most words are learned from context. In *The Acquisition of Word Meanings*, eds. M. G. McKeown and M. E. Curtis.

Storch, S. A., and Whitehurst, G. J. 2002. Oral language and code-related precursors to reading: Evidence from a longitudinal structural model. *Developmental Psychology* 38:937–47.

Wechsler, D. 1974. *Wechsler Intelligence Scale for Children-Revised.* San Antonio, TX: Psychological Corporation.

White, T. G., Graves, M .F., and Slater, W. H. 1990. Growth of reading vocabulary in diverse elementary schools: Decoding and word meaning. *Journal of Educational Psychology* 82: 281–89.

Woodcock, R. W., and Johnson, M. B. 1989. *Woodcock-Johnson Psychoeducational Battery-Revised.* Allen, TX: DLM Teaching Resources.

Section • VI

CODA

Chapter • 16

Scaling Reading Interventions

Carolyn A. Denton and Jack M. Fletcher

Perhaps the greatest tragedy in education today is that we are not adequately exploiting what is known about how effective instruction could reduce the incidence of reading failure. In our information-oriented culture, the demand for literacy is high and continues to rise. The recent consensus report of the Rand Reading Study Group (RAND 2002) outlined some of the factors behind the commonly expressed concerns about the number of individuals with inadequate literacy in our country. First, the overall growth of reading skills on national assessments such as the National Assessment of Educational Progress has been relatively flat over the past 30 years (U.S. Department of Education 2001).

The Rand group also noted that, in some international comparisons, older students in the United States have placed near the bottom, behind countries like the Philippines, Brazil, and Indonesia. This level of performance contrasts with higher international rankings for U.S. fourth graders. The disparity between the international rankings of older and younger U.S. students may be related to the ineffective nature of typical reading comprehension instruction. Many educators assume that students will develop proficient comprehension skills just by reading, which is clearly not the case (Knapp 1995; Pressley 1998). For many students, instruction in reading comprehension must be explicit and integrated with content-area instruction (National Reading Panel 2000). Not surprisingly, the Rand report cited inadequate teacher preparation as an issue underlying ineffective instructional practices.

Similarly, there is a persistent gap in test performance between students of various ethnic, socio-economic, and linguistic backgrounds, a disparity that has not lessened despite a significant Federal investment in compensatory education programs. Large investments by federal and state governments in education and research indicate few gains that have been substantiated, and there is little evidence that students served in compensatory education programs make significant progress in reading (Birman et al. 1987). Although the research base on the effectiveness of compensatory programs is not adequate due to lack of accountability for results in Title I programs, the available data indicate that effectiveness is limited to school reform models, such as Success for All, whole-school curriculum reforms, such as Project Follow Through, and some small group tutorial programs (Birman et al. 1987; Slavin, Karweit, and Wasik 1994).

Many of the students who experience reading difficulties are served by special education. The number of children identified as having learning disabilities has increased dramatically since 1975. These children now represent about half of the 6.2 million children identified for special education services in the United States (U.S. Department of Education 2002). Of all the children identified as learning disabled in our schools, 80% to 90% are served primarily because they have not learned to read well (Lerner 1989; Kavale and Resse 1992). The recent report of the President's Commission on Excellence in Special Education (2002) estimated that two of every five children in special education were placed because of difficulties with reading. Yet, there is little evidence that students in special education programs make significant gains in reading after they are placed in special education. Hanuchek, Cain, and Rivkin (1998) evaluated the reading progress of children in Grades 3 to 6 placed in special education and found gains of .04 standard deviations a year, clearly a trivial amount of improvement. In Torgesen et al. (2001) and Blachman et al. (this volume), children with reading difficulties who were receiving intervention only through special education showed either no change in reading standard scores (Torgesen et al. 2001) or a decline (Blachman et al. this volume) over a 1 to 2 year time period. A similar lack of progress has been observed in studies that have documented the ineffective nature of reading instruction commonly provided through typical special education service delivery models (Moody et al. 2000, Vaughn, Moody, and Schumm 1998, Zigmond et al. 1995). Hence the call from the President's Commission on Special Education (2002) and other reports (e.g., Donovan and Cross 2002; National Center for Learning Disabilities 2002) for more focus on the achievement outcomes of special education programs.

THE CONTRIBUTIONS OF RESEARCH

Partly in response to these factors involving reading achievement, research has been conducted that has demonstrated that the percentage of students with severe reading difficulties could be dramatically reduced through the provision of high-quality intervention to children in Kindergarten through second grade (see Denton and Mathes this volume; Lyon et al. 2001; Torgesen 2000). Most reading problems become apparent in the initial phases of beginning to read. Recent consensus reports suggest that we know how to teach most children to read at this level (Donovan and Cross 2002; RAND 2002; Snow, Burns, and Griffin 1998). The report of the National Research Council (NRC) (Snow et al. 1998), based on a review of research in early reading instruction and intervention, established the essential components of effective early literacy instruction, which included (a) explicit instruction in the alphabetic principle, (b) teaching students to read for meaning, and (c) providing extended opportunities for practice reading connected text. The NRC elaborated on this finding, noting that effective instruction is best characterized as the integration of these three components, rather than a balance between phonics and whole language. In fact, the most successful primary level reading teachers integrate the attractive features of whole language with explicit skills instruction, providing a literate environment, along with instruction in multiple competencies related to early reading, including concepts of print, the alphabetic principle, comprehension strategies, and writing. They offer this instruction both in the context of explicit instruction in reading and writing and in decontextualized formats (Pressley 1998; Snow et al. 1998).

Other research initiatives have demonstrated the effectiveness of intensive intervention offered to struggling readers early in their school careers (see Mathes and Denton 2002). For example, Torgesen et al. (1997) identified children in kindergarten who had poor phonological awareness, that is, they had difficulty blending and segmenting sounds in speech. By second grade, intervention brought 75% of these children to grade-level reading. Vellutino and colleagues (1996) identified middle-class children with very low word recognition skills at the beginning of Grade 1. After one semester of intervention, 70% were reading at grade level. After two semesters, over 90% were at grade level.

Given what we know about effective reading instruction and intervention, how is it that so many students continue to fail? How can the findings of research be scaled into widespread practice?

BRINGING RESEARCH-BASED PROGRAMS AND PRACTICES TO SCALE

As noted in the "No Child Left Behind" educational legislation (PL 107-110, 2002), all too often research findings have little influence on instructional practice. Systemic barriers exist that limit progress toward the goal of widespread use of empirically supported practices. First of all, not all agree that scientifically based research should come to scale (Allington 2002; Pressley and Allington 1999). There are assertions by some that the research base is not adequate, that research should not be the basis for scaling, or that the underlying epistemology of scientifically based research is inappropriate for school-based practices. As recent legislative initiatives and consensus documents indicate, these views are in the minority and do not enjoy wide acceptance.   Perhaps more significantly, there is a limited research base that explicitly addresses effective methods of scaling up and sustaining educational innovations. If we are to overcome obstacles to the widespread implementation of effective models of early literacy instruction, the process of bridging the research-to-practice gap must be explicitly studied. Well-articulated theoretical models of scaling and sustainability must be developed and empirically validated.

PREVIOUS THEORY AND RESEARCH ON SCALING

In the next section, we review research and theoretical papers that might be used to support scaling. Presently, the knowledge base on scaling up educational interventions is composed largely of anecdotal commentaries and researcher impressions. These have produced converging recommendations concerning factors that may impede or facilitate scaling and sustaining research-based innovations in practice. However, we found no examples of fully articulated scaling models in the literature, although some authors have suggested models that describe certain aspects of the process.

Elmore's Theoretical Models

Elmore (1996) proposed five theoretical models for replicating successful educational interventions: (a) Incremental Growth, in which a given number of teachers are provided professional development in the educational innovation each year, incrementally increasing the total number of teachers using the methods; (b) Cumulative Growth, which includes provisions for monitoring the effects of the innovation on the actual practice of teachers who receive the professional development, with additional training provided to those who do not implement with high fidelity, (c) Discontinuous

Growth, a "trainer-of-trainer" model, in which one group of teachers are trained in the innovation, and they provide training to subsequent groups, (d) Unbalanced Growth, in which several high-performing teachers are concentrated in a few schools, in order to assist each other in the implementation of the reforms, later providing support to other teachers who would be placed in the same schools; and (e) Cell Division or Reproduction, in which a core group of model schools nurtures leaders in the reforms, who later form another school and mentor a new group of teachers there. The later two models are specifically relevant to reforms that involve effective classroom practices. They are less applicable to the scaling of small-group specialized interventions.

The Fuchs and Fuchs Model

Fuchs and Fuchs (1998) proposed a model of scaling that includes three major stages: pilot research, formal evaluation, and scaling up. Each of these stages is reiterative, in that revision of the educational intervention is possible, based on teacher input. The model also emphasizes the continuum of support from grant funding in the early stages to school funding in the later.

Disseminating Curricular Materials

The dissemination of curricular materials has been used as a vehicle for scaling. Some authors have attempted to have a wide impact on educational practices primarily through the publication and dissemination of such materials (i.e., Fountas and Pinnell 1996). Ball and Cohen (1996) discuss the critical importance of high-quality professional development related to the implementation of novel curricular materials, observing that high-quality implementation of instructional directives found in materials such as basal readers depends on factors such as the teacher's knowledge of the subject matter and the way it is presented in the materials; their beliefs about instructional priorities; and their personal teaching philosophy and style. Although thoughtfully constructed instructional materials are key to quality implementation of educational programs, merely disseminating these materials is unlikely to have a strong impact on teachers' behavior, without attention to their attitudes, goals, and knowledge base.

Models Implemented by Successfully Disseminated Programs

Another source of insight into scaling could be based on programs that have been scaled with some success. For example, consider Reading Recovery (see Clay 1993), Success for All (see Slavin et al.

1996), and the Comer School Development Program (School Development Program 2001). Reading Recovery and Success for All are similar in that trainers from the central institution provide training to teacher leaders or facilitators within the school district, then continue contact with these trainers and hold schools and teachers accountable for high-fidelity implementation of the interventions (Reading Recovery Council of North America 1998; Slavin and Madden 1999). The Comer School Development Program is a school-restructuring model based on the theory that enhancing the interpersonal relationships and social climate in a school will ultimately result in enhanced learning for its students (School Development Program 2001). The blueprint for the dissemination of this model includes five phases: (a) planning and preorientation, including the establishment of the school/program partnership, commitments, and selection of a district facilitator; (b) orientation, including baseline data collection, training of school personnel, and the establishment of teams; (c) transition, in which the program is in place, the process is documented, and follow-up consultations are provided by the program staff; (d) operation, characterized by increased self-sufficiency, continued process documentation, and assessment of outcomes; and (e) institutionalization, in which the program is integrated into the routine operation of the school.

Diffusion Theory

Social science disciplines other than education have documented success in scaling interventions. Particularly impressive are public health endeavors, some of which work through schools to provide interventions addressing issues such as physical fitness, nutrition, and information related to the prevention of obesity, heart disease, and other health risks. The programs have been subjected to large-scale clinical trials with budgets much larger than those typically seen in education, and a research base on scaling has emerged in efforts to scale the results of these trials.

A model that has emerged from this program of research is diffusion theory, which bears striking similarity to the phases of dissemination in the Comer project. According to this theory, individuals and organizations choose to accept or reject innovations in a process termed diffusion, which includes the stages of dissemination, adoption, implementation, and institutionalization (Brink et al. 1995). In this model, dissemination is the process of informing potential stakeholders about the innovation and persuading them to try it (related to the Comer planning and preorientation stage). Adoption is the decision by an entity to commit to a program, often defined as the purchase of program materials. Implementation is the process by which the entity actually carries out the program (incorporating the Comer stages of orientation, transition, and operation), while institutionalization is the integration of the intervention into an institution's culture through policy and practice. Another conceptualization of the diffusion process includes a stage in which the decision to implement must be reaffirmed or rejected (Confirmation), occurring prior to institutionalization (Rogers 1995). Institutionalization occurs when a program becomes an integral part of an organization, incorporated into its standard operations and annual budget (Goodman and Steckler 1989; Goodman et al. 1993). When institutionalization occurs, the program is continued beyond the research agency's funding, with the intent to sustain or extend the program's positive effects.

Factors Influencing Sustained High-Quality Implementation

Cooper (1998) investigated the impact of socio-cultural and within-school factors on the quality of implementation, replicability, and sustainability in the Success for All (SFA) Program. Cooper analyzed data from surveys completed by about 500 principals and SFA site facilitators in 350 schools, examining the variation in social and school factors between high- and low-implementation sites. He found that a school's student mobility and attendance rates were significantly related to successful implementation, as were factors related to ethnic diversity. Within-school factors that had statistically significant relationships with sustained high-quality implementation included a supportive culture for institutional change ($d = 1.13$), program resistance ($d = 1.30$), commitment to program structures ($d = .66$), and a strong school site facilitator ($d = .51$). Other factors yielding medium, although not statistically significant, effects included early success experienced by teachers in the program and student-teacher ratio. We observe that the first three of the significant within-school factors appear to be derived from the same construct, that of teacher acceptance and commitment to the implementation of the program. Cooper, stating that the success of SFA in a school is strongly related to high-fidelity, high-quality implementation, concluded that successful replication of the program depends on "unambiguous buy-in on the part of all staff at the school" (p.16), and that schools in his study that were more able to obtain and sustain this level of commitment were able to empower teachers to take ownership and responsibility for the process of school change related to high-quality implementation. Thus, feelings of professionalism and self-determination among the faculty and staff in the SFA schools appear to be a critical component of successful replication and sustained implementation of the program.

Klingner and her colleagues (1999) observed the sustained implementation by seven teachers of reading-related interventions they had learned in a year-long professional development program (see Vaughn et al. 1998). Three years after completing the professional development, the teachers were still implementing some of the strategies they had learned. The teachers described factors that supported the continued use of the innovations, most often citing (a) their students' acceptance of a strategy, (b) professional development that included the demonstration of the strategies by one of the researchers or facilitators in the teachers' own classes, (c) having access to the materials needed for the intervention, and (d) the instructional needs of their students. In sum, teachers tended to continue to implement interventions that benefitted their students, that their students liked, and that they felt they had adequate preparation to implement with confidence. Teachers in this study also noted the importance of a support network to the continued implementation of an innovation, both the support of an on-site facilitator and the support of their colleagues who were also engaged in the project. One teacher noted that continuing to implement the strategies was easier "because we are all doing it" (p.269). This indicates that innovations that become the norm for the school or for a subgroup of teachers in a school may achieve a status of widespread acceptance and respect that encourage continued implementation.

These conclusions are reinforced by Gersten and his colleagues (1997), who reviewed existing literature on the subject of sustainability. They suggest that sustainable interventions are practical, concrete, and have a high degree of specificity, reflecting the realities of implementation by teachers whose time and attention are consumed by multiple demands. As in the study by Klingner and her colleagues (1999), the Gersten et al. review noted the importance of professional development in which teachers are provided with multiple opportunities to practice new procedures and receive helpful feedback, and in which the professionalism of teachers is emphasized through engagement in joint problem solving activities. Likewise, it is important that teachers maintain continuing supportive interactions within collegial support networks, providing them with opportunities to discuss connections between research and their real everyday classroom situations. Above all, sustainable instructional innovations must result in the recognition by teachers that their efforts have paid off in the form of increased student learning.

A MODEL FOR SCALING AND SUSTAINING EDUCATIONAL INTERVENTIONS

Based on our examination of these models, and on our review of the literature on scaling and sustaining educational innovations and reform initiatives, we propose a five-phase model of the process of scaling and sustaining interventions in our schools. Each component of the model includes key factors affecting implementation of the innovation, key participants in the process, and the role of the research team in that phase. Like the Fuchs and Fuchs (1998) model, this model provides for the regular revision and adaptation of the intervention, in response to teacher feedback and the results of each stage in the process.

The five phases of the model are (a) development of the intervention, (b) empirical evaluation of the intervention, (c) tests of robustness and generalizability, (d) scaling up and sustaining, and (e) networking. Within the scaling phase, we include the stages of (a) dissemination, (b) decision, (c) implementation, (d) transition, (e) confirmation, and (f) institutionalization.

Development

In the development phase, instructional interventions are designed, extending from a solid base of empirical research, grounded theory, and practical experience in schools (Stone 1998). Although some literature suggests that these will be most effective when developed cooperatively by researchers and teachers (Abbot, Walton, and Tapia 1999), there are examples of successfully scaled programs that were developed primarily or solely by researchers (e.g., Reading Recovery; Success for All).

Empirical Evaluation

During the empirical evaluation of the interventions, researchers establish a partnership with schools to examine the efficacy of the interventions, applying rigorous scientific methods. The research team has a dual role, providing resources and ongoing professional development and support for the implementation of the intervention in the schools, and assuring that the intervention is implemented with suitable fidelity and the research is conducted with suitably high standards. In this phase, the school stakeholders are the teachers (both intervention teachers and classroom teachers, if the intervention involves activity outside of the regular classroom), administrators, students, and parents. During this period of empirical evaluation, and throughout the remainder of the model, the degree of support and cooperation of these stakeholders are shaped primarily by five factors: (a) stakeholders' backgrounds, defined as their prior knowledge, beliefs, feelings of self-efficacy, school culture, and routine practices (the nature of "business as usual") (Berends et al. 2001; Borman et al. 2000; Cooper 1998; Gersten, Chard, and Baker 2000; Showers, Joyce, and Bennett 1987; Wong 1997); (b) stakeholders' perception of benefits and costs of the program (Berends et al. 2001; Borman et al. 2000; Cohen 1995; Elmore 1996; Fuchs and Fuchs 2001; Klingner et al. 1999; Stone 1998); (c) socio-cultural factors such as socio-economic status and cultural norms of the community (Borman et al. 2000; Cooper 1998), (d) the quality and quantity of staff development and ongoing support (Berends et al. 2001; Fullan, 2000; Gersten et al. 1997; Klingner et al. 1999; Schorr 1997; Showers et al. 1987); and (e) the nature of the intervention itself (i.e., its scope, level of prescriptiveness, and practicality), and particularly its perceived effectiveness for students in the school (Borman et al. 2000; Gersten et al. 2000; LeFevre and Richardson 2000; Stanovich and Stanovich 1997). The analysis of data in the evaluation stage indicates the degree to which the intervention can be implemented with high fidelity, and, ultimately, its effect on student outcomes. Based on feedback from teachers and administrators, and on the empirical results, the intervention can be revised somewhat, staying well within the parameters of its empirical and theoretical support.

Tests of Robustness and Generalizability

The factors described above continue to exert influence on school stakeholders during the tests of robustness and generalizability. In this phase, the goal is to examine the effectiveness of the intervention among large, diverse student populations and in varying educational contexts. Factors related to these diverse contexts take on critical importance. Socio-cultural factors that have been found to affect the degree of implementation of educational interventions include the socio-economic status of the community served by the school, and the school's student mobility and attendance rates (Cooper 1998). Policy and political contexts that can exert strong influence include perceptions and pressures emanating from parents and community members, along with mandates and accountability policies from local and state entities governing education. For example, teachers and administrators need to perceive that the intervention will result in better outcomes on high-stakes testing, if that is the tool used to evaluate the school's performance (Klingner et al. 1999). Factors such as these influence the perception of costs and benefits of the intervention among administrators, parents, and teachers. During the tests of robustness and generalizability, the research team continues to provide a large contribution to the project, contributing resources and considerable coaching, mentoring, and support. Once again, the intervention is adapted according to teacher feedback and to the results of the implementation in multiple contexts.

Scaling and Sustaining

If the intervention is found to be sufficiently robust and generalizable, the scaling and sustaining phase is begun. In this phase, it is critical that the research entity establish strong partnerships with the schools (Fuchs and Fuchs 2001). The schools take on primary responsibility for the implementation of the intervention, and the research team assumes a much different role. In this phase, the model takes on a trainer of trainer approach, as in Elmore's (1996) Discontinuous Growth model. Former teachers, who acquired experience in the interventions during the empirical evaluation and test of robustness stages, provide professional development and become coaches and facilitators for schools that are implementing the program. As the scaling phase continues, school district personnel are provided with training to assume increasing responsibility for these roles.

Dissemination and Decision.   During the initial dissemination, the team informs schools of the availability of the intervention, helps them to understand the nature of the intervention, and tries to convince them to adopt it. This phase includes delivering presentations to school stakeholders on the nature and benefits of the intervention. This leads schools to the decision phase, in which they decide whether to commit to the implementation. During this time, the research team acts as a resource, answering any questions, and revisiting schools as needed. The decision is heavily influenced by the prior knowledge and beliefs of the stakeholders, particularly their beliefs about the nature of teaching and learning, and by their perception of the costs and benefits of the program. Administrators must determine whether they can commit sufficient resources to the program, including fiscal resources, time, space, materials, and personnel. These costs must be explained sufficiently by the resource team so that an informed decision by the school is possible. The school should be asked to make a multi-year commitment to the program, so that they can increasingly integrate it into their everyday practice (institutionalization). True change takes time to develop, as teachers must accept the innovation, develop mastery in the practices and techniques associated with it, and integrate it with their personal teaching style (Stone 1998). Showers et al. (1987) estimate that it takes about 25 teaching episodes implementing a new practice before transfer is complete and maintenance is likely.

Implementation. If a school decides to adopt the program, they enter the stage of implementation. At this point, they begin to deal with the practical aspects of implementing the program in real educational contexts. The role of the research team is critical at this time, as they not only provide professional development to the teachers, but also assist the schools as they grapple with situations that could derail the implementation. This is particularly critical in pull-out supplemental interventions, since the school must establish schedules for removing the students from their regular classrooms, policies regarding making up work missed, grading policies, and resolve issues regarding adequate space and materials. These factors may be compounded by the absence of immediate effects from the interventions.

Transition. After initial difficulties have been overcome, the process enters a period of transition, and the technical support provided to the school is decreased. However, the research team must always be available to them as needed on a consulting basis. Some of the ongoing support is provided in the form of collegial networks, peer coaching, and computer technologies. During this transition stage, the research team continues to monitor the quality and fidelity of implementation, and assists the school in the collection of valid student outcome data.

Confirmation. The school continues to implement the intervention with this lowered level of support during the period of their initial multi-year commitment. At this point, sustainability becomes an issue, as they enter the phase of confirmation, or the decision whether to continue or discontinue the program. The aspects of perceived costs and benefits take on critical importance (Stone 1998). The most motivating benefit to the school is the perception that student learning has occurred as a result of the intervention (Cooper 1998; Fuchs and Fuchs 2001; Gersten et al. 2000; Stanovich and Stanovich 1997). The research team continues to assist the school personnel in the analysis and interpretation of student outcome data (Stone 1998).

Institutionalization. Finally, if a school opts to continue the intervention program, it becomes institutionalized. At this point, the innovation is accepted as common practice in the school. It is integrated into the budget, and scheduling for the intervention is routinely done. Even at this point, the research team must provide continuing technical support, contracting with the schools to provide staff development and consultation, assisting them in the evaluation of their programs, and providing technology support. To guard against program drift, or the tendency for a program to change over time, often resulting in reduced effectiveness, members of the research team or their representatives must make periodic visits to the schools, collecting data on the quality and fidelity of implementation of the intervention, and engaging in discussions with teachers and administrators about issues related to the program.

Widespread Diffusion: Networking. The model we have described pertains to the dissemination of educational innovations from a research setting into multiple schools. If this phase of scaling is successful, and the educational practices are sufficiently robust to maintain their effectiveness under this model, widespread diffusion of the innovations is possible.

This type of large-scale dissemination requires an extension of our model to include a phase consisting of networking. Related to Elmore's (1996) theoretical model of Discontinuous Growth, networking refers to the establishment of an increasingly large cadre of professional trainers and coaches who provide professional development and ongoing technical support for the implementation of the innovation in schools in widely separated geographic areas.

Building networks. Implementation networks may be constructed through a system in which (a) the entity originally responsible for the innovation provides extensive training to persons who will, in turn, become trainers of school personnel, and (b) the original entity continually monitors the professional development and coaching provided by the new group of trainers. The successful dissemination model implemented by the Reading Recovery intervention follows this format. A small number of university sites in countries in which Reading Recovery is implemented offer an extended program of training for cohorts of teacher leaders, who, in turn, train teachers in their school districts and monitor the implementation of the program by those teachers. While the prospective teacher leaders are learning to implement the program, they are engaged in a type of internship, in which they themselves are teaching Reading Recovery students. Thus, the trainers receive experience as teachers in the intervention, along with extensive instruction in the theoretical bases and technical components of program implementation. After the training period for the teacher leader is complete, he or she continues to have contact with the university program, in order to receive updates and assure continued high-fidelity implementation.

Accessing existing networks. Several states have implemented initiatives to encourage the implementation of research-based practices in the teaching of reading (see, for example, Limon 2002). Strategies commonly used by states to promote improved student outcomes in reading include (but are not restricted to) (a) instituting requirements for the implementation of practices or programs related to prevention or intervention for reading difficulties, or promoting these practices through grants, and (b) providing, or requiring school districts to provide, professional development on research-supported practices related to prevention or intervention programs or practices (Education Commission of the States 2001). Some state models include the preparation and employment of reading coaches who work continually with teachers to promote advances in student learning (see, for example, State Board for Educator Certification 2000). In addition, some states have networks of regional education centers, with staff members who provide professional development and support in schools in their areas. This type of existing network may be accessed in some situations for the widespread dissemination of innovative practices.

In any case, the challenge for any widespread diffusion of research-based practices or programs is the maintenance of program fidelity. It is critical that the originating organization address questions relating to the level of fidelity required in order to assure outcomes comparable to those attained in research implementations. This level of required fidelity will ultimately determine both the extent to which the innovation can be disseminated successfully, and the nature of the network required to support its extended implementation.

CONTINUED CHALLENGES

The model we have described must be validated through empirical research that explicitly addresses its effectiveness in promoting widespread high-quality, sustained implementation of instructional practices. But it is research that is needed. Policy has pushed literacy-based research to the forefront, but there has been little empirical research on scaling in education. The models that we have discussed need to be evaluated. To do these evaluations, a commitment to funding research on scaling is essential. This research will require large budgets because of the number of schools that must be involved. The Interagency Educational Research Initiative is an excellent start, but there is little happening with scaling for special education initiatives. Given the linking of Part D and Part B in IDEA, this lack of emphasis is puzzling. The President's Commission on Special Education (2002) noted specifically that special education was not part of the Interagency Education Research Initiative and called for a research emphasis on scaling. This emphasis will require a change in philosophy for the research programs in the Office of Special Education Programs and a significant increase in the Research to Practice budget.

Before research can investigate the validity of models of scaling reading intervention, there is a need for criterion-based studies of the validity of benchmarks that denote the practical success or failure of intervention efforts. Simply put, how do we know when we have truly succeeded in our efforts to teach children to read at levels that are sufficient to ensure their continued success in school? Benchmarks based on oral reading fluency levels may be the most valid indicators of future success (see Denton and Mathes this volume), but there is at present a lack of research to support this hypotheses or to validate particular fluency levels as adequate predictors of continued growth. These measurement issues have not been adequately funded.

The negative consequences of reading difficulties remain high. The widespread implementation of high-quality, scientifically validated reading instruction is not a luxury, but a necessity that we simply cannot afford to neglect. Accomplishing the goals set out in recent policy initiatives, including "No Child Left Behind," will require partnerships among educators, local and state educational agencies, and researchers. It has not been a simple process so far and managing these complex partnerships will continue to be a struggle amidst the language of scrutiny and criticism. The essential scaling of literacy research will not happen quickly and it will be essential for all partners to stay focused and directed to the end goals. All children can learn to read if provided appropriate and timely instruction. Its time to scale what is known from research.

ACKNOWLEDGMENTS

Supported by a grant from the Interagency Education Research Initiative, NSF 9979968

REFERENCES

Abbott, M., Walton, C., and Tapia, Y. 1999. Research to practice: A "blueprint" for closing the gap in local schools. *Exceptional Children* 65:339–52.

Allington, R. A. 2002. *Big Brother and the National Reading Curriculum: How Ideology Trumped Evidence.* New York: Heinemann.

Ball, D. L., and Cohen, D. K. 1996. Reform by the book: What is—or might be—the role of curriculum materials in teacher learning and instructional reform? *Educational Researcher* 25:6–8, 14.

Berends, M., Kirby, S. N., Naftel, S., and McKelvey, C. 2001. *Implementation and Performance in New American Schools: Three Years into Scale-up.* Santa Monica, CA: Rand Education.

Birman, B. F., Orland, M. E., Jung, R. K., Anson, R. J., Garcia, G. N., Moore, M. T., et al. 1987. *The Current Operation of the Chapter 1 Program.* Washington, DC: U.S. Government Printing Office.

Borman, G. D., Rachuba, L., Datnow, A. Alberg M., MacIver, M., Stringfield, S., and Ross, S. 2000. *Four Models of School Improvement: Successes and Challenges in Reforming Low-performing, High-poverty Title 1 Schools* (Tech Rep. No 48). Ann Arbor, MI: University of Michigan, Center for Improvement of Early Reading Achievement.

Brink, S. G., Basen-Engsquist, K., O'Hara-Tompkins, N. M., Parcel, G. S., Gottlieb, N. H, and Lovato, C. Y. 1995. Diffusion of an effective tobacco prevention program. Part I: Evaluation of the dissemination phase. *Health Education Research* 10:282–96.

Clay, M. M. 1993. *Reading Recovery: A Guidebook for Teachers in Training.* Portsmouth, NH: Heinemann.

Cohen, D. K. 1995. Rewarding teachers for student performance. In *Rewards and Reforms: Creating Educational Incentives That Work*, eds. S. Fuhrman and J. O'Day. San Francisco, CA: Jossey Bass.

Cooper, R. 1998. *Socio-cultural and Within-school Factors that Affect the Quality of Implementation of School-wide Programs* (Tech. Rep. No. 28). Baltimore, MD: Johns Hopkins University, Center for Research on the Education of Students Placed At-Risk.

Donovan, M. S., and Cross, C. T. 2002. *Minority Students in Special and Gifted Education.* Washington, DC: National Academy Press.

Education Commission of the States. 2001. Common state strategies to improve student reading. Denver, CO. Accessed on August 20, 2002, from www.ecs.org.

Elmore, R. F. 1996. Getting to scale with good educational practice. *Harvard Educational Review* 66:1–26.

Fountas, I. C., and Pinnell, G. S. 1996. *Guided Reading.* Portsmouth, NH: Heinemann.

Fuchs, D., and Fuchs, L. S. 1998. Researchers and teachers working together to adapt instruction for diverse learners. *Learning Disabilities Research and Practice* 13:126–37.

Fuchs, L. S., and Fuchs, D. 2001. Principles for sustaining research-based practice in the schools: A case study. *Focus on Exceptional Children* 33:1–14.

Fullan, M. 2000. The return of large-scale reform. *Journal of Educational Change* 1:1–25.

Gersten, R., Chard, D., and Baker, S. 2000. Factors enhancing sustained use of research-based instructional practices. *Journal of Learning Disabilities* 33:445–57.

Gersten, R., Vaughn, S., Deshler, D., and Schiller, E. 1997. What we know about using research findings: Implications for improving special education practice. *Journal of Learning Disabilities* 30:466–76.

Goodman, R. M., and Steckler, A. 1989. A model for the institutionalization of health promotion programs. *Family and Community Health* 11:63–78.

Goodman, R. M., Steckler, A., Hoover, S., and Schwartz, R. 1993. A critique of contemporary community health promotion approaches: Based on a qualitative review of six programs in Maine. *American Journal of Health Promotion* 7:208–21.

Hanushek, E. A., Kain, J. F., and Rivkin, S. G. 1998. *Does Special Education Raise Academic Achievement for Students with Disabilities?* National Bureau of Economic Research, Working Paper No. 6690, Cambridge, MA. Accessed on September 6, 2002, from http://www.nber.org/papers/w6690.

Kavale, K. A., and Reese, L. 1992. The character of learning disabilities: An Iowa profile. *Learning Disability Quarterly* 15:74–94.

Klingner, J. K., Vaughn, S., Hughes, M. T., and Arguelles, M. E. 1999. Sustaining research-based practices in reading: A 3-year follow-up. *Remedial and Special Education* 20:263–74, 287.

Knapp, M. S., Adelman, N. E., Marder, C., McCollum, H., Needels, M. C., Padilla, C., Shields, P. M., Turnbull, B. J., and Zucker, A. A. 1995. *Teaching for Meaning in High-Poverty Classrooms.* New York, NY: Teachers College Press.

LeFevre, D., and Richardson, V. 2000. *Staff Development in Early Reading Intervention Programs: The Facilitator* (Tech. Rep. No. 3-011). Ann Arbor, MI: University of Michigan, Center for the Improvement of Early Reading Achievement.

Lerner, J. 1989. Educational intervention in learning disabilities. *Journal of the American Academy of Child and Adolescent Psychiatry* 28: 326–31.

Lyon, G. R., Fletcher, J. M., Shaywitz, S. E., Shaywitz, B. A., Torgeson, J. K., Wood, F. B., Schutle, A., and Olson, R. 2001. Rethinking learning disabilities. In *Rethinking Special Education for a New Century*, eds. C. E. Finn, Jr., R. A. J. Rotherham, and C. R. Hokanson, Jr. Washington, DC: Thomas B. Fordham Foundation and Progressive Policy Institute.

Mathes, P. G., and Denton, C. A. 2002. The prevention and identification of reading disability, *Seminars in Pediatric Neurology* 9:185–91.

Moody, S. W., Vaughn, S. R. Hughes, M. T., and Fischer, M. 2000. Reading instruction in the resource room: Set up for failure. *Exceptional Children* 16:305–16.

National Reading Panel 2000. *Report of the National Reading Panel: Teaching Students to Read: An Evidence-based Assessment of the Scientific Research Literature on Reading and its Implications for Reading Instruction: Reports of the Subgroups.* Bethesda, MD: National Institute of Child Health and Human Development, National Institutes of Health.

President's Commission on Excellence in Special Education 2002. A new era: Revitalizing special education for children and their families. Retrieved on August 6, 2002, from http://www.ed.gov/inits/commissionsboards

Pressley, M. 1998. *Elementary Reading Instruction That Works: Why Balanced Literacy Instruction Makes More Sense Than Whole Language or Phonics and Skills.* New York: Guilford Press.

Pressley, M., and Allington, R. 1999. What should reading instructional research be the research of? *Issues in Education* 5:1–35.

Rand Reading Study Group 2002. *Reading for Understanding.* Santa Monica, CA: RAND.

Reading Recovery Council of North America 1998. *Standards and Guidelines of the Reading Recovery Council of North America.* Columbus, OH: author.

Rogers, E. M. 1995. *Diffusion of Innovations (4th ed.).* New York: Free Press.

School Development Program, Yale Child Study Center 2001. Overview of the school development program. Retrieved April 9, 2002, from http://www.info.med.yale.edu/comer/about/overview.html

Schorr, L. B. 1997. *Common Purpose: Strengthening Families and Neighborhoods to Rebuild America.* New York: Doubleday.

Showers, B., Joyce, B., and Bennett, B. 1987. Synthesis of research on staff development: A framework for future study and a state-of-the-art analysis. *Educational Leadership* 45:77–87.

Slavin, R. E., Karweit, N. L., and Wasik, B. A. 1994. *Preventing Early School Failure: Research on Effective Strategies.* Boston: Allyn and Bacon.

Slavin, R. E., and Madden, N. A. 1999. *Disseminating Success For All: Lessons for Policy and Practice* (Tech. Rep. No. 30). Baltimore, MD: Johns Hopkins University, Center for Research on the Education of Students Placed At-Risk.

Slavin, R. E., Madden, N. A., Dolan, L. J., and Wasik, B. A. 1996. *Every Child Every School: Success for All.* Thousand Oaks, CA: Corwin Press.

Snow, C., Burns, M. S., and Griffin, P., eds. 1998. *Preventing Reading Difficulties in Young Children.* Washington, DC: National Academy Press.

Stanovich, P. J., and Stanovich, K. E. 1997. Research into practice in special education. *Journal of Learning Disabilities* 30:477–81.

State Board for Educator Certification 2000. Master Reading Teacher. Austin, TX. Accessed on August 20, 2002 from http://www.sbec.state.tx.us.

Stone, C. A. 1998. Moving validated instructional practices into the classroom: Learning from examples about the rough road to success. *Learning Disabilities Research and Practice* 13:121–25.

Torgeson, J. K. 2000. Individual differences in response to early interventions in reading: The lingering problem of treatment resisters. *Learning Disabilities Research and Practice* 15:55–64.

Torgesen, J. K., Wagner, R. K., Rashotte, C. A., Alexander, A. W., and Conway, T. 1997. Preventive and remedial interventions for children with severe disabilities. *Learning Disabilities: A Multidisciplinary Journal* 8:51–61

Torgesen, J. K., Alexander, A. W., Wagner, R. K., Rashotte, C. A., Voeller, K. K. S., and Conway, T. 2001. Intensive remedial instruction for children with severe reading disabilities: Immediate and long-term outcomes from two instructional approaches. *Journal of Learning Disabilities* 34:33–58.

Vaughn, S., Moody, S. W., and Schumm, J. S. 1998. Broken promises: Reading instruction in the resource room. *Exceptional Children* 64:211–25.

Vellutino, F. R., Scanlon, D. M., Sipay, E. R., Small, S. G., Pratt, A., Chen, R., and Denckla, M. B. 1996. Cognitive profiles of difficult-to-remediate and readily remediated poor readers: Early intervention as a vehicle for distinguishing between cognitive and experiential deficits as basic causes of specific reading disability. *Journal of Educational Psychology* 88, 601–38.

United States Department of Education. 2001. *The Nation's Report Card: Fourth-Grade Reading 2000.* Washington, DC: National Center for Education Statistics.

United States Department of Education. 2002. *Twenty-third Annual Report to Congress on the Implementation of the Individuals with Disabilities in Education.* Washington, DC: author.

Wong, B. Y. L. 1997. Clearing hurdles in teacher adoption and sustained use of research-based instruction. *Journal of Learning Disabilities* 30:482–85.

Zigmond, N., Jenkins, J., Fuchs, L. S., Deno, S., Fuchs, D., Baker, J. N., Jenkins, L., and Couthino, M. 1995. Special education in restructured schools: Findings from three multi-year studies. *Phi Delta Kappan* 76:531–40.

INDEX